CW01336998

THE PEARL OF KHORASAN

C. P. W. GAMMELL

The Pearl of Khorasan

A History of Herat

HURST & COMPANY, LONDON

First published in the United Kingdom in 2016 by
C. Hurst & Co. (Publishers) Ltd.,
41 Great Russell Street, London, WC1B 3PL
© C. P. W Gammell, 2016
All rights reserved.

Distributed in the United States, Canada and Latin America by
Oxford University Press, 198 Madison Avenue, New York, NY 10016,
United States of America.

The right of C. P. W. Gammell to be identified as the author
of this publication is asserted by him in accordance with the
Copyright, Designs and Patents Act, 1988.

A Cataloguing-in-Publication data record for this book
is available from the British Library.

ISBN: 9781849046541

This book is printed using paper from registered sustainable
and managed sources.

www.hurstpublishers.com

For my father, without whom this journey could never have been begun, and without whose continued love and support it could never have reached this point.

For Charlie Cox, without whose generosity and friendship I simply wouldn't have finished this book when I did.

CONTENTS

ACKNOWLEDGEMENTS

This book is the result of three years of research and writing, and therefore the list of those to whom I owe thanks is a long one. For anyone I have missed off, I apologise. It has felt at times to have been as much a collaboration with friends and family as it has a product of my own work, and many of the people thanked here have been essential cogs in the machine that has produced what you hold in your hand today. I am indebted to Christine Noelle-Karimi's scholarship and erudition; her book *The Pearl in its Midst* is an extraordinary feat of learning and research, a lifetime's understanding of Herat and Afghanistan telling many stories of Herat's inclusion and exclusion in Persian and Afghan states. It fills many gaps that I could never even hope to approach, and was a great help to me as I wrote this book. For those seeking more detail and depth, I can highly recommend her excellent study. Thank you to Charles Moore for introducing me to Lord Salisbury, who was of enormous help in his insight and memories of the Afghan conflict of the 1980s and beyond. Also to Christina Lamb for telling me about her experiences of Afghanistan during the Soviet war and beyond; meeting up with Christina in Kabul was always fascinating. Professor Charles Melville taught me so much about Iran and the study of history in general, and I am indebted to his friendship, support and expertise in so much of what I have done—thank you, Charles. Ladan Akbarni and St John Simpson at the British Museum gave me helpful tips and put me in touch with so many wonderful people connected with Herat. Dr Jonathan Lee in New Zealand sent me emails of extraordinary comprehensiveness and detail, in which were invariably to be found real gems of research and analysis; thank you.

ACKNOWLEDGEMENTS

John and Veronica Baily generously gave of their time in describing Herat in its pre-Soviet Golden Age of music, plays and laughter; it was a real joy to sit with you and hear your stories of a city we both love so much—thank you for lunch as well. To Sue Gaisford who read the manuscript in its most garbled form: thank you for reading through and suggesting ways to make it better; your advice so helped me to get the book into shape. To my friends in the British Library—Tobie Mathew, Felix Lowe, Chris Cowell, Cleo Roberts, Ed Posnett and Christopher de Bellaigue—thank you for sanity-saving cups of coffee and chats. To the staff of the British Library, who are always professional and courteous, thank you.

Thanks to the International Committee of the Red Cross (ICRC) for employing me in 2009 to go to Herat as a Persian interpreter, and for the excellent work they do around the world, and especially in Afghanistan. The ICRC is by far the most extraordinary organisation working in war zones across the world, and long may its work continue; in many ways, this book is a great big thank you to the ICRC for showing faith in me as a young and dangerously inexperienced Farsi interpreter. To Peter Guigni, Abdul Wali Zazai, Mukhtar Tannai, Taleb Jan Bashari Zadran, Hazrat Gul, Mobin and the office in Khost, thank you for making my Afghan experiences so fun-filled and rich; I have the fondest memories from the time I spent with you all. To Alberto Cairo, Gregory Halford Jones and the ICRC Ortho team who would drop me off near to Kabul University in the winter of 2014, thank you for that and for saving me extra journeys through Kabul in a frozen and cramped yellow taxi. Thank you to Hajji Abdul Wahhab Qattali for sparing an afternoon to discuss Herat's recent history and for showing me around your extraordinary museum in Herat. The coat you bought me is still doing excellent work in keeping me warm. To Ismail Khan, for giving generously of your time whilst planning an election campaign, thank you so very much for talking to me about your experiences in Herat as the city's ruler and saviour. To my trusted taxi driver and friend, Tareq Jan; thank you for making me laugh and for the thermos of tea that always awaited me when I left a meeting or a frozen stint in the library. To Jolyon Leslie, one of the most knowledgeable people on Herat and Afghanistan that I have ever met, thank you for letting me stay in your guesthouse in Herat and for giving freely of your time and your considerable wisdom. Your team in Herat—Khalil and Habib and co.—is a credit to you and what you are working towards. I have very fond memories of spending time with them all in the city. In Tehran, thank you to Mrs Ettehadieh for her generosity and for giving me a copy of Bagher Kazemi's journals.

Thank you to Tommy Wide, without whom so much of this simply would not have been done, your first edit of the first chapter prevented this book from becoming a fog of footnotes and research, and helped me to see the light of a story and a narrative that could sustain the reader throughout. Thank you for that and for offering up your expertise and advice throughout the project; it has always been hugely appreciated. Your example of heading out to Afghanistan in 2007 was the inspiration I needed to start learning Persian and to head to Iran to begin this journey; your edits, friendship, support, library and knowledge have always been generously given and hugely appreciated. His Excellency Dr Yaar, Afghanistan's ambassador to the UK, was a great help in so many ways, and along with the team at the Afghan Consulate in London helped ensure a steady stream of successful visa applications for research trips to Afghanistan. To Bruce Wannell for his peerless knowledge, endless advice and all his kindness in helping me understand those many aspects of Afghanistan that I'd never have mastered without his help. Thank you, Bruce, for editing the manuscript in its rough and ready form, for advising me where I might improve the writing and for pointing out the many instances where I erred. I will always be grateful to Antony Wynn for giving me his time and an endless stream of advice and understanding of Iran, not to mention countless edits and advice, and prompting me in useful research directions in Iran; also to the Iran Society and the British Institute of Persian Studies for their generous funding, without which much-needed research trips to Afghanistan and Iran would not have been possible. To Michael and Jon at Hurst: thank you for your patience and your hard work in getting this book over the line, finally. Your help has always been gratefully appreciated. Thank you to Melissa Neckar for reading through drafts, and for your love and support.

In Herat, I was lucky enough to come under the guidance of Engineer Salahi, a great man who knows Herat and loves the city as well as anyone I have met; to have made friends with him over the

ACKNOWLEDGEMENTS

course of the research and writing of this book was a real pleasure. To Rafiq Shahir for giving me his time in Herat and for explaining to me so much about Herat's recent history. Likewise, Dr Nik Seyar, and all those from the Cultural Shurah in Herat: thank you for all your time and knowledge. To my good friend and former ICRC colleague, Hedyatullah, for showing me the genius, humour, compassion of Herat's people; so much of this book is indebted to you, as you taught me not just my Herati accent, but you gave me an understanding of what makes this wonderful city tick; your generosity of spirit and your kindness were the best welcome to me in my first year in Herat. To Yousufi, Sagharwal, Shakib and Yusouf, thank you for being good friends and patient colleagues. I have so many fond memories of ICRC Herat: Eric, David, Judy, Anne Marie, Tomassina, Patrick, Arnaud, Omar Sharif, Philippe and Dietrich and all those who came after—so much of this book begins and ends with those memories. In Kabul, thank you to the staff at UNESCO for employing me and putting up with my occasional unlicensed forays to libraries and meetings and houses. Kouki, Sarah, Masanori and Paolo: it was excellent to get to know you. Thank you to Robert Knox for sending me to UNESCO and for offering a sounding board at times of stress and strain. Habib Rasa must also be thanked for answering my out of the blue queries on Herat's geography and mythology so promptly. To Rohullah Amin at the American Institute of Afghan Studies, a great thank you must go for putting me in touch with so many of Herat's most important and influential figures. It was excellent to get to know you in Kabul and I thank you for your time. Thank you to Matthew Leeming for talking to me about Herat as you know it and as you remembered it. Bijan Omrani, thank you for putting me in touch with useful people and for asking me to write for the Royal Society of Asian Affairs. In Kabul perhaps the biggest thanks must go to Nancy Hatch Dupree and her wonderful team at the Afghan Centre at Kabul University; it was a real privilege to have access to the archives there and to be able to talk to you about your memories of Afghanistan and Herat. There are few people alive who understand the country as well as you do, and with as much common sense and compassion. It was an honour to have chatted with you, and your support for this project has always been timely and well received. To Melissa Emery for being such a rock and a companion through my near constant absences—so much of this book is thanks to your love and support; I can never thank you enough.

Thank you to my family and friends for listening to me complain, muse and rant about the book over the three years that it has been making its way from sources, to my head and then onto the page; I am in awe of your tolerance and understanding and cannot thank you enough for listening, offering advice and generally being there for me. Ned and Philipa, you kept me sane and kept me laughing. Two other special thanks have to go to Charlie Cox for giving me use of his house in London for the whole of 2015; that I could stay there and work away meant this book could see the light of day in 2016. And to my father, without whose support and encouragement I could never have begun this adventure back in 2008. You have enabled me to pursue this journey, begun rather hopefully with a Persian grammar book and a flight to Iran.

GLOSSARY

Abdali	Pashtun tribal grouping that settled in Herat and whose subdivision, the Sadozai Abdalis, ruled over a semi-independent enclave in Herat during the nineteenth century.
Akhund	a title of respect given to eminent religious figures or teachers.
Amir	a military commander, and the title of Afghan rulers in the nineteenth century until the arrival of Amanullah, who preferred the title Shah, or King.
Anjoman	society or grouping, often cultural but also, in Iran, a collective or guild.
Bakhshi	Turkic scribes in the service of the Timurid court.
Boluk	district or taxable rural area.
Caliph	a person considered to be a religious successor to the Prophet Muhammad.
Chahar Suq or Su	literally 'four bazaars', a place where Herat's city quarters met, under one great covered bazaar.
Dervish	religious mendicant preacher, associated with Sufism.
Durrani	Pashtun tribal grouping, originally Abdali Sadozai, who ruled Afghanistan during the nineteenth century.
Diwan	administrative offices or court.
Dawlatkhana	a hall in a royal or aristocratic garden from which official business was conducted.

GLOSSARY

Eid	Islamic festivals celebrating the end of the holy month of Ramadan.
Fetnah	a revolt, disturbance or uprising which bred schism within the Islamic community and which threatens the purity of Islamic faith.
Farsiwan	Persian speaker.
Firman	royal edict or warrant.
Ghazi	those who take part in ghaza, raids against infidels; it is used to confer respect on those who take part in religious conflicts against apostates or non-Muslims.
Ghulam	slave, referring to the cadre of loyal military and bureaucratic figures created by Shah Abbas I and around whom he built his great Safavid state.
Guy, Juy or Gui	canal or irrigation stream, cf. karez.
Hadith	a written record of the words, actions or habits of the Prophet Muhammad.
Hajj	pilgrimage to Mecca, the fifth of the five pillars of Islam.
Hajji	someone who has taken part in a pilgrimage to Mecca.
Harem	a forbidden place, a sacrosanct sanctuary, an enclosed female space largely forbidden to men.
Hazara	Shia Afghans most likely of Mongol descent who originate from the Hazarajat in Central Afghanistan; many have moved to Herat since the Taliban persecution of the 1990s.
Iraq-e Ajam	medieval and early medieval geographical term referring to the region of central and western Iran as it is today.
Iraq-e Arab	medieval and early medieval geographical term referring to the ancient province of Babylonia, stretching over central and southern provinces of Iraq as it exists today.
Imam	prayer leader at Friday Mosques, a descendant of Ali.
Il-Khanate	the Persian branch of the Mongol empire, founded

	by Great Khan Hulagu on the ruins of the Abbasid empire, and ruled by Il-Khans. It fell in 1335.
Iwan	a covered hall in a mosque or palace, usually open at one end.
Jihad	signifies an effort towards a determined objective, a struggle; a form of physical or spiritual struggle against non-believers or apostates.
Kalantar	police-chief.
Karez	irrigation channel, often underground, also known as qanaat. These were the lifeblood of Herat's urban existence, and were fed by the waters of the Hari Rud.
Kart	local Ghurid dynasty that ruled Herat in the wake of the Mongol atrocities, 1245–1381.
Khalq	in Pashtu, 'masses', or 'people'. This refers to a faction of the People's Democratic Party of Afghanistan. Khalq traditionally represented Pashtuns from rural and non-elite sections of Afghan society. They advocated a radical over-throw of Afghan society to set it on an immediate path to a communist utopia.
Khan	a title similar to Lord or Prince, used mainly amongst Mongol and Turkic nomadic tribal group-ings. Khanate and Khanid derives from this, as does the term the Il-Khans, the Persian Mongol empire established by Hulagu Khan in the wake of the destruction of the Abbasid Caliphate in 1258.
Khaneqah	a building reserved for Muslim mystics and Sufis belonging to a Sufi brotherhood.
Kharwar	measure of weight.
Khelat	a robe of honour usually given in the course of diplomatic negotiations, to confer submission on the recipient.
Khiaban	a wide street, or boulevard.
Khorasan	a pre-Islamic and medieval geographical term referring to an area whose four great cities were Balkh, Herat, Nishapur and Merv. The term means

GLOSSARY

'Land where the sun rises' and was in use well into the later nineteenth century; it continues to have meaning for present-day Salafi Islamic fundamentalist groups such as ISIL.

Khutbah — a Friday sermon given by the khatib, or spokesman, in the mosque in which the name of the ruler is mentioned.

Kufic — the oldest calligraphic form of various Arabic scripts. It is a modified form of the old Nabataean script and appears in strikingly angular form.

Khwaja — a patrilineal descendant of Abu Bakr, the first Caliph.

Lala — royal tutor to Safavid princes in Herat, or uncle. The phrase can still be heard on the streets of Herat to this day.

Malek — an aristocratic title with which the Kart dynasty styled themselves during their rule over Herat as Mongol vassals, later changed to the more important title of Sultan.

Madrasa — institution in which Islamic sciences and jurisprudence are taught.

Maidan — town square, often flanked by shops and with a mosque at one end.

Masjed — mosque.

Masjed-e Jam'e — Friday Mosque, or Congregational Mosque.

Masnawi — a formal description of a style of Persian poetry which takes the form of rhyming couplets, literally translated as 'constellation.' Also, a celebrated and lengthy Persian poem written by Jalal al-Din Muhammad Balkhi also known as Rumi, the renowned Persian Sufi saint and poet.

Mawlana — religious scholar of theology and jurisprudence.

Mirza — Persian prince.

Mosalla — an open space outside a mosque in which Muslims pray and congregate. In Herat's Timurid century, this referred to large open courtyards which were surrounded by theological colleges and mosques.

Muezzin — call to prayer.

GLOSSARY

Muhtaseb	one charged with the maintenance of moral virtue, hisba, which indicates the duty of each Muslim to 'promote good and forbid evil'.
Mufti	Islamic legal authority giving an opinion, or fatwa, when asked his opinion on a matter of faith.
Mujahed	one who wages jihad, pl. Mujahideen.
Muqarnas	stalactite-like architectural features which visually support the ribbed dome of a cupola.
Murid	a novice, or disciple, in a Sufi brotherhood.
Nawruz	Persian New Year beginning on 21 March.
Parcham	meaning 'flag' or 'banner' in Persian, this refers to the Parcham faction of the People's Democratic Party of Afghanistan. The Parcham faction traditionally represented a gradual shift towards communism and represented Afghanistan's urban and middle and upper classes.
Paizeh	Ceremonial gift to Mongol vassal allowing rule in Mongol territories in the name of the empire. See also Yarligh.
Pashtunwali	societal code of the Pashtun tribal grouping.
Pir	elder, or, in Sufism, Murshid.
Pirhan tonban	traditional Afghan and Pakistani dress consisting of baggy trousers and knee-length long-sleeved shirt.
Qalah	fortress or citadel. Qalah-ye Ekhtiar al-Din is the name of Herat's famous and ancient citadel, named after a prominent Kart military figure from the fourteenth century.
Qanun	law, secular code of regulations related to Western political systems.
Qasida	an ode in poetic form.
Qazi	judge who applies the Sharia law.
Qiyam	insurrection or uprising.
Quiriltai	Mongol great meeting convened to choose a new khan or ruler at which subjects were required to attend.
Ramadan	Islamic month of fasting.
Safavid	Shia Persian dynasty which ruled over Herat inter-

	mittently 1510–1717, and which is credited with founding the modern Persian state.
Sanad	royal proclamation or warrant which demands action of its subjects.
Sardar	a prince, or leader of the royal house.
Sayyed	patrilineal descendant of the Prophet Muhammad via the sons of his daughter, Fatima.
Shabnama	'night-letter', clandestine publication.
Shah	king.
Shahid	a martyr who dies in the defence of his or her faith against infidels or apostates.
Shahr	town, city.
Sharia	sacred law of Islam.
Shaybanids	Uzbek dynasty claiming descent from a grandson of Chingiz Khan. They threatened and occasionally ruled Herat for much of the sixteenth century, based in Bukhara and Samarqand.
Shaykh	a superior to dervishes.
Shaykh al-Islam	highest legal authority in Islam, who in theory presides over the whole judicial and theological hierarchy.
Shurah	gathering of tribal or religious elders.
Sikka	minting of coins in the name of the ruler—a symbolic gesture of royal prerogative.
Taarof	Persian system of etiquette governing behaviour.
Tariqat	way, path, road; the system of training and rights within a Sufi order.
Timurid	dynasty which ruled in Herat 1381–1510, and under which Herat reached the heights of cultural, architectural and intellectual sophistication.
Ulema	the possessors of knowledge, ilm, religious scholars.
Umma	the Islamic community.
Ustad	a master in a craft or profession.
Waqf	pious foundation, or state land conquered or taken over by the religious community; basis for much Timurid wealth in fifteenth-century Herat.

Watan	fatherland.
Yarligh	ceremonial offering from Mongol Khans to subject conferring authority to rule in the name of the Mongol empire.
Yasa	Mongol law code which is said to have originated with Chingiz Khan and was codified under Mongke Khan.
Zikr	the recitation of esoteric names of Allah, to moving, chanting, rhythms through which the adherents will reach mystical union with God.
Ziyarat	a sacred shrine or tomb visited in the course of a ziyara, a religious visit or pilgrimage.

Map 1: Afghanistan

Map 2: Khorasan

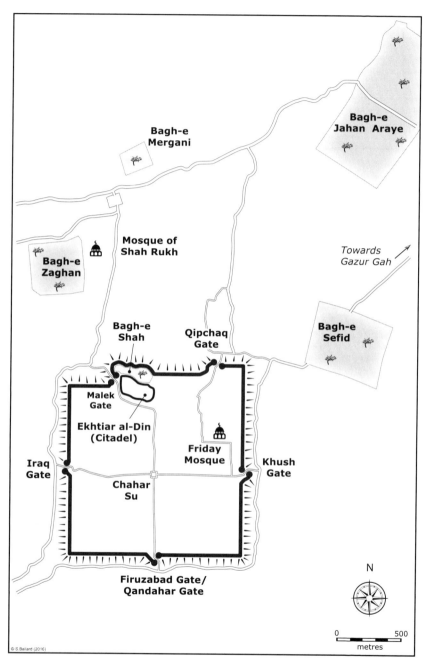

Map 3: Medieval Herat

INTRODUCTION

If anyone should ask which is the pleasantest of cities, you may answer him that it is Herat.
For if the world is like the sea, and the province of Khorasan the oyster contained within,
Then the city of Herat is as the pearl in the middle of that oyster.

Hamdullah Mostowfi, fourteenth-century Persian poet and mystic

In Persia in the year 330 BC, Alexander the Great of Macedon was in a quandary, fretting about the security of his armies. Like so many who followed him, Alexander found himself harassed by those who plundered supply lines from north of the Oxus; his troops were in need of pasture and sustenance, and he longed for the security of high walls. Writing in fourteenth-century Herat, Sayf Ibn Mohammad Ibn Yaqub al-Heravi (known as Sayfi), the city's first great medieval chronicler, notes that Alexander sought to build a fortress which might protect him from raiding tribesmen from over the Oxus. Alexander asked his mother's permission to travel to the unknown lands of Sistan and Khorasan, where he wished to construct his walled city and a strong fortress. Venturing further east into Khorasan, to an oasis watered by the Hari Rud (*Rud* means river in Persian), Alexander drew up plans for the construction of his new fortification and city. He began discussing this project with the local tribes. This site, according to the mythmakers, would become Herat.

Alexander the Great's arrival into the Hari Rud oasis was not well received; potential conquerors rarely are. Against his mother's advice,

1

he remained for two years, trying to win the people of the fertile plain to his cause. During this period Alexander received a missive from Macedon requesting that he leave Herat, for it was feared he would be killed whilst trying to build his fortress. In an attempt to assure the doubters of the viability of this new fortress, Alexander sent home soil samples from each corner of the fertile plain that would one day become Herat. Some parts were hard, some soft, some white, some black: diverse and enigmatic like Herat itself. The soil was duly placed under a carpet, and members of Macedon's elites came to discuss the prospect of founding a city in Khorasan, whilst sitting, unbeknownst to them, on the very same soil on which this city would eventually be built.[1] At first, the nobles were in disagreement; one group said that Herat's geographical isolation would give its inhabitants a rebellious cast of mind; another group countered by saying that Alexander would surely be able to subdue a rabble of Persian tribesmen. These disputing figures had assumed Herat's own contrariness. The following day, when they returned to discuss the matter, miraculously all were in agreement. This was not, however, taken to be a good omen, for Alexander's mother saw in this sudden volte-face a sign of Herat's lack of constancy and the changeable whim of its people. She advised against its construction. Alexander, headstrong, went ahead despite these warnings, setting thousands to work on the four corners of this new city. In a concession to Alexandrian prudence, on the final day of construction he put to death 1,700 local workers and soldiers, and populated the city instead with tribes from Mesopotamia, Persia and the northern reaches of Khorasan.[2]

This apocryphal story is just one of many foundation myths of Herat. Others are equally far-fetched, drawing on characters from Persia's earliest histories: Bahman, Lorhasp, Gushtap and Zohak. Like the city itself, the stories are ambiguous, mysterious even, yet they are preserved in outline through constant retelling to subsequent generations. Despite lacking corroboration, the story of Alexander the Great and his mother at least contains some eternal truths about Herat: the lure which the Hari Rud oasis holds for conquering armies, the changeable, even fickle, nature of its citizens, and the geographical problem of Herat's distance from imperial capitals. During the eight centuries covered by this book, we shall see that Herat is invariably unpredictable, impossible to pin down and repeatedly misunderstood by foreign empires, be they Mongol, Persian, Russian, British or Soviet. We shall also see played out again and again the province's ability to recover from calamitous conquests and to regenerate itself. The story of Alexander, his mother and the soil samples also hints at Herat's calamitous interaction with empire, suggesting that it was the city's fate to mix, clash, rise and fall with imperial whim. When we hear of Herat's soil beneath the carpet in Macedonia, we glimpse the central role that earth will play in this story, even if we are looking back through a biased fourteenth-century lens. Whilst this tale is one amongst many, the story of Alexander and his mother and their role in the founding of Herat is a leitmotif for the city's identity and story, drawing in the great themes that run through this book.

The earliest empirical beginnings of Herat are difficult to pinpoint with any certainty, and certainly less interesting than the myths that have sprung up in place of real facts. The ancient Aryan Zoroastrian text, the *Avesta*, refers to a city named Haraewa (from the Old Persian *harayu*, meaning 'with velocity'),[3] and it is thought that we derive Aria, Arianna and ultimately Herat from this single ancient source.[4] It is entirely fitting, therefore, that the Hari Rud and its oasis are the ontological beginnings of this story. There is no life without water, and Herat's waters are famed for their purity and abundance. It is thought that early Aryan settlers moving to Herat in roughly 1500 BC left their mark on Khorasan's rivers and meadows, but it is not until the Achaemenid era (*c.*550–330 BC) that we hear with any certainty of Herat paying taxes to a fixed empire, thus beginning its story as a liminal outpost in a contested region, and suggesting that Alexander's founding of the city might be a far-fetched tale, even if there is evidence of his having built citadels in Herat and Farah. It is likely, for example, that the city of Areia to which Alexander's chroniclers refer is in fact Herat, suggesting that prior to his arrival in Persia, the Hari Rud oasis had been cultivated and populated for centuries. Given how this strip of watered land, 150 kilometres long and rarely more than 25 kilometres wide, is so suited to inhabitants, it can be said with some certainty that Herat has long been a home to both nomads and sedentary tribes alike.

In Khorasan, from its earliest beginnings to the present day, the ability to produce food to sell and eat and handicrafts to sell and use has been essential to the continued existence of a functioning and flourishing province and city. When we say 'fertility', we are talking about the production of crops, animals, healthy populations and prosperous settled villages and towns. It might be better to think of this as resilience in the face of natural and man-made disasters that are routinely visited upon the city. To understand the significance of Herat's ability to produce crops, to feed its inhabitants, and the armies that periodically marched through the province, we must first acknowledge the precariousness of the tax base—the people—and the fragility of the medieval world. Pestilence, floods, plagues, earthquakes and military conquest all threatened a province's ability to survive and repopulate, and a fertile oasis and plentiful rivers were the only way of ensuring survival. Medieval political systems and dynasties were essentially fragile institutions, just one untimely death of a monarch away from widespread chaos and destruction. Stability stretching out over long periods was a luxury; chaos was the rule. In this vein, Herat's ability to produce fruit and corn, to mine for minerals and precious stones and to irrigate its fields and villages through systems of canals and rivers lends a deeply practical aspect to its legendary fecundity. Fertility and resilience, throughout Herat's history, are one and the same.

For the ancient Greek historian Herodotus, Herat was the bread basket of Asia. From Ibn Haukal, the tenth-century Arab geographer, to a generation of Victorian adventurers and beyond, everyone (this author included) has marvelled at the sweetness of its waters, the lushness of its gardens and its temperate climate. Fruits abound in Herat, fertility incarnate. One tenth-century ruler from Bukhara was so entranced by Herat's grapes, 'as black as pitch and sweet as sugar', that he was distinctly unhappy at the prospect of heading back northwards over the Oxus to resume his patrimony in Central Asia.[5] So sweet are its melons that they were even used as currency in medieval diplomatic exchange. I have vivid memories of wandering through Herat's outlying villages in the spring and summer months, entranced by the overpowering sense of abundance: a cornucopia of fruit, green and water. This fertility is a reliable trope for the province's equally enchanting poetry, and lush green valleys and sweet fruits are a stock refrain for the province's poets and historians. Every time that the city has been sacked and spoiled by wave after wave of conquest, Herat's fertility assumes a reviving role, asserting the province's resilience. A perspicacious nineteenth-century British diplomat, touching on this theme, noted that 'Herat, however, has always displayed a recuperative power in recovering from blows which would entirely have obliterated any place that did not possess great advantages in natural productiveness and commercial development.'[6]

The Hari Rud begins its journey in the Baba mountains of the Hindu Kush range, heading west before it skirts Herat to the south, and then flows towards Jam; after bordering the Islamic Republic of Iran, it disappears into the Kara Kum desert of Turkmenistan on its way north into oblivion. This river is the ultimate victor over conquest, for it has enabled Herat to recover from the deleterious effects of the sieges and conquests which pockmarked the city's history for at least 700 of the 800 years covered in this book. It is no wonder that Heratis refer to themselves as fish swimming in a clear sea of their province; they suffer when they are forced to leave the riverine valley of Herat, as so much in Herat's history takes its cue from its waters and meadows. As a result, we can justifiably read Herat's history as a paean to nature and its indestructability; the river remains, flowing through, giving life and ebbing away like the seasons, long after dynasties and empires have fallen.

To fertility we can add geography as a factor to explain Herat's history of conquest, revival and culture. Perched at the edge of natural frontiers, Herat has long been a city caught between different geographical and cultural zones. The frayed edges of Khorasan, the deserts of Sistan (present-day Helmand, Baluchistan and Farah), the Persian plateau and the Hindu Kush all sit within striking distance of Herat. Not quite on the Silk Road, but close enough to profit from its trade, Herat province lies where desert and mountain give way to pasture and river, making it both protected and isolated; self-sufficient yet vulnerable. Herat has always attracted and repelled forces, from the local raiders against whom Alexander the Great sought protection, to the armies of Chingiz Khan, Shah Ismail I Safavid and nineteenth-century British and Russian empires (for whom Herat became an unhealthy obsession). As a consequence of these factors, Herat's history is a regional story, the history of Central Asia, Persia and beyond.

Given its existence as a fertile oasis city on routes linking the Indus to Persia, it is not surprising to note that Herat has suffered through the centuries. Citing every sacking of the city would take space and time, yet without acknowledging these frequent episodes of sack, siege and regeneration, we would be doing Herat's history a disservice. How Herat attracts and recovers from conquest is as much a part of its story as the Hari Rud itself. As one would expect, the city's population has mirrored its fortunes, rising and falling as different empires came and went. One chronicler estimated that 190,000 soldiers fought for the city in 1221, and over a million souls died during the conflict of 1222.[7] Although these figures represent a chronicler's exaggeration, they put the population many times above the meagre 6,000–7,000 estimated by one nineteenth-century traveller to Herat when the city was at one of its lowest ebbs.[8] Herat's population later rose to around 22,000, before settling somewhere between 45,000 and 50,000 for the nineteenth and early twentieth centuries. Timurid Herat, when the city was at its very height of regional and international renown, was a city of some 150,000 inhabitants, flourishing shops and villages and fertile meadows which skirted the edges of the Hari Rud. Today, it is estimated that roughly 1 million souls live in Herat province.

* * *

Amidst the moving empires and rising powers, geographical terms are paramount throughout this book; they are the shifting frames in which the story hangs and moves.[9] Khorasan itself is a geographical concept dating back to the pre-Islamic and early-Islamic eras. The Middle Persian name means 'Land where the sun rises', referring to its eastern orientation in relation to the lands of present-day Iraq and Iran. Originally brought into being by the Sassanid empire, Khorasan has shrunk and expanded over time, but we can broadly say that its four leading cities have consistently been Merv, Balkh, Herat and Nishapur. These were designated as the four capitals of the Umayyad and Abbasid empires when these dynasties ruled over Khorasan and this has proved the most durable geographical concept of Khorasan. Its eastern borders give onto Hindustan, roughly following a line south from present-day Afghanistan's Hindu Kush mountain range into Baluchistan. Its western edges run through present-day Iran; Baluchistan in the south and the Oxus to the north complete the roughest of outlines. Khorasan's close association with early Islamic dynasties has given it a certain cachet amongst modern Salafi Jihadi groups, such as al-Qaeda and the Islamic State of Iraq and the Levant (ISIL). Their implicit rejection of the concept of the modern nation state has helped to resurrect Khorasan's contemporary importance as a historical seat of insurrectionary Islam and millenarianism. There is a saying of the Prophet, a *hadith*, in which Khorasan is afforded special status in millenarian Jihadism: 'If you see the black flags coming from Khorasan, join that army, even if you have to crawl over ice, for this is the army of the Caliph, the Mahdi and no one can stop that army until it reaches Jerusalem.'[10] This has been used as a rallying cry for militant groups in Khorasan for decades, and it is no accident that Abu Musa Zarqawi, a key figure in al-Qaeda in Iraq until his death in 2006, spent time in Herat prior to the al-Qaeda attacks on the World Trade Center buildings and the Pentagon. Khorasan is, however, more famous for its cultural achievements, producing mystics, poets, philosophers, scientists and artists for centuries.[11] Those who claim a special place in their violent millenarianism and nihilistic slaughter for Khorasan do the province's culture and art a great disservice.

Aside from Khorasan, under early Islamic dynasties from the eighth century, Iraq-e Ajam and Iraq-e Arab were significant provinces in the Islamic world. Iraq-e Ajam (Greater Iraq, or Persian Iraq) covered the space of central and western Iran as it is today, and was a development of the ancient territories of ancient Media. Iraq-e Arab covered the ancient province of Babylonia, stretching over central and southern provinces of Iraq as it exists today. When I use the term Iraq-e Ajam, I am referring to this Persian Iraq, covering the cities of Esfahan, Ray, Qazvin and Kashan. Timurid and Seljukid empires divided their administrations between the broad territories of Iraq-e Ajam and Arab and also Khorasan. These two Islamic geographical entities were separated by the Zagros mountains, which still provide the same function to this day, dividing the modern nation states of the Islamic Republic of Iran and Iraq.

In Herat's medieval period, it remains a great city of Khorasan, a central bureaucratic and trading pillar in the region, along with Merv, Balkh and Nishapur. As this story moves into the Safavid era, Herat continues to be an important city of Khorasan, but is increasingly drawn into the Afghan sphere by the arrival of Pashtun tribes into positions of influence and power on the borders between Mughal India and the eastern reaches of the Persian Safavid empire: present-day Helmand, Qandahar and the city of Multan. With the arrival of Pashtun rulers, Herat begins to shift within an Afghan 'nation', but we must at all times be aware that localism and Herat's sense of itself as an independent city is of the upmost importance to its self-image. Herat's early entry into the Afghan nation was by no means smooth. Even the notion of an 'Afghan' nation is a contested one, for historically the word Afghan, or *Aughan* in its Herati pronunciation, refers to the Pashtun tribes, and as such is a term fraught with disputed meanings. (For clarity's sake, when I use the term Afghanistan I am referring to the nation created by Ahmad Shah Durrani in 1747, an entity which stretched from Herat in the west to Peshawar in the east.) In the nineteenth century, as European empires descended on the region, Khorasan was a more useful geographical term than the hazy notions of Persia, Afghanistan or Iraq; the Persian Qajar dynasty's 'Governor of Khorasan' occupied a prestigious position at court. For much of the nineteenth century, Afghanistan was referred to as Khorasan; Ahmad Shah Durrani (1747–72), the first ruler of a roughly united nation, referred to himself as King of Khorasan. Although the notion of Khorasan was officially rendered obsolete by the emergence of nation states, it persists as a powerful concept for Iran and Afghanistan to this day.

Herat has played host to Zoroastrians, Arabs, Christians, Jews, Hindus, Mongols and tribes from north of the Oxus. The tenth-century Arab geographer Ibn Haukal talks of Nestorian Christian churches in and around the city, and Jewish and Hindu figures appear in significant yet minority roles in the city's story well into the twentieth century. Herat's Zoroastrian communities, before Sunni Islam took hold in the tenth century, were the bedrock of Herat's faith community, but slid from prominence in the tenth century when its Muslims were urged on by the city's chief mullah to burn the Zoroastrian temple to the ground. When a petition to have it rebuilt came before the city's authorities, 4,000 Herati Muslims testified that no such temple had ever existed, thus denying the fire worshippers the chance to rebuild what fire had destroyed.

Herat spent almost two centuries avoiding wholesale conversion to Islam, but succumbed in AD 870 to soldiers who would later found the

Saffarid dynasty. It has never questioned its faith since that point, and at its core Herat is a city of Islam, a city of Hanafi Islamic legalistic traditions and a stronghold of Sunni orthodoxy.[12] Herat's Sunni Muslims are predominantly Hanafi, adherents of one of the four major schools of Islam, the others being Hanbali, Shaafi and Maliki. Hanafi jurisprudence is the most widely followed amongst the world's Sunni Muslims, and its allowance of analogy and discussion of matters of Islamic law mean that this school is seen as more moderate than, for example, Hanbali Islamic jurisprudence. Although Herat has always been a city of Hanafi traditions, this has not been to the exclusion of other schools. Indeed, the city's patron saint, Abdullah Ansari, was an adherent of the Hanbali school of Sunni Islamic jurisprudence. Shia Islam, too, has long had a place within Herat's walls, especially from the time of the Shia Safavid empire's early-sixteenth-century conquests into Khorasan. Herat's Shia have long occupied the best places in the bazaar, the most prosperous of the city's four quarters. Herat's Shia Muslims have traditionally been jewellers, tinsmiths, shoemakers and shopkeepers, but have also been targeted for their faith; Herat's Sunni pride can sometimes boil over into anti-Shia words and deeds, as one early-twentieth-century Iranian diplomat found in Herat, almost to his mortal cost.[13]

Herat's Friday Mosque, within the Old City walls, is the city's focal point, its orthodox soul. It has been a home for scholars and theologians, yet judging by its east–west orientation, as opposed to facing Mecca, it is likely that this was already a sacred space in pre-Islamic times, possibly a Buddhist monastery or even the torched Zoroastrian temple. The Friday Mosque's main structures were built under the Ghurid dynasty, whose greatest ruler Ghias al-Din Ghuri (r.1163–1202) reigned in the decades before the Mongol apocalypse burned its way through Khorasan. The stunning blue inscriptions on a Ghurid portal to the south of the main entrance in a tucked away space bear eloquent testament to Herat's long-standing artistic genius. They are a beautiful turquoise blue and they rise with geometric precision and grace towards the tip of the *iwan*. The mosque experienced restoration in the fifteenth century, when Herat assumed its place as a global capital of culture and refinement under the Timurids, and again during Herat's sleepy mid-twentieth century.

Nancy Dupree's peerless guidebook on Afghanistan from the 1960s, packed with fascinating history and photos revealing a magical world now lost to conflict, describes entering the courtyard of Herat's Friday Mosque in the following terms: 'The blaze of colour and wealth of design which delights the eye upon entering the courtyard is a sight never to be forgotten.'[14] I remember my first visit there on a hot and shimmering afternoon in August 2009. Walking through the corridor which leads into the courtyard was like advancing down a tunnel of light, as the marble floor of the courtyard shone at the end of the darkened passage; a few beggars lined the edges and silhouettes dressed in *burkha*s or *pirhan tonban* (Afghan clothing for men consisting of loose trousers and long shirt) moved towards me, shadows against the reflected light of the marble floor. On that day, the courtyard did dazzle and render speechless, all around was a wonderful tension between the intricacy of tile-work and motif and the serene majesty of a calming place of God. Students were reading Qurans and a few dozed in the shadow of the niches which run along the edges of the courtyard. Late-summer lethargy hung over the place, yet a quiet industry was discernable from the hushed comings and goings of students, mullahs and those who had come to pray.

Alongside Herat's Sunni orthodoxy is a city of shrines and saints, a valley of Sufis whose brotherhoods have played key roles in the city's history from the tenth century onwards. Herat as a whole is famed for its Sufi heritage, and it for this reason that it is often referred to as the 'Dust of the Saints', so imbued is the place with Sufism and Sufi masters. For centuries Herat's Sufi and Sunni Islamic traditions existed in near total harmony; the Sunni suspicion of Sufi movements we associate with contemporary Islam was not a factor for the majority of the period covered by this book. Sufism has long existed alongside orthodox Sunni schools of jurisprudence and worship. Sufi saints occupied positions from mediators between Mongol and Herati nobles in the thirteenth century, to freedom fighters in the 1980s; Sufism runs in Herat's very blood, and shrines dot the city and countryside and go deep into its people's consciousness.[15] Sufis are a constant refrain in Herat's story, always there in the background to provide a check against hubris, to mediate between imperial powers, to work miracles when needed and to resist tyranny at all times.

Herat's most famous son or daughter, secular or spiritual, must surely be the eleventh-century Sufi mystic, poet, theologian and intellect, Khwajah Abdullah Ansari.[16] Ansari was born in AD 1006 in Herat, where he spent the majority of his life, barring the occasional exile. Ansari is said to have been precocious beyond words; he was his father's assistant when aged five, and a figure of standing in Herat's council of Sufis when aged fourteen; he memorised over 100,000 verses and wrote on subjects ranging from mysticism to theology to poetry and philosophy. The twentieth-century travel writer Robert Byron's pithy summation of this saint surely does the man an injustice, but is amusing nonetheless: 'Khoja [sic] Abdullah Ansari died in the year 1088 at the age of eighty-four, because some boys threw stones at him while he was at penance. One sympathises with those boys: even among saints he was a prodigious bore.'[17] As a Shaykh al-Islam of the Abbasid empire, Ansari brought international renown to Herat and cemented it as a place of global religious standing. Today many see Ansari as Herat's patron saint, conscience and father, and stories of his intercession on Herat's behalf are commonplace.

Ansari's shrine is at Gazur Gah—literally, 'Bleaching Ground'—a site to the north-east of the Old City walls. This space is a monument to his precocious genius, to his paternal care for the city of Herat, a place where Herat's holy and illustrious offspring come to die and be buried. Gazur Gah is Herat's heart, its soul and its conscience all in one, embracing Sufi traditions and offering pilgrims a chance to pray at the tomb of the city's patron saint. The first ruler over a broadly united Afghanistan, Dost Mohammad Khan (d.1863), is buried here, bringing Herat's story very much into line with the Afghan nation as it currently exists. Today Gazur Gah still functions as a working shrine complex, with tombstones and prayer spots and the steady stream of visitors. Buses wait outside the shrine complex, disgorging respectfully chatter-ing schoolchildren who mingle with the venerable Sufi *pirs* tending the tombstones to Herat's fallen heroes. It is invariably a calming and respectful place, despite the children and tourists. The inner courtyard is a sea of gleaming white tombstones, faded blue tiles clinging to walls worn down by devotion, footfall and years. Whether summer or win-ter, old men brush dust or snow or water or leaves from the tomb-stones, and pilgrims come to pay their respects to Herat's ultimate protector or to the city's many great figures.

If geography and the fertility of the Hari Rud define Herat's evolu-tion as a city, and religion gives it a conscience and a soul, then it is through culture, poetry, textiles and arts that the city has traditionally made sense of the passage of time. Herat has long been seen as a seat of learning, be it theological, scientific or philosophical. It has played host to philosophers, artists, scientists and some of the most beguiling poets and painters the medieval world ever saw. Herat's reputation as a place of poets and artists lives on to this day; dating from the mosque's restoration in 1943, a calligraphy of lines of poetry runs across tiles on the columns of the arcades in the mosque's main courtyard: Jami, Ansari, Saadi. This is as eloquent a tribute as can be made to Herat's complementary traditions of poetry and Islam, orthodox and Sufi, which have coexisted for so long. Cultural brilliance provided a function throughout the city's history, for it seduced invaders, persuading them to adopt Persian cultural and artistic norms, and thus ensured that it was Herati, Persian culture that would outlive the conqueror's imported customs. Culture, poetry and learning sustained Herat throughout its torturous history of sack and siege, destruction and renewal. These artistic achievements are, like the Hari Rud, the victors over ambitious conquerors and hubristic emperors. It is only natural therefore that this book should take its title from a line of medieval poetry in which poetry and fertility are celebrated as one.

Yet however much we seek to define Herat, the city remains an enigma. A popular saying about Herat and its people is 'Herat has neither water nor weather, currency nor rate, friend nor acquaintance.'[18] Contradictions abound in Herat: pious and hedonistic, orthodox and Sufi, warlike and peaceful, strong and vulnerable. So many world conquerors have misunderstood its importance, overestimated or underestimated its strengths. Mongol leaders periodically sacked the city for some act of disobedience on the part of the local ruling dynasty, and then withdrew, confused, having set the rebellious vassal back on the throne; they often achieved little more than repeated promises of loyalty from the leader whom they had set out to crush. British diplomats and politicians would spend a century debating whether Herat was, or wasn't, the definitive 'key' to India through which Russian armies would march on their way to take Britain's own imperial jewel. Herat struggled to find a place for itself in the emergent Afghan nation of the nineteenth-century, remaining an embattled and semi-independent enclave, menaced by Persia and Britain, Russia and Pashtun ruling dynasts from Kabul and Qandahar. British and Russian diplomats wrestled with Herat's identity and geography in the late nineteenth-century, and the Afghan Boundary Commission drew up the borders which largely define Herat's western edges to this day; the result of this was a twentieth-century obsolescence and political irrelevance from which Herat has not recovered. During the post-2001 conflict against the Taliban, fevered European and US speculation surrounded Herat's supposed links to the Islamic Republic of Iran; Kabul, too, suspected nefarious dealings between mullahs of Tehran and warlords of Herat. Herat's enigma endures to this day. One of the city's foremost academics and historians, Ali Kaveh, sat with me in his house in the summer of 2014 discussing this very issue, consumed with the question of why Herat was not more closely involved in Afghanistan's political life, not better represented in Kabul, and so often eyed suspiciously by the capital when it has always played such a central role in the history of the nation. How can a city that is so patriotic be so misunderstood by its capital and by its neighbours? Unpicking various strands of Herat's history will go some way towards a better understanding of Herat's place in a modern Afghanistan.

For a long time I wanted to pinpoint Herat, to bend a city's identity to my will and find a pithy phrase to set the definitive seal on an understanding of Khorasan's pearl. Yet the more I read, spoke and listened, the more I realised that this is a city whose very energy, heterogeneous nature, vibrancy and contrariness make that task a fool's errand. When living in Herat, I was often just as shocked as prudish Victorian gentlemen at Herat's life force and energy, as censorious of the ruling classes as the Mughal emperor Babur when he noted the decadence and debauchery of its Timurid princes, as transfixed as Robert Byron when looking at the crumbling remains of a truly great civilisation, and as horrified as so many others at the violence which lurks under the surface, which has shaped it over the centuries. Yet the city always draws me, and others, back. Religion, fertility, violence, greed, lust, art, poetry, independence chaos, generosity, kindness and beauty; these all form indelible parts of a complicated city, and when we layer on the vicissitudes of conquest and geography, we might, just might, come close to understanding Herat.

* * *

Herat's basic geometric plan was dictated by its Greek conquerors from the fourth century BC. Through centuries of struggle this plan remained largely intact until the early twentieth century. The walls were its protection from the very real threat of invasion. So too were the gates, and yet they also welcomed traders, diplomats and intellectuals who had come to visit Herat, or to seek shelter within its walls. One English visitor to the city, writing in the 1960s, noted how Herat's 'walls both isolated and insulated the city', going on to describe how 'all contacts with the outer world were carefully filtered through the five gates, and the gates themselves became the meeting points of urbanites and rural people'.[19] Herat's gates once marked these points of ingress and egress (gate names have altered over the ages, but I use the most durable and current of the names): the Qandahar Gate (south, and known in medieval times as the Firuzabad Gate), the Khush Gate (east), the Iraq Gate (west) and the Malek Gate (north), corresponding with bazaars which bore these same names. The eastern gate, the Khush Gate, takes its name from the happiness that awaited those who left through that portal to the pleasant meadows and garden lying to the east of the Old City walls.[20] There is also a fifth gate, the Qipchaq Gate, which sits at the north-eastern part of the Old City. Huge towers sat at the four corners of the city, and Abdul Wasay Najimi, an expert on Herat, notes that there were around 150 towers and bastions in and around the Old City.[21] The walls and gates and towers were once ringed by moats, as deep as 5 metres and as wide as 15 metres. Today, these walls, which had once struck fear into Chingiz Khan himself, are crumbled, barely visible. Its gates have been replaced by roundabouts, no longer the heavy portals that had repelled invaders from the steppe.

The Old City of Herat, as distinct from its modern suburbs which lie to its north-east, occupies a near perfect one-mile square. It is oriented north–south, east–west. This square itself sits on a lateral north-east–south-east pattern of surrounding fields and villages, which slope with the land and the distributaries of the Hari Rud.[22] The Old City plan is divided into quarters, bazaars, with each edge of the city having a gate through which it would take from and give to the outside world. The Malek Bazaar is in the north, the Khush Bazaar to the east, the Qandahar Bazaar to the south, the Iraq Bazaar to the west; they met in the centre, the Chahar Su (literally, four ways), traditionally the hub of the city's trading. The bazaars were once a profusion of covered buildings selling bejewelled swords, bows inset with tourmaline and jade, vessels of coral, illuminated manuscripts and silks. Today, Herat's bazaars are no longer covered, save for one restored by the Agha Khan Trust for Culture, but instead the city is served by shops lining the streets where the city walls once stood and in and around the remains of the Old City. Herat has always been a proud trading hub for the region and the province, and one visitor to the city in the 1960s noted how 'There are 5,500 shops located within easy walking distance of 80,000 people, and the organization of commercial space is such that any bazaar is within ten minutes' walk of any home.'[23]

The Old City still retains some of its pleasingly confusing warren-like maze of streets, streets that appalled nineteenth-century European visitors to the city for their filth and lack of coherence. This compact maze of streets provides a form of protection against Herat's wind that lasts 120 days, blowing hot and dusty through the summer months. The wind is a blessing as the heat of July and August hangs over the city. When the wide boulevards of the new city were constructed in the 1930s, smart Heratis co-opted unwitting Qandahari cloth merchants to set up stall where the hot wind howled up and down dusty avenues.[24] Getting revenge on Pashtuns from Qandahar for centuries of supposed tyranny would have been sweet indeed for Herat's merchant classes.

In the Old City, as elsewhere, water is the guiding principle for life. The alleyways follow strange cambers and contours, channelling sewage and water down to culverts. Quarters are numbered according to when at what point they receive water from the Injil canal, inextricably tying Herat's Old City to nature and water. The north-eastern quarter of the Old City is called *Awwal*, meaning first in Persian, because it is this quarter that receives water first from the Injil canal. It is no surprise to learn that this is the most prosperous quarter, home to the city's Friday Mosque. Herat's most squalid quarter of the Old City has always been the quarter which received the least and the last water.[25] Urban and nature are one and the same in Herat.

The imposing Qalah-ye Ekhtiar al-Din citadel (*qalah* means citadel in Persian), named after a fourteenth-century Herati governor, still dominates the Old City. It sits on a mound of previous iterations, built up over centuries by various conquerors. The citadel had its own entry port in the north-west, called the Malek Gate, and a second gate provided access to the mosque quarter; the availability of water probably explains the location of these main structures in the northern part of the Old City. Herat's citadel has seen Arab, Kurdish, Greek, Mongol, Persian, Russian, British and Soviet imperial armies; medieval would-be conquerors trembled when faced with the sight of its walls, and countless would-be resisters sought sanctuary within its walls. In Taliban times the citadel functioned as a home for government, of sorts: a prison and a fortress. Today it is neutered: a museum.

As befitting a city which is both connected and isolated, it is natural that one of Herat's most enduring and celebrated monuments is a bridge, the Pul-e Malan. The bridge, whose twenty-six arches are graceful and solid, if slightly dilapidated today, is said to have been built by Bibi Nur, a female saint of Herat from over a thousand years ago. Her mixture of clay with eggshells gave the bridge its legendary durability. That it has ferried traffic south, armies, traders, spies, emperors and so many in between, for over a millennium, says a lot for Bibi Nur's building techniques. (Her shrine in the city is famously able to grant whatever wishes one requests, so long as one visits on a Tuesday evening).[26] Herat is by no means closed or parochial, despite strong strains of localism; it greets and welcomes visitors with the grace one would expect of a city of whispering canals, rose gardens and plentiful fruit. Fleeing emperors have sought refuge in Herat; fleeing soldiers too. With the arrival of each nomadic tribe and conquering army, its tribesmen and women would become seduced by the easy life of the city and by Herat's charms of 'zephyr-like sweet breezes' that take the edge off the heat of summer, and the sweet waters that run along the oasis.[27] Their attraction to Herat dulled their martial vigour, lulling them into a pleasing existence of gardens, artistic patronage, an easy life of luxury. Herat attracts, seduces, collapses, recovers and then repeats.

* * *

This book is both a narrative history of the city of Herat and also a personal story, for it was in Herat that I worked with the International Committee of the Red Cross (ICRC) and United Nations Educational, Scientific and Cultural Organization (UNESCO) between 2009 and 2014. Herat will always have a special place in my heart. I first went there in the late summer of 2009, when the city toiled and slumbered, stoically, through the holy month of Ramadan. It was quiet and slow and my job was to interpret Persian in the prisons. Initially, I had almost no idea what the Heratis were saying as I'd studied Iranian Farsi, and in Herat the dialect spoken is Dari, which, although close to its Iranian cousin, is far enough away to have kept me up at night in fear of the next day of interpreting. Gratifyingly, I was not alone in struggling to decipher Herati Dari. A twentieth-century Persian diplomat spent a year in Herat in 1929–30, and at the end of his account of his time in the city he added a glossary of Herati phrases, translated into Farsi. I was pleased to read that he too had struggled with Herat's beautifully rounded and comforting dialect; he even made a few mistakes in his translations from Herati to Farsi. Herat was my first taste of Afghanistan, and I have always enjoyed walking its streets and meeting its witty, charming, proud, intelligent, cunning, helpful, compassionate and generous people; I have come to love Herat as a second home.

This book is not a complete narrative account of the province and the city's history, and neither is it thematic; through events it tries to answer what makes Herat the city it is today, and why. I have used seminal events as set pieces through which to tell a city's story, through which to make some sense of Herat's complex identity, and I have structured the book along dynastic lines, charting their rise and fall as seen from Herat. I have used Persian sources as far as possible, but not exclusively, as foreign travellers' accounts are excellent sources for seeing what the Heratis cannot, or for admitting what they won't. I begin this book in the early thirteenth century with the arrival of Mongol armies into Khorasan, and end with the arrival of the US empire to Afghanistan in the chaotic days of hope and despair that gathered around the fall of the Taliban in the autumn of 2001. Herat is a city defined by interaction with empires, and as such it felt correct that it should be cast in an imperial frame.

At the dawn of the thirteenth century, Khorasan was a wealthy and prosperous trading region and Herat was one of its four great cities, alongside Balkh, Nishapur and Merv. Herat had flitted in and out of various imperial grasps since the Arab conquests of the eighth and ninth centuries, repelling and attracting in equal measure.[28] In the early thirteenth century, a Ghurid puppet in the service of the Khwarazmian dynasty ruled Herat; in 1221 it would face its most destructive foe: Chingiz Khan.[29]

1

DESTRUCTION AND RENEWAL

HERAT IN THE SHADOW OF THE MONGOLS AND BEYOND,
1221–1381

In 1218, a caravan of 400 Mongol traders arrived at the Silk Road oasis town of Otrar in present-day Kazakhstan. They were representatives of the emerging Mongol empire, a military force of terrifying power and ruthlessness then under the leadership of Chingiz Khan, and they had come to Otrar to trade.[1] Now a ghost town, in the thirteenth century Otrar was an eastern outpost of the Khwarazm dynasty with whom the Mongols enjoyed cordial relations. These relations were informed by a pragmatic recognition of regional power and a mutual desire for wealth and trade. Yet beneath these practicalities lay suspicion and thrusting regional ambition. It was here, in this oasis town, that the fates of Herat and Khorasan were sealed.[2]

The governor of Otrar quickly arrested the Mongol merchants on suspicion of spying for Chingiz Khan: most likely a well-founded suspicion, for this was a time when merchants, moving between cities, often worked as information gatherers. Otrar's governor accordingly had all but one of the merchants executed. The lone survivor brought news to Chingiz Khan, who in turn sent envoys to Otrar to demand retribution for the merchants' execution. The subsequent execution of these emissaries was a more than sufficient *casus belli* for Chingiz Khan.

He launched a mighty Mongol conquest from the steppe, a conquest that would scar the landscape of Khorasan and Herat for centuries. In the words of the thirteenth-century Persian historian Juvaini: 'For every drop of their [the merchants'] blood, there flowed a whole Oxus.'[3] Otrar fell in February 1220. Juvaini noted that the Mongol army forced the governor of Otrar to 'drink the cup of annihilation and don the garb of eternity'.[4] Moving through what is now Central Asia, Chingiz Khan, with his son Tolui at his side and the Mongol army behind him, announced himself to the people of Bokhara as 'the punishment of God'. They blazed a trail of destruction through Central Asia and beyond.[5] The province of Khorasan was 'rendered like the palm of a hand' as its cities, Balkh, Merv and Nishapur, all suffered appalling devastation.[6] The fourteenth-century Herati historian Sayfi, in his *Tarikh namah-ye Herat* (History Book of Herat), recounts the cruel destruction of one province to the east of Herat in which every single living thing was ordered to be executed in revenge for the death of Chingiz's favoured grandson, Tumaki.[7]

Tolui's army of Mongols and captured conscripts entered Herat from the lush northern pasturelands of Badghis in the early spring of 1221, encircling the city and camping in the meadows of Beshuran to the south of Herat's walls. The governor of Herat had already prepared for war, building walls and ramparts and 'raising the banner of Islam' against the infidel Mongols.[8] With 190,000 men at arms gathered within the city, as per Sayfi's account, Herat felt confident enough to murder the Mongols' first envoy in a surprising show of defiance. Herat had very publicly refused the offer of surrender in return for submission to the Mongol yoke, and had chosen to resist. The Mongols replied with a fierce assault; any Herati caught was to be killed. The Mongol invaders set up catapults and mangonels at the four corners of the walled city, and they began to batter Herat into submission. On the first day of real fighting, Sayfi writes of around 30,000 losing their lives, amongst whom were 1,700 Mongol nobles. Skirmishes and fighting continued for seven days and nights; on the eighth day, the governor of Herat fell in battle, leaving the city without a leader. In an atmosphere of desperation, and facing the threat of further destruction, cracks appeared within Herat's hitherto united resistance. Some wished to surrender; others wished to defend their city against the Mongol army.[9] Tolui, sensing division, rode to beneath Herat's southern gate, flanked by his most trusted horsemen. On reaching the outer moat, he dismounted and cried out to the besieged city, his voice striking the walls, 'O, people of Herat! If you wish to find safety, lay aside your arms from the fight, turn your faces towards submission and obedience; be tame so that you can fully appreciate the dignity and order of the Mongols.'[10]

Tolui's words placated Herat, and won the day for those who had sought peace, yet rumours of previous Mongol atrocities Khorasan would surely have made this an uneasy surrender. It fell to Herat's chief weaver, Ezz al-Din Moqaddam Heravi, to lead a delegation of a hundred weavers and tailors from within the city to parlay with the Mongols, offering as tokens of their submission 'nine robes of expensive cloth'.[11] By choosing weavers and tailors to represent the city, Herat hoped to dazzle the invaders with beautiful clothes. Herat was then, and still is, widely famed for its tailors and weavers, silk spinners and dyers, and the artisans' pleas and gifts were accepted. Save for 12,000 local soldiers, whose loyalty to the Khwarazm Shah earned them death in the citadel, the population of Herat was saved from execution. After stripping Herat of its transportable wealth and carting away its prominent artists and nobles, the Mongols left the city under the dual control of the Mongol governor, Monketai, and a Herati named Abu Bakr Maruchaq. Despite this simulacrum of control, Herat remained tense. In reality it was by no means submissive.

The anger of a conquered city soon erupted in an uprising that caused Herat's total devastation. Some at the time suggested that a defeat of the Mongol army in Parwan, near the site of today's US military base at Bagram, was the cause of the rebellion. Yet Sayfi, citing his source as a venerable local Sufi shaykh, claims that the uprising was in fact instigated by the residents of Kalyoun, one of the few citadels in Herat province not conquered by Chingiz Khan.[12] When 'spring was at the edge of its beauty', Kalyoun's undefeated soldiery infiltrated Herat disguised as merchants, their weapons concealed under heavy clothing worn for crisp spring mornings.[13] They sold their wares in the covered bazaars, and when the opportunity presented itself they killed the hated puppet governor, Abu Bakr Maruchaq, at the foot of the citadel. This was the signal for an uprising. Each Mongol soldier found was executed on the spot; the citizenry rushed out from windows, roofs and doors and hurtled down blind tangled alleys to take part in a spate of revenge killing, hoping to drive the Mongols from Herat for good. These rebels took their city back from the Mongols, and appointed two local men to rule over a liberated Herat: a man of arms, Malek Mobarez al-Din Sabzawar, and a man of God, Khwajah Abdul Rahman Ghizani. Their rule was to be short-lived, and would end as it had begun, through force of arms and bloodshed.

'The dead have become living. This time, cut off heads; you must slaughter the entire city of Herat.'[14] With these words, Chingiz Khan dispatched the Mongol general, 'the accursed' Eljigidei, at the head of 80,000 men, to take his revenge on Herat in November 1221. Eljigidei arrived at the northern banks of the Hari Rud and began raising levies from 'the surrounds of Khorasan, the mountainous hamlets of Turkestan, from Shiburghan and Afghanistan' (this refers to areas to the south of Herat—Farah, Sistan and Helmand).[15] The brutal eight-month siege ran through a frozen winter; the resistance was heroic. Yet in June 1222 Herat was taken after a furious assault on the southern walls of the city. As the Mongol troops stormed the city, Chingiz Khan's orders were carried out to the letter. Sayfi wrote that 'Inside and outside, the canals ran red with blood; no being was left alive.'[16] Moats were filled in with earth, the citadel was razed to the ground, and for eight days the Mongol troops did nothing but slaughter, burn, pillage and sack. Sayfi gives the final figure of those dead as over 1.5 million. Although this figure is a vast exaggeration, we should see it as the chronicler's response to the incomprehensible tragedy that had been visited on Herat: a whole city destroyed. In an act of vindictiveness, on reaching the village of Obeh, to the east of Herat, Eljigidei sent back 2,000 Mongols to hunt down and kill any remaining survivors who might have hidden amongst the ruins. Legend has it that as these last Mongol troops left the city, their slaughter complete, an old Herati man crawled out of his hiding place, sat down amidst the ruins and rubble, and said, 'Phew, thank God that's over. Now at last we can have some peace and quiet.'

* * *

Of Herat's pre-1221 population, some sixteen men are said to have remained.[17] A band of survivors, led by a local religious figure, a *Khatib* (religious preacher) from the village of Jaghartan, returned from their ruined villages to an equally ruined Herat to find death in the charred remains of every house and street. There was nothing left of their city. It is little wonder that Sayfi wrote that 'For twenty days they did little but wail and lament their loss.'[18] For the next few years, these men and women camped first in a bathhouse in the east of the city and then, when their numbers swelled, they moved to take refuge under the cupola of the mausoleum of Herat's Ghurid king, Ghias al-Din (r.1157–1202), located in the Friday Mosque. They survived a famine in 1225 and endured a winter of appalling bleakness. These unlucky survivors eked out an existence through scavenging and banditry, sending out raiding parties in all directions to look for signs of life. Robbing an Egyptian caravan of silk and sugar on its way to northern China provided some sustenance. It was said that 'Each man took five *kharwar*s [one *kharwar* is roughly what one can expect to fit on the back of a pack-animal] of sugar cane and one of fine pure silk. To this day they are known as the sugar-eaters.'[19] Many amongst this group of desperate survivors wanted to leave Herat and head elsewhere, but were told by the *Khatib* of Jaghartan (hereafter *Khatib*), their guide and leader, that the whole of Khorasan was desolate: 'From here to Mazandaran, no one can live.'[20]

For sixteen years, Herat remained stricken and barely populated. It was not until 1236 that Chingiz Khan's son and successor, the Great Khan Ogodei, whom Sayfi praises for his kindness to Muslims, set about rebuilding the city and its surrounds.[21] As was the Mongol custom in the aftermath of conquest, Herat's urban craftsmen and artisans had been taken to the Mongol court at Karakorum in 1221 to add lustre and sophistication to an expanding world empire.[22] Herat's weavers, silk makers and artisans soon found themselves spinning and weaving at the Mongol court, and it was their skill which would be Herat's salvation. One of Chingiz Khan's wives had given her son, the then Prince Ogodei, a Herati suit of finely wrought silk and gold; its fine beauty attracted no little attention at the Mongol court. Prince Ogodei ordered Herat's exiled weavers to produce more silk garments. Herat's chief weaver, Ezz al-Din Moqaddam, did as ordered, but the quality disappointed Ogodei. He asked, 'How could such beautiful cloth be so lacking in the skill and lustre of those which I have from Herat?' The reply from the cunning Herati weaver was that the freshness of Herat's water and its temperate climate were the key ingredients that gave its silks the beauty which had so captivated the Mongol court.[23] Consequently, the weaver and fifty of his family and friends were allowed to return to Herat. *Khatib* and his sugar eaters met their arrival with joy and relief, rushing out some five *farsangs* (one *farsang* is roughly 4 miles) from the city to meet their old townsfolk, and ending a celebratory homecoming with a joyous celebration in Herat's Friday Mosque. These two groups—the hardy survivors, and the tailors and silk spinners—set about rebuilding Herat, aided by the fertile Hari Rud oasis.

Sayfi's account of these years of rebuilding and regeneration has a harmonious and egalitarian quality to it. It is a tribute to the importance of water, the life-giving properties of Herat's climate and the strength of community fostered in the dark days of the Mongol apocalypse. He talks of rich and poor joining together two-by-two to yoke the plough and scatter the seeds, and he describes how the people gathered together to divert the northern canal of Injil, as old as Herat itself, into a meadow.[24] These canals, *karez* or *qanat* in Persian, are the man-made underground irrigation channels which gave water to the meadows outside the urban spaces, delivering water from nearby rivers to crops and gardens and villages. Herat's recovery from the Mongol destruction is a tale of gradual renewal in which the motifs of water, silk and religion all play their part, as they continue to do to this very day. Herat could be sacked and burned, pillaged and plundered, yet its waters would never fail to revive the city in times of the darkest despair.

In 1239, Ezz al-Din Moqaddam died. On his deathbed, he advised his son, Amir Mohammad, to 'be kind and compassionate with the people', and urged him to head east to the Mongol court to obtain a *yarligh* (a patent of Mongol authority) so as to rule as a legitimate Mongol vassal in a world then under the sway of Mongol power.[25] Amir Mohammad was paired with a Mongol named Kharlegh, and they were sent to govern Herat as dual representatives of local and global power. Kharlegh so feared the Heratis as 'experts in deception, perfidy and masters of treachery' that he asked to have his brother appointed to accompany him on the journey to Herat.[26] They reached Khorasan in 1240, pitching their felt tents to the east of Herat amidst an atmosphere of suspicion and resentment. Kharlegh more than once, along with his 'corrupt and wicked' son, deeply offended the people of Herat, as conquerors so often seem to do.[27] Herat's elders complained bitterly about Mongol arrogance and abuse, 'the violence, theft and rape', and urged *Khatib* to set in motion an uprising to overthrow the Mongol infidels.[28] Yet in a remarkable display of restraint and sagacity, *Khatib* reminded the assembled men of the futility of bloodshed, of the appalling suffering the city had seen since 1221. He chose words as his weapon when confronting the Mongols:

> When a country is empty of its people
> What good are all the nobles and kings?[29]

Sayfi tells us that these words had the desired effect. At a banquet a few days later, Kharlegh repented and spoke eloquently about his desire to bring Herat back to life and restore the city and its surroundings. The rapacious Mongol administrator was duly thrown out of the government, his place being taken by a native of Herat.

As Herat climbed out of the ruins of desolation, its strategic importance to the various Mongol empires became apparent, along with the notion that this was a city which sat awkwardly at the edge of empires. Herat was far from the traditional power centres of Tabriz, Karakorum, Baghdad and the lands of the Indus, and this made it difficult to hold with any certainty; its inclusion in the various competing Mongol factions was not geographically obvious. Ezz al-Din Moqaddam had sought *yarligh*s from the Mongols in the east, yet Herat's total destruction in 1222 at the hands of Eljigidai placed the city naturally within the sphere of the Golden Horde to the north-west. Herat soon attracted the attention of Chingiz Khan's other sons, Great Khan Ogodei in Karakorum and Chagatai Khan, whose own lands in Central Asia abutted the fertile province of Badghis to the north and east of Herat. Wealthy and ambitious sons of Chingiz Khan surrounded Herat. *Yarligh*s came and went, as did puppet rulers in a succession of plots and assassinations. The 1240s saw delegations from different corners of the Mongol empire come to Herat, all bidding to secure its allegiance.[30] The stage was set for the Kart *malek*s, a local dynasty that would outlast the Mongols in Khorasan, and rule Herat for more than 140 years.[31]

* * *

The death of the Mongol Great Khan Guyuk, killed whilst brawling in April 1248, unleashed a bloody and violent family feud for the throne and soul of the Mongol empire. In what is commonly referred to by historians as the 'Toluid Coup', the house of Tolui, with the backing of Batu from the Golden Horde, prevailed and put the houses of Ogodei and Chagatai to flight. This war put Mongke Khan on the Mongol throne. Mongke, an astute and intelligent man, looked to expand further than the bounds set by Chingiz Khan's conquests, sending armies to conquer Persia, Iraq and beyond. It was against this chaotic background that Shams al-Din Kart (r.1245–78) had taken his chance to head east and stake a claim amidst the chaos.[32] Shams al-Din Kart, a minor Herati prince from Kheisar near Herat, was famed for his hot-headed impetuosity. He reached Karkorum in July 1251 with twenty Herati horsemen. There he inflicted a heavy and showy defeat on Mongke Khan's enemies. Such was the impact he made that he was granted a personal audience with Mongke, and there given a *yarligh* to rule Herat and its surrounds. Shams al-Din now possessed a fiefdom stretching from the Indus to western Khorasan, from Sistan to Shiburghan. He also had the backing of the world's most powerful military force.[33] Sayfi might well have exaggerated Shams al-Din's prodigious feats on the battlefield, but the extent of the lands granted to him do suggest that here was a man whom the Mongols trusted to rule over a province at the edge of competing Mongol principalities, a man to bring order to a city that had so troubled Karakorum. He left the Great Khan's court with swords, gold and jewel-encrusted belts to return a hero, a local ruler set to bring the city back to life.[34] Herat would be his capital.

Yet for all Shams al-Din's valour and skill, he was powerless to halt the fragmentation of the Mongol empire. In 1270, as the unwieldy political patchwork created by Chingiz Khan began to disintegrate, Herat became the centre of a conflict between the Chagataid prince of the Golden Horde, Baraq Khan (r.1266–71), and Il-Khan Abaqa (r.1265–82) of the Mongol's Persian empire, the Il-Khanate, whose lands stretched from Iraq-e Ajam to the Indus and included parts of Azerbaijan. The Chagataid princes saw the Il-Khanate as a direct threat to their own power. Herat itself, owing to its place in Khorasan, was loyal to the Il-Khanate and its capital at Tabriz, but also coveted by the

Chagataids of the Golden Horde. It was from this struggle that Baraq's designs on Herat emerged.[35] A tribute-gathering envoy from Baraq to the Il-Khanid court in 1268 brought home enough intelligence to convince the Golden Horde that Il-Khanid lands around Herat could be theirs by force of arms. Baraq simply stated: 'our pasture, hunting parks and pleasure palaces have become too small. Thus we should turn our armies to Khorasan and Iraq [Iraq-e Ajam, Persia] to conquer those lands.'[36] A band of 30,000 Chagataid troops duly marched to the pasturelands of Badghis, where Baraq's forces routed the Il-Khanid army. The vanquished Il-Khanids fled to Mazandaran with the news that Khorasan was now at Baraq's mercy. The conquest of Nishapur left the road to Jam and Herat defenceless.

Baraq's envoy travelled south to sound out Shams al-Din Kart as to the colour of his loyalty: Chagataid or Il-Khanid? Baraq's ministers advised against simply reducing Herat to ashes, arguing instead that Shams al-Din's loyalty, achieved through 'seduction and temptation', would hand them Khorasan and its *malek*s on a plate.[37] Finding Shams al-Din in his ancestral fortress at Kheisar, the envoy flattered, promised and cajoled him into joining the insurrection against the Il-Khans. It worked. Shams al-Din, after taking two days to think the matter over with his viziers, went over to Baraq Khan's side, betraying the Il-Khans. He soon regretted his betrayal. Eight days spent in the Chagataid military camp in Badghis, where he observed the soldiers plundering the surrounding countryside, led him to the conclusion that these soldiers 'were not here for conquest, but simply for wanton destruction'.[38] Shams al-Din feared for his city. He engineered a swift return from Badghis, hastily excusing himself on the grounds that he really should be in Herat preparing for battle, making sure that Il-Khanid propaganda wasn't sapping the morale of its citizenry. His return was preceded by the arrival there of three of Baraq's men, who emptied the city of 'fruit, flour and wine', setting ruinous taxes over the gates, the mint and the people, and announcing that Herat must recite prayers in his honour.[39] Herat again faced ruin, and Sayfi noted that 'from peasant to king, the people sank into the slough of despair'.[40] Shams al-Din fled to the secure walls of Kheisar, yet not before ordering that Herat's gates be closed to Baraq's armies: a futile show of loyalty to the jilted Il-Khans. For the Il-Khan Abaqa, the desertion of this erstwhile bright light in Khorasan's military firmament was a cause for rage, and he gathered an army and set out to attack Baraq Khan. Abaqa gave the order that Shams al-Din be captured along with his family.

The Battle of Herat, fought between the Il-Khans and Baraq on 22 July 1270 amidst Herat's fierce summer winds that swirled around the plains of Ghurian, ended in a decisive victory for the Il-Khanids. This victory was achieved, in large part, through a masterstroke of disinformation in which three of Baraq's spies were captured at night-time in a small village outside Herat. They were beaten and tortured for information, left to sit in the corner of the tent, tied to a pole, while the Il-Khanid generals caroused and drank wine. At a pre-determined point, an Il-Khanid solider rushed in to say that trouble in the west had erupted; their army was to abandon Herat immediately. Yet this was a trick, for there was no such crisis in the west and no need to abandon their siege of Herat. An order was given to kill two of the spies, but to let one go as if by accident, with the aim that this 'escaped' spy would carry back to his masters the false information that their enemies were soon to leave the battleground. The ruse worked: the Il-Khans remained where they were and the element of surprise this trick created was key to their triumph.[41] Yet as impressive as the victory was, it represented something of a problem for Shams al-Din and Herat. A serious question now hung over his loyalty to Herat's Il-Khanid masters.

The Il-Khanid army were aggrieved that Herat had cost them countless thousands of dinars and many lives in the last ten months; was it not the city's wealth and fertility which had attracted Baraq in the first place? Herat should be made to pay for what it had forced upon the Il-Khanid armies. The nomadic impulse to pillage sedentary dwellings, 'to destroy each narrow street and lane so that no king could ever build a dwelling there again', rose to the surface amongst the conquering army, and they gave the people of Herat three days in which to evacuate the city.[42] On the fourth day, a Friday in the autumn of 1270, 500 Mongol soldiers entered Herat, driving the remaining citizens out 'with great blows from wooden clubs'.[43] Yet a repeat of 1222 was averted through diplomacy, and Herat's saviours were an Il-Khanid royal, Prince Tubsin, and the *sahib divan* (leading official) of the court.[44] When these two men heard of Herat's predicament, they rushed to their ruler's side with urgent appeals to let Herat be, for they had, as Sayfi tells us, 'read in books of old by the elders of another age' that any man who destroys Herat does so at his peril and with a stain on his honour, for the city is 'a place of sacred value, of abundant saints, shrines without number and of great efficacy, and holy men of inestimable fame'.[45] Herat's natural wealth had doomed it; its reputation for holiness and shrines had saved it. The looting ceased, and a team of Il-Khanid officials was sent to Herat, then alive with rumours of an imminent Kartid return, to put the people back to work and rebuild the city. Herat's place as a frontier post at the eastern edge of the Il-Khanate, far from the capital in Tabriz, yet clearly essential to securing the frontiers of that empire, was now clearly established.

Shams al-Din never returned to Herat. His son governed in his stead, bringing peace of a sort. This peace, however, could not gloss over Shams al-Din's momentary act of treachery when he had pledged his allegiance to Baraq Khan. In 1273 Baha al-Din Juvaini, nephew of the Persian historian Ata al-Malek Juvaini, entered Herat, ostensibly to add to the rebuilding and oversee its progress, but also to punish Shams al-Din for his indiscretion. Yet a way had to be found to lure Shams al-Din from his stronghold in Kheisar, to coax him out of self-imposed exile. There followed between Kheisar and Herat, Herat and Tabriz, an exchange of letters as one side probed and the other resisted; Shams al-Din replied to the promises of jewel-studded belts, lands stretching from the Indus to Iraq-e Ajam and from Shiburghan to Sistan with diplomatic parries. He cited old age and a desire to escape from the world's inconstancy and fickleness.[46] Given the Il-Khanids' anger with him, Shams al-Din was wise to remain shut up behind strong walls. Yet in 1275, on the strength of a missive from Herat assuring him of his good standing at the Il-Khanid court, Shams al-Din decided to leave Kheisar for Esfahan and the court of the Il-Khans, bypassing Herat. In Esfahan, however, there was to be no hero's welcome, or even considered forgiveness. Il-Khan Abaqa ignored Shams al-Din and took his sons prisoner. Shams al-Din himself was then sent to Tabriz to await his fate. Despite the strident intercessions of a Mongol noble named Amir Tekneh whose livestock Shams al-Din had saved from some form of disease, in January 1278 Herat's first Kart *malek* was poisoned with a watermelon in a Tabriz bathhouse. Such was the mistrust that the

Il-Khan had for the 'perfidious and cunning Tajik', even in death, that he ordered the coffin to be wrapped in heavy chains before being sent away to its burial place in Jam, west of Herat.[47] Shams al-Din Kart, reckless, impetuous, brilliant and unlucky, had paid the price for Herat's position at the frontier of squabbling empires, a fate that would befall so many who followed him.

* * *

Herat had evidently suffered since the comparative recovery of the early 1270s; a description of the city in the spring of 1278 is of a place turned upside down, its people scattered amid anarchy and lawless-ness.[48] An Il-Khanid prince asked the people of Herat why the weak were trodden under foot, why laws had vanished and why crime was so rampant? The rather predictable answer, so Sayfi tells us, was that without the strength of the Karts and their firm hand on the tiller of government, Herat was going to ruin. For all the frustrations that Shams al-Din had caused, it was clear that his local dynasty provided a semblance of stability on the outposts of the Il-Khanid lands. The Il-Khans accordingly chose Rokn al-Din Kart (r.1278–1305), a young man who had proved himself whilst fighting with the Il-Khanids Darband on the western shores of the Caspian. Rokn al-Din Kart took the name Shams al-Din *Kehin* (The Smaller), and began his task of 'renewing the territories of Herat'.[49] Kehin, 'whose knowledge shone like the radiance of the sun in matters of learning and religion', was a man of excellent intentions and, if we credit accounts of his valour in the Caucasus, of rare military skill.[50] And yet despite these strengths, Kehin would spend little time in Herat, preferring to shut himself up in Kheisar, like his father. It is probable that amidst the uncertainty of thirteenth-century Khorasan, Kehin felt safer with large tracts of masonry separating him from the world outside. His absence from Herat did not, however, hamper his ability to project Kartid power in the city, to create a semi-independent political entity.

Kehin sought to put Herat back on a firm footing, to emphasise its reputation as a home of Islamic orthodoxy, for this was a time when Islam appeared to be under attack from infidel Mongols. The Mongol sack of Baghdad in 1258 and the end of the Abbasid Caliphate had inflicted deep psychological wounds on the Muslim world, which needed its champions, local and regional, to reassert Islamic notions of justice, governance and culture in the face of an invading force. These Persian and Islamic values would endure long after the Mongols had been absorbed into the fabric of their conquered nations. Sayfi's description of Kehin as bringing the 'sun of Islam [*shams* means sun or solar in Persian] shining into the province of Khorasan and opening people's eyes to the glory of his justice' is thus no empty rhetoric, for he sought to place Herat at the front of this struggle for the soul of Islam in an uncertain and fragmented world.[51] Kehin's brief return to the city in 1282 gave Herat a year of peace and stability: a year in which trade flourished and the light of Islamic justice is said to have provided the backdrop to daily life in Herat. Peace meant crops being gathered in, traders coming to the city and Herat's Muslims being allowed to worship without the fear of imminent exile or invasion.

* * *

The tribe of the Nikudaris, Negudaris or Qaraunas, represent something of a mystery for historians and anthropologists; few agree on their origins.[52] Whatever the truth of the matter, be they Mongols or Persians, the Nikudaris would come to play a decisive role in Herat's history, shaping the way the city related to Il-Khanid authority. In 1284 a Mongol military commander named Hindu Noyin sought refuge with Kehin at the fort of Kheisar. Hindu Noyin had earlier made enemies at the Il-Khan's court in Tabriz; he had clashed with a powerful man named Ta Temur. To avoid all-out war, Hindu Noyin was forced to hide his hatred of his enemy, yet the ingenious Hindu Noyin soon found an opportunity to slaughter Ta Temur and his clan. The murdered Ta Temur was a native of Badghis, and his supporters in that province 'turned to gathering armies', readying themselves for war.[53] The ensuing hostilities forced Hindu Noyin to flee to Kheisar with no more than 800 men. Kehin now faced the difficult decision of whether to hand over the rebellious Mongol and risk troubles closer to home, or to side with him and thus incur the wrath of his Il-Khanid masters: a lose–lose situation. Kehin chose the former, handing over Hindu Noyin. Extravagant praise from the Il-Khans soon followed, as did drums and robes of honour.[54] Whilst these gifts and honeyed words of congratulation were well received at Kheisar and Herat, the predicament which the event created was problematic for Kehin and his city, for in handing over Hindu Noyin to face Mongol justice, he had created powerful local enemies in the province of Badghis to the north of Herat. In the tense atmosphere that ensued, as false rumours swirled around the city and Herat's reputation was savaged at the Il-Khanid court by Hindu Noyin's acolytes, a nervy Kehin recalled his son to Kheisar, leaving Herat without a titular sovereign.[55] It was into this precarious situation that the Nikudaris stepped.

Proving the theory that medieval politics abhors a power vacuum, contemporary chroniclers saw the appearance of the 'accursed' Nikudari hordes in Herat in 1288 as directly linked to an empty throne, echoing familiar themes in Persian and Islamic political theory that strong governance, in the shape of a visible and present lawgiver and enforcer, are key to social harmony.[56] Bands of Nikudari fighters soon set upon a leaderless Herat. They separated mothers from children, destroyed homes and took prisoners by the thousand. They did not seek to rule, but rather to plunder, much as the Vikings of Medieval European history had done to a prosperous England. Sayfi's account of these events is particularly personal, for he, as a six-year-old boy, witnessed the Nikudari assaults on Herat first-hand. He writes vividly of the mass exodus of bedraggled and starving families of all classes and professions, trooping out on foot from Herat to begin new lives in surrounding countryside villages in Esfezar, Jam, Ghur and Badghis.[57] Herat was too alluring to be left alone, yet not powerful enough to fend for itself, so was doomed to swing from peace to war, from exile to return.

The Nikudaris returned in 1289 in league with a rebellious Il-Khanid general, Amir Nawruz (r.1291–5). Kehin advised Herat to refrain from resistance so as not to draw Nawruz's rebellion further towards Herat, yet this advice proved futile, and the Nikudaris set upon the city with a fresh vigour, again scattering its inhabitants.[58] Some Heratis sought refuge in the citadel, while others, mindful no doubt of their ancestors who had found sanctuary there in 1222, headed for the cupola of the Friday Mosque in the hope of history repeating itself, or not. A band of 500 Nikudari horsemen were sent in pursuit of those Heratis who had escaped. The ruin which the city suffered must have been significant, for Sayfi records in his chronicle that for one whole year it was totally empty of people, and that the immediate aftermath of this sacking saw the city's population stand at a mere one hundred souls.[59]

In the spring of 1291, Amir Nawruz, now restored to Mongol favour with his rebellion having run its course, reached Herat. He came with the express intention of restoring the city and province to its former glory after the horrors of the Nikudari attacks and the instability which had arisen as Herat languished without a protector. It is something of an irony that Nawruz was sent to fix Herat, for it was his rebellion which had caused so much trouble to the province in the first place.[60] His entry to Herat was announced in the following terms: 'I am Nawruz, come with a *yarligh* from the Il-Khan Arghun the Just, to return Herat to her former glories, to gather the people from Khorasan and its surrounds.'[61] Herat and its people were to be spared any injury or molestation, 'be that by Mongol or Muslim', for a period of two years, so that its people might once again enjoy a life free from war.[62] Nawruz was given licence to pillage south and east of Herat, summoning to his cause the maleks of Esfezar, Farah and Sistan, so as to bring back money and arms and men with which to regenerate a damaged city. The countryside was scarified to regenerate the city, and in a short space of time it returned to prosperity, once again taking its rightful place alongside the wonders of Samarqand and Baghdad.[63]

As with earlier Il-Khanid missions to Herat, there existed motives other than simple urban and rural regeneration. Kehin and his family were still inexplicably hiding in Kheisar, shirking duties accepted by them from the Il-Khanid court in Tabriz. Yet Nawruz did not just seek Kehin's loyalty to an empire; he needed Kehin to burnish his own legitimacy in Khorasan as a military commander. Nawruz needed the support of a stable Muslim dynasty to protect him against the hostility that many shaman Mongols held towards him as a Muslim convert. He sought powerful friends in Khorasan, and a fortress with high walls. On Friday 19 December 1292 Kehin received a letter from Herat, written by Nawruz, imploring him to return to the city and to accede to his hereditary title as Herat's *malek*.[64] Whilst ostensibly similar in nature to the diplomatic niceties exchanged prior to the eventual death of Shams al-Din, these entreaties differed in that they were genuine; Nawruz was sincere in his wish for an alliance and had no designs on Kehin's life. Kehin's response was cagey. It demonstrated caution, born no doubt of experience. His ornately worded refusal to budge brought into focus the possibility of Kehin's eldest son, Fakhr al-Din Kart, ruling in Herat. Yet Fakhr al-Din had been a prisoner of his paranoid father since 1285, shut up in the citadel of Kheisar. The sources do not relate why he was locked up, but subsequent events reveal mutual fear and suspicion to have been the defining features of this uneasy father–son relationship.

Kehin is said to have acted 'maliciously and without manners' in his dealings at this point, and in an allusion to the now lost *Kart Namah* (Kart History) of the Herati poet Rabii Fushanj, Sayfi wrote that should readers wish to know more about these events, they should simply consult Rabii's excellent account.[65] Luckily, Sayfi gives us enough evidence to construct the story. Fakhr al-Din had escaped his captors in the upper fort of Kheisar, killing many in the process, and then took refuge in the same citadel.[66] On hearing this, Nawruz asked his advisers, some of whom were important Herati nobles, if they thought that an approach to Fakhr al-Din would be advisable, to which their simpering response was that such an approach represented the very height of sagacity.[67] Nawruz then sent an envoy to persuade Kehin to release his son back to Herat. Understandably, a father who had imprisoned his son for seven years feared the consequences, and accordingly Kehin replied that his son was 'mad', that the initial arrest had been merely out of fear of what the young prince might do to his aged father.

Negotiations continued in a similar vein, with both Kehin and Fakhr al-Din seeking assurances that they would be safe from each other; Kehin, fearful of his wayward son, begged the Mongol envoy to promise him that should his son be freed and allowed to take control of Herat, he would bear no responsibility for his son's actions. Fakhr al-Din, for his part, was simply scared of his enemies and wary of his father's violence; he, too, sought personal assurances from Nawruz that he would be protected.[68] As a way to break the deadlock, and in an incident highly revealing of the role of religious men as powerbrokers and intermediaries in thirteenth-century Khorasan, Nawruz called on Herat's two most senior Sufi clerics, Shaykh al-Islam Khwajah Shahab al-Din Jami and Grand Shaykh Qotb al-Din Chishti, to mediate a truce and find a solution.[69] The two shaykhs succeeded in their task, bringing Fakhr al-Din round, assuring him of his safety under the Mongol yoke and gently reminding him of his duties: 'O Prince, your time has come, the hour has arrived.'[70] Fakhr al-Din duly accepted the offer, and returned to Herat, refusing even to glimpse his father as he left Kheisar. A portentous coda to this episode, told through some beautiful lines from the chronicle of Rabii of Fushanj, is a description of Fakhr al-Din swearing that he is bound in loyalty to Nawruz, and that he would never betray his saviour.[71]

Meanwhile, Nawruz's rebellious instincts soon reappeared. His détente with the Il-Khan Ghazan (r.1295–1304) fell to pieces in spectacular fashion, and Il-Khanid armies chased him all the way from Iraq-e Ajam to Herat in the summer of 1297. Nawruz had made dozens of powerful enemies at the Il-Khanid court through his persecution of Christians, his proselytising Islamic ways and, of course, his frequent rebellions. Herat's chroniclers simply state that he had 'raised sedition in the Il-Khanate', at a time when the Il-Khans were facing a near constant battle with the Middle East's regional hegemon, the Mamluk Sultanate of Egypt.[72] It was this conflict that provided the backdrop for his downfall.[73] One evening in a Persian tavern, an Il-Khanid messenger had spent a heavy night of drinking, egged on by a group of mysterious and unknown men. On waking, the messenger was arrested and during his interrogation were found fabricated letters, of which he was totally unaware, sewn into his coat. These false missives detailed supposed correspondence between Nawruz and the Mamluk Sultans, cast-iron evidence of Nawruz's desire to join forces with his co-religionists in Egypt and Syria so as to overthrow the Il-Khanate and rid Muslim Khorasan of the 'infidel Mongol yoke'. This was to be the final nail in Nawruz's coffin, proof positive that here was a man more interested in serving his own ambitions than fighting for the Il-Khan. Even though the evidence used to frame Nawruz was false, such was the hatred many held for him that his demise would be ordered on the slightest pretext.

Nawruz, then at Nishapur, fled south east to Jam, 150 kilometres north-west of Herat. There he fought a battle with Il-Khanid forces from morning prayers until dusk prayers. His force of 1,000 iron-clad men was reduced to 400. They limped on to Kousieh, from where Nawruz mooted the idea of heading to Herat, where his 'long-standing friend and ally' Fakhr al-Din was then holding court.[74] The remainder of his supporters, to a man, advised him against this, citing the Heratis' reputation for treachery; some of Nawruz's men even fled to Badghis out of fear of the mere mention of Herat and its imposing citadel. Ignoring the advice of his camp and trusting the man he had saved from Kheisar who had sworn to remain loyal, Nawruz left for Herat in July 1297. Fakhr al-Din housed and welcomed him with all outward appearances of loyalty and kindness. Four days later an Il-Khanid army, 70,000-strong, appeared at the foot of the walls of Herat, demanding that Fakhr al-Din surrender Nawruz. Once again Herat had to choose between personal and imperial loyalties: Nawruz or the Il-Khans?

For eighteen days Fakhr al-Din remained true to his promise and refused to surrender Nawruz, despite the threat of soldiers camped on the banks of the Hari Rud. Yet skirmishes soon broke out in the villages and fields outside the city walls between Heratis and the encamped army. It then came to Fakhr al-Din's attention that Nawruz, his guest, was planning to take Herat for himself; he had even chosen the men to seize the gates and carry out the operation.[75] Fakhr al-Din was shocked at the news, and accordingly advised his most trusted men, amongst whom were Taj al-Din Yeldez and Jamal al-Din Mohammad Sam, to capture Nawruz. A dramatic scene ensued in which the former strongman of the Il-Khanate was arrested on a roof of the citadel. His supporters were all cut down in flight, thrown into wells, or consigned to its dungeon.[76] Nawruz was bound hand and foot, bareheaded (a great insult in medieval Khorasan) and killed. On 16 August 1297, as news of Nawruz's execution filtered out to the besieging army, their siege was called off. Fakhr al-Din, however, remained under suspicion for his wavering loyalty and for sheltering Nawruz in the first place. A weary Fakhr al-Din travelled to the Il-Khanid court in Tabriz, where he was nevertheless given extravagant gifts and yet another *yarligh* to govern Herat from the Oxus to the Indus.[77]

* * *

Nawruz's death in Herat is often portrayed as evidence of the Karts' supposed perfidy and their fickle nature, echoing themes that have dotted the city's story from its very inception. Whilst there is little doubt that Fakhr al-Din did renege on his promises, his initial impulse was to welcome his friend into Herat. It was Nawruz's own treachery, his desire to betray Fakhr al-Din and take Herat for himself, that led to his death. Nawruz, not Fakhr al-Din, broke the oaths binding the two together. Yet this incident is important for revealing a deeper and more important pattern, one which goes to the very heart of Herat's identity. As a result its geography and prosperity, Herat would repeatedly be forced to choose between competing imperial and local interests, and as a result it would constantly face dilemmas of this sort; it was forced into fickleness. Consequently, a finely honed and ruthless self-interest emerged, giving Herat a reputation for inconstancy and treachery. But behind these shifting alliances and opportunistic executions is a city looking after its own interests at the frontier of unpredictable political powers. An oath is important, but staying alive is, surely, more important?

* * *

Domestic interests and regional alliances once again collided in 1298, this time in the shape of the Nikudaris, who appeared at the city gates with a band of 3,000 men, all seeking asylum with Fakhr al-Din.[78] Mindful of the recent momentous events with Nawruz, Fakhr al-Din's actions here hint at a reckless streak and suggest an imprudent understanding of either the role ascribed to him by the Il-Khans in Tabriz, or the regional power dynamics in which he existed. It is surprising that Fakhr al-Din, flush with imperial favour, chose to receive the Nikudaris, given the latter group's pillaging of Il-Khanate lands, and their leader Buqa, with such pomp and goodwill, giving each man a horse, arms and clothing. They were allowed to plunder at will. This was unadvisable on many counts, not least because the Karts were answerable for taxes to the Mongol court; and a pillaged province, emptied of its people, would be in no position to pay those taxes. As Herat and its surrounds bled and burned, a group of Herat's nobility, gathered from Farah, Sistan and the city's outlying villages, took tales of captured children, destroyed villages and crops to Il-Khan Ghazan. Ghazan, given his obsession with bureaucratic reform and taxation, was highly receptive to these complaints. He was also justifiably alarmed at the rebellious actions of a man he had so recently covered in gold.[79] He placed his brother, Prince Oljeitu (r.1280–1316), at the head of a 10,000-strong army with orders to invest Herat if needs must, but with the clear order that Oljeitu refrain from harming the people of Herat or their religious classes.[80] While still at Nishapur, Oljeitu sent a messenger to Herat requiring Fakhr al-Din to surrender Buqa and the

Nikudaris. Fakhr al-Din replied, untruthfully, that the Nikudaris had left for Helmand a month before. They were in fact still camped in the provinces surrounding the city. Oljeitu did not believe Fakhr al-Din, and with the impetuosity common to young imperial princes he decided to take Herat for himself. Fearing for his life, Fakhr al-Din fled north-east to the fortress of Aman Koh and was pursued by Oljeitu's heavily armed forces. Oljeitu set up camp outside Aman Koh and a siege was set in motion, occasionally broken up by intermittent sallies from the citadel and small skirmishes. Under cover of darkness, Fakhr al-Din escaped from Aman Koh and rode the distance back to Herat. That same night he inspected the city's fortifications before again flee-ing, this time into the mountainous heartlands of Ghur to the east. A native dynasty the Karts might have been, but hands on they were not.

Oljeitu's forces turned their attention to Herat. Camped in the lush villages and vineyards surrounding its walls, they began an eighteen-day siege of intense fighting.[81] Once again, the warring parties called upon Sufi shaykhs to negotiate peace, they who understood better than most the transient nature of existence and the futility of war. A delegation from Herat led by Shaykh al-Islam Shahab al-Din Jami, who had once negotiated the release of Fakhr al-Din from Kheisar, came to Oljeitu and implored the prince to call off the siege. He pleaded with Oljeitu, 'Fakhr al-Din is not here and the Nikudaris have left the city. Why are you fight-ing and unjustly spilling the blood of innocent Muslims? Spare us.'[82] These entreaties, as well as his warnings that Herat would not fall with-out a long and costly fight, had the intended effect and the two sides agreed terms in which Herat would pay 100,000 dinars as compensation for the deaths of the Mongol soldiers and the ravages of the Nikudaris. The Il-Khanid armies headed away westwards. Fakhr al-Din duly returned to Herat in the dubious guise of a victor, showering the city's defenders with gold and money and robes of honour, unperturbed at how his maladroit political calculations had caused Herat such ruin.

In the autumn of 1299, with the situation calm, Fakhr al-Din set about restoring his shattered city. He called in 'all the workers and rabble' from the surrounds of Ghur, Sistan, Fushanj, Kousieh and Jam to strengthen the ramparts of the citadel and repair the moats sur-rounding the city walls.[83] The towers guarding the four corners of the citadel were repaired and enlarged to such an extent that Sayfi could boast that the city was rendered so strong as to be now impregnable, a boast which more or less rang true for the remainder of Fakhr al-Din's reign. He added a walled *maidan* (square) to its west to serve as an open-air mosque, and ordered the construction at the southern foot of the citadel of the Malek Bazaar and an extravagantly painted *khaneqah* (buildings designed for gatherings of Sufi brotherhoods, places of spiritual retreat and meditation, also serving as hospices for travellers). Both of these were still standing in the fifteenth century.[84] Fakhr al-Din decreed that travellers and the needy be cared for, and he made a point of making weekly visits to the *khaneqah* to debate points of religion and mysticism with the dervishes, giving these men the large sum of 1,000 dinars.[85] Fakhr al-Din's good works extended to helping orphans, religious mendicants and *sayyeds*—descendants of the Prophet Muhammad—with donations of quilted coats and the slaughtering of sheep.[86] Mosques were repaired, notably the Abdul Amir Mosque (Khorasan's 'first Amir') and the mosque of Tera Foroush. Peace had brought revenue into the city's coffers through good harvests and secure roads, along which trade could pass safely.

Yet it wasn't solely in the spheres of mosques, walls and bazaars that the ambitious Fakhr al-Din sought regeneration; Herat's souls had also to be saved. He set about this task enthusiastically. Anticipating legislation that would be brought into force by the Taliban almost 700 years later, he commanded that females should not leave their homes alone under any circumstance, and that those who did so would be punished; their guilty menfolk would be paraded bareheaded through the different quarters of the city as examples to others. Gamblers and dice-throwers fared scarcely any better: their heads and beards were also shaved as a punishment for transgressing the *sharia*. Drunkards were shackled when caught, and pressed into hard labour of gathering mud and baking bricks to rebuild the city, a punitive *corvée* system. This latter scenario raises the intriguing possibility that many of Herat's Kartid buildings were actually the work of recovering alcoholics. Even female ululations at funerals were deemed to be un-Islamic, and therefore banned.[87] Yet despite these laws we are told that 'every night the clamour of drunken brawling and licentiousness could be heard in the city of Herat'.[88] Peacetime was used to wash away Herat's sins and patch up a city shaken by incessant conquest and siege.

The courtly life of Fakhr al-Din's Herat was no less riotous than the bubbling underbelly of the city's taverns. One contemporary Afghan historian refers to Fakhr al-Din's court as a 'sea of cultured tranquility existing in a time of blood and fire, of oppression and tyranny', but the reality may have been less than tranquil.[89] Fakhr al-Din was himself a poet and a cannabis addict who wrote more than a few beautiful lines about that green plant and its relaxing properties.[90] Forty poets, all said to have been addicted to wine, song and pleasures of the flesh, were the bright cultural lights of Fakhr al-Din's cultured Herat. They were employed solely to write eulogies to their ruler and his extravagant court. Typical of the hedonistic life of a Herati courtly poet was Mawlana Sadr al-Din 'Rabii' of Fushanj. Rabii was from the village of Fushanj, the son of a *khatib* (religious preacher). He rose to prominence as a man of poetic talent and merciless wit and Sayfi's own epic history rarely goes a few pages without praising Rabii's *oeuvre*. His talents quickly brought him to the attention of Fakhr al-Din, who commissioned the poet to write the epic history of the Karts in the metre of Firdausi's epic *Shah Namah* (The Deeds of Kings): the *Kart Namah*. For this he was paid the handsome sum of 1,000 gold dirhams a month, which he promptly spent on 'wine, women and boys'.[91] It is a miracle that he managed to write anything at all.

The cannabis-eating Fakhr al-Din soon grew tired of the alcoholic poet, and exiled him. After eventful wanderings in Helmand and Sistan, Rabii wound up at the court of the Il-Khans, Herat's ultimate sovereigns, in Tabriz. Fakhr al-Din became anxious about the very real damage a jilted and unpredictable poet could do to his reputation at a court where Herat's own reputation was by no means unblemished. Fakhr al-Din thus coaxed Rabii back to Herat with flattery and disingenuous protestations that he had no designs on the head of the poet.[92] Rabii was duly reinstated with pomp and ceremony. The flattery, however, was merely a front, for Fakhr al-Din was simply waiting for a chance to arrest Rabii and silence him for good. He would get his opportunity to do so shortly after his return, as Rabii and his friends partied in Fushanj. High on drink and cannabis, the poets began to make extravagant boasts. One man claimed to be 'a lion-overthrowing elephant', and stated that 'with one stroke, I can lift the mountains from the earth'. Another poet exclaimed, 'My mind is the sun and the top of heaven is beneath my feet.'[93] Rabii's own boast was that he could control any province he so desired and bend its people to his will simply by the force of his poetry. This caused the assembled party to pledge their loyalty to the poet, a move possibly placing Fakhr al-Din's sovereignty in hazy abeyance. It laid Rabii open to the charge of treason. The next day one of Rabii's disciples went to Fakhr al-Din and confessed all. Fakhr al-Din's soldiers seized the men. Rabii, possibly unaware of the harsh edicts against alcohol, simply said, 'I was drunk; I spoke from the height of drunkenness.'[94] In retribution for their drunken treachery, some of the poets were skinned, some thrown down wells and others had their ears and noses cut from their faces. Rabii himself was imprisoned, despite sending many very beautiful eulogies in honour of the *malek*. He died a prisoner, 'and no one ever knew the circumstances of his death'.[95] Cultural life in Herat was, largely, service to the ruling dynasty, and drunken diversions would not be tolerated.

Herat's cultural flowering was short-lived. In 1303 Sultan Oljeitu acceded to the throne, and his previous skirmishes with Fakhr al-Din threatened to puncture Herat's semi-independence.[96] Oljeitu was not fully confident of Fakhr al-Din's loyalty to the Il-Khanate, and the tension to which this gave rise would again suck Herat back into regional conflict, producing a rebellion and forcing Herat's leaders to make difficult choices. Herat would suffer for it. Oljeitu had invited Fakhr al-Din to take part in the coronation ceremony, a requirement of every dutiful Mongol vassal. Fakhr al-Din refused, choosing to remain in Herat instead. As if to compound this slip of loyalty, Fakhr al-Din had also chosen to ally himself with the Nikduaris. This forced Sultan Oljeitu to send Amir Daneshmand Bahador, the most famous military commander of his time, from Persia to Herat along with 10,000 men at arms so as to bring order back to that troublesome part of Khorasan. Daneshmand was ordered to defeat Fakhr al-Din and his Nikudari allies.[97] When the Il-Khanid army arrived at Badghis in the summer of 1306, they sent envoys to Herat demanding that Fakhr al-Din give up his Nikudari allies. An illustration of the extent of Fakhr al-Din's disobedience to the Il-Khanids was the ancillary request that Herat pay up to three years' worth of taxes still owed to the Il-Khanid court, and that Fakhr al-Din mint coins bearing the name of Sultan Oljeitu; here was a vassal behaving like an independent prince.[98] Fakhr al-Din's response to these entreaties was spiteful, proud and uncooperative. Herat, so the Kart *malek* said, would not surrender, even to Daneshmand Bahador. Rather, it was content to hide behind its high walls and hope that geography and politics might save it from conquest.

In the autumn of 1306, Daneshmand Bahador drew his troops up to face the walls of the city from their positions in Badghis, eventually arriving at the eastern Khush Gate. Camped beneath the city, Daneshmand, like Chingiz Khan before him, was astonished at the strength of the ramparts, the height of the walls and the depth of the moat. The summer had been spent in diplomacy, negotiating terms and feeling for weaknesses, but aside from Fakhr al-Din quitting Herat for the safety of Aman Koh and leaving the citadel in the hands of a local figure named Jamal al-Din Mohammad Sam, no real conclusions were reached. Both sides implicitly acknowledged a state of unresolved resistance. Daneshmand, seeking to bring the stalemate to a close, decided to send his son, Laghri, into the city with a party of men, under the guise of conducting an agreement for Herat's submission. Yet the men entered the city with the intention of killing Mohammad Sam and taking the citadel for Daneshmand Bahador. Like so many before him, Daneshmand was seduced by the idea of establishing himself as the sovereign ruler of Herat.

Despite the advice of a highly perceptive Indian necromancer, who saw in this venture rivers of blood and hastily drawn swords, eighty Mongol nobles were allowed into the citadel's highest rooms to attend a feast where terms might be discussed with Mohammad Sam.[99] One Mongol, 'half-drunk', left the raucous feast to relieve himself outside the great hall, and as he did so he noticed heavily armed Herati soldiers moving through the shadows to line the exits. At this point, Daneshmand Bahador, accompanied by 180 men at arms, entered the citadel to join the feast and put into plan his conquest. Having dismounted from his horse to greet some Herati soldiers, one Herati noble, Taj al-Din Yeldez, allowed Daneshmand to pass in front of him up some stairs leading to the upper enclave of the citadel. In the darkness, Taj al-Din struck Daneshmand on the back of the head and hurled his lifeless body into the courtyard below. The carnage that followed rendered Herat's citadel red like a field of tulips, soaked in Il-Khanid and Mongol blood.[100] Mongol soldiers were killed and many more taken prisoner, including Daneshmand Bahador's wife, Shirin Khatun. A handful of Il-Khanid nobles managed to escape through the southern gate after breaking the locks, but all around them their friends and fellow soldiers lost their lives.[101] The carnage continued for three days. When it ended, Mohammad Sam built a fire on top of the citadel to alert Fakhr al-Din, then safely ensconced in Aman Koh, of Daneshmand's death. This seems likely to have been a pre-arranged signal, and one which forever seals Fakhr al-Din's reputation. Yet more damning was his subsequent request that word be put out amongst the people and notables of Herat that 'Fakhr al-Din Kart was saddened by the death of Daneshmand Bahador'.[102]

In the depths of January 2014, I stood, spine tingling, in the citadel on the exact same spot on which Daneshmand Bahador was hacked to death, looking up at the heights above and the steep path leading down to the lower citadel as the snow fell softly about me and the darkness gathered around. History has never felt so alive as it did in that moment. I remained rooted to the spot for some minutes, lost in a reverie of early-fourteenth-century Herat.

This treacherous rout of Il-Khanid troops soon brought a response in the shape of Daneshmand Bahador's descendants and an army of 40,000 men camped in Herat's pasturelands and meadows. Fakhr al-Din denied his role in the plot, citing the power of Mohammad Sam to act independently and the sheer distances involved between Aman Koh and Herat as evidence of his innocence. Yet Bujai, a descendant of Daneshmand Bahador, saw past this. Here was an opportunity to avenge his relative and take Herat in the process. Bujai ordered mangonels manned by European soldiers, possibly the first Europeans to visit Herat, to be trained on the city's walls and set up shops for his troops on the banks of a small river to the south, ordering the vendors to fix their prices at an acceptable rate.[103] (Having seen the prices of Afghan goods for sale in American and British military camps in Afghanistan, I would like to know what passed for 'acceptable' rates in 1307.) Proving that loyalty gravitates towards strong armies, men from all around came to join the Il-Khanid army in their attack: Sarakhs, Farah, Helmand, Esfezar, as well as nobles of the Hari Rud oasis and Kousieh.

On 13 February 1307, Fakhr al-Din died at Aman Koh as his city was starved into submission and frozen into misery. He was buried with pomp in the Friday Mosque in Herat, his funeral rites attended to by his black-robed retinue and court. His rule would be mourned neither by the Il-Khans, nor, one presumes, by the people of Herat on whose heads he had brought so much misery. Yet Afghan historians are quick to admire the feats of this unlikable figure who so stubbornly resisted the Il-Khans. He was a man who, in the words of one prominent Afghan historian, 'did not surrender his homeland to foreign enemies'.[104] He epitomised a reckless independence, typical of so many of Herat's rulers, yet it is his less admirable traits that stand out against his brave resistance, nearly always waged from the safety of a distant citadel.

Turning away from the deeds and whims of powerful men, it is famine and hunger that speak loudest from the chronicles describing the siege, as the people of Herat suffered blockades on trade routes into the city. Sayfi notes how a 'grain of wheat became more precious than a pearl and a grain of barley than a jewel', before going on to describe how 'granaries became as empty as the houses of the poor and destitute'.[105] Men were said to have thrown themselves from the walls of the city, if they had the strength to do so, in a bid to end their hunger. Parents pleaded with Herat's rulers to save their children from starvation. Some civilians were allowed out of the city, but on leaving they were repulsed, beaten back with sticks by the besieging forces; hundreds died in the rivulet of Ab-e Kartbar under the shadows of the southern walls of the city.[106] Sayfi describes a landscape of nothingness and remarks that some Kartid building projects, in particular the *khaneqah* and reception hall of the citadel, were rendered into dust, along with bazaars and mosques.[107] The siege ended in July 1307 with surrender to Bujai, and Herat's rebellious ruler, Mohammad Sam, was dragged in chains across Khorasan.[108]

* * *

While these momentous events shook Herat, while Fakhr al-Din plotted from afar, Ghias al-Din Kart (r. 1307–29), son of Kehin, fled Herat to the Il-Khanid court at Baghdad where he professed his loyalty to the Il-Khans and sought sanctuary from the turbulence of his native province. Ghias al-Din's loyalties are difficult to gauge, for prior to leaving for the Il-Khanid court he spent time with both Fakhr al-Din and

Daneshmand Bahador only a few days before the latter was killed. He even acted as something of an intermediary between the two sides. Perhaps he saw that this was a game in which there were few victors, and reasoned that the shelter of imperial power was preferable to an uncertain life in Khorasan?[109] Whatever the truth of the matter, his stay in Baghdad would prove an uncomfortable one. He arrived at court in the autumn of 1306, as word of his brother's murderous rebellion was reaching Baghdad. It is not clear whether he already knew of the carnage that would engulf Herat, but Ghias al-Din was soon confronted with the news. Talk quickly turned to the seemingly permanent state of rebellion in Herat and to the Karts' pathological unreliability. These were an uncomfortable few months for Ghias al-Din, no doubt with the fate of his ancestor Shams al-Din Kart, poisoned by a watermelon in a Tabriz bathhouse, at the front of his mind.[110] Yet news of Herat's submission to the Il-Khanid armies becalmed Oljeitu, and he granted a nervy Ghias al-Din a *yarligh* reaffirming Kart control over Herat. It seems that Oljeitu simply wanted order to return to the province, and with it some taxes to the imperial coffers.

Ghias al-Din, no doubt relieved, now returned to Herat, where he was received with great ceremony. He soon set about rebuilding the city's damaged fortifications and restoring order in the surrounding areas, for he was flush with gold from Baghdad. Herat knew 'the upmost peace and prosperity, no injury befalling any of the people from Iran to Turan in the year of 1308'.[111] ('Iran to Turan' conveys the meaning of 'from far and wide'.) Yet the accusations that Herat was a magnet for treachery refused to disappear. Ruling Herat without creating enemies was an impossible task, and before long these enemies came to the attention of Sultan Oljeitu, a man whose almost permanent state of drunkenness made him paranoid, angry and impetuous. Tales of Herat's disloyalty resonated with Oljeitu and his absolutist attitude to power, and it was not long before Ghias al-Din's loyalties were called into question in the court in Baghdad. A noble of Khorasan named Hindu Kah, who had once paid Ghias al-Din homage in Herat in 1308, but who secretly 'nursed jealousy in his heart', took his chance to advance his own cause and injure Ghias al-Din's reputation. When Oljeitu was particularly drunk, Hindu Kah related to him the frantic building programmes then going on in Herat to strengthen its walls, the city's crazed drive to make weapons and the gathering of soldiers from Khorasan. This was, Hindu Kah whispered to the drunken sultan, little more than a pre-emptive act of rebellion against the Il-Khanids, yet more evidence of the Karts' rebellious cast of mind.[112] No doubt allies of the slain Daneshmand Bahador supported this line of reasoning; his sons, in particular, were eager for a chance to bring this troublesome city to heel.[113]

These were tense times for Herat; threats mounted. Accordingly an Il-Khanid envoy travelled to Herat to arrest Ghias al-Din and bring him back to court where he would answer charges of rebellion and face his accusers in the flesh. Fearing nothing, Ghias al-Din set out from Herat for Iraq on 13 August 1311, leaving the levers of power—the treasury, the citadel and the bureaucracy—in the hands of Herati nobles and bureaucrats, a telling indication of Herat's effective independence from the Il-Khanate. Sayfi, using first-hand accounts, renders the account of Ghias al-Din at court in Baghdad with much emotion and pride at Herat's importance and political clout. Yet the reality was that Ghias al-Din spent almost five years in limbo at court awaiting his fate. It seems that there he had as many enemies as friends, for the impassioned defence of Ghias al-Din and his rule over Herat by important men at the Il-Khanid court reveal Herat's standing on the regional stage and the power the Karts had accrued. One venerable holy man of Khorasan pleaded with the sultan in the following terms: 'It is four years since Ghias al-Din has been wasting away at this court. As a result of his absence, the people of Herat have suffered many wrongs.'[114] Ghias al-Din, clearly a persuasive man with friends in the right places, personally pleaded with Sultan Oljeitu that his drive to make Herat strong and safe was purely motivated by unstinting loyalty to the Il-Khan, and assured the court that he was a devoted servant, not a rebel waiting to throw off the imperial yoke. Oljeitu relented, no doubt eager to be rid of a problem city and a problem vassal, and Ghias al-Din was made to swear to Sultan Oljeitu that his 'heart would be given to no other' in matters of government. In an attempt to deepen his loyalty, he gave Ghias al-Din tunics of golden cloth, his own robe, jewelled caps, golden belts, arms and weapons from Egypt, silken dragon standards, kettledrums large and small, and musical instruments.[115] Herat's loyalty clearly had a price.

Ghias al-Din made his way to Herat via Jam in the autumn of 1315. Whilst in Jam, in one of many overt displays of piety, he spent three days 'in the service of the Shaykh al-Islam Shahab al-Din', before being welcomed by the nobles and *ulema* of Herat and the surrounding areas.[116] Such was the significance of this homecoming, we are told, that even the sons of Daneshmand Bahador, who had so violently enriched themselves during his absence, made the journey from Obeh and Kousieh to come and welcome the new Kart *malek*. In the 1330s, the Moroccan traveller and geographer Ibn Batuta described Ghias al-Din as 'a man of notorious bravery'. He went on to say that he was also 'favoured by divine aid and felicity'.[117] Given Ghias al-Din's ability, time and time again, to escape the most difficult situations with his head and the crown upon it intact, it would be difficult to disagree.

What is most remarkable about this brief period in Herat's history, from Ghias al-Din's initial accession to his return in shaky triumph, is the sense that no one really knew what to do with Herat. Was it an impossibly rebellious province, or was it just unfortunate to be plagued by jealous enemies at court? Was it a province to be ruled and taxed, or should it simply be plundered for its fertility? That the Il-Khans, time after time, put rebellious Karts back on the throne of Herat reveals a helplessness about their Herat policies, if they ever existed as a coherent whole. What on earth were they going to do with this prosperous but problematic city? Who could control it?

Yet for all the confusion and opacity of Herat-Il-Khanid relations, there are indications that the Il-Khans were actively involved in the city on a more intimate level: that Karts' independence was not total. One such indication is the story about a petition from Herat to the Il-Khans about the case of an unlettered cleric. During the reign of Ghias al-Din, the *ulema* of Herat were unhappy with their *qazi* (head judge). He was deficient in scholarship and experience required for the role, so they said, and they petitioned Sultan Oljeitu that Herat be given a *qazi* worthy of the city's name. Sultan Oljeitu decreed that Mawlana Sadr al-Din of Kheisar, then residing in Baghdad, should be sent back to Herat to perform the duties of a *qazi*. The man was given a *yarligh* of wide-ranging proportions, indicating the vast extent of his territorial jurisdiction from Farah to Badghis and from Herat to the Indus. It outlined his role as *qazi*, a role which included legal duties as a judge, yet which also covered tasks relating to the supervision of Herat's morals, overseeing the content of the sermons in the region's mosques, *madrasas* and Sufi houses. He was the conscience, lawgiver and moral arbiter of a vast tract of land covering present-day Afghanistan. The *yarligh* also stipulated that Sadr al-Din should have responsibility for overseeing the sap harvest from Herat's willow trees, which appears as a somewhat isolated task amidst the mosques and morals.[118] The personal involvement of Oljeitu in this evidently detailed decision and the presence of Sadr al-Din at Baghdad show us a different and more integrated side of Herat's relations with the Il-Khanids. We see Herat as a city linked to the world around it, an ease of relations between Herat and Baghdad and a city of real regional significance, belying so much of its troublesome politics. In an age of precious little information on the daily life of the city, it is fascinating to see glimpses of a leading theologian and lawgiver inspecting Herat's willow trees. It adds a wonderful layer of texture to Herat's story and suggests a strong sense of community within the city that could stand up for itself and bypass the local strongman.

* * *

After five years of fighting off threats from the Chagataid north, and victorious battles in which 'the roar of the drums made the very earth tremble', Ghias al-Din's control over Herat was supreme.[119] A bewildering cycle of conflict and betrayal had shown the importance and desirability of Herat to all corners of the region, yet it had also shown just how difficult it was to take and keep the city. These were turbulent and difficult times as sultan replaced sultan in Baghdad, and regional strongmen looked for weak points in Herat's defences. Ghias al-Din and Herat managed to survive. The city was exempted from paying taxes for three years from 1320 as a reward for its heroic resistance against predatory neighbours.[120]

Ghias al-Din could now turn to rebuilding a broken city, incarnating his successes in the permanence of bricks, gardens and the written word. Being a renowned man of God, he first turned his attentions to the Friday Mosque, the eastern and southern flanks of which lay ruined by war and neglect. In a touching echo of the collective effort which had rebuilt Herat from rubble after 1222, its people, from peasant to noble and even Ghias al-Din himself, laboured shovel in hand to repair the Friday

Mosque. For fifty days they camped in the ruins of broken cupolas and niches, working day and night to restore the Friday Mosque to its former glories.[121] The pages of Sayfi positively sing with a sense of community and civic pride in Herat, his beloved city. For all that we must allow medieval chroniclers latitude in praising their paymasters and idealising their deeds, it is hard to ignore this heartfelt picture of *malek* and peasant working hand in hand to rebuild the Friday Mosque.

The Timurid chronicler Esfezari writes that bathhouses, whose beauty easily compared with that of 'Syria or Iraq', were constructed in the citadel. They remained in use well into the fifteenth century.[122] There were caravanserais, a bazaar which abutted the Chahar Su and a cistern within the city walls which all date to the reign of the energetic Ghias al-Din. The mention, with such admiration, of these buildings by Timurid historians is significant, for it shows that Herat's glorious Timurid architectural and cultural fluorescence sprang from this period, and suggests that Kartid Herat was every bit as sophisticated and majestic as the century that followed. Yet Ghias al-Din's civic munificence did not end within the walls of the city; he gave the order that all destroyed villages and hamlets be rebuilt so as to be more magnificent than they had ever been. The countryside, Herat's lifeblood, was restored to its previous levels of fertility and productivity, proving that peace is the best aid to prosperity.

Ghias al-Din wisely also chose to pay homage to the Il-Khans in his building spree. He commissioned celebrated artists of the day to paint a mural in a newly built reception hall at the northern end of the citadel. On the hall's western wall the artists were tasked with depicting the heroic scenes of the forces of the Il-Khans in their finest hours, glorifying the alliance between the Karts and the Il-Khans. On the eastern wall, they painted the defeat of the Chagataid army in 1319 in all the gory detail one might expect.[123] Nothing now remains of these murals.

As the summer of 1320 gave way to autumn, with the city secure and thriving, Ghias al-Din could fulfil his most heartfelt desire of going on the Hajj to Mecca (the birthplace of the Prophet Muhammad and the place of Mohammad's first revelation of the Quran). The holy men of Herat chose an auspicious date for his departure, and Ghias al-Din set out on pilgrimage, wrapped in a white shroud and accompanied by nobles from his territories of Jam, Fushang, Badghis. He left the reins

49

of government in the hands of his son, Shams al-Din, a dissolute young prince whose achievements fell well short of his father's. Ghias al-Din's arrival in the Hejaz was greeted with gifts and an extravagant welcome, and whilst in Mecca he discussed the finer points of the *sharia* with holy men from Egypt, and talked politics with leading political figures of the age.[124] Leaving Mecca, Ghias al-Din and his party returned via Medina and Baghdad, where they met with the last Il-Khan, Abu Said (r.1316–35), for more lavish entertainments and extravagant gifts. The Hajj was a moment of triumph for Ghias al-Din; with his city secure and his loyalty assured he could enjoy the perks of high office on a lofty stage.

It was at this point that Herat's first chronicler of real significance, Sayfi, died. His chronicle trails off with an uncharacteristically plodding account of military operations in Farah in the summer of 1321 after Ghias al-Din's glorious Hajj.[125] Ghias al-Din had commissioned Sayfi to write Herat's history, as he felt that Herat's reputation in the world was not commensurate with the city's cultural excellence and its regional standing in the fourteenth century. Through Sayfi's history of Herat, which stretches back into the mists of Herat's foundation myths, details the Karts' extravagant building programmes and highlights Ghias al-Din's displays of loyalty to the Il-Khans, Ghias al-Din strove to rescue Herat's reputation for perfidy from the dark days of Fakhr al-Din and Mohammad Sam. Sayfi's account of Ghias al-Din's reign shows it to be a mini Golden Age for Herat; Sayfi departed when Herat's stock was very much in the ascendant. Yet for all the beauty of Ghias al-Din's mosques, his dazzling eloquence, his piety on the Hajj, or the brilliance of his court in Herat, his reign would end with a shadow over his house. Herat's reputation for perfidy and trickery would be reinforced by the death of yet another Il-Khanid amir in its citadel.

* * *

Amir Chupan (d.1327) was a powerful military figure. He was feared throughout the Il-Khanate. During the reign of the last Il-Khan, Abu Said, Chupan's power over the vast Il-Khanid territories from modern-day Afghanistan to the Middle East and further afield into the Caucasus and Transoxania was almost unrivalled.[126] He had a ravishingly beautiful daughter named Baghdad Khatun, whose looks were said to have made roses appear ugly in comparison. Il-Khan Abu Said, his imperial power already emasculated by Chupan's omnipotence, had the added misfortune of falling helplessly in love with Baghdad Khatun. But she was already betrothed, so Abu Said decided to retreat to his tent to pine and wail. The Timurid chronicler, Hafez Abru, describes a young man in the very depths of a broken heart, noting that at this moment Abu Said was not 'an all-powerful Il-Khan of Iran, but rather a poor wretch, tortured by passion and unjustly condemned by cruel fate'.[127] Crushed by his broken heart, Abu Said took refuge in power; surely the Il-Khan should be able to have what he so desired? Citing a decree of Chingiz Khan that Mongol Khans were allowed to take for their own any wife or daughter of a subject, he demanded that Baghdad Khatun be brought to his *harem*. Chupan delicately sidestepped the issue by spiriting his beautiful daughter away from the court, and putting on hunting parties for Abu Said to distract him from his broken heart. Yet Chupan's efforts were in vain and Abu Said remained steadfast in his passion and determined to defeat the man who had defied him both in matters of the heart and in affairs of state. Il-Khan Abu Said's frustrations were given fresh impetus by the wild excesses of Chupan's son, whose chaotic control of royal finances and intrigues with royal concubines gave Abu Said the perfect pretext on which to move against this over powerful family.[128] An order was given to eradicate Chupan's family, beginning a monumental purge that shook Khorasan and Persia. Chupan retaliated with his own lightning purges, yet his forces deserted him at Sultaniyeh in northern Persia, leaving him in a state of rebellion, hounded by Abu Said. He was forced to drive his men back into the comparative safety of Khorasan, and he settled on the banks of the Murghab.

Chupan's arrival in Badghis was not an auspicious one, for the vast majority of his troops had fled from their once mighty master.[129] Assessing his options, he abandoned the idea of heading north into Chagataid lands to seek asylum with Abu Said's enemies. Eventually he struck upon the dubious notion of heading to Herat with what remained of his once powerful army and camp. Chupan's wife and son begged him to abandon the plan of seeking refuge in Herat with Ghias al-Din, citing the fates of Nawruz and Daneshmand Bahador at the hands of the Heratis. Chupan reasoned that having supported Ghias al-Din's cause at the Il-Khanid court, he would surely be kept safe behind Herat's walls and would surely find a friend within. Once again,

Herat and its leaders found themselves in an uncomfortable position, forced to choose between personal friendship and an all-powerful empire. Amir Chupan was initially welcomed by Ghias al-Din, but the latter's political conscience soon got the better of him and, mindful both of his obligations as Abu Said's vassal and also of Chupan's ongoing insurrection, he executed his guest.[130] One of Chupan's deformed fingers was sent to Abu Said as proof of death.[131] Yet another Mongol amir had met his death in contested circumstances within Herat's walls, and as Herat braced itself for a response, the death of the city's *malek* pushed it further into contested uncertainty. Ghias al-Din Kart's death in 1329 left Herat in an uneasy state, yet aside from two reigns of disastrous ineptitude, one by an alcoholic and one by an ineffectual aesthete more concerned with pigeon fancying than politics, rackety life within the walls of Herat continued with no major disasters.

* * *

On 1 December 1335, Il-Khan Abu Said died of heatstroke in a bathhouse.[132] With him went the Il-Khanate, gradually and violently withering away, heirless, confused and in turmoil. This marked the extinction of the line of Hulagu, and although a Chingizid puppet ruler, Arpa Keun, was hurriedly placed on the Il-Khanid throne, the fatal splits were clearly visible. When Arpa Keun fell, defeated in battle in April 1336 by another claimant to the throne, no semblance of unity within the Il-Khanate remained.[133] Consequent on the fall of the Il-Khanids, the Karts of Herat became, by default, an independent Khorasani political dynasty. They had outlived the descendants of Chingiz Khan. Moezz al-Din Kart (r.1332–70) was the last of his line to collect a *yarligh*, and when Il-Khanid pretenders to the throne came calling to subdue the city, he felt assured enough to dismiss them. He did, however, take a Chingizid bride, hedging his bets in an uncertain world.[134] This independence from the Il-Khans gave Herat's rulers the highly symbolic royal prerogatives of *khutbah*, mentioning the ruler's name in the Friday prayers, and the right to strike coins, *sikka*.[135] Herat's mosques rang out with the names of the Kart dynasty, and coins bearing their inscriptions passed through bazaars and to the edges of the lands they controlled. Kart *maleks* now bore the more elevated title Sultans of Herat, and invitations to submit to a Chingizid puppet were politely declined. A cursory glance at the chaotic state of other cities of this period, such as the turbulent Shiraz or the flattened Bokhara, only serves to highlight Herat's relative stability.[136]

It is a mark of Herat's pre-eminence that as the known political world crashed around Khorasan, Persia and into Iraq, artists, philosophers and scientists flocked to its court. It was a beacon of civility and sanctity, becoming a refuge for the 'grandees and nobles of the world', all of whom descended on the Hari Rud so that they might profit from Moezz al-Din's reputation for justice and equity.[137] The durable and independent Karts and their court had become two bright lights in a region of clouded political fragmentation. Herat and its newly independent sultans, a local Islamic dynasty that had outlived the Mongols, stood for unbroken ideals of stability, continuity and permanence. Their heritage reached back into the pre-1221 days, to a time before the parvenu Mongol infidels. It is little wonder that contemporary Iranian and Afghan historians, reflecting their own views on the negative consequences of foreign interference, see Moezz al-Din's reign as an unbroken and glorious time of Persian sovereignty.[138]

As the Il-Khanids descended further into family squabbles, Herat unfortunately did not enter into a particularly lengthy period of unbroken peace and tranquility, but instead had to live with the consequences of imperial collapse. It was soon confronted with the uprising of the Sarbedars of Sabzevar. The Sarbedars were a millenarian Shia force who sought the creation of a theocratic state of sorts; they arose from amongst the disorders thrown up by the fall of the Il-Khanate. For the Sarbedars, eschatology provided the driving force for social and political change in a world corrupted by evil and made uncertain by conflict. In many ways they occupy similar ground to their Bohemian Hussite contemporaries in Europe: a heady fusion of eschatological slogans, millenarian tendencies and real popular support. Because of its roots in political turmoil, and its concomitant message of equality, the Sarbedars have since been infused with anachronistic proto-socialist interpretations as a class-based revolution; its Marxist sheen in Iranian historiography says more about Cold War Iran than it does about the movement itself.[139] The group took their name from a pronouncement of a disgruntled man named Abdul Razzaq, who railed against the corruption and wickedness of those who ruled Khorasan. Abdul Razzaq fulminated that 'by God's grace we will succeed in doing away with the oppression of these tyrants, or else we will submit to having our heads on the gallows (*sar be dar*)'.[140] The injustices to which Abdul Razzaq alluded were most likely tax hikes placed over Khorasan by Il-Khanids in the dying days of their rule.[141]

When the opportunity presented itself, the Sarbedars executed a tax official in an uprising in Sabzevar, clearly announcing their intentions to the world. They then set Khorasan ablaze with the help of the preaching of a mystic from Mazandaran. These were not simply 'doers of evil and creators of disorder', as the anti-Shia Moroccan Ibn Batuta would have us believe, but rather they created a functioning state at Sabzevar, and ruled over large swathes of Khorasan, minting their own coinage and becoming genuine regional dynasts in the process.[142] Common to all expanding political dynasties, especially those with a religious or millenarian bent, it was not long before the Sarbedars aroused the suspicion and hostility of their neighbours. The Sarbedars' ability to inflame revolutionary ardour amongst the masses and their strong alliances with Herat's long-standing enemies, Chupan's still-aggrieved descendants, meant that Kartid Herat was right to worry about the threat they posed. Some have suggested that the Karts had aroused the ire of the Sarbedars through aggressively spreading the Sunni faith, but this is a difficult position to sustain, given that the Karts had not previously shown any real tendencies to religious persecution, terms such as 'infidel' being reserved for Mongols and Chagataids.[143] The simple explanation for the conflict between Herat and the Sarbedars, as given by Hafez Abru, that 'they had gathered a large army' and were marching on Herat, buoyed by the news of the Karts' military reverse in Kerman in 1340, is more plausible.[144]

In June 1342, at Zaveh, south-east of Nishapur, Moezz al-Din arranged his 'bloodthirsty' armies of Helmandis, Ghurids, Nikudaris and Baluch against the Sarbedars. Although his enemies, said to have been 'as numerous as the rain and seemingly propelled by a storm', initially had the upper hand, Moezz al-Din quickly moved his troops to higher ground and there set up his kettledrums and standards to encourage his men below.[145] The tactic worked and on the death of their leader Shaykh Hassan Juri the crazed assassins and dervishes of the Sarbedars fled, giving Herat a victory which would keep the two enemies at arms' length for almost thirty years.[146] The battle of Zaveh was both a triumph and a disaster for Herat. Filled with the zeal of victory, Moezz al-Din pushed his gains north, well into Shiburghan and Balkh where he routed enemies and sacked cities. He returned to Herat laden with skulls and the hubris of conquest. This wanton provocation caused the Chagataid princes and amirs of northern Afghanistan to seek revenge. Some speculated that Herat's leader had become overblown with conceit since his victory in 1342 against the Sarbedars. By building towers of skulls to line the northern approaches to the Old City of Herat, Moezz al-Din did little to refute this speculation.[147]

These amirs of northern Afghanistan, 'fed up with Ghurid [Kartid] adventurism', distressed at an upstart Herati minting his own coins and pronouncing his own *khutbah*, and no doubt peeved at the piling of skulls in Herat (traditionally a Mongol spectacle), marched on Badghis in 1350 alongside the descendants of Herat's enemies and the last flickering remnants of the Il-Khanid empire.[148] Raging at the dying of the Mongol light, they demanded, 'Has the race of Genghis [*sic*] Khan collapsed that there is no one to destroy this shah?'[149] Proving worthy successors to their ancestor, they routed the Kart army outside Herat. The Kartid troops were blinded by light and swirling dust and Herat once more found itself under siege, and once more it held out. Moezz al-Din ordered that a wide wall be constructed from the village of Boy Margh to the Kahdistan meadow, and that the eastern entrances and exits to Herat be sealed and that all weapons be taken from the city to the defensive wall. These defensive measures were all in vain, for Herat was forced to sue for peace and send gold to placate their tormentors. It was a ruinous peace that contained in it an ominous promise that the Chagataids would return to Herat that winter to take what they considered theirs by right.[150] This defeat proved to be Moezz al-Din's temporary undoing in Herat, for tensions amongst the ruling classes, exacerbated by defeat and hunger, came to the surface. Intrigues amongst the Sufi shaykhs of Jam against Moezz al-Din climaxed in dramatic fashion, causing a temporary exile.

One day in 1351 in the bazaar of Herat, Moezz al-Din was surrounded by a group of Ghurids. He sensed that their intentions were not friendly. Yet he had the presence of mind to point his would-be assassins in the direction of some Mongols, come to Herat from Badghis to sell horses, and politely suggested that the Ghurids pillage the available merchandise as opposed to killing him. No doubt the Ghurids, if what we are told about their state of mind is true, were caught between a desire for pillage and their duties as potential regicides, and in the commotion that followed, Moezz al-Din fled first to Aman Koh and then to Transoxania.[151] During his flight, Moezz al-Din struck up an alliance wtih a Chagataid amir who had previously sacked Herat. This enabled Moezz al-Din to return and enter the citadel under disguise. He quickly arrested the plotters whilst they held court, and on the same day reassumed his role as sovereign of Herat.

Moezz al-Din's return in 1352 marked the beginning of a period of tranquil prosperity for Herat. The sunny uplands of political independence and stability found a mirror image in a vibrant courtly life. Herat flourished with a strong king at the helm of government, and scheming nobles from Ghur retreated back to the shadows of power; the rightful Sultan of Herat had returned to his throne in the *qalah*. Herat's court once again became a refuge for those fleeing the fall-out from the declining Il-Khanate, and the presence at court of the famous Ibn Yamin, captured at Zaveh in 1342, provided Herat with a poet of truly regional renown. Moezz al-Din is not known to have built on such a grand scale as his predecessors, perhaps feeling more secure in the outward trappings of real independence, but his work on restoring and renewing Herat's irrigation canals is to be added to the long list of Kart contributions to Herat. Clearly a man with a passion for irrigation, early on in his reign Moezz al-Din devised a system for dividing up the irrigation canals, a fact which is noted by the twentieth-century historian of Herat, Mayel Heravi, when he notes, 'With regards the division of the water canals, we have no earlier indications on the division of Herat's canal network than from the time of the Karts.'[152] Yet no amount of flowing water could protect Herat from the earthquake of 1364, an earthquake so severe that an arch of the Friday Mosque, 'such as no other city in the world contains', was destroyed.[153]

With Moezz al-Din at the helm, Herat could look east to India and the Delhi Sultanate in search of trade, patronage and bouts of mutual diplomatic flattery. Herat had become the centre of a booming regional trade in horses, from Iran to India and north into Central Asia.[154] Horses reared in Badghis' fertile plains were sent south to Qandahar, from where they would travel to Delhi via Multan, north to Merv and south-west to Kerman in Iran. Cultural exchanges between Delhi and Herat showed those two cities to be the brightest lights in in the region, as poets and artists and musicians travelled freely back and forth. Herat now represented a significant political, commercial and cultural regional power, a fact which would have seemed impossible after Eljigidei Noyin had reduced it to rubble and massacred its people. Yet stability in medieval Khorasan was a precious and fleeting commodity. To the north of Herat, a Chagataid of extreme ruthlessness by the name of Timur, or Tamerlane, was making striking military advances in a bid to resuscitate the former glories of Chingiz Khan's empire. These were the dark clouds appearing on an otherwise clear horizon.

* * *

In the early spring of 1370, Moezz al-Din fell ill. Sensing that his time was almost upon him, he gathered together his sons and Herat's nobles to read his last will and testament. He demanded that the peasants, on whose shoulders rested so much, were not to be harmed, and that their place in society would be respected.[155] From Herat's court he demanded that they align their conduct with the dictates of religious law, that they rule Herat with justice.[156] He enjoined loyalty to the Kart name and gave his principal lands and title to his eldest son, Ghias al-Din Pir Ali (hereafter Pir Ali). In an unusual move, Moezz al-Din gave Sarakhs, a town and citadel to the north-east of Herat, to his other son, Mohammad.[157] The decision was unorthodox, for it divided Herat's territorial unity, previously such a feature of the dynasty's strength. It is difficult to discern any obvious strategic benefit from the division, save possibly reinforcing northern trade routes. As a coda to this bequest, Moezz al-Din expressly stated that his sons should remain united, and forbade them to fight over their respective inheritances. They should consult each other on how best to govern in the interests of Herat, not in the interests of personal ambition.

Moezz al-Din died on 29 May 1370, and although his dynasty would limp on for another decade, a death knell for the Karts was clearly sounded with his passing. The body of this immensely significant ruler of Herat was buried according to the necessary rites and traditions in the septentrionale of Herat's Friday Mosque, close by his father's tomb. Moezz al-Din's legacy as an independent ruler over Herat and Khorasan was assured and it endures to this day: a respected, powerful and wise ruler. A prominent Afghan intellectual of the 1950s simply stated: 'Until his death, he remained an independent ruler.'[158] For Afghanistan in the fourteenth century, as in the 1950s when the country was caught up in the Cold War, independence was a prized asset, and those who achieved it were praised accordingly.

For all Moezz al-Din's advice and well-meaning deathbed speeches, the inevitable fraternal conflict came to pass. And yet it was not through Pir Ali's desire for more land or power that this uneasy coalition came crashing down, but rather through the intrigues of 'perfidious and corrupted advisers' close to the court at Sarakhs. These advisers planted the seed of 'sedition, the thorn of satanic delusions and mad fictions' between the two brothers, bringing Mohammad to the point of dividing his lands from Herat, breaking up the patrimony his father had created.[159] Mohammad soon turned his back on the oaths of alliance he had sworn in the spring of 1370, and he removed Pir Ali's name from coins and from prayers, thus splitting Herat from Sarakhs. Mohammad was clearly ruthless and opportunistic, always out to ally with anyone who might help his cause. By way of revenge, Pir Ali marched on Sarakhs to subdue his rebellious brother and re-establish Herat's territorial unity with Sarakhs. After a brief campaign in the biting cold of a brutal winter which claimed the lives of more soldiers than did the fighting, Pir Ali brokered a peace deal with his brother and then departed for Herat with the opaque status quo ante having been restored.[160] The scorn with which Hafez Abru describes Mohammad's inclination to go against his father's deathbed commands clearly reflects a Timurid chronicler's abhorrence at the thought of sedition and the division of Herat's lands. The expanse of territory the Karts had ruled as Il-Khanid vassals and now as independent sovereigns was being gradually broken up by ambition and infighting.

As Mohammad's loyalties were being mended, events dragged back the Sarbedarid threat, long dormant, into Herat's sphere of influence. Their rule in Sabzevar and Nishapur was by now well established and they sought to flex their muscles in the name of a Shia theocracy. Pir Ali countered by pushing Herat's armies north-east in an attempt to check the Sarbedars' advances into Khorasan. Herat's *ulema* duly issued a *fatwa* in 1371 enjoining its Sunni Muslims to fight the infidel Shia, providing the gloss of *jihad* to what was little more than a simple display of political expansion on Pir Ali's part.[161] The use of religion in this context as a way of masking political ambition and expansion is reflected by Hafez Abru, the Herati chronicler, who uses the phrase '*wa sabab-e dige…*', which roughly translates as 'and another reason', when describing the religions motivation for this particular campaign; religion was a secondary, tertiary motivation for protecting Herat's territorial unity. Herat's reaction to the Sarbedarid threat was, in essence, part of a regional and local political struggle in which Mohammad's questionable loyalty at Sarakhs and the proximity of that citadel to Sarbedarid strongholds in Khorasan played key roles. Politics and context, as ever, trumped all.[162]

Pir Ali drew up his troops in 1371 for the first of three attacks on Nishapur in an attempt to dislodge the Sarbedars from Khorasan. He would eventually take the city in 1375, after both sides had endured terrible losses. Sabzevar fell in 1376–7 and Herat's domination of the Shia revolutionaries was momentarily complete. Nishapur suffered heavily, many of its canals and mosques destroyed in the fighting. Acres of walnut trees lay ruined and charred as the Sunni Herati troops departed for the Hari Rud.[163] A popular anecdote told by the Timurid historian Esfezari relates that during his conquests Pir Ali came across a Shia man from Nishapur, and asked him to name the main tenets of Islam. The old man replied, unaware of his audience: 'They are three, according to Pir Ali. One, grazing horses on the corn crops of Muslims; two, destroying their canals for cultivation; three, sacking their forests.'[164] Pir Ali was, so the chronicle went, ashamed of the part he had played in the ruin of Nishapur, and he returned to Herat with a heavy conscience, abandoning the idea of permanently controlling Nishapur and its surrounds. Despite this story, it is worth asking whether his decision effectively to abandon the city he had so recently conquered was solely a result of a guilty conscience. Perhaps he also sensed the perils of territorial overreach in a time of instability and uncertainty as Timur made lightening conquests across Central Asia?[165]

* * *

As the Sarbedars' fortunes declined, Timur's entry into Khorasan demanded the attention of Herat and its rulers. Timur had been making inroads into Central Asia with steady, and often brutal, military victories, and in the spring of 1372 he granted Kabul and Kunduz to his followers, a significant event, for these cities had previously belonged to Herat. The Karts had entertained diplomatic relations with Timur earlier in the century, a time when envoys moved back and forth over the Oxus in displays of respect and probing diplomacy. Initially, it had been Timur who had feared the Karts; he was wary of their reputation for executing powerful Mongol generals and of the prodigious height of the citadel, Qalah-ye Ekhtiar al-Din. Timur even struck a treaty of friendship with Moezz al-Din, and it is likely that Timur assisted Moezz al-Din in his triumphant return to Herat after the latter's escape from Ghurid assassins. As if to repay this deed, Timur and his family lived for a period under effective Kart protection near to Merv. Yet despite these shared moments, Timur coveted Herat, and Herat in turn lived in fear of one of the world's most ruthless conquerors.

In 1376, a messenger reached Herat from Timur's court at Samarqand. He brought with him renewed expressions of a desire that Herat and Samarqand might be bound by ties of loyalty and friendship. The Karts and Timur were to be friends, not enemies.[166] The messenger also came with a proposal of marriage between Timur's own niece, Sevenich Qutlugh Agha, and the grandson of Moezz al-Din, Pir Mohammad. In Timur's mind the alliance would bring Herat one stage closer to being his vassal. For Herat, this was a difficult proposal to refuse, and yet its acceptance brought with it expectations of loyalty and hints of submission. Accepting the proposal, the young couple were married in Samarqand, and Timur himself lavished gifts and honours on Pir Mohammad. The newly married couple returned to Herat in 1378 for yet more betrothal feasts, and the city received the returning prince along with a wedding party of Timurid and Chagataid nobles with 'joy unbounded'. On hearing of the party's approach, Pir Ali ordered the city to be made 'like the Garden of Eden'. Herat's arches and pillars at the north of the city were festooned with beautifully decorated silk banners. These fine materials were draped along the tops of buildings, running all the way to the central bazaar, the Chahar Su. Each guild of Herat's craftsmen was instructed to create something beautiful in their own traditional fashion: silk, metalwork, carpentry and woven banners or silken signs. Herat's bakers baked towers of bread inside which it was said a grown man could walk, and the walls and gates of the city of Herat were adorned with gold-embroidered silk hangings brought from as far afield as Europe and China.[167]

This celebration marked the high watermark of Herat's Kartid history: cultural, urban and artistic majesty seamlessly intertwined with a political match of mutual benefit. Herat was once again a player on the global stage, shining bright. Yet even the most naïve observer would have discerned the storm clouds gathering. Timur's ruthless expansionism had found human form in the beautiful young bride, and this match simply set Herat on a collision course with the megalomaniac ambitions of the region's latest would-be Chingiz Khan. The city's hard-won place at the high table of Khorasan's political power game was fatally threatened, but nevertheless Herat burned bright and happy before its extinction. The fluttering of the silken flags and embroidered drapery foreshadowed a city in flames.

Echoing the Mongol custom of convening meetings, *quiriltais*, to mark territorial expansion and to choose a new khan, in the winter of 1379–80 a Timurid envoy brought word to Herat of a *quiriltai* to be convened in Samarqand: a recognition of Timur's regional power. The diplomatic niceties of weddings and treaties had been replaced by cold requests for recognition of suzerainty. The Karts must now officially recognise Timur's power in the region and thus submit themselves to vassal status, a process they knew would end either in war or capitulation.[168] Pir Ali's year-long building of fortifications in Herat and his strengthening the city's outer walls to a distance of 8 miles give us an indication of how Herat intended to face these requests for submission.[169] Despite Timur's emphasis of the strength of their bond and the closeness of their ties, Herat sent the envoy back to Samarqand empty-handed. In retribution for this snub, Prince Miranshah, Timur's son, was sent to the lands to the north and east of Herat at the head of 50,000 troops to challenge Pir Ali's brazen refusal. Miranshah spent three months in Badghis in the winter of 1380–81, pillaging and harrying in preparation for an assault on Herat.[170] At the tender age of fourteen, Miranshah was in the very best tradition of precocious young princes sent to Khorasan to learn the arts of governance, warfare and pillage. As a teenager, he was prodigious in his appetite for booty; in later life, he became a cruel and violent man.

Herat now lay at the mercy of a Timurid army gathered from the conquered tribes of Central Asia, and a very angry teenager. Timur soon joined his son in the spring of 1381, and from there they headed to Sarakhs, where they met with Mohammad Kart, whose previous proclivity for political opportunism resurfaced. Mohammad, sensing the arrival of a conqueror of rare skill, aligned himself with Timur against his brother and against Herat. This alliance now secured, Timur travelled to Jam where he visited the venerable Sufi Pir, Mawlana Zayn al-Din. The two men, as per Hafez Abru's account, discussed the state of affairs at Herat. Timur asked the holy man why he did not scold Pir Ali, a man described as a negligent, soft-hearted and weak-willed ruler, for indulging in vices, alcohol and pleasures forbidden in Islamic law.[171] The holy man replied that he had done so, but that no heed was paid to it, and consequently God had brought Timur as divine vengeance for the sins of Herat's rulers. As if to prove he was no push-over or toadying courtier, the Sufi is said to have finished the meeting with the ominous warning to Timur: 'Your punishment will be the same if you do not heed the advice to govern well and within the precepts of justice and Islamic law.'[172] Whilst this is a convenient way for Hafez Abru, a Timurid chronicler, to portray Timur as a divinely sanctioned conqueror of Herat, the emphasis on justice and ruling according to the precepts of Islamic law is a wonderful indication of political currents in Herat and Iran at this time. Absent is any specific appeal to a Chingizid legacy, or the illustrious deeds of the Il-Khanids. Instead we get a sense of continuity within change. The enduring justice of ruling in accordance with Islam and its precepts provides the ultimate sense of legitimacy for Timur; those who flout these laws essentially commit political suicide.[173]

Having razed Kousieh and Fushang, Timur now arrived at Herat in the late spring of 1381. Pir Ali had been building up his defences since 1379, and he set about bringing people from outside Herat into the city, exhorting Herat to stand firm in the face of the likely onslaught. Pir Ali demanded that 'every man should fight for the protection of his wife and children and give everything of himself' in the defence of their beloved city.[174] So confident was Pir Ali of the impregnability of the city walls, the citadel within and the courage and loyalty of his subjects that he took to the bottle, seeking 'in wine blissful ignorance of the dangers by which he was presently menaced'.[175] Given Timur's reputation for military genius and ruthlessness, it is not surprising that Herat's rulers chose to drown their sorrows before attempting to resist. On arrival at Herat, Timur ordered the moat ringing the city's defences to be crossed and that all walls outside Herat be torn down. Herat's garrison attempted a surprise attack from within the city whilst Timur's army set up camp; fighting continued until nightfall. The following day, a Friday, a Chagataid prince led an attack on the Kartid positions at the point where the Injil canal enters the city, and in this exchange Timur's forces took nearly 2,000 Herati prisoners. Timur spared the lives of the prisoners as a signal to Herat's inhabitants that surrender would not automatically be met with execution. Some within Herat's impregnable citadel even refused to fight; others close to Pir Ali advised that he execute those who wanted peace, so as to set an example. In a display of humanity and common sense, Pir Ali replied that he was not prepared to shed any more of his city's blood in vain. To which his advisers replied simply, 'Then you can no longer hope to hold onto this city.'[176]

Negotiations for peace followed. Timur assumed the position of a traditional Mongol conqueror, offering the Karts either submission and their lives, or destruction. His reminder to Pir Ali that Herat had always been a Mongol city must have irked such a proud and independent Herati ruler. Pir Ali sent out his son and his wife to discuss terms with Timur, then residing in the luxurious Bagh-e Zaghan (The Garden of Ravens). The discussions were cordial, but Timur eventually forced Pir Ali into issuing orders to destroy the walls and fortifications he had so assiduously built up over the years. The vast iron gates which had guarded Herat for nearly a century, and on which the names of successive Kart *maleks* were inscribed, were placed on carts and disappeared over the Oxus; they were never found or heard of again. The treasury in the citadel was emptied of all its vast treasures, and Hafez Abru's account of this episode contains a note of sadness despite his obvious Timurid loyalties. Herat's past glories that had been created by an indigenous dynasty of Khorasan and Herat were summarily dismantled. Two hundred of Herat's leading nobles were then taken away, after three or four days spent rounding them up. Herat had been neutered, its defences torn down, its coffers emptied. It was stripped of men of influence and wealth, and Pir Ali himself was forced to march to

Samarqand. His son, along with a pathetic shell of a Kartid court, were left to rule over a desolated Herat under the watchful eye of Miranshah. Prayers were said and coins were struck in the name of Timur, Herat's new overlord; the Kartid rule as independent sovereigns of Herat came to an abrupt end.[177]

Today all that remains intact of Kartid Herat's artistic contribution to Herat is a large bronze bowl, beautifully inscribed with the names of the Kart rulers up to Fakhr al-Din; it sits behind a perspex box in a corner of the Friday Mosque. I used to make a point of examining it each time I visited the mosque, awestruck at being in the immediate presence of the past: so close to an object that the Kart dynasty family and Herat's fourteenth-century coppersmiths would have touched and seen. Quite how it has remained in Herat through centuries of conquest is something of a mystery, although it did disappear from Herat during the 1980s when conflict raged against the occupying Soviets. During Herat's famine of 1970–71, it was used as a vessel from which to dispense food to the starving and needy.

Much as in 1221, in 1381 Herat was left in a state of uncertainty and tension, having been taken by force of arms but not totally destroyed. In the absence of utter desolation, there always remains a glimmer of hope. As the wagons of gold and treasure, nobles, princes, princesses and craftsmen made their way to exile in Samarqand and Central Asia, two disgruntled and disinherited Kartid sons plotted a rebellion which would, they thought, land them on the throne of Herat. They had been prisoners in the citadel for a decade, and were itching to take revenge on the world. The two men had managed to persuade Timur that they should be set free and allowed into positions of power; and in a rare lapse of judgement, Timur granted the men their freedom. They decided to attempt to take power for themselves instead of submission to one of the world's greatest and most ruthless conquerors. It was a costly miscalculation which underestimated both the swiftness of Timur's vengeance and his son's efficiency as a conduit for it. In the spring of 1383 they forced the garrison within the citadel to admit them and their rabble of men. As fighting erupted, the men started a fire which not only destroyed much of the citadel and its buildings, but also spread to the districts of the province. Hundreds of Timurid soldiers died in this opportunistic and entirely chaotic uprising. The ghosts of 1221 had come back to haunt its conquerors. Herat had once again become a charnel house of destruction; and as was the case in 1221, vengeance would be swift and furious.

Herat's Timurid chroniclers write of this brief and futile rebellion in a damning fashion; this was not heroic resistance, but brainless larceny. The chroniclers' ire reflects both their loyalty to Timurid patrons, but also to the city of Herat itself. It was the city which suffered the most, and this is as much lamented as the act of sedition that had caused it. Timur's response was predictable. He executed Pir Ali in Samarqand and then ordered Miranshah, camped in Badghis, to march south on the rebels and to send out advance parties to clear the way. Herat was now leaderless and in chaos, at the mercy of Timur's vengeance. While the first conquest had offered glimpses of humanity, in these changed circumstances, Miranshah manifested a cruelty beyond belief. The initial fighting took place in Herat's main street, the *khiaban*, which runs from the Old City north to Gazur Gah. There, mounds of Herati skulls were piled high in the wide streets where silken ribbons had previously hung from arch to arch to celebrate the Kartid–Timurid marriage alliance. Timur himself reached Herat in November 1383 and ordered a further massacre, taking whatever of value he could find. Tales of streets piled with bodies and houses desolate from destruction are the depressing coda to the Kartid dynasty's hold over Herat.

* * *

The Karts had been rightly famed for their cultural achievements, their patronage of the arts and their sheer obstinate durability in the face of Mongol rule; they had rescued Herat from the despair of 1222, and dragged it back to life as a place of culture and a refuge for fleeing artists. They had ruled for nearly 150 years, far longer than their erstwhile Il-Khanid patrons; they had given Herat back its soul after the apocalypse of 1222, resisting in deed and word through the strength of the city's walls and the lifeblood of its cultural brilliance. It was a resistance at the centre of which stood the city of Herat, its canals, silk factories, citadel, Friday Mosque and the reputation it had as a pious, independent and indomitable fortress. Their story is interwoven into the fabric of Herat, the streams and the blood of the city; they had embodied its recklessness, its toughness and its enigmatic charm. Yet above all, the Karts bequeathed to Khorasan and the region a legacy of architectural and artistic excellence. It was a legacy from which the Timurids would fashion Herat into one the world's most captivatingly beautiful cities.

2

HERAT IN AN AGE OF HIGH ART, IMPERIAL FAVOUR AND LOW POLITICS, 1381–1510

In 1404 Timur's empire was secure; Herat was a pliant and conquered vassal. Timurid forces had sacked Delhi in 1398, and in the autumn of 1400 these troops pushed further into Arab territories, crushing the Mamluk Sultans, taking major cities one by one: Aleppo, Hama, Baalbek and Damascus. In the summer of 1402, Timur's armies pushed north and defeated the Ottoman ruler, Bayezid I (r.1389–1402). At this point, Timur's empire stretched from Egypt to the borders of China, and in a nod to the global ambitions of his hero, Chingiz Khan, Timur then launched a campaign into China. This was to be his last, however.[1] Timur succumbed to a fever after an energetic drinking bout on 18 February 1405 in the town of Otrar, where Khorasan's fate had been sealed in 1218.

Some mourned Timur's passing: others did not.[2] The unity provided by his leadership of such a vast empire was gone in an instant, resulting in furious internecine conflict.[3] Khorasan and Central Asia had fought bitter wars for he scraps of Chingiz Khan's legacy in the thirteenth century; Herat now feared that history would repeat itself. On hearing of Timur's death, Herat's then governor, Shah Rukh, a son of Timur, made preparations to safeguard the province and city. He raised money and ordered the armies of Badghis to Herat. He sent emissaries to Samarqand in pursuit of intelligence.[4] Herat's ramparts were restored to the 'apogee of their height', and the moats were sunk to the 'very nadir of depth'.[5] With Herat's fortifications more secure and its treasure gathered in the citadel, Shah Rukh set out for Samarqand to stake his claim to the Timurid throne.

In Samarqand, Timur had been succeeded by his grandson, the young prince and noted romantic, Khalil Sultan (r. 1405–7). Khalil Sultan presided over a brief rule of rare profligacy. A chronicler noted how Khalil Sultan 'threw open the treasury that Amir Timur had amassed throughout his reign from the taxes on Iran and Turan and, like the April rain, nay the mines of Badakhshan and the sea of Oman, scattered silver and pearls over soldiers and civilians'.[6] On account of this liberality, and his deep infatuation with the courtesan Shad Malek Agha, Khalil Sultan's rule and his liberty were cut short by a rebellious coup. Meanwhile, Shah Rukh was marching his army from Herat, and owing to the chaos unfolding in Samarqand he faced little in the way of stiff resistance. He conquered with relative ease, and with all the major claimants to the imperial throne dead or in chains, Shah Rukh became the ruler of a fractured Timurid empire. Shah Rukh resolved to govern his newly won lands not from Samarqand, where his son assumed the role of governor, but from Herat, the 'dome of Islam'.

Shah Rukh's decision to move his capital south represented a desire to appeal to an Islamic heritage which would burnish his religious credentials in the eyes of those over whom and through whom he would rule.[7] He wished to cloak himself in a blanket of Sunni orthodoxy and to do away with the Mongol heritage that had so defined Timur's imperial ambitions. Timur's tombstone in Samarqand carries an inscription which directly links his ancestry to Alanqoa, a mythical Mongol queen whose offspring were said to include Chingiz Khan himself, and Timur married his sons to Chingizid princesses (NB this tombstone was erected in the 1430s by Prince Baysanghur). Timur's empire had seen a continuation of legal traditions in the name of the Mongol *yasa* (Mongol law code which is said to have originated with Chingiz Khan and was codified under Mongke Khan). This uneasy balance he had struck between Islamic and Mongol traditions would be reversed by Shah Rukh's conscious move towards a more Islamic self-image.[8]

For Shah Rukh the old steppe notions of legitimacy seemed to be of little use as he built his imperial edifice on self-consciously Islamic foundations, but still the tension between the urban and the nomadic, the shamanistic and the Islamic persisted through artistic expression and the actions of the Timurid military elites residing in Herat. In many ways this tension defines Shah Rukh's rule over Herat, for whilst he is portrayed as the 'Emperor of Islam', and not the hybrid amalgam of Mongol and Muslim preferred by other Mongol or Timurid rulers, hints at the survival of Mongol practices can be found up until the Timurid dynasty's fall.[9] Shah Rukh quickly restored the *sharia* as the legal code of his empire, dispensing with the Mongol *yasa*, so beloved of Timur, and his coinage, minted in Herat and exhibiting the phrase *Khallada Allahu khilafatahu* (May God perpetuate his caliphate), are evidence of intentions to create an Islamic imperial capital at Herat.[10] Shah Rukh's very first actions in Herat on assuming imperial power were to build religious institutions through which he could promulgate and codify his Sunni religious credentials.[11] Indeed, such was Shah Rukh's Islamic piety that Herat's chroniclers portrayed him as a saint, describing how miracles occurred around him.[12] Herat's fame as a city of Sufi shrines, a valley lined with the dust of the saints, and its upstanding Sunni orthodoxy—and yet the distinctly fluid boundaries between Sunni and Sufi, Shia and Alid—meant that it was the perfect place on which to construct Shah Rukh's imperial edifice.

Yet Shah Rukh could never totally discard his Mongol ancestry, or the language and imagery of earlier histories. Indeed, one chronicler observed that such was the strength of Mongol traditions amongst Herat's Timurid elites that were Shah Rukh to have outlawed Mongol law, his followers would 'flee like assess to the gate'.[13] A genealogy commissioned in Herat during Shah Rukh's rule, the *Muizz al-ansab* (The Glorifier of Genealogies), is an extension of a work begun under Chingiz Khan. In this work, the Timurid line is traced directly back to Chingiz Khan and beyond, showing how Herat played host to a broader struggle for identity between Timurid nobles who embraced their past and those who rejected it in favour of Islamic legitimation.[14] Perhaps it was a sop to some Timurid aristocrats who felt that Shah Rukh was in danger of forgetting his history? From this we get the distinct image that all is not as it appears in Timurid Herat, subtly undermining the glorious Islamic edifice its rulers created for the city.

In regional political terms, the greatest challenge facing Shah Rukh came in the form of the Qara Qoyunlu tribe (Black Sheep), described by one historian as 'the great unresolved problem of the Timurid empire'.[15] The Qara Qoyunlu were a Shia Turcoman tribe who exercised control over present-day Azerbaijan, northern Persia and Iraq-e Arab. The Qara Qoyunlu had earlier taken Baghdad from the Jalayirid dynasty and had subdued territories from the Caucasus to Qazvin. In battle they had killed Miranshah, Herat's erstwhile governor and one-time destroyer. Although the campaigns outside Herat were frequent and costly and Shah Rukh's control of his fragmentary empire was tenuous, he could be assured of Herat's internal stability and was more or less confident of his control over it.[16] One Timurid chronicler wrote how Herat's peasantry enjoyed peace and prosperity that 'have never been known in any other epoch from the time of Adam until today'.[17] Shah Rukh could thus present himself as the very ideal of a just Islamic ruler who provided peace in his territories, allowing life to function, Islam to flourish and his lands to prosper. Peace is also good for the historian, for aside from providing a welcome break from an endless cycle of siege and conflict, it affords us the luxury to look at Herat in a more or less thematic fashion, albeit within the framework of a dynasty of roughly two parts: the stability and prosperity of Shah Rukh's reign, and then—with a messy interlude—the bright lights of Husain Bayqara's Herat.

With his authority secured, Shah Rukh could turn his attention to creating a capital worthy of the great Timurid name, and a city to rival the ostentation and scale of ambition of Timur's Samarqand.[18] It was thus in 1410 that a great Timurid building boom began, given impetus by access to imperial coffers and taking its lead from the Kartid city of the previous century. In the same year, Shah Rukh ordered the construction of his own *madrasa* and *khaneqah* within Herat's city walls, to the east of the citadel, in an area on which the Kartids had themselves built.[19] Timur had embodied the tension between sedentary and nomadic. He was a man who spent vast sums making Samarqand a city of breathtaking scale and beauty, yet who also roundly chastised a fellow steppe warrior for fortifying the city of Balkh and thus violating nomadic traditions.[20] For Shah Rukh, however, it seemed there was no such tension. His architectural additions to Herat were a clear affirmation of his assimilation to Persianate urban life and his desire to leave behind the ways of the steppe. His early endeavours were designed to consolidate Herat and to establish power; this was the building of the utilitarian spaces—mosque, *madrasa*, defences and bazaars—as if Shah Rukh were somehow preparing Herat for the explosion of culture and brilliance that Husain Bayqara would later unleash on Herat. This was Shah Rukh, the conservative pious ruler bringing order to spaces which had seen so much chaos. Timurid power and wealth met Herat's religious repute and cultural sophistication: mutually assured seduction.

In these endeavours Shah Rukh was assisted by his wife, the most extraordinary woman to have graced Herat, Queen Gawhar Shad. Gawhar Shad means 'joyous jewel' in Persian, and her contributions to Herat and Mashhad—mosques, colleges, gardens and so much more— were on a scale to rival any of the region's great medieval patrons. Gawhar Shad was a daughter of a Chagataid noble, and as a patron of art and architecture ranks alongside the most cultured Medici or stylish Renaissance pontiff.[21] Were her talents to have ended simply at architectural magnificence, she would still deserve a place in history, but she was also a political operator of great skill and ruthlessness, qualities which sit uneasily with her exquisite taste for beautiful floral motifs on sky-high minarets. Her great patronage was largely directed towards monumental structures, most notably the *Masjed-e Gawhar Shad* (Gawhar Shad Mosque) which now abuts the shrine to Imam Reza, the eighth Shia Imam, in the Khorasanian city of Mashhad. Her greatest gift to Herat was the Gawhar Shad *madrasa* and her own mausoleum, whose crumbling remains can be found to the north of the Old City walls. She was aided in her great building projects by a native of Shiraz, Qawam al-Din Shirazi, the most brilliant of a number of Shirazi architects of the period. Shirazi was responsible for some of the most significant additions to a glittering Timurid skyline in Herat.[22] Now they are all but gone, ruined by centuries of conflict.

The remains of these buildings, their scale so characteristic of a bombastic Timurid architectural style, give tantalising glimpses of the ambition, expertise and thinking of Timurid Herat. Gawhar Shad's *mosalla* (this term refers to a large complex of religious buildings, often situated outside city walls and centred upon an *idgah*, a large space used for Ramadan prayers in particular) acted as a place where those from the surrounding districts came to pay their respects to God. Yet it seems that paying homage to the munificence and charity of Herat's ruling elite surely was not far from the minds of those who commissioned and

designed these edifices; it was not just God who was to be worshipped
in Timurid Herat. Gawhar Shad's famous structure was framed by an
entrance portal of over 80 feet in height; four minarets of real beauty
and scale sat in the corners of the inner courtyard. A visitor to the city
in the late nineteenth century made the following observations:

> The main building consists of a lofty dome some 75 feet in diameter, with
> a smaller dome behind it, and any number of rooms and buildings around
> it. The entrance to this dome is through a lofty archway on the east, some
> 80 feet in height, the face of which is entirely covered with tile-work and
> huge inscriptions in gilt; while above the archway is a lot of curious little
> rooms and passages, the use of which I cannot tell. To the east of this arch
> is a large courtyard some 80 yards square, surrounded with corridors and
> rooms several storeys in height—all covered with tile-work. The main
> entrance of all is on the eastern side of this court, through another huge
> archway, also some 80 feet in height, but though the inside of the arch is
> all lined with tiles, or rather mosaic-work in regular patterns, the outside
> is bare, and looks as if it had never been finished. Four minarets, some 120
> feet in height, form the four corners of the building: a good deal of the
> tile-work has been worn off by the weather… but when they were new,
> they must have been marvelously handsome.[23]

This courtyard played host to large numbers of worshippers who
came into Herat for the feasts marking special dates in the Islamic
calendar. Gawhar Shad's *madrasa* was a monumental vehicle for the
propagation of Timurid legitimacy, combining the Persian and Islamic
with the Timurid obsession with powerful and sizeable architectural
features. It was a space to impress Herat's visiting imperial dignitaries,
but also a place in which to educate Herat's next generation of scholars
and clerics.

The mausoleum itself—in which Baysanghur and Gawhar Shad,
among others, are buried, their tombs still visible today—resembles the
Gur-e Amir in Samarqand, the resting place of Timur, in that 'the ribbed
bulbous dome is supported on a high drum which rises from the cubical
structure with no visible transitional zone'.[24] As the English travel writer
Robert Byron remarked, with his customary wit, 'Few architectural
devices can equal a ribbed dome for blind, monumental ostentation.'[25]
The monumental ostentation Byron remarked on is sadly no longer in
evidence and the cupola is scarred with shoddy repairs, weather damage
and the odd bullet hole. To the east of Gawhar Shad's crumbling mauso-

leum, and within the confines of this once great complex, is one minaret. It leans precariously, saved from falling by cabling. It is now home to pigeons. The stump of another minaret stands at the south-west corner of the garden, kept company by an equally destroyed Soviet tank. Today, the use of the area as a garden for picnics has saved it from total ruin, and there is a nice resonance that this garden abutting Gawhar Shad's mausoleum is known today as the *bagh-e zananeh*, the ladies' garden, for it is reserved for women and small children on Fridays.

The architecture of Herat at this time was of a scale and precision that would have astounded everyone who saw it: imperial envoys, tradesmen, poets and the everyday Herati passing by. For size and grandeur, it was revolutionary; for its veneration of the ruling house and Timur, it was unsurpassed. Even today the mausoleum, or what remains of it, and the leaning minaret to its east make a mockery of the tacky architecture—Pakistani-style 'palaces'—that has begun to engulf Herat's Old City; the solidity and elegance of the Timurid architecture will outlast the hastily and poorly built high-rises that make up Herat's present-day shiny urban skyline.

During 2014, I had the great privilege to work with UNESCO on conservation projects relating to Gawhar Shad's mausoleum. I spent many afternoons inspecting the tiles and discussing glazings with European architects and ceramicists and talking with Herat's own craftsmen on the buildings that UNESCO hoped to conserve and restore. The quality of the glaze on the Timurid tiles and the precision of the motifs astound the world's leading experts on architecture, ceramics and tile glazing. The same level of accuracy and consistency, the tile-works on the ribbed dome, the *muqaranas* (the stalactite features which visually support the ribbed dome of the cupola) and the *kufic* (Quranic verses) band which encircles the drum, still partially visible, might never be reproduced in Herat. Herat's depleted stock of ceramicists and glazers can do little but shrug at the beauty and complexity of their ancestors' craftsmanship. Yet they continue to work, inheritors of a tradition in the Friday Mosque, chipping away, glazing and always aiming to reach the heights of achievement of the fifteenth century. Experienced and renowned Italian ceramicists with whom I worked could not believe the consistency of glaze and colour, made even more extraordinary for the fact that it has withstood the passage of time and conflict. Herat's 120-

day hot summer winds, blowing through the city year after year, have also worn away the exposed sides of remaining minarets and Gawhar Shad's mausoleum. These staggeringly beautiful faience patterns of flower and geometry that one can still see on the minarets and parts of the drum surrounding Gawhar Shad's mausoleum are a distinctively 'Timurid' architectural feature. To have held them in my hands was humbling and exhilarating at the same time.

While our UNESCO team worked on the dome, I used the mausoleum as an 'office', setting up a laptop each morning on a rickety table, with Gawhar Shad and Husain Bayqara's tombs visible over the top of my screen. The temptation to label it 'surreal' was to be avoided at all times; everything and nothing in Herat is surreal. The beautiful deep reds and heavenly blues of the colouring of the inside of the mausoleum and the interwoven meshed stalactite arches reaching upwards to support the ribbed dome create a sense of space and even motion which is truly captivating; it is a space in which it is a pleasure to exist. The walls and arches are now faded, blues and reds no longer as brilliant, but the glories of the architecture and its intentions still strike anyone who enters.[26] In the fifteenth century the mausoleum held no official Islamic function (and its veneration of a non-religious figure is not without its controversies amongst Herat's conservative religious elites), yet it is a space in which the sacred is palpable and calm is everywhere. In a poignant reminder of the decline of this all but destroyed seat of learning, this monument to one of Herat's greatest patrons of the art and the sciences, at the back of the mausoleum currently stand three book cabinets in which are kept a bizarre assortment of obscure English textbooks (on, variously, computer programming and maths), Persian poetry and books on Afghan politics. There is a computer, long broken, that sits as some sort of a trophy behind the desk. We would eat our lunch next to the tombstones.

A popular story relating to Gawhar Shad and the *madrasa* she founded is told today in Herat, although owing to its scandalous nature, it currently gets a poorer reception than it might have done in the fifteenth century. When Gawhar Shad went to inspect her college upon its completion, she arrived at the building on what might well have been a glorious summer's afternoon, along with over 200 ladies in waiting. The young men studying in the school had all been sent away for fear of any impropriety should they come into contact with the ladies of the royal court. Yet one young student had remained behind, having fallen asleep in an alcove of the college. He woke to see a 'ruby-lipped lady'. Desire overwhelmed both the student and the lady in waiting and their lustful tryst was betrayed when the young lady returned to the royal inspection as her clothes were askew and her face flushed. Gawhar Shad, in her infinite wisdom and compassion, decided to bless this happening, not condemn it. Every one of her 200 ladies in waiting was married off to a young seminary to whom she gave a salary, a bed and clothes. Husband and wife could meet once a week, but the students were required to continue their studies. Whether Gawhar Shad really did this to 'arrest the progress of adultery', or not, we shall never know, but it speaks of real humanity and no little common sense.[27] It is little wonder that Heratis still sang ballads in praise of Gawhar Shad and her wondrous works well into the early twentieth century, and today she is a hero for Herat's young girls. One Indian visitor to the city in the early nineteenth century was so moved by tales of her genius and artistic patronage that he described her as 'the most incomparable woman in the world'.[28]

The area on which this building boom took place in Timurid Herat was an expanse of irrigated fields to the north of the Old City, the *khiaban*.[29] The *khiaban*, which roughly translates as 'boulevard', became the 'architectural focus' of the Timurid building project, stretching to the foothills of the shrine of Herat's most famous mystic, Abdullah Ansari, at Gazur Gah.[30] The area took its water from the Juy-e Naw, a canal running east to west around the north of the Old City walls, and was a place in which Timurid Herat's rulers and powerful men and women would live, play and work. Here their power could be incarnated in the beauty of gardens and tiled surfaces. The settlement of royal and non-royal figures of note in the newly-populated areas along the *khiaban* contains in it a nice example of the tensions between sedentary and nomadic, and how they were possibly being broken down in Herat as the Timurid elites were gradually seduced by Persianate urban culture. The nomadic attitude to urban spaces traditionally bordered on the disdainful, but Herat seemed to break down these barriers with charming ease. Sedentary life was something to which some of the Timurid elites had evidently taken, but strictly on their terms—

outside the city, and in gardens which glorified, tamed and harnessed the power of nature. They had chosen to rule from the irrigated spaces to the north of the city, removed from the sedentary bustle of the urban masses.

This stretch of land also played practical functions of power and diplomacy. It functioned as a route which carried trade and political emissaries from north to south, a route on which visitors would pass Herat's architectural riches and marvel at its power and wealth. Travellers on this route, down the *khiaban* and into the city, passing south again through the Firuzabad Gate onwards south to Farah, Qandahar and then India, would have seen Timurid Herat in all its architectural glory. This function was a must for an imperial capital, drawing the visitor to the Bagh-e Zaghan, or into the city for official business, past the blue-tiled domes behind which Timurid princes and princesses played at Persian kings and queens. Similarly, Heratis heading north from the city to Gazur Gah or the Shia shrine at Kuh-e Mukhtar, north-east to the *Takht-e Safar* (Throne of Travellers) for prayers or picnics, would have been reminded of the ruling dynasty's power and majesty.

This strip of land running north was a living affirmation of Herat's fertility and prosperity, a monument to its resilience, manifesting age-old themes of the province's life-giving water and its rich soil. The canals which had aided Herat's recovery after Chingizid destruction were now elevating the city to new heights. At the end of one particularly cold and snow-covered winter and after a ride to Sarakhs and Badghis, one prominent Timurid prince, along with his retinue, repaired to the Bagh-e Sefid, to the north-east of the city walls, to see out the cold months before spring covered the city and the garden with colour.[31]

* * *

In October 1414, a Chinese man by the name of Chen Cheng, diplomat and experienced troubleshooter at the Ming court, arrived in Herat.[32] During his eight-month journey he had traversed much of Central Asia in the paths of ancient caravan routes north of the Takla Makan desert, before heading south through Samarqand, Balkh and into Herat, down the *khiaban*. On this epic adventure he underwent privations and faced extreme danger. Herat was the seventeenth place of note he had visited.

Clearly an adventurous man who 'saw [a trip of] 10,000 *li* [one *li* was approximately a third of a mile] as but going out of the door', Cheng came to Herat as a trade envoy, information gatherer and adventurer.[33]

Timurid relations with Ming China had not always been harmonious. Previous encounters between the two powers featured ugly diplomatic feuding, detained ambassadors and threats of forcible conversion to Islam. Yet with Cheng's arrival in Herat it was clear that both sides sought to improve the situation and to increase trade between their nations. Two trading empires, so the theory went, were less likely to wage war on each other. The Ming desired horses for battle and intelligence on the lands of the 'west'; Herat wanted silks, porcelain and money from trade to fuel their luxurious imperial capital. Chinese influences would later inform Herat's artistic renaissance during this Timurid century, bringing with it a cultural exchange visible in pottery, tilework and the work of Herat's famed miniaturist painters. As Cheng made his way from China to Herat, he was assured a favourable reception, albeit one not totally free from suspicion.

Cheng's observations are witty and comprehensive: an official report, a diplomatic handbook and language primer featuring a small number of Persian words transcribed for future imperial visitors to Herat. His account is far more plausible than that of a German counterpart, Johann Schiltberger, who clearly did not visit Herat, but did travel through Iraq-e Ajam. Schiltberger talks of a Herati man of 'three hundred and fifty years old' and describes how the 'nails on his hands were one in length, his eyebrows hung down from his eyes over his cheeks'.[34] Confucian Cheng stuck to the more empirical fields of bricks, mortar and the observable facts of daily life. Much of Cheng's work is taken up with descriptions of the city's architecture and buildings. He describes the citadel, Qalah-ye Ekhtiar al-Din, as the place where the ruler resides (a strange confusion, owing to Shah Rukh's residence in the Bagh-e Zaghan) in a 'house made of bricks'. Its doors are carved with floral patterns, 'inlaid with bones and horns', and inside Shah Rukh's bedchamber there is a gold mattress piled up with blankets.[35] These observations occurred prior to Herat's building boom described above, and this explains his description of simple 'earthen' buildings, contrasting with the stone buildings of Cheng's homeland.[36] It is thus unlikely that he would have seen much, or any, of the extraordinary tile-work or faience which later adorned the city's royal and aristocratic residences. Cheng describes the walls of the houses of the elite as being decorated with white and flowered silk, and notes that the 'inferior and petty men lived in flat-topped earthen houses or in felt tents'.[37] Clearly, nomadic habits died hard. His description of Herat's Friday Mosque as a 'big earthen temple' possibly did the structure some injustice, although the mosque had suffered greatly when the dispossessed and disaffected Kart scions burned and sacked the city in the dying days of Kartid Herat.

Cheng shows us a city of busy prosperity, of exchange and vibrancy, and of no little humour. Herat's bazaars are described as having the customary holes bored in the roofs through which light, and sometimes rain, flood in. They sell items for hunting, 'bows and arrows, saddles and reins, and clothing', and the bazaar, most likely the Malek Bazaar near to the citadel, is divided into sections based on produce, as is very much the case today. Taxes were charged at purchase in the bazaar at a rate of 20 per cent, something which surprises Cheng. The harvests are described as 'abundant' owing to the fertility of Herat's soil, and Cheng tells us of sweet grapes, which 'shine like crystal', walnuts, plums and various different varieties of tree that were then to be found in Herat.[38] We hear of Herat's handicrafts, with special mention of the province's still famous production of blue glass, both for windows and as vessels from which to drink.[39] He also grudgingly accepts the city's silk as being of good quality. Whilst Cheng was surprised at those Heratis whose headdresses were bejewelled, grotesquely extravagant in his eyes, his description of an abundance of 'gold, silver, gems, coral, amber, crystal, diamonds, cinnabar' suggests that finding jewels and gems for one's turban or hat was not an impossible task.[40] Reflecting Herat's mineral, agricultural and artistic prosperity, it is also not surprising that he describes the city's people, great and small, as dressed in clean, colourful clothing. Such is Herat's fondness for displays of wealth that we hear that even the 'saddles and the harnesses of the horses and mules are decorated with gold, silver and rich colours', and that bells are suspended from the felt mats which cover the animals' backs.[41] Money and wealth had descended upon the city; Herat was enjoying its time as an imperial capital. Whilst the Herat of today has fewer bejewelled heads or decorated donkeys in the bazaar, the fondness for colourful and intricately woven clothing is still as strong as it was in the autumn of 1414.

During the two months Cheng spent in Herat, he made close observations of almost every aspect of Herat's life, from bathing to windmills, from doctors to animals. We hear, for example, of the people's careful tending of their horses, keeping them cool in summer and warm in winter; we hear of Herat's windmills, and the trips he made to Herat's numerous bathhouses, wherein the pinching and shaking of the bones and the squashing of the flesh caused 'men to be happy', for a very reasonable price of 'one or two copper cash, and that's it.'[42] He is disdainful of the doctors who practise in the bazaars, assembling patients at their feet and, after long discussions on health, dispensing medicines of extremely dubious efficacy.[43] Medical men of dubious efficacy are still, unfortunately, a feature of Herat's bazaars, where one can buy counterfeit sleeping pills and receive questionable health advice.[44] In Cheng's account, there is an intriguing reference to a group of running messengers, employed for the most urgent tasks, who could run nearly a hundred miles in a day; round their legs were tied small bells and round their hands tiny bunches of flowers. Cheng, obviously entranced by these running messengers, states that 'They run as if they were flying.'[45] This must truly have been an extraordinary sight— winged messengers gliding in and out of Timurid Herat to the sound of tinkling bells. The twentieth-century German spy and adventurer Oscar von Niedermayer photographed a 'Läufer' in his wonderful book of photos from 1915, although it is not possible to make out any bells on his ankles.[46] Yet perhaps the most amusing anecdote of Cheng's account is the following rather mystifying description of a group of people that can only be described as Herat's rabble-rousers:

> There are men who like to meddle around in the city. In dense crowds, they shake big halberds and battle axes and gesticulate with their hands and feet. Boasting loudly, they shock everyone and frighten the commoners. They cannot explain the reasons they do so, but they believe that it is a good idea to startle people.[47]

Exactly who these angry men are, and what purpose they served, is a mystery to me, and also to those Heratis I asked about the shouting Timurid men.

Another area of Herat's daily life confused the efficient Chinese diplomat: dervishes.[48] Cheng describes these mystics and wanderers in terms which indicate that he mistook them for vagrants, unaware of their religious and spiritual significance, or the degree to which their orders were patronised by the Timurid elites. The description of the dervishes and Sufi mystics as 'people who abandon their homes and possessions, have dishevelled hair, walk around bare-foot, wearing sheepskin and other distressing clothes' is accurate as *prima facie* observation, but it misses the importance these figures played in medieval Herat as dream interpreters, preachers, inspirations and much more.[49] Yet in saying that for these men it is 'extremely difficult ... to establish themselves in life', he did at least encapsulate the mystic's disdain for the things of this world.

A fascinating aspect of Cheng's report is the extent to which the Timurid elite were willing to go to present themselves as strict Muslim and Persian sovereigns. Cheng must have met Shah Rukh, as is clear from his description of his bedchamber, and it is likely that the Chinese diplomat was given an official tour in which Timurid Herat was portrayed in as orthodox and upright a fashion as possible. Was this a report of what Cheng saw, or a report of what the Timurid elites wanted him to see? Having been on tours of prisons, villages and ministries in Herat, I am only too familiar with the city authorities' desire to show the visitor what they feel he or she really should see. Nowhere is this clearer than in descriptions of the place of wine among Herat's citizens. Cheng's account states categorically that 'the prohibition against wine is extremely strict. Those who violate it are punished with a leather whip.'[50] And yet there are later references to its production, and the plain assertion that 'at feasts the honoured ones drink wine'.[51] Whilst this could easily be referring to Timurid military elites who had remained true to their shamanistic beliefs, or to Herat's small non-Muslim population, it does hint that wine-drinking was more widespread than the edict suggests. This was the riotous underbelly to the almost perfectly constructed edifice of Sunni orthodoxy and imperial piety that Shah Rukh so assiduously created. I am even tempted to see the following, wonderfully evocative observation in this vein. Cheng notes that in 'the city and in the villages, people live peacefully'. He goes on to describe how villagers 'can travel alone in the densest wilderness';

there are no tigers, wolves or demons to harass Herat's population.[52] This description feeds into the well-established notion that one of the tasks of a just Islamic sovereign is to provide peace and stability, at whatever cost, to his flock so as to create conditions in which Islam can flourish. Were a Timurid courtier, or Shah Rukh himself, to have discussed security and the situation in the outlying areas of Herat with Cheng, it is surely the picture of a secure, stable and peaceful province they would have presented to the Chinese diplomat. In an inherently unstable and precarious world, peace and stability were precious commodities and their attainment was a noteworthy achievement which reflected well both on the ruler himself and also on the ideology, or religion, through which he claimed to rule. For Cheng to take home tales of peaceful Timurid villages would have been clear evidence of the light of Islamic justice and the legitimacy of the Timurid imperial project.

Cheng's descriptions of Herat are of a city in which Turk and Tajik (Timurid and Herati) seemed to get along, existing between the accepted bounds of sedentary and urban, where Ramadan and strict Islamic principles vied with traditions from the steppe. The bubbling undercurrents of chaos and excess exist beneath the party line of a strictly Islamic city paying its dues to all the right Persian and Islamic traditions. The Ramadan fast, for example, was broken by mock hunting rituals and boozy feasts.[53] Cheng shows us an abundance of life and of the material and spiritual needs necessary to sustain such a city and its inhabitants. He might have missed the dervishes, but in his own way he perfectly encapsulated a city ruled by an elite unsure of its place and yet determined to get it right.[54]

* * *

In the summer of 1989, as Herat suffered under Soviet bombs and Mujahideen mines, an exhibition opened in the Smithsonian Institution in Washington, DC, entitled 'Timur and the Princely Vision: Persian Art and Culture in the Fifteenth Century'. The exhibition highlighted the Timurid cultural legacy to the world in their extraordinary contributions to the visual arts. Through a seminal eponymous publication, this flowering of cultural genius was placed firmly in its urban and political contexts: a dynasty's desire to be respected, accepted and loved. The publication illustrates some of the most beautiful works of painting and calligraphy the world has seen. Subtlety and motion, dynamism and elegance infuse these paintings of scenes from Persian poems and the depictions of historical narratives, yet in reality it is the city itself which is the undisputed star of the show, albeit a reluctant and enigmatic star. Herat's Timurid imperial court had become a magnet for talented artists, poets and musicians, who flocked there in search of patronage and work, much as was the case in Renaissance Europe's flashier urban centres. It was the fertile and shining backdrop from which this cultural explosion burst forth.

Under the Karts, it had been the poets and mystics who were lauded in the chronicles; now it was the turn of those who painted and illustrated as well as those who wrote and thought. The most influential figure in this first renaissance of the visual arts (the second will take place later in the chapter) was Prince Baysanghur, whose death in 1433 from a surfeit of alcohol belied the stringency with which Shah Rukh's religious edicts were enforced from top to bottom.[55] No later than 1421, Baysanghur founded an artistic atelier, the *ketabkhana*, in Herat. Here he placed the scribes and artists captured from Samarqand as well as Herat's own talented calligraphers, and it is from within this space that the majority of these illuminated manuscripts and other works of art were produced.[56] In the *ketabkhana*, Timurid Herat's artistic talents were commissioned to produce works glorifying the royal household and celebrating the Persian heritage and sophistication of the Timurid dynasty.[57] We have no idea where the physical building of the *ketabkhana* was, or if indeed it was a physical building and not simply a term used to describe a grouping of like-minded souls all of whom reported to Baysanghur.[58] My personal opinion is that this was a physical entity, and most likely a building close to one of the royal *bagh*s on the exterior of the city walls. My reasoning is simple: chronicles refer to this space as a fixed space by using the term *khana*; it would be unusual to refer to a *ketabkhana* if there were no *khana*, 'house' in Persian, as a physical entity. Nonetheless, it seems to have functioned as a coherent entity producing works to glorify the Timurid dynasty.

To get an idea of the types of works being commissioned and the extent of the projects being carried out in the *ketabkhana*, a surviving document gives us an intriguing glimpse into the day-to-day workings of this central cultural institution. The document, written by a senior

Herati calligrapher named Jaafar Tabrizi, is entitled *arzadasht* (collection of petitions). It begins as follows: 'Petition from the most humble servants of the royal library, whose eyes are as expectant of the dust from the hoofs of the regal steed as the ears of those who fast are for the cry of Alla-u Akbar.'[59]

The rhetoric then moves down a notch with the entirely prosaic line, 'Amir Khalil has finished the waves in two sea scenes of the *Gulistan* [a prose work by the Persian mystic and poet, Saadi] and will begin to apply colour.'[60] The *arzadasht* discusses a variety of projects on which the *ketabkhana* is working. We hear of Khwaja Abdul Rahim working on 'designs for binders, illuminators, tentmakers and tilemakers', and a Mawlana Saduddin working on a small box for a lady of the royal house.[61] There were no fewer than twenty-two projects underway, all of which were likely to have been known to the patron Baysanghur. We hear of works ongoing on building structures and on tents and of numerous documents being illuminated and repaired.[62] This was an active atelier which branched out in different artistic directions—not simply pictorial illuminations. Given the efficiency of this report, its formal tone, it would suggest a coherent and single organisation, probably housed under one roof. Baysanghur's patronage was intimately concerned with the day-to-day workings of his artistic projects; he was alive to the welfare of his artistic protégés: Mawlana Ali, for example, has sore eyes from over work; Ustad Sayfuddin is now well again.[63]

Between 1421 and 1433, the production of the *ketabkhana* was of a quality and beauty which far outstrips works done in Shiraz at the same time, proving that Herat was the region's foremost cultural hub, and every bit the equal of Renaissance Europe. Perhaps the most luminous, and politically interesting, of these productions is an edition of Firdausi's *Shahnama* (Book of Kings).[64] The *Shahnama* is an epic poem written in the late-tenth or early-eleventh centuries, and its themes are timeless: of kings and queens, of morality and of good governance. The images in Baysanghur's *Shahnama* illustrate these issues of governance and the responsibilities of the prince or sultan, and to this day in Iran and Afghanistan it is recited and used as an allegory for how those in power should behave. One contemporary academic perfectly encapsulates the scope and reach of this document when she describes the functions of the *Shahnama* as 'the teaching of a people in their earliest years as a nation, the courting of princesses to ensure posterity, the education of heirs, the ordering of battles against invaders and usurpers'.[65] To choose the *Shahnama* for production in his atelier, Baysanghur was sending a message to the people of Herat, all of whom would have been familiar with these tales of heroism and deceit by heart, that he understood their language of legitimation and their rules of kingship. Baysanghur wanted to fit into his surroundings. The reproduction is beautiful in the extreme, the illustrations full of drama, elegance and subtlety, and a colour scheme which is rich and powerful. It was the perfect tool for legitimation, and a timeless vehicle for Herat's wealth and artistic skill.[66]

My personal favourite illustration from this period is 'A Prince Seated in a Garden', from a now lost manuscript completed in Herat during 1425–30.[67] The setting is a prince seated on a beautiful carpet of geometric design, surrounded by musicians and courtiers in a garden and being offered a glass of wine. The musicians play and sing, slightly nervously looking on, and courtiers in the opposite plate argue about something, one raising a staff of some sort about his head in a menacing fashion. The background is elegant, formulaic and suggesting a spring afternoon in one of Herat's many gardens. The trees in the background are in bloom and two small clouds drift away towards the edge of the picture. This is a scene of playful seriousness tinged with uncertainty. The musicians seem unsure as to what they are playing and the courtiers appear nervous. The seated prince is earnest, questioning and expectant. He seems isolated, alone and very much apart from his companions.[68] Was this, within strict guidelines of form, the faintest suggestion of a Timurid prince, a son of the steppe, separated from his more cultured urbane Herati courtiers, sat alone on a carpet, drinking wine? Is the joke on the Timurid? Herat excels in subtlety and wit, and to see an uncertain prince stranded on his fine carpet with a jug of wine for company is surely no accident.

Babur Mirza, who later founded the Mughal Empire, visited Herat in 1506 while the city's cultural flame was burning the brightest. He wrote the following words about Prince Baysanghur's cultural achievements:

> Alike in talent and encouragement of talent, he was famous throughout the world. Calligraphy and poetry were highly esteemed in his time, and

scholars and men of talent, attracted by his renown, flocked from all regions and quarters to enter his service. He showed favour to men of talent, loved poets, strove after refinement and luxury, and entertained witty courtiers and boon companions. Of all the kings since Khusrau Parviz none lived so joyous and splendid a life as Baysanghur Sultan.[69]

This explosion of the visual arts in Herat had a literary counterpart. The Timurids commissioned histories glorifying their dynasty, putting an Islamic gloss on their line whilst simultaneously showcasing Herat's wealth and imperial majesty. Historians such as Hafez Abru, who wrote widely on the region's geography as well as its history, told the story of the Timurid century through a local and dynastic lens. Reading these chronicles, we get the impression that whilst the patrons, the Timurid elite, were theoretically 'in charge', the subtle and pervasive influence of the local Persian men of letters and learning added an element of subversion to Herat's creative output. Perhaps, once again, the joke was on the Timurids for their perceived lack of sophistication and urban wit, something for which Herat was, and still is, famed. A story illustrating this concerns Mawlana Maruf, a calligrapher of extraordinary skill brought to Herat by Shah Rukh in the aftermath of the latter's conquest of Shiraz in 1409. Maruf was said to have been 'self-confident and lordly in his bearing' and a trifle arrogant as well. He had the temerity to return to Shah Rukh a whole bundle of blank manuscript papers on which he had been commissioned to copy out some Persian poetry for the Timurid royal library. His disdain for royal authority is clear from the fact that it took him over a year to do precisely nothing, and his later suspected involvement in a plot to assassinate Shah Rukh tells us something of his loyalties.[70] Another prominent literary figure was the poet and mystic, Qasim al-Anwar. Qasim Al-Anwar perfectly encompassed this sense of Herat's cultural elites thumbing their cultured noses at unlettered patrons. He became more popular and influential than his royal Timurid patrons, and because of this he was driven from the city, forced to live out his days in the village of Jam. He too was suspected along with Maruf in the plot to kill Shah Rukh, but it is likely that this was a convenient pretext on which to exile a potentially troublesome figure. The message was that for all the Timurids' power, wealth and military might, real cultural and apolitical clout rested with those local Persians who wielded fine brushes and quills, those who drew portraits or wrote verse. There is more than a hint of snobbery from the educated elites towards their steppe overlords. It is almost as if these sultans and world princes were still somehow learning the ropes, learning the art of good governance, Islamic probity and the subtleties of a Persian urban existence, and as if the city's poets and artists were always ready to remind the Timurids of their status as nomadic interlopers. Perhaps this condescension can explain the vast output, the sheer energy and enthusiasm with which the Timurid princes threw themselves into an extraordinary programme of cultural patronage? There was, they felt, a credibility vacuum that should be filled with acres of beautiful tiles, pages of intricate manuscript illustration and stories upon stories of a shared and glorious Persian past.

Much like the city's architectural achievements, Herat's literary and illustrative output also served imperial diplomatic purposes. By showcasing Herat's ability to attract the brightest talents of Khorasan, Herat projected to their imperial neighbours and subjects alike an image of sophistication and wealth. In 1439, a newly appointed ambassador from the Egyptian Mamluk court came to Herat. The ambassador specifically requested for the Mamluk Sultan in Egypt five 'highly esteemed books from the emperor's library' in Herat.[71] These were works of Islamic exegesis and poetry, and Shah Rukh ordered that they be copied from the royal library immediately and presented to the Mamluk.

Educating the next generation of Timurid princes in the ways of sophisticated urban Persian elites became a way to overcome this perceived lack of sophistication. Shah Rukh's sons—Baysanghur, Mohammad Juki and Ibrahim Sultan—were educated at Samarqand in the arts and sciences, but it was Persian literature which fascinated these young princes. Baysanghur and Ulugh Beg had heated debates on the subject of whose *Khamsa* (a collection of five works of poetry, covering subjects of morality, love and including traditional Persian epics)—Khusraw or Nizami—was the superior. The two men compared the poems 'line by line'.[72] They also exchanged correspondence on wider issues relating to artistic and poetic excellence, showing that while their patronage served political purposes, it was not a totally empty vessel in which they themselves were little involved. Although their native tongue was Chagatai Turkish, Persian was the undoubted language of the court, the language of sophistication and elegance. Embracing Herat's literary

culture was a central pillar of the Timurid artistic programme of legitimation and assimilation.

Yet it was not solely in the content of artistic output that competition and rivalry existed between these Timurid princes. Differing
Timurid courts dotted around the empire all competed for the best
poets, calligraphers and artists, elevating the place of the artist in
Timurid society to a hitherto unattained level, much as was the case in
Renaissance European cities. A court could be made more splendid
with the addition of some bright jewels: artists, poets and calligraphers. One such patronage tug of war concerned a singer named Yusuf
Andigani, who lived in Herat during Shah Rukh's reign. Andigani was
an artist who 'had no equal in the world in recitation and singing', and
his voice is said to have 'augmented the agony of passion'.[73] It is not
surprising that Andigani, then resident in Baysanghur's aesthetic orbit
of Herat, was coveted by the Timurid prince, Ibrahim Sultan of Shiraz.
Such was Ibrahim Sultan's desire to attract Andigani to his court that
he sent 100,000 dinars in cash to Herat in an attempt to lure the singer
and his melodies away from Baysanghur. Baysanghur replied as follows:
'We do not sell our Joseph. You keep your black silver.'[74]

* * *

'If you have doubts about our grandeur, look at our edifice.'[75] So goes
a line from an official Timurid historian of Herat. Artistic and architectural patronage provided Herat with this glittering and magnificent
edifice; it coated Shah Rukh with an air of religious and political credibility which in turn connected the Timurid imperial house to Herat's
Islamic history.[76] Yet looking closer at Timurid Herat, to the contested
spaces of religion and politics, we see that Shah Rukh's control over the
minds and hearts of his citizens, even those he patronised, was far from
total. In the dangerous atmosphere of courtly sophistication, religious
and mystical heterodoxy, and along the opaque strands of politico-
religious loyalty, Shah Rukh saw rivals to his sovereignty.

Herat in the early fifteenth century was a city of shaykhs, Sufis and
dervishes. Sunni orthodoxy was only part of the story, for it hid from
view an intellectual and spiritual community at once curious and
troublesome for royal authority. The vibrancy of Herat's religious communities, its shrine culture and the interaction between Sufis and ordi-

nary Heratis is all too apparent from the sources. This was a time of shrines, of dream interpretations and of the visiting of graves, all avenues through which the ordinary Herati could access the world of the spirit. The very distinctions between life and death were blurred by the culture of saintly shrines, devotion to dead family members and a disdain for the affairs of the political and temporal world. Dream interpretation functioned as a particularly powerful and popular form of maintaining contact between the living and the dead; and in medieval Khorasan, such figures could attain a quasi-divine status. Herat's daily life was thus at once ordered and orthodox—its shining blue faience a testament to this—yet simultaneously heterodox and subversive. Herat's artistic, intellectual and spiritual luminaries embodied these tensions, and were conduits for anti-Timurid feelings which bubbled beneath the beautiful exterior of the court. Fazlullah Astarabadi, founder of the Hurufiya movement (see below), was adept at interpreting dreams, as was the other renowned mystic of fifteenth-century Herat, Zayn al-Din Khwafi. These skills gave these men a popularity and fame to rival Timurid sultans. They hinted at a spirit world which could not be controlled or awestruck by vast buildings or by the finest calligraphic achievements; they spoke of a world outside good, bad or drunken princes. Here was a world removed from Timurid majesty. This was the real Herat, with healing springs which revealed strong connections to worlds of the soil and the spirit, transcending the messy compromises of political power. Charms, amulets and exorcism of evil spirits were services provided by Sufi shaykhs for the cure of ailments of those visiting these healing springs.[77] A more visceral, primordial and nebulous world existed among Herat's ordinary people, the total antithesis to hollow courtly refinement and the elites in gardens or ornate tents.

This parallel Sufi existence played out much of its drama in the bazaar, wonderfully described by a contemporary academic as the 'stage and recruiting ground for the Sufi community'.[78] Potential Sufis would be paraded through the bazaar as a form of ritual humiliation in an attempt to cure them of their attachment to society's expectations and norms. Cheng's description of the dervishes wandering Herat's bazaars is a nice illustration of this ramshackle space of spiritually sanctioned chaos achieved through a renunciation of the here and now. To a cautious and strictly orthodox elite, striving to get their message across, a city running wild with necromancers, shaykhs, Sufis and dream interpreters would have been cause for concern.

In the realm of the spiritual in Herat, the Timurids were clearly on the back foot in this sea of Sufis and saints and shrines; they were as hesitant and nervous as the prince on the carpet. Might we see Herat's Timurid Renaissance a reaction to these perceived inadequacies? Episodes appear in sources where Herat's Timurid elites were gently mocked or belittled by men of religious or local standing, reinforcing the notion that Herat conquered the Timurids, not the other way round. Sufi shaykhs disdained, outwardly at least, the world of politics. They were concerned that the requirement of the sovereign to provide the necessary stability in which the *sharia* can be properly enforced often drifted into grey areas of un-Islamic practices: taxation being one. Accordingly, food from a ruler or politician was seen to be suspect because of the potentially sinful methods which might have led to its procurement. On one occasion, Shah Rukh sought to puncture the religious pomposity of one of Herat's most prominent Sufi figures, Shah Ni'mattullah Wali. Ni'mattullah wrote poetry, performed miracles and had a large following of faithful devotees.[79] Shah Rukh set out to test the assertion that the Sufis only ate uncorrupted meat, and so ordered one of his men to rob an old lady of a lamb. The royal kitchen cooked the lamb and served it to Ni'mattullah. After he had eaten the stolen lamb, Shah Rukh crowed over his apparent exposure of a religious fraud. A local chronicle describes the following exchange that took place: "'Sultan of the world," said Ni'mattullah, "order an investigation into this, for God must have a [hidden] purpose herein.'"[80] Shah Rukh in his pique duly ordered an investigation, which subsequently proved that the old lady had intended the sheep to be slaughtered in honour of Ni'mattullah, thanks to whose intercession she believed her son had returned safely from a difficult journey. The meat was therefore uncorrupted and Ni'mattullah's saintliness was triumphant and intact.

Yet the Timurids were not totally out of their depth when it came to Sufis. Herat's greatest shrine dates to the Timurid century and celebrates the city's most famous and cherished saint. In 1425 Shah Rukh rebuilt the shrine at Gazur Gah to the eleventh-century Islamic scholar, Sufi poet and mystic, Abdullah Ansari. One seventeenth-century Herati poet, Beheshti Heravi, described Gazur Gah in the early seventeenth century as 'the envy of Paradise itself', as part of a loving and gratify-ingly flowery description of a functioning shrine which had seen all manner of invaders troop past into the city.[81] Gazur Gah is a central part of Herat's story and soul, and Ansari is considered by Heratis as a patron saint of the city, who protects the city in times of crisis. Today the shrine welcomes flocks of tourists, children and pilgrims of all ages. I have been lucky enough to spend afternoons there, in the boiling heat of high summer and on days when the snow piled up around the tombstones and doughty old theologians heaved and shovelled snow from the entrances and roofs; it is always tranquil and peaceful. It is where Herat's most famous sons are buried, beneath tombstones of brilliant white marble.

Ansari's role as theological mediator between strict Islamic ortho-doxy and the development of Sufism within this tradition marked him out as a man who could transcend the worlds of the spirit and the Islamic schools of jurisprudence: much as Herat itself moved between the two worlds. Ansari's shrine was not excessively patronised by the Kart *malek*s, but Shah Rukh gave it a new lease of life, very possibly because of Ansari's famous piety and his 'strict adherence to the *sunna*'.[82] A patron saint who embodied both Sufism and Islamic juris-prudence as well as protection of the city was an extremely attractive proposition for Herat's outsider imperial sultan. In this vein, Shah Rukh preferred to patronise Herat's institutions, its shrines, rather than to forge links, as Timur had done, with individual Sufis or members of the clerical elites, the *ulema*.[83] Individual clerics were potential rivals for power, as the story of Ni'mattullah and the lamb suggests. Dead saints, however, could not threaten his authority. This assiduous court-ing of the spirit world, particularly through Ansari's shrine at Gazur Gah, suggests once again that the Timurids did not conquer Herat; if anything, Herat conquered the Timurids.[84]

Yet politics, top-down legitimation, eschatology and religion are uneasy bedfellows. Add to this mixture an over-enthusiastic royal patronage of artists and poets, many of whom happen to be mystics and religious figures, and the potential for high drama is almost limitless.

On 21 February 1427, Shah Rukh, 'most particular in attending to his religious duties', was attending Friday prayers in Herat's Friday

Mosque. Whilst at the mosque, 'he rubbed the forehead of needfulness on the ground of devotion'.[85] Exactly what happened next is open to interpretation. Each courtly account offers a different version of events, but consensus exists on the main facts, as follows.[86] A man by the name of Ahmad Lur, a known disciple of the radical Sufi Hurufiya movement, approached Shah Rukh with the apparent intention of handing him a petition as the latter was leaving the mosque. The Hurufiya sect was a Shia-oriented Sufi movement which saw in the words of the Arabic and Persian alphabets the basis for divine and human beauty. It was founded by Fazlullah Astarabadi in the reign of Timur, and occupied a similar space to the more famous Sarbedars of Sabzevar; and they occupied a space opened up by the repeated crises of a post-Mongol Khorasan: famine, pestilence, warfare and a crisis of religious identity. Millenarian striving for the end of days makes more sense when we understand the precarious situation in which Herat and Khorasan repeatedly found themselves. Fazlullah Astarabadi had once tried to convert Timur to Hurufism but was executed by Timur's son, Miranshah, for his temerity in attempting such a conversion. The group was only short-lived in Khorasan, but it left its mark on Herat. As Ahmad Lur approached the royal party, he stabbed Shah Rukh in the stomach. The would-be assassin was killed on the spot by one of Shah Rukh's attendants and the injured sultan was spirited away to the Bagh-e Zaghan where he was treated for his wounds, eventually making a full recovery. On the surface this assassination attempt appears to be little more than the work of a religious fanatic, unhinged and from the margins of society; it was not successful. Yet as is the case with so much in Timurid Herat, it is beneath the edifice of courtly chronicles and shrine patronage that the truth of the matter lies.

The eagerness with which Ahmad Lur was executed presented those close to Shah Rukh with an evidential problem: how to find more information about the intentions, links and views of this sect? Some accounts suggest that a key to a guesthouse in Herat, frequented by known religious subversives, was found on the person of the potential assassin. This pushed the investigation, of which Prince Baysanghur had taken charge, towards the Hurufiya movement. Yet I feel that the detail of a key found in a pocket does not ring true; religious fanatics on suicide missions rarely bring their house keys. Nonetheless, this link to the guesthouse brought Mawlana Maruf, a calligrapher of skill and fame, to the attention of Prince Baysanghur and his fellow-investigators—the same Mawlana Maruf who had once been so disdainful of a royal commission from Shah Rukh. Mawlana Maruf, who 'wore a felt cloak of the highest quality and on his head a tall cap of the same type' (this latter detail being important as the Hurufiya sect were known to have recruited their members from among Herat's felt-making and drapery guilds), was said to have had dealings with Ahmad Lur, for which he was imprisoned in the dungeon of Herat's citadel. In the purge that followed, associates of Ahmad Lur and a relation of Fazlullah Astarabadi were all put to death. Qasim al-Anwar, the charismatic Sufi mystic with a fondness for attractive young boys, was also a victim of this purge; he was exiled. The investigation had found its suspects and had handed out justice. The net cast by the authorities had caught a surprising number of the city's most prominent poets and intellectuals, suggesting that the Timurid response to this event might have been a pretext on which to rid the city of troublesome figures.

This was not, however, where the matter ended, for the case went much deeper than a simple investigation into an unhinged marginal fanatic. The academic Ilkber Evrim Brinbas shows us that a letter from one Ghias al-Din Mohammad to a Mawlana Hassan in January 1433, both of whom had been disciples of Fazlullah Astarabadi, indicates that arrests relating to the assassination attempt were still ongoing in 1429, and that the investigation into the matter had stretched as far as Mazandaran in present-day Iran. In the early 1430s, nearly five years after the attempt, Shah Rukh's officials hauled two men back to Herat for questioning about their links to Ahmad Lur and the assassination attempt of 1427. After a number of unsuccessful interrogations, the two suspects, Amir Nurullah and Ghias al-Din Mohammad, were cross-examined about both their religious beliefs and their involvement in the assassination attempt in a gathering in Herat's Gawhar Shad *madrasa*. This monument to Timurid orthodoxy played host to a trial of these two men, religious and political dissidents who had allegedly been in league with Shah Rukh's would-be assassin. To think of the glittering minarets and the vast tiled spaces of greens, whites, blues and turquoise being the stage for this most intriguing drama is quite exhilarating. With no definitive verdict of either involvement in the assassination attempt or concrete proof of heresy, the men were then sent to Samarqand to an exile of sorts.[87] This collision of political drama and radical religious preachers, of earthly power and intellectual prestige, aired in the vast monuments of Timurid Herat, shows a regime on the back foot, threatened by existing and pre-existing indigenous currents of radical thought swirling around Herat.

As the spirit world and its collision with high politics consumed Herat, the city still could not escape the more mundane travails of plague and pestilence. Khorasan remained essentially a fragile place, never far from the deleterious effects of a disastrous famine or a disputed succession. Peace and tranquillity were highly esteemed for very practical reasons. In 1435 Herat was struck down by a plague, most likely a variant of the Black Death which had decimated Chinese and European populations from the fourteenth century onwards. Necromancers and astrologers had earlier predicted that in Khorasan such a phenomenon 'would burst forth, especially in the area of Herat'; they were correct.[88] Urban and rural populations alike made the appropriate arrangements for flight, out of fear of a horrible death. Those who could escape fled north to the pasturelands of Badghis, the mountains and hills where the air might be purer. For those who remained, the resulting sickness was an incendiary fire which scorched its way through Herat and the surrounding areas, killing indiscriminately.[89] The city was emptied of its nobles and officials, its peasants and artisans. Estimates for the numbers of deaths reach into the hundreds of thousands; Esfezari estimated 600,000 died in the province of Herat, and Samarqandi noted that in one single day 400,000 coffins were taken out of the city gates.[90] Both of these figures, however, are clearly extravagant exaggerations for it is likely that Herat's urban population at this point was somewhere around 150,000 to 200,000.[91] Yet the deaths of so many leading lights at Baysanghur and Shah Rukh's court are a telling indication of the scale and force of the plague. It claimed the lives of three of Herat's most important cultural, legal and religious figures: the famous saint and mystic, Shaykh Zayn al-Din Abul Bakr Khwafi; Herat's chief judge, Sadruddin Mohammad; and the preacher in the Friday Mosque, Mawlana Zia al-Din Nurullah al-Khwarazmi. As the world around them crashed and burned, it is little wonder that mystics and millenarian figures such as Ahmad Lur held such appeal for the people of Herat. Yet as the plague subsided, Herat's scattered people gradually returned, and the city recovered, displaying its essential resilience.

* * *

Shah Rukh's rule had brought Herat to a genuine pitch of imperial splendour, secured its borders and made Herat wealthy as it had never been before. The latter part of his tenure, however, saw corruption, rebellions and a slipping of Timurid power at the margins of empire. His last years were spent stamping out the fires of familial rebellion and uprising. When subduing opposition he was characteristically ruthless, often urged on by his faithful wife, Gawhar Shad, on whose orders more than one mass killing occurred as retribution for rebellion or resistance. On an expedition to crush an uprising in Shiraz in March 1447, Shah Rukh died of abdominal pains.[92] Shah Rukh's death was initially kept a secret amongst those in the know, his corpse hidden in the baggage train of the imperial army. It was feared that his death could be the trigger for violence and civil war. Yet before long, word spread; the soldiers sacked the baggage train and each line of the imperial family fell to fighting for his or her share of the spoils.[93] Shah Rukh's corpse was then taken away to Samarqand along with many of Herat's artists, all captured in the scuffle for his body by the forces of Ulugh Beg of Samarqand.

The fragility of medieval dynasties should not be underestimated, no matter how shining the faience or how brilliant the cultural output. Peace was a rare and precious commodity, and often skin deep. Whilst Shah Rukh excelled at the provision of peace within the confines of Herat, despite the threats to his rule, in one aspect of crucial importance to the medieval sovereign he was an abject failure: the provision of a designated heir through whom to continue stability and prosperity. Shah Rukh's long rule meant that his offspring, and their offspring in turn, had become restless and especially eager to access power and wealth they felt long overdue, creating the perfect conditions for a disputed succession. It was for this reason that Shah Rukh's grandson, Sultan Mohammad, a coarse man who once urinated on the beard of an adviser in a fit of drunken exuberance, rebelled against his grandfather, for he sensed an opportunity in a weakened imperial polity with no fixed heir.[94] The chaos of a post-Timurid Khorasan was to be revisited on Herat. After the peace and prosperity of Shah Rukh's reign, it was to return to the days of cyclical sieges.[95] A pithy summation of these intensely complicated years of familial strife goes as follows: 'The history of the next several years is not an heroic one. Few of Shah Rukh's descendants survived the succession struggle and many lost their reputations along with their lives.'[96]

The years 1448–50 were a blur of skirmish and battle during which Herat changed hands a number of times. An escaped Turcoman prince, Yar Ali, besieged the city in 1448. He had managed to enlist the support of a frightened populace, and the siege he set in motion was the occasion for heroic resistance from Herat's Sufis, artisans and judges; one Mawlana Imad al-Din '*Karezi*' so excelled in acts of bravery in stopping the invaders from breaching the moat of Herat that the epithet *Karezi*, meaning moat, was added to his name. Ulugh Beg arrived from Samarqand in time to save the city from further conflict, and proceeded to punish Herat's outlying areas for the assistance they gave to the escaped prince, Yar Ali.[97] Ulugh Beg, however, was arrested on his way home to his seat at Samarqand along with Shah Rukh's corpse by a son of Baysanghur, Abul Qasim Babur. The latter sent his men to Herat to oust yet another Timurid claimant, Abdu Latif, whose own rule in the city had lasted a mere fifteen days. Fifteen days would come to seem a comparative lifetime in this appallingly congested year; the Timurid prince, Abul Qasim Babur ruled for a matter of days, yet still he found the time to set a tax over the city. The escaped Turcoman prince, Yar Ali, also made a dash for very well worn throne of Herat. He ruled for an alcohol-soaked haze of twenty days; his hedonism left little time for proper rule, thus making Abul Qasim Babur's reentry into Herat in early 1449, relatively easy to accomplish.[98] A period of nine months followed in which Abul Qasim Babur found time to build a beautiful marble column, which stands to this day, in Gazur Gah. This column aside, the region continued to fragment violently. All the while, Gawhar Shad's favourite, her grandson Ala al-Dawla, the pleasure loving, effete prince, was still in Khorasan, well supported, popular and with the backing of his powerful grandmother.[99]

In this moment of Herat's rapid slide into anarchy, there occurred a brief shift in the locus of imperial power; it moved to Esfahan with

Sultan Mohammad's appropriation of that city and its surrounding lands. As if to confirm this, in the spring of 1449, Abul Qasim Babur sought protection from Sultan Mohammad, offering the latter submission and implicitly surrendering Herat's claim to imperial capital status. Herat had, in a few short years, become subordinate to Esfahan.[100] Esfahan's pre-eminence vis-à-vis Herat was helped by the fact that its residents at this time included Gawhar Shad and Ala al-Dawla, yet their presence in Esfahan did manage to retain a sheen of imperial prestige for Herat.

Nowhere were the divisions and contradictions of a post-Shah Rukhid world more clearly apparent than in the incessant rebellions of Herat's castellan. On more than one occasion, as new rulers came and went with new loyalties and heightened expectations, the castellan would lock himself up in the citadel in a show of defiance, leaving the new ruler to appropriate the imperial and aristocratic *bagh*s which ringed the city. On occasion conquerors would simply ignore the citadel for being too difficult to capture. Two different political entities would thus exist side by side in Herat, separated by tracts of masonry: citadel and town. In the maddeningly complicated years of 1456–8, as Herat changed hands back and forth, back and forth, one castellan by the name of Ahmad Yasaoul seemed determined to provide an iota of continuity in a sea of violent change, staying put as the chaos erupted around him.[101] In July 1457, Mirza Sultan Abu Said entered Herat province as a conqueror. Ahmad Yasaoul was then in charge of the citadel, and the city was controlled by Qara Bahadur, both of whom were loyal to another claimant, Ala al-Dawla, despite being in opposition to each other. Abu Said, after having taken the city and its *bagh*s, asked Yasaoul to open the gates of the citadel. Yasaoul in turn gave a predictably flowery response, but one which indicated a steadfast commitment to the cause of defending the citadel against those who were enemies of his patron, Ala al-Dawla. Abu Said simply allowed life to go on, tolerating this act of rebellion and continuing life in and around the city. As Yasaoul continued his resistance within the walls of Herat's citadel, political life in the Bagh-e Zaghan, which then contained Gawhar Shad and her retinue, also continued as usual. On 25 December 1457, yet another prince, Mirza Ibrahim Sultan, himself loyal to Ala al-Dawla, entered Herat in an approximation of triumph, having briefly ousted

Abu Said. Upon his entry, a dervish warned him that one more campaign into Herat by sons of Timur (clearly anticipating historians' frustrations at this deeply complicated period) would result in the extinction of the Chagataid race. Yet for the revolting castellan, Yasaoul, the return of Ibrahim Sultan was a cause for celebration as it meant that he was reconciled to a friendly party. But Yasaoul, clearly a sensitive character, felt that Ibrahim had not been fulsome enough in his praise at how steadfastly he had retained control of the citadel, and he therefore returned to the citadel, locked himself in and began a new phase of resistance against a man to whom he was supposedly loyal. Ibrahim, wisely, chose to ignore Yasaoul.

During these years of bewilderingly frequent changes of ruler, Herat was effectively divided into three different stages on which politics were played out: the citadel, the various royal *bagh*s and the city itself (also, on one occasion, Shah Rukh's *madrasa* was used as a space from which to plot and in which to hide potential claimants to the throne).[102] Royal authority was gained in the *bagh*s, the citadel provided protection and the city was a space in which popular acclaim might be found.

Perhaps one of the most significant tragedies of these years was Gawhar Shad's death in 1457 at the hands of Abu Said, for her part in attempting to influence the succession crisis in favour of her favourite grandson, Ala al-Dawla. Within the tensions of this stand-off, opportunities for personal advancement presented themselves; Gawhar Shad was implicated in a plot to associate with Abu Said's enemies, and on 31 July 1457 she was put to death as a makeweight in a deal to lure a corrupt official, Amir Shir Hajji, back to the retinue of Abu Said at a time when the latter had just taken Herat. Gawhar Shad was made to endure humiliation when marched around Khorasan as a prisoner, and her death at the age of 74 deprived the world of one its most fascinating figures. This episode was, in the words of one chronicler, 'the one blemish on the face of that praiseworthy padisahah's [Abu Said] career'.[103] Herat's greatest woman, 'that Queen of Sheba of the age', the city's most durable politician and patron of the arts was yet another casualty of this period of turbulence. Her death occurred, ironically, at a point at which some semblance of stability was returning to Herat.[104] The city would never see her like again, and today her reputation as an inspirational woman still shines through the dismal years of war and corruption that have engulfed the city. Her tomb still attracts gaggles of schoolgirls hoping to find out more about her life and benefit from her example and strength.

In December 1458, Abu Said returned to Herat to make his conquest permanent, after having temporarily taken the city in 1457. His return to Khorasan from Balkh in the autumn of 1458 was intended to remove the Qara Qoyunlu leader, Jahan Shah, who had himself become Herat's sovereign in June 1458 after putting Ala al-Dawla to flight and sacking much of the city's surrounds. During Jahan Shah's brief rule in Herat, he had even managed to coax Ahmad Yasaoul from the citadel. Yet this ambitious raid into Khorasan was not destined to last; Jahan Shah's capital at Tabriz was many miles away, and a rebellion in Azerbaijan forced him to relinquish control over Herat, allowing the return of Abu Said to the city of his grandfather. Referring to the status quo ante under Shah Rukh, Abu Said drew up an agreement whereby Jahan Shah would control Azerbaijan, leaving Iraq, Fars and Khorasan to the Timurids. Accordingly, Jahan Shah left Herat in December 1458. In an ever so slightly wearied description of Abu Said's early days, we hear of Herat's latest sovereign unfurling the 'banners of justice and equity' and being crowned in the Bagh-e Shah, 'the envy of paradise'.[105]

Owing to the Mongol-esque destruction which had befallen Herat and Khorasan, Abu Said turned to mitigating the conflicts' disastrous consequences by opening up royal stores of grain and food to feed the starving. Famine hung over the province, a legacy of the fighting which had laid so much to waste. The Timurid army was sent away from Khorasan to Transoxania to ease the pressure on Herat's meadows, which had for so long provided for their welfare and sustenance. Yet whilst Abu Said was away on campaign in 1459–60, Herat was further despoiled by an avaricious vizier, Khwaja Moezz al-Din. The vizier taxed the people under the guise of collecting money for the imperial army. Needless to say, the money lined his own pockets, rather than paying for a phantom army. Abu Said's punishment was to throw the vizier into a cauldron of boiling water. He then took the step of relieving taxation over Herat's people for military purposes, an edict he enshrined with a stone carving placed in the Friday Mosque.[106] Khwandamir's descriptions of a city once again playing host to talented craftsmen and excelling in the world of the arts are an eloquent testament to Abu Said's genuine efforts to restore his broken lands. Such was the speed and scope of Herat's recovery, relatively unscathed by a vicious bout of plague in 1462, that in 1466 Herat even saw fit to let off steam in a city-wide gathering to celebrate its fecundity and prosperity: 'Silvery-limbed cupbearers illuminated the assemblies of intimacy with the radiance of their cheeks, which were the envy of the Garden of Iran, and with brimful goblets they intoxicated bowed-backed old men and clothed with the garments of the days of youth.'[107]

Perhaps the most important initiative implemented by the proactive Abu Said, or indeed any Timurid sultan, was in the sphere of the city's irrigation channels. Abu Said's vizier, Qotb al-Din Taus, was a man of vision and intelligence, and in 1467–8 he put this vision and intelligence to good use, altering Herat's canals and water channels in a way which allowed irrigation of the areas between the *khiaban* and the foothills of the Koh-e Mukhtar, to the north of the Old City:

> He brought forth the excellent design of bringing into use the water of the Guy-e [*sic*] Soltani, and created the *guy* [bringing it] from the east of the city for a distance of four *farsang*s through the middle of mountains and rocks. In many places stone was cut through, and artificial channels parted the earth and in many places bridges were installed. After several months a great deal of water was brought to the waist [foothills] of Kuh-e Mokhtar.[108]

The already fertile oasis city was given a new lease of life, thus expanding the scope for building, gardens and for the growth of the city. This initiative had a profound impact on the urban morphology of Herat, pushing the life-giving water of the Hari Rud oasis into the northern reaches beyond the Old City, a move which both enabled the building of royal *bagh*s to rival those begun under the patronage of Shah Rukh and Gawhar Shad, and also increased the revenue of the city through the produce which could be grown there. The building programmes of Husain Bayqara would never have been possible without this stroke of genius from Abu Said and his vizier. One seventeenth-century Herati poet would describe these fertile areas to the north of the Old City as the very epitome of an earthly paradise, yet today only the vaguest hints of their glory remain. Abu Said himself never lived to see the fruits of his project, as at the time of its completion he was engaged in a 'pointless war' in Azerbaijan, a war in which he was killed on 6 February 1469.[109] He had steadied a decidedly rocky ship, which though rackety and menaced was still beautiful, and was about to embark on its most glorious era under the celebrated Timurid ruler, Sultan Husain Bayqara.

* * *

On the morning of 15 August 1470, Sultan Husain Bayqara, grandson of Shah Rukh, along with his retinue of soldiers, marched south from their mountain hideout on the outskirts of Herat. After gradual military successes in Khorasan they were now poised to rule over Khorasan's pearl.[110] They paused, like all good conquerors, to pay their respects at the shrine of Abdullah Ansari at Gazur Gah before entering the *khiaban*, as dawn broke on the minarets of Gawhar Shad's mausoleum and the *muezzin* rang out over the city. On reaching the Bagh-e Zaghan, Husain Bayqara found Herat's ruler, a Timurid puppet ruling at the behest of the Qara Qoyunlu, slumped in a corner of the garden, drunk in the arms of his mistress. Husain Bayqara shamed the prince for allowing the Qara Qoyunlu, traditionally Herat's vassals, to place him on the throne of Herat as a puppet, roundly insulted him for his weakness and castigated him, slightly hypocritically, for his drunkenness.[111] The prince was then executed.

It was during the reign of Husain Bayqara (r. 1470–1506) that Herat reached the very zenith of cultural and artistic glory, a saturated apogee during which the city's craftsmen, poets and artists would rise to levels not reached since, and during which architecture scaled heights of beauty and elegance. Shah Rukh and Baysanghur's renaissance would be elevated and intensified, as if it had simply been a forerunner to the main event of Herat in the age of Jami, Behzad and Ali Shir Nawai. The brightness with which Herat shone at this time was somehow made all the more poignant when we appreciate that this fluorescence was taking place as the city and what remained of the Timurid empire were menaced by forces which would eventually topple the tipsy Timurids from gilded thrones. These forces, Uzbeks and Safavids, called to mind Timur and Chingiz for their zeal, hardiness and devotion, far removed from the pleasure-loving later Timurids of whom Husain Bayqara is a prime specimen. Despite these crumbling edges, Timurid Herat during these years under Husain Bayqara kept a carapace of political order and provided the stability necessary for the economy to flourish. Husain

Bayqara, echoing his forbears' pride in keeping the peace, saw this as one of his major achievements in Herat:

> If, in former days, traveling merchants, other strangers and wayfarers had insurmountable difficulty going from their homes to their destinations because of brigands and highway robbers, now swift retribution has reduced that God-forsaken group to chaff and despatched them to hellfire. At every stage there are lofty caravanseraies for travelers and exalted fortresses providing safety for wayfarers in which they may find protection from the cold and shade from the heat.[112]

Sultan Husain Bayqara was born in Herat in the high summer of 1438 at the time of Herat's first Timurid cultural renaissance: stamped with the mark of a great royal patron.[113] His exposure to the power of royal patronage, its limitless possibilities for shaping a dynasty and a city happened early in his life. Yet Husain Bayqara's formative adult years took place in the service of Abul Qasim Babur at a time when Herat and Khorasan were experiencing one of their most tumultuous periods. The contrasts with his idyllic childhood in Shah Rukh's Herat could not have been starker. His subsequent desires to rule over a manageable territory, resisting the temptation to expand beyond the Oxus, reflect these early experiences of political instability, and speak of his admiration of Shah Rukh's utopian Herat. A small, functioning, quasi-imperial city-state with manageable domains was preferable to a sprawling and restless empire.

In his youth Husain Bayqara was a soldier of renown; sources linger over his military exploits.[114] He had 'the build of a lion, slender from the waist down', and despite his apparent piety, he was prevented from regular prayer by arthritis.[115] What prevented him from fasting is not mentioned.[116] But like many disciplined alcoholics, Husain Bayqara managed some form of abstinence: 'he never had a morning draught', preferring to begin his drinking after midday prayers.[117] It therefore should come as no surprise that we hear from his cousin Babur, a fastidious diary-keeper, that Husain Bayqara presided over a 'lively court'. His offspring, wives and concubines were many and varied; he was a man with a vigorous appetite for all things on offer to a medieval prince or sultan. The ever so slightly prudish Babur is lost between admiration and condemnation of his cousin, the urbane Timurid libertine, detailing his virtues but also telling us that in Husain Bayqara's Herat, 'vice and debauchery were rife and rampant'.[118] Yet Husain Bayqara was every bit the renaissance prince, keenly aware of his duties as a ruling Muslim. He was also aware of his responsibilities to Sufis, poets and the traditions of courtly life in Herat.[119]

In matters of legitimation, Husain Bayqara combined Shah Rukh's Islamic piety and Timur's consciously 'Mongol' outlook. He sought legitimacy in Islamic tropes, and historians of the court were ordered to stick to the party line by trotting out the regular Persian and Islamic epithets and titles. Reminiscent of a doctrinal indecision which typified his Mongol forefathers, Husain Bayqara showed leanings towards certain devotional practices more commonly associated with Shia Islam, and took the distinctly unorthodox step of attempting to sneak into Herat's *khutbah* the names of the Twelve Imams (highly unorthodox in Sunni Herat), a venture from which he was dissuaded by Abdul Rahman Jami (1414–92), Herat's most celebrated poet and scholar. It must, however, be noted that Islamic practices in medieval Khorasan were fluid, moving between Shia, Sunni, Sufi and tribal customs with a facility and ease which has all but disappeared from contemporary Islam. Yet in other ways Husain Bayqara represented a throwback to the roots of his Chagataid past, and his rule was a highpoint for Chagataid literature and culture.[120] His close friend, Herat's most powerful non-royal, Ali Shir Nawai, presided over a revival of Chagataid literature at court, and accounts from the period, Babur's in particular, give us the strong sense that Islam was by no means unassailable amongst Timurid elites in Husain Bayqara's Herat. Had the Timurids grown tired of assuming an Islamic persona? Or did they feel secure enough, both in their own skin and within Herat's walls, to embrace their Mongol past?

Artistic genius and cultural brilliance had outstripped the prosaic concerns of politics and war, but unfortunately such concerns would not go away, no matter how much Timurid sultans and princes wished they would. Weakened political power consequent on the fragmentation of Shah Rukh's empire meant that Herat as an imperial capital would no longer project outwards into the world; instead it sought sanctuary in the finer points of cultural expression, in the glories of their ancestors, and in wine. The Timurid empire was projected inwards, on itself. If Herat could not be the centre of powerful imperial domains, it could at least be the absolute arbiter of what passed for wit, sophistication and high culture, and as such it became an exquisite bubble, temporarily protected from the residual currents of succession and conflict, isolated from the religious revolution emanating from Iran with the rise of the Shia Safavid tribe who would later conquer Khorasan. The martial vigour of the Uzbek Shaybanid powers from over the Oxus also went largely unnoticed. Late-Timurid Herat proved the truism that a city is at its most recklessly brilliant and chaotically productive as the world is crashing around it: excesses feed off impending disaster, and decay acts as a powerful stimulus to art. Indeed, as Herat stood on the brink of conquest in the dying years of Timurid power, its leaders repaired to a garden where the following couplet was uttered:

> Make the most of any good time that presents itself:
> no one knows what the end will be.[121]

* * *

On a cloudless morning in late summer 2014, as the rising sun struck the dome on Gawhar Shad's crumbling mausoleum, I stood at the foot of a minaret to the north of Gawhar Shad's *madrasa*. While motorbikes and cycles roared and clattered past, and heroin addicts woke from their slumbers in the craters near another crumbling minaret, I marvelled at this relic to the late flowering of Timurid Herat. The minaret beneath which I stood, gazing up, had once marked the south-east corner of Husain Bayqara's *madrasa*, a building whose majesty is difficult to imagine from the ruins which remain. A slow-moving canal, clogged with refuse, winds its way around the remaining four minarets, bisecting east and west; rubbish piles up in the corners. A surrounding wall built when the Taliban ruled Herat is all but destroyed. These buildings once formed part of a complex of similar constructions, stretching for miles to the north of the Old City, running alongside Gawhar Shad's masterpiece. Throughout 2014 I spent days walking the site, gazing in awe at the remaining minarets and the buildings they must have cornered, trying to picture just how magnificent this complex would really have been. On the surfaces that remain, the geometric precision of the tiles is astounding and the quality of the glazes is quite extraordinary; even in this skeletal form it is impossible not to get lost in historical fantasies, imagining Timurid ministers, princes, princesses, poets, intellectuals and clerics going about their daily business in the rose gardens, to the refreshing sound of running fountains. The minarets climb into the sky, more like smoke stacks now than the imposing architectural marvels they once were, and occasionally one glimpses the shimmering of the faience, glinting from a long-ago era. When complete, there may well have been up to thirty minarets, educational colleges, hospitals and gardens all rising from this structure, all covered in blue, green, white and yellow glazed tiles arranged as verses from the Quran, flowers and beautifully patterned motifs. It is not difficult to understand why this period in Herat's history is so widely famed and mourned.

Nineteenth-century British hubris and the paranoia of high empire played their part in the final destruction of Husain Bayqara's greatest monument, tearing down what the intervening centuries of weather and neglect had not destroyed. Much of the site was demolished at the behest of British officials in 1885 at the high point of the Anglo-Russian tensions we now call the Great Game (see Chapters 4 and 5). The British feared that Russian soldiers attacking Herat, a city then seen as the key to the security of Britain's Indian empire, would use the decaying buildings as cover for their troops. Needless to say, the invasion never materialised and Herat's workmen were left to clean up the rubble as British officials left the city. The demolition left eleven minarets standing, a number which was reduced to nine by earthquakes, as described in the account of German spy and historian, Oscar von Niedermeyer. Yet another earthquake in 1931 left seven; now there are five, including the leaning minaret in Gawhar Shad's garden. A nineteenth-century British diplomat in Herat, there as part of the Afghan Boundary Commission (see Chapter 5), described the crumbling majesty of Husain Bayqara's complex in the following terms, giving us an idea as to the scale of this lost wonder of the world:

> The main building consists of a lofty dome some 75 feet in diameter, with a smaller dome behind it, and any number of rooms and buildings around it. The entrance to this dome is through a lofty archway on the east, some 80 feet in height, the face of which is entirely covered with tile-work and huge inscriptions in gilt; while above the archway is a lot of curious little rooms and passages, the use of which I cannot tell. To the east of this arch is a large courtyard some 80 yards square, surrounded with corridors and rooms several storeys in height—all covered with tile-work. The main entrance of all is on the eastern side of this court, through another huge

archway, also some 80 feet in height, but though the inside of the arch is all lined with tiles, or rather mosaic-work in regular patterns, the outside is bare, and looks as if it had never been finished. Four minarets, some 120 feet in height, form the four corners of the building: a good deal of the tile-work has been worn off by the weather… but when they were new, they must have been marvelously handsome. [122]

Their further decline is a sorry symbol of the city itself and the many years of invasion it has endured; few in Herat are aware of their significance, and failed efforts on the part of UNESCO and successive Afghan governments to have Herat listed as a World Heritage Site reflect an almost total historical amnesia which centuries of war have stamped on the city. Yet it would be doing the relics a disservice to say that they have lost their power to inspire awe. I felt a tangible sense of wonder on that glorious summer's morning, as did the English travel writer Robert Byron, who visited Herat in 1933 and 1934. Byron wrote:

No photograph can convey their colour of grape-blue with an azure bloom, or the intricate convolutions that make it so deep and luminous. On the bases, eight sides are supported by white marble panels carved with a baroque Kufic, yellow, white, olive green and rusty red mingle with the two blues in a maze of flowers, arabesques and texts as fine as the pattern on a tea-cup. [123]

He went on to describe the scene as a whole, including Gawhar Shad's mausoleum:

I see seven sky-blue pillars rise out of the bare fields against the delicate heather-coloured mountains. Down each the dawn casts a highlight of pale gold. In their midst shines a blue melon dome with the top bitten off. Their beauty is more than scenic, depending on light or landscape. On closer view, every tile, every flower, every petal of mosaic contributes its genius to the whole. [124]

In a tragic irony, the Husain Bayqara *madrasa*, once home to serious Islamic scholars, now plays host to a ragged collection of drug addicts who cower in the holed out pits beneath the minarets, smoking opium and injecting heroin. The sadness of cultural loss is compounded by the individual human tragedy of lives wasted to drug addiction and poverty. Each day tiles fall off the minarets, lying in a broken jumble around their base. Some of this fallen tile-work has been salvaged by the Afghan government, yet it piles up like rubble outside, or inside covered with old army or police uniforms and even the odd broken bicycle frame in a back room of the Qalah-ye Ekhtiar al-Din. I once spent an afternoon sifting through the rubble in search of major extant pieces of the tile-work that UNESCO had catalogued in 2006, and other important pieces; they could not be found anywhere, and had possibly been sold off on the black market.

Husain Bayqara's *madrasa* complex was just a small part of the extraordinary building programme, both royal and aristocratic, undertaken in Herat during his reign. These initiatives utterly transformed the areas to the north and north east of the Old City walls. Herat became an imperial capital of verve and grandeur at a time when its territories were more modest in scale and ambition. Terry Allen, historian of Timurid Herat, talks of a 'wholesale renewal of Herat's shrines and mosques', and sources from the period give us indications that Husain Bayqara and his aristocracy built on a truly epic scale.[125] Allen's painstaking research on Timurid Herat gives us some idea of the sheer number of buildings constructed during this period, far eclipsing the efforts of Shah Rukh and Gawhar Shad: eight mosques, eight *madrasa*s and twelve residences, or *bagh*s, speak of activity and wealth. One noble, Hajji Afzal al-Din Kermani, built an impressive grouping of a Friday Mosque, a *madrasa*, a *khaneqah* and baths outside Herat's Iraq Gate, to the west of the city walls. Yet Husain Bayqara's building was not limited to grand Islamic structures. Pleasure gardens, combining the business of rule with the fun of the feast, were also built widely during this period. This was suburban sprawl, but with aesthetics, not necessarily demography, leading the way.

Of especial note in this regard during Husain Bayqara's Herat was the Bagh-e Jahan Aray (World Adorning Garden), begun in 1469 and built making use of the newly irrigated land of the *khiaban*.[126] The *bagh* housed Husain Bayqara's residence, a lake and a hall which functioned as a court, a *dawlatkhana*, and also as a place for feasts and events at which formal governance, the intricacies of courtly ritual and pleasure might mix. Here the experience of pleasure was highly ritualised, lending to evenings of hedonism, high politics and high art an edge familiar to many medieval courtly settings. The lines between power and play were blurred, often literally as well as metaphorically. Pictorial representations of Husain Bayqara at play in his gardens show us an atmosphere of licensed chaos, with hints and nudges towards the doom which awaited this reckless last Timurid generation: political senescence met hedonistic abandon, head on.

In one such image, entitled 'A Party at the Court of Sultan Husayn [*sic*] Mirza', and accompanying a work of the Persian poet Saadi, dated 1488, it is difficult to see if the protagonists are enjoying themselves or not. Drunken figures stumble hazily across the neat geometry of the tiled floors in a thrilling contrast of order and disorder; more wine is brought by obedient servants; jugs lie cracked and prone, spilling onto painted patterns and tiles; men beat their breasts and others cry and wail whilst a musician plays what appears to be an extremely sad tune. One man appears to be vomiting; another faints in the lap of a friend, also overcome with an overwhelming sense of grief.[127] One can almost feel the hangover that would hit these revellers. The image, colourful and bold, is a wonderful portrayal both of the heady rush of intoxication, but also the more debilitating torpor of inebriation and the depression which often follows. It shows us Herat as it peaked, as its star reached the arc of its trajectory. Simultaneously an apogee and a nadir, the ascent and descent, this image perfectly encapsulates the final days of Timurid Herat.

Much as Gawhar Shad and Shah Rukh, Qasim al-Anwar and Shah Wali Ni'mattullah had been bright lights in the century's first period, its second iteration was studded with genius and epoch-defining personalities, all going about their business in an elegantly expanding city. Famous personages define Herat at this time. Few figures better embody the glories of Husain Bayqara's Herat, its wit and sophistication, wealth and charm, than Mir Ali Shir Nawai, a nobleman of Chagataid descent and childhood friend of Husain Bayqara. When E. G. Browne, Britain's foremost scholar of all things Persian, wrote that 'he may without exaggeration be described as the Maecenas of his time and country', this was no empty claim.[128] Babur, a man not given to undeserved praise, is unstinting in his admiration for Ali Shir's poetry, his peerless composition of *ghazals* and *diwans*, although he is more critical when it comes to the patron's mastery of metre.[129] Nawai's patronage of the pictorial artists Behzad and Shah Muzaffar enabled two of the world's finest painters to flourish and produce work of incomparable beauty. The musicians Qul Mohammad and Shaykh Nai owed their careers to Mir Ali Shir, and his contributions to Herat's urban landscape were no less impressive.

Born in Herat in 1441 into a cultured and connected family of Uighur *bakhshi*s, Turkic chancery scribes long in the service of the Timurids, he cut his teeth in the maelstrom of the years of disputed succession, and this no doubt made him nostalgic, as it did his close friend Husain Bayqara, for the more or less peaceful and cultured days of Shah Rukh. He occupied the role of keeper of the great seal, and in 1472 became a member of the Great State Council, Herat's ultimate political body.[130] Ali Shir's political career was, however, not without controversy, and at one point he suffered an exile of sorts, being sent away to govern a distant province for unknown reasons.[131] This seemed to prompt a retreat from the world of politics, enabling Ali Shir to devote himself to the pursuit of spending his Croesus-like wealth and developing his considerable talents as a musician, painter and poet. He ran his own *ketabkhana*, in which he trained and sponsored artists, much as Baysanghur had done in the 1430s, and he gathered around him the best talent and liveliest wits. Such was the sophistication of this *ketabkhana* that it even boasted a clock containing a mechanised figure which on the hour would strike its chest to indicate the time, astounding all those who saw it.[132] Much like his European counterparts the Medici, Ali Shir's wealth enabled him to loan the state large sums of money, a tactic he used to ensure that he remained in favour with government officials as well as the sovereign.

Ali Shir was totally devoted to service; he never married and no offspring are recorded from him. He was an aesthete who found satisfaction in poetry, witticism and art, in money and in the magnificence of buildings and patronage. Yet by no means did he lack edge; he was no unworldly aesthete. Rather, it seems that, as a man of 'extreme delicacy and elegance' who desired others to reach his own exalted standards of sophistication, he was forever destined to be let down by others' shortcomings, and he wasn't afraid of letting this be known.[133] This manifested itself in haughtiness and an urge to prove his supremacy in all areas of courtly life, for these were the pillars of his claim to be the leading light in a city famous for its cultural brilliance. He could also be a bully, on occasion. At Husain Bayqara's court there was a brilliant poet called Bannai, whose name came from his father's profession, that of a builder. Bannai's *ghazal*s are said to have contained 'verve and ecstasy', and he was renowned for his skill at court: a possible rival to Ali Shir. Yet one chink in his creative armoury was a lack of musical skill. Ali Shir mercilessly taunted the mason's son for this creative deficiency.[134] One winter, Ali Shir and Husain Bayqara left for Merv, and Bannai resolved to remain in Herat and use the absence of his nemesis to master the art of music. Over the winter Bannai became an accomplished musician, able to compose his own pieces, and when Ali Shir returned, he was piqued no end by Bannai's new-found accomplishments. Their rivalry continued to such an extent that Bannai felt compelled to leave Herat for Iraq, where he was welcomed at the cultured court in Baghdad. He returned briefly to Herat, but was once more driven from the city, again as a result of Ali Shir's taunting. Yet the end of the story suggests that Bannai might have had the last laugh. Given the popularity and fame of Ali Shir in Herat, it became a custom to give his name to fashions in vogue, to popular items of clothing. For example, a fashionable way of wearing one's scarf would be termed an 'Alishiri', and so on. As Bannai was preparing to depart for Samarqand, he prepared a saddlebag for his donkey. When asked what this was called, he named this extremely prosaic travelling ornament, highly unflatteringly to the sophisticate of the age, an 'Alishiri'.[135] Bannai's exile might have saved him from further ridicule, but it could not save him from being executed by Shia fanatics in the Uzbek city of Qarshi in 1512.[136]

Ali Shir also built widely, commissioning over fifty caravanserais and twenty mosques.[137] Perhaps his most notable achievement, alongside his renovation of the Friday Mosque, was his construction of a group of buildings named the *Ikhlasiyya* (sincerity) site; opposite and to the north-east of Gawhar Shad's *mosalla*, it consisted of a mosque, *madrasa*, *khaneqah*, bath house, hospital and a place for Quran recitations. It was a monument of real beauty, and built on a scale usually reserved for the royal family. Its existence took advantage of Abu Said having laid out the Juy-e Sultan on the now habitable slopes to the north of the Old City, leading up to Gazur Gah. On a clear winter's afternoon in 2014, I stood on the roof of Gawhar Shad's mausoleum and looked north towards Gazur Gah, over an area now filled with new buildings or scrubland. I tried to picture the quite otherworldly beauty of Ali Shir's Herat: the intricate faience of the geometric tiles which covered minarets and mosques; the running water; the green of the gardens and the many colours of the produce within. Unfortunately in today's Herat one has to make do with imagination and the scraps of tiles which still cling to the minarets of Husain Bayqara's own monumental structure.

One of Ali Shir's gifts to cosmopolitan Herat, and to literature in general, was to raise Chagatai Turkic to the level of a literary language, fostering a Persian–Turkic literary tradition of competition. He even saw fit to write a treatise arbitrating between the two languages, the *Mukhakamat al-Lughatayn* (The Arbitration Between Two Languages), in which he concluded that Chagatai was superior to Persian for its greater expressiveness. His love of Chagatai is clear from his history of literature, dwelling on the notable Chagataid writers of the *Majalis al-nafais*.[138] This revival in Turkic literature at the courts of Husain Bayqara and Ali Shir was by no means an isolated phenomenon; Babur's own diary, the *Baburnama*, was written in Turkic, and Husain Bayqara himself also wrote poems in Turkic, some of which were translated into Persian by an Afghan scholar of the 1960s.[139] It seems that Persian never fully conquered the hearts and minds of the Timurid elites of Herat, no matter how much Shah Rukh and his ilk would have us believe. Yet we should be careful not to overplay this Chagataid seam running through Herat's Timurid autumn, for it was an elite phenomenon and did not overly influence the province as a whole.

Ali Shir died on 3 January 1501. Khwandamir's moving eulogy of Herat's greatest patron is the best indication we have of the high esteem in which he was held. 'On Sunday morning, the bird of his pure light broke the bondage of its cage and took flight from the strictures of corporeality for eternal gardens of paradise.'[140] Even in an age well-stocked with brilliant patrons who moved seamlessly between the realms of high politics and high culture, Ali Shir Nawai, Herat's Chagataid aesthete, remains peerless. His tomb, close by to Gawhar Shad's mausoleum, attracts curious visitors every day, and is housed in a beautiful and newly built domed building. A carved marble slab next to the entrance contains a fitting description of his life and work.

Persian poetry also flourished in later Timurid Herat, proving that Ali Shir and his Chagataid ilk were not simply longing for the sounds of their ancestors. Herat was awash with poetic talent, eager to catch the ear, or eye, of Herat's patrons. One could not move for poets in Herat. One story from this era, beloved by Heratis and Afghans, concerns a poet and a recital. Ali Shir Nawai was playing chess whilst a poetry recital went on in the background and the wine flowed. Mid game, Ali Shir stretched out his leg in repose, and unintentionally struck the poet Bannai. Ali Shir remarked, half in jest, 'What a sad state this is—that in Herat one cannot stretch out a leg without poking a poet in the ass.' Bannai's reply was equally witty, 'Yes, and if you pull your leg back in, you'll poke another!'[141]

Culturally, the autumn of Timurid rule in Herat was one of subtlety, hidden meaning and an obsession with mysticism and complex circles of wit: the brilliance of a city both rising and falling. That an artist's celebrated talent was the delicacy and intricacy of his painting gives us an idea as to the introspective and highly refined atmosphere of the time. Similarly, the poetry of late Timurid Herat was inward looking, complex and often disappeared down alleyways of intricacy and artifice. The focus became glued to 'purely technical challenges in ever more dazzling displays of complexity'.[142] Poems became stages on which to showcase an ability to write complex puns and elaborate riddles and acrostics. Chronograms, sentences whose word values would add up to give the date of a particular event, had been popular in previous centuries, but in Husain Bayqara and Ali Shir's Herat they moved into more abstruse and refined territory. Also enigmas, containing secret allusions to letters of the Arabic alphabet, which when assembled yielded a name or word, became intensely popular. Solving all these was a valued skill at court. The esoteric genre did not age well, however; E. H. Gibb, the noted Orientalist scholar of Persian literature, is less than complimentary about the tendency to literary parlour games which infected the higher echelons of Timurid courtly life:

> This all-absorbing passion for rhetoric was the most fatal pitfall on the path of these old poets; many an otherwise sublime passage is degraded by the obtrusion of some infantile conceit, and many a verse, beautiful in all else, disfigured by the presence of some extravagant simile or grotesque metaphor.[143]

It would be doing Timurid Herat a disservice, however, to castigate its entire later poetic output for the reasons noted above. Poetry, and culture in general, were social filters, dividers marking out the elites from the bureaucrats, whilst also serving as a way of passing the time. Their position and status in society afforded the wealthy elites of Timurid Khorasan time and money; by enjoying poetry and philosophy, however recondite and esoteric, Timurid elites in Herat and beyond were marking themselves out from their bureaucratic and clerical inferiors: the clergy and the scribes. Parlour games are not, by their nature, high cultural achievements, but rather ways to amuse and entertain. As Timurid imperial life moved further into the recesses of courtly ritual and cultural sophistication, it is no wonder that this was reflected in the output of those courts and the poets and artists employed to serve them.

Of all Herat's late Timurid poets, Mawlana Nur al-Din Abd al-Rahman Jami is the most celebrated. Born in Jam on 7 November 1414, outstanding also as a mystic, a scholar in various disciplines and as a powerful personality. E. G. Browne goes so far as to describe Jami as 'one of the most remarkable geniuses whom Persia ever produced'.[144] It was Babur's opinion that Jami's genius was such that it rendered praise obsolete. His fame was such that the Ottoman ruler, Sultan Bayazid II, begged him to come and adorn his court. A Sufi by training and inclination, Jami was also a close friend of Ali Shir Nawai, with whom he shared a disdain for mere mortals and those who did not appreciate or match his extraordinary intellectual gifts. Jami was not without humour, however, as the following story indicates. One day, Jami was found repeating the following lines to himself, an elegy for a lost lover:

So constantly art thou in my stricken soul and sleepless eye
That whosoever should appear from afar, I should think that it was thee.

An 'irreverent bystander' cut short Jami's poetical reverie with the question, 'Suppose it were an ass?' To which Jami responded, 'I should that it was thee.'[145]

Jami's poetic output was prodigious and his range of subject matter equally so, from the mystical and theological to the political, the elegiac and the romantic. His poetry included seven long poems whose name *Haft Aurang* (Seven Thrones—a name in Persian given for the Great Bear constellation) was given to a publication of twentieth-century poetry in Herat under Taliban rule. Jami's hold over the hearts and minds of Herat's poets is as strong today as it was in the late fifteenth century. One poem in particular, the fifth of the 'Seven Thrones', in which the romance of Joseph and Potiphar's wife is described, is a particularly beautiful rendition of that well-known staple of romantic poetry in the Persian canon. Mystical discussions of how to approach God through love of another and musings on the nature of beauty come together in Jami's writings. Jami's prose output included commentaries on existing poetical traditions, yet also touched on issues of justice and kingship. He was a polymath on a par with Ali Shir.[146]

In the sphere of Herat's pictorial arts under Husain Bayqara, one can see a softening of the Islamic strictness observed under Shah Rukh and Baysanghur, a lessening of the focus on legitimacy and Islamo-Persian heritage. Compared with the earlier figures described above, these later Timurid figures depicted in illustrated manuscripts appear more alive, more human and more at ease. Whilst the later-fifteenth-century illus-trated manuscripts respect traditional forms and themes, it seems that something of a shift has taken place; the colours are warmer, less forced somehow, more more human. Gone is the forlorn Timurid in a garden, alone and surrounded by nervous courtiers, and in their place we see Timurid princes and princesses who are confident, daring and clearly more comfortable with their place in a Persian setting. A beautiful example of this later approach can be seen in the folio from the *Khamsa* (literally, Five Poems, a work in *mathnawi* rhyming couplets covering Persian folktales and romance stories) by the twelfth-century Persian poet Nizami, entitled 'Shirin Views Khusraw's portrait'. This image, dated 1494–5, was undertaken at the very height of Herat's splen-dour.[147] The scene depicts the moment when the Persian princess Shirin is inspecting an image of her suitor, Khusraw, and is seated on a carpet of red and blues whose geometric design echoes that of Herat's Timurid buildings and mosques. Her ladies in waiting are variously playing music and conversing with each other, and the image is set against the back-drop of a lush garden which gives onto stylised scrubland and rocks. Wine jugs sit close to the rug. The effect draws the viewer into the garden and into the emotional intrigue which is clearly unfolding; we are part of the drama in a way that might not have been the case in those paintings of the Baysanghurid era. These are images wonderfully detailed in their observation of the everyday at the court of these powerful men and women; the details humanise figures who had previously appeared to us in stiff, formulaic poses, surrounded by nervous flunkeys anticipat-ing the needs of their masters and mistresses.

Often claimed as the era's ultimate artistic genius was Kamaluddin Behzad. He painted in Herat under Husain Bayqara, and later found fame at the Safavid court. His talents span the later Timurid era and into the Safavid empire. A protégé of Ali Shir Nawai, Behzad's paintings are of breathtaking detail, sumptuous colour and no little dynamism, but he was by no means Herat's single greatest artistic luminary. Babur, reflecting a justified criticism of Behzad's Herat work, felt that whilst Behzad painted 'delicately', his depiction of the beardless was defective as he gave them all double chins. In contrast, 'He drew the faces of bearded people quite well.'[148]

I have purposefully used words indicating light, or stars, or fluorescence to describe this period of Herat's story, its second Timurid Renaissance. This truly was a period of light, the light of Persian and Chagataid cultural genius refracted through the fertile oasis city of Herat. The Timurid chronicler Esfezari describes the accession of his patron, Husain Bayqara, in terms which resonate with Herat as a shining light of high-medieval Khorasan; he is 'the world-illuminating ruler' who is banishing the darkness of the previous years, a ray of light shining after the decades of chaos which had followed from the death of Shah Rukh.[149] Amidst the essential fragility of medieval Khorasan, cultural highpoints and peace were to be celebrated for what they were. A potential return to chaos was never far from the surface. Much as the European Renaissance saw a collision of the medieval and the 'modern', Herat's own Renaissance was a collision of Turk and Tajik, sedentary and urban, and the light it produced was every bit as worthy of our appreciation and wonder as Europe's cultural apogee, even if Herat's lights were to be almost totally eclipsed with the passing of time.

* * *

The year 1501 ushered in a new era for both Central Asia and the Middle East. Great power shifts were taking place in the region. Herat's cultured bubble was at risk. To the north and east, Uzbek power arising from Mohammad Shaybani's final conquests of Samarqand was consolidated and strengthened; to the west, the accession of Shah Ismail I, the first Safavid ruler of Persia, betokened the arrival of another regional dynasty, a Shia powerhouse that changed the region forever.[150] Husain Bayqara, now a pale imitation of the vigorous and martial youth he had once been, was prevented by advanced age and protracted illness from taking necessary decisions to secure his empire. He was at pains to avoid the coming conflict with Shah Ismail Safavid I, and for a long time—too long—he closed his eyes to the immediate threat of a massive attack from the Shaybanid Uzbeks, whose successes in Transoxania were, of course, no secret in Herat. Correspondence with the emergent Safavid dynasty reveals Husain Bayqara's desire for friendly relations at all costs.[151] Like many before him, he chose to place his trust in Herat's Ekhtiar al-Din fortress and to seek solace in wine. His decision in 1506 to confront the Uzbek menace threatening Khorasan smacked of too little too late: a token gesture.

In May 1506, at the very beginning of this ill-fated campaign, Husain Bayqara died. He had been ill for a number of years, reportedly stricken with palsy and no doubt suffering from that ubiquitous Timurid ailment, gout. Herat now lay open, beset by internal weakness and faced with a determined enemy. Such was the lack of certainty that followed his passing, echoing previous instances of a divided house in Herat, that two princes were installed on Herat's threadbare imperial throne: Badiuzzman Mirza and Mozaffar Mirza Sultan. One contemporary reaction to news of this royal coalition, calling to mind the final days of the Kartid dynasty, was to quote the following lines from Saadi's *Gulistan*:

Ten poor men can sleep under one blanket,
but two kings cannot fit into one clime.[152]

It was into this divided city that Babur, founder of the Mughal empire, wandering Timurid prince and grandson of Abu Said, entered in the autumn of 1506. At the time of Husain's death, Babur had been marching an army from Kabul to Herat to aid his Timurid cousins in the fight against the Shaybanid Uzbeks.[153] Babur had heeded Husain Bayqara's call to arms out of a sense of dynastic loyalty and pride in his Timurid heritage.[154] Even though Herat was divided between two princes, it was still the capital of the Timurid empire. Babur's retinue reached Herat just as Shaybani Khan, the eponymous leader of the Shaybanid Uzbeks, was besieging Balkh. Babur's account of Shaybani Khan was scathing, reckoning his only praiseworthy act was to beat up a precocious lutenist by the name of Husain. Shaybani Khan felt that the lutenist was not putting enough into his performance, and as Babur had no patience for artistic types, he was in no doubt that 'such temperamental fellows' deserve what they have coming to them.[155] There

115

was talk amongst Babur's troops of heading back to Kabul, possibly fearing Herat to be a lost cause, but Babur was adamant that they see Herat, 'which has no equal in the world'.[156] As they approached the outskirts of Herat, passing irrigated and *bagh*-laden meadows, the expected royal greeting from Herat's nobles was delayed as their Timurid hosts were suffering from hangovers. This was a sign of things to come.

The memoirs of Babur's travels, the *Baburnama*, written in Chagataid Turkish, contain lively, witty and perceptive observations of the Timurid elite at work and play in the *fin de siècle* atmosphere of a post-Husain Bayqara Herat. Babur shows us a dynasty bordering on senility, undone by excesses, and almost completely out of touch with their Mongol and Timurid heritage. The wandering prince is shocked at a seeming obsolescence of courtly rituals and Mongol protocol, alarmed at a court more interested in wine and song than politics and military strategy. On one occasion, in the presence of Badiuzzman Mirza, Babur felt his status as a Timurid noble who had done more than anyone else to defend the realm from outsiders was not afforded the requisite respect; words were exchanged, and an apology accepted.[157]

Babur shows us a comically decadent Herat, fading into torpor. One of Abu Said's sons is described as addicted to sodomy; his sons all died young of 'shameful immoderation and debauchery'.[158] Another prince instructed 'clowns and buffoons' to perform 'lewd acts' in front of the assembled court. Babur is wary of these witty and sophisticated aesthetes running amok in Herat's urbane and sophisticated palaces and *bagh*s. Occasionally, when discussing religious figures, he casts aspersions on their claims to be either Sufis or *sayyed*s, doubting that piety can exist side by side with such decadence. An eminent *sadr* (religious scholar) in Husain Bayqara's court, Mir Sarbirahna, is described in withering terms as someone who 'most likely pretends' to be a *sayyed*, and whose poetic and literary output amounts to 'a lengthy, overlong pack of lies'.[159] We hear of an amir who was so addicted to playing chess that he would grab the skirt of another man so as to corner him for his next game, even whilst he was in the middle of playing another. We hear of feasts on the banks of the Murghab, gold and silver vessels from which limitless wine was poured. Babur himself was not himself fond of drinking, but his cousins were. On one occasion, however,

Babur did allow himself to drink, asking himself the perfectly reasonable question, 'if not, in Herat, then when would I?' His 'leap into drink' was accompanied by recitations of Khorasani music and poetry, after which the evening descended into 'tasteless impertinences'.[160]

Yet for all Babur's superficial admiration of the luxury of Herat's nobles, behind his prose is a tangible unease at the senescence, military and social, which looms large over Herat. After one particularly lavish banquet, Babur is moved to remark, 'Although these mirzas were outstanding in the social graces, they were strangers to the actuality of military command and the rough and tumble of battle.'[161] The alarmingly serious political background against which this account was set—Herat menaced from east and west—makes this behaviour and raucousness even more intriguing. Babur eventually took his leave of Herat, reluctantly one imagines (perhaps he knew the Timurids of Herat were irrevocably doomed?), on 23 December 1506, marching north to Badghis to begin his journey back to Kabul.

It would be doing Herat's Timurid elites a disservice, however, to pin on them the entire blame for the collapse of their empire. The Timurid empire had become divided internally, by this point: split along lines of an expanding family, as was its wont. As news of Shaybani Khan's victory over Balkh, a city 'swept clean', reached Herat, a discussion took place amongst Herat's leading military and political figures.[162] As was always the case, there were doves and there were hawks. The hawks favoured a swift attack, with troops pushing up to Badghis and further north-east to confront Shaybani Khan between Balkh and Herat. The doves favoured consolidation of the surrounding provinces, sending commanders to Khorasan so that they could deal with the Uzbek invaders from a place of internal strength, as necessary. They favoured preparing for a conflict as opposed to initiating one. Those in favour of this line of reasoning cited two main fears: were an army to set off from Herat to confront Shaybani Khan, they would leave Herat open to attack from disaffected Timurid princes Kipchiq Mirza and Mohammad Mushin Mirza. Then, any such attack on Herat, were it successful, would attract back to Herat those native Herati noblemen who would be tasked with fighting the Uzbeks, thus weakening the Timurid army in the surrounding provinces. The doves, unsurprisingly, won the day and military commanders dispersed to the surrounding provinces of Timurid Khorasan to prepare the surrounds for the invasion which would surely come.

For all the Timurid amirs' dovish prudence, and it was sensible advice, winter gave way to spring and events moved faster than expected, hastening the fall of Herat to the Uzbeks. In early May 1507, 'when the crescent moon of Muharram 913 [13 May 1507] rose from the east of fortune and magnificence over the green sea of celestial sphere, news was received that Mohammad Khan Shaybani had crossed at Kirki and was headed for Khorasan'.[163] Four days later, Herat's military leaders once again convened, although this time the consensus was reached that Herat and Khorasan were simply unable to resist the advancing Uzbeks, and masterly inaction was declared the best course of action. In the words of one eyewitness chronicler:

> The next day [17 May 1507] they were honored to pay homage, and in the company of all the great amirs they spread the carpet of counsel, thinking that they could repel the arrow of fate with the shield of machination and hold back the torrent of the Great Effector's will with a handful of chaff.[164]

On 17 May 1507 Shaybani Khan's armies poured south, quickly reaching the banks of the Murghab river, gaining allegiance and troops as they went. On 19 May battle was joined, a battle in which Herat's greatest amirs, Dhul Nun and Muzaffar Husain Mirza, were unable to hold back the Uzbeks. Khwandamir likens the Timurid resistance to a bunch of sticks being used to stem the flow of a flood. The brave, but crazed, Amir Dhul Nun refused to surrender, fighting to his last breath, but to no avail. Many of Herat's nobles, native and Timurid, fled in all directions: some south, some to Mashhad. Sultan Badiuzzman Mirza escaped to a royal *bagh* outside Herat's city walls. Muzaffar Husain Mirza sneaked into Herat under the cover of darkness, heading to the Bagh-e Shahi, where he unsuccessfully begged various religious and political figures from amongst those who had remained in Herat to assist him in one last defence of the city. We next see the downcast prince leaving Herat through its southerly gate, heading for Astarabad on the Turshiz road. Herat had all but fallen to the Uzbeks.

Proving that *madrasa*s combined political and religious functions, on the morning of 20 May 1507 the *sayyed*s, judges, dignitaries and grandees of Herat assembled in Herat's Shaykh al-Islam *madrasa* to discuss their response to the invasion of the Shaybanids. As Herat experienced

the abundant promise of spring, the light of Timurid peace and prosperity was rapidly fading. The chronicler Khwandamir, an eyewitness
to the proceedings, was tasked with preparing a petition for surrender
which would be submitted to the Shaybanids in the hope of leniency.
Ominously, the young holy man sent to deliver the petition was robbed
on his way out to the Shaybanid camp, for Herat's surrounding areas
had already submitted to the Uzbeks and pillage and plunder had begun
in earnest. Yet he somehow managed to deliver the missive to the
Shaybanid camp in Herat's meadows.

The message had its intended effect and diplomatic wheels were set
in motion for Herat's submission to the Shaybanids. Herat's most
important figures, the *Qazi*, Ekhtiar al-Din Hassan, and the Shaykh al-
Islam, Mawlana Sayfuddin Ahmad al-Taftazani, received a document
from Mohammad Shaybani promising good terms for peace and an end
to the pillaging that devastated the countryside. Herat duly sent men
of standing out to Mohammad Shaybani, the majority of whom were
ulema (clerics).[165] Herat's delegation met with the leading figure at
Mohammad Shaybani's court (Mawlana Nizam al-Din Abdul-Rahim
Turkistani), and began to talk money: what price would Herat put on
peace and survival? Punitive terms were reached and Shaybanid nobles
were placed in positions of power, effectively setting a military and
bureaucratic seal over the conquest of Khorasan. It now fell to their tax
collectors to empty Herat's coffers. If the parlay had been ordered,
measured even, then what followed was little more than licensed pillage. One eyewitness describes the appalling scenes which brought an
end to the Timurid century:

> So many lustrous pearls, emeralds, Badakhshan rubies and other gems and
> gold vessels were obtained in that not a decimal of a tenth could be con-
> tained in the imagination of any emperor. From the personal possessions
> of the amirs and ministers of that dynasty much cash and goods were
> taken, and the Uzbek soldiery seized every one of the rectors of Khurasan's
> [*sic*] benefices and endowments of Khurasan [*sic*] on some pretext and
> tormented and tortured them until they got from them what they could
> get. Indeed the meaning of the Koranic verse, 'Verily kings, when they
> enter a city by force, waste the same, and abase the most powerful of the
> inhabitants thereof' [*Koran* 27:34], was fully realized [*sic*]. And the cries of
> many people of quality and station, reduced to misery and degradation,
> rose to the celestial spheres. The delicate beauties of the inner sanctum of

inviolability were taken captive and tormented by the merciless Uzbekz, and Venuses of the chambers of chastity were left by ravaging Mughals to wander destitute in the lanes and the bazaars.[166]

The citadel stood fast, for a brief time, until a successful tunneling operation caused the tower facing the Bagh-e Shahr to topple, at which point the fort's defenders decided to bow to the seemingly inevitable. Prayers rang out over Herat in the name of Mohammad Shaybani; Herat's conquest was complete. After the Uzbek storm had settled, Herat's leading men, many of whom were hiding in the mountains around Herat, decided to return to the city to seek employment under the Shaybanids, much as the vestiges of the Kartid administration had done when Timur became supreme ruler of Khorasan at the end of the fourteenth century.

Timurid Herat had stood at the very centre of Khorasan as the ultimate in high culture, elegance and sophistication. Once a capital of a powerful empire, by 1510 its lands had shrunk following inheritance squabbles, administrative mismanagement and political fragmentation. And yet still, in the face of this, Herat had refused to compromise on its unstinting pursuit of excellence in the sphere of architecture, poetry, art and philosophy as the political world crashed around them. The wobbling and drunken courtiers of later Timurid art are a beautiful testament to this. To this very day, when one thinks of Herat as a centre of cultural and artistic excellence, it is to this period that one points, the age of poets, painters and cultured drunken sultans, rose gardens and shimmering blue faience. It is from this period that Herat's cultural reputation truly begins. Yet it was a time of complexity, too, for an enduring irony of that century is that to the very end, Herat's greatest patrons, those who did more to mould the city's identity than many other rulers, considered themselves somehow outsiders, fearful of the real Heratis. Herat had played host to a Mazdakite struggle between the forces of light—represented by Gawhar Shad, Ali Shir, Jami, Behzad and Baysanghur; and the forces of darkness—represented by instability and pathological tendencies to familial squabbles. The fall of the Timurids in Herat can be seen as a perverse victory of these forces of instability and chaos, the unfortunate but logical end to a dynasty that saw achievements of art, culture and beauty as more important than the more immediate concerns of defence of the realm.

3

SAFAVIDS TO PASHTUNS AND THE DECLINE
OF A TIMURID JEWEL, 1510–1747

In the early fourteenth century, when Mongol Il-Khans ruled Iraq-e Ajam and Khorasan and Kart *malek*s oscillated between vassalage and rebellion, a pious and charismatic Sufi preacher named Shaykh Safiuddin Ishaq appeared in the town of Ardebil. This Sufi preacher would give his name to the Safavid empire, a dynasty which did much to create the Shia powerhouse nation we know today as the Islamic Republic of Iran. At its height, the Safavid empire stretched from Anatolia in the west to Qandahar and Sistan in the east, yet its beginnings were with Shaykh Safi's small Sufi order. This Sufi order was to grow from a body of Turkic men gathered to his cause of mystical spiritual enlightenment into a formidable and wealthy empire of trade and politics which professed to rule in the name of Shia Islam's Twelve Imams. One fifteenth-century Herati chronicler describes Shaykh Safi as:

> a sun rising from the orient of sainthood, shedding the illumination of divine grace over the expanse of the world. In the treasury of his breast he held jewels of divine knowledge, his pearls of wisdom adorned the ears of great sultans and kings, the dust under the feet of his retinue was collyrium for the eyes of ascetics, and the heaven-scraping dome of his hermitage was a focus of divine light.[1]

Besides holding jewels of knowledge in his divine breast, Shaykh Safi was a Sufi dervish who sought mystical enlightenment throughout the lands of present-day Iran, fasting and seeking truth from holy men. He earned his Sufi spurs under a shaykh named Zahid, marrying the latter's daughter and taking over this line of Sufis from the Caspian region of Gilan.[2] Shaykh Safi combined his asceticism with a practical understanding of the world and military affairs, skills which marked him out for greatness, in a manner reminiscent of the Prophet Muhammad's own martial, spiritual and bureaucratic talents.

Shaykh Safi's Sufi movement emerged in an Islamic world still rocked by the 1258 sack of Baghdad by the Mongols and the resulting collapse of the Abbasid Caliphate. Millenarian revolutionary movements such as the Hurufiya, whose disciple Ahmad Lur almost succeeded in killing Shah Rukh in Herat, are perfect illustrations of the milieu from which Shaykh Safi came: Islam in crisis, a region in flux. Sultan Husain Bayqara's abortive attempt to have the *khutbah* recited in the name of the Twelve Imams shows how the lines between Sunni, Shia and Sufi had been blurred in the search for meaning in a turbulent world. Herat was bursting with shrine cults, popular saints and dream interpreters, existing side by side with the prevailing Sunni orthodoxy which Shah Rukh had so assiduously cultivated. As we shall see, despite the arrival of the Shia Safavids, Herat remained true to its soul as a bastion of orthodox Sunni learning and jurisprudence, whilst also retaining its place as a valley of saints, shrines and mystics.[3] In Iraq-e Ajam the Safavids found support from Turcoman tribal groups who would later be known as the Qizilbash, 'red heads'. This appellation came into usage under the rule of the Safavid leader Haidar (1460–88), son of Shaykh Junaid (d.1460), and it refers to the characteristic twelve-gored red turban (each gore representing one of the Twelve Imams) worn by these Turcoman soldiers who functioned as the Safavids' praetorian guard. Haidar's claim that each of the twelve gores signified one of the Twelve Imams was said to have been inspired by a vision from Imam Ali, and still to this day the word Qizilbash is used to refer to Shia communities in Afghanistan. As mystical union with God via contemplation and initiation into mystical rites gave way to the more prosaic requirements of soldiering and dying for God, under a later Safavid leader, Shaykh Junaid, military training to his Turcoman adherents became a standard part of their initiation into the Safavid order: the muscle behind the millenarianism. The Qizilbash became known as *ghazis*, warriors for a *jihad*, a title which elevated the Safavids' military conquests from mere political expansion to the level of divinely sanctioned conquest in the name of the Twelve Imams.[4] One sixteenth-century Italian merchant described how the Safavid leader Ismail I (r. 1501–24) inspired such loyalty and veneration amongst the Qizilbash that they entered battle with no armour.[5]

The chaos of post-Timurid Khorasan and the emergence of Safavid, Mughal and Ottoman empires would once again place Herat at the margins of empire, far from the womb-like sanctity that imperial status confers on a city. The following two centuries drag Herat in various uncomfortable directions, into contested political spaces, giving rise to sectarian disputes and a prolonged identity crisis which would continue well into the twentieth century. As a province, Herat would almost constantly find itself at the mercy of imperial whim or neglect; it was a magnet for Central Asian tribal confederacies who saw easy loot, fresh fodder and grazing grounds. Herat comes off badly in this grand tug of war, and the city that emerges into the eighteenth century is significantly altered from the one so vividly portrayed by the awestruck and censorious Babur.

* * *

On 8 December 1510, a Safavid emissary flanked by Qizilbash troops reached Herat's walls. They had come to claim Khorasan's pearl in the wake of their decisive victory over a ragged Shaybanid Uzbek army near Merv.[6] Herat's citizens initially gave the Shia soldiers a cautious welcome, albeit one preceded by an uprising of a 'seditious rabble' in which a number of Herat's prominent figures lost their lives.[7] For some, the threat of Shia rulers sacking Herat was too much to bear. When the Safavid officials entered the city walls, bringing with them promises of leniency, if not religious tolerance, for those who submitted, it seemed as if Herat might enjoy a peaceful transition from Sunni Uzbek to Shia Safavid. These hopes were short-lived, however. The following day a Safavid general forced Herat's leading mullah at the Friday Mosque, Hafiz Zaynuddin Ziaratgahi, to read a royal proclamation from the pulpit in the name of Herat's Safavid overlords. Ziaratgahi was compelled to denigrate the city's Sunni creed as well as the Four Caliphs on whose authority so much order and orthodoxy rested. He refused. As a consequence of his refusal, he was seized by an armed group of Qizilbash, dragged from the pulpit and executed in the mosque. Khorasan's most venerable Islamic scholar, too, 'the first of his age in matters of *hadith* and exegesis, having occupied the position of Shaykh al-Islam in Khorasan for thirty years', suffered the same fate in this sectarian bloodletting. The lines of Sunni–Shia conflict in Herat were now drawn in blood across the floor of the Friday Mosque. The 'entire population' of the mosque fled for their lives.[8]

For a city famed for its Sunni orthodoxy, its venerable traditions of religious disputation and its Sufi shrines, dream interpreters and mystics it is difficult to overstate the significance of these acts. As if to cement this first step in a sectarian conflict, yet another Safavid emissary was sent to Herat to conciliate the nobles and propagate their version of the Shia faith.[9] Good sense or pragmatism prevailed, and Herat's *ulema* consented to read the *khutbah* in the name of the Safavids and Shah Ismail I, along with a rowdy although possibly half-hearted celebration of the qualities of the Twelve Imams. Herat then gave itself over to offering gifts to the new Safavid emissaries, doubtless secretly hoping that their reign would be short-lived. Timurid *bagh*s were given over to celebration of the Safavid line, and the new rulers even managed to coax Herat's castellan from the citadel with promises of continued employment. Everything changes and yet everything remains the same. As if to cement his rule, Shah Ismail I chose Herat as his winter quarters; he governed from the Bagh-e Jahan Aray, where Husain Bayqara had once hosted notoriously riotous gatherings. Shah Ismail I set to work dispensing justice and governing with all the severity one would expect from a monarch of a freshly created radical religious dynasty. Certain Herati nobles who had enjoyed alcohol under the Timurids and the Shaybanids were accordingly hung upside down before being executed.[10]

In past centuries, Herat had seen the trial of politico-religious agitators who had attempted to assassinate Shah Rukh, in the name of a millenarian Sufi ideology and had even in the Kartid times waged a war against the Shia Sarbedars and their millenarian movement. Yet the execution of important figures of Sunni orthodoxy on the floor of the Friday Mosque caused waves of fear and uncertainty to ripple out to the corners of Khorasan. It was as if a line had been crossed in Herat.

The politico-religious foundations on which Herat relied for so much were now threatened by a new and powerful Shia empire, albeit one whose Shiism was a mix of tribal customs and millenarianism.[11] Gone was the Timurid aping of Herat's existing Sunni religious traditions, their desire to sit within Herat's accepted religious parameters. In its place was a ruthlessly enforced Shia Islam which aimed at ideological supremacy over a fluid religious landscape. Whereas previous conquerors of Herat had sought simply money and power, the Safavids wanted to change even the most intimate aspects of the lives of Herat's citizens and elites.

* * *

As the winter of 1511 turned to spring, Herat gave a banquet in honour of the Persian festival of Nawruz, a pre-Islamic celebration of the return of warmth and life after the winter months and a celebration of the new Persian year. The oasis was decorated to a pitch of imperial majesty, the fields north of the *khiaban* covered in tents and pavilions, silver beakers brimful with wine (exactly how this was squared with the previous year's execution of Herat's wine-drinking nobles is not clear). Food was prepared in abundance. The city and its surrounds would have looked beautiful in the extreme, if a little ragged from Shaybanid rule and Safavid conquest. Shah Ismail I sat on a throne prepared for him in the Bagh-e Jahan Aray; he was flanked by extravagantly dressed military and spiritual advisers, and there he received gifts from Herat's chastened and defeated nobility. One Herati noble presented Ismail I with 'purses of gold and silver, strings of rubies, turquoise and pearls, vessels of gold and silver, china ware, precious textiles from Egypt, Syria, Europe and China, horses with jewel-studded reins and swords in gilded scabbards...'[12] The bounty was said to have been so great that it took a thousand people to convey it all to the seated Safavid.

Herat's fading Timurid glory had come face to face with the rising splendour of the imperial ambitions of a still-young Safavid empire. This event both hinted at the luxury with which Safavid Esfahan would become synonymous in later years, yet also clearly contained a strong echo of the excesses and wealth of Timurid Herat. A baton was being passed from the flickering remains of Timurid Herat to another warlike tribal grouping with a fondness for ceremony in a process on which Ibn

Khaldun would have looked with a knowing smile; one united, warlike tribal dynasty replaced another once united, warlike tribal dynasty now gone to seed in excesses and corruption. Echoes of Ali Shir Nawai's celebrations would have been hard to ignore for those Heratis present who had witnessed Timurid Herat's demise. Despite the symbolism and luxury of this feast, the religious persecution which had shadowed these first months of Safavid rule in Herat meant that this was a nervous celebration for Herat's people. The Uzbek threat remained, and Herat's pliant elites who had chosen to side with the Safavid dynasty would have either hoped or feared for their return.

Vanquished Uzbek forces had retreated back over the Oxus, ready to invade again when the opportunity presented itself. In many ways, the Shaybanid Uzbek threat defined Herat in the early sixteenth century, stuck between a preoccupied and adolescent Safavid empire and a highly mobile and extremely greedy Shaybanid Uzbek force from Transoxania, always eager to cross the Oxus and flood south into Herat in search of quick riches.[13] Yet it was not simply a naked lust for loot that propelled the Uzbeks over the Oxus to Herat. Sectarian beliefs also motivated the Uzbeks in their desire to capture Herat. The Sunni Shaybanid Uzbeks saw the Shia Safavids as mortal sectarian foes, and enmity between the warring factions ran very deep indeed. So deep that after Shaybani Khan's death at Safavid hands in battle in 1510, his limbs were sent to different parts of the kingdom. His headless neck was stuffed with straw and sent to the Sunni Ottoman Sultan Bayazid II in Constantinople; his skull was turned into a gold-plated drinking cup for Ismail I's personal use.[14] The Safavids' rise to power had ignited region-wide as well as local Sunni–Shia tensions, and sectarian conflict was now widespread. To the west, the rise of the Ottoman empire gave the Safavids their bitterest sectarian enemy at a time when the region was entering an age of rising Islamic 'gunpowder' empires: Safavid, Mughal and Ottoman. Khorasan had the distinct misfortune to find itself at the edge of two of these: Safavid and Mughal. Unfortunately for Herat, the Safavids' preoccupation with fighting the Ottomans often came at the expense of defending the city against Uzbek predations from north of the Oxus. Accordingly, this period is as much a story of Herat's geopolitical vulnerability to predatory empires as the fifteenth century was a story of the city's brilliance.

The innumerable Uzbek sieges of the early sixteenth century blur into one another in an unhealthy jumble of famine, musket fire, castellans and blockades.[15] Herat suffered. Ruinous running battles were fought in the religious and educational establishments built by the Timurids. The beautiful gardens created by Ali Shir Nawai and Husain Bayqara were reduced to quasi-military camps in which Uzbek forces stopped at the edges of the city, whilst within the city walls preparations were hurriedly made to resist and fight.[16] In these years of siege, the *khiaban* and the madrassas, once places of highbrow theoretical religious disputation, came to know more of religiously motivated physical violence than of peaceful debate or scholarly endeavour. As is so often the case, the horrors of scarcity and want forced groups of Heratis to seek salvation in opportunism and audacious but desperate reaches for power, for it was clear that neither Uzbek nor Safavid seemed to be able to control the city for any length of time. Calling to mind the divisions which Il-Khanid rule had brought to the surface in Herat, spaces opened up for ambitious or ruthless Heratis to stake a claim to the fragments of power that remained to be grabbed. Yet given the precariousness of the political situation and the regularity with which Herat was attacked, one senses that these speculative coups from within Herat's elites were little more than aimless punts into the political middle distance.

In 1513, Abdul Qasim Bakhshi, a local scribe from the days of Husain Bayqara, attempted such a coup in the wake of an Uzbek capture of the city. Bakhshi had transferred his allegiance to Herat's Uzbek rulers so as to maintain employment in the court's administration. After their capture of Herat, the Uzbeks departed for Transoxania, leaving the city in limbo after a desultory three months of rule and pillage. Bakhshi, amidst the ruin, saw an opportunity. He vied with certain Herati amirs and nobles who had chosen Safavid protection for control of the city. As if to make this situation more complicated, Bakhshi was aided by a number of Uzbeks who also saw themselves as potential independent rulers of Herat. Bakhshi gathered supporters to his cause, and Herat began to tear itself apart from within. A ruinous few days of skirmish and siege ensued during which both sides fought for possession of the city and the citadel. The arrival of Safavid enforcements to restore order led to the provision of a Safavid governor, which in turn led to the death of Herat's ambitious scribe and would-be sultan, Abdul Qasim Bakhshi. There were few winners and no heroes at this time as power lurched back and forth between Safavid and Uzbek.[17]

Famine, too, came to Herat. From the spring of 1513 to February 1514 scarcity and starvation moved through villages and the city itself. Two poor harvests had been compounded by three years of Uzbek sieges, and misery ruled the city and its fertile surrounding villages. Bread was nowhere to be found; people ate cats and dogs, or even boiled leather for the slightest form of sustenance that might leak into the water. Inflation made food a luxury only very few could afford. Such was the seriousness of the situation that bands of criminals roved Herat's streets, capturing passers-by and killing them before boiling the flesh and selling whatever fat they found on the ragged bones. Herat's new Safavid governor Zaynal Khan attempted to clamp down on these profiteering cannibals, executing the guilty wherever he could, but such was the extent of their crimes and the hunger and scarcity in Herat that they simply could not be stopped. Dead bodies lay in the streets and parents lacked both the energy and the money to prepare their own offspring and relatives for burial.[18]

In 1529 Herat found itself yet again at the mercy of an Uzbek leader: Ubaidullah Khan. The Safavid shah Tahmasp I (r. 1524–76) was then at court in Baghdad, and Ubaidullah Khan had faced little resistance in conquering the city. Herat suffered mismanagement and looting, and in an event which must have deeply offended Herat's aristocracy and elites, Ubaidullah Khan submitted a famous Herati poet, Mawlana Hilali, who wrote 'simple and elegant' *mathnawi*s and odes, to a series of gruesome tortures followed by public execution. The poet's crime was to have written verses critical of Ubaidullah Khan, a fact not miti-gated by his having also written complimentary ones.[19] The Uzbeks were not the cultured Timurid sultans of Husain Bayqara's day. Stretching out a foot in sixteenth-century Herat, one was more likely to strike a corpse or a starved animal than the backside of a poet.

As Herat's poets and wits bit their collective tongue, Shah Tahmasp I marched a Safavid army east from Persia to Khorasan to deal with the Uzbek threat then menacing the eastern frontier of his empire. On his march he received envoys sent from Ubaidullah Khan Shaybani, then in Herat. The envoys brought with them a letter warning the invading

Safavid Shia army that in returning to Khorasan they were now engaged in a bitter sectarian war in which there would be only one winner, Sunni Islam. The Uzbek envoy said that Khorasan was troubled because it had been forced to accept the Shia faith, and the people of the province of Herat, the *dar al-saltana* (the abode of sultans), longed to return to Sunni rule. Khorasan could no longer tolerate Shia sovereignty or the threat of Shia armies marching east. Ubaidullah Khan claimed to have the best interests of the region at heart, remaining true to Herat's Sunni traditions and placing the Safavids in the position of unlawful interloper, a position which in reality they both occupied. The missive also made the slightly exaggerated claim that such was Ubaidullah's beneficence that he had restored all of Herat's mosques to their proper Sunni usage, adding, confusingly, that they had been used as stables in the time of Sultan Husain Bayqara. As if to round off this aggressive diplomacy, he further rubbished the Safavids by asserting, correctly, that the people of Khorasan had no desire to embrace the Shia faith or those who ruled in its name. If only Tahmasp I would embrace Sunni Islam, there would be no conflict in Khorasan, according to Ubaidullah's reasoning. In the Safavids' defence, history suggests that Ubaidullah Khan and the Uzbeks were not the beneficent protectors of Herat they claimed to be. They also rarely needed an excuse to invade Khorasan.

Ubaidullah displayed an easy familiarity with the language of legitimation beloved of Shah Rukh, and this missive gives us an insight into what drove conflict over Herat in this precarious age. No doubt this anti-Shia vitriol would have been popular amongst members of Herat's Sunni *ulema* and nobility, and it is highly likely that it was written from within Herat's *madrasa*s and theological colleges as a way of warding off the Safavids. Yet behind the bombast of ideology and rhetoric lay a more pragmatic business interest: the Hajj. The Uzbeks were in alliance with the Mughals of India against the Safavid Shia for control over taxes and pilgrims who made their way from India and Transoxania to the holy cities of Medina and Mecca. Herat was a key stop-over on this journey to the Hejaz, and a Shia empire was bad for business as much as anything else. This supply line of pilgrims not only saved souls but also provided intelligence to Mughal and Uzbek courts on the military strength or otherwise of Safavid armies.

Ultimately, despite the impressive-sounding threats of innumerable Sunni armies marching south from beyond the Oxus, Ubaidullah Khan's diplomatic posturing in this instance proved little more than ideological bluster. On hearing that the Safavid forces were 70,000 strong, the Uzbek army fled back to the safety of Bukhara, and in November 1529 Shah Tahmasp I marched into Herat and handed control to his brother Bahram Mirza and a Qizilbash adviser.[20] Bahram Mirza's hold over the city would prove as precarious as his forefathers'.

* * *

Herat's internal crises, its disaffection with the Safavid governors and viziers, bubbled over in armed rebellion in 1536, a rebellion from within and without the city in whose tortured beginnings we can see the complex city Herat had become as Uzbeks, Heratis and Safavids competed with one another for control. The early 1530s had seen siege, occupation, starvation and destruction, and at times Herat had been forced to revisit the horrors of cannibalism. In 1536 Khorasan found itself under the control of a Safavid prince by the name of Sam Mirza, and his Qizilbash adviser Aghziwar. The latter sought to improve Herat's military capabilities, training local and Qizilbash troops, but it was not long before the temptations of plunder and extortion—aided by the distances between Herat and the Safavid capital of Tabriz—trumped any attempts at building up the local military forces.

Successes in the field of vice and racketeering convinced the Safavid governors that they might expand their influence and deepen their pockets further by heading south to conquer Qandahar. In their absence, control of Herat was given to a Qizilbash named Khalifa Sultan Shamlu, and two others. Khalifa Sultan Shamlu was an eighty-year-old with questionable competence and motives; the others were bandits. Evidence of 'the weakness of the first and the wickedness of the other two' soon reached Transoxania, bringing with it to Khorasan avenging and opportunistic Uzbek forces. In an ominous sign of coming internal crises, the local forces mustered by the Safavids which set out from Herat to confront the Uzbek army in Esfezar were not in the slightest motivated to fight their co-religionist Sunni Uzbeks; each one of them deserted, leaving almost a thousand Qizilbash to be slaughtered by the Uzbeks. Despite this victory, the Uzbeks did not see fit to continue to Herat. They pulled back, and Safavid reinforcements were called for in the shape of the governor of Mashhad, Sufiyan Rumlu.

When Sufiyan Rumlu arrived in Herat, 'tired from the rigours of the road', he too quickly found that a life of easy pillage and extortion was far easier than governance, and so fell into racketeering with an enthusiasm particular to his class. As if to put at least a veneer of legitimacy on his lust for money, he claimed that he had been guided by the Hidden Imam in a dream as to where the loot could be found, from whom and how much.[21] Tensions within the city began to build amidst this cycle of divinely sanctioned extortion and corruption. Sufiyan Rumlu's departure to Mashhad on political business in early 1536 gave Herat yet another Qizilbash, Khizr Chalabi, and 'the fool' Nuruddin Esfahani. In a sign of the febrile atmosphere that pervaded the city, Esfahani was himself murdered by an angry Herati mob as he took a bath.[22] When news of Sufiyan Rumlu's defeat and death in battle near Fushanj reached Herat, Khizr Chalabi began to make preparations to withstand the inevitable Uzbek siege which so often followed in the wake of political disturbances in that century. Yet Khizr Chalabi's efforts at raising an army from Herat's surrounding villages were met with total failure, as they had been at the beginning of this sixteenth-century saga; no one in Herat was willing to fight for the Safavids or their Shia empire. Sedition began to pick at Safavid control over a fractious city and province.

These currents of opposition, often motivated by personal opportunism coated in sectarian hatred, soon came to the attention of Herat's Sunni *ulema*, such as Khwajah Ziaratgah (a descendant of Herat's Friday Mosque leader who was publicly executed in 1510) and his brothers. A group of plotters began to gather in secret, determined to stake a claim to a Sunni Herat. Sensing the coming unrest, Qizilbash troops set up a gibbet in the main square on which to hang the insurrectionary *ulema*, and in warning to others who might be contemplating resistance. The opportunity never arose to put the gibbet to use, and it remained little more than a pre-emptive strike in a psychological war.[23] These Qizilbash attempts to frighten Herat into submission did not deter the city's *kalantar* (police chief), however. He sent a secret messenger to the plotters to suggest the viability of a grand Sunni alliance between Herat and Uzbek against Qizilbash tyranny. Safavid spies, along with most of Herat, soon got wind of this plan and Herat's *kalantar* was apprehended and executed in a 'vile' fashion, according to a Safavid chronicler.[24] Many fled the city in terror, and such was the fear of a ruinous uprising that Khizr Chalabi indiscriminately rounded up Herat's noblemen and *ulema*; as tension continued to build, the Safavids had only coercion and execution with which to head it off.

Then the rebellion came, erupting after years of frustration and repression. Men from the surrounding areas of Herat, *bolukian* (literally, 'those of the districts'), descended on the southern Firuzabad Gate, armed with muskets and swords, and even as Khizr Chalabi moved to quell the unrest, more Heratis, *bolukians*, rallied to the cause of the rebels. The image of a Sunni Herati 'smiting the gates with his sword', as one local miller did in an attempt to take control of their own city from Shia Safavid invaders, encapsulates the chaos of early-sixteenth-century Khorasan: a tableau of inverted allegiances and self-defeating alliances.[25] Yet one aspect, at least, provided some certainty: rule by Shia did not appeal to parts of Herat. That much was apparent from the overtures that Herat's disaffected made to the Uzbek leader Ubaidullah Khan in the aftermath of this first assault. The Safavids retained their control over the city, but the Uzbeks looked on in expectation of an opportunity to seize the city. It is not surprising to read that 'Ubaidullah Khan harvested a variety of information concerning these events.'[26] Clearly, the Uzbeks retained some support within the city amongst those who could not abide Shia rule.

On 28 February 1536, Ubaidullah Khan marched his troops to the outskirts of Herat, appropriating a vacant Timurid *bagh* as a resting place prior to an assault. The city was vulnerable; Safavid resolve was wearing thin. Musket fire from within the city walls initially drove the Uzbeks back amongst gardens and villages surrounding the city walls. Herat fought hard in the bitter cold for a day and a night before a siege was set in motion. Months of Uzbek pressure soon told, and internal divisions inevitably caused the fall of the city to the Uzbeks. One ambitious Herati stuck inside the city, Abu Tahir, tired of starvation and siege, had smuggled a secret messenger to the Uzbek camp with the message that were a favourable position offered to him in Uzbek government, he would be willing to hand the city over to the Uzbeks. The famed 'perfidy' of Heratis was soon to rid them of hated Safavid Shias. In the early hours of 16 August 1536, Abu Tahir, on cue, destroyed the battlements at Herat's Khush Gate, setting a ladder up over which nearly 300 Uzbek fighters, along with Herat's rebellious *boloukian*, could scramble, entering the city walls of Herat and defeating the Qizilbash defenders of the fort. Safavid chronicler Hassan Rumlu described the entry of this army of opportunism and anger as follows:

> From far and wide the army fell upon the city,
> Heads filled with vengeance, hearts filled with hatred.[27]

Men were tortured to reveal the hiding places of jewels and money; women were raped. Those Heratis who had risen up took the opportunity to seize a Safavid amir; they burned him alive.[28] It is of a piece with the bewildering, and often cripplingly ironic, turbulence of Herat's history in this century that the Uzbek invaders, with whom Herat's disaffected and persecuted Sunnis should have had common cause, plundered the city of their nominal allies. This episode, and the difficult position Herat found itself in within this new world of escalated Sunni–Shia tensions, in some senses marks the start of an identity crisis, born of geography, religion and politics, which continues well into the nineteenth century and beyond. The city resented Shia Safavid overlordship, but chafed under the rule of uncivilised Uzbeks from over the Oxus; Persianate and Sunni was a difficult concept to reconcile with the realities of a world dominated by Safavids, Uzbeks and Ottomans. Herat had all the qualities to be an independent city-state of sorts—fertility, resilience, culture, religious standing—yet precisely for these reasons, it proved fatally attractive to those empires on whose edges it was unfortunate enough to sit, and a complex identity began to emerge in Herat.

If the looting had been mindless, the settling of scores which came to Herat as Ubaidullah Khan proclaimed his rule took on a distinctly sectarian hue. Sunnis persecuted Shias in a grim reversal of the events of 1510. The punishments were beyond barbaric, and included death by burning in cages, being pushed from high minarets or skinning alive, much as Europe's own religious wars had showcased humanity at its worst. Each day in Herat's Chahar Su 'five or six' Shia were executed for their allegiance to the Twelve Imams. Such was the alacrity with which Shia, real or suspected, were executed in Herat in the late summer of 1536 that it was possible for treacherous Heratis to settle per-sonal feuds by 'bringing such men to the *qazi* and claiming that in the days of the Qizilbash, this man had cursed Abu Bakr, Umar and Uthman [the Sunni Caliphs]'.[29] Questions were never asked; execution always followed denunciations of this kind. One wealthy Herati man was accused of having Shia leanings; he was forced to flee Herat to find sanctuary in Fushanj, leaving his family utterly at the mercy of ruthless criminals who plundered his property and even stole the doors from his house.[30] As Maria Szuppe's excellent work on Herat at this time shows, religious ideals were often less of a motivating factor than personal gain and score settling.[31] Her extensive research paints the elites of this time in an unflattering light: motivated solely by power and money, and using religion as a cover for theft. This tactic of using political power shifts to settle personal scores is one that occurs frequently in Afghanistan's his-tory. It was a feature of the Soviet conflict, and it continues to this very day. In prisons all over Afghanistan I heard countless such stories of personal feuds being settled by a call to the US military claiming so and so to be a Talib or member of al-Qaeda. The arrest or air-strike which inevitably and unquestioningly followed removed rivals and enemies, placing ruthless men in unassailable positions of power.

It was not until January 1537 that the entry into Khorasan of a Safavid army forced the Uzbeks to abandon Herat and flee to Bukhara. On the final day of January 1537, a young Safavid prince, triumphant in battle, sat, wearily one presumes, on the increasingly bloody and threadbare throne of Khorasan.[32]

* * *

The *Resale-ye tariq-e qesmat-e qoloub-e ab* (A Treaty on the Ways of Water) was written in early-sixteenth-century Herat by a native of Herat, Qasim b. Yusuf Abu Nasri Heravi. Essentially a factual rendering of Herat's irrigation channels and waterways, it is better read, however, as an elegy to a world that was threatened, and eventually destroyed, by the political vicissitudes and regional fragmentation described above and below. This unintentional ode tells of a world before Uzbek inva-sions, before Safavid neglect. The author writes of small villages and their populations and describes in detail the province's irrigation sys-tems and agriculture in the final days of Sultan Husain Bayqara's rule.

The quantity of water that flows through villages is meticulously measured and recorded, almost as if the author can sense the impending decline and seeks to put down in writing the fertility of the province before it is ruined by conflict.

We see ordered prosperity and a precious eco-system of water, humans and crops which had sustained Herat for centuries, albeit with a Mongol interlude. Heravi's work is a paean to fertility and resilience: the natural order of things in which nature and people are in harmony. One example of this is Karokh, a village which would suffer during the Soviet occupation of Afghanistan. But on the eve of the Safavid dynasty's march into Khorasan, Karokh was a place of considerable prosperity. The district remitted 5,000 Tabrizi dinars to Herat's divan and produced 20 *khawar*s of corn; its many villages were well supplied with water and healthily populated.[33] At the heart of this prosperity and natural abundance were Herat's waterways and irrigation channels. The patterns and courses of these canals and rivers, both man-made and natural, were the veins which ran across the province, around the city. The contrast with cycle after cycle of Uzbek and Safavid destructive siege could not be greater, for Herat's waterways are its lifeblood, the essence which helped both to repopulate and to regenerate the city after the Mongol disaster; they were a byword for all that is resilient and pure in the oasis and rivers of the province and city.

Precious little was achieved in these decades during which Safavid and Uzbek duelled for Khorasan. Neither power could be said to have 'won'; Uzbeks had enriched themselves materially, but had also drastically reduced the province's productivity; Safavids had seen internal tensions in their military and bureaucracy exploited by distance and sectarianism, and their empire found itself sorely in need of the political genius of Shah Abbas I (r. 1588–1629). Herat itself had suffered the deleterious effects of conflict and famine. Even those who took power were rarely safe from revenge and assassination. Yet in the shape of Mohammad Khan Sharaf al-Din Takkalu, a Qizilbash vizier who spent over three decades in Herat as the province's governor, the city found some stability and a patron who was at least partly worthy of his more illustrious predecessors.[34] The 1540s accordingly were spent restoring mosques, *madrasa*s and hospitals, and bringing some life back to the city and countryside. In keeping with the Safavids' keen appreciation of the values of trade and commerce, Sharaf al-Din brought prosperity to the areas of land to the north of the Bagh-e Shahr, creating a space in which shops could flourish and which could attract Heratis from the districts to sell and buy in a stable and safe city; this area soon became a central hub for trading on Fridays. A governor who realised that a safe and secure Herat was a profitable Herat provided a brief flicker of renewal, and with it came a temporary withering away of the Uzbek threat.

* * *

In the biting cold of late January 1544, the second Mughal emperor, Humayoun (r. 1530–40), arrived at Herat's southern outskirts by way of Helmand and Farah. He was a refugee from succession crises which had engulfed his territories in India and forced a westward retreat, first to Kabul and then south to Qandahar. In December 1530 Babur, the first Mughal emperor, had on his deathbed divided his territories amongst his sons. This was a Chingizid and Timurid practice which never failed to cause conflict. Humayoun had been granted Mughal territories in present-day India, whilst his half-brother Kamran Mirza was given Kabul and Lahore. Humayoun was menaced by rivals in Gujarat to the south-west and by Pashtun tribal raiders along the banks of the river Ganges.[35] He was forced to withdraw to Kabul in the summer of 1543, and from there he marched from Qandahar to Herat with a smallish retinue of roughly forty, living on scraps of meat boiled in the helmets of his soldiers. Given the hardships endured on his forced flight to Herat, it is little wonder that he chose to discuss the 'world's faithlessness and the instability of external circumstances' with the locals of Qandahar and Sistan.[36]

The welcome they would receive in Herat would banish their hunger, if not their apprehension. Mughals were, after all, sectarian rivals of the Safavids, and the fear of the unknown would surely have informed the early exchanges. Was Humayoun a prisoner, asylum-seeker or guest? In all likelihood he was a bit of everything, as well as a potential ally yet to realise his loyalties to the Safavid empire. Disaffected or captured princes and kings could always be hidden away for use as bargaining chips further down the line. Whatever the reality of Humayoun's status, his visit is gloriously described by a *firman* (order or edict) from the Safavid chancellery, written out whilst Humayoun was making his way from Qandahar to Khorasan and discussing fickle fate. The *firman* is a diplomatic edict setting out how the Mughal refugees should be received in Herat. It offers us rare glimpses into Herat's fading Timurid courtly culture and its continuing importance as a place of cultural and artistic excellence. It hints at daily life in the city and suggests how it had evolved since the Timurid century of princes. In preparing for Humayoun's arrival, an event of enormous regional significance, the Safavid empire wanted to make a good impression on a potentially useful ally or hostage, and Herat proved the perfect stage on which to do so. Indeed, in 1544 Herat was the only stage on which to do so.[37]

The *firman*, drafted by Persian scribes in Qazvin, divides proceedings into two distinct parts: the meetings which would occur outside the city walls to welcome the Mughals, and then the entertainments which would take place within Herat, at which issues of a more political nature would be discussed.[38] Reflecting the language of diplomatic protocols of all ages, Humayoun is described as the 'sphere rider, sun cupola, pearl of consciousness and sovereignty's ocean, goodly tree ornamenting the garden of government and worldly sway…'[39] Yet behind this ornate language, the formulaic diplomatic correspondence, we see a document of precision which plans Humayoun's reception in quite stunning detail.[40] In an age of rapid and bewildering change, it is the continuity this *firman* suggests, its conscious links to a Timurid past, which is most interesting for our understanding of Herat's evolution.

A royal procession was set in order to greet the party from the south, with orders sent out to Sabzevar to gather suitably beautiful horses with ornamental bridling to welcome imperial Mughal refugees. These horses were fitted with embroidered saddles with 'housings of gold brocade and gold thread',[41] and were to be 'fit for the riding of that royal cavalier of the field of glory and success'.[42] Four hundred robes of velvet and European and Yazdi satin were to be prepared, and Safavid heirlooms, including a jewelled weapon said to have been used by Shah Ismail I, would be presented as tokens of the esteem in which the Mughals were held. To welcome the retinue's entry into Herat from the Malan bridge, the roads had been swept and watered and were lined with Herat's young and old, presumably press-ganged into cheering on the Mughals. Late January in Herat can be a cold and unforgiving place, but the Safavids were determined not to let something as trivial as the weather interfere with their spectacle. (By far the coldest experience ever in this author's life was in late-January Herat, shuffling through its snow-strewn streets to conduct interviews, and sitting in the doorless, heaterless Public Library reading dog-eared editions of Herat's old newspapers.) Silk and golden-threaded carpets were to be sent out to greet the party, along with twelve tents of differing colours. Awnings of silk and velvet were ordered to adorn the *bagh* in which the Mughals would stay outside the city walls.[43] The visiting party was to be met with rose-water sherbet and sweet-smelling lemon juice; they would eat fennel and poppy-seeded bread, apples from Mashhad and watermelons and grapes from Herat. The drinks were to be examined by the imperial drink-taster prior to drinking; the food was to amount to no fewer than 1,500 dishes and to be of the highest quality. Each local noble entrusted with entertaining the Mughals was required to give lavish gifts to their newly arrived guests. These same nobles were also ordered to behave in a manner befitting the majesty of their Mughal guests and in the best traditions of Timurid diplomacy that the Safavids so clearly sought to emulate. Even the winter flowers were ordered to be appearing at their finest.[44]

After a few days of 'heart-inflaming' entertainment, no doubt necessary in the freezing temperatures, the Mughals would be brought to the seat of governance inside the city walls and in the colleges along the *khiaban* where the meetings took on a more serious nature.[45] Troops numbering 30,000 were mustered to welcome the procession to within the city walls, in a show of respect to Humayoun, but also as a clear hint at Safavid military prowess. The two parties held discussions in tents at the head of the *khiaban*, tents set up with 'crimson satin on the inside, fine linen in between and Isfahan linen on the top'. The Mughals were to spend three days in the *khiaban*, seeing artisans, being guided around the bazaars and *bagh*s and sung to by 'masters of melody', a Safavid courtier close at hand to answer any questions Humayoun might have. The *firman* required of its Safavid princes and aristocrats that the conversation with which the Mughals were to be entertained was reassuring and of a pleasing nature: a fitting accompaniment to wandering amongst the streets and gardens of Herat. A Safavid prince was to be brought out from the court in Persia, and dressed in a set of clothes he was given in March 1543. The stipulations for diplomatic protocol even prescribed the distances at which it was permissible for the Safavid prince to dismount from his horse when faced with the Mughal retinue.[46] Humayoun wandered the city's bazaars, admiring Herat's crafts: glass-blowing, silk-weaving, jewellery and carpet-making, as so many tourists have done over the centuries. Singing and playing of music provided a constant background, and Herat's famous musicians—Hafez Sabir Qaq, Mawlana Qasim Qaq the harpist and Hafiz Dost Mohammad Khwafi—were specifically requested to accompany the Mughal visit. A final celebration in the Bagh-e Shahi was planned before the Mughals left Herat: yet more carpets, more silk, more awnings, sweetmeats, fruits, female camels and so on.

Intelligence would be gathered, also; every word that passed between Mughal lips had to make its way to Qazvin. This was not simply Persian etiquette on an imperial scale, for behind the protocol and silk, leverage was being gained in Safavid-Mughal affairs. For example, in the bestowal of gifts and their acceptance there was more than the kindness of one empire offering an exiled prince trinkets in times of hardship; power flowed from giver to recipient and submission flowed back along the same channel. Much as had been the case with the Mongol Il-Khanid takeover of Khorasan, it was the giver of these ceremonial robes, *khelats*, who held the power; the recipient showed his or her submission to the imperial order of the giver and implicitly acknowledged the wealth and majesty of the giver.

In the winter of 2014, I believe I was the unwitting recipient of such a *khelat*. After a long lunch with the ex-*mujahed* and now successful businessman Hajji Abdul Wahhab Qattali (see Chapter 6), he told me he wanted to give me a gift to honour my visit and to thank me for the work I was doing on Herat's history. I parried, saying that it had been my pleasure to learn about the city's recent history from someone who had played such an important role. A quasi-diplomatic exchange went back and forth for a few minutes, with me refusing, Hajji Qattali pressing. His eyes soon took in my torn winter coat, and he told me with a degree of certainty, in the face of which resistance was futile, that he would be buying me a better coat for the cold weather. After some more toing and froing and a large amount of Afghanis being thrust into the hand of one of his aides, I consented to be taken to the bazaar by his armed guards to seek out a replacement coat. Surrounded by men in balaclavas wielding AK-47s, I chose my own *khelat*. My Chinese/ Italian/Japanese fake-fur-lined winter coat is a prized possession, and exceptionally useful in a cold Herati winter

Reading the exhausting itinerary laid out for Humayoun's visit, one gets an idea of the lengths to which Safavid diplomacy wished to go to impress upon the Mughals the courtly sophistication of their Safavid hosts. The hope was that word might reach India, eventually, that Herat still shone as brightly as it had under Sultan Husain Bayqara. In many ways, this quasi-exile in Herat would have been something of a return home for Humayoun. For as he savoured Persian and Timurid architecture, the fine beauty of the miniature paintings, the richness of the illuminated manuscripts and the beauty of the buildings which housed him, he would have been reminded of the wondrous tales of Timurid Herat at its height, no doubt told to him as a child. Such was his enthusiasm for all things Herati and Persian that he managed to persuade a number of Herat's artists to return with him to Mughal India should he ever regain his throne. Indeed, Herati musicians fleeing the chaos that Safavid and Uzbek wars had produced in Khorasan would later appear at the Mughal court during the reign of Akbar (r.1542–1602).[47] Herat and Humayoun's experience there played their part in the later explosion of Persianate sophistication at the Mughal court, much as it would also for the Safavids in Esfahan. Even when in decline, Timurid Herat spread its wings from India to Khorasan to Persia.

Where does this episode fit within the broader notion of Herat's gradual decline in the context of a damaging Safavid–Uzbek 'Duel for Khorasan'? The *firman* suggests anything but decline, drawing as it does on Herat's seemingly well-established prosperity, showing a city flourishing, profitable and still beautiful enough to entertain and awe putative allies. Despite Herat's suffering since the early sixteenth century, it had clearly not lost its power to impress a visiting audience, and it is beyond doubt that its links to a Timurid past had not been severed, despite the sectarian and ideological turmoil it had experienced. If anything, this visit was a conscious re-run of a distinctly Timurid diplomatic spectacle, showing the endurance of Herat as a city of sophistication and elegance. As the historian Colin Mitchell notes, by giving Humayoun 'plush red velvet' made in Samarqand, the Safavids were aping a particularly Timurid gesture, something which would have been clear to all those present. Indeed, by consciously linking themselves with the Timurid past of Herat, the Safavids were using Herat's architectural and cultural brilliance to enhance the prestige of their own dynasty.[48]

Against the backdrop of a general decline in the visual arts which had taken place in Khorasan since the fall of the Timurids, Herat had managed to retain some of its genius for poetry and music during the Uzbek–Safavid wars.[49] Culture and the arts had suffered under the Safavids, largely due to Shah Tahmasp I's strict decrees banning music in the 1520s and early 1530s, but also linked to political upheavals forcing poets and musicians to scatter. Tahmasp I had been concerned that by associating with musicians, the royal princes 'might begin to pay too much attention to music, and that they [musicians] might corrupt the amirs who were their moral tutors and guardians and thus generate an uncontrollable demand at court for forbidden pleasures'.[50] In reality, Safavid princes needed little help from music or poetry to corrupt themselves or those around them. Yet despite this, a number of Herat's prominent poets and musicians were specifically called upon by name to entertain the Mughals, proving that for all the revolutionary Shiism of Tahmasp I and his Safavid courtiers, Herat's cultural life remained very much intact, thriving even.

Historical processes rarely stop dead; momentum pushes from one dynasty to the next, despite the violence of upheaval or change. Whatever changes were brought about by the arrival of a radical millenarian Shia empire and the cycle of conflict which engulfed Khorasan, the rhythms of life and the city had managed somehow to endure, helped in no small part by the retention of Heratis within the administration of the Safavid state. As had long been the case, whilst dynasties changed, bureaucracies and official positions largely remained in the same hands, in the interests of continuity. This mitigated the upheaval caused by a change in dynast or ruling family. There were, therefore, limits on the extent to which a Safavid revolution could take place while those in charge of the paperwork were opposed to wholesale religious and societal revolution. Evidence of this continuity within change can be seen from this episode in which the dominant motifs were Timurid, Sunni, Perso-Islamic. These events took place against an imposing physical backdrop of Gawhar Shad's mausoleum, Ali Shir Nawai's complex and the Friday Mosque he restored, all of which placed continuity, rather than change, at the centre of imperial projection. Radical Shia theology was absent, conspicuously so, and it was not until the party arrived in Esfahan that significant pressure was brought to bear on the Mughals to convert to Shia Islam.

For some weeks, this now well-fed group of political refugees remained in Herat, fortunate enough to see winter turn to spring, and blossom adorning the trees that lined the streets and bazaars through which the processions marched and dotting the gardens in which they ate and drank. Like all diligent tourists, they visited Abdullah Ansari's shrine at Gazur Gah and travelled east to the village of Jam to see its intriguingly mysterious minaret.[51] A stay of three glorious and clearly very expensive months came to an end, and in late March 1544 the retinue left Herat heading west through the Iraq Gate to the shrine city of Mashhad. Herat had suffered, that much is clear, but it had also survived in its guise as city of splendour and imperial majesty, fit to entertain, impress and subjugate its visitors with wealth and excess.

* * *

The last years of Shah Tahmasp I's reign had been a study in waning Safavid power; the outbreak of the Ottoman–Venetian war of 1570–73 and the eruption of rebellions in Anatolia had caused the flow of currency and trade between the Ottoman Empire and Persia to dry up. The Safavid state had not been able to pay its troops during the last fourteen years of Tahmasp I's reign, and coinage stopped altogether in the years 1573–6. Tahmasp I's death in 1576 led to instability and ruinous inter-familial power-grabs. A successor, Shah Ismail II, was little able to control the extent of the Safavid empire, and fearful of the potential for rival claimants to be found within the royal family, Ismail II executed anyone and everyone within reach. Five of his own children were either blinded or executed, yet his rule was mercifully short. Rivalries amongst Qizilbash amirs seethed at court and seeped into the edges of the empire. Khorasan, too, fell into infighting and tension; Herat fought Safavid Qizilbash in Mashhad whilst Uzbeks looked on, waiting for an opportunity to invade.[52]

In 1580 Khorasan was in rebellion. Herat's governor, Ali Quli Khan Shamlu (r. 1577–88), ruled over a fiefdom of almost total independence from the Safavid capital in Qazvin, fighting with his fellow Qizilbash amirs in Mashhad and engaging in a game of 'snatch the prince', competing for possession of a young Safavid prince, Abbas Mirza. Abbas Mirza would become a pawn in the inter-Qizilbash rivalries, which threatened the existence of the Safavid empire.[53] Ali Quli Khan Shamlu's wilful resistance to the imperial capital called to mind the Karts and their opportunistic politics. Like many before him, Ali Quli placed his trust in the strength of Herat's walls, reckoning that any siege, even if headed by a Safavid army as happened in 1582, would be unlikely to succeed in taking the city. Ottoman threats to the Safavids' western and northern flanks would not remain quiet for the time it would take to subdue Herat, he imagined, leaving him alone to rule a city which had evidently seduced him.

The post of Governor of Herat was coveted amongst aspiring Qizilbash. The role included the duties of tutor, or *lala*, to the royal prince, a role for which the reward was the potential patronage and loyalty of a young Safavid prince, soon to become shah. Correct moves made in this regard could ensure transition from *lala* to imperial adviser. Herat had long served as the centre for Safavid royal tutors-cum-governors, and so when dynastic struggles erupted, as they did in the late 1570s and early 1580s, Herat naturally became a centre for intrigue and strife: young princes and their guardians made for an explosive combination. Tutoring the scions of the rich and powerful can be a thankless task, as this author knows too well, yet for Qizilbash *lala*s there was a sense of danger added to the tedium, for this was a role for which many were prepared to kill, or abduct. Ali Quli was keenly aware of this, and in 1577 he had left the then imperial capital of Qazvin for Herat under orders from Shah Ismail II to execute the latter's nephew, the young prince Abbas Mirza. Abbas was at this point emotionally vulnerable, having had the misfortune to witness the murder of a number of his own Qizilbash protectors on Shah Ismail II's orders.

Had Ali Quli Shamlu succeeded in his task, he would have been rewarded with marriage ties at court, and money. As it stood, things did not look good for the young prince as, on 7 December 1577, Ali Quli arrived at Herat from Qazvin. Yet his arrival coincided with an auspicious date in the holy month of Ramadan, the eve of the *Laylat al-Qadr*, The Night of Power, a feast which celebrates the night of the revelation of the first verses of the Quran to the Prophet Muhammad. Owing to this divinely ordained or accidental calendric coincidence, it was deemed unwise to execute a young *sayyed* (the Safavids claimed direct descent from the Prophet Muhammad) and royal prince. The women of the royal household begged Ali Quli to spare the young boy, and he did. Abbas was allowed to live. Meanwhile in Esfahan, in the unlikely setting of the house of a disreputable sweet-maker, Shah Ismail II nodded off and then expired from a combination of alcohol and opium.[54] News of his death took a week or so to reach Herat, by which time the young Abbas was still alive; his execution was thus put off for good.[55] The young prince would go on to become Shah Abbas I, or Shah Abbas the Great, and is widely accepted to be have been the most talented ruler Iran has ever had. He would take the Safavid dynasty to unrivalled heights of cultural excellence and territorial expansion. His experiences of Herat's architectural glories as a young boy no doubt inspired his building project, the magnificent city of Esfahan.

Yet despite saving the life of Abbas, Ali Quli could not prevent wave after wave of succession crises from engulfing Khorasan. Hiding behind Herat's walls, Ali Quli remained true to his duties in Khorasan, and resisted Safavid entreaties to move the young prince to the imperial capital at Qazvin, citing the dangers of leaving Herat and Khorasan without a Safavid protector. In reality, however, notions of the unity of the Safavid empire at this point were largely fictional, as Herat had been functioning as a semi-independent city-state for some time. It is likely that Ali Quli was simply buying time: waiting to see if the empire could last the year, sitting tight and hoping for a disaster in Persia. Yet no such disaster befell the Safavids, and Ali Quli's continued residence in Herat with the young Abbas caused him to be summoned to Qazvin to answer the charges of disobeying imperial orders. He was threatened with exile should he remain in Khorasan.[56] Such was the confidence the post of *lala* conferred on its occupant that in 1581 Ali Quli felt secure enough to crown the young prince Shah Abbas I in Herat in total defiance of the Safavid court at Qazvin. Perhaps he sensed that the empire's fragmentation was irreversible, and that now was the chance for him to push his own claims to the position of imperial protector. What better place to do so than Herat? Coins were minted, prayers were read, and for a brief moment Herat again became an imperial capital.

Herat's claim to imperial status did not last. Different Qizilbash factions fought a bitter civil war amongst themselves for the heart of the Safavid empire.[57] The young prince Abbas was taken to Mashhad in 1585 after a flaky truce between two different branches of Qizilbash factions (the Ustajlu and Shamlu) fell apart. Ali Quli sulked back to Herat, presumably in the knowledge that with the departure of his bargaining chip, Abbas, his fate was surely sealed.

It is not therefore surprising that early in 1587 intelligence reached Bukhara of a weak and divided Khorasan whose bickering Qizilbash amirs had fallen to kidnapping princes in Herat. On 9 May 1587, an Uzbek army with Mughal support crossed the Oxus and set in motion yet another ruinous siege, beginning with the obligatory skirmishes outside the city walls. Before long, Herat was surrounded. The Uzbek leader, Abdullah Khan II, was a man famed for his conquests on the battlefield, so much so that tales of his military prowess even reached the ears of the English queen, Elizabeth I.[58] Poised to take the city, Abdullah Khan II busied himself with finding a religious pretext to justify yet another siege of Herat. Unsurprisingly, this was to be found in Islam's oldest conflict: Sunni vs Shia. The Shia Qizilbash, so his edict went, were heretics for their condemnation of the caliphs, Abu Bakr, Othman and Umar and the prophet's wife, Ayesha. On the other hand, the Uzbeks were the upholders of Islamic Sunni orthodoxy. This edict, however, was little more than a tired refrain from a bitter war, and it was of little genuine significance.

Of more practical relevance was Herat's ability to withstand the Uzbeks. Small Qizilbash garrisons dotted the land to the west of Herat in 'fortified villages', designed to protect the routes linking Herat with Khorasan's other trading centres, and they proved difficult to subdue (with the exception of Ghurian).[59] Attempting to capture these outlying fortresses consumed Uzbek time and manpower, and in the chaos that resulted from the sieges, local garrisons took to raiding the countryside, further upsetting the Uzbek plans and further depleting the province's ability to supply provisions for a stationary army of some 80,000 men.[60] The summer of 1587 dragged on for the Uzbeks; they suffered in the fierce summer storms. Herat repulsed numerous attacks—mortar bombardments and assaults—and it was not until February 1588 that Ali Quli sought terms, feeling his position utterly hopeless. In reality, both sides had become locked in a stalemate of thirst and want and gunfire.[61]

The reasons for the eventual fall of the city in 1588 divide historians and chroniclers: some saw Shamlu or Herati betrayal as assisting the entrance of the Uzbek forces; others saw starvation as the principal cause; others simply saw a victory of superior military muscle.[62] Whatever the reason, Shah Abbas I's *lala*, Ali Quli and his Shamlu Qizilbash fighters were disarmed as the Uzbeks entered the city. After a scuffle in which an Uzbek had attempted to steal some precious cloth from the head of a Shamlu noble, Ali Quli Khan Shamlu was stabbed to death by an Uzbek high on alcohol and opium.[63] Herat could have been saved at any point had the Safavid army been sent from Mashhad, but so deep were Qizilbash tensions that no such army was ever sent. The fall of Herat to the Uzbeks reignited a familiar and tragic cycle of sectarian persecution and vengeance; pliant Sunni religious judges passed down sentences of execution by burning or hanging to those fingered by their local enemies.[64] Ten years of Uzbek rule in Herat would yield little of note, save petty personal retribution under the flimsy pretext of Sunni–Shia enmity.

It was not until 1598 that Herat returned to the Safavid fold. Shah Abbas I's accession to the throne in 1588 had given Iran a ruler of real intelligence and no little practical nous. Shah Abbas I had learned his political trade in Herat during the tumult of Uzbek–Qizilbash–Safavid tensions and these experiences hardened him to rule ruthlessly but also to rule with wisdom. He first settled the conflict with the Ottoman empire through the humiliating but tactically astute Peace of Istanbul of 21 March 1590, by which the Safavids lost large tracts of lands in Azerbaijan and Qarabagh; even the old Safavid capital at Tabriz was handed over. Ideological concessions, too, were made to the Ottomans, doing untold damage to an already brittle Safavid self-esteem. Yet the Peace of Istanbul allowed Abbas I to address matters in Khorasan by building up his army in peacetime and waiting for a suitable opportunity to move east against his Uzbek enemies. Owing to internal Qizilbash fighting, Abbas I's accession to the throne was stamped with a commitment to impose his own authority on over-mighty Qizilbash nobles, even if that meant creating enemies in the short term. He was hamstrung by the political reality that it was from amongst the Qizilbash amirs that real power came, real power in a weakened empire. Accordingly, he sought to establish his own standing army made up of slaves (*ghulam*) taken from amongst Georgian, Armenian and Circassian Christians, prisoners from Safavid campaigns in the Caucasus. He wanted to create his own cadre of loyal soldiers, bound to the Safavid state, much as the Qizilbash had been to Shah Ismail I. These new *ghulam*s converted to Islam and provided a valuable makeweight in internal Safavid power games. Indeed, it was the most famous of all *ghulam*s, Allahverdi Khan, a Georgian who later went on to achieve a high rank in the Safavid military, to whom the Safavids gave the sensitive task of executing Mashhad's governor, because his refusal to send reinforcements to Herat in 1588 had effectively handed the city to the Uzbeks. The imperial army was reordered along these lines, creating a new third force in the Safavid empire.[65] *Ghulam*s soon moved into positions of power, and with the rise of a centralised and loyal bureaucracy, the Safavid dynasty moved away from its Sufi and theocratic stances; Shah Abbas I even shunned Sufis as worthy holders of office. These policies targeted the short-term gains of stability and order, yet they failed to mask more serious internal weaknesses in the Safavid state.

Meanwhile in Herat, the Uzbek polity had begun to fragment; family rivalries picked apart a fragile cohesion previously sustained by conquest. Herat found itself in the hands of an Uzbek commander who had previously been granted a Safavid military alliance as insurance against his own unpredictable family, but who later forgot this alliance and accordingly suffered the consequences.[66] Herat's torrid sixteenth century was drawing to a close in a tumultuous fashion.

Suitably revitalised and reformed, Shah Abbas I set out to wrest Khorasan from the Uzbeks on 9 April 1598, the third day of the holy month of Ramadan. His progress east was more of a stately ramble through Khorasan than a determined march of conquest. He stopped at Mashhad in July, 'seeing to the affairs of the shrine', and then made his unhurried way to Jam, circulating through Herat and heading east into Ghur and the village of Jam. There he met with Qizilbash amirs who had been forced to flee to Mughal India when Herat had fallen to the Uzbeks in 1588.[67] One of these amirs passed on valuable information to Shah Abbas I on the state of Herat's defences. Uzbek Herat was apparently busy preparing for conflict with the Safavids, and the assembled military commanders told Shah Abbas I of thousands of Uzbeks, along with Hazara troops, garrisoned near to the city. Yet despite the impressive troop numbers, Herat's Uzbeks were not fully apprised of the situation, and they lacked precise information on exactly how far the Safavid camp was from Herat. Abbas I saw this as an opportunity he could use to his advantage, and he thus sent ahead a secret emissary in the advance party to spread false rumours around Herat that a crisis had arisen to the west and north which necessitated his urgent attention and the departure of the Safavid army from Herat. This ruse, reminiscent of that which had decided the Battle of Herat in 1270, aimed to lull the Uzbeks into neglecting Herat's defences and riding out to attack the rump of a fleeing Safavid force. It worked perfectly. The Uzbeks gave battle 15 miles from the city walls under the impression that they held a distinct numerical advantage. On 9 August 1598, as the wind kicked up dust into the faces of parched Safavid and Uzbek soldiers alike, the Uzbek troops suffered a decisive defeat, bringing to a close their decade of rule over Herat. Most of their army fled north to Transoxania, while Herat's indigenous tribes—the Timuri, Hazaras, Qipchaq and Jamshidi—saw fit to tender their allegiance to the Safavid Shah in the political merry-go-round that was sixteenth-century Khorasan. Herat was once again under Safavid control and in the hands of a Shamlu governor, Hussein Khan Shamlu.

After this Safavid victory, Shah Abbas I transferred his capital from Qazvin to Esfahan. He transformed Esfahan into one of the most captivating cities the world has seen. Esfahan's position roughly in the centre of the Iranian plateau placed it at a suitable distance from Ottoman and Uzbek threats. It lay in an oasis of cultivation surrounded by arid landscape and was thus fortified by nature, much like Herat. Abbas I's inspiration for an imperial building programme would have surely been Timurid Herat, where he had grown up in troubling circumstances. Contemporary descriptions of Esfahan depict a setting of extraordinary charm, with facades and gardens to rival those which Gawhar Shad, Ali Shir Nawai and Husain Bayqara had built. I have spent many afternoons in its main square, the Maidan-e Imam, or Maidan-e Naqsh-e Jahan, revelling in the peace of the space, wandering through the bazaars down to the Friday Mosque and then back again to hear the rising and falling cadences of the call to prayer as they sound across the city. Three masterpieces of Persian architecture flank the square: the Ali Qapu Palace, the Shaykh Lotfullah Mosque and the Masjed-e Shah. Pietro Della Valle, an aristocratic seventeenth-century Italian traveller, wrote that Esfahan's *maidan* outshone Rome's own Piazza Navona, an assertion with which it is difficult to disagree. Another seventeenth-century traveller, the German diplomat Olearius, gave a lively description of the wonderfully cosmopolitan nature of the city and its main square, in which 'Tartars, from the Provinces of *Chuaressem* [Khwarazm], *Chattai* and *Buchar*, *Turks, Jews, Armenians, Georgians, English, Dutch, French, Italians* and *Spaniards*' all traded, no doubt marvelling at the majesty of its spaces and architecture.[68] The Persian proverb '*Esfahan nesf-e jahan ast*' (Esfahan is half the world) could not have been more apposite during its energetic seventeenth century.[69] Abbas's Esfahan was varied and lively: prostitutes, jugglers, dervishes, traders, preachers, poets, thieves and spies all competed for space and life. Textiles, carpets, miniature painting, architecture all poured forth from Esfahan, eagerly purchased by traders from around the world or copied by architects and artists. English adventurers, such as the Shirley brothers who traded and trained the Shah's armies in modern military techniques, were but a few such characters who added so much to Esfahan and the Safavid empire. Indeed, so strong were relations between the Safavids and the seventeenth-century monarchs of England that the English assisted the Safavids in fighting and defeating Portuguese pirates in Hormuz, for which the English were handsomely rewarded.[70] Esfahan's flourishing would have important consequences for Herat.

The significance of Esfahan as an imperial capital, Mashhad as a Shia shrine city to rival Najaf and Kerbela (both then under Ottoman dominion), and the rise in importance of Qandahar as a trading hub connecting the Indus and Persia, all contrived to deal something of a body blow to Herat. If the previous century had been one in which Herat had retained its importance—diplomatic missions, royal princes and strategic centrality as a way of soaking up Uzbek advances—the seventeenth century would see a gradual fall from Timurid heights. No longer the home of Qizilbash *lala*s with princely wards to tutor, and now competing with Mashhad for religious significance and Qandahar and Esfahan for trade, Herat began to lose out. Whilst still technically the *dar al-saltana* (the seat of governance) and still required to fulfil legal and executive functions, the reality was that Herat had become a once great imperial capital with a precarious future.

* * *

In the heat of July 1631, a 29-year-old Balkhi man of letters, poet and information gather, Mahmud bin Amir Wali, rode into Herat on his way home to Balkh, after travelling north from Farah to complete an epic journey of six years, in which he visited Peshawar, Kabul, Vijaynagra and Bijapur amongst many other cities and provinces.[71] The aims of Mahmud's journey were simple; 'observation, sight-seeing and amusement.' We know that he was also something of a mystic, writing poetry and musings on spiritual and mystical enlightenment, jotted down as he went.[72] Mahmud's observations on Herat are pragmatic and cursory, running only to a few pages in what is a vast body of work. Farah in the summertime, we are told, had weather 'at the very limits of bearable heat', an experience with which this author would totally concur, and its people divined auspicious events through the flowing waters of the river of that province, praying at the foot of arches of stone. Mahmud passed a few days idly wandering around the bazaars and streets of Herat, recording relatively little.[73] Yet it is clear that since the horrors of conflict which had marked the late sixteenth century, Herat had at the very least seen a modest recovery: two Shamlu governors, Hussein Khan Shamlu (r. 1598–1619) and Hassan Khan Shamlu (r. 1619–41) brought stability to the city, despite the oasis being mulcted to pay for imperial Safavid campaigns into Transoxania, and later Qandahar.[74]

Herat pushed its own scholars and dervishes out into the world to report back, and Mahmud bin Wali was not the only such wandering poet of this time. The extravagantly named Beheshti Heravi (Heavenly Heravi, though his real name was the more prosaic Abdullah Sani) wrote a beautiful account of his travels in the Safavid and Mughal empires in the form of a long poem of rhyming couplets chronicling a journey to the edges of empire whilst also praising Herat's own architectural, natural and spiritual abundance.[75] The account, entitled *Nur al-mashreqain* (The Light of the Two Easts), tells of Beheshti's Safavid-sanctioned journey from Herat to the Persian cities of Esfahan, Hamadan, Tehran, and back through the southern provinces of present-day Afghanistan and into Mughal India via Qandahar. On his travels Beheshti fell helplessly in love with Kashmir, a country whose lush valleys and verdant meadows he describes with real feeling. Beheshti's poem is in the very best traditions of adventure writing: tales of hitching lifts with merchants and fellow poets, quitting Hamadan precipitously out of fear of an Ottoman advance and fighting with Pashtun bandits all feature in this ode to life and travel.[76] Above all, however, this is a ballad to natural, man-made and spiritual beauty, an account which sings with the joy of discovery and travel. *Nur al-mashreqain* showcases Herat's most subtle and enterprising poetical traditions, all harnessed to tell the story of a pilgrimage of aesthetics through Persia and India. It is a glimpse into daily life in Safavid Herat, hinting at a city not yet ready for total obsolescence, elegantly raging at the dying of the Timurid light.

Beheshti was born in 1597 to a noble Shia family of Herat's religious elite, a family loyal to the Safavid dynasty. As a child, he suffered from such a serious bout of measles that his parents despaired of his living beyond six months; Beheshti himself wrote that his parents anxiously looked on as he 'burned in the heat of a fever'.[77] Thanks to a visit to one of Herat's many shrines (most likely the celebrated Shia Sufi shrine on the Kuh-e Mukhtar, close to Gazur Gah), the young Beheshti survived his youthful illnesses, but was left with a withered foot and lasting weakness. It is touching to see the faith shown by Beheshti's father in the ability of the shrine to cure his son, an indication of the power of Herat's faith in shrines. Beheshti was a bright child with a quick mind, and when he reached the age of four or five he was given a pen and taught to read and write. As a young boy his skills of reading both the Quran and the classics of Persian poetry were prodigious. Within six months he had mastered religious and literary exegesis, calling to mind Herat's other precocious literary talent, Jami; and indeed, Beheshti's account of his own youth, consciously or unconsciously, apes Jami's own lack of modesty. For Beheshti, school was a 'treasure trove' of knowledge and learning, most likely a distraction from the tedium of illness and injury. He learned his poetical craft under Fasihi Khwafi (an itinerant Herati poet who had travelled widely throughout India), and Khwafi saw in his young protégé a rare talent for making sense of the world around him through the medium of words.

In his early twenties Beheshti was accepted into the order of poets in Herat after having impressed the right people, and in particular the Safavid governor, Hassan Khan Shamlu. Beheshti's formative years as a poet were not solely spent in Herat, however, for he travelled to India, a destination much in vogue for early-seventeenth-century poets. In India he saw the patronage of the Mughal princes in Lahore, Kabul and the Deccan as more attractive propositions than Herat's chaotic courts, or the more crowded courts of Safavid shahs in Esfahan.[78] He would spend over thirty years in India at the courts of various Mughal princes, writing odes and getting by. India remained his true love, right up until his death. He even wrote a panegyric poem entitled the *Morad Namah* for a minor Mughal prince, Moradbakhsh Mirza, celebrating his patron's Persian sophistication and princely qualities; it seems that life as a mendicant poet clearly suited Beheshti, travelling from court to court, to Kashmir, Lahore and Multan, to seek patronage, living off the speed of his wits and the beauty of his rhyme. During his Indian dotage, Beheshti wrote *Nur al-mashreqain*.

It was in the late 1630s that Beheshti had set out from Herat on this journey—part fact-finding, part poetic wandering and part nature tourism. *Nur al-mashreqain* starts with an elucidation of the lives of the Twelve Imams and some miracles attributed to them, and then gives the reader a brief account of Herat as it appeared in the 1630s. Beheshti begins with a rather feeble proclamation that he feels duty-bound to record the life of his city, but the ebullience with which he launches into descriptions of Herat's fertility suggests something stronger than obligation. Herat is not a city but a worldly paradise, he reminds the reader almost immediately.[79] The citadel competes with the very heavens for majesty and glory; Herat's four main bazaars, linked together at the city's centre, the Chahar Su, are filled to bursting with foods and fruits from the far corners of Herat's known world, stocking clothes and jewels too. Herat's shoppers want for little. Apples, pears, peaches and grapes can be found throughout the city, and gentle streams trickle throughout; the gardens will most certainly steal your heart, he says.[80] We read awestruck descriptions of the dimensions of the Friday Mosque, declaring it peerless and estimating its size at over 2,000 square metres; it is the 'pure light of the city'.[81] Its *iwans* rise majestically into the sky, imposing and beautiful.

Beheshti cites the myth of Herat's creation at the hands of Alexander the Great, and writes that the city is created from the very 'earth of paradise and the running streams of *Kosar*' (a river in Persian paradise from which all other rivers flow).[82] The fertile grounds which run north from the city towards Gazur Gah are alluded to in breathless couplets, lightly touching on the *madrasa*s and the meadows beloved of Timurid Sultans and their military amirs. Gazur Gah still shines as bright as ever, its function as a Sunni shrine still intact, its gardens still rich and green; *madrasa*s still teach and inspire, filled with young scholars of angelic countenance. The princely gardens still house shahs, Beheshti tell us, and each event of significance begins life in one of these gardens.[83] Any Sunni–Shia tensions that may have erupted in violence in the previous century are absent from Beheshti's harmonious Herat. The poem is littered with words indicating heaven, paradise or transcendence, and when the author turns to leave Herat's people and its paradisiacal earth, setting off west for Khorasan's city of Tus, one imagines it was with a sense of reluctance mingled with the excitement of a new adventure.

The backdrop for Beheshti's work is the fertility and resilience of the Herat oasis, the tableau on which this idyll is created. One couplet sings with Herat's beauty as a lush oasis:

Few Padishahs have seen the like,
this green pasture, unrivalled in the seven climes.[84]

The word *khizr*, green, is used often, not simply to echo Herat's lush fertility, but also as a way of suggesting the ancient prophet Khizr who discovered and drank from the water of life, after which he became immortal. Herat's essential attributes are thus linked to the most ancient traditions and deities of Khorasan and Iran. The house of the governor and the head judge are similarly described as abodes of flowers, their fecundity possibly a reflection of the supposed moral fibre of those who occupy their positions.

Poetry, too, naturally brightens Beheshti's Herat as a life-affirming force through which the city lives and breathes. Even its scholars of mysticism (*erfan*) are skilled orators (*sokhan sanj*). Music, Beheshti suggests, is simply another form of poetry, an offshoot of the basic art by which the city makes sense of the world around it. As one Herati intellectual told me, when he was a young boy in Herat respect was gained through an intimate knowledge of Persian poets from across Persia and Khorasan who embodied centuries of traditions. Poetry in Herat, both then and today, is not just a passport to greater understanding of this world, but also to a more elevated place within it.

These strands of Islam, poetry, water and fertility, drift in and out of each other, just like the streams that run through the city. The fertility of the oasis alongside the city feeds directly into the prosperity of the city, serving as a link between city and country, creating a sense of fluidity and ease between rural and urban, which scarcely needs to be said in these lines of poetry. The eastern Khush Gate, through which urban and rural interacted, was so-called because it gave onto beautiful fields and gardens. Such was this fluidity of interaction that Herat's urban–rural populations were largely in harmony, not in opposition to each other; Beheshti's poem is a lovely example of this. That is not to say that Herat was free of such tensions, however. Instances of rural areas venting their opposition to the urban population can be found in Herat's history: one only has to think of the repeated use of the phrase *bolukian* by Rumlu to refer to those Heratis who joined in an anti-Safavid and possibly anti-urban revolt in 1537. But it is the harmony created by Herat's oasis, the functioning natural order of things, which is noteworthy in Beheshti's account. *Nur al-mashreqain* echoes the Timurid ode to the fertility of Herat's waters and oasis: canals and channels from the districts flow into the city, from Injil to Ghurian, Karokh to Gozarah. Water and nature sit at the heart of Herat's identity, urban and rural, and fertility, whether creative, natural or spiritual, binds the oasis with the city and vice-versa.

It is one of the many tragedies of Afghanistan's recent past that these routes and canals and meadows have been blighted by war. Yet while walking through Injil on a warm evening in the late summer of 2010, eating ripe figs from the trees and drinking sweet pure water from a well so deep I couldn't see the bottom, one had the sense that Herat's oasis can overcome almost anything that people throw at it. Water, light, agricultural fertility, poetry and Islam—these notions encapsulate Herat's identity, and Beheshti's wonderful ode perfectly channels these themes in just fifty-one lines.

The remainder of his journey is no less fascinating. Uzbeks, rather uncharitably, are 'the unclean', almost constantly engaged in pillage and conquest. Fellow Khorasanis of Nishapur are clever, quick-witted and studious, whilst those of Sabzevar, like the Uzbeks, are almost constantly at war. For Herat's wandering poet, Esfahan is a veritable feast for the eyes; its shops are the epitome of a trading empire. Beheshti riffs and rhymes on his Esfahan experiences in a manner which evokes the clattering and bustling industry of horses' hooves sounding around Esfahan's greatest square; he encapsulates the abundance of its bazaars, the bloody industry of its butchers, 'covered in innocent blood', and the greed of its money changers.[85] The rhythms and ordered chaos of these lines present a welcome counterpoint to the occasionally staid and lengthy European accounts of seventeenth-century Esfahan.[86] This is not the embattled traveller slogging their way through a perpetual warzone, but the relaxed jaunt of an aesthete feasting on the visual and olfactory delights of a prosperous Safavid empire. A fulsome and beautiful account of Beheshti's time in Kashmir, and the poet's appreciation of Kashmir's green-covered valleys, beautiful flowers and sweet waters complete this little-known gem of a travelogue.

It is difficult to square Beheshti's account with a more accepted narrative of death and destruction which hangs over early-seventeenth-century Khorasan and Persia. Perhaps I am inclined to prefer Beheshti's take on life after reading a constant stream of sack and siege? Perhaps his Kashmiri retirement had blanked out memories of the hardships of early life in Herat and the rigours of the road? Even if only in his memory, Herat still flourished.

Common to these accounts is the sense that one is reading a celebration of the ways and roads along which the poet and the mystic travelled during their journeys. The conquests and sackings of Khorasan had left urban centres crippled for months without being rebuilt, but the arteries on which trade flowed were quickly rehabilitated so as to facilitate money and troops, information and trade being ferried from one corner of the empire to the other. One of the first acts of the first Safavid shah, Ismail I, was to stamp out looting on the roads in Khorasan, and despite the turbulence of early-sixteenth-century Khorasan and Transoxania, trade continued largely unabated; in 1522 merchants even received tax exemptions on their way south from Transoxania.[87] Shah Abbas I was equally fastidious about the health of his trading empire; the presence of all manner of nationalities in Esfahan was no accident. Whilst also being a staple trope of good governance, security on the roads was a practical necessity for empires wishing to survive and prosper.

* * *

It is difficult to pinpoint the moment at which the Safavid empire began its hurtle or stumble downhill (and here is not the place to enter into detail), but the apogee of Shah Abbas I's reign might be a logical starting point.[88] One French observer, roughly contemporaneous with events, correctly noted that '*Dès que ce grand et bon prince eut cessé de vivre, la Perse cessa de prospérer*' (When this great prince ceased to live, Persia ceased to prosper).[89] At the beginning of his reign, Shah Abbas I had issued edicts to ban the practice of princes learning their trade in the real world of political courts, in Herat. Perhaps his negative experiences of political intrigue during his own accession to power had made him paranoid. From his reign onwards, young princes were banished to the *harem* for fear of courtiers poisoning their minds or their food. Consequently, subsequent generations of Safavid princes grew up with little experience of the world outside and were barely acquainted with the practical requirements of statecraft, beyond simply executing their rivals. After Shah Abbas I, there were no rulers with his breadth of experience or wisdom. Instead, lust, alcohol and indolence took over the dynasty as it retreated further and further away from the realities of governance and into pleasure, and further and further into the *harem*. A cycle of paranoia was thus set in motion in which wholesale massacres of family members, or at the very least the blinding of children became *de rigueur*.

As a young man, Shah Abbas II (r.1642–66) would devote two or three days a week to the supervision of the government of Safavid lands and administrative structures, occasionally intervening with spectacular brutality. Sources write of a young man adept at theological disputation. Yet Shah Abbas II died in 1666. He was a noted roué, with a passion for his female *harem*, and one historian noted, wryly, that 'it would seem that his early death was not unconnected with his lack of restraint in this regard'.[90] Like many medieval monarchs, Shah Abbas II had made no real provision for the succession. It was his eldest son, Shafi Mirza, who in the end ascended to the throne in November 1666 after having spent his adolescence in the *harem*. He was unprepared for life as a monarch. Indeed, he felt it necessary to crown himself again, with a different name, Shah Suleiman I, in the hope of having better luck the second time round; he did not. Suleiman I was a paranoid and fearful ruler, but his fears stemmed from the justifiable suspicion that each time he left the sanctity of the *harem* he might be blinded, or worse. As his rule dragged on, Suleiman I retreated into the *harem*, cutting off daily meetings with his ministers and speaking to his viziers through servants sent out from within. Affairs of state became the preserve of eunuchs and royal wives, not ministers; government shrank to a small clique. Yet as the state declined as a functioning bureaucratic system, pomp and ceremony continued unabated. On some occasions, up to 800 of the shah's wives would be paraded through the streets, from where ordinary people had been forbidden on pain of death.[91] The army, too, was a dwindling institution, collecting money from the divan and contributing little in the way of real military strength. Some divisions merely existed on paper as a ruse to defraud the treasury. So depleted was the army, and so removed from affairs of state was the court, that during a troop parade the same soldiers were forced to march past Suleiman I again and again to create the illusion of a larger force. When faced with the prospect of losing his entire empire to the Ottomans, Suleiman replied that as long as they let him keep Esfahan, he wasn't really too bothered either way.[92]

Yet the Safavids were also beset by contingencies beyond their control. The decline in the quality of Safavid rulers was mirrored by the emergence of new and vigorous empires that might capitalise on Esfahan's weaknesses: the Russian empire, conquering Safavid lands in the Caucasus, Astrakhan and Georgia; and the British East India Company, whose naval dominance effectively cut the Safavids off from overseas links to East Africa and the Arabian Peninsula and South Asia. Trade, once the source of Safavid power, had slipped; the silk industry of Gilan and the north-west of Iran suffered a slump in quality in the later seventeenth century, and the dominance of Indian silk relegated Iran's produce further. Aside from horses, Safavid Iran simply was not exporting enough; currency crises inevitably followed.

* * *

The effects of the break-up of Safavid control over Khorasan would have profound consequences for Herat's orientation. This decline would effectively bring Herat kicking and screaming into the orbit of a new group of tribal warriors who would claim the city for their own fledgling polity. These were the Abdali Pashtuns of Multan, Qandahar and Herat. A new generation of tribal fighters would now target Khorasan's pearl with the same intensity as Alexander the Great, Chingiz Khan, Timur, Ubaidullah Khan and Shah Ismail I had all done before. The conflicts this caused brought into being a three-century-long tug of war over the city's soul. As a Persian city, Herat would be claimed by Safavids and those who followed them on the Iranian plateau; and yet as a Sunni city, it would also be claimed by the rising tide of Pashtun power. The British empire, too, would come to claim Herat as the key to their imperial security architecture. Herat itself wanted to exist as a semi-independent city-state and be left alone.

* * *

I was attending the wedding of a friend's cousin in the furnace heat of August 2009, sitting in a small village to the north of the provincial capital of Badghis, Qala-ye Naw, and wearing my relatively new and altogether too pristine *pirhan tonban*. I was busy pretending to be an Afghan, put up to the task by some Afghan Red Cross friends. This was a game I would play throughout Afghanistan, and whilst it was mostly harmless fun, it sometimes had distinctly un-humorous consequences. Linguistically, this particular attempt was proving a cautious success. The *salam*s, the chitchat about weather and so on and even the Islamic phrases I uttered somehow masked my European appearance, as well as the frayed espadrilles (footwear invariably gives the game away) which I had taken off my feet before entering. My Afghan friend, Nader Jan, a large bear of a Pashtun man from a village in Bala Murghab, gave me support where needed, having earlier fixed on my being an ethnic Pashtun who spoke Dari (many ethnic Pashtuns who grow up in Persian-speaking cities do not speak Pashtu). As the group of Qalai Nawis pressed me on the tribe to which I belonged—its sub-tribes, and so on—my Pashtun edifice began to crumble; even Nader got a bit lost after a few too many tribal declensions. Luckily the group fell about laughing when I confessed to being an English colleague of Nader's from the Red Cross.

The time I was fortunate enough to spend in the provinces of Khost, Paktiya and Jalalabad as a Pashtu-interpreter gave me an insight into

Pashtun history, culture and society. Pashtun life is culturally rich, filled with stories, traditions and poems, songs and dancing. My understanding of Pashtuns is largely drawn from experiences of living and working amongst them—farmers, prisoners, fighters, IT experts, cooks and cleaners—and speaking their language.[93] The poetic and musical canon of Pashtun life self-consciously celebrates and castigates intra-familial conflicts. Revenge, *badal*, drives these conflicts and is a pillar of Pashtun life, echoing themes found in Greek tragedy; it is both a source of pride and a source of sadness. Sometimes these intra-familial feuds stretch back generations, and they are invariably informed by the Pashtun concerns of women, gold and land: *zan, zar, zamin*. I learned that hospitality and kindness are deeply embedded hallmarks of this multi-layered tribal system of etiquette and mores. Pashtun culture places the guest above all others, defends the pride of females and males alike, and this is all expressed in poems and songs and dances. Speaking Pashtu, *Pashtu wayel*, doing Pashtu, *Pashtu kawel*, and having Pashtu, *Pashtu larel*, form the core tenets of what it means to be a Pashtun, and much of Pashtun life is governed by an unbreakable system of etiquette and behavioural norms, *Pashtunwali*. It is similar to the Persian customary system of *taarof*, which also governs issues such as how one treats guests. *Pashtunwali* dictates, as I was often reminded, that when someone, friend or foe, crosses their threshold, that person or persons become honoured guests to whom it is required to show respect and civility. The guest, at all costs, must be protected from any threats they might be facing at the time of seeking shelter in the host's house. I was always made to feel welcome by Pashtuns, be it in a prison cell or at a wedding ceremony. Osama bin Laden's largely unpopular time in Afghanistan was governed by this principle of *melmastiya* (hospitality), by which guests are protected, no matter how much they are disliked. Indeed, US attempts in the weeks after the 11 September 2001 attacks to spare the Afghan people a conflict by persuading the Taliban to hand over Osama bin Laden fell flat on this principle; bin Laden was a guest, and as such his betrayal would irreparably damage the honour of the Pashtun Taliban.

Pashtun tribal groupings present a complex network of familial ties which cut many ways and along which flow a myriad of alliances and enmities. Pashtun tribes split into tributaries and deltas, each line carrying its own customs and legends. They are largely divided into Abdali (later to become Durrani with the accession of Ahmad Shah Durrani to the throne in 1747—we will refer to them as Abdali until Chapter 4) and Ghilzai. It is from these two main Pashtun lines that innumerable subdivisions and clans trickle down into Afghanistan and Pakistan's towns and villages, but for the purposes of Herat it is the Abdali tribes and their subdivisions which are of most importance.

Abdali Pashtuns hailed from the west and south of present-day Afghanistan, as opposed to the Ghilzai to be found to the east of Sistan, close to Indian trading towns beyond the Indus. One Afghan source suggests, in the course of a wonderfully detailed account of Pashtun history, that the 'first' Afghan tribe is the Abdali tribe with its roots spreading across from Qandahar, Herat, Multan, Kashmir, and Balkh.[94] Etymological claims on the name Abdali are obscure, with descent claimed from a 'common patrilineal ancestor, Abdal, who himself, it is further claimed, was descended from Qays Abd-al-Rashid [Qays Abdur Rashid], the ultimate ancestor of all Pashtun tribes'.[95] The Afghan scholar, English deserter from the Bengal Artillery and father of Afghan archeology, Charles Masson (his real name was James Lewis), suggested a link between Abdal and the pre-Islamic Hephthalite nomadic dynasty of Central Asia. This theory reaches back into the ninth century BC with the King of Israel, Saul Talut, whose grandson, Afghana, was said to have built the holy temple at Jerusalem within forty years.[96] It was during the reign of Nebuchadnezzar that Afghana's descendants were supposed to have been scattered throughout Iraq and the Levant, eventually finding their way into Khorasan and Ghur. One such descendant who settled in Ghur was Qays Abdur Rashid. Abdur Rashid travelled to Medina on hearing of the Prophet Muhammad's revelation, and is credited with spreading the word of Islam in Ghur and Khorasan. Linking the Pashtuns to a lost tribe of Israel, however, is rarely a popular move amongst the fiercely conservative Muslims one finds amongst Pashtuns of Afghanistan and Pakistan. This theory has in turn been discredited by genetic analysis of Pashtun DNA, ruling out a connection to Israel's tribes. The DNA analysis suggests Indo-European or Aryan origins, which might give Masson's claim some credibility. Abdali subdivisions run into two main branches, the Zirak, from whom flow Popalzai, Alikozai, Barakzai and the Achezai, and the Panjpao, from whom flow the Nurzai, Alizai, Sakzai and Eshaqzai, and whose number are mostly found in the west and south-west of Afghanistan.[97] Popalzai Pashtuns who have risen to prominence include Afghanistan's recent president, Hamid Karzai, as well as the nineteenth-century plaything of British imperial ambitions, Shah Shujah (see Chapter 4). Ghilzai Pashtuns subdivide into Ahmadzai (of whom Afghanistan's current president, Ashraf Ghani, is one), Hotaki and Kharoti.

Given the uncertainty that dogged the origins of the Pashtun nation, it is not surprising that the Abdalis in Herat sought to link their confederacy with the Chishti Sufi saints, and in particular Abu Ahmad of Herat (d.966), and by so doing tapped into Herat's religious past in search of local legitimacy. Using Sufi networks and appealing to Herat's Islamic heritage shows a flexible, and opportunistic, attitude to lineage.[98] Like other ambitious dynasties in waiting that sought to rule in Herat, the Abdalis realised that legitimacy within the context of the city's history was vital to their cause.

During the earlier Safavid era, the time of Shah Abbas I, Pashtun tribes had first made a distinctive entrance into Herat's history, and that of the region. For the Safavids, the Pashtuns occupied a space beyond Khorasan's frontiers; it was Pashtuns who had pushed Emperor Humayoun to his refuge in Herat, and it was Pashtun tribes who defended Qandahar against Safavid incursions in the winter of 1648–9. To the east, for the Mughals the Pashtuns were convenient soldiers or mercenaries, and sometimes enemies. Emperor Babur had struggled to control their looting and brigandage in and around Kabul, and the most famous Pashtu poet, Khushal Khan Khattak (1613–89), widely considered to be the father of Pashtu literature, argued for armed resistance against Mughal dominance, preaching a Pashtun nation throughout his poems. In this vein, Abdali Pashtuns can be said to resemble the Karts as independent actors who impressed themselves upon the powers of the day, treading a fine line between mercenary and vassal.

Safavid and Mughal rivalry for Qandahar was the backdrop against which the Abdalis emerged into Herat's politics in the seventeenth century, offering their assistance and wealth, depending on the direction of political travel. Indeed, contemporary sources often highlight the Pashtuns' talent for opportunism. One first-hand observer with many years' experience in Persia remarked that the Pashtuns 'served whoever offers them most'. He went on to remark that '[Safavid] Persia treats them with caution and grants them such privileges and advantages that even if she cannot attach them fully to her cause, she at least reduces their inclination for doing harm.'[99] Similarly, the French traveller and historian Thevenot, visiting India in 1666, described the Pashtuns as 'small Rajas in the Mountains, who are suffered to live in liberty, paying some easie [sic] Tributes'.[100] This notion of a warring and opportunistic Pashtun mentality endured into the following centuries, and one late-eighteenth-century British traveller slightly uncharitably described Afghanistan's Pashtuns as being 'generally addicted to a state of predatory warfare'.[101] Yet despite this sentiment, one with which many Pashtuns today would not disagree, it was trade between Safavid Persia and Mughal India which gave sixteenth- and seventeenth-century Pashtuns the opportunity to move from a tribal grouping of mercenaries to a force that would change the region for good. The mass movement of Abdali Pashtuns to Multan in the mid sixteenth century had enabled them to seek Mughal patronage and gave them a fixed urban backdrop against which to push for greater conquests into Khorasan and Sistan. There the nomads found urban stability and the prosperity it can give to trading communities. Multan linked directly to Qandahar, and was a prosperous stop on the route west to Herat and north to Kabul and beyond the Oxus.

Herat played an important role in the expansion of Pashtun tribes, for it sent horses east, much as it had done over the centuries. These horses had been bought from Herat and Khorasan, reared and fed in the meadows surrounding Kabul and Qandahar, before being sent east for sale in Mughal India.[102] This was a lucrative and widespread trade in the seventeenth century, which reached as far as the Arabian Sea and down into India's south. As Christine Noelle-Karimi shows, there were tens of thousands of Central Asian horses coming into India in the eighteenth century, the vast majority of which had come from Herat's fertile oasis overland along the ways and routes which had long sustained travellers and poets and mystics.[103] Through this trade from Herat in horses, as well as textiles and fruits, the Abdali Pashtuns could enrich themselves to become indispensable to two competing empires, both of which were in need of military assistance. Naturally, Abdali Pashtun traders settled in and around Herat. Their settling in Herat added yet another layer of complexity to that city's ethnic and sectarian make-up, confusing matters and unwittingly giving rise to centuries of ethnic and sectarian tensions. They were non-Persian, but Sunni Muslims and as such occupied an uneasy place in Herat's ethnic and religious landscape. These Abdali Pashtuns would later claim to have occupied the province since time immemorial, but even well into the late nineteenth century (and beyond), Herat's snooty Persians would see Pashtun tribes as uncultured interlopers, parvenu trading bandits.

Herat's first prominent Abdali Pashtun, Assadullah (1558–1627), rose as a tax collector during the reign of the Mughal emperor, Akbar (r. 1556–1605). His royal connections gave to extortion a veneer of legitimacy, and Assadullah's rise was thus protected by Mughal might. He was ambitious for power as well wealth, and not content with solely looking east to the Mughal court for patronage. The opportunism which so many sources mention was never far from Assadullah's political calculus, and as Safavid power revived, slightly, in the region, he sought out the Safavid, Shah Abbas I, travelling to Herat to show off his archery skills. This was a tactic that Shams al-Din Kart had once used to win a powerful Mongol patron in the thirteenth century, and it worked for Assadullah three centuries later.[104] Martial prowess was still a ticket to success in an uncertain world. Aligning themselves with the Safavid shah whilst simultaneously serving the Mughal emperor would pay dividends for Herat's Abdalis. For many, Assadullah is a father figure of the Pashtun royal line, a line from which descended Afghanistan's first king, Ahmad Shah Durrani (r. 1747–72). Assadullah's important role in Pashtun history gives Herat a central role in the Pashtun story of Afghanistan, despite the fact that Qandahar is today seen as the heartland of the Pashtun, and Afghan, nation. Yet for Herat this would be of little comfort, for the emergence of Pashtun power in Khorasan brought with it serious problems, giving to the city yet another royal household who wished to claim the city as their own through recourse to real military power and imagined family trees.

A Safavid source written in Bengal by Mohammad Khalil Marashi, the great grandson of a Safavid prince and once a guardian of the Imam Reza shrine in Mashhad, gives an excellent account of the rise of the Abdalis in Herat from obscure beginnings to their Afghan, and Herati, pre-eminence.[105] Marashi puts the date of the Abdalis' emergence in Herat at 1591; they had arrived from the mountainous regions surrounding Kabul after being driven west by 'some events'.[106] Of the subdivisions of Abdali Pashtuns, it was the Sadozais who became most prominent in Herat, beginning a line of nobles who would rule Herat like a semi-independent fief and fight intra-familial wars with Qandahar and Kabul. These Sadozai Abdalis chose the fertile meadows of Badghis as their summer pasture, and for their winter pasture they chose Shindand and areas to the east and south-east of Herat. Shindand is today still home to the majority of Herat's ethnic Pashtuns. In 1682 the Sadozai chief, Hayat Sultan (d.1728), was forced into exile in Multan after clashing with the Safavids over a dispute relating to revenue owed to Esfahan; and the ease with which Hayat Sultan found a welcome in Multan is a telling indication of the respect the Abdalis had begun to command: they could be useful makeweights in regional power games. As control of Multan slipped from Mughal hands, it was the Sadozais who stepped in and effectively governed the province, making profits as traders and taxers and cementing their hold on the city of Herat and eastern Khorasan. In the early eighteenth century there were around 60,000 Sadozai/Abdali houses in Herat. As a military and economic force, the Pashtuns had arrived.

In 1717 Herat's Sadozais finally expelled the city's last Safavid governor, eight years after Qandahar was decisively conquered in the name of Ghilzai Pashtun forces under the rule of Mirwais (d.1715). Herat's hungry and expanding Sadozai forces, political, economic and military, proved too strong for a Safavid state crippled by indecision, drink and distance. The distances between Herat and the Safavid capital at Esfahan finally told on the Safavids' hold over Khorasan, and proved the point that Herat was a difficult city to govern from a secluded court in the middle of Persia.

In 1715 a leading Herati Sadozai, Hayat Sultan, a talented robber of caravans equally adept at hightailing it with the loot, learned of the imminent arrival in Khorasan of a Safavid general, Khusraw Khan. Khusraw Khan's mission was to punish Qandahar for its insurrection of 1709 in which Mirwais had taken power. The army was to pass through Herat on its way to exacting retribution from Qandahar. Herat's Sadozais saw this as an opportune moment to rise up and rid the city of the Safavid authority under which it, or they, chafed. Herat and its people, at this time in the hands of a Safavid governor, Abbas Quli Khan

Shamlu, had quickly learned of the declining powers of the Safavid empire. At a meeting between the heads of the Sadozai tribe and Abbas Quli Khan, the Sadozais were arrested; Abbas Quli Khan suspected their insurrectionary intentions and placed them in the citadel, hoping the problem would disappear. Proving that torture and ill treatment rarely produce anything other than lasting enmity, their ill treatment at the hands of the Safavid vizier shocked the Qizilbash amirs of Herat to such an extent that they chose to back the Sadozai cause against a weakened Safavid power. The Qizilbash evidently saw opportunities in the shifting political fortunes of the day; they wanted to be on the right side of history. Qizilbash envoys thus sent an official complaint to the Safavid court in Esfahan requesting that Abbas Quli Khan be fired and another appointed in his stead. They got their wish, and a new appointee, Jaafar Khan Ustajlu, was quickly despatched to Herat; yet during the time it took for him to arrive, the industrious Sadozais managed to engineer an uprising to take power, ditching their erstwhile Qizilbash allies.

Sadozai prisoners were sprung from within the citadel, and the jailbirds fled to join their families amongst the Do Shakh mountains to the west of the city. No doubt the escapees were aided by their Sunni coreligionists within Herat's prisons and on its highways. From Do Shakh, they regrouped before attacking and subduing Esfezar, to the south of Herat. Next, they moved on Khorasan's pearl. Qizilbash defences had been alert enough to attempt to head off the approach, and they met the Sadozais in battle a few miles from Herat's southerly walls. But these preparations proved insufficient to defend the city, and the Sadozai forces quickly triumphed over Safavid–Qizilbash power; they arrested the governor as soon as they could. At this point the Sadozais would have been forgiven for thinking that they had done enough to secure victory and eventual control of Herat. Yet this was not to be the victorious homecoming they expected, for when news of this reverse reached Herat's people, they 'turned away from obedience to the Afghans' and shut the doors of the city.[107] The appalling siege and limitless appetite for plunder shown by the Sadozais when they eventually broke through wearied Safavid and local defences were, if anything, a validation of the city's initial decision to bolt heavy doors and refuse entry.

The Sadozai Abdalis were the first near-local military forces to conquer Herat since the thirteenth century, when Kart *malek*s, with characteristic insouciance, had thumbed their noses at Il-Khanid power and ruled the city as semi- and eventually fully-independent sovereigns. Sadozai control now stretched into Herat's districts, to the banks of the river Murghab in Badghis and south into Sistan, east to Ghur. Herat's new rulers were titled 'Sultans', acceding to a throne which was theirs by dint of force and force alone. Their rule was firm enough to keep the erstwhile Safavid governor of Herat a prisoner under watch in the citadel, and then to execute him along with a number of Qizilbash prisoners, all in defiance of a neutered Safavid empire. As if to prove that their conquest of Herat was not merely a combination of luck and opportunism, they routed two armies sent to Khorasan from Esfahan, smashing Safavid military pride comprehensively. One particularly humiliating defeat, at Islam Qala, saw the Safavid commander climb onto a barrel of explosives and blow himself up, 'preferring death to disgrace'.[108] Such was the confidence of Herat's Pashtun overlords that in 1726 its leader marched to Mashhad and subdued that bastion of Shia Islam in the name of a Pashtun and Sunni Khorasan.

The years separating the Abdali takeover of Herat and the arrival in Herat in 1732 of the Persian conqueror Nader Shah Afshar (r.1736–47) saw Pashtun tribal infighting at its most sanguinary and confusing.[109] In the service of settling family feuds, Pashtun soldiers tore Herat apart with a fury reminiscent of Greek tragedy. The city was tossed back and forth between rival cousins in running conflicts which damaged the Sadozais' ability to rule as a unified dynasty, foreshadowing later conflicts amongst different Pashtun tribes and sub-tribes, confederacies and subdivisions. This had the effect of weakening the city and province and opening Herat to the possibility of further conquest at the hands of Nader Shah Afshar's military genius.[110] Nader Shah sought to recreate a Safavid empire in Persia and Khorasan; he defeated the Ghilzai Pashtuns who had sacked Esfahan in 1709, and he set up a short-lived but wide-ranging empire which ran from India to Iran, trailing blood and loot wherever they went.[111] For Herat, Nader's rule was in no way glorious. Information is scarce as to how Herat experienced this whirlwind of conquest. What is clear, however, is that Herat's importance continued to dwindle during these years, owing largely to the fact that Nader Shah chose Mashhad as a logistical base, not Herat, further relegating Herat to the status of a forgotten frontier town with pretty ruins. Nader took Pashtun soldiers with him on his lightning conquests to India, co-opting Pashtun military might to serve his imperial ambitions, much as Safavids and Mughals had done before him. In doing so he effectively robbed Herat of military men of prestige and wealth, rendering the city almost totally defenceless.

* * *

As the spring of 1740 moved into summer, and the fields and gardens of Herat's oasis were in full bloom, a native Indian of Nader Shah's army passed through Herat on a march west, returning from Indian campaigns. I have erred on the side of caution when stating the case for Herat's decline, possibly a reflection of some deep sadness that it had slipped from Timurid heights, but the observations made by this Indian soldier leave the reader with no doubt as to the extent of Herat's descent. He paints a depressing picture of a region gone to seed, and a once great city all but ruined. It is worth quoting in full:

> From Qandahar to Herat, most of the villages and towns are utterly ruined. You will meet with some that resemble cities; but only at a distance of five to seven farsakh. To be fair, Herat was truly a fine city; but, because of the extreme oppression exercised by ill-fated governors, it is now in such a state of desolation that the courtyards of the houses are used for agriculture. The other affairs are in a similar state. Even so, it is proverbial for its fine fruits. The melons of Karez near Herat are inimitable in fragrance, sweetness, juiciness and fleshiness. A good melon should have these characteristics. The former princes and wealthy men have built enormous, magnificently ornamented and lofty mosques and graves for the pious and their attendants. But the majority of these buildings are decaying because their walls and roofs have not been repaired and their attendants have been harassed.[112]

Safavid decline, Pashtun infighting and Afsharid conquests had left Herat a broken city. Yet despite this picture of decay, the legendary quality of Herat's fruits still constituted currency for diplomatic exchange; in these apocalyptic days, its melons and grapes had been deemed suitably delicious to form part of diplomatic gifts between sultans and shahs in the eighteenth century, flitting back and forth from Iran to India as tokens of respect and favour. Reading diplomatic exchanges between Safavids and Mughals can be a tedious affair, but when obsequious courtiers and diplomats pause from politics and troop movements to praise the qualities of Herat's melons, a note of levity and humanity enters into the exchanges.[113] I remember listening to odes to the sweetness of Herat's melons, sitting by shops, in fields, small mud huts or air-conditioned rooms, and can see how such a topic is fit both for diplomatic exchange and for elevated prose. Yet beyond these glimmers of bright yellow hope, decline was winning out. Despite the optimism of *firmans* and poets and historians, a sense of senescence is unavoidable in these years. Beheshti described an idealised utopian Herat of his memory, but it is an Indian soldier's account which gives us the starker reality.

The Herat of 1747 had become a complicated space; there were more claimants seeking to control its walls and tax its lush surrounds. The introduction of Pashtun rulers altered the province, introducing elements of uncertainty in its citizens' identity. Persian and Afghan each felt Herat was theirs by right of culture, language, ethnicity or sect, but as a result of this complexity, few would fully grasp the city.

The two hundred years or more of history that this chapter has covered take Herat away from a Chingizid and Timurid past and into a changed present in which Afghan, British, Russian and Persian will squabble for control of the city and its surrounds. Nader Shah's conquests had ripped up Chingizid, Timurid or Safavid notions of geopolitics, bridging Khorasan to India, and inadvertently laying the foundations for the emergence of an Afghan state stretching from Peshawar in the east to Herat in the west, from Bukhara in the north to Sistan and its capital, Qandahar, in the south. Herat's attraction, from now on, would lie in its geographical setting more than the fame of its courtly life or the genius of its artistic output. It would be reduced to its barest utilitarian bones, a city on a route linking warring empires and aspirational nation states. The eighteenth century had begun, in typically robust and martial fashion, with the emergence of the Sadozai Abdalis, hinting at the emergence of an Afghan nation. Persia, under the Qajar successors to the Safavid dynasty, was clamouring to reclaim its lost Safavid patrimony. Further east, the British East India Company flourished, and to the north, the Russian empire was beginning to show signs of expansion. The clashing of these two European empires would form the backdrop against which Herat's history played out in the eighteenth and nineteenth centuries. As it had done so many times before, Herat once again found itself at uncertain margins of emerging empires and nations.

4

HERAT, THE KEY TO INDIA

HERAT, KHORASAN'S BROKEN PEARL, 1747–1863

On the night of 19–20 June 1747 in a military camp in Khabushan (in northern Khorasan), the life of Nader Shah Afshar came to an end in bloodletting and messy confusion. The pillage and looting of Nader's Persian campaigns of 1747 had caused rebellions from within his own family, moving some to contemplate regicide. Nader's grip on reality gradually slipped amidst a descent into insanity.[1] His death would have profound consequences for Herat's orientation in the nineteenth century and for the city's eventual inclusion in the earliest beginnings of the Afghan nation. It gave rise to a Pashtun dynasty based on the Abdali Sadozai line which had previously ruled Herat in the dying days of Safavid Khorasan. This Pashtun empire would lay claim to territories stretching from Herat to Peshawar.

According to the account of a Jesuit priest in his camp, Nader had so feared the loyalty of his Persian troops that he ordered an Afghan by the name of Ahmad Khan Abdali (1722–72) to arrest the suspected Persian plotters on the morning of 20 June, a morning Nader would never live to see.[2] Ahmad Khan Abdali was the son of a former governor of Herat and the leader of 4,000 Abdali Pashtuns who formed a highly effective fighting group within Nader Shah's army. That evening Ahmad Khan Abdali gathered his men in readiness to carry out his

169

king's orders. But news quickly reached the plotting Persians of their impending arrest, and they hastened their plan to execute Nader Shah. A group of thirteen Persian and Uzbek chiefs entered Nader Shah's tent and killed him, bringing to an end one of the most feared and mercurial military talents of that, or any, era.[3]

Ahmad Khan and his Pashtuns were too late to save Nader Shah. A lady of the royal camp informed them of Nader's death, and as dawn broke his Afghan contingent rushed to the royal tent where he found the dead body of their former patron. We are told that Ahmad Khan 'stood guard until morning over the royal harem', ostensibly with the aim of preventing further chaos breaking out, but possibly so as to buy some time and evaluate the opportunities that such an event presented to an ambitious military leader.[4] On the morning after the regicide of the night before, fighting erupted; Ahmad Khan and his entourage of Uzbek and Pashtun fighters so distinguished themselves that Nader Shah's wife granted him the Koh-e Nur, a diamond of prodigious dimensions which would be passed back and forth amongst aspirant potentates of Afghanistan and India in the nineteenth century before ending up in the crown of the British monarch, where it sits to this day.[5] Within four hours after sunrise, the entire camp of Persian, Uzbek and Afghan soldiers had been dismantled, stripped bare and routed; soldiers scattered towards homes and pastures with immeasurable treasures taken from years of relentless conquest.[6] Desultory skirmishes and looting rippled outwards across Khorasan.

* * *

Compromise and contradiction define Herat and its entry into Afghan history as the nation's liminal soul. After the regicide of Nader Shah, Ahmad Khan was given a humble coronation as 'Ahmad Shah Durrani' (hereafter referred to as Ahmad Shah) in Qandahar, with a sheaf of barley, which still forms part of the Afghan flag to this day, being placed in his turban. The Pashtun chiefs declared a stated intention to seek their own nation, and independence from Shia Persian sovereignty.[7] Ahmad Shah's descent from Assadullah Khan, the Sadozai clan's patriarch, and the latter's role in Herat's seventeenth-century history stretched his patrimonial ambitions into Khorasan and to Herat. The Pashtuns' natural political inclination was to look east into the rich and fertile lands of the Indus, to Multan. Ahmad Shah's Sadozai lineage, however, meant that for him Herat would always mark the western edge of a Sadozai and 'Afghan' identity, as it continues to do so today.[8]

Ahmad Shah Durrani's capture of Herat in 1750 and the subsequent successful forays into what is today northern and central Afghanistan to subdue Uzbek, Tajik and Hazara tribes set the seal on his conquests into Khorasan and the lands to its east and north. Herat now formed a strategically important part of the Durrani empire, which stretched from the Oxus in the north, to include Punjab and Kashmir in the east and the lands of Sabzevar to the south-west; its southern borders ran through Baluchistan. Herat was, for Ahmad Shah Durrani, the gateway to Khorasan and Iraq in the east, the gateway to Turkestan in the north and linked to the capital, Qandahar, by passable roads and tracks. In the words of one Afghan historian, 'Ahmad Shah, bearing in mind that whoever became ruler of Iran would find Khurasan a barrier between Afghanistan and Iran, undertook to guarantee the independence of Khurasan [sic]...'[9] Herat's conquest thus placed it in a unique and complicated position, again at the blurred edges of expanding empires. On top of Herat's existing tensions and complications, the incorporation of the city into this Pashtun Sunni empire added yet more ethnic and sectarian complexities. Herat's Pashtun rulers never became fully accepted in Herat, for whilst they were Sunni Muslims, they were very much seen as uncultured non-Persian barbarians, whom Herat felt were totally unsuited to rule over the Pearl of Khorasan. Herat now had a Persianate foot in the Shia camp, but a Sunni foot in the Pashtun camp.

Accordingly, this chapter explores a very fundamental dichotomy which sits at the heart of Herat's modern identity. Historically and culturally a Persian city of Jami, Beheshti, Behzad and Bayqara, Herat sat on the western fringe of a Pashtun empire. It was divided from Kabul and Qandahar by mountains, brigands, language and custom, and yet it was a largely Sunni province perched at the eastern edge of a Persian Shia empire. To this day it is both united with and divided from each of its neighbours, echoing themes brought into being by Alexander the Great's own conundrum in the Hari Rud oasis. These contradictions, incarnate with the flesh and blood shed in trying to resolve them, became the driving force in upheavals of the years in question. To this situation, we must add European imperial ambitions, a factor which, more than any, shaped the region's political evolution and doomed Herat to a century of misguided strategic and political scrutiny. Our gaze, accordingly, must flit from capital to capital, from camp to camp, to show Herat's changing fortunes, evolving identity and shifting boundaries within the context from which they arose.

The Pashtun unity and consensus formed in the aftermath of Nader Shah's assassination proved difficult to sustain, and a propensity for feuding soon asserted itself. The struggles from these feuds further isolated Herat, locking the city in a precarious state of semi-independence. In 1775 Timur Shah (r.1772–93) had designated the capital of the nation of Afghanistan to be Kabul, with the winter quarters of its court to be to the east, in Peshawar. Herat was now effectively cut off from both the capital and the winter court. Geographically, it was clear that Herat was not well suited to being an Afghan city; a journey from Kabul or Peshawar to Herat could take a matter of months. Internal feuding punctuated the reign of Timur's successor, Shah Zaman (1793–1800/1), hampering any attempts to build territorial, administrative or political unity from Herat to Peshawar. Shah Zaman's brothers, Mahmud Mirza in Herat and Humayoun Mirza in Qandahar, showed the colour of their loyalty by choosing to rebel against Kabul as it marched its armies east to capture the territories of the Punjab, territories which were essential to their empire's long-term economic prosperity. In one such campaign against the Sikhs of the Punjab in 1795, Shah Zaman's efforts were cut short when he heard news that Mahmud Mirza had assembled troops in Herat to attack Qandahar. Shah Zaman was obliged to return and defeat Mahmud Mirza. Despite this, Shah Zaman placed Mahmud Mirza back on the throne of Herat, requesting that his rebellious relative show more obedience in future.[10] Personal gain trumped the more elusive notions of national unity, or even prosperity. This inability of the Durrani monarchs to capture and hold the rich Indian territories, on which Ahmad Shah Durrani had so relied for money and grain, compounded the internal weakness brought about by damaging tendencies to civil war. Enclaves, principalities, breakaway provinces are bywords for this era of Afghan history; it produced fragmented states menaced by internal feuding, and the relentless warring deprived Afghanistan of the riches of India and Kashmir.[11] Herat, consequently, remained a semi-independent Sadozai–

Durrani enclave, true to its seventeenth-century traditions until the mid nineteenth century. It was governed by a succession of princes, a shah and a vizier, all of varying competence and authority, but all distanced from the capital in Kabul and protected by geography and tribe. As the eighteenth century gave way to the nineteenth, this position on the western fringe of the fragmented Durrani empire was secure enough, yet surrounded by a troubled Khorasan and a contested Afghan nation. Coveted by the Persian Qajar empire and yet nominally part of a feuding Afghan state, it is little wonder that Herat proved to be difficult to understand, or place.

* * *

Into this Sadozai enclave, on 2 November 1781, strode George Forster, an East India Company civil servant. His approach was from the south, and as he neared the city he noted 'light and sandy soil' and the 'remains of some tombs or religious edifices' which dotted the way.[12] Forster was then employed in Madras but returning to England from Bengal, and is the first recorded English visitor to Herat; his account of this twenty-day visit is a remarkably leisurely opening salvo for a century of intense European involvement in Herat which would shape the city's destiny and end up destroying many of its antiquities. Forster's first impressions were of a piece with so many who had made this journey before him:

> The city of Herat stands on a spacious plan, which is intersected with many springs of running water, some of which are supplied with bridges; and the numerous villages surrounded with plantations, must afford a pleasant view to the traveller, whose eye has been wearied with the deserts of Afghanistan.[13]

The young civil servant's observations allow us to glimpse daily life in Herat at this time, offering a picture not painted in courtly Persian chronicles which more often detail the great deeds of noble men of questionable morals. This is an outsider's impression of a city as it shuffled and surged from day to day; and Forster adopted the custom of English nineteenth-century adventurers by travelling in disguise, as an Armenian trader.

On entering one of Herat's caravanserais, Forster sought a real Armenian through whom to convey a message of introduction to another, whose house was some 40 miles from Herat. His advances were rebuffed, and the man walked away from him 'without even expressing the common terms of civility'. Forster then attempted to 'slide into the Mahometan community', an endeavour he undertook with fear of his life, imagining himself becoming a martyr for his troubles. Perhaps he thus relished the romanticism such a prospect presented? Forster noted two caravanserais at Herat, 'about one hundred Hindoo [sic] merchants, chiefly natives of Moultan [sic], who by the maintenance of a brisk commerce, and extending a long chain of credit, have become valuable subjects to the government'. Their lives in Herat were far from blissful, however, for 'discouraged by the insolent and often oppressive treatment of the Persians, they are rarely induced to bring their women into this country'.[14] With this observation begins a century-long complaint from within Herat's non-Muslim mercantile community at the derision and unfair treatment they received at the hands of their Muslim rulers. Every single British visitor to Herat in the long nineteenth century would hear this refrain, and each British official in Herat would be pressed to make life easier for Herat's Hindus, Christians and Jews.

Despite Forster's intentions to observe Herat unnoticed, word of his Christian beliefs escaped the small group of Armenians with whom he had made contact. Herat soon penetrated his disguise, and his unmasking had unpleasant consequences. Forster was greeted some days before his departure by a mullah who exclaimed with 'sensible emotions of joy' that he had now obtained a 'favourable opportunity of revenging the grievous injuries sustained by many of his holy ancestors at the hands of infidels'. The practicalities of this opportunity required Forster to pay a fine of 500 rupees, 'repeat the creed of Mahomet and be circumcised'.[15] Forster feigned ignorance and sent for Persian-speaking Armenian Christians of Herat to assist him in avoiding on-the-spot circumcision and conversion. This only emboldened the mullah, whose actions suggest he might have been a direct descendant of those holy men whom Babur had dismissed as charlatans. Forster continues his narrative by relating:

> When the hungry Afghan perceived that, instead of one Christian, he had found five, his exultation had no bounds. He swore by his beard, that we should all incur the fine or circumcision. Oh! what a glorious sight, cried

he, will be displayed to our prophet, when these hardened infidels, renouncing their heresy and impunities, shall become a portion of the faithful: what a triumph to our holy religion![16]

Forster managed to escape with his foreskin and his life; the mullah was eventually bought off for a smaller sum than the one demanded, and a rabble which had joined the spectacle first shouted a little and then dispersed.

This incident did not prevent Forster, evidently enterprising and adventurous, from exploring Herat; we hear of trips to the 'eating houses, where all the talk of the day is circulated, and chiefly fabricated', and his admiration of the neatness of Herat's barber's shop and its gleaming mirrors.[17] We also hear, surprising when set against Forster's own experiences, of tolerance amongst Afghan and Persian, Sunni and Shia: 'In the division of Khorasan, subject to the Afghan empire, the Persians enjoy a fair portion of civil and religious liberty, and are rarely treated with insults.'[18] The covered bazaars of the Old City were well stocked, and bread, rice, meats and fruit and vegetables of all kinds could be found in these markets for good prices. Within the city, prosperity of a sort was clearly in evidence, for Forster writes that the Friday market, possibly held in the Bagh-e Shahi area, 'is so crouded [sic] with the produce of the neighbouring villages, that a passage through it is difficult and fatiguing'. There were sheepskin garments, much worn in the winter, then and now, by Heratis of all social and economic classes; and he mentions a small quantity of European goods—cloths, cutlery, glasses and prints—but concludes that the low prices wanted for such goods must surely be an indication of their unpopularity. Herat's security affairs were well in hand, it seems, for he describes the administration of justice as 'vigorous'. Evidence of this is seen from two thieves, 'apparently above the ordinary class', who had been suspended by their ankles for over an hour, watched by Heratis milling about at the foot of the citadel. Forster concluded that this spectacle of men suspended by their ankles made him, and his gold, feel a little safer in Herat than he had felt on Khorasan's roads and byways.[19] Aside from being England's first visitor to Herat, Forster also distinguishes himself as an early advocate of a vegetarian diet, for he noted that 'Having witnessed the robust activity of the people of this country [Persia] and Afghanistan, I am induced to think, that the human body may sustain the most laborious [*sic*] services, without the aid of animal food.'[20]

* * *

Scamming religious leaders were the least of Herat's worries at the beginning of the nineteenth century. Political tensions and family rivalries which had marked relations between Kabul, Herat and Qandahar in the late eighteenth century produced a quarter of a century of near constant civil war, further isolating Herat from Qandahar and Kabul. In the early nineteenth century the Durrani empire disintegrated into a number of small regional states, with power splitting and fragmenting amongst descendants of the various branches of the ruling Pashtun families. The 1818 execution in Herat of Fath Mohammadzai, a leading Pashtun, caused twenty of his brothers to advance separate claims to authority, simultaneously competing against each other from their local bases in Peshawar, Kabul and Qandahar. Further weakening the Afghan state by depriving it of the wealth of lush Indian territories, the region east of the Khyber Pass fell to the Sikh empire in 1834, and the years 1826–37 saw Dost Mohammad Khan (r. 1826–39 and 1845–63) carve out a power base for himself in Kabul, Bamiyan, Jalalabad and Ghazni. Meanwhile, his half-brothers, the 'del' (*del* means heart in Persian) Sardars of Qandahar, controlled a principality in southern Afghanistan and found themselves allying with Persia against enemies in Kabul and Herat. By 1818 Herat had retreated further into its isolation as a Sadozai enclave in which Kamran Mirza Sadozai (d. 1842) held sway, having ousted his father, blinded his rivals and entered into a variety of shaky alliances and agreements with his predatory neighbours.

For Herat these years were marked by frequent conflicts as the warring Pashtun brothers sought to establish workable limits of control. Echoes of Herat's citadel existing as an almost separate political space in the sixteenth century can be seen at this time. In one early-twentieth-century history of Afghanistan, written by a charismatic Herati opium dealer and sometime historian, Riyazi Heravi, the year 1822 is dealt with simply by reference to 'other related events that occurred in Herat and its surrounds'.[21] He records a siege of 6 June 1822 in which two local tribal notables were besieging the town with the help of either Persian or Pashtun money and arms, surrounding Herat's walls.

They fought here and there, and looted as they went. During skirmishes at the foot of the citadel both men were injured by gunshot wounds; they later died of these wounds, and on their death the troops scattered into the countryside to return to their homes, and most likely to fight for another master.[22] Although this was a relatively inconsequential episode in a century bursting with events of importance for Herat, it somehow captures the processional nature of so much of the infighting that Afghanistan saw in that century, and into the next two. One temporary, and unsuccessful, insurrectionary and ruler of Herat, in the summer of 1821, was crowned with a paper crown and boiling oil was poured over him before he was executed.[23] As a result of the fighting, famine scoured the countryside and the natural rhythms of real life fell apart. Herat, its city and province, suffered from Turcoman raiders and slave traders. Pilgrim routes to Mashhad were regularly targeted and few were safe from the gangs.

Yet Herat, by dint of language and history, was more than simply a Sadozai enclave. Set against the ambitions of Afghanistan's Pashtun chiefs were those of the Shia Qajar empire of Iran. The Qajars were doggedly determined to incorporate Herat into a revanchist Safavid imperial project, reclaiming lands once controlled by Shah Ismail I and his descendants. As Ahmad Shah Durrani was heading to Qandahar to found his Pashtun dynasty in the summer of 1747, regicides from the Qajar tribe who had assassinated Nader Shah Afshar made their way back into Iran to form an eponymous dynasty that would last until they were swept from power in 1925. The Qajar dynasty was part of a long tradition of Turkic nomads turned sedentary rulers, yet their rule over Iran lacked the military brilliance of their Safavid forefathers, proving a near constant struggle to regain lands lost either to Russian forces, or to protect eastern Khorasan from rebellious Turcoman slavers. It is true that the Qajars had established themselves on the ruins of the Safavid empire, yet history alone was not a strong enough justification for a unified kingdom which incorporated a variety of tribal, ethnic and sectarian groupings spanning Iran, Afghanistan and into India.[24]

The conquest in 1796 of Mashhad by the first Qajar leader, Agha Mohammad Khan (d.1797), had heralded a revival of Qajar dominance into eastern Khorasan. Early diplomatic exchanges between Qajar and Sadozai representatives from Herat in the late eighteenth century suggested that Safavid rule by proxy over Herat might be a possibility, and in 1800 a Sadozai diplomat from Herat headed to the Qajar court to discuss the centuries-old issue of Herat's allegiances. Herat's emissary based Sadozai claims to the city on the twin claims of military supremacy and recent history, remarking, 'If it befits my Alexander-like standing, it [Herat] will be mine, bound to the essence of my perseverance and resolve. I have occupied this region by merit of military strength and intrepidity. It was my blessed forefathers who obtained this realm by means of the sword.'[25] The Qajar counter-claims reached back into the Safavid past to establish an imagined sovereignty over Herat. Both sides evidently felt that they had a strong claim to the city, yet within Herat it was possible to find those in favour of Persian dominance and totally opposed to Pashtun hegemony, and those for whom the Shia of Iran were hated infidels. The *impasse*s of ethnicity and religion blocked every which way, and a sustainable *modus vivendi* proved elusive.

Herat's Sadozai rulers bristled at having to offer shows of fealty to the Qajars, whose claims, they felt, rested on tenuous appeals to a long-vanished Safavid Golden Age. Yet despite this, the city's Sunni Sadozai leaders paid lip service to Qajar sovereignty in a bid to secure their city against aggression from Qandahar or Kabul. Prince Kamran Sadozai in Herat was outwardly loyal to the Persians, striking coins (sikka) and having Friday prayers (khutbah) sung in the name of the Qajar monarchy, but in reality his hatred of the Persians was widely known. Echoing, and entrenching, Herat's own isolation, Kamran's hatred of the Persians was equalled by his aversion to his Pashtun enemies in Kabul and Qandahar and Dost Mohammad's family. The reason for this aversion relates in part to an incident in Herat involving Dost Mohammad. During one expedition there to subdue the city, 'Dost [Mohammad] himself tore off a sash ornamented with precious stones which supported the trousers of the daughter of Shah Mahmood.'[26] Taking down the trousers of a female member of a Pashtun household, and stealing jewels in the process, is more than enough to earn eternal hatred in Afghanistan. Yet neither party, Pashtun or Persian, could hope to hold Herat decisively for themselves, and so compromise and deception continued to define Herat's dealings with its neighbours.

Much as had been the case during its Safavid centuries, Herat's frequent rebellions against Qajar sovereignty were couched in terms of religion: Sunni against Shia. One such rebellion of 1807 against the Qajars was carried out in collaboration with a messianic Sunni leader named Sufi Islam. Sufi Islam had previously worked as a dyer at the foot of Herat's Iraq Gate, and rose to prominence as an itinerant Sufi preacher, gaining adherents as he went around Herat. In 1807 he found himself carried into battle against the Shia Qajar forces seated in a golden *howdah*. His clarion declaration of a *jihad* against the Shia infidels of Persia had made him the figurehead of Herat's anti-Qajar force, and 366 bodyguards protected him and his golden *howdah* in battle. Unfortunately for Sufi Islam, the Qajar troops slaughtered Sufi Islam and his army in their thousands, and 'slashed his [Sufi Islam] corpse to bits' before building a fire in which to burn his remaining body parts, possibly to prevent a shrine cult growing up around the martyred Herati Sufi, but possibly out of spite.[27] So deep were the lines of enmity and so strong the power of storytelling in Herat and Khorasan that Riyazi wrote in the early twentieth century that in Sufi Islam's adopted home of Karokh, no more than a few kilometres from the centre of Herat, 12,000 families were still loyal to the martyred Herati and his Sufi order.[28] (Well into the late twentieth century, Sufis and those seeking his intercession in daily life still visited his shrine at Karokh.) Total Qajar dominance was prevented, however, in a deal by which Herat paid Mohammad Khan Qajar 'an elephant, 100 bolts of Kashmiri shawl-cloth, and 100,000 rupees cash' and in which one of Herat's noble sons was sent to the Qajar court as surety against good behaviour.[29] Herat in the grasp of the Qajar ruling house was content to protect itself with an elephant, some cloth and bags of rupees, belying the notion that Herat formed an ineluctable part of Qajar territorial ambitions, and suggesting that few really knew what to do with Herat.

It is in these years that we begin to glimpse the city's identity, or its identity crisis, a crisis whose echoes still sound in the twenty-first century. Herat had become an orphan of history and geography, and yet it longed for the security and protection that a large power, such as Qajar Persia, could provide. It was too far from Qajar Tehran to be a meaningful part of that state, however, and yet its distance from Afghanistan's feuding capitals, Kabul and Qandahar, rendered it independent by accident and default. It both chafed under Shia sovereignty but welcomed the protection it provided against internal Afghan feuding.

Herat still suffers from this orphan complex: seen to be too close to Iran to be trusted by Kabul, and too Sunni to be trusted by Tehran, and too complicated to be understood by the West. Today's Heratis feel a sense of injustice that they are sidelined, when they feel strongly that their city has done so much to define the Afghan nation, and its citizens are so central to Afghanistan's cultural identity. The more I study and discuss the city's history, the more I understand how Herat still inhabits this identity crisis, and, paradoxically, the more central Herat appears to my understanding of the Afghan nation. It is clear that this stems from its turbulent eighteenth and nineteenth centuries: denied the ethnic or sectarian certainty of, say, Qandahar or Mashhad or Kabul, it had its own identity which proved difficult to place with ease in a box marked 'Afghan' or 'Persian'.

* * *

The nineteenth century was the century of European imperial intrigue in Central Asia. It was also the century of Afghan, Persian and Indian intrigue; this was not a passive century of imperial domination.[30] Herat, for its part, was a stage for the Great Game, a political struggle conducted in the shadows as Russia and Britain fought a war of information in which geographical and political knowledge, mapping the territories that separated Qajar Iran from India, were its ways and means.[31] Adventurous British and Russian spies, diplomats, chancers and soldiers sought out alliances at the courts of Central Asia, India and Persia so as to gain an advantage that might further imperial aims and lead to lasting personal fame and fortune. The prize in this war was the jewel that was British India. Many who played this game met lonely and horrendous deaths; others made their careers through it. Despite the popular image of the Great Game as an Anglo-Russian conflict set against a regional backdrop, its genesis was grounded in fear of Britain's oldest foe, 'those villainous but active democrats the French'.[32] The East India Company was petrified at possible Franco-Russian alliances aimed at wrestling India from British hands. A British diplomat sent to the courts of Baghdad and Persia in the early nineteenth century to ascertain the extent of French designs on India made the following pithy observations: 'I have not the smallest doubt but that Bonaparte designed to form a *point d'appui* in Persia, from whence, when the time came, he might either persuade or force another great power to join him in the invasion of British India.' He went on to explain France's training of Persian troops by reference to a line from Horace's *Epistles*: '*Condo et compono quae mox depromere possim*'[33] (I am putting down and preserving the stores on which I may someday draw), a comparison with the principles for storing good wine.[34] As early as 1808, whilst Herat mourned the death of Sufi Islam, the British sent to Peshawar Mountstuart Elphinstone, a man who would later play a calamitous role in Britain's first Afghan war, but was now bidden to negotiate a defensive treaty with Afghan leaders directed against Napoleon's oriental ambitions.

Russia, too, had long harboured ambitions in the direction of the Indus. Catherine the Great toyed with the idea of an invasion of India; her son, Tsar Paul I, even sent troops southwards on such an expedition in 1801, only for the force to be recalled to Russia shortly afterwards. British fears were not therefore fantastical. Ultimately, it was a combination of French and Russian ambitions that presented the most frightening of all prospects for the British empire in India. The Great Game's most eloquent historian, Peter Hopkirk, sets out the planned Russo-French alliance which aimed at taking India from the British; Napoleon's 'breathtaking plan was to march 50,000 French troops across Persia and Afghanistan, and there join forces with [Tsar] Alexander's Cossacks for the final thrust across the Indus into India'.[35] Thankfully for British interests, Napoleon and the Russians would never have the opportunity to divide up the world as they saw fit, but instead set about attempting to destroy each other in the early years of the nineteenth century, leading to ruinous defeats for each side, and Napoleon's ultimate military humiliation in the frozen wasteland of December 1812.

In the late eighteenth and early nineteenth centuries, policy-makers in London and the East India Company became increasingly convinced of the utility of a strong alliance with the Qajars to secure their western Indian borders. One British diplomat, posted to Tehran to shore up British interests at the Qajar court during the first decade of the nineteenth century, noted the following assessment of Persia's usefulness to Britain: Qajar Persia was 'one of the greatest outworks of that precious citadel', India.[36] Herat very quickly became central to the metaphors of gates and keys and outworks. The Qajars sought to control Herat; the British, in turn, would seek to control the Qajars, to prevent them from falling under the sway of the Russians. Captain John Malcolm, a fluent Persian speaker, was sent to the Qajar court in Tehran in 1800 with gifts and promises of more gold and more gifts, aimed at winning the Qajar assent to a defensive treaty protecting India from Russian military actions through Persia. The terms of this treaty bound the shah to assist the British should the Afghans make aggressive moves on India; in return, the British would assist Persia in the event of a Russian or French attack on the Qajars. Yet in 1801 the Russians annexed Georgia, a territory that Qajar Persia considered formed part of their Safavid patrimony, and when in 1804 the Russians laid siege to the Armenian capital Yerevan, the Qajars felt entitled to invoke the terms of Malcolm's treaty of 1800. European political life, however, had long since evolved on its own terms: Britain and Russia were now in alliance against Napoleon, who was in turn seeking to tempt the Qajar court into allying with him against the British as a stopping-off point for his own triumphal entry into India. A treaty was therefore signed between France and Persia on 4 May 1807, giving French troops the right of passage through Iran and severing British commercial interests with Persia. For Britain this was nothing short of disastrous. Napoleon's defeat of the Russians in the summer of 1807 at Friedland and the subsequent naval blockade caused yet more diplomatic pressure to be heaped on the confused head of the Persian court; desperate envoys from France and Britain hovered at its edges, promising fidelity and protection against the Russians, gently reminding the Qajar monarch of his obligations to two diametrically opposed treaties. The Shah was 'desperately looking for friends' in an uncertain region; at least Herat was nominally a Qajar city.[37]

Herat assumed a place at the centre of the Great Game, a red dot on all the era's most important maps. Strategically, Herat sits on the easiest approach to Afghanistan from the west by way of roads running between Mashhad and Qandahar, roads along which most invaders from Persia to India have passed. As one British report surmised, 'together with Mashhad and Marv, it [Herat] stands guard against incursion from the north across the only real gap in the mountains which straddle Asia from China to the Black Sea'.[38] This quirk of geopolitics, this axiom of geography, gave to nineteenth-century Herat an inversion of the Timurid century, when the city sat proudly at the centre of power. In the nineteenth century, power did not radiate outwards from Herat's tiled walls, but rather converged upon it, destroying instead of building. Herat, with its innumerable spellings, would be seared on the nineteenth-century British consciousness in much the same way as Sangin, Nadir Ali and Helmand province in the twenty-first century. Herat would be claimed as central to the security of British interests, discussed publicly and privately *ad nauseam*, and later abandoned with guarded justifications of success amidst changing domestic political agendas. For a generation of diplomats, Herat was the 'Key to India'. The British empire, mindful of its interests in India, would send armies, spies dressed as mullahs, diplomats and money into Herat to ensure its loyalty and to gain an understanding of the country which separated Qajar Persia from British India. These were the passes through which Russian and French armies were feared to be plotting to march; Herat was the fertile plain in which their armies would rest before pouring into Qandahar and Quetta. During this time, Herat remained as phlegmatically enigmatic as before: too Sunni for Qajar Persia, too far from Qandahar and Kabul for the Pashtun nation of 'Afghanistan', yet always somehow the 'Key to India' for Britain. Refracted through a variety of different interpretive lenses, Herat's customs, the habits of its leaders and the state of repair of its urban fabric were meticulously described by all those who passed through its gates; the city comes alive in all its faded and chaotic glory, shocking and entrancing in equal measure. If the Great Game were to have had a capital city, it would surely be Herat.

A succession of intelligent, linguistically adept British, French and Russian officials set out to map the lands separating India from Persia, to curry favour with local chiefs and to document everything and anything they saw. The results are fascinating for the historian, for the details recorded on village life, politics, trade, crops and tribal affiliations are remarkably detailed and, if one takes the trouble to read them in their entirety, perceptively balanced. The first British visitor to Herat in the guise of an active player of the Great Game was a young Englishman named Captain Christie.[39] He rode into Herat in 1810 and stayed for a few weeks. Whereas the walls of Herat's citadel had struck fear into the heart of Chingiz Khan and Timur, Christie thought them merely 'contemptible'. There is little in his account to hint at the anxieties that Herat would cause to prime ministers and foreign secretaries, let alone the lives that would be lost in trying to bend it to British or Persian will.[40]

By 1830 the fear of Russian advances into India via Herat had gained striking new momentum, helped along by Russian–Persian alliances, and the concomitant Russophobia in London and India. Russian–Persian diplomatic proximity was the worrying background to all of Britain's fears for India and for Herat. Russian military success in the Caucasus in a succession of wars against Qajar Persia, and the humiliating Treaty of Turkmanchai of 1828 which effectively rendered Persia 'delivered, bound hand foot, to the Court of St. Petersburg', forced the Qajars to look to Khorasan and Herat in pursuit of their Safavid legacy now that the Caucasus was in Russian hands. The Russian diplomat Prince Menshikov was anxious to keep hold of lands taken in the Caucasus, and so he encouraged this eastward expansion; Persian designs on Herat kept them away from Russia's newly won territories in the Caucasus.[41] In 1830 the Qajar Crown Prince, Abbas Mirza, looked east to Khorasan in the context of his government's difficult relations with Russia (a Russian ambassador had not long before been hacked to death in Tehran by a Persian mob for perceived insults to Islam) and indifferent ones with Britain. Kerman was in uproar, and Turcoman raiding blighted Khorasan and kidnapped Shia pilgrims on their way to Mashhad. Khorasan had not seen peace since the beginning of the nineteenth century, and the question of Herat was nowhere near being settled amicably between those who coveted it. In the early 1830s Sir John Macdonald, British India's resident envoy at Tehran, was sounding the alarm bells at the Qajar court to anyone who might listen; an invasion was forthcoming, a Perso-Russian invasion of British India by way of Herat. Meanwhile, Afghanistan's own internal chaos troubled further the quickened pulses of policy-makers in London and India, and their conclusion was that Russian forays had to be stopped at all costs.[42]

In September 1830, Arthur Conolly entered Herat in disguise. A young Captain in the 6th Bengal Light Cavalry, it was Conolly who had coined the phrase 'The Great Game', and his death, executed in

Bukhara in 1842 after months in a vermin-infested pit, was be a seminal event in its history. The tone of his appraisal of Herat's fortress and the ability of the fertile plains to hold and feed an army is a stark indicator of the rise in British fears for Herat. Yet Conolly's was a simple reconnaissance mission, undertaken simply to ascertain and observe, and he had no power to make or break alliances. He repeatedly assured Herat's ruler, Kamran Shah, that he was simply a traveller, with no official function, and unable to influence events. Kamran evidently believed Conolly, 'for the only subsequent communication that I received was, an inquiry whether I possessed, or could prepare, a liquor which would make his Majesty drunk at once'.[43] The young Englishman's observations of the city itself were a far cry from Babur's awestruck account; he described Herat as 'one of the dirtiest [towns] in the world'. Dark tunnels within the Old City ran in all directions from the main Chahar Su and the streets were littered with dead animals and rotting rubbish. Gambling houses and wine dens thrived, providing the morality police with work to do, and opportunities to make money from fines and penalties. The once-great mercantile hub that had been Herat was no longer, for its traders were so heavily taxed and harshly treated by Kamran Shah that they were said to be 'ruined'.[44]

Yet whilst within the city walls Herat had been harshly hit by war and famine, 'without the walls all is beauty'.[45] Conolly, like so many before him, is struck by the beauty of Herat's suburbs, describing them as 'one beautiful extent of little fortified villages, gardens, vineyards and corn-fields', a lush scene 'lightened by small streams of shining water, which cut the plain in all directions'.[46] The waterways had survived the early nineteenth century's civil wars, for Conolly writes of a dam 'thrown over the Heri-rood [*sic*]' which, through the canals and *kareze*s, watered the city and its surrounds. The fruits and bread of Herat were 'a proverb for their excellence'.[47] As one might expect, it was the water of Herat's oasis which brought Conolly's prose to a slightly tangled peak: 'I really never in England even tasted more delicious water than that of the Herirood [*sic*]: it is "as clear as tears," as the natives say, only equaled by the waters of Cashmere, which make those who drink them beautiful.'[48] Conolly was privileged to see the remains of Timurid Herat, in particular Husain Bayqara's Mosalla site, and could even ascend one of the twenty minarets to survey the city and countryside from on high. He notes how 'We ascended by one hundred and forty steps to the top of the highest minaret, and thence looked down upon the city and the rich gardens and vineyards round and beyond it; a scene so varied and beautiful, that I can fancy nothing like it, except, perhaps, in Italy.'[49] His assessment that there are seventeen varieties of grape in the Herat oasis, however, would surely have disappointed Herat's proud grape farmers, for it is well known that Herat's varieties of grapes stretch well beyond that number. Conolly left Herat after his brief stay, and like Forster before him, it is difficult to see in his report the alarm and consternation that Herat would cause.

* * *

In 1832 the Qajars had launched a series of attacks on Khorasan, ostensibly to curb the flourishing trade in slaves which targeted defenceless Shia pilgrims making their way south-west and west from Central Asia and Herat. Tensions between Herat's vizier, Yar Mohammad Khan Alikozai, and the Qajars in Tehran were on the rise. The Qajars, for their part, felt that Herat was not doing enough to curb the slave trade. For Yar Mohammad Khan, trading in slaves was a lucrative business. Indeed, Yar Mohammad was at one point taken prisoner at the court of the Qajars and pressured to bring Herat into line, back under the Qajar yoke, and to refrain from kidnapping Shia pilgrims. One Afghan source describes a Qajar minister explaining to Yar Mohammad the region's history and power dynamics in the following, slightly condescending, terms:

> In olden days, Afghanistan was part of Iran. But following the assassination of Nadir Shah, Ahmad Shah Saduzai established an independent regime there. Up to now Herat has been in Saduzai [sic] hands, presently Prince Kamran's, but the rest of the kingdom is under the control of the sons of Sardar Payandah Khan. The prince, therefore, ought to vacate Herat and come to the shah of Iran. Or he should have the khutbah read and coinage minted in the name of the shah of Iran and should collect and send the revenues agreed on by treaty and also send his son as bond. He would thereby obtain peace of mind. Otherwise, we will take Herat by force.[50]

However, peace of mind, of any kind, was hard to come by in Herat. As a result of Yar Mohammad's incarceration at the hands of the Qajars, a treaty emerged which required that Kamran in Herat should perform *sikka* and *khutbah* in the name of the Persian shah, submit 15,000 tuman and fifty bolts of cashmere cloth as gifts, and send over one of his sons as hostage.[51] By agreeing to the terms of this treaty, Herat kept itself safe; and in many ways this was a typical compromise that Herat had to make so as to retain its precarious state of semi-independence.

As the signs of Persian designs on Khorasan increased, the British sought more substantive relations with Herat and firmer assurances of its independence to head off potential Russian and Persian ventures into the Hari Rud. Thus it was that Mohan Lal, an India Office official, interpreter and general fixer, entered Herat in the frozen depths of 1833, with Dr Gerard and a retinue of mappers and camp followers. Lal's team sought assurances from Kamran Shah that Herat would remain neutral in the face of Persian pressure. Lal also set out to inspect the city's defences, to map its supply lines and assess its suitability for hosting the phantom Russian army that kept British politicians and East India Company officials awake at night. Yet despite the seriousness of his mission, Lal's observations have a remarkably personal touch, seeking out detail in the most unlikely places and offering the reader a rich portrait of the famed Kamran Shah Sadozai. Kamran was, we read in Lal's meticulous accounts, a 'decrepit gloomy prince' who 'excites the pity of mankind', being 'destitute of the signs of royalty'. Kamran, so Lal tells us, lacked both money and a palace. Lal's first meeting with Kamran, the man who supposedly held the keys to the future safety of British India, was only a partial success:

> We were summoned by the king inside of the arg [Qalah-ye Ekhtiar al-Din], in a very narrow and dirty room where he [Kamran] was sitting on a rotten carpet. He had a large quantity of wood, with an iron plate full of fire, before him. He was drunk or stupefied with opium and bhang. Three miserable candles were burning on each side. He was in such a senseless condition, that I could hardly understand his half-broken and lazy conversation, the substance of which was, that we were welcome in his country, and that he was much pleased to see us.[52]

During subsequent audiences, one conducted whilst Kamran bathed, and another with six goldfish in a fountain placed on the floor between the two men as they discussed the future of the region, Kamran professed his friendship to the British, stressing that Herat was neither a friend to the Persians nor to the Russians. This was a subtle contradiction of Kamran's long-standing ties to the Qajar court, clearly manifested in coins and Friday prayers: *sikka* and *khutbah*. It was for such questionable assurances that Lal had made this long journey to Herat.[53] A subsequent audience with Kamran was interrupted by the latter's regular pauses for vomiting.

It is easy to paint Kamran's political outlook as deceitful and opportunistic, but we must temper this assessment with an understanding of the situation in which he found himself: faced between the Scylla of Kabul and Qandahar and the Charybdis of the Qajars, totally unable to pursue an independent policy for want of money and firm allies, he could be forgiven for dissembling at every turn. Lal himself noted this unenviable situation when he correctly observed: 'Being afraid of the Persian Government, he is very anxious to make an alliance with the English power, and is extremely afraid of his ministers, of the Alikozi [*sic*] family [the family of Yar Mohammad], and never dares to feed his horse without their sanction.'[54] By offering the outward symbols of loyalty to Tehran, some shawls, money and the occasional elephant, Kamran could largely avoid military conflict with Persia, whilst also being sufficiently protected against attack from Qandahar or Kabul. With the arrival of a British official offering assistance, it is not therefore surprising that Kamran saw fit simultaneously to extract promises of assistance from Lal through a pension, yet then also to continue a policy of flexible opportunism with the Qajars to save his skin. It is in these audiences that we see Herat's uneasy independence, the tendency of those who ruled it to hide behind the strength of its walls and the city's ability to play one power off against the other. What else could it do?

Much as twenty-first-century observers of Herat obsess over the substance of Herat's ties to the Islamic Republic of Iran, Herat's nineteenth-century leaders faced the same scrutiny. The substance of those ties, in both centuries, should be seen through a lens of pragmatism as much as anything else. Herat was a complicated place, multi-ethnic and home to Sunni and Shia alike, not to mention Hindu, Armenian and Jewish populations. Loyalty to either Afghan or Persian was broadly shared, divided on confessional lines, between the Persian Shia and the Afghan Sunnis, and the policy of its rulers had to navigate a myriad of concerns, alliances and vested interests. The safety of its ruling family's skin, invariably, trumped any other concerns.

An example of Herat's complications can be seen in the following brief anecdote. When Mohan Lal was on a journey from Mashhad back to Herat, having gone to the shrine city to pick up medicines for an English colleague who had fallen sick in Herat, he was mistaken for a Qajar Persian by a group of villagers who lived to the south of Herat city. Lal was asked when the Persian governor of Khorasan would come to take Herat 'and release them from the oppressive yoke of the Afghans'.[55]

Lal, like Conolly before him, shows us a city of depressing poverty, strikingly contrasted with the fertile oasis which rings its edges. Lal, familiar with Indian cities, writes that Herat's material conditions compare unfavourably with Delhi and Calcutta. As if to prove his point, he describes a procession through Herat in celebration of Eid-e Qurban (a Muslim festival celebrating Abraham's willingness to sacrifice his son, Ismail), an occasion on which celebrations and the giving of alms are the norm. Yet in this retelling Shah Kamran scorned Herat's destitute population as he rode by, giving one old woman a worthless copper coin. In a further damning assessment of royal life in Herat, Kamran's court and palace 'bore but a caricature semblance of the ancient royal court'.[56] Herat's mosque had all but gone to total decay, and even the palace in which Lal met Kamran for his audiences is described as having 'so little of the character of a regal residence, that the gaols in British India are much superior to the palace of Kamran, not only in architectural beauty, but even in cleanliness'.[57] We hear of the custom at court by which men of rank would scrabble around on the floor for scraps of sweetmeats and food to honour the king, directly echoing the descriptions of the mystified fifteenth-century Chinese diplomat who observed exactly the same custom, with equal bewilderment.[58] Through the gloom of a bitingly cold winter and the poverty of the city, Lal shows us Herat on the cusp of taking its place as the Great Game's lightning rod.

In 1833 Herat remained the most fertile country in the whole of Khorasan. Lal writes that its outlying villages, most likely directly outside the city walls, were full of rich green orchards producing considerable quantities of fruits, no doubt sprouting up amidst the ruins of former Timurid and Kartid *bagh*s. The district of Obeh abounded with mines of different metals, and was famous for a hot fountain in which sick people bathed themselves and immediately recovered.[59] Lal notes the abundance of mineral wealth to be found around Herat—copper, lead, marble, sulphur, silver, tin and ruby—all drawn from Herat's hills, but he laments the fact that they had so much unrealised potential, as 'the rudeness of the people, and the oppression and indifference of the Government, have caused them to be neglected'.[60] Not quite the breathless reports which surfaced in twenty-first-century Western newspapers detailing Afghanistan's supposedly inexhaustible lithium reserves, but close.[61] Echoing centuries of observations on Herat and hinting at the exquisite melons which once formed part of diplomatic exchanges, Lal lists twenty-four different types of grape in Herat, seven better than Conolly, but still not the full quota of upwards of seventy.[62] Herat's people, Lal tell us, 'though reduced to poverty by oppressive government, are fond of pleasure', and he goes on to describe how they 'go daily to meadows, and pass their time in firing from horseback, racing, singing, joking, dancing, drinking and sleeping'.[63] The slightly bawdy nature of Herat's womenfolk when outside the city—whereas inside the city walls they were veiled, even their feet covered for the sake of modesty—is also commented upon; 'some of them sing ballads, and others, abusing slightly the passers-by, burst into a laugh, which makes them move on, hanging down their heads with shame'.[64] I sorely regret that I never had the opportunity to witness a bold Herati woman hurl jesting insults at me. Years of Islamic extremism and conflict have beaten down the feisty pride of Herat's womenfolk. Yet Lal's observations in published form lose some of the innocence seen in his hand-written notes from Herat in March 1838 which can be accessed in the British Library; these notes might almost be a postcard from a diligent and observant tourist, entranced by the country he was visiting.[65]

In an unwelcome coda to his political tasks, Lal found himself the subject of an attempted, and entirely unappreciated seduction. An attractive young Herati man of twenty or so was brought into his presence with the aim of persuading Lal into taking him away to India for a better sort of employment. The Herati shamelessly fluttered his eyelids and gestured suggestively, but Mohan Lal, one of British India's foremost civil servants, sent the would-be scribe away with flustered reproaches against his brazen behaviour.[66] There was too much life in Herat for a neat and punctilious India Office official; his censorious responses, his mystification at the chaos of what went on within its walls, are of a piece with Cheng and Babur, both of whom were over-whelmed by a city going about its way noisily, dangerously and not always honestly. In so many ways Herat had altered beyond belief since 1221, and yet the same raucous energy, the chaos which had bubbled under the surface in the Timurid era, still gave the city its drive and character. The citadel's walls are still said to reach the sky, vice still picks at the seams of courtly life, madness infects its rulers and yet life continues, its women still laugh, people revel in the province's water, its fruits and the simple pleasures of being alive. It is with this intoxi-cating chaos, brilliant when set against such hardship, that I was so entranced; Herat is not for the easily shocked, for it offers life at its most real and its most unpredictable.

* * *

Qajar Persia sought Herat as an inalienable part of their revanchist Safavid project; Britain was terrified that should Herat fall into the hands of Persia, the way to India would lie open to a pitiless Russian army; Sadozai Herat wanted to deter members of its own family from taking the province for themselves. It is not difficult, therefore, to understand why these tensions should have erupted into open warfare in the autumn of 1837 with the advance of the Qajar army from Tehran to Mashhad, Ghurian and then to a camp outside Herat, where they were joined by various representatives, some willingly, others coerced, of different powers with a stake in the fate of Herat. Persia, with Russian prompting, had returned to take what they felt was theirs by dint of history.

Some Persian chronicles, however, are vague as to the reasoning for the Qajar assault on Herat. One chronicle offers us one wholly uncon-vincing sentence on the subject: 'When Mohammad Shah celebrated the feast [of Nawruz, March 1837], he decided to conquer Herat and, there-fore, mobilized the army of the empire.'[67] One Afghan history prefers the safer territory of poetry to express the horrors of the siege that would later unfold. These lines are essentially a plea from Herat's Shia to their Afghan rulers in Herat to spare them what was surely coming:

Oh you gardener, when you expel the birds from the garden,
spare the nests of the nightingales which long made their home within.[68]

The fate of nightingales was the least of Herat's worries as a 30,000-strong Qajar army (Riyazi, however, has the figure at 80,000)[69] proceeded from Mashhad to Ghurian, sacking it with ominous ease in the early autumn of 1837. Their camp followers numbered over 90,000. Riyazi notes that three sides of the fort at Ghurian still bore the marks of this terrible bombardment over three quarters of a century later.[70]

On the morning of 21 November 1837, Mullah Abdul Haq Pushtaki, a leading member of Herat's Sunni *ulema*, rose to the pulpit of Herat's then crumbling Friday Mosque. He proclaimed a call to arms, a *fatwa* demanding that Herat's people fight the heretic Shia from Tehran, Esfahan, Azerbaijan and Mashhad. The mullah roused his flock as follows:

> O men, this was the command of God and the prophet that you heard. Here is the Qajar army present and ready for battle. If it defeats you and occupies the city, your lives, property, and honor [*sic*] will be subject to devastation with impunity. Your duty is to defend your lives, property and honor. Fighting the Qajars is a jihad in the way of God. If you are killed you become a martyr and enter eternal paradise. If you kill any of them you become a ghazi and make Paradise for yourself out of that.[71]

Those present duly 'performed their ablutions, clipped their fingernails, and wound themselves in their burial shrouds'.[72] Similarly, in May 1837, the *ulema* of Mashhad had sent demands to Mohammad Shah Qajar that he do more to protect Khorasan's Shia population from the oppression of the Turcoman slavers who preyed upon pilgrims to Mashhad, and the Pashtun rulers of Herat who had allowed this trade to flourish unpunished. Angry diplomatic missives had been sent between the two powers—Persian and Afghan, Sunni and Shia. Yet to view this conflict solely through a sectarian lens would be to do its significance a disservice, for it had also an imperial, a global dimension. It was a conflict which brought empires into confrontation, threw up tales of heroism and intrigue and whose fate was decided not within the impregnable four walls of Herat, but in a small port in the Persian Gulf.

The urban fortress facing the Persians was formidable: thick ramparts rose 90 feet in the air, giving the impression of a 'long hill surrounding the city' on which further walls were built 32 feet high, a structure at the corners of which were large towers facing the invaders.[73] The insides of the walls were fortified by counterforts of masonry, made strong by earth brought from outside the walls. Ringing the walls was an area of boggy marsh giving onto the wooded villages, shaded by poplar, vines, cypresses, willows and fir trees. It was here that the Persians set up camp. Amongst them, windmills dotted the southern approaches to the Qandahar Gate, reminders of more prosperous and peaceful times. Mohammad Shah Qajar commanded his assorted troops of Persian mercenaries and Russian deserters to fortify the city from all sides, although curiously his troops didn't seal all the gates. This proved to be a costly error. Qajar soldiers, camped in squalid, ruined mosques near to the Qandahar Gate, were harried by incessant Afghan attacks; fights even broke out within the Qajar camp. Nightly raids from within the city boosted Herati morale, but inflicted few decisive blows on the invaders. Yar Mohammad stripped the countryside of provisions and men, partly to deny the Persians, but also to bring such provisions and men into the walls of the city; the areas surrounding Herat for a distance of 20 miles had been plundered even before the siege had begun, emptied of people, crops and animals.[74] A determined army camped outside Herat's walls faced an equally determined force within, and the rhythm of siege and skirmish set in, as autumn gave way to winter. A hard frost settled over the Herat oasis, causing Heratis to pray that a severe winter would come to their aid and freeze the Persians into withdrawing their siege. The frost did not come to Herat's rescue, but instead the news of the fall of the reputedly impregnable fortress of Ghurian reached the city on 15 November 1837, dealing a sore blow to morale.[75]

Prince Kamran, no doubt urged on by his less intoxicated adviser Yar Mohammad, did what so many besieged Herati rulers had done throughout the centuries: he 'bolted the city gates and sat tight'.[76] The initial skirmishes, as Afghan 'braves' rushed out to harry the Persian troops camped in once-great *bagh*s and lush villages, resulted in a few dead elephants, some dead Persians and many dead Afghans, but only served to convince Herat that it would be better to place their faith in the walls of the citadel, as their troops, estimated at 4,000–12,000 strong, were outnumbered. But the initial Qajar sallies were more concerned with personal glory than with the overall success of concerted military action against the city. Promising positions were not built upon with concerted military action, for each commander wanted the spoils all for himself.[77] A Russian eyewitness observed this trait, describing how the Qajar commanders saw that if they could be seen to capture the city for themselves, they would be covered in gold and rewards; failure of the overall siege was a price worth paying for the possibility of personal glory. Yet although individualistic acts of heroism were the yardstick by which Qajar military generals sought to be judged, one British eyewitness, Britain's ambassador to the Qajar court, Sir John McNeill, saw in the Qajars' futile attempts to subdue Herat, privations aside, one of the finest examples of its kind in the military history of Central Asia. Against all the odds, the Qajar troops, under questionable leadership, managed to remain true to their objectives of attacking Herat's walls again and again, despite being effectively trapped in squalid, freezing and rotting camps and with vainglorious commanders leading them on, from behind.[78] Meanwhile, Afghan soldiers continued to launch countless 'sallies of lightning speed and ferocity' and fell on the Qajar soldiers like a 'nighttime robber' inflicting numberless casualties on the Qajar soldiers.[79] These attacks were so merciless that, according to one Afghan chronicler, 'days of leisure and nights of rest became unlawful' to the Qajar troops stationed in squalid camps at the feet of the walls of the city.[80]

Alongside their punishing assaults, the Qajars employed a tactic of bombardment from the very start. This was a questionable strategy, given the strength of Herat's walls. Indeed, one eyewitness describes how the Persian artillery 'played without judgment on the whole circumference of the place, and wasted their shot in a point-blank fire against the rampart, which all the cannon-balls in the world could not destroy'.[81] Owing to the scarcity of ammunition, the Persians would launch the cannon balls over the city to frighten its inhabitants, and then send their soldiers over to the other side to retrieve the ordnance and re-use them for re-firing: shock and awe, on a shoestring. As the siege wore on and Qajar military provisions became scarcer still, they took to uprooting Herat's gravestones and fashioning cannon balls from tombstones. For those unfortunate enough to be within its walls, being killed by the hurtling spherical gravestone of an ancestor would have been darkly comic, even by Herat's standards.

Herat quickly became a beleaguered city; the price of salt and meat rocketed, horses, camels, mules, asses and dogs were eaten. As water became scarcer, Herat began to die of thirst. Yar Mohammad put sentries on the cisterns so as to ration water consumption. Ammunition was scarce too, and not only did Herat have to survive against Persian troops, but also against rafts of sedition from within. Kamran himself was shut up in the citadel precisely because of that fear of sedition, but also because there he could cause the least trouble, and devote himself fully to wine and opium. Yar Mohammad, seeking to inspire his soldiers to further acts of heroism, offered cash rewards for the heads of any Persian soldiers that could be brought to him. This unquestionably had the effect of spurring Herat's defenders on to a point, but it also meant that the sorties would end in a frenzy of beheading, and with each man returning within the walls with their captured heads, more eager to rush from the battlefield and exchange severed heads for money than to pursue the attack further. One man even brought the head of a fallen comrade to Yar Mohammad in the hope of a reward.[82]

At the outset of the Qajar siege, Yar Mohammad Khan received a letter from his brother who was then a hostage in the Qajar camp. The letter strongly advised him to surrender, for 'there is an European [*sic*] officer with it [the Qajar Army] who can in forty-eight hours raze Herat to the ground'.[83] Yar Mohammad's response was fittingly defiant, stating that as long he had a sword in his hand and a cartridge left to fire, he would resist to the very last. Yet it was not simply Yar Mohammad's resolve and unbending will that would protect the city. Herat, too, had a European within its walls and this European would prove more decisive than the Qajars' European. Lieutenant Eldred Pottinger, twenty-six years old and of the Bombay Artillery, a relative of another Great Game luminary, Henry Pottinger, happened to be in Afghanistan in the summer of 1837, mapping the routes, gathering information and assessing Russian influence in the country with a view to reporting back to India. He was the very archetype of a Great Game player: adventurous, idealistic, staunchly Christian and attracted by romantic notions of glory in far-flung imperial outposts. As he would have seen it, it was just his good luck that the Persians were preparing an attack as he slipped into Herat disguised as an Indian holy man on 18 August 1837. Pottinger's stay in Herat and his role in successfully defending the city from a monumental Qajar siege is legendary within British, Persian and Afghan history. His life was made into a best-selling early-twentieth-century book, *The Hero of Herat*, and his exploits as the city's saviour are feted in English and Afghan sources, albeit with more gusto in the former, and despised in Persian accounts.[84] One Afghan source refers to Pottinger as 'Sir Pottinger the Brave', and describes how he put his military expertise towards repairing the foundations of the 'sky high citadel of Herat'.[85] Another gives the following description:

> Sometime earlier, a certain Mr. Pottinger went to Herat dressed as an Islamic mulla [*sic*]. There, calling himself an Indian mawlawi [religious scholar], he opened a school, and began teaching students. He so ingratiated himself with Prince Kamran and Wazir Yar Muhammad Khan that whatever he suggested they listened to with the ear of acceptance and whatever he proposed they would not reject but would carry out. Besides conducting classes, he became the prayer leader at the Congregational Mosque of Herat and would guide the people in their prayers.[86]

The above suggestion that Pottinger preached sermons from the pulpit of the Friday Mosque in Herat is, unfortunately, not borne out by his own account, extracts of which appear in Kaye's epic three-volume *History of the War in Afghanistan* (Pottinger's original journal was lost in a fire). Yet the above assessment does give some indication as to the god-like status that his abilities and actions conferred upon his reputation. Pottinger himself admits to having some problems with both language and Islamic prayer rituals, and during the first weeks he spent in Herat he cut a cautious figure in the caravanserais which Forster and Conolly had occupied before him. The role he would play is one of sometime mediator, cajoler to battle, military strategist par excellence, and go-between for Herat and British interests. His diplomatic skills enabled him to secure loans from Herat's forty-family Jewish community, and his name would live on in Herat's nineteenth-century memory. One Afghan source, hostile to him in general, has him simply placing 'the foot of reconciliation between the different parties within the city'.[87] Whatever the truth of his actions, it is beyond doubt that Pottinger played a crucial role in Herat's defence. So crucial, in fact, that the Persians grew increasingly tired of his heroics, to the point where they cited his removal from Herat as a condition for negotiations. The city Pottinger would defend was, at the time of the arrival of the Persian troops into Khorasan, in a parlous state. His first impressions of the city were hardly encouraging:

The general appearance of the inhabitants was that of a poor and oppressed people. Dirty and ill-clad, they went about in a hurried, anxious manner, each man looking with suspicion into his neighbour's face. Few women were to be seen in the streets. It was hardly safe for a stranger to be abroad after sunset. Unless protected by an armed escort, there was too great a likelihood of being seized and sold into slavery. There was no protection for life, liberty or property. They who should have protected the people were the foremost of their oppressors. In 1837, such was the frightful misrule—such the reign of terror that had been established by the chartered violence of the rulers of the city, that the shops were closed before sunset, and all through the night the noise and uproar, the challengings [sic] and the cries for help were such as could scarcely have been exceeded if the place had been actually besieged.[88]

There is some confusion as to the exact point at which Pottinger made the transition from Indian impersonator to English saviour of Herat. One version has his disguise rumbled in the bazaar by a doctor who had known Conolly on his trip to Herat in 1830, whilst Kaye's account, drawing on Pottinger's own journal, suggests that his disguise was quickly, and intentionally, cast aside when he became aware of the advance of Persian troops, and that he began his audiences with Kamran and Yar Mohammad a matter of weeks after his entry into the city.[89] Another version can be found in British archival sources, letters to Pottinger from McNeill during the summer of 1838, as the siege became an intolerable blockade and entered its final stages. McNeill wrote the following, suggesting Pottinger had initially, like Conolly, announced himself as simply a journeyman soldier, not yet admitting the official nature of his business in Herat: 'I think the time is come when you may advantageously use the permission you have received, to announce yourself to Shah Kamran and his Minister as attached for the present to Captain Burnes' mission [then in Kabul, conducting ill-fated diplomacy with Dost Mohammad Khan], and employed here in a civil capacity to your own Government.' Ever the diplomat, and with a keen eye for protocol, McNeill also thinks Pottinger's elevated diplomatic status should entitle him to 'apartments in the citadel'.[90] In a coda to the letter McNeill added the following instruction, slightly confusing given Pottinger's role throughout the siege: 'You will of course abstain from taking any share in the military proceedings in Herat.'[91] Irony? Humour? Whatever the truth of the matter, the siege wore on into December, frozen and miserable, few decisive military victories being scored. Heratis concerned themselves with bounties on severed heads, and Persian generals' lust for personal glory provided a barrier to conclusive military action.

26 December 1837 was a day of bitter cold and incessant rain. The siege had entered into a harsh winter and provisions within the city were running low; sewers were blocked with refuse and corpses; Heratis tore down lintels and doors for firewood. Yar Mohammad sent Persian Shia prisoners from within Herat to Karokh for sale into the slave markets of Central Asia to raise money for the defence of the city. Most would die of starvation or cold before reaching their intended destination. In retaliation, the Qajars set about executing every single Herati prisoner in their care: the tragic back and forth of siege and resistance.[92] Eid festivities marking the end of Ramadan took place on 30 December inside Herat's Friday Mosque, but it was a sombre and depressing affair for the huddled masses who took part, the triumphalism of the earlier call to *jihad* totally absent. Rarely can Eid have been so pitifully celebrated in Herat.

If 1837 had seen almost constant fighting and bombardments, 1838 would herald negotiations and European political pressure brought to bear on all sides.[93] Britain sought an independent Herat; Persia coveted the symbols and realities of power over eastern Khorasan; and Russia sought to increase its influence throughout Central Asia. Herat simply wished to be left alone. Yet the city became the world's diplomatic problem. Representatives from two world powers, Britain and Russia, set up home in the Persian camp, occasionally making trips within the city's walls, and debating its future.[94] Sufi mystics were no longer the preferred medium of choice for diplomatic exchanges or hostage negotiations, and in their place professional diplomats and courtiers thrashed out the framework of sovereignty. The points debated between Qajar and Herati courts reflect a logical continuation, or possibly conclusion, of the themes raised with the entry of the Safavid army to Herat in December 1508, and in untangling these different skeins—Persian, Shia, Sunni, Afghan—we can again glimpse the complex identity of the city: a city both at the frontline of conflict and geopolitics and yet totally isolated. This paradox resurfaces as a key theme in Herat's history from the Russian invasion of 1979 to the present day.

Whilst the manners, tactics and political context clearly changed, the immutability of Herat's place at the edge of empires or nation states remains stubbornly the same. It is entirely typical of Herat's troubling enigma that these debates were less concerned with Herat itself than they were with wider strategic concerns: India, the Baltic, the Caucasus and Tehran. Even when Herat was the centre of the world, it still managed to remain ambiguous, impossible to pin down. Thousands would die from starvation, hypothermia and fighting as negotiations stretched from winter to spring and from summer to autumn.

On the frozen morning of 8 February 1838, Lieutenant Eldred Pottinger, sometime financier, occasional Indian mullah, intended defender of the city and now potential negotiator, made his way from the bomb-wrecked shell of a house he shared with a small family to one of Herat's twenty public baths. Within, Prince Kamran was seated almost entirely naked before some breakfast. He gave Pottinger instructions needed for a visit to the Qajar camp to discuss terms. Pottinger's return into Herat, however, as a storm broke overhead, brought with it no solution, no terms and no movement on the position of either party. The Qajars would not countenance Herat's independence, and Herat saw little point in surrender if it would mean Qajar revenge on the city and the concomitant loss of pride that such a capitulation would entail.[95] Yet more envoys came and went, and the Shah's demands slipped from their former position; by 20 February it was merely the outward signs of sovereignty that interested the Qajar camp: *khutbah* and *sikka*. The Herati response indicated a willingness to continue down an avenue of superficialities, but fighting trumped all and these overtures were swiftly forgotten. Faintly echoing the earlier artistic glories of Herat, one of the first Qajar requests of Kamran and Yar Mohammad was that the Heratis release the prominent calligrapher, Amir Abdul Rahman, 'for whom life is very difficult in Herat'.[96] It is not clear why exactly life was difficult for Abdul Rahman, but Herat still clearly held some vestigial allure for calligraphers and artists, and he refused to leave the walls of the city.

In March 1838, Qajar military ambitions, urged on by Russian advice from Count Simonich, had taken an alarming lurch to the east. Qandahar now became a target for the Persians' eastward push. Evidence for this was found in an intercepted draft of a treaty between the Qajar Shah and the ruler of Qandahar, Kohandel Khan, drafted under the auspices of Russian power. The treaty proposed a total restoration of the old Safavid territories encompassing Qandahar and Herat through an alliance between Qandahar and Tehran which would effectively deliver Herat to the Persians and Russia. Far from being Britain's defensive bulwark against Russian expansion, Herat could become the feared Trojan horse through which Russian and Persian troops would flood, eventually crossing into British India via Qandahar and Quetta. British alarm at this diplomatic smoking gun positively leaps from the thinning pages of the intelligence reports and diplomatic missives. Handwritten notes in the margin of the intercepted draft treaty, which now sits in the British Library, are shrill and hysterical. For the British, this was everything they had feared since they became aware of Herat's strategic importance. One diplomat writes that Herat's capitulation to the Persians and Russians 'would destroy our position in Afghanistan and place all or nearly all that country under the influence or authority of Russia and Persia'.[97] As the negotiations crawled along in the early spring of 1838, the importance of Herat to British security concerns seemed to increase just as the perceived danger of losing the city increased. A British diplomat present in camp noted confidently, 'If I could succeed by any means in preserving the independence of Herat, I should have secure from danger our influence in all the countries between the frontiers of Persia and the Indus.'[98] And yet the siege dragged on, with neither side making discernible headway.

That the Qajars enjoyed Russian support should be in no in doubt, as per an extremely flowery but steely missive from the Russian Ambassador Count Simonich to Mohammad Shah Qajar, in which an obsequious Simonich lauds Persia's rights over Khorasan, but simply asks them to put off the attack for at least two months until the weather improves so that the Russians could furnish the Qajars with more suitable and lasting assistance.[99] A collection of Persian letters between the various parties contains instances of the Qandahar ruler, Kohandel Khan, sending the Qajar court information on the British, their morale, their troop numbers, and showing clearly that Qandahar remains at the service of the Qajar courts in their attempts to capture Herat. Herat was effectively sandwiched. The British may have had their man in Herat, but the Persians had men and alliances throughout Afghanistan, to such an extent that both Yar Mohammad and Dost Mohammad, one an 'enemy' of Persia and the other its 'friend', were both sending letters of obedience to the Qajars at the same time.[100]

The arrival of spring in 1838, a joyous event in Herat in which the fertile Hari Rud oasis comes to life with purpose and beauty, also welcomed on 6 April 1838 the British diplomat John McNeill. McNeill, in the words of a French contemporary, belonged 'to that school of diplomatist who are perfectly happy in the midst of agitation'.[101] A phlegmatic approach to diplomacy would most definitely come in useful if the British were to remain true to their plan of an independent Herat in the pay of India Company rupees and as British India's first line of defence. McNeill's arrival, however, heralded a Qajar bombardment, as if to present to him Qajar intentions with regard to a negotiated settlement. The bombardment was immense, the fighting fierce, but somehow Herat still held on, fighting off disconnected Persian attacks. The following day, Major D'Arcy Todd, a Persian-speaking officer of the Bengal Artillery, entered Herat seeking to boost Herat's resolve, to assure Kamran of Britain's continued support for the principle and reality of an independent Herat and to get an idea of how long the city might hold out. It was, however, his uniform which had the greatest impact on proceedings. Pottinger notes how Todd's 'tight-fitting coat, the glittering epaulettes, and the cocked hat all excited unbounded admiration'.[102] Sartorial excellence was all very well and good, but the city needed concrete assurances and the tangible succour of money, food and weapons. But Pottinger and McNeill were adept at convincing Yar Mohammad to stick to his task of resisting the Persian attacks.[103] McNeill's visits, and those of Todd, within the city walls were conducted ostensibly to mediate between the parties, but in reality they sought to buy time for their own aims of securing India, all the while reassuring Herat of Britain's good intentions vis-à-vis its continued existence as an independent entity.

With the coming and going of the envoys and messengers within the city, Yar Mohammad Khan took advantage of the opportunity this presented to send out his own envoys, often his sons, to seek help from the northern provinces of Maimana and Shiburghan and Badghis. His efforts were mostly in vain.[104] These were infuriating months of diplomatic solipsism; back and forth went promises, all fruitless. McNeill, so comfortable in the midst of agitation, noted plaintively in April how those laying siege to the city suffered, and the countryside with them: 'This country is nearly exhausted of its supplies of every kind and the Persian troops are suffering great privations, many of them subsisting on the herbs which at this season spring up in this fertile soil.'[105]

Yet from it all, the faint outline of a treaty emerged: Qajar demands were that Herat, and Yar Mohammad Khan, desist from plundering trade and pilgrim routes into Persian Khorasan; that the remaining Persian and Shia prisoners not be executed; and that Kamran's status change from shah to prince, or *mirza*. Kamran, in turn, demanded to be on an equal footing with the Qajars, a 'brother'; that Herat remain politically independent; that the Qajars desist from sending troops to Herat; and that they desist from the notion of installing a Qajar garrison within the walls of Herat. These were the positions entrusted to McNeill and Todd in his brilliant epaulettes. Amidst it all, McNeill noted, perceptively, how the people of Herat were 'fighting for their independence' against the Persians, and he seems to have taken pity on the 'frail old man', Kamran, forced into possibly making yet another act of submission to the Qajars.[106] Yar Mohammad, acting in Kamran's place, for Kamran was constantly drunk, cautiously agreed to the treaty proposals, save those in which Herat gave up her independence, and promised to desist from plunder and the kidnapping of Shia pilgrims. Yet on 20 April, as McNeill exited Herat's walls, he heard news of the arrival in the shah's camp of Count Simonich—his Russian counterpart and Great Game nemesis. This had the effect of emboldening the Qajars in their dealings with the English, giving to their military weakness a misplaced sense of strength. Whilst McNeill urged caution and restraint, with an eye on a negotiated solution, Count Simonich advised the Persians on how to proceed with 'offensive operations against the town'.[107] Negotiations had been sabotaged by Russian imperial hubris.

At the height of the negotiations, a delegation of prisoners from within Herat's citadel approached Yar Mohammad and Kamran, pleading that they be allowed to leave for fear of death by starvation. Yar Mohammad Khan was left with no option but to allow them to leave, and in a moment of humanity Mohammad Shah Qajar allowed around 12,000 men, women and children to leave the city 'in a state of extreme hunger' and make their way to the Persians' camp, where they were fed and clothed and allowed to start new lives in and around Mashhad.[108]

The negotiations were essentially concerned with Herat's position in Khorasan, whether it marked the edge of Qajar Khorasan, or the eastern outpost of the Pashtun nation. Qajar Khorasan was a historical fiction, and the Pashtun, or Afghan, nation was in reality divided into three separate principalities, each bitterly opposed to the other. Even the notion that Herat formed such an inalienable part of Britain's security architecture is a contested one, and it seems that the different parties were all fighting for reasons and causes which had little relation to reality. The Qajar insistence on its inalienable right to Herat produced the following withering response from McNeill:

> It is stated that in histories and maps, Herat is described and laid down as belonging to the territory of Persia. The statement is correct; but Georgia, Shukkee, Erivan, Karabaugh, and even Mosul and Bagdad [all *sic*], have been also numbered amongst the hereditary dominions of Persia; but these places are now in the possession of others and no longer belong to the Persian Government.[109]

Definitely condescending, but undeniably true, McNeill had hit upon a sore point in the Qajar psyche. Meanwhile, amidst petty and taunting missives to frustrated Qajars, McNeill was writing in less assured tones to Lord Palmerston in London, nervous at the possibility of India's supposed gate being unpicked:

> If Persia should succeed in taking Herat, while Russia subdues Khiva and overawes Bokhara into submission, I conceive that it would be hopeless for us to attempt to preserve a footing in Afghanistan, or in Persia. But if we save Herat, and secure it, as it is now completely at our disposal, all Afghanistan will be tolerably secure behind it.[110]

In the early summer of 1838, the Governor General of India, Lord Auckland, had put in motion a plan which would lead to the lifting of the siege, cutting through interminable diplomacy. This was not an overland army setting out over Afghanistan, and nor was it subtle diplomatic pressure from afar on the courts of Tehran and St Petersburg. It was a naval–military expedition to the Persian Gulf. The British empire despatched the *Semiramis* and *Hugh Lindsay* steamer ships, and some 'vessels of war, with detachments of the 15th, 23rd and 24th Regiments, and the Marine battalion' to the Persian Gulf with the express intention of landing on the island of Kharg and subduing it.[111]

The theory was that naval pressure on the Persian Gulf might persuade the Qajars to lift the siege of Herat. The landing was a smooth one; on 19 June Captain Hennell was greeted by the island's governor and the troops disembarked, effectively setting the seal on a painless conquest of sorts. News of the British arrival in the Persian Gulf travelled fast to Herat and the Persian camp, and in a manner which totally distorted the truth of the landing. A naval landing had quickly become a massed land assault, and Persian fears of British troops marauding through the port city of Bandar Abbas, flooding down to Shiraz, the home of Hafez, and poised to subdue Fars soon became accepted fact. The expedition had been sent 'with a view to the maintenance of our interests in Persia', but the results were proving spectacular beyond British expectations.[112] The Qajar resolve to take Herat wilted dramatically in the face of these rumours, and one Persian account even claimed that the British had threatened to occupy Fars and might thus be in a position to overthrow the Qajar dynasty itself.[113] The effect of this diplomatic and military stranglehold over the Qajars was that they abandoned the siege of Herat and headed home.

On the night of 27 August 1839, the Persian army sounded the drums of retreat and called a halt to the siege of ten months and six days. A missive from a British official at camp near Herat, written at '8 am, September 9th, 1838' has 'the honour to report that the Persian Army has marched from this [Herat]'.[114] Qajar diplomatic reaction to this strategic reverse was a masterstroke of understatement. One Persian diplomat wrote that 'Had we known that our coming here might risk the loss of their [British] friendship, we certainly would not have come at all.'[115] An Afghan historian surveying the wreckage of a futile siege chose to put a poetic gloss on the Persian loss when he noted that the 'Qajar army departed marked with the pimple of regret'.[116] Pimple of regret or not, it appeared that the British had scored a strategic victory.

At the time it was assumed that the departure of Persian troops from Herat in the late summer of 1838 was a triumph for British interests; it proved the unassailable power of the British Navy, warned the Qajar forces against further meddling with British interests in the region, dealt the Russians a strategic defeat in Central Asia and, so the theory of Herat's importance went, saved British India from invasion.

Yet the aftermath of the siege was anything but glorious or successful for the British. The very same can be said for the Heratis who had been ejected from their city on the pretexts of sectarian conflict and a half-baked imperial security policy which did not stand up to reasoning. The departure of Persian troops settled little for Herat, or for Persia, and dragged the British into a war in Afghanistan from which few would emerge alive. For a triumphant success, 1838 achieved precious little. Those in Herat fortunate enough to survive were afflicted with many different types of diseases, paralysis and strokes on account of the suffering and the mental anguish that they were forced to endure; 'still to this day [1905] the memory of this time lives on in the minds of the people of Herat'.[117]

Herat was a desolate plain after the departure of Qajar and Russian troops, devastated from months of conflict; the 'great emporium of Asia' was reduced to its very barest bones.[118] Around 8,000 people had remained in the city, a dramatic fall from the 45,000–70,000 estimated in the years prior to the siege. Major Todd noted in 1839 that 'not more than one tenth of the houses in the city are inhabited'. He went on to describe how the remaining houses were 'deserted and ruined: the bazaar consists of about one hundred shops, chiefly of the necessaries of life, beyond which there is scarcely anything procurable in the place'. The city's population was made up mostly of 'soldiers, retainers and dependents of the Vizier [Yar Mohammad]'.[119] It is with no little irony that Todd notes that the fortifications of Herat had been so badly damaged that he estimated that it would take only 'a few hundred resolute men' to attack and hold this weakened city and fortress.[120] The French scholar and wanderer Joseph Ferrier passed through Herat in 1845 and noted that it was 'impossible to conceive the reckless devastation committed by the Persian soldiers in the principality of Herat during the ten months of the siege of its capital: they made a perfect desert of that once rich and fertile country'. The city was 'nothing but a mass of shapeless ruins; it was in fact a heap of cinders, ruin and desolation'.[121]

* * *

It was around the time when Qajar siege guns were battering the ancient citadel of Herat, messengers were scuttling in and out of the city walls and phlegmatic diplomats were debating the future of the world that the British began their first of four ill-fated entries into Afghanistan. Using reasoning—Russophobia and the defence of India—which had been applied to Herat, British policy edged towards a military expedition to replace Afghanistan's king, Dost Mohammad, with an exiled Sadozai of Herat, Shah Shujah al-Molk.[122] The English believed that an alliance with Shah Shujah would forestall the Persians at Herat, prevent the spread of Russian influence southwards and keep Dost Mohammad Khan out of the Punjab. British victory in Herat, surprisingly, did little to shift them from these policies.

Accordingly, in the summer of 1838, Sir William Macnaghten, Secretary to the Secret and Political Department in Calcutta and a well-connected linguist, put forward a plan by which Ranjit Singh (1780–1839), the Sikh ruler of the Punjab and an avowed enemy of Dost Mohammad, might assist in overthrowing Dost Mohammad and retaking Afghanistan for the Sadozai ruling house.[123] Shah Shujah, in return for Ranjit Singh's help, would abandon his claims to Peshawar, thus shrinking Afghanistan and denying it a winter capital. Few saw this as a sensible idea; Arthur Conolly had prophetically remarked in 1830 that Dost Mohammad is 'widely famed for the excellence of his rule', adding with prophetic understatement that 'the inhabitants of Caubul [sic] would probably be sorry to see him supplanted'.[124] The charming Scot, talented diplomat, Afghan veteran and explorer Alexander Burnes, better informed than most on Afghan politics at that time (he had spent time with each of the main protagonists: Shah Shujah, Dost Mohammad and Ranjit Singh), was adamant that any such move against Dost Mohammad would only end in disaster.[125] With the siege of Herat in full swing in June 1838, and Ranjit Singh more than happy to wave goodbye to Afghan claims on Peshawar in exchange for tacit approval of the British plan, a secret deal was struck in Lahore amongst British representatives, Ranjit Singh and Shah Shujah, setting the seal on British plans to invade Afghanistan and place Shah Shujah on the throne.[126] Herat was to be left alone, and in an implicit admission of its effective isolation, the parties to the treaty promised that 'When Shah Shuja [sic] gains full control over Kabul and Qandahar, he will in no way interfere or meddle in the lands subject to his nephew, the wali of Herat [Prince Kamran].'[127] Lord Auckland, with more than a hint of hyperbole, stated that so long as Dost Mohammad was in power in

Kabul, there remained no hope that 'the interests of our Indian empire would be preserved inviolate'.[128] Afghanistan was to become a British dependency, in theory.

The Army of the Indus, in Lord Auckland's grand phrasing, marched over the Bolan Pass: 15,000 troops and 30,000 hangers on, 'bearers, grooms, dhobi-wallahs, cooks and farriers', and very few Afghans amongst them heralding the return of Shah Shujah to Afghanistan.[129] There was a touch of hubris and a touch of farce to the British entry into Afghanistan: one officer had two camels laden with nothing but cigars; others brought their foxhounds.

In late June 1839, Shah Shujah made what must surely rank as one of the least popular returns to the throne of an exiled monarch. He paraded through Kabul wearing robes that shone and sparkled with the lustre of precious stones, robes which covered a distinct lack of tangible regal lustre. British observations of this re-entry into Kabul were withering in their assessment, and equally alarmed at the new king's unpopularity. Whispers of rural resistance from Baluchi tribesmen and Shah Shujah's hostile welcome back to the throne were all ominous signs of the difficulties that the British would face in Afghanistan. Infuriatingly for the British, the man whom they had come to depose, Dost Mohammad, was nowhere to be found. He eventually handed himself in to the British only to be shipped off to India where a comfortable, and temporary, exile awaited him. The 'del' brothers and cousins of Qandahar fled to the court of the Qajars, where they were received with open arms.

Herat, a Sadozai enclave, jealously independent and cautiously pragmatic, saw the influx of English troops as a threat, but a distant threat all the same. One Herati chronicler described these events with something approaching indifference, but in the same breath, and with a nod to various literary conceits, also described Herat's furious spring floods erupting from the Hari Rud, the water racing towards the town with a tumultuous energy. Stories began to swirl around the country telling of British soldiers interfering with Afghan women, and in these actions, Riyazi notes, 'the seeds of revenge had been planted in the fertile breasts of that honor-conscious and brave group of Afghans'.[130]

Herat's courtiers hurried to Tehran to complain of the English troops' lusty behaviour, and local mosques duly proclaimed the name

of the Qajar monarch, making a mockery of the British 'victory' of a
year previous. Allegiances could, it seems, change in the blink of an
eye. Riyazi wrote that 'the majority of people in Afghanistan prepared
themselves to align their interests and thoughts with the nation and
government of Iran, and to resist the English'.[131] Given Riyazi's Shia
beliefs, we might take that last point with a pinch of salt; Afghanistan's
Sunnis loathed the Qajars largely because of the latter's Shia beliefs. Yar
Mohammad's and Herat's preciously guarded independence now
seemed under serious threat, especially if the British saw fit to renege
on their earlier promise to leave Herat alone, and instead incorporate
the city in a greater Afghan nation under the rule of the puppet Sadozai
king, Shah Shujah. A new alliance would have to be forced, between
Herat and Qajar Persia against the British. Yar Mohammad, between a
rock and a hard place, would rather ally himself with those who had
battered and starved his city into near submission not eighteen months
ago than embrace the British invaders.

D'Arcy Todd, he of the brilliant epaulettes, made another entry into
the city in the spring of 1839 to prevent Herat falling under the sway
of the Qajars. Britain sought a political dependency in Herat; Herat had
just fought a bitter siege for its independence; Persia's laissez-faire
hands-off approach was just about tolerable, but direct interference in
Herat would not be tolerated. Todd's instructions were to sign a treaty
with Kamran binding the latter to Britain, to repair the city's defences,
and to regenerate livestock and agriculture. This was nineteenth-century nation-building to get Herat back on its feet. (Critics of Western
intervention who blithely argue for more 'specialist' knowledge as a
panacea to cure all developmental and political ills in Afghanistan
would do well to read of Todd's experiences in Herat.) In an attempt
to kick-start Herat's recovery, taxes of all kind were postponed until
the harvest of 1840, and this alleviated a measure of discomfort for the
ravaged province.[132] On reflection, it seems that attempting a new
beginning with the old guard—Yar Mohammad and Kamran Shah—
was a foolish undertaking, but with few other options available, the
British felt that with gold, good intentions and 'right' on their side,
little could go wrong. They were to be proved that much could go
wrong; from the very beginning, scuffles, tension and threats were the
currency of diplomatic exchanges at this time, as well as a prodigious

flow of East India Company rupees. Pottinger sounded an early note of caution against simply buying one's way out of trouble: 'however profuse might be our liberality, we could never hope to satisfy the unbounded expectations of a greedy government, and an impoverished people'. He continued, prophetically: 'When we ceased to give [money], our friendship would be looked upon as worthless, and our presence would cease to be desired.'[133] As so many would later find, myself included, once the payments began, scaling them down was a very difficult task. Yar Mohammad too remedied his situation with money and security. His first action was to turn to the slave trade to replenish Herat's coffers; he sold criminals to the Uzbeks for a profit. Unfortunately, this had the effect of driving down crime and thus shrinking the pool of potential slaves, so he sent his men into the bazaars to stir up trouble, consequent upon which men were arrested, giving him fresh criminals for the slave markets of Central Asia.[134]

Palmerston's dictum, 'whilst enemies come and go and friends change, it is interests that remain constant', could well have been written about Herat at this or any time. It was as if the war against the Qajars had never happened; Herat turned back to the Persians for protection, in opposition to the British who had been their erstwhile saviours from the Persians. Kamran Shah wrote to Mohammad Shah Qajar in the spring of 1841 that 'It is clear and evident to all men that Herat is in Khorasan, and is part of the kingdom of Persia.'[135] In the same breath, Kamran paints a picture of ruinous subjection to the British, as Afghanistan suffered miseries under the oppression of infidel foreigners; infidel foreigners who were trying to rebuild the city's fortifications, revive trade and agriculture and put a stop to the slave trade. Kamran stressed to Mohammad Shah Qajar that 'my heart is with Persia and with Islam' and professed that his 'hands will never be loosened from the skirts of the Government of His Majesty'.[136] Yar Mohammad wrote to Mohammad Shah in the same tone, describing Todd as 'one who walks in the way of fraud, deceit and treachery'; he invited the Qajars to come to Herat to deliver him from the English.[137]

Reading the different letters and proclamations of the time, those going into Herat and those leaving the city, it is possible to be confused by Yar Mohammad's baffling inconsistency: one minute a friend of the British and an implacable foe of the Shia Persians, and the next a staunch ally in faith with Tehran, the 'protector of the Muslim faith against the infidel English'. Yet for Herat to pursue a policy which permanently alienated a global empire, the British, or to make an avowed enemy of their neighbour, Qajar Persia, would have been unthinkable. Yet it is the constancy of Yar Mohammad's ruthless opportunism, his dogged determination to survive at all costs, that is the thread running through these years, reflecting Herat's own need to be flexible in navigating a course through this intensely complicated period. McNeill's rather elegant assessment of Yar Mohammad's politics encapsulates this, the core of Herat's enigma: 'His love of independence is gratified by the very act of his submission.'[138]

Herat accordingly once again became a hotbed of intrigue, some of which was geared towards killing Todd, but most of which was geared towards killing various members of Herat's ruling families. At one formal dinner Yar Mohammad became so drunk that he fell senseless under the table, at which point the assembled nobles, enemies to a man, sought Todd's permission to cut off Yar Mohammad's lolling head. Todd denied them such permission, 'being obliged to sit up with him the whole night to save his life'.[139] In the burning summer of 1840, daily intrigues of impending arrests of the British and their informants hung over the city; few would leave their houses for fear of arrest. No matter how much money the English spent in Herat, they could not secure Herat's allegiance or cooperation. In January 1841 Yar Mohammad sent a confidential emissary to the court of Tehran with a request for guns to enable him to march on Helmand.[140]

Despite the many difficulties faced by the resilient Todd, he continued to be beguiled by the city's strategic importance, firing off memoranda by the day on its commanding regional position, its fertile oasis and the importance it retained for the defence of British India. Britain should occupy Herat, for it 'would be impregnable to an Asiatic Army, and to a European army it would offer an opposition so protracted and embarrassing, as would probably lead to his discomfiture'.[141] One cannot help but admire Todd's optimism and his unshakable faith in Herat's fortress, but the daily problems that faced him should surely at some point have hinted at the practical difficulties of holding Herat for a protracted period of time, or Afghanistan for that matter. It is true that British possession of Herat might 'put Russian and France off a possible invasion' of Afghanistan, but it might also destroy Britain in the process.

In one missive of 8 December 1840, Todd finishes his report on a very positive note indeed, by declaring that the 'aspect of affairs at Heraut [*sic*] is tranquil and I have every reason to believe that the authorities of this place will accede to any requests which may be proposed to them by the British Government'.[142] Todd would not get a chance to solve the Herat crisis, for in March 1841 he was hounded out of the city by Yar Mohammad. Only a few days after his departure from Herat to Qandahar, his former residence was attacked by a mob, foreshadowing more serious events yet to take place in Kabul. Todd's failings in Herat contained serious warning signs for the British and their involvement in Afghanistan in 1841 and onwards. He could only watch as British policies in Afghanistan unravelled with prodigious speed.[143] Parallels with the most recent conflict in Afghanistan are too obvious to pass without comment, but too complex a field to enter without courting controversy. Suffice to say, the frustrations at corruption and deceit that dot Todd and Pottinger's letters from Herat to Kabul, Calcutta and London are almost direct replicas of those I have heard in so many embassies and offices throughout Afghanistan; corruption will destroy Afghanistan faster than fundamentalist Islam or Western interventions ever could. Similarly, the frustrations of Yar Mohammad at being dictated to by infidel foreigners read like so many snippets of conversations I have overheard at the edges of meetings in which the protagonists assumed me not to understand what they were saying, being myself an infidel foreigner.

From the sanctity of Herat, Todd had estimated that the news of the advance of the British army into India would 'strengthen our position in this place'.[144] The effect, however, was the polar opposite. Stories of British soldiers' dealings with Afghan women spread throughout the country, and news from Khiva, via a resident British agent there, said that the British were widely accused of 'having cast the Koran into the gutters of Cabool'.[145] Riyazi was in no doubt that it was Britain's transgressions into the sphere of Islam and Afghan customs that caused the uprisings which drove the British from Afghanistan in 1841: 'The English showed the hand of tyranny to the Afghan people, and it came to light that they had committed grave trespasses on the holy law of the *sharia*.'[146]

Somehow, Herat remained calm as tension in Kabul and the lands to its east and south rose to an uncomfortable pitch for the British.

The massacre of British troops and the 'bearers, grooms, dhobi-wallahs, cooks and farriers' who had accompanied the Army of the Indus over the Bolan Pass in the spring of 1839 is a well-told story: women and children sold into slavery, one lone figure, Dr Brydon, making his way, tottering half-dead on an emaciated horse, to the cantonment at Jalalabad and an army eviscerated, an empire humbled.[147] The Afghan defeat of the British and their massacre in the frozen passes on the way to Jalalabad affected matters little in Herat, for the seemingly eternal question as to whom Herat should be sovereign still endured. Ever-changing displays of loyalty and intrigue, skirmish and retreat, pockmarked the 1840s. Herat's status as a Sadozai enclave protected it from the worst of the Anglo-Afghan war, and geography shielded it, temporarily, from the return to power of Dost Mohammad.[148]

* * *

In 1851, the British diplomat Justin Sheil noted with frustration that 'The affairs of Herat appear to be involved in greater confusion from day to day.'[149] Proving Herat's reckless independence, as the English were being massacred by their hundreds in the passes on the way to Jalalabad, Yar Mohammad had celebrated his new-found power by resolving to conquer Ghur and Maimana for Herat, disdainful of the reality that Herat was a smallish state menaced on all sides by predatory powers. The taxes of Maimana and Ghur were diverted to Herat, and their princely offspring found themselves uneasy guests at Herat's once-great court.[150] The Sadozai line, so long inextricably linked with Pashtun rule over Herat and Afghanistan, had been extinguished by Yar Mohammad in 1842, although in reality it had for some years been little more than a stupefied fiction: a king under house arrest. An Afghan chronicler described the event with characteristic panache: 'Yar Mohammad threw Prince Kamran from the felicitous [*kamrani*] throne of Herat, and crowned him on the throne of imprisonment.'[151] Yar Mohammad at least had the decency to bury his ineffectual nemesis within the city. One of Shah Kamran's sons was later found in the poorer parts of Tehran, surrounded by Berber tribesmen and in a state of almost total destitution, living off strong spirits and opium, 'completely brutalised', on a small pension from the Qajar court.[152]

Yar Mohammad's rule was in part reform-minded. A functioning city was a prosperous one; a stable province could trade. His forceful rebuilding efforts, along with English gold, restored some of a city almost ruined by the siege of 1837. The poor and criminal classes, as so often before, were set to work rebuilding the citadel; and Yar Mohammad clamped down on the pillaging and looting that had so menaced Herat in the previous decades, after having allowed it to flourish whilst it suited his purposes. Corn duties were relaxed; agriculture was encouraged, along with better commerce. The account of Joseph Ferrier, a visiting Frenchman to Herat and Afghanistan in the mid 1840s, is one of the most fascinating and detailed accounts of Herat, full of insight and detail. His stay there convinced him that Yar Mohammad had put the government of Herat back on a firm, if not necessarily compassionate, footing. Yar Mohammad presaged a Stalinist approach to law and order, for:

> the means that he employed to attain this end [safe roads] were so terrible that to this day, when any article is by accident dropped on the roads, or even in the fields, no one dares to take it up; the first person who finds it informs, with the utmost speed, the nearest officer of police of the fact, whose duty it is to seek out the owner, and return it to him.[153]

Echoes of this strain of thinking can be found throughout Herat's history, a justification of harsh rule by strong men. I heard so many times, in prison and taxis or tea houses, that under the Taliban one could 'drop a gold bar on the street at night, and find it there in the morning', or how one could walk from Herat to Farah unmolested. These were fond retellings of tropes that reach back into Herat's deepest history, prizing strong rulers in times of crisis. At such times, stability and security trump all, and it is no surprise that as Herat faces a distinctly troubling future, some will idealise the security of Taliban Herat.

Yar Mohammad died in 1851, simultaneously reviled and revered on his death. Herat's shops shut in mourning; people wailed in the streets. A visitor to his tomb in 1857 found it 'desecrated', the head stone 'broken and thrown down'.[154] Public mourning had clearly given way to a more accurate assessment of his rule. His son, Sayyed Mohammad, succeeded to power, yet he lacked his father's authority, a fact strongly suggested by his immediate decision to head for the interior of the citadel and find some thick walls behind which to rule. A British description of him as 'profoundly incapacitated' does not differ from the Persian accounts, or indeed from an objective reading of his actions.[155] It was not long before he 'opened the hand of oppression' to the people of Herat, and he took to arranging the soldiers in the parade ground of Herat's citadel so that he might hurl abuse at their commanders. He also interfered with the pay of the soldiers, and fired large cannon balls at the side of the citadel in which royal prisoners were kept.[156] Exiling important members of his father's court only served to add more people to the already prodigiously long list of Herat's enemies.[157]

Politically, Sayyed Mohammad was in a delicate position. One British official reflected this when he wrote: 'This Chief [Sayyed Mohammad] has to fear not only the machinations of Kamran Shah's family, but of Kohendil Khan, and probably Dost Mahomed Khan [*sic*], and he may even be in doubt on the designs of Great Britain.'[158] It was only natural, therefore, that he would seek an alliance with Tehran. Amongst the many predatory powers hovering around Herat, at least Tehran showed some constancy in their desires. Sayyed Mohammad sent some special horses to Tehran, and in return he received 'some Austrian military tunics', which he then distributed to his soldiers in Herat.[159] Herat's soldiery were not best pleased with the tunics, nor with the requirement for them to shave their beards, and only deigned to wear them when the nobles of Sayyed Mohammad agreed to do so.

Britain's humiliating reverse at the hands of Dost Mohammad Khan had altered little as regards Herat's claim to be a 'key', a 'gate' or any other portal to India. Britain's relations with Tehran, in a similar vein, remained fraught with tension and mistrust. The Treaty of Peshawar, conducted between Dost Mohammad Khan and Britain in March 1855, caused Persia agitation, fearing as it did a united Afghanistan gathering strength in eastern Khorasan. A repeat of 1837–8 became increasingly likely, despite the fact that the addition of Sindh and the Punjab to the India dominions (1834 and 1849 respectively) had given India a naturally protected frontier to its north-west and possibly rendered obsolete Herat's claims to strategic pre-eminence. Yet Britain remained doggedly preoccupied with Herat, spooked at the appearance of Qajar troops in Mashhad and anti-British sermons in Tehran. British diplomatic files and intelligence reports from 1851–2 are full of erroneous reports of Persian annexations of Herat, and speculation, strenuously denied by the Qajars, that the Qajars sought to retake the city. Persian diplomatic letters, in turn, stress that Herat has *ab antiquo* formed part of eastern Khorasan, a Persian domain; whilst in the background, the Qajars made preparations to take Herat. British responses contained the vague threats and hints common to powerful empires. They expressed continued British support for an independent Herat, to be achieved, confusingly, 'by cultivating Affghan [*sic*] national feeling'.[160] As Sayyed Mohammad Khan struck coins and said prayers in the name the Qajar Shah Nasr al-Din shah in late 1852, a repeat of 1838 seemed increasingly likely.

In January 1853, Justin Sheil responded to the uncertainty by concluding a treaty with the Qajars, by which Tehran would refrain from interfering in the affairs of Herat, regardless of provocation from Qandahar or pleading from Herat.[161] Yet on 11 December 1855, the Qajars received just such a request from Herat: that Qajar troops head to the city to save it from the advances of Dost Mohammad, who had taken Qandahar in November of that year and was poised to attack. Nine days later, Persian troops made their way to Herat, with a logistical haste strongly suggestive of forward planning, to press their claims over eastern Khorasan. Meanwhile, a Persian diplomat was sent to Europe to negotiate a peaceful settlement with the British, to seek help from the French and to bargain for a loan from the Americans. Each side cast around for allies and leverage. The fall of the fortress of Ghurian in March 1856 to the Qajar troops indicated that an attack on Herat was imminent.

Some in London saw the causes of the siege as an unfortunate offshoot of an alleged affair conducted by a British diplomat in Tehran, Charles Augustus Murray, a quarrelsome and difficult man unsuited to diplomacy, with a Persian royal lady in waiting. An editorial in *The Times* concluded as follows: 'While the broadsheet at breakfast proceeds on the solemn supposition that it is all about Herat, the talk of the dinner table equally takes for granted that it is about a Persian courtier's runaway mistress.'[162] Despite the neat and enticingly romantic reasoning, this Anglo-Afghan-Persian war had very little to do with a Persian mistress, and much more to do with Britain's preoccupation with the role that Herat might play for the security of British India.

On the eve of the siege, Herat was divided into different factions, all competing for power. Riyazi's retelling of the chaos is tinged with sarcasm, as he noted that 'three and a half sultans were crowned in the city in one day'.[163] One, near to the Timurid era *burj-e khakestar*, the Tower of Cinders, 'beat the drums of kingship in his own name', whilst another announced his political office in his own quarter of the bazaar. In the Shia quarter of the city, near to the Shia shrine of Abdullah Mesri, a group of Qizilbash took for themselves independent authority. From the chaos of a threeway urban brawl, the fighters looked up to see an advancing Qajar army.[164]

The Afghan vizier who rallied the resistance against the Persians was in no doubt as to the parameters of this conflict: Afghan Sunni against Persian Shia. He stated simply that 'the Afghans, as good Sunnis, would never submit to the supremacy of the Persian Shia'.[165] A report from within Herat at the time quotes a Herati man opining that 'we esteem Sadozais better than Barakzais, but between Shias and Sunnis, there can be no question'.[166] Sides were taken along these lines, and early attempts by *farsiwans* (Persian-speaking Shia) to allow the Qajars into the city resulted in a first assault on the city, ropes and turbans hung over the city walls to allow the Persians to scale them and briefly take the bazaar on 28 August 1856; the reprisals, after the attack had been beaten off, were swift and merciless.[167] Herat's then leader, the Pashtun Essan Khan, wrote to Charles Murray in Tehran of desolation and want in Herat. The letter recalls with fondness the twin saviours of Herat: Eldred Pottinger and the British. Essan Khan begged the British to send another agent to guide the city through this difficult period, taking on the guise of subservient vassal in describing himself as 'your slave' and imploring Murray to 'send your Commissioners quickly, that they may assume the control over your country and people, and let them rescue them from the bond of death, disgrace and infamy'.[168] Such was the desperation within Herat for British assistance that certain members of the city hoisted the Union Jack in Major Todd's former garden, hoping it might frighten the Persians into retreat.[169] A man named Mullah Omar, who was said to have been of service to the British in the late 1830s, was ready to do the same in 1856. As if to cap the confusion, as the Persians moved in on the city and the skirmishes retreated to under the outer walls, an ammunition dump exploded killing over 360 Qajar soldiers. Herat's governor, Mohammad Yusuf, was betrayed and handed over; he would later end up in one of Tehran's very worst prisons.[170]

1. A Timurid Prince seated in the garden. Herat, 1425–30. Smithsonian Unrestricted Trust Funds, Smithsonian Collections Acquisition Program, and Dr Arthur M. Sackler.

2. Iskandar visits the wise man in the cave, Kamaluddin Behzad, Herat, 1494/5. © The British Library Board, Or.6810, f.273.

3. Gawhar Shad Mausoleum and Minarets. 1935, from A. Scheibe (1937): *Deutsche im Hindukusch*, © Stiftung Bibliotheca Afghanica, CH-4416 Bubendorf.

4. Sketch of Mosalla Complex on the eve of its destruction, Afghan Boundary Commission, July 1885, © Stiftung Bibliotheca Afghanica, CH-4416 Bubendorf.

5. Ekhtiar al-Din citadel and city scene, c. 1934, © Stiftung Bibliotheca Afghanica, CH-4416 Bubendorf.

6. Man standing at prayer close to City Walls, 1942, from R. Stuckert (1942): *Brief an Herrn und Frau Rietmann-Haak vom 5.Oktober 1942*, © Stiftung Bibliotheca Afghanica, CH-4416 Bubendorf.

7. Herat's Timurid ruins, Winter 2014. Author's own.

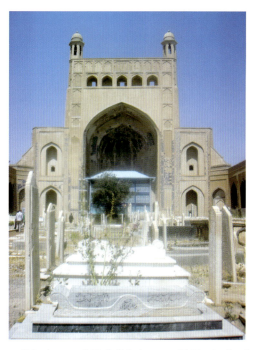

8. Gazur Gah shrine of Abdullah Ansari, 2009. Author's own.

9. Shopkeeper within Herat's Old City walls, Summer 2010. Author's own.

10. Friday Mosque, Herat, 2014. Author's own.

11. Ismail Khan depicted, radio in hand, on the celebratory front cover of *Ettefaq Islam*, 21 April 1992, Herat. Author's own.

12. Monument to mujahideen soldiers in Herat, Qandahar gate, 2014. Author's own.

13. Sayfuddin, glass blower, 2014. Author's own.

14. Ekhtiar al-Din citadel, 2014. Author's own.

15. Gravestones in Gazur Gah, 2014. Author's own.

16. Ekhtiar al-Din citadel, 2014. Author's own.

Turcoman tribes raided the hinterlands with impunity, embracing the commercial opportunities offered to them by chaos. Within Herat, 7,000 men at arms huddled together under a tattered Union Jack.[171]

On the occasion of the Qajar shah's birthday on 8 October 1856, Nasr al-Din Shah spoke at length about his attempts to take Herat. Responding to queries from his courtiers as to why it was taking so long for Herat to fall, he pointed out that it had taken Nader Shah Afshar over a year to take the city. Yet despite this apparent wavering at court, there is a definite sense that the Persians had resolved to take Herat for good, as if they sensed British weakness against the backdrop of British struggles in the Crimean War and the Charles Murray affair. In these endeavours, French military advisers assisted the Qajars, offering advice and insight both in Tehran and in the field. A British official had intercepted a letter from a French military figure advising the Qajars in their efforts to take Herat, in which the Frenchman states decisively that '*Nos travaux de siège avancent, et dans une dixaine de jours nous arriverons au fosse.*' It seemed as if this might be the moment when Persian troops finally subdued Herat. Meanwhile, Herat had taken to sending frantic appeals to their erstwhile enemy Dost Mohammad in Qandahar requesting assistance, pleading for anything he could spare. This was both a surprising and yet not surprising reversal from the previous overtures to the British earlier in the summer.[172] If 1837–8 had been long drawn out, this crisis was to have a reckless quality to it, speeding along with undue haste and confused abandon. The siege itself was bitter and ruinous. Tunnels dug under the city's outer walls and towers under the supervision of a French military expert, Bohler, had the desired effect of weakening its defences. Herat ceded to the Qajar troops on 25 October 1856. The Qajars had finally retaken Herat, a city which had eluded them since the seventeenth century, dominated by Pashtun Sunnis and cut off from its perceived home in a Persian state built on the ruins of the Safavid empire.

After their conquest, the Qajars sent an agent to sound out possible alliances with Dost Mohammad in Qandahar, for they wished to expand their influence right to the eastern edges once ruled by the Safavid predecessors. Meanwhile, a French diplomat tried to wrong-foot the British by stating confidently that 'the Persians have no intention to retain Herat even if they succeed in capturing it'.[173] This could

217

not have been further from the truth: Husam al-Saltanah, the Qajar governor of Khorasan, turned his guns towards Qandahar. For the Persians, the conquest of Herat was an exercise in *khelat pushi*, 'placing the robe of submission', and this phrase, used by Riayzi, is a clear indication that the Qajars had come to claim what they felt to be theirs by right.[174] They were restoring the region to its Safavid status quo ante, and they did not intend to give it up. A British agent in Herat, a trader named Sayyed Husain, confirmed these intentions through overheard gossip doing the rounds of Herat's teahouses and bazaars. He could note with certainty that the Qajars were looking for alliances with different Afghan and Persian tribes 'who may be said to hold the keys of Herat', for they wished to consolidate their hold over it.[175] The fall of Herat to the Persians dealt such a serious blow to Anglo-Persian relations that British agents in Persia were either expelled or felt the need to leave of their own accord.[176]

British policy-makers were caught out and confused as to the mass of conflicting reports flooding into offices in Tehran and India. Britain still desired an independent Herat against Persian designs, yet worried about siding with Dost Mohammad for fear that his death might unleash unmanageable chaos in Afghanistan and undo the very stability that they sought. The British Prime Minister duly warned the Qajar court that unless the Persians withdrew, Britain would 'adopt such measures as a regard for its own honour and its own interests may prescribe; and will hold itself absolved from any responsibility for the consequences of those measures however disastrous for Persia they may prove'.[177] This was as close as they could get to a declaration of war without actually making one. Bursts of diplomacy shot across Europe and the region; Charles Murray, seething in Baghdad, urged war on Persia, possibly for personal reasons. Dost Mohammad, unsurprisingly, would not come to the aid of the British. A declaration of war eventually came from Calcutta on 1 November 1856. The corresponding declaration of a *jihad* against the British from the Shia *ulema* of Persia set the seal on a war. Once again, naval power held the key, and Britain sent warships and soldiers into the Persian Gulf to attack Persia on its own soil, to squeeze it into abandoning the occupation of Herat.

The appropriately named Major General Stalker occupied the island of Kharg on 4 December 1856, and on 10 December the port of Bushire in the Persian Gulf surrendered to the British ships. When news of the fall of Bushire and Kharg reached Persian diplomats in Paris, negotiations moved up a gear and were conducted alongside real fighting between Qajar troops and the East India Company's soldiers in Khoramshahr and the southern provinces of Qajar Persia. British naval power subdued Khoramshahr in March, and East India Company soldiers came ashore to face abandoned posts. In Paris, Persian diplomats urgently sought peace at any price for fear that their nation was on the verge of being overrun by the British empire. With the mediation of Napoleon III, and after reaching terms which were as ruinous as the 1828 Treaty of Turkmanchai, the Persians and the British signed the Treaty of Paris on 4 March 1857. Once again, Herat had been saved by British naval interventions in the Persian Gulf, and Qajar Persia had been humiliated. It is difficult not to feel some sympathy for the Qajars, whose claim on Herat was at least as strong as that of the Pashtun tribes who had moved to the city in the seventeenth century, and clearly stronger than that of the East India Company.

The Treaty of Paris effectively barred Persia from Herat, beginning with the disingenuous preamble that the treaty was 'sincerely animated by a desire to put a stop to the evils of a war which is contrary to their friendly wishes and dispositions, and to re-establish on a solid basis the relations of amity which had so long existed between the two Exalted States'.[178] Articles 5 and 6, respectively, required the Qajars to withdraw from Herat within three months of signing the treaty, and demanded that Qajars 'relinquish all claims to sovereignty over the territory and the city of Herat or the countries of Afghanistan, and never to demand from the Chiefs of Herat, or of the countries of Afghanistan, any mark of obedience, such as coinage or "Khootbeh" [khutbah] or tribute'. Nasr al-Din Shah further promised 'to abstain hereafter from all interference with the internal affairs of Afghanistan' and to 'recognise the independence of Herat and the whole of Afghanistan, and never to attempt to interfere with the independence of that state'. Any problems arising between Herat and Tehran would be mediated by Britain, presumably in the interests of the East India Company. The scars of this loss ran deep for Qajar Persia. A Qajar diplomat writing over two decades later in 1880, as Herat again began to occupy acres of newsprint, said that the loss of Herat in 1857 'has

left a festering wound in the heart of Persia which hitherto has seemed
to defy cure'.[179] The minister went on to say that without Herat, it was
impossible for Persia to exist. With such sentiments still pulsing
through diplomacy so long after 1857, it is easy to see how a simple
treaty would not stop Persian longing for the Pearl of Khorasan.

* * *

The year 1838 changed little; neither did 1842; nor was 1857 any different. In many ways the Treaty of Paris was little more than a clerical
blot, soon to be wiped away by the momentum of events. In its immediate aftermath, Herat had the misfortune to be engulfed by successive
floods, heaping natural disaster on man-made ruin; the resulting famine
of 1858 was a catastrophe for the people of the province and city.[180]
The Qajar appointment of Sultan Ahmad Khan, a Pashtun with opportunistic loyalties to Qajar Persia, had clearly shown their intentions
vis-à-vis treaty obligations of neutrality. Within two years, Herat was
minting coins with the name of the Qajar shah, Nasr al-Din Shah
(r. 1848–96), on one side, displaying Herat as the *Dar al-Nasrat*, 'The
Abode of Victory'; while the other side bore an inscription glorifying
Nasr al-Din Shah Qajar.[181] Prayers rang out in the name of the Qajar
sovereigns, and life continued largely as before. Yet some within Herat
felt abandoned by the Qajars, left to endure rule under the Pashtun
yoke. Shortly after the treaty was concluded, a collection of prominent
ulema, political and society figures sent letters to Tehran signalling their
displeasure at the Qajars' abandonment of Herat. Herat's aristocrats,
religious leaders and military chiefs requested that 'they be placed
under the shadow of a God-fearing government in which the people of
Herat are protected from tyranny', presumably Pashtun tyranny.[182]
Persian documents detailing Turcoman and tribal raiding blighting
Herat and its surrounds, and European accounts of crippling and often
arbitrary taxation on merchant and citizen alike, all lent some credence
to the notion that paternal, and distant, protection from Qajar Tehran
was preferable to the more uncertain future of total independence
under Pashtun governance.

In the years following 1857, Britain gradually came to the conclusion that Herat was a headache, and one from which they benefited
little. Yet they persisted in the old theory of Herat as India's phantom

portal. There is a disparity between briefing notes which acknowledge the city as the Gate to India, and the turbulent realities of political life in Khorasan, which showed how difficult it would be for an army to take Herat, restock and replenish itself and then march peacefully through Sistan and Qandahar, onwards into India. British experiences in Afghanistan and Persia had surely demonstrated that Afghanistan is a difficult country through which to march an army of any size. By subduing Persia with naval attacks on the Persian Gulf, the British had shown that Herat might not be the 'key' to India, and that there were many ways to secure India's security, few of which were to be found in Herat. The pithy summation of one English diplomat in Tehran is worth quoting in full as a window into Britain's troubling strategic relationship with Herat as it stood in 1859:

> Of all the schemes that England has ever undertaken, none have cost her proportionately more, or have been altogether so unsuccessful, as her attempts at establishing an independent state in Herat. Two wars, the first the most disastrous on record, together with an expenditure of some seventeen millions of money, have been the result of the project; and the effect produced is, that while a Persian nominee, supported by Persian money and Russian counsels, acknowledges in words that Herat is independent (although he himself openly once a week confesses the sovereignty of Persia, by having the 'Khutbah' read in the name of the Shah and sees two provinces of Herat occupied by the Russians), we are content. Surely it requires no demonstration to prove that a continuance of such a policy would be an error.[183]

Yet continuance was exactly the path pursued. Presumably the price of ignoring Herat was far too high to contemplate.[184] London and Calcutta duly returned to well-worn discussions of equally well-worn routes linking Persia to India, Herat to India, and came to similarly drastic conclusions about the dangers of letting Herat fall, either to the Persians or to Dost Mohammad, whose advanced age and infirmity promised upheavals should he die whilst trying to take the city. Diplomats in London and India worried incessantly about the Herat–Qandahar route along which 'Alexander the Macedonian' had so successfully marched. Yet another cause for alarm and panic was the lavishly expensive visit to Herat in 1858 of a Russian academic, N. V. Khanikov, during which he spent his way around the city's bazaars and courts, scattering gold in the hope of trade and political alliances. A loan was promised and a treaty was negotiated between Russia and Herat, providing for a permanent Russian presence there; all the while Count Anichkov, the Russian minister in Tehran, courted Sultan Ahmad. Britain was reluctant to send another man to Afghanistan for fear of him being hacked to pieces in the mode of Alexander Burnes in Kabul in 1842; but as fear increased out of all proportion to political prudence and history, something clearly had to be done—again.

In October 1860, Britain and India decided to send another 'plain dealing Englishman' to Herat: Lieutenant General Sir Lewis Pelly, Secretary to the British Legation at the Court of the Shah of Persia. He set out from Tehran for Herat on 10 September 1860. A Persian-speaking diplomat, Pelly was tasked with discovering what Herat felt towards Persia and Russia, while armed with the dictum that the English government wished to see Herat's sovereign 'independent and prosperous within the limits of his own territory'.[185] Pelly's early assessments of Afghanistan were not promising, however; he refers to Afghanistan as a 'combustible tract of country… between Meshed and our frontier of India'.[186]

Pelly's letters to London, Calcutta and Tehran bristle with unease as a result of information gleaned from discussions with Afghan ministers in Herat and bits and pieces picked up from gossip and chatter in the city's bazaars. Afghanistan, he felt, was on the precipice of another round of internal fighting, and with the uncertainty surrounding Dost Mohammad's looming succession (he was over seventy and increasingly ill) it was not surprising that Herat practically begged Pelly to remain in Herat and put the weight of the British behind an independent city.[187] But as Qajar armies fought Turcoman tribes north of Herat and Dost Mohammad plotted to unseat his son in law, Sultan Ahmad, from the throne, the notion that an English presence in Herat could keep it independent went very much against the grain of history and logic.[188] This assessment, however, was not solely the hubris of empire and strategic folly; merchants in Herat, and particularly Hindu merchants, had long sought out the protection of the British empire and welcomed Britain's perceived fairness in mediating between different parties, be it in political or commercial disputes.[189] Conolly, Lal and Todd all fielded the same requests. From a political standpoint, much as had been the case

earlier in the century, it is not surprising that Herat sought British protection at this point. After all, had not the British effectively saved Herat
from direct Persian occupation on two separate occasions?

Qajar relations with Herat were similarly complicated, and Persian
displays of affection towards Herat hid a very real frustration with the
tendencies of Herat's nobilities in the direction of creative accounting.
Nasr al-Din Shah Qajar, always willing to involve himself in the minu-
tiae of policy and diplomacy and a keen practitioner of the art of marginalia, wades into a discussion on the debts of a certain Sardar Sultan
Naail Khan. The frustrations with their sometime allies, sometime
enemies are palpable, whilst also being amusing. Nasr al-Din Shah ful-
minates: 'I have recently had Afghans at our court, and I can tell you
that aside from idle bragging and exorbitant claims, you will get nothing from them—you are in no way to give them any more money as if
you do it will be as good as lost from you the moment you hand it
over.'[190] (When I told this story to a Herati friend as we discussed
Herat's recent history over a cup of tea in his office, we both saw its
comic potential.) Yet the Qajars also played an active part in the running of the province at this time, through the granting of land and
supervision over appointments to positions within the Shia clergy. One
edict from Nasr al-Din Shah concerned the land of a Sayyed Abu al-
Hassan Khan in late August 1860; the document praised the activities
of this Herati holy man and advised that his lot should be increased.[191]
This is a pleasing insight into Nasr al-Din Shah's deeply personal
involvement in the running of Herat, an indication of the depth of
feeling the Qajar court attached to the city and what it represented.
Qajar Persia's roots in Herat were, it seems, deep and founded on sect
and patronage from afar.

* * *

In the high summer of 1862, Herat's defences were manned to resist
attack; grain had been gathered to within the city walls and troops
rallied to the nominal Qajar–Pashtun alliance that shakily ruled over
the city. Meanwhile, the Afghan old guard that had routed the British
two decades ago now geared up for one last assault on their nation, one
final attempt to unify the country under a Pashtun flag. Dost Mohammad
had been picking at the fringes of Khorasan since the departure of

Persian troops in 1858, but now he was camped around the city with 4,000 men at arms. His force was divided into two sections and poised to attack the city from the north and south. Herat's capture of Farah in the spring of 1862 had convinced Dost Mohammad that he must move now to bring Herat back into the fold of Kabul and Qandahar. Herat burned in the heat of a fierce summer; its defenders surveyed the foot-hills of Gazur Gah from the tall towers of the Old City, and south from the Qandahar Gate, over the tracts of land leading into Baluchistan. There, according to Riyazi, 'their enemies dressed in red tunics, flooded the plains like a field of tulips, and towards Firuzabad flags of red and gold and other hues fluttered with the intention of conquering the city of Herat'.[192] In a show of sectarian bravura, Dost Mohammad had brought with him the Four Friends Cannon, a reference to the four caliphs of Sunni Islam. Dost Mohammad hoped that this canon would subdue Herat in the name of Sunni Islam. For all the city's proud his-tory as a bastion of Sunni orthodoxy, Herat in the late nineteenth cen-tury could not quite escape the suspicion of being a Shia Persian city, suspicions which continue to this day.[193]

Persia and Britain squabbled: Persia had the moral high ground; Britain had the muscle; Herat suffered. The British chose to help Dost Mohammad financially, for its policy at that moment could be reduced to the slogan, 'anyone but the Persians to rule over Herat'. Herat had sleepwalked into yet another diplomatic crisis of global proportions into which even the French orientalist and scholar Comte de Gobineau saw fit to wade and remind Britain, with no little glee, of its obligations under the Treaty of Paris to assist Persia in securing its eastern frontiers against instability. Persia sent emissaries to Dost Mohammad urging him to call off the siege; they protested to Britain in the strongest terms at what they saw to be Britain's disregard for Article 6 of the Treaty of Paris, which demanded English assistance to Qajar Persia to resolve issues of security in Khorasan and Herat. Nasr al-Din Molk, Tehran's ambassador to the Court of St James, wrote to the British government as Dost Mohammad laid waste to Khorasan, stating that the Qajars had no problem with an independent Herat, and stressed that even the awful state of affairs under Sayyed Mohammad would be preferable to a Herat under the control of Dost Mohammad. These were not extravagant claims, and nor did they seem to be totally at odds with British desires for tranquility at the so-called gates of India.[194] A controlled or pliant Herat was vital to the Qajar interests for trade and security on the eastern frontier. The plains of Merv, as a Qajar prince wrote to a British diplomat, Edward Eastwick, 'are the homeland of the Qajar monarchs, a symbol of our royal might and lineage; Iran depends upon it'. Yet this road to Merv was then, as a result of Turcoman raiders and the conflicts with Herat, a grassless wasteland.[195] Persian alarm only increased with reports of British warships hovering in the Persian Gulf. Diplomacy and debate once again moved around the globe's leading capital cities: London, Tehran, Calcutta, Paris and St Petersburg. Persian diplomatic correspondence is as alarmist as British correspondence from the dark days of the Anglo-Afghan war, or from the time of the 1837–8 Herat crisis.

The British sent Edward Eastwick, a latter-day Pottinger or Todd, ostensibly to mediate between the parties, but in reality to ensure that Herat did not fall to the Qajars, but rather to Dost Mohammad. Persian historians rightly see through the neutral surface of his mission, to the vested interests of the British empire.[196] Meanwhile, Sultan Ahmad assured the people of Herat that Nasr al-Din Shah would surely send assistance at any moment, yet official Persian correspondence paints a picture of Sultan Ahmad, Herat's rightful ruler (by some assessments), being slowly squeezed into submission by wilful diplomatic inertia on the part of the British.[197] Herat was being left open to Dost Mohammad simply because it suited Britain's imperial security strategy.[198] Nasr al-Din Shah sent a missive to the Qajar ambassador in London urging him to press Persia's claims on Herat in the very strongest terms to the British, with a good deal of logic and common sense so often lacking in British policy in Afghanistan. It is worth quoting his exhortations in full to understand Persia's justifiable frustrations:

> Wherever you are in England, go to London and report on the fall of Herat to Dost Mohammad, a fall which threatens Iran's security greatly and relate that Iran is prepared to sacrifice its last soldier and last *tuman* to save Herat from falling further under the control of Dost Mohammad Khan and Kabul. As far as you understand this danger, so why can you tolerate it? We are not saying that Herat belongs to the Iranian government; we are saying that Herat should have a separate government that is in no way joined Dost Mohammad Khan. Why is the English government so concerned that Herat should be out of Iranian hands? Iran has that right

to control Herat, and why are you [the British government] not afraid of what the Afghans might do to Herat? Try to make them see some sense that Kabul should be happy with what they have, and repeat that Iran has no malicious intentions towards on Herat, just the natural desire to keep the borders of Khorasan and Kerman safe and tranquil.[199]

Nasr al-Din's scrawled and heartfelt marginalia stress how serious this issue would be for the British and their security interests in the region. He even wrote to Queen Victoria in the summer of 1862, and at one point threatened to withdraw Persian diplomats from London.[200] Persia repeatedly warned Britain of the dangers of a united and reckless Afghanistan, sure to dissolve into uncontrollable chaos after the death of Dost Mohammad, possibly even into the arms of the Russians. Qajar Persia felt that they should frighten the British with the threat of Dost Mohammad aligning himself with the Russians, and Nasr al-Din warned, deliciously provocatively, that 'of course the English know better than us that the Afghans are covetous, untrustworthy and greedy, and that they will do a deal with the Russians, which will in turn be a cause for sedition and political unrest'. The orders continue: 'Tell them that right now, we are not interfering in Afghanistan, but that their peace is our peace and that it would never ever be in the interests of the British that Afghanistan become one country united under a single leader.' The missive suggests that Afghanistan be divided into three separate political blocs, with Dost Mohammad controlling Kabul, and Qandahar being wrested from his grasp by the British. The bearer of the note is warned, intriguingly, that under no circumstances should its contents come to the attention of the Russians.[201] Countless meetings took place in London between Lord Russell, Foreign Secretary, and Nasr al-Din Molk, Iran's ambassador to London, yet none could persuade Britain to pull back from its position of tacitly supporting Dost Mohammad's attack on Herat. Persian diplomats, however rattled, never lost their wit. In February 1863, with Dost Mohammad Khan's armies massed around Farah, Ghur and perilously close to the gates of Herat, a letter from the Persian Foreign Ministry to the British ambassador noted drily that 'we doubt that the Amir's intentions are confined to the protection of Qandahar'.[202]

* * *

Herat fell to Dost Mohammad on 27 May 1863, uniting under one ruler the three main cities of Afghanistan: Herat, Kabul and Qandahar. As the siege had intensified, Herat's soldiers deserted the city 'in their tens, in their hundreds', by night, down the towers, over the ditches and moats and into the camp of Herat's latest conqueror.[203] Dost Mohammad's soldiers, and possibly some deserters, flooded into the city to plunder and sack in a grimly apposite beginning to Herat's incorporation in a unified Afghan nation. The siege had worn Herat further into the ground, breaking only for a sombre funeral cortège to snake its way up a ruined *khiaban* to Gazur Gah, where a relative of Sultan Ahmad and Dost Mohammad was buried; the two warring parties, temporarily united in grief, ate sweets under the trees at Gazur Gah before returning to fight each other. Was the city to rejoice at its liberation from Qajar yoke, or simply to weep at the never-ending cycle of destruction that continued to be its lot?

Dost Mohammad's youthful, and more reckless, actions in Herat had seen him tearing diamond-encrusted trousers from the legs of young princesses and being sent away in shame; now it was where he had come to die. On 9 June 1863, Dost Mohammad Khan Barakzai died at the age of seventy-two, emaciated and broken by fighting. He was buried in Gazur Gah, where the father of the Afghan nation finally found peace in a Herati graveyard. His death in Herat is somehow fitting as a signal for the beginning of Herat's incorporation into an Afghan state, whose boundaries are much the same then as they are now. Herat is unfairly viewed by many in the east as somehow not part of Afghanistan, too Persian, and yet this could not be further from the truth. Abdali and Sadozai Afghans who came to power in Herat in the dying days of the Safavid empire represent the first stirrings of the western frontier of the Afghan nation. Yet I remember sitting talking to a mullah in Khost, eastern Afghanistan, after I had given him an ICRC calendar with images from around Afghanistan marking the months. The mullah looked at the calendar, with no real enthusiasm, and said, 'It's rubbish; it doesn't have any photos of Khost or Paktiya. Herat!? Who gives a toss about Herat? It's not even part of Afghanistan!'

* * *

The Hungarian academic, traveller and sometime dervish in disguise, Arminius Vambéry, met with Nasr al-Din Shah Qajar in December

1863, four months after Dost Mohammad's sack of Herat. Nasr al-Din Shah tried to hide his dismay at having lost Herat, with the elegant phrase, 'I have no taste for such ruined cities.'[204] Yet behind this outward insouciance lay deep pain at having lost a city which so many Persians coveted for its cultural brilliance, the fertility of its oasis and the evidently impenetrable walls which surrounded it. Herat was part of Persia's rich cultural and political heritage, and Nasr al-Din's casual resignation at having lost the city is at odds with the emotive and defiant tone of his flurry of handwritten notes to Persia's ambassador in London at the height of the crisis, and his carefully considered praise of a holy man of Herat. It is also at odds with his aggressive posture when seeking to claim Qajar rights to Herat, his stated intention to fight to the very last *tuman* to place the city back within touching distance of Qajar sovereignty. Like Vambéry, whose own account of Herat in these early days of the new Afghan nation is troublingly prophetic, Nasr al-Din Shah knew that Herat's Persian-speaking population had no love for the Pashtuns from Kabul and Qandahar.

5

HERAT IN AN EMERGING AFGHANISTAN

ISOLATED, SLEEPY AND REVOLUTIONARY, 1863–1978

For almost 800 years Herat had been contested and fought over. Now it could sit back and enjoy the questionable fruits of obsolescence. The losses suffered in the nineteenth century rendered Herat impotent as a place from which to launch anything other than the most desultory of garrison-led uprisings; it had been neutered by war and effectively rendered irrelevant by its distance from Kabul and Qandahar. Qajar Persia would not dare go near it, for it had problems of its own—notably the millenarian Babi movement of the late nineteenth century, creeping erosion of its powers and the lead-in to the Constitutional Revolution of 1905–6—and Britain and Russia had largely, although not entirely, ceased to fight over it. Herat was suspended in peace: the very antithesis of so much of its history. Histories written during this period rarely pay Herat much attention, and consequently the historian is frustrated by the lack of continuous information coming out of the city. The modernisation which would grip Afghanistan in the early twentieth century barely touched Herat, and the city remained something of a cultural backwater until the late 1960s and beyond. And yet, despite this, Herat in its time of drift was gradually, cautiously, connected to the world outside. Abdur Rahman Khan repaired the road from Herat to Qandahar, and a functioning post office came into being linking Qandahar and Kabul in communication, effectively making the business of government between these cities more manageable, yet still difficult. Regional and international powers discussed trade links from Herat to Persia, spurred on by the grand vision of railways opening up between India and Paris, running through Khorasan and into Russia, but ultimately these came to little.[1] Herat, a city of roughly 25,000 in the late nineteenth century, had fallen from its Timurid, and even Safavid, peaks to the status of a lowly garrison town in a forgotten corner of Afghanistan.[2]

Dost Mohammad's death in the summer of 1863 had left Herat part of a tottering nation soon to descend into chaos. The fleeting moment of national unity scarcely lasted beyond the time it took to bury him in Gazur Gah.[3] A contemporary remark might be all that is required for this period of civil war: 'Any detailed narrative of the internecine struggle which ensued between the Ameer [Dost Mohammad's successor, Shir Ali Khan, r.1863–66 and 1868–79] and his brothers would be alike tedious and unprofitable.'[4] These are complicated years, difficult to follow and not entirely relevant to our story as they concern themselves mainly with a fight for control of Qandahar and Kabul. These years of war culminated in 1870–71 with a famine that surged through Herat, starving and killing those who had only recently felt secure enough to return to their villages and homes. Herat, as is so often the case, was simultaneously an onlooker and a victim.

In the summer of 1880, the British diplomat and noted Afghan expert Sir Henry Rawlinson made the following observation about the turbulent decades which Herat experienced in the wake of Dost Mohammad's death in 1863: 'Herat unfortunately would seem to have been left hitherto out in the cold. Matters there have been allowed to drift as chance directed. The present anarchy is the result.'[5] Late-nineteenth-century Herat was struggling to define its role in a fledgling and uncertain Afghan nation, if such a thing could be said to exist at this point. The events of the next century should be seen as an extended attempt to answer the question of Herat's place, its inclusion or exclusion, in Afghanistan's story. What role should this awkward and glorious city of culture and conflict assume within the Afghan nation, if any? This chapter covers a century in which the defining characteristic is Herat's isolation within Afghanistan. Yet this century is also a story of the triumph and durability of Herat's culture and its extraordinary ability to rebuild and survive.

Herat might have been something of a sideshow in Afghanistan's late-nineteenth-century internal chaos, but the city did not entirely lose its appeal to international policy-makers and intriguers. It was and would forever be to a generation of Victorian statesmen the key or gate to India, and as such it had to be protected, or locked. A Persian diplomat gently mocked Britain's obsession with Herat when he wrote in 1880 that 'there is hardly an Englishman who does not seem perfectly satisfied with his personal knowledge of it [Herat]'.[6] These satisfied men, and their Russian counterparts, remained true in their admiration for Herat's strategic and geopolitical charms. Russian intrigue, in particular, hardly moved from the forefront of British policies towards Herat. British informants kept a keen look out for Russian activity in Herat, their agents in Mashhad working overtime. One Russian officer, for example, was spotted in Herat in November 1878 with a large escort of Afghan horses, sending word to his superiors in Tashkent that his stay in Herat had passed in a 'most satisfactory and cordial manner'.[7]

Russia, fresh from victories over the Ottoman empire, had been humiliated at the Congress of Berlin of 1878 by Europe's creation of an Austro-Hungarian entity on Russia's Balkan doorstep. This remained a festering sore in international relations until the end of World War I, for it threatened Russian naval interests and hurt Russian pride. British tensions with Russia, which lay at the root of the congress's convening, did not subside at its conclusion, and it would not be long before they spilled over into Afghanistan and, by ways and means, into Herat. Russia, piqued at the slight she felt to her European doorstep, decided to turn its attentions to Central Asia, and to the cities of Bokhara, Tashkent, Khiva and areas perilously close to Herat's northern borders. Khiva had fallen to the Russians on 10 June 1873, and a subsequent treaty between Khiva and Russia gave the Russians the right bank of the Oxus, and Russian vessels free and exclusive right of navigating that river. In the summer of 1873 Lord Northbrook in London and the Viceroy in India fielded panicked requests for assistance from Kabul, and it was deemed opportune to send a British officer to assess and examine the status of Afghanistan's western and northern borders.[8]

In the summer of 1878, Russia sent an uninvited envoy to Kabul as a response to British military moves in Malta. The envoy duly arrived in

August, seeking alliances to offset the reverses suffered at the Congress of Berlin and with a view to testing the mettle of Britain's own alliances in Kabul. Shir Ali received the Russians cordially, and with enough friendliness to terrify London and Calcutta, both of whom had been trying, with little success, to get an envoy into the country since 1876. British ultimata demanding the expulsion of the Russian mission were ignored, and the Afghan refusal to allow a British counter-envoy across the Khyber Pass in September 1878 was the signal for the British to send in 40,000 troops to occupy Afghanistan in November. The Second Anglo-Afghan War had thus begun with the familiar initial success of an easy British occupation of Afghanistan. The death of Shir Ali in February 1879 and the lack of help from Russia convinced Mohammad Yaqub Khan, Shir Ali's successor, to sue for peace with the then all-conquering British, a peace which resulted in the Treaty of Gandamak. The treaty was signed in May 1879, and through it Yaqub Khan accepted British control of Afghanistan's foreign policy, agreed to a permanent British envoy in Kabul, permitted Britain to control the passes into Afghanistan from the south and the east and, to prove that it was not all totally humiliating, accepted an annual subsidy of 60,000 rupees. Despite Afghanistan's famed ability to ward off predatory empires, it was now effectively a British protectorate and would not be able to claim itself officially independent of outside interference until 1919.[9] Yet within a few months, the tide had turned against British presence in the country, much as it had done in the mid-nineteenth century with such disastrous consequences. The state which the British sponsored proved unruly, especially in out of the way Herat.

In summer 1879 a group of soldiers stationed in Herat made a plundering march across Afghanistan to reach Kabul on 4 August. They sacked and burned their way through Helmand, and then up through Qandahar. Their grievances were simple: they had not been paid and they resented rule by the British. When in Kabul they protested at their lack of pay from the government and hovered nervously at the edges of garrisons and bazaars. Two weeks later, after kicking their heels in frustration, dressed in fading red British-issue military tunics, penniless and bored, the soldiers' anger turned to revolt. A bloody uprising followed in September 1879 in which the British envoy, Sir Louis Cavagnari, and most of the British mission in Kabul were massacred.

The British response was to send the following message to the Afghans: 'We wish one thing from you, and that is friendship, but whether we get this or not, we will have your obedience, you may chafe as much as you please, but we will be your masters, and you will find that the only escape from our heavy hand will be your entire submission.'[10] The British sent another army of retribution back into Afghanistan to crush the rebels in a lightning raid on Kabul in which they executed anyone with even a hint of a link to the uprising. The British had clawed back the advantage, for the moment, through the slaughter of innocents in Kabul. A stunning Afghan victory at the Battle of Maiwand in July 1880, in which Herati troops excelled under the leadership of its governor Ayyub Khan, could not hide the fact that Afghanistan was again the victim of imperial intrigue.[11] Nor could it hide the fact that Afghanistan was still bound by the Treaty of Gandamak, and as such was a puppet state. Nearly 10,000 British troops and many more Afghans died in this short and nasty conflict: it ended militarily in 1880 with a decisive British victory at the Battle of Qandahar, and concluded politically with the coming to power of Afghanistan's 'Iron Amir', Abdur Rahman Khan.

Effectively placed on the throne by British imperial design, Abdur Rahman was a sovereign who built up his nation by cherry-picking what he thought appropriate from European technological advancements, whilst also ruling as a traditional Afghan khan. He felt that railways and telegraphs, for example, threatened his control over Afghanistan, and so were avoided; guns and tunics and soldiers and ammunition, on the other hand, strengthened his hand, and were ordered by the trunkload. Riyazi's account of his rule laments the harsh treatment meted out to Afghanistan's Hazara population in Abdur Rahman's expeditions to subdue and coerce Afghanistan into a unified nation. The state that Abdur Rahman Khan brought into being was one ruled by fear, by informants and by the forcible resettlement of Pashtun tribes in Persian-speaking areas so as to have eyes and ears in areas he felt to be potential sources of rebellion. Many of Herat and Badghis' Pashtun enclaves date from this time, and yet these villages still think fondly of the Iron Amir, his crimes against humanity having passed into nostalgia. Some see Abdur Rahman as a strongman who brought order where chaos once ruled, which is undeniably true, but we should never overlook the tyranny and misery he brought to the people of Afghanistan. Eyewitness reports of Abdur Rahman's torture methods and the severity of his punishments are often disturbing in the extreme, especially the following story. A gardener in the royal palace had one day not swept the leaves from the drive. Abdur Rahman sent for him, but in his place his heavily pregnant wife arrived to explain the situation: her husband had been ill with fever while she was with child and tending to her sick husband. Abdur Rahman replied that he would 'relieve her of her burden', and so he ordered her to lie on the floor on her back, at which point he ordered several men to beat her stomach with heavy wooden bars. She lost her child, and died soon after the beating.[12]

* * *

The impact of Russian moves north of Herat, British concerns about the city's vulnerability and Abdur Rahman's comparative lack of concern for Khorasan's Pearl would very nearly take the world to war. In 1878 a Russian staff officer, Colonel Grodekov, rode from Samarqand to Herat in order to survey the passes and assess the city's defences. In 1881 a Russian army under General Mikhael Skobelev captured the fortress of Geok Tepe (Blue Hill) at Akhal, defeating the powerful Tekke tribe of Central Asia in present-day Turkmenistan. In 1884 the Russians completed their pacification of the Tekke tribe by annexing the oasis of Merv and moving the Russian frontier even closer to Herat, terrifying British India in the process. Advancing in a line from the eastern shore of the Caspian towards the Murghab river, paralleling the course of a nascent Trans-Caspian Railroad, the Russians had annexed sections of the Yamut, Salor and Tekke, making a clear claim on the Turcoman tribes who harried and plundered to Herat's north; Russia was bearing down on Herat at a time when the city was beset by garrison riots of unpaid Kabul and Qandahar troops.

By 1884 cartographers in St Petersburg had printed maps showing Russian borders to lie a mere 20 miles from the northern outskirts of Herat. Russian advances into Afghanistan once again became real, and Herat again geared itself up to play the role of India's key, or gate or door. Although this time it seemed that war for Herat might be avoided, for in 1884 the British and Russian governments agreed that a joint boundary commission should survey and delimit the northern border of Afghanistan, a 400-mile stretch between the Hari Rud and Oxus rivers. The theory was that the certainty of a clearly marked border would deter any further opportunistic land grabs or conflicts. The two powers accordingly set up the Afghan Boundary Commission to address thorny and age-old problems on Herat's frontiers, and in the process possibly solve some as well. Afghanistan's sovereign, Abdur Rahman, was at once preoccupied and ill-informed with regard to Herat's boundaries. As long as Herat did not cause him too much trouble and remained out of the hands of the Persians, he was happy. The logic of this tactic ran as follows: the presence of a boundary, arrived at by Britain and Russia, would be a line beyond which Russia could not advance south without the British coming to Afghanistan's aid, for free. He had effectively outsourced the defence of his eastern frontier to the world's great superpower, and been paid in the process. In an indication of his almost total lack of knowledge of the western edges of his nation, Abdur Rahman had earlier requested from the British in India an accurate map to show him the extent of his western territories and the borders they shared with Imperial Russia.[13] Britain's response was that a treaty had been worked out between Britain and Russia in 1873, but that at present no one really knew the extent of the boundaries. Britain and Russia, therefore, set to work trying to mark out the boundaries between them, and for this task, no Afghans were required.

And so it was that after another Anglo-Afghan war in which Herat had again played a minimal role, despite supplying troops for the famous victory at Maiwand, the British returned to the city in search of the mythical Russian menace, hoping to bring order to borders and ballast to the city's crumbling walls. The arrival in Herat and the surrounds of the city in 1884 of spies, intriguers, yet more 'plain dealing Englishmen', cartographers, soldiers, doctors and camp followers brought with it a slew of artists, photographers and accounts which again bring the city to life, albeit through the lens of paranoid civil servants and the sketches of military artists. The Afghan Boundary Commission photographed their expeditions, and it is through their images that we see the first photos of Herat. These images, photos and sketches, hint at former glories, giving us elegant images of Heratis going about their business.

The Commission's discussions focused on the frontiers dividing Herat from the territories of Merv and Badghis, a line running from east to west between the rivers of the Murghab and the Hari Rud. Russia sought to push this line south, and Britain and Afghanistan to push it north. In a century where Herat was the 'key to India', it is interesting that one contemporary English writer describes Sarakhs and Merv as the keys to Herat.[14] The phraseology of keys and portals was again in full swing. Qajar Persia, for its part, wished to occupy Herat again, as well as Merv, for without Herat the Qajars felt they could not control Merv, or so the increasingly intricate logic went. The small village of Pul-e Khatun, 90 miles north-west of Herat, became one of many focal points which Russian Cossack troops occupied in the early 1880s as they based themselves north of a line running roughly from Sarakhs to Merv. British positions stood to the south of this line. Afghan troops, in turn, occupied the village of Panjdeh and a post at the Zulfikar pass which sits on the Hari Rud, some 60 miles north of Herat city. By the time of the arrival of the Boundary Commission, despite its noble and peaceful intentions, tensions were already running high, and it seemed as if Herat was set for a conflict of some sort.

Sheltering from the elements atop the hills overlooking the northern parts of Herat, Charles Yate, soldier, diplomat, politician and son of a Yorkshire vicar, described Herat's wind as 'boisterous'; it forced his party to seek cover.[15] Yate and his colleagues of artists, map-makers, soldiers and hangers-on were then surveying the valleys of Karokh, on the upper banks of the Hari Rud, as part of the Afghan Boundary Commission. He records meetings with men of Badghis of Arab descent, part of a thousand-strong settlement of Arabs north of Herat. These tribesmen were termed *siah khanah* (black house), a reference to the black felt tents under which they camped from season to season, rolling them up as the weather and pasture took them. These were most likely Kuchi nomads, a tribe apart, itinerant farmers who roamed across rural Afghanistan, occasionally coming into cities to sell and buy.

Just like Yate's descriptions of Kuchi settlements in and around Herat, I remember driving through Badghis and Herat and Farah, and seeing Kuchi signs of occupation, those stretched black felt tents slanting low over the ground. I observed villages of a few houses surrounded by grassy plains and black tents, glinting with the colour of children chasing tyres with sticks, riding donkeys and stopping to stare at the visitors with blond hair and blue eyes. Dogs would roam about looking for scraps. There was invariably a sense of peace in these villages, despite having suffered centuries of near constant interruption, right up to the present day. Each time I found myself in rural Herat or Farah or Badghis, I felt this sense of peace at the passage of life's most basic and essential events: harvest, animals, birth, life, death, winter, spring. A triumph of simplicity, removed from the conflict or politics, as if one were back in a 1960s hippie dream of an unspoiled Afghanistan. One picnic in particular in Badghis will never be forgotten: we rode out of the city, northwards, to the hills which were then green and lush. A small house in a remote village, the home of our cook, was the scene for a lunch of steaming rice, meat, ripe fruits and green tea, followed by an afternoon-long walk through the pistachio groves and up onto the highest points we could find. We drank more tea, looking down over Qalai Naw and then north to the Murghab and beyond. We barely discussed prisons or war or the Taliban. Yate's account encapsulates this scene of rural calm which would have enchanted generations of travellers to Herat down the centuries in which he notes, 'In the centre of the valley the waters of the Heri Rud [sic] glistened in the setting sun; while on every side, interspersed amongst the numerous villages and orchards, were lying the heaps of freshly cut corn, waiting to be threshed.'[16]

Yet conflict hovers at the edge of these occasional forays into the lyrical. The Russian menace of Central Asia and Britain's vigorous attempts to keep Herat as part of Afghanistan are, unsurprisingly, the point to which he always returns. One chapter is even entitled 'Preparations for War', in which he discusses at length the possibility of setting up a sanatorium to deal with the expected casualties of a global war that was surely just a matter of time.[17]

Within the Old City walls, Herat's troubles had continued. It was divided on itself and in a poor state of repair. Yate and his colleagues were fortunate to visit within the city walls, for Herat's governor later banned any foreigner from coming within 12 miles of the city walls. Yate estimated that there were not more than 2,000 families within the city walls, as so many had fled to rural hideaways where they might think themselves safe from Turcoman slavers and Russian ambition. A further 4,000–5,000 soldiers were stationed in the garrison of the citadel. Like so many before him, Yate bemoaned the poor state of repair of the city's defences, and described the city's attempts to restore Herat's walls to their former military glories. Those forced to work on repairing the citadels were most likely the descendants of the gamblers and drinkers and criminals who had once repaired Herat's fortifications in the thirteenth century under a *corvée* system of forced labour.[18] The tensions between Persian and Pashtun appeared as striking as ever in this account, and Yate's observations are a good indication of just how divided Herat had become. During four years spent on the border of Afghanistan and Qajar Persia, Yate could observe 'how intensely the Afghans [Pashtuns] are hated by the population of the Herat valley, irrespective of faith, they being almost equally unpopular with the Sunnis and Shiahs [*sic*]'.[19] Typically contrary, the people of Herat wanted independent rule under a Herati sovereign and were united in their dislike of rule by one of Dost Mohammad's sons. Yate concludes on this enigma that 'they will not have a Kabul rule—they are unanimous on that point—they would prefer to be under English rule and after that Russian rule'.[20] The city was also divided linguistically, for it was only the soldiers of the garrison who spoke Pashtu and they were consequently unintelligible to the Persian-speaking Heratis (this was a foreshadowing of the time when the Pashtun Taliban would populate the citadel and the streets). Yate's description of the difference between Heratis—those who spoke Persian and identified as Heratis—and Afghans is, despite its generalising tone, worth quoting in full both for its humour and also for its exploration of a sense of a Herati's natural calm, as opposed to the more warlike urges of the Pashtuns, or 'Afghans':

> Nothing can be more marked than the difference between the Herati and the Afghan. The former is far quieter and more subdued in manner—a cultivator, as a rule, pure and simple, rarely or never armed, nor apparently trained to the use of arms. Even the local *sowars* [local forces], when called out on duty have scarcely a weapon amongst them, and when they do possess one, it is of the oldest and rottenest description; whereas the Kabulis swagger about armed to the teeth, with knives half as long as themselves, and weapons of every sort and shape.[21]

Herat's Friday Mosque, once reckoned by Ibn Haukal as one of the very greatest of Central Asia and Khorasan, barely merited a mention

in Yate's otherwise detailed account of Herat's antiquities. His interpreter translated a slab dating to 1462 which had been set up to mark
the end of a repressive tax by Sultan Abu Said (see Chapter 2), but in
the whole this monument slips beneath Yate's otherwise eager eyes.[22]
Herat's shops were only half-occupied, many of their occupants having
fled in anticipation of the coming conflict. Inside the city walls it was a
desolate scene, occupied almost solely by soldiers 'lounging about',
whilst Herat sat emptied of its people and life.[23] Gawhar Shad's tombstone was half buried in rubbish.

In March 1885 Yate's quasi idyll was punctured by a highly significant
skirmish between Russian and Afghan forces in the village of Panjdeh,
a small hamlet on the banks of the Kushk river. In a fierce battle lasting
from 3 a.m. on 30 March till mid-morning, Russian troops decisively
defeated Afghan sentries drawn from the garrison at Herat. Russian
troops killed over 600 Afghans, leaving the survivors to straggle back
into Herat, wounded and terrified of what was to come.[24] Russian military might seemed unassailable against Herat's pitiful defences, and the
Afghan sentries who defended Herat's northern villages were an
underfunded and underfed force; they used their rifles, when ammunition could be found, for foraging and hunting so as to have enough food
to stay alive. A British observer described these outposts, set to guard
against the invading Russian empire, as practically useless.[25] An imperial Russian force was bearing down on a series of crumbling forts,
faced by equally crumbling and starved Afghan troops; the British
looked on helplessly as Heratis fled to the countryside. Riyazi, for his
part, thought that this skirmish portended instant and global calamity;
for the Afghan Boundary Commission, it was their worst nightmare:
Cossack and Sepoy potentially coming to blows in the contested passes
of Central Asia and Khorasan and sparking off a world war.

As the world reacted with fear and anger to the Panjdeh incident,
the Russian military leader, General Komaroff, then in northern Herat,
pleaded that the presence of Afghan troops on the left bank of the
Kushk violated terms agreed at the setting up of the Afghan Boundary
Commission. Russia claimed that its possession of Merv gave it rights
over Panjdeh. But Panjdeh, according to the Russian defence, was
merely a part of the Merv oasis (which it was not), and should therefore fall within Russian territory. Afghan representatives in turn pro-

tested that the Sarik Turcoman tribes who populated Panjdeh had for centuries paid tribute to Herat's rulers in a show of submission which indicated Herat's possession of Panjdeh (which they had). On the available evidence, the Afghans were well within their rights to withstand Russian encroachments, but their military capabilities indicated that they might not be in a position to resist an advancing Russian force. Since mid March tensions had been high, producing a tense stand-off. The Russians had promised not to attack as long as the Afghan troops remained where they were, and an agreement of 16 March regarding the possession of this stretch of land had kept things in precarious check. Russian reconnaissance missions along the banks of the river had made Afghan forces fear an attack, and these moves had effectively goaded the Afghans into giving the Russians a pretext for a skirmish. A Russian ultimatum demanding an Afghan withdrawal south further into the heart of Herat province was ignored, giving the Russians their green light to attack—which they did at 3 a.m. on 30 March.

When the news of this skirmish reached Afghanistan's amir, Abdur Rahman Khan, he was in Rawalpindi with the British viceroy, Lord Dufferin, attending a conference. In a flustered fit of angst, Lord Dufferin proposed British military intervention. Abdur Rahman advised caution. The Afghan sovereign, we are told, was 'determined that his country should not be a battleground of several nations'.[26] Abdur Rahman's hands-off attitude stretched to his opinion of Panjdeh and Badghis, for he felt the Sarik Turkomans [who populated Panjdeh] to be 'a lot of thieving ruffians'.[27] Perhaps Abdur Rahman had also assumed that the Panjdeh incident was not his problem, but a Herati, British and Russian one. His relaxed response was certainly at odds with the angry reaction in Herat and its surrounds, where local tribes and citizens of Herat, in the words of one Afghan historian, had little love for the 'idol worshipping Russian infidel'.[28]

Leaflets denouncing the Russian raid on Panjdeh circulated throughout the province, telling inflated stories of the infidel Russians and their atrocities against the people of Herat and Panjdeh, much as the Russians in London had earlier tried to circulate stories of Afghan atrocities against Panjdeh.[29] A document entitled *Targhib al-Jihad* (Path of Jihad) was handed out, Riyazi tells us, to all the tribes and elders of Herat and its surrounds, so as to exhort Afghanistan to a *jihad* against the Russians and help the British to drive them back over the lines running from the Hari Rud to the Murghab to the Oxus.[30] Reflecting Herat's global pretensions, this inflammatory document harboured wider ambitions than a simple domestic *jihad*. It urged Afghans to throw their religious support behind the Ottomans in the latter's war against the Russians, and thus draw Afghanistan into the global conflict which Panjdeh would surely create. The seductive lure of martyrdom was trumpeted to the rooftops in this potentially incendiary leaflet, and Afghanistan braced itself for yet another siege in which two empires would collide on Herat.[31] It is little wonder that, with two armies flexing their muscles in and around Herat, its people decided that fleeing to the countryside was a better bet. Yate's description of a deserted city makes perfect sense in this context.

* * *

As the Hari Rud turns north, having left Herat on its way west, it runs up towards the Zulfikar pass and then again north to Pul-e Khatun before it reaches Sarakhs, a garrison town which had once caused war between the last Kart *malek*s of Herat. Sarakhs lies 120 miles north-west of Herat as the crow flies, and is in turn overlooked by Merv, 60 miles to its north-east, at the point where the Murghab river splits into tributaries. In 1881 the Russian General Staff had drawn a line east from Sarakhs to the banks of the Murghab. It was this line which had once marked an accepted northern frontier of Herat and Russia. Panjdeh lies some 50 miles south, on the Murghab river, overlooking the towns of Maruchaq and Bala Murghab. The skirmish at Panjdeh effectively dropped this border 60 miles closer to Herat, poised above the Paropamisus hills. Russia had now advanced 40 miles to the north of Herat, and with over 5,000 troops at Merv facing sporadic Afghan sentry postings, ill-equipped and demoralised. The fertility of Herat and Badghis' pasture, so necessary if an imperial army were to survive for a season in Herat before making an attack on India, now lay open to Russia. One British eyewitness noted, a few days after the incident, that 'a defence of Herat now seems hopeless… In three weeks at the least the Russians can enter Herat.'[32] Conditions for Russian expansion into Herat were now ominously favourable. The British contemplated abandoning Herat to a fate so many had predicted, and as bedraggled Afghan soldiers trickled back into Herat from Panjdeh, ill-feeling towards the British began to increase.[33] The Afghans' erstwhile protectors had, it seemed, turned agitators, and it was the British presence, so Herat thought, that had encouraged Russia to make advances into Panjdeh.

The Panjdeh incident shook the international order. Here was the conflict that had for so long hovered at the edge of British and Russian forays into Afghanistan, and which had placed Herat as the key to India. Russian incursion into what the British regarded as territories of a pro-British Herat and Afghanistan represented a serious international incident, and very possibly a legitimate *casus belli* between the two empires. Contemporary observers considered the event as 'the greatest disaster that has befallen Britain since the occupation of India', and the same writer noted that the fight at Panjdeh 'sent a great thrill throughout Asia'.[34] When we add to this the Afghan response of incitement to a global *jihad* against the Russians, we get some idea of the magnitude of this skirmish at Panjdeh. The fact that, even before the skirmish itself, 50,000 troops had been mobilised in British India in alarm at Russia's southerly encroachments towards Herat is an indication of how much concern the Russian presence in Khorasan was causing British India. In response to Panjdeh, the British Navy went so far as to occupy Port Hamilton in Korea as a potential base of operations against Vladivostok and Russian bases in the North Pacific. As news of the conflict reached London, the Stock Exchange was rocked and Britain's Prime Minister, William Gladstone, then reeling from the Sudan crisis which had claimed the life of General Gordon, immediately sought assurances from the Russian ambassador that this was a mistake on the part of over-zealous Russian commanders in Khorasan. For its part, Qajar Persia largely stayed out of the crisis, but strongly urged the British to take Herat before the Russians did.

Yet when global conflict became a reality, Britain and Russia decided that diplomacy was a more fitting way to solve what was essentially a boundary dispute. Envoys duly rushed back and forth across the globe so as to avoid all-out war. In Herat, meanwhile, British and Russian representatives met in November 1885 at the British camp in the village of Zulfikar as a recognition of this reconciliation of sorts. Boundary pillars were laid in the ground to signify permanence and the beginning of a solution. On the evening in question, in the hills to the north of

Herat, British and Russian officers made their way through vodka, port, madeira, claret, Caucasian wine and champagne before finishing, in Russian fashion, with jam. The celebrations helped to ease the wheels of diplomacy, and after fifteen months in camp, the British were happy to hear some music, provided by a Cossack guard who sang for the entire evening.[35]

The diplomacy that led to the final demarcation of Herat's borders is complex beyond the scope of this book. Inch by inch, the different sides worked out lines and surveyed villages with a thoroughness whose results are quite breathtaking and which ended up with a tortuous line starting from the Zulfikar Pass on the Hari Rud, snaking its way south-east to the village of Chehel Dukhtaran, 100 miles north of Herat, before arcing north-east towards the Oxus at Khojeh Saleh.[36] The British reports from this time, stacked up now in the British Library, are monuments to thoroughness; one such report describes in great detail the ethnic and sectarian make-up of villages of no more than one hundred people around Herat, and tabulates the crop yields and water flow of every single populated dwelling in Herat. The Afghan Boundary Commission had succeeded in setting down frontiers for Herat and Persia and Russia, but more importantly it left the testimony of some of the most complete surveys of Afghanistan ever to have been carried out; they were a Great Gamer's dream, although in reality half a century late.[37] The eventual demarcation took place in August 1887, after four more years of political debate and diplomatic brinkmanship. Herat's borders were finally secured and the Russian threat seen off. The city was, if not loyal to Abdur Rahman, at least fixed within the borders of his despotic state.

Britain's continued fears of a Russian military invasion occasioned one of the most startling pieces of cultural vandalism that Afghanistan has ever seen. Orders were given for Herat's Timurid ruins, which dominated the northern approaches to the city along which British politicians so feared a Russian army might march into Herat, to be torn down to clear a sight-line for the guns and weapons that would be trained on the phantom Russian army, should it decide to invade. In July 1885 Yate noted, despairingly, the following:

> the Amir's [Abdur Rahman Khan] orders for the demolition of both the Musalla and the still older Madrasah close by are being rapidly carried into

effect, and a few days, or at most weeks, will see the last of this famous relic of bygone grandeur. The rooms and habitations have mostly disappeared, but the massive arches, some 80 feet in height, the still higher minarets, and the large dome, all of which bear traces of the beautiful tile-work with which they were covered, attest its former magnificence.[38]

Riyazi, by contrast, tells us that it was the British who ordered the destruction of Herat's Timurid antiquities. Petitions were sent to British and Herati authorities in an attempt to stop them demolishing the buildings, but the depressing refrain of 'national security', as so often, rode roughshod over the claims of common sense and decency. Riyazi laments that the buildings the British destroyed, Husain Bayqara's *madrasa* and Gowhar Shad's *mosalla* complex, were 'covered in blue and green tiles of a skill and beauty whose like cannot be replicated in Herat today'.[39] When I was working on the remains of these buildings in 2014, I remember hearing this sad lament from craftsmen and poets and mullahs alike. In this act of destruction masquerading as strategic prudence, Kartid-era buildings were also destroyed, along with priceless remains of Timurid arches, mosques and gardens. As Yate left Herat, his work done, he noted the piles of rubble amongst which donkeys were being led so as to clear away the debris of one of the world's most beautiful architectural structures. One of the guns used to destroy this architectural vista was later pressed into service as a way of sounding midday to the city, booming out from Herat, close to the minarets whose rooms it had destroyed. Ironically, the gun was moved from where it stood close to the minarets, for fear that the vibrations from its loud noise might cause the minarets to fall down.[40]

An idea of the beauty of the tiles that the guns destroyed can be seen in a collection of watercolours painted by artists from the commission, depicting the different tiles they saw in Herat. The geometry and colour depicted are rich and varied, and looking at them one gets a sense of the tragedy of their destruction. White marble shades compete with majestic reds and olive greens in intricate patterns: geometric, floral, diamond-shaped lozenges surrounding flower motifs and azure.[41] This is as close as we can come to some of the patterns whose effects Robert Byron would later describe as wrapping the minarets in a 'glittering net'.[42] As the buildings fell under the weight of bombardment, so fell Herat's greatest monuments to an era whose grandeur and genius now left only faint traces on a disfigured and tired city. Red-coated Afghan troops from Qandahar and Kabul flooded into the city; lookouts and redoubts were dug around the city's centre. Yate and his troupe of mappers, sketchers and camp followers later drifted out of Herat to the sounds and sights of donkeys clearing priceless Timurid rubble from the northern approaches to the city. In Herat the Great Game petered out in a flurry of sextons, treaties and destroyed Timurid artifacts.

Now that Herat was just a pitiful collection of ruins, had it ever been the Gate to India? Had it been worth all the lives lost and treasure expended to keep it out of Persian hands, Russian hands, in Afghan hands and occasionally in British hands? Herat's place in these nine-teenth-century imperial war games is a difficult one to assess with any certainty. Yet on balance it seems that Herat continuously offered the fiction of belonging to Britain, Persia or Kabul, whilst in reality remaining loyal to itself, or to whoever directly ruled and taxed and robbed it. It held out the promise of so much, but proved elusive and stubborn. It would be easy to dismiss the British policy-makers as obsessive and paranoid with regard to Herat's importance for India's security, but the events at Panjdeh and Russia's gradual movements into Central Asia, as well as the secret missions to Kabul and the courting of the Qajar state, do indicate that Russia was serious in its desire to launch attacks into Afghanistan and most likely India too. Russian assis-tance to Persian troops besieging Herat is also proof that the Conollys and the Lals and the Stoddarts of the nineteenth century, the Russophobes, were not entirely deluded about the intentions of St Petersburg. Intentions, however, are one thing; realities are another. Surely the British difficulties in subduing Afghanistan, especially the troublesome post-1838 years when D'Arcy Todd was so comprehen-sively outwitted and subsequently driven out of Herat, would have shown London that the theory of Russian advances into Afghanistan came very much undone when faced with the realities of campaigning in Afghanistan, of securing alliances and of taking Herat in a short enough time to avoid British retaliation and Afghan resistance? Herat was a key to India in the minds of many, but I feel there was too much assumption in this theory. To assume that Russia's advance would be far smoother than that of Britain's own experiences, which had been little

short of disastrous, bloody and ruinously expensive, was a miscalculation. Why should Russian armies fare any better in subduing
Afghanistan than British ones? One possible theory is that Russia could
have promised Afghan leaders spoils of Indian conquests. This does not
add up, however, for the Afghan leaders were already recipients of
Indian gold from the British in any case, so why swap a steady flow of
riches for the uncertain promise of a glut?

If Herat were a gate to anywhere, I would suggest that it had once
been a natural gate into Persia, out of whose hands the British were
steadfastly determined to keep it. Qajar Persia's claims over Herat
made themselves known in *khutbah* and *sikka*, cashmere bolts and elephants; Herat's rulers, for their part, were clear that their loyalty to
Persia stopped at the symbols of submission and went no further. This
impasse of sovereignty, a legacy of Herat's turbulent history, further
complicates the matter, making it impossible to ascertain with any
certainty to or from where Herat was a gate. A highly perceptive article
written by a Persian diplomat in London in 1880 sets out Persian
claims on Herat, but also highlights the folly of British determination
to keep it out of Tehran's hands; true, Herat is fertile and was once a
strong city, but why does this mean that it would be safer in the hands
of the Afghans than in the hands of the Persians if the Russians were so
determined to take it for themselves? Addressing Herat's strategic suitability and Russian intentions in India, the unnamed minister writes:
'are not Samarkand, Cabul and, above all, Kandahar, more advantageously situated for such a purpose than Herat?'[43] Mashhad, Astarabad
and Merv might all have been gates to India, yet it was Herat's fertility,
its command of passes down to Qandahar and through Afghanistan to
Kabul which gave it its strategic importance and which so seduced the
early-nineteenth-century adventurers and policy-makers of British
India. Perhaps British policy-makers were on balance right about
Herat's importance, but wrong about the feasibility of Russian troops
executing the type of invasion which the British themselves had repeatedly tried, and failed, to achieve?

For all the miles of print written on Herat's status, perhaps the
most pithy expression of the frustrations of English policy towards
Herat can be found in a report from 1859. In one of many such
reports on Herat's strategic importance to British India, Sir Peter

Lumsden, who would later take charge of the Afghan Boundary Commission, notes that:

> With Peshawar, Kohat, and Sindh in our possession, and the communication with our Indian provinces open by rails and steamers on the Indus and a strong force of Europeans located in healthy cantonments all over the country, supported by a well-organized Native army, I consider that we should really have the keys of India in our own pockets, and be in a position to lock the doors in the face of all enemies.[44]

* * *

If the boundaries separating Afghanistan from Russia can be said to have been decisively marked in 1887, as pillars plotted across tracts of Khorasan and dotted through villages and meadows, then Herat's actual inclusion in this nation was less fixed. In a post-1887 world, Herat slips almost entirely from view. Even Riyazi's faithful account shifts its focus from Herat to central, northern and eastern Afghanistan, occasionally returning to Herat to tell of a dead mullah or a garrison revolt. It seems that with the demarcation of Herat's borders, and the effective peace that this guaranteed, Abdur Rahman could afford to leave Herat to its own devices, safe in the knowledge that should anyone threaten its frontiers, the British would surely come to the rescue.

Previous treaties and supposedly epoch-defining moments—1838, 1842 and 1857—had changed little. The Afghan Boundary Commission, however, left a lasting legacy to Herat and its inclusion in Afghanistan. It gave to Herat an isolated, quiet and even crumbling political irrelevance. Herat could now remain calm in the face of further enemies, but forgotten as far as Kabul was concerned. The year 1887 was accordingly the end of Herat's turbulent nineteenth century. It was also the beginning of Herat's sequestered seclusion within Afghan borders, heralding an isolation which characterises the city for much of the twentieth century.

Abdur Rahman died on 1 October 1901, and the peaceful transition of power to his son, Habibullah Khan (r.1901–19), belied the violence which had informed his rule. Habibullah Khan, a reform-minded ruler with vague secular leanings and a penchant for Rolls Royce cars, was to introduce reforms and begin an overhaul of Afghanistan's bureaucracy. Habibullah was an enthusiastic proponent of reform and education, and his was a simple approach to the subject: 'In a single sentence, I give you my whole exhortation. Acquire knowledge.'[45] Habibullah set up Kabul's first high school, the *Habibya*, and its teachers taught the scions of Kabul's elites subjects from French to science to literature to mathematics. Habibullah felt that education would bring Afghanistan out of its slumber and be the cure for all Afghanistan's ills; by creating a national identity, surely a dynamic and forward-looking society and nation built on science, progress and exploration would emerge. Graduates of the *Habibya* school effectively ran the country, but corruption menaced the efficiency of the Civil Service. Requiring all civil servants to list their property holdings did little to stop this.[46] A list of names of prominent teachers at this school at Kabul in the early years of Habibullah's reign features men with appellations indicating the provinces of Logar, Laghman, Nangahar and Qandahar, but no one who can be identified as 'Herati'.[47] Habibullah also sought to undo some of the despotic tendencies of his father, Abdur Rahman Khan, and rule with a lighter touch and fewer acts of genocide. He also welcomed back exiled intellectuals and whole sections of the royal family who had fled in terror during the terror of his father's rule. Accordingly, under Habibullah's rule, pockets of Afghanistan were pitched forward into the twentieth century through the advent of printing presses, factories, science, photographs, Western clothes and an influx of new ideas. Turkish doctors, printers and military experts came to Kabul, vying with British interests in the capital and setting up tensions and rivalries that would explode in conflicts which still echo today. Histories, notably the unsurpassable *Siraj al-Tawarikh* of Fayz Mohammad Kateb, were written embracing Afghanistan's history as a unified nation.

These Turkish-leaning intellectuals would be the bedrock on which Habibullah's modernisation process took place. With these figures came new ideas from the Young Turks and from Persia's own burgeoning constitutional movement. One returning intellectual, Mahmud Tarzi, a Mohammadzai aristocrat who had spent his exile in Ottoman Turkey, would attempt to change the face of Afghanistan with his reforming zeal, nationalism and strident anti-British sentiments. Yet in reality this zeal would prove more significant for the tensions to which it gave rise than the material success it delivered. During his exile, Tarzi had worked in bureaucratic roles within the Ottoman administration, giving him a firm faith in bureaucratic excellence and the importance of solidarity, be it achieved through nationalism, faith or education. Tarzi's themes also reflected those of Mohammad Abduh in Egypt and his protégé, Mohammad Rashid Rida, in espousing ideas of nationalism, pan-Islamism and education through reform as being the basis on which Islamic nations could compete with the West. Nationalism, modernism and Pan-Islamism thus all combined to inform an ideology of dynamic change in Afghanistan. This was a task to which all of Afghanistan must turn its efforts; it was the responsibility of 'an enlightened Muslim religious leadership, the Afghan scholars, and the ruling elites'.[48]

The mouthpiece of Afghanistan's modernist dream was the newspaper *Siraj al-Akhbar Afghaniyah* (The Lamp of the News of Afghanistan), a bi-weekly Persian publication which ran from October 1911 to January 1919. It was a publication which 'promised to be the tribune of an ideology, first and foremost modernistic, pan-Islamic and nationalistic'.[49] *Siraj al-Akhbar*'s leading figure, and editor, was Mahmud Tarzi. The narrative that Afghanistan had fallen behind the West because of its rejection of science in favour of superstition and outmoded tradition propelled Tarzi and his group of reformers in Kabul. The country, he said, lacked unity and national purpose or feeling; it was the role of his paper to provide this. *Siraj al-Akhbar* featured news from around the world, strident articles on modern themes and photos of Turkish cities and Islamic mosques.[50] Its themes were nationalism, independence and modernisation for Afghanistan. Amongst the subjects addressed in the paper were 'the natural and evolutionary progress of humanity; the causes of cyclones; the human circulatory system; meteorology; geology and cosmology; archaeology, geography, and historiography; international law, political science, and municipal government; and the importance of joint stock companies'.[51] Public health was a particular topic of concern, and a mania for medicine and hygiene gripped the pages of Afghanistan's modernist mouthpiece. Ghoulish photos of facial and bodily disfigurements before operations—vast tumours, cleft lips and rotting legs—all featured in this bi-weekly paean to the wonders of Western medicine and science. It was, and still is, a total inspiration, a marvellous historical document full of possibility and the heady seduction of revolutionary change. European books, such as Jules

Verne's *Around theWorld in Eighty Days*, were translated into Persian and serialised in its pages.

Yet this was a distinctly Kabul-centric phenomenon. Its reach into Herat was sketchy at best. The crumbling ruins of Khorasan's pearl were not suited to a modernist dream of science, factories, Western medicine and the harsh ideals of Pan-Islamism or Pan-Asianism. Herat's history was, if anything, pan-Herati in its outlook, despite having experienced the unwanted attentions of so many empires. In an ominous warning to Herat, *Siraj al-Akhbar* thundered, 'Times of poetry are bygone. It is now the time of action and effort. The era is that of motor, rail and electricity. The time of camels, oxen and donkeys is bygone.'[52] It seemed that Herat was also bygone as well. Across the pages of *Siraj al-Akhbar* it is rarely mentioned; articles reporting events there are scarce. One article, from 17 March 1915, simply reports on the snow and rain which for that apparently incessant winter had battered Herat; it had frozen its waterfalls mid-flow. Snow blindness and the cold seem to have been the most important events in a city which had once been at the forefront of global events.[53] Herat was left to kick its cultured heels and recite poetry, although quietly, for poetry was, according to Tarzi, the enemy of progress and a sure sign of Afghanistan's backwardness. At the dawn of a new Afghanistan, Herat was yesterday's metropolis.

These reforming strains, this dynamic nationalism beloved of Tarzi, are difficult to wrestle into Herat's identity; the city itself was still unsure of its own place in the Afghan nation, isolated as it was. Perhaps it welcomed the comforting umbrella of an Afghan nation; perhaps it was uneasy about such a phenomenon? Yet there was a practical logic to this, for owing to the poor quality of the roads linking Herat to the capital, it was unlikely to profit from anything more than the most rudimentary benefits that modernisation might confer. Hardened as it was by years of suffering, it surely viewed any grandiose nationwide plans with a healthy dose of scepticism. Nationalism, too, was a contested point in Herat, for nations are traditionally bound together by common ties of heritage, soil, climate, language and way of life. Herat, however, had its own climate, the 'wind of 120 days', its own fabled customs and history; it spoke Persian, unlike many of Kabul's Pashtun ruling elites, and saw itself as distant from the Pashtuns of Kabul, Farah and Qandahar and distinct from the Uzbeks in the north, or even the Nuristanis over the Hindu Kush. The tangled skeins of its history—Sunni, Shia, Persian, Pashtun—placed Herat in a sort of limbo.

Yet as far as the British were concerned, Herat and the city's strategic importance had not been entirely forgotten. Reports from 1904 from an agent in Herat tell that Herat's governors were opening his letters to the British. The agent writes that he found himself under grave suspicion, watched day and night, with a guard outside his house. Herat's governor, for his part, was worried the British would 'convert Afghanistan into a Native State of India' if information on his province were known to London and India.[54] Surely, however, this fear had been rendered obsolete by the quite extraordinary amount of information collected during the years of the Afghan Boundary Commission? The Great Game still flickered, just.

* * *

When World War I came, it was something of a miracle that Habibullah managed to keep Afghanistan neutral and not under the German–Ottoman alliance, as so many wanted. Afghanistan had become a hotbed of anti-British sentiment. The Dean Treaty of 1905, described by one Afghan historian as a treaty forced upon Afghanistan 'without so much as a what or a why', had reaffirmed Afghanistan's status as a British protectorate, and in the process strengthened Kabul's growing dislike for all things British.[55] Two years later, the Anglo-Russian Convention of 1907 was conducted exclusively between British and Russian diplomats in St Petersburg, cementing British pre-eminence in Afghanistan whilst effectively dividing up Persia between the two superpowers. Afghanistan and Persia reacted with justified horror at this diplomatic fiat, and anti-British sentiments in the region rose accordingly. The catastrophe of the 1907 Anglo-Russian Convention gave credence to those, such as Tarzi, who argued for reform as a way to strengthen and make their nation independent from foreign intrigue, yet it also alarmed the conservative religious and political elites who feared that more European meddling in Afghanistan would change their country for good by removing religious elites from positions of control in the spheres of education and the law.

As World War I wore on, the pages of *Siraj al-Akhbar* hummed with letters tending towards cooperation with the Germans and the

Ottomans against the Allies. There was a growing feeling, at odds with official policy, that the British should be forced to leave Afghanistan; the desire to throw Afghanistan's lot in with the German–Ottoman forces became a real one, growing at court. The clamour to reject British support caused Habibullah to rebuke Tarzi for his provocatively anti-British stance; Habibullah set great store by his alliance with the British, no matter how distasteful it might appear to his court.[56] Just how distasteful British and European involvement in Afghanistan appeared to the royal court can be seen in an article written in 1915 for *Harper's Weekly* by a royal nephew. In this article prince Ahmad Abdullah gave vent to a rich seam of anti-British feeling:

> The common basis of our steadily growing Asian solidarity is hatred of the whites, the Christians. We hate the European because we consider him an intolerable barbarian, who bullies where his wheedling is unsuccessful. We hate him because, according to us, he is torturous and cannot speak the truth; because he prates about his new-found hygiene, but is personally unclean compared to the majority of the Asians.[57]

For Herat, it was external events which would propel it back into the limelight for a brief few weeks in the summer of 1915. A new Great Game was taking hold of Afghanistan, testing Habibullah's mettle and the strength of his alliance with the British. This iteration of the Great Game, however, was not aimed at controlling gates or keys, but at inflaming the minds of Afghanistan and India's Muslims against British India. Its backdrop was World War I. This wildly ambitious scheme produced some of the most fascinating, flawed and unfathomable characters to have ever graced a region with a long history of putative and actual world conquerors.[58] As per the Treaty of Gandamak, reaffirmed in 1905, Afghanistan had pledged to be neutral in World War I, but a German–Turkish alliance aimed to topple the British from India by calling a *jihad* to inflame the hearts and minds of the region's Muslims, and thus begin a war against British rule in India, weakening the British irrevocably. Leaflets, written in Urdu, Pashtu, Persian and Hindi, proclaimed a *jihad* against the British empire in India; Indian revolutionaries from Japan, to New York, to South Africa agitated against British rule in India. For these figures the starting point of their plan for world domination was Afghanistan. In London and India, Russophobia was now replaced by the menace of this German–Turkish alliance whose grandiose ambitions seem in hindsight to have been hopelessly ambitious. The German Kaiser even claimed, in letters and leaflets to be distributed around the region, that he had converted to Islam and preformed the Hajj. This was to be a war in India, in Afghanistan and anywhere that a restless Muslim population could be roused from their slumber to throw off the yoke of British imperialism. This era of megalomania was immortalised in John Buchan's 1916 novel, *Greenmantle*.

On 19 August 1915 a group of German spies, doctors, a few Indian revolutionaries and some very tired, thirsty and sick hangers-on crossed over the Persian border into Afghanistan. Leading the group were two charismatic German soldier–adventurers, an Indian Hindu revolutionary and an Indian Muslim revolutionary named Barakatullah, who had spent time in New York and once said that 'the firing of an Afghan gun will give the signal for the rising of all of Islam'.[59] The Germans, Oscar von Niedermayer and Werner Otto von Hentig, were Persian-speaking soldier–adventurer–spies for whom the term 'iron-willed' could well have been invented. Their journey from Constantinople to Baghdad and through Persia had outwitted British and Russian armies, respectively in the south and north; they had travelled through neutral central Persia and eventually made it to the relative safety of Afghanistan as 'parched skeletons', having lost roughly a third of their manpower and animals.[60] Niedermayer describes his reception into the lush fields which ran along the Hari Rud oasis as something close to paradise. Gleaming mosques and running water in lush gardens made Herat a welcome break from tortured flight through parched desert. Hentig wrote of 'a light Viennese spirit' pervading the city, 'with exotic flowers and upwardly pointing shoes' being one of many visual feasts for bodies scourged by desert and hounded by imperial armies.[61] Hentig donned his spiked helmet and put on his best blue military cuffs of his regiment, the Prussian 3rd Cuirassiers, for the occasion of their reception into the city. Herat's governor, Mahmud Sarwar Khan, gave the group an enthusiastic welcome, and the German emissaries con-vened meetings in which they promised the Afghans swathes of land, gold and men at arms if they decided to rally to the Ottoman–German *jihad*. Herat's governor demurred, saying that he would have to get Kabul's permission before accepting these wild offers, conscious that the days of rebellious abandon were long gone. Herat might have still been isolated, but it could no longer afford to pursue its own independent policy as it had once done in the nineteenth century. Yet despite this, the group was given licence to roam the city, explore its ruins and luxuriate in eating the melons and other fruits that stocked the bazaars. Sarwar Khan entertained the emissaries with surprising liberality, even stretching to buy them new clothes and their horses new saddles. After two weeks of meetings, eating and entertainments, the group went on their way to meet Amir Habibullah in Kabul in pursuit of their *jihad*, having been given enough by way of encouragement from Herat to make them hopeful that they might, through Afghanistan, topple British India in a hail of *jihadi* pamphlets and unified insurrection.

One Afghan historian sees the group's positive reception in Herat as an example of the positive feeling the Niedermayer mission produced amongst Afghans, not simply because of the pro-Turkish sentiments which informed many of Kabul's elites, but also because of its distinctly anti-British stance.[62] It is true that Germany's increasing power represented an attractive makeweight against the tired empires of Britain and Russia, and this is what attracted so many Afghans to the success of this mission. But surely these schemes would have appeared ludicrous to Herat, a city so used to imperial hubris and megalomania? Yet given what was at stake, it is no wonder that British alarm peaked as these men crossed Persia, into Afghanistan and eventually into Kabul. Ultimately, however, the mission hit the wall of Habibullah's neutrality in Kabul, where the Germans and their Indian colleagues were effectively put under house arrest. Despite promises of money, arms and India, Niedermayer and Hentig could not move Habibullah from his position of pro-British neutrality. They left Kabul empty-handed to face difficult journeys home.

For their mission, Herat was nothing more than a stopover, a rest on the way to more serious business in Kabul. Yet during the short weeks that Niedermayer was in Herat, he took some of the most beautiful photos of the city that have ever been taken. He recorded haunting images of nomads on the way from Herat to Kabul, huddling under their slanting black felt tents, children staring directly into his camera lens with a curious intensity, and a whole city at prayer. Niedermayer's photos of Herat show a peaceful, even slumbering town, bathed in late summer heat. Walled compounds enclose houses with domed roofs and beautiful gardens; the city walls appear proud yet crumbling, and men and horses mill around arches and shops. The Qalah-ye Ekhtiar al-Din still appears imposing and magnificent, if crumbling; stiff-backed troops shuffle out from within, rifles leaning against their shoulders, while some watch on; and a flock of sheep graze as the troops file past. It is possible to see the vast scale of the citadel from one of the photos, taken from the south-west: it rises away from the viewer into a heaped mass of solid masonry built upon centuries of previous iterations that have been torn down and rebuilt, torn down and rebuilt. Its heft sits almost apologetically alongside images of the delicate and complex tiled motifs still extant on minarets and crumbling Timurid ruins. Inside the Friday Mosque, the Kartid bowl stands amidst rubble, proudly placed in the centre of the main courtyard, and Niedermayer shows us remaining bands of Kufic inscriptions, Ghurid glazed tiles and the intricacy of the tiles cloaking the faces of the mosque.

The best photos, however, are reserved for the northern meadows of Herat, where the Timurid architectural project had once reached such heights. Nine minarets stand against the heat. Gawhar Shad's mausoleum still gives flashes of its former magnificence and an image of one of the minarets in her *madrasa* give us an idea of how imposing and affecting this space would have been. Men on horseback gaze at the ruins, while one German figure stands next to a ruin, hands on hips in admiration. Another image has a man next to his horse in the shadow of a minaret from Gawhar Shad's *madrasa*, with her mausoleum behind, to the man's right; he is dwarfed by the sheer scale of the buildings, and despite their ruined state, it is impossible not to be awestruck by the beauty of this spectacle and what it suggests. Niedermayer shows us Gazur Gah much as it appears today, complete with a wizened gate-keeper at the entrance.

An image of Herat at prayer is especially moving; thousands upon thousands stand in massed ranks, offering up Friday prayers on a large open space to the north of the Old City walls, possibly where Husain Bayqara's *mosalla* complex had once stood. A sea of white turbans prepare to kneel in prayer, watched over by the Old City walls. The images are evocative of Herat's essential charm, its casual elegance and the lively curiosity of its children's faces.[63] The simplicity of these images hints at so much of the city's history, and yet they also perfectly encapsulate Herat in its state of enforced isolation: a relic of previous imperial ages. Looking back at the photos, in the cold of an approaching London winter, I become homesick for Herat and its crumbling minarets, its imposing citadel and the energy of its bazaars, and all the joy the city gives to those who spend even a few weeks there, as Niedermayer did.

German intrigue in Herat, however, did not stop with the departure of Niedermayer and his diminished troop of would-be global revolutionaries. Herat still played host to echoes of German intrigue; in the high summer of 1919 two mysterious Germans, von Gruden and Dimitrovich, were shot dead in Herat as they tried to escape their Afghan pursuers, most likely tipped off by the British. Their intentions in Herat were unknown, but it is likely that they sought to succeed where Niedermayer and Hentig had failed. In a gruesome coda to an otherwise perfunctory intelligence report, the British agent at Herat writes that 'their black box is still in Herat'.[64]

* * *

On 21 February 1919, Habibullah was out hunting in Laghman. On that morning, however, he was the hunted. An assassin's bullet brought his sometimes exciting, definitely transformative and largely peaceful rule to an end. The assassination manifested the clash between his politics of gradual change, and the intellectuals', or Young Afghans', drive for speedy national modernisation and independence. His reign had shown Afghanistan the advantages and disadvantages of reform and nationalism, the tensions between an absolutist and traditional monarchy and an intellectual elite demanding a national transformation, a transformation which had alienated the nation's dominant conservative Islamic classes. Above all, however, what had been clear from Habibullah's reign was that it was independence from Britain that Afghanistan desired. After a five-day reign in Jalalabad of a royal prince, another of his sons, Amanullah Khan (r.1919–29), a son-in-law of the reformer Mahmud Tarzi, was crowned amir in Kabul. Amanullah was a nationalist in the mould of his father-in-law, Tarzi, and the new king soon sought Afghanistan's independence as a way of freeing his nation from its status as a protectorate. He immediately demanded independence from the British, and then marched troops to Afghanistan's shared borders with India. On 4 May the Third Anglo-Afghan War broke out. Afghan troops attacked the British base at Thal, but after only a matter of weeks of fighting, both sides sought terms. Britain could ill afford yet another Afghan disaster. By the terms of the Treaty of Rawalpindi, signed on 8 August 1919, Afghanistan ended its hated submission to British India.[65] With Afghanistan's third victory over the might of imperial Britain in under a century, they could at last celebrate their national day of independence, still commemorated on 8 August every year.

With independence now assured, the country could turn to reform and progress: a hail of treaties of alliance and a flood of experts, diplomats and advisers. Tarzi and his 'Young Afghan' movement of intellectuals now had its moment. On 24 August 1919, the first edition of a publication called *Ettefaq-e Islam* (Islamic Solidarity) appeared in Herat.[66] It was a celebrated event, and it runs to this day. *Ettefaq-e Islam* was a weekly publication of news from Afghanistan and abroad, and published on a 'yellowy' paper by a lithograph printing press in Herat.[67] In 1919 it was part of a boom in Afghanistan's publishing industry, a legacy of *Siraj al-Akhbar*, bleeding into the provinces. The unifying cry of Amanullah's first months as amir seems to have reached Herat, for the strapline of poetry which sat at its head praised national unity as the cornerstone of a happy nation:

That which makes a nation happy and joyful,
Is unity, is unity, is unity.[68]

Ettefaq-e Islam carried news sections, from Afghanistan and abroad, and had poetry, culture and history sections, giving Herat a window into a world that had forgotten it. *Ettefaq-e Islam* also translated diplomatic treaties, in particular the Treaty of Rawalpindi, bringing news of outside events to Khorasan in a way not seen since the nineteenth century when Herat was the news itself. Possibly by way of Persia, *Ettefaq-e Islam* even managed the occasional scoop. One story in particular reported on a 'raging fire in London' that was translated into Persian for the readers of Herat.[69] Herat's yearning for inclusion in an Afghan nation is clear from the poetry which ran across the top of *Ettefaq-e Islam*, but the reality was often different, for Herat remained isolated from Kabul and cut adrift, despite the good intentions of its intelligen-tsia. Despite this, *Ettefaq-e Islam*'s appearance in Herat should be seen as an indication of the strength of nationalist feeling created by 1919 and the Treaty of Rawalpindi.

Herat's experience of these years of Amanullah's energetic drives for reform and free expression, as enshrined in Article 11 of Afghanistan's first constitution of 1924, did not stop at its citizens reading about fires in London, uprisings in India and, presumably, floods in Kabul.[70] The Knowledge Printing House (*Motabeh-ye Danesh*) was one of a number of non-state printing houses in Afghanistan, which was opened in Herat in 1927 by a group of private Heratis. It satisfied a growing elite thirst for news, literature, history and connections. Little is known about this printing house—it was privately run, featured poetry and literature with a nationalist orientation and was sorely in need of funds—but there exists a letter signed by its editor in chief, Soror Juya, which was sent to an important publication in Kabul, *Anis Journal*, in 1927. The letter was from 'a small number of knowledgeable and insightful [*ahl-e danesh wa fahm*] people of Herat' who for some years had been labour-ing in the pursuit of a national dream; they were in need of some assis-tance from Kabul and elsewhere to keep this dream alive in the form of a publication which embraced nationalist dreams and elegant lines of poetry.[71] Any committee of poets that might be sent to Herat would be of use, as would paper, technical and other assistance. The letter was dotted with references to a beautiful and prosperous nation, and is very much of a piece with the line of poetry which heralded the beginning of the publication of *Ettefaq-e Islam* and so many other similar publica-tions around Afghanistan at the time. This private printing house was no doubt driven by a nationalist sentiment, but it did not want for influ-ences from abroad: its founder had made a number of trips to the Soviet Union and Persia to gather expertise and understanding about how such an endeavour should be put into practice, before returning to Herat to begin work. The echoes with Herat's private magazines and journals of today are impossible to ignore, and the Knowledge Printing House of Herat was the first in a long, yet occasionally broken, line of private initiatives in the cultural sphere which mark out Herat as a city of independent cultural and artistic action. Today, private-led publica-tions proliferate in Herat, covering culture, science and news and offering employment and expression to its people. Yet unfortunately Herat's private Knowledge Printing House faded away in the chaos of the later 1920s and disappeared completely, along with Amanullah Khan. It was most likely merged with the city's government printing house.

Ghulam Muhi al-Din *Anis* (d.1938) was a native of Herat who had published books in Herat on the importance of education for an enlightened and unified nation; he had experienced life in Cairo and travelled throughout the Islamic world. An intellectual, nationalist, historian, poet and free-thinker, he sought to change Afghanistan for the better by chipping away at the entrenched conservatism that he felt held his country back. Accordingly, in the early spring of 1926, he left Herat 'with a few books and magazines', most likely his own, for Kabul, where he set up a magazine in which he could push ideas of political, social and legal reform to a more enlightened public than the one he felt resided in Herat.[72] This publication was called *Anis*.

Ghulam Muhi al-Din had thought of starting up this modernist publication in Herat, but, as one of his close friends recounted, one particular event convinced him of the need to leave his home city and head to Kabul, hoping one day to return to Herat where he might reform and reshape the city according to his enlightened vision. For the time being, he felt that Herat was beyond redemption. This was the winter of 1926, and he was in Herat's bazaar. He heard a scuffle erupting on the streets. A young man, Ibrahim, was in a heated argument with a group of men with whom he 'had a private problem', and the group was in the process of dragging Ibrahim to the courthouse, where presumably he would be punished for this imagined crime, and the score between the two families would be settled by Ibrahim's imprisonment, or worse. Ghulam Muhi al-Din fell in with the group and asked them what the problem was; to which they replied, 'He was saying infidel slogans [*kufar amiz*], and slandering us.' Muhi al-Din used his eloquence to defuse the situation and effect a reconciliation, saving the young boy from an unpleasant and undeserved fate. He took the boy to one side, sent him to a *madrasa* for a few days and then instructed him to leave Herat for a while to let the problem subside. This event convinced Muhi al-Din, more than anything else, that Herat and Afghanistan were in need of reform, of laws, of education and of enlightened thinking. Muhi al-Din concluded that as long as 'this nation doesn't see the light of education and its guidance, it will forever remain in ignorance and darkness'.[73] The paper that he founded in Kabul, *Anis*, sought to provide 'a service to society and to people' in educating Afghanistan on the values of enlightened thinking, literature and freedom of expression; it ran until the 1980s.

Amanullah, too, sought to open up Herat to the world outside, and to expand Afghanistan's telephone and communication systems. A telegraph system was introduced during his reign, and it was under Amanullah that Herat's first hotels opened, descendants of the old caravanserais that had once welcomed British travellers in disguise. The city became the capital of one of the five administrative provinces into which Amanullah divided the country, the others being Kabul, Qandahar, Afghan Turkestan and Badakhshan; this gives us a faint sense of Herat's gradual absorption into an Afghan nation from this time.[74] Amanullah improved the roads that Habibullah had built linking Kabul to Qandahar and Herat, and Herat gradually became less the isolated Persian enclave it had been under earlier Afghan rulers. In the sphere of trade Herat also saw improvements, reaping the benefits of its place at the edge of empires. Between 1928 and 1932, the Soviet Union gained a greater share of the Afghan market; in Herat and northern Afghanistan, goods made in Bukhara and Tashkent became dominant, replacing British monopolies on bazaar goods and clothing.[75] Yet despite all this, Herat could not shake the notion that it was a city apart, a legacy of its turbulent eighteenth and nineteenth centuries as a Sadozai enclave, menaced from all sides.

Amanullah's reign had brought to Afghanistan printing presses, a smattering of education (one school in Herat), some hotels and greater connections with the outside world. Although mostly a Kabul phenomenon, his reign had also brought social reforms addressing polygamy, the veiling of women and had introduced notions of secular education. Yet these reforms stirred up resentment and mistrust amongst the country's conservative Muslim elites; the spheres of law, society and education were theirs, not to be tampered with. The backlash would be every bit as revolutionary for Herat and Afghanistan as what had gone before, and it came in the form of Amanullah's abdication, a nationwide uprising and a nine-month reign of chaos by an illiterate Tajik bandit named Habibullah Kalakani. His nickname, Bache-ye Saqao (son of the water carrier), is an indication of how history has judged Kalakani. Whilst it is fashionable amongst Pashtuns and Persians alike to deride Kalakani and his governance as an aberration, a historical anomaly, it cannot be denied that he enjoyed the support of scores of important religious and tribal figures, and even by some Ghilzai Pashtuns, who felt that he was the man to stem the tide of modernisation that so threatened Afghanistan's conservative Muslim values. Ghulam Muhi al-Din *Anis* even edited Kalakani's official paper, *Habib al-Islam*. Kalakani enjoyed genuine popularity and credibility, if only as a counterweight to the revolutionary rate of reforms of Amanullah and the 'Young Afghans'. He was a Robin Hood type of figure, whose brigandage in and around the north of Kabul appealed to the poor, to whom he often gave the spoils.[76] Afghanistan's conservative elites were particularly scandalised by photos of Amanullah and his wife in European clothing; Kalakani was the man to right these wrongs, and he took Kabul in January 1929, desecrating the capital through looting and violence. Schools closed, mullahs took the place of secular teachers and education shrank back to its barest Islamic bones. These were chaotic times in Afghanistan, its eastern tribes in a state of revolt, its treasury empty. Such was the fiscal disaster facing the new ruler that Kalakani tried to issue leather coins in the place of real silver or metal ones.[77] To mark Afghanistan's independence day in 1929, he gave a speech to the assembled Afghans praising their efforts to free the country from foreign control and promising never to give up the fight in the name of Islam and Afghanistan; he finished with the ambitious promise that 'next Eid, we shall be saying our prayers in London!'[78]

One eyewitness account of Herat during Habibullah Kalakani's ill-fated rule over Afghanistan gives us a different view to the blood and thunder which so much of the country experienced. The memoirs of Bagher Kazemi, a Persian diplomat who had postings in Paris and New York and later became Foreign Minister, show us Herat at its most down at heel and politically irrelevant. Kazemi arrived in Herat in early March 1929, as Afghanistan was scorching in the fire of Kalakani's revolutionary surge throughout the east and south. He spent a frustrating few hours waiting for a car to take him into the city from its outskirts. When he finally arrived, he described the city as 'deplorable', and as a Shia he felt immediately menaced and threatened by the conservative Sunni Muslims of Herat.[79] Discussing the situation with soldiers at the Perso-Afghan border, he was shocked to hear glib boasts about how many men they had each killed, to see their simple manners and to imagine the horrors that both these things might portend for his mission to Herat. After the joys of his airplane flight, brilliantly described, from Tehran to Mashhad, a tense and febrile Afghanistan was not the welcome this cultured diplomat expected (Kazemi's descriptions of Herat's minarets, mud walls and fertile plains from an airplane are perhaps the first of their kind). Kazemi enters into great detail about the altitude, distance covered and every little sensation connected with flying; the shaking of the airplane gave his legs and arms a warm feeling. His head touched the roof of the inside of the cabin.[80]

On 23 February 1929, Kazemi had been told by his diplomatic superiors that he was going to Herat; it hit him 'like a thunderbolt', and he even considered disobeying his orders.[81] Kazemi met his superiors, and asked what on earth Persia had to do with Afghanistan any more? He was told that Persia had received reports that Amanullah was planning to move his capital to Herat, after a retreat to Qandahar, and that he was to fly immediately to Herat so as to be a welcoming party there for the returning Amanullah.[82] Quite where the Qajars got this information from is unclear, as it seems unlikely that Herat was being considered as a capital of a post-Kalakani Afghanistan. Kazemi's account of this meeting is in the very best traditions of adventure writing: 'take anything and anyone you need, and do as you see fit'. Ultimately, Kazemi did not meet Amanullah in Herat, and neither did the latter transfer his capital to that city. Wishful thinking on the part of Tehran, perhaps? Yet all the same, this was an important mission, and one for which Kazemi was seemingly well suited.

When Kazemi arrived in March 1929, Herat prayers were still being read in the name of Amanullah Khan, although this required the city's military chief, Mohammad Ghaws Khan, to be standing next to the mosque's minaret and threatening Herat's chief mullah with a gun before he would agree to announce prayers in the name of Amanullah Khan.[83] The city did not surrender to Kalakani's troops until May, but from Kazemi's journal, one would be hard pressed to notice the changes. Within the city, Kazemi tells us, life under Kalakani was largely the same. A new governor, but not much else. Accordingly, he talks of his time in Herat, as Kabul fell to pieces and Afghanistan was in the midst of a veritable revolution, as 'boredom, disorder, idleness and gloom'.[84] Clearly Kalakani's edicts on clamping down on *Ettefaq-e Islam* were far exaggerated, for although Kazemi talks of Afghanistan's papers undergoing name changes, Herat's *Ettefaq-e Islam* seems to have continued much as before. Kazemi even met its proprietor, a man he described as being 'warm hearted and a great patriot'.[85] His entries describe the occasional fearful rumour, a brief coup attempt, from which he hid out of fear of his life, but then always a return to the familiar and the quiet. Kazemi even gently mocks Herat's independence, its isolation from Kabul, when he refers to Abdul Karim Khan, the city's governor, as Herat's Bismarck, surely waspish irony, but clearly making the point that Herat was largely seen to do as it pleased, although without the pomp of a nineteenth-century German imperialist.

The reality of Kazemi's time in the city was diametrically opposed to the adventures he was promised. Life in Herat was for the cultured diplomat a boring, frustrating, difficult time. Anti-Shia feelings stalked him wherever he went, and no visit to a mullah in Herat was complete without some anti-Shia invective being thrown his way. When he was not vomiting from dysentery, or being eaten alive by mosquitoes, he was homesick, tired and fed up. Herat's virulent strain of anti-Shia feeling was a depressing refrain for Kazemi's time there, and it is hardly surprising that he chose to summarise Afghanistan's problematic relationship with modernisation in the following manner: until such a time as each Afghan can refrain from killing 'thirty of forty' Shia, the country will never reform in the slightest.[86] He did enjoy sightseeing, however, and derived some pleasure from examining the Timurid remains, no doubt lamenting a vanished Persian Golden Age. His quarters in the *khiaban*, once host to diplomats at the global court of the Timurid sultans, were poorly built and run down; Kazemi was, one senses, 500 years late. Whereas the nineteenth century had barely progressed without some sort of a conflagration, real or imagined, in and around Herat, at this point history was passing Herat by. In the absence of white-hot political intrigue, sightseeing and picnics were a welcome distraction for this bored diplomat. During the Nawruz (Persian New Year) festivities of March 1929, Kazemi managed to go sightseeing to the Malan bridge and have a picnic on the Takht-e Safar; a convivial meeting with various religious figures, and tea and sweets with Herat's Persian population capped a relaxing and trouble-free celebration of the New Year.[87]

He passed his time in sleepy Herat by reading news of events in Persia, and his account is notable for the fact that he was more concerned with events in his home country and the outside world than he was with Afghanistan's own momentous shifts and evolutions. He even described his time in Herat as 'imprisonment and obsolescence', and his homesickness jumps from the page when he mentions reading letters from home about parties and picnics in Tehran.[88] Kazemi's observations on Herat's healthcare system border on the comical: 'Perhaps no one will believe me when I say that a city like Herat has no pharmacy or decent doctor...'[89] There were two old doctors who, according to Kazemi, had read Avicenna, but for the rest the city was a mess of dirty water and poor hygiene. Clearly the healthcare drive under Habibullah Khan had not reached into Khorasan. Like all visitors to Herat, Kazemi toured the bathhouses, and on their dirty walls he was surprised to see photos of Persian soldiers and the Qajar governor of Khorasan. As a conclusion to this surprising observation, he writes that the city's sanitation was appalling.[90] The citadel was a heinous big lump, the centre of politics and daily life; the mosque was falling down, with ruins visible everywhere, and the roof was caving in.[91] To fill a cultural void which Herat's post-apocalyptic landscape seemed to have created, Kazemi would spend one evening a week at the Russian consulate, listening to music concerts on the radio and catching up on world news. His account is notable for the fact that news from outside Herat takes up far more space than news from the city itself. A senior figure in Herat's military establishment, Shojah al-Dawlah, welcomed Kazemi for supper on the night of 27 March 1929 with shouts of hoorays and a few shots fired in the air. Kazemi felt the man was a charlatan who was pathologically unable to speak the truth, but the supper was nonetheless convivial.[92] As if to break the tedium of Kazemi's Herati life, a Japanese man came to Herat in September 1929 along with a delegation from the Japanese embassy in Tehran; they spoke a little English with Kazemi and provided a distraction or two. Meanwhile, life continued much as normal: hunting, trips to mosques, radio evenings with the Russians.[93]

In August 1929, rumours were circulating round Herat of Nader Khan's increased power in the east of the country. Herat was calm, and its military leaders were neither 'openly or privately' (*zaheran ya bat-enan*) in favour of Kalakani, preferring to remain neutral and stay out of any military revolutions for the time being.[94] In keeping with Herat's falling off the political map, they were afforded the luxury of remaining 'neutral' and waiting to see what happened. Herat's people feared more war if its governor opposed the man who would take Kalakani's place on the throne, Nader Khan of the Mushahebin dynasty. Consequently, Herat's soldiers were gathered together in the citadel and forced to recant their loyalty to Kalakani in favour of neutrality. Some with suspected Kalakani sympathies were dismissed, although this seems to have been a token gesture. Kazemi wrote that the military commander of Herat, Abdul Karim Khan, spoke the following words to the assembled, possibly confused, soldiery: 'In the centre and south of Afghanistan, it is a field of revolution; it is still not clear who will become shah, and so it is best for Herat that we remain totally neutral in light of what may transpire.'[95] For those assembled in the citadel, so long as conflict did not erupt into Herat, a change of government could be seen as a positive development.

On 3 September 1929, news came to Herat that Habibullah Kalakani, Afghanistan's Tajik king, had fled his throne in the face of the returning armies of Nader Khan and his brothers.[96] Herat was confused and not entirely sure what was transpiring in Kabul. Kazemi himself was much more optimistic about a Nader Khan-led Afghanistan than the chaos that had erupted under Kalakani, even if Herat had mostly escaped unscathed save for an increase in anti-Shia violence. Kazemi wrote that 'the revolutionary period in Afghanistan is at an end', but one cannot help feeling that this was more in hope than anything else. What comes through in his memoirs of Herat is the unpredictability of that city, and its utter removal from, and irrelevance to, what was going on to the east.[97] The end came on 23 October 1929, when the government of Nader Khan was announced throughout Herat, bringing to a close the reign of Afghanistan's first and last Tajik king, Habibullah Kalakani. Kazemi went sightseeing as Kabul was looted and sacked in the chaos that followed.[98] Even though Herat had suffered little, it welcomed the certainty that Nader Khan's rule brought; life could return to its previous pedestrian pace after the briefest of ripples.

Aside from the occasional scare of a Kalakani revival, Herat largely remained peaceful and calm as the news-loving, radio-listening, home-sick Persian diplomat departed the province in the late winter of 1930. On leaving Herat, Kazemi's final hope for Herat was that it could rise above its appalling hatred of the Shia and that Herat's Shia might live in peace and prosperity in Afghanistan.[99]

* * *

By the early 1930s, Herat had slipped further into a state of slumber. A British intelligence report of early 1932 described a 'general air of peace and contentment amongst the populace' of Herat.[100] Soldiers around the city, the report said, were rare, and Herat went about its business in a calm, tranquil and ordered fashion: a continuation of Kazemi's world, minus the ennui and stomach cramps. Even troops on the road from Herat to Qandahar numbered single figures, suggesting peaceful roads and way of life. Herat's trade with India, which followed that road, continued as normal. Persian coins circulated in the bazaar, much as they do today, and the cotton mills set up in Amanullah's time stood unmanned, testament to the stagnated modernisation drive that he had begun. The new city that Amanullah had begun to build outside the northern walls of the Old City was not yet finished, and little work was being done on it at the time of the 1932 report, which notes that 'It consists of one broad street parallel to the north wall with side streets running north about every hundred yards with a second mains street parallel to the first.'[101] The USSR had a few officials in their consulate, and the report noted that the Kabul post left Herat on Wednesdays, taking twenty days to reach the capital: quiet, ordered, isolated.[102] In the spring of 1933, two Americans, a Dr Sproull and a Mr Pease, passed through Herat on their way to Qandahar, but had to turn back because of spring floods, and they remained in Herat a few days. No more than thirty cars or trucks moved about the city, and sleepy life rumbled on.

On 8 November 1933, a Hazara activist murdered Nader Shah as he visited the Nejat High School in Kabul. Nader Shah's death brought to the throne his son, Zaher Shah (r.1933–73). Zaher Shah would preside over one of the most peaceful and prosperous times in Afghanistan's history, ushering in gradual modernisation, a thriving tourist industry and recognition of Afghanistan on the regional stage.[103] Little changed in Herat in the aftermath of Nader Shah's assassination: a few more rifles on the streets, and some tension in the air, but life carried on very much as before. This crumbling yet historically significant city was the perfect setting for the arrival of the English travel writer and architectural historian, Robert Byron. In a few words Byron succeeded in summing up Herat's confidence, its wit, its intelligence and its sense of its own worth when he remarked, 'here at last is Asia without the inferiority complex'.[104] Herat's isolation from the modernising zeal of Kabul and Tehran meant that it could retain its casually confident insouciance.

Byron spent two stints of a week or so in Herat: in the autumn of 1933 and then the spring of 1934. His observations stand alongside the most amusing and fascinating accounts to have been written on the city throughout its long history. Characteristically poetic and witty, his initial summation of Herat reads as follows:

> Herat stands in a long cultivated plain, stretching east and west, being three miles equidistant from the Hari river on the south and the last spurs of the Paropamisus mountains on the north. There are two towns. The old is a maze of narrow and twisting streets enclosed by square ramparts, and bisected diagonally by the tunnel of the main bazaar, which is two miles long; on the north stands the Citadel, an imposing medieval fortress built on a mound, whence it dominates the surrounding plain. Opposite this lies the New Town, which consists of one broad street leading northward from the bazaar entrance, and a similar street intersecting it at right angles. These streets are lined with open fronted shops. Above then towers the second storey of the hotel, situated among the coppersmiths, whose clang between dawn and sunset deters the guests from sloth. Further on, at the crossroads, is the ticket office for lorries, where passengers assemble daily among bales of merchandise and vats of Russian petrol in wooden crates.[105]

Byron's writing captures Herat's gentle torpor, showing us the down at heel charm of this cultured outpost forgotten by time. He writes of false rumours that were half-heartedly circulated around the bazaars of the death of the young Zaher Shah, ostensibly put about to stir up anti-Shia feelings, but he then notes that order quickly returned to Herat's tranquil streets. It seems that Herat had not totally lost a simulacrum of martial vigour; Byron's apposite descriptions of Afghans carrying 'rifles to go shopping as Londoners carry umbrellas' finds a nice echo in Bruce Chatwin's later (1970) observation that Herati men 'storm about with artificial ferocity, flashing dark and disdainful glances'.[106] (Such men were the possibly descendants of the halberd-wielding town criers that Cheng observed in the fifteenth century.) Byron's description of Herat in springtime, 'now a sea of varying greens and silver streams', is a worthy, albeit unwitting successor to Beheshti Heravi's poetry.[107] In Byron's Herat, the 'lush emerald corn' that flanked the remains of the *mosalla* complex and the Gawhar Shad mausoleum contrasts beautifully with the azure bloom of the glittering minarets which he describes as rising into the heat of a temperate spring sky. Byron writes of a group of young religious students sitting in the shade of Gawhar Shad's mausoleum, hoping to catch some inspiration from Ali Shir Nawai or Gawhar Shad herself, engrossed in a lesson from a mullah. Reading this whilst in Herat was amusing for me, as I too saw young boys and girls walking around, books in hand, revising for exams or learning poems in those same gardens. I once stopped to speak to a young boy as he walked around the garden, head rocking back and forth in concentration, book in hand. I asked what he was learning and expected him to reply that these were verses from the Quran, or, at the very least, some Sufi poetry. He showed me the Periodic Table, and told me that it was almost impossible to learn all those strange-sounding names.

* * *

Cautious is a word one might use to describe the modernisation that was taking place in Herat at this time. As Byron and Kazemi's accounts illustrate, Herat was still wedded to its isolation. Yet change, nonetheless, did take place. To the north and east of the Old City walls, the city saw expansion: the main bazaars were enlarged, and the avenue which runs north to the Friday Mosque was expanded to create a wide boulevard space, much as would have existed in Timurid times; residential quarters were built to the east of the Old City, complete with banks, government buildings, hospitals, schools, a theatre and, later, a cinema. Herat city was moving outwards, onwards; a prosecutorial house, and exchequer's office, an office for the foreign ministry, and a customs office on the border with Persia all date from the 1930s. A hotel with a garage for cars and a caravanserai signalled Herat's intent to welcome dignitaries and tourists. Never a city to forget aesthetics, flower pots were ordered to line the roads in and out of the New City, to the north of the old walls. A Kabul almanac of 1937–8 features photos from Herat of these newly built, austere and unpopulated, buildings—hotels, government buildings and the governor's residence.[108] These buildings appear to have been dropped into Herat, bearing little or no resemblance to their nineteenth-century ancestors. They are stark and have no windows; one can see the earth which was dug for the foundations curling up around the base of the walls as if the walls had been forced into the earth from above.

Across Afghanistan, the 1930s was a time of literary societies, or *anjomans*, through which poetry, prose and academic discourse were discussed, published and embraced. Herat's Literary Anjoman (*Anjoman-e Adabi*) was set up in Herat in 1932, and its first publication appeared off the press on Monday 4 April 1932. This monthly publication was called *Majale-ye Herat* (Herat Magazine), and it ran until 1969. It published articles on history, society and literature. Under its auspices a literary magazine, *Mojale-ye adabi-ye Herat* (Literary Magazine of Herat), was published as a monthly discussion of literary themes and featuring contemporary poets.[109] According to its preamble it aimed at spreading the word of Herat and Afghanistan's literature and culture to its neighbours in Tajikistan and Persia, whilst also providing a forum for Herat's poets and historians to discuss and write. The magazine's main contributor and editor was Hajji Mohammad Ismail Khan Siyah, a poet of nationwide repute whose poetry touched on themes from mysticism to politics to Herat's plight as an isolated outcrop. His interactions with royalty and those in power are strongly reminiscent of the gently mocking tone that Timurid poets took with their unlettered patrons. One story concerns a trip by Siyah to Kabul, where Nader Shah asked why Herat contributed so little to the treasury in terms of taxes. Siyah replied that Herat was broke, but agreed to find a way to send tribute to Kabul, reflecting what Herat could pay. The chest which arrived in Kabul contained just one grain of rice, making the eloquent point that how could Herat expect to contribute to the Afghan nation if it were so cut off, isolated, poor and ignored?[110]

From the late 1930s onwards, it seems that everyone was passing through Herat to get to Kabul, stopping for a few days or weeks to taste the fruits, stroll amongst the ruins and admire the faded glories of an architectural museum. Bagher Kazemi's account shows better than almost any the political irrelevance of Herat at one of the most inflammatory periods of Afghanistan's recent history; this sense of a quiet backwater continues well into the twentieth century. And yet, the two themes of isolation and increasing nationalism are both in evidence from this quiet period of Herat's history. Nationalism competed with Herat's localism and isolation, and vice versa. For example, between 1933 and 1946, nearly 2,000 miles of roads were laid, and for the first time the trip from the northern provinces to Kabul could be made by motor vehicle. Buses, bicycles and trucks were imported in their thousands; a trip from Kabul to Herat could be made within three days, via Qandahar. Kabul hoped to join Herat to a larger Afghan project and strengthen national ties. In some ways this was achieved, as can be seen in the strains of nationalism which crept into Herat's musical sphere. As John Baily, the noted ethno-musicologist and Herat lover, shows in the 1920s, Herat had absorbed Persian musical styles into performances; but as the 1930s evolved, a conscious shift towards a Kabuli style of music can be discerned. Whilst the New City was being built to the north and east of the Old City, new music was being sung with a nationalist and 'Afghan' drive; musical innovation brought in Pashtun instrumentation and mixed this with Herati songs, in tune with the roads being built to link Herat to its capital city, Kabul.[111]

* * *

World War II came and went; Afghanistan once more remained neutral, much to the chagrin of pro-German factions in Kabul. Old habits died hard, however, and the threat of Russian influence in Afghanistan lingered on in the minds of the British well into the 1950s. This was more of a political reflex than active policy, however. A half-hearted musing on the possibility of setting up a consulate at Herat in the early 1950s on the part of the British embassy in Kabul gives us an idea of quite how far Herat had fallen since the heady days of the nineteenth century. It was a 'God forsaken' city with the air of a 'lesser capital', an opinion which contrasted slightly with that of the Persian consul in Herat, who saw Herat as 'a beautiful city but with no people in it'.[112]

A new war came: the Cold War. Russia and the United States competed for influence in Afghanistan, at first with a cautious sense of decorum and a desire to help Afghanistan. Russian influence was long-standing, and now in the Cold War the Soviet Union again saw Afghanistan as their imperialist forefathers had done, as a way into India and a geopolitical hedge in a strategically important part of the world. America's dominance in Iran and Pakistan meant that Afghanistan would assume an extra importance not seen since the nineteenth century. Soviet agents flitted in and out of Kabul, and very occasionally Herat, and trade with the Soviet Union was brisk in post-World War II Afghanistan. The US, for their part, built Herat's airport and flooded the country with engineers and advisers, concentrating on irrigation and engineering projects mainly in the southern province of Helmand. But US interest waned when their relationship with Pakistan was threatened because of Afghanistan's insistence on pushing the issue of Pashtun irredentism along the Durand Line, the border separating Afghanistan from Pakistan. This left Soviet influence slightly in the ascendancy.

Gradually, Kabul became a hotbed of dynamic new ideologies, from Pashtun nationalism to hard-left Marxism, all surging through the campus of Kabul University. Herat, for its part, remained relatively unscathed: its journals, *Herat Bastan* (Ancient Herat), and its literary societies continued. Poetry, tile work and calligraphy still moved the city's cultural life forwards as they had always done; still the forgotten city. Even its trade with Iran slipped, and most of those crossing the border to Mashhad were doing so for pilgrimage to the Imam Reza shrine, not to sell and buy.[113] Yet In Cold War Herat, optimism and opportunity were not hard to find. From the 1960s, hippies came to Herat to smoke weed and opium, shuffle around the city and, as one visitor to the city told me, sit inside and listen to music by The Doors.[114] Informal guesthouses sprung up among Herat's wealthy youth as a way of making money on the side, but mostly to have a chance to hang out with those long-haired students from Europe. Practising their English was another boon for Herat's young at this time, as the city took on its guise as the Hippy Trail's prize destination. One decidedly un-hippyish visitor to Herat in the summer of 1962 was the traveller and noted cyclist Dervla Murphy. Although she only spent a few days there, Dervla Murphy captured the sense of timeless elegance and unapologetic charm that Herat impresses on every visitor:

> This is a city of absolute enchantment in the literal sense of the word. It loosens all the bonds binding the traveller to his own age and sets him free

271

to live in a past that is vital and crude but never ugly. Herat is as old as history and as moving as a great epic poem—if Afghanistan had nothing else, it would have been worth coming to experience this.[115]

The city attracted hippies and cyclists, but also scholars and those determined to see the Timurid monuments that had caused Robert Byron to feel like a child on Christmas Eve before he set out to gaze at the blues and grape greens and cool whites that still clung to these edifices in 1933 and 1934. One such figure was the poet and historian Peter Levi, who wrote of the 'endearing grandiosity' of the wide streets built by Amanullah Khan earlier in the century. Unfortunately his visit was cut short by rumours of a cholera outbreak, but not before he managed to fit in a visit to Gazur Gah, where he saw a blind Sufi singer chanting the Quran in the main courtyard.[116] Levi's description of a 'luminescent, wind-startled pine tree of knotty age and great size' standing outside Gazur Gah's courtyard which 'streamed light and energy' is as elegiac as a visit to the shrine itself.[117]

On 31 May 1973 an article appeared in the *Kabul Times*, simply entitled 'Herat'. It was intended for a Western audience, and most likely written to attract tourists to the city: diplomats and advisers working in Kabul or elsewhere, or possibly hippies passing through on their way to India. Accompanying the piece are photos of camels festooned with colourful ribbons and a smiling but resolute young boy driving a horse-drawn cart through the streets of the Old City. The prose is romantic, promising visitors to Herat peaceful strolls along dusty lanes and thriving bazaars, echoing the charming peace and quiet evoked by Byron, Kazemi and Murphy. Warming rice and tea could be found in the city's many teahouses, and the glassblowing factory, Herati silks and rugs were a must for any visitor to this 'ancient, aristocratic town'.[118] Hotels were plentiful, and the offices of the Afghan Tourist Organization were more than willing to help in any way they could. These descriptions of a peaceful liminal oasis town, with its fresh fruits and vegetable markets, show a relatively prosperous border town: isolated, yet at peace with itself and its traditions.

If Herat were frozen in time, as seems to have been the case, few capture this better than Nancy Hatch Dupree in her guidebook from the 1960s. Hotels, restaurants, trips to the bazaar and sightseeing are all packed into the pages of this wonderful work. Herat's charm is perfectly translated onto the page. Herat is rightly portrayed as an enchanting resting-point for travellers or truck drivers to rest their weary limbs and recharge on tea, bread and fruit, all set against the stunning backdrop of an elegantly fading Timurid capital. Bright photographs of nomads, festivals and lush valleys give this guidebook the quality of a rare historical artifact, a relic from a time of peace when Herat could flourish away from the prying eyes of political interference, or the wild political ideologies of Islamists and Leftists which were then sweeping through Kabul's university campuses.[119]

Meanwhile in Kabul, as Herat slumbered, on 17 July 1973 Prime Minister Daoud Khan, with the support of a cadre of loyal army officers, enacted a palace coup. Daoud removed his cousin, Zaher Shah, then on holiday in Rome, from the throne of Afghanistan and established a Central Committee; he then elected himself President of the Republic of Afghanistan, Minister of Foreign Affairs and Minister of Defence.[120] Overnight, a president had replaced a monarch and Afghanistan became a republic, albeit the type of republic which disbands parliament and muzzles or imprisons political opposition. Herat's theatres were closed down and the city moved to the edges of an era of repression from which it never recovered. Daoud rubber-stamped his accession to power with a radio broadcast, a staple of any respectable coup, in which he promised a new future, especially for 'the oppressed and the young generation'. Still following protocol, he talked of his steadfast commitment to creating a brighter future in Afghanistan.[121] In that other trademark ploy of dictatorships of all political stripes, Daoud took over the public sphere with photos of himself. Allah was conspicuously absent from these political upheavals.

Daoud began his rule with cabinet purges and police crackdowns on Islamist groups. Kabul became a battleground of ideas and dissent, with rallies and fights breaking out on university campuses between leftists and Islamists. My research in Herat suggests that Herat had at first rather ignored the coup, seeing it as a family squabble of little relevance, highlighting the indifference that many held for Kabul's courtly life. As the pre-eminent scholar of Afghanistan, Thomas Barfield, puts it, 'The Afghans had already experienced the autocratic rule of Zahir [sic] Shah's uncles and his cousin Daud [sic] from 1933 to 1963, so having the puppet masters return to retire the puppet hardly shocked the audience.'[122]

But after the initial shrugging of shoulders, something of an optimistic reaction in Herat could be discerned. A good friend told me:

> I heard it on the radio and wasn't particularly interested at first, as the events in Kabul so often had no impact on our lives in Herat, but we did see Daoud as someone smart enough to play the Cold War game, and defeat the radicals in Kabul. After discussing it with my family and friends we felt hope and optimism that Herat would now open up more to other countries. [123]

Perhaps this was a new future, free from cronyism and nepotistic commercial and political cabals? Even Herat's Mujahideen leader and later governor of the city, Ismail Khan, then a captain in the 17th Division of the Afghan army, himself told me that he was cautiously sympathetic to Daoud Khan's government in Kabul, seeing this as a legitimate government of the Afghan people; he admired Daoud's assertion on the world stage, his unwillingness to be cowed by Moscow and his desire to link Afghanistan positively to other nations in relations of equality rather than dependence. Others in Herat viewed his leftist links with more suspicion. Yet whatever his political leanings, it is clear that Daoud sought to link Afghanistan to the wider world. One clear indication of this was Daoud's visit in April 1975 to Iran to the Shah of Iran, Mohammad Reza Pahlavi, to seek financial assistance as a make-weight against Soviet domination. On his way to Tehran, Daoud made a rousing speech in Herat in which he championed his own policies of opening Afghanistan to the world. [124] Daoud left Tehran with a credit extension of $2 billion, of which $1.7 billion was to be devoted to a rail system linking Herat, Qandahar and Kabul to Iranian lines extending to the Persian Gulf. There were also promises of agriculture and infrastructure projects, and of oil exploration. [125] Whilst these plans were never realised—victims of revolution, war and a crashed oil market—this was a tangible indication of what many saw as a new and energetic Afghanistan, and a Herat once again linked from east to west to ports and cities of importance.

Yet during these years Herat largely remained in its own cultured and peaceful bubble, little affected by Daoud's posturing dynamism. The musicologists John and Veronica Baily spent years in Herat during the 1970s, living amongst Herat's musicians and artists and chronicling their experiences through videos and books. John Baily's videos from this period show Herat's cultural life as vibrant, alive and dynamic as ever. The cycle of music festivals to celebrate weddings, Ramadan, New Year and other celebrated days and period ensured colourful and joyful occasions at regular intervals; comedic troupes, dancing, musicians and theatre productions fed into this varied and rich cultural life. Footage of comedians and bands of musicians (some of whom moonlighted as prostitutes), in the city to sell their music and humour, and dancing boys and Ferris wheels on sunny spring and summer afternoons show us Herat's living and breathing chaotic charm, its humour and its joy. This was the living antidote to the ruins and crumbling edifices of centuries gone by; its heartbeat lived on in songs and comedic sketches. John and Veronica Baily were privileged, through force of their own talent and skill, to live in this world of Herat before the war, and to see Herat experiencing something of a Golden Age. Their experience was not listening to The Doors in a hotel, stoned and shuttered; it was very much in the heart of the city's ongoing cultural traditions, which had sustained the city for centuries.

In a similar vein, *The Glassblowers of Herat*, a video shot in the summer of 1977, links the city back to the ancient craft of glassblowing, a skill which was thought to have long since disappeared with the ancient world.[126] The film shows Sayfullah and his brother Saydullah, two master craftsmen, blowing glass after gathering the raw materials, plant ash and pebbles, from the riverbed in Herat's surrounding areas, and using ancient techniques. Handicrafts, as we have seen throughout the city's history, have always played a central part in Herat's identity and self-image. From the weavers who parlayed with the Mongols in 1221 to the glassblowers of the twentieth century and beyond, it has always been a city of craftsmen and artists. One afternoon in the summer of 2014, I was walking around the gardens of Gawhar Shad's mausoleum, and in the north-western corner of the garden, tucked up against the inner walls, I came across Sayfullah and his son, working on new glass in a small mud hut, with a burning fire in the centre. He is now an old man, but his posture, stance and the technique he uses for blowing the glass and whirling it around his head to mould it into shape is unchanged. Still handsome and with a broad smile, his craft is timeless, linking Herat back centuries into the past. Watching him make glass after glass, candlestick after vase was a true pleasure, hinting at the glories of the city at its height. Sayfullah still longs for the 1960s and 1970s when tourists came and went and peace prevailed, and when he had a larger shop. In 2014, he desperately wanted a new workshop in which to sell his goods. A small boy, possibly five or six, sat next to the fire and gave a helping hand here and there, hoping to keep the tradition alive. Isolation might have deprived Herat of space on the briefing notes and front pages of the world's great powers, but in the twentieth century it gave the city space and time to thrive and embrace its cultural legacies and to come alive through the arts.

Glassblowing, silk spinning, instrument making, tailoring, carpet weaving, calligraphy, history, literature, archeology and poetry all contributed to a vibrant cultural life in Herat during the 1960s and 1970s. Magazines such as *Herat Bastan* (Ancient Herat) and *Majale-ye Herat* (Herat Journal) provided outlets for poetry, history and archeological studies to be published and read in Herat. Histories of the citadel and the mosque regularly appeared, citing Sayfi and Khwandamir, and foreign contributors wrote articles on Afghanistan and Herat's ancient history. In the 1970s, UNESCO teams carried out studies on Herat's archeological remains in the northern reaches of the *khiaban* and the minarets themselves. Other examples are the poet and historian Fekri Seljuki and the musician Aziz Heravi, who all added to Herat's wonderful cultural life at this time, elevating it from a sleepy tourist attraction to a self-contained dynamic centre of ideas and history.

Yet Herat's cultural effervescence by no means impinged upon its naturally conservative reflexes. These were by no means the ruinous Timurid parties of the late fifteenth century, and conservative Islamic values still informed rural and urban society and their mores. Photos and videos from this time show a sea of white turbaned men and women in cornflower blue burkhas gliding through the bazaars. Traditional Herati dress was the norm, with only a few wearing suits or trousers and shirts. John and Veronica Baily talk of a strain of deeply conservative values existing alongside Herat's musical and artistic milieus; Islam and music and dancing were by no means contradictory in the eyes of Herat's conservative cultural elites. Preserving cultural traditions was every bit as important as staying true to the Islamic values that regulated so much of life in the city and surrounding areas.

Islamic edicts had, however, once sought to ban music earlier in the century, on the pretext that music and dancing led to all sorts of vice and immorality, but in the 1960s and 1970s music became once again socially acceptable, and Herat's musicians saw themselves as conservative in matters of faith and practice. Sufi traditions have always helped to maintain the special status of music in Herat, through Zikr, the recitation of esoteric names of Allah, to moving, chanting, rhythms through which the adherents will reach mystical union with God. John Baily's footage of various Sufi and Shia practices captures these traditions, with insightful running commentary. In one section on Herat's shrines, we see hundreds of Shia pilgrims troop up to the Kuh-e Mukhtar, a Shia shrine in the city's northern outskirts, to pay their respects whilst listening to passion plays commemorating the suffering of Imam Ali at the battle of Kerbela. Karokh is shown as a paradise of shaded groves and Sufis, simple villages existing as they had done for centuries: music, Sufism and the rhythms of nature. Sheep skulls lie in the alcoves of the shrine to Sufi Islam at Karokh, and votive balls of mud are hurled at the mud ceiling, where they stick, with prayers attached on pieces of paper creating the effect of intercessions dancing in the breeze within the cool shrine to Sufi Islam, the nineteenth-century Sufi mystic who died at the hands of the Qajars.[127]

Given what we know about what followed, we should see these videos and accounts as images of a Golden Age of peace in Herat. It is impossible not to watch these videos without feeling a nostalgia for an age I never knew, and cannot ever know. A place of festivals, musical recitals, comic turns, bright clothing and the joys of the seasons: a place of Sufis, birdsong and the *muezzin*. They show us Herat's thriving local traditions—weddings, festivities for the New Year, Ramadan feasts and passion plays at Shia shrines—at a time before so much was washed away by conflict and exile.

And yet, these visions of Herat as a closed world, somehow stuck in time, do not tell the whole story. It would be wrong to say that Kabul's political vibrancy totally passed Herat by during these sleepy decades of music, mysticism and hippies. Global politics could not ignore Herat forever, and nor could the strains of Cold War ideology that had infected Kabul's university campuses. Whilst never a hotbed of political activism, Herat's youth communities did debate currents of political ideology, but there was no university through which to articulate any coherent response to President Daoud Khan's republic. Schools, instead, became Herat's political petri dishes. My good friend and Herati mentor, Engineer Salahi, a pillar of Herat's business and cultural communities, told me that there was a sense of excitement amongst Herat's youth during the 1970s. Students and teachers would meet after school at the Cinema Roundabout to the north of the Friday Mosque and hurl slogans at each other, splitting hairs on the leftist divide: 'materialist', 'Marxist' and so on. (In 1972, the slogan shouting and student activism caused Herat's schools to be closed for four months because of rioting and striking students.) Most supported the Maoist group, Shola-ye Jawid (Eternal Flame), but some others supported the Khalq (Masses) or Parcham (Flag) wings of Afghanistan's communist party, the People's Democratic Party of Afghanistan (PDPA). In these inchoate beginnings of leftist ideology in Herat, Khalq and Parcham factions were not well represented, and Herat took to the Maoist group Shola-ye Jawid; most of its young firebrands were adherents of this otherwise poorly represented Maoist group of revolutionaries.[128]

Yet many saw these revolutionaries or idealists as arrogant and out of touch with what it meant to be a Herati. The accusations ran that they were uncouth youngsters who looked down on all that was good and traditional in the name of an atheistic creed. Herat's proto-revolutionaries therefore occupied their own space in the city's life, and John and Veronica Baily remember traditional musical, Sufi and artistic circles as being largely untouched by the avowedly 'modern' thinking of the radical left which was so popular in Kabul, yet which had made comparatively little impact on the fabric of Herat's society or culture. Musical, artistic, literary and theatrical circles represented a conservative and devotional Herati, for whom local traditions and superstitions were embraced in their religious and societal outlook. This proud sense of local tradition, allowing for creativity, music, theatre and the arts and strongly rooted in Islam, was offended by the arrogance of youthful ideological certainty which saw Herat's traditions as a barrier to progress. Herat, as we shall see in Chapter 6, was not generally excited by the sloganeering and empty leftist rhetoric of Marxism–Leninism, partly because of its isolation, and partly, Heratis tell me, because of their good sense. Many in the city saw government or military figures who returned from 'brainwashing' trips to Moscow or St Petersburg as insufferably arrogant and condescending. They would come back to Herat proclaiming the future: a godless, classless, perfect future.

As Herat's youth hurled slogans at each other across roundabouts, and returning government officials from the Soviet Union looked down their noses at those they had left behind, Daoud tested the international waters by playing all possible ends of the Cold War against the middle in an optimistic bid to outsmart the US and the Soviet Union. This was Daoud's challenge to the idea that Afghanistan was a passive nation through which others marched their armies. He travelled non-stop to Tehran, Cairo, Moscow and Islamabad in an attempt to raise money and build alliances that might offset his over-reliance on Moscow. Daoud's energetic policy-making and alliance-building caused no end of confusion, leading CIA analysts to refer to the direction of his policies simply as 'Daoudward'.[129] These new regional entanglements and loan deals, however, betokened a different sense of involvement with foreign powers; it was not just power plants, loans or tanks that were for sale, but ideas and obedience. Ideological debts were being built up in Moscow, Cairo, Tehran and Islamabad which Daoud would struggle to pay. For each promise of aid from Saudi Arabia, America or Iran, there was a corresponding reaffirmation of ties to Moscow or an influx of Soviet military advisers. It was a game for which Daoud would pay with his life.

Internally, Daoud's own–ism, opportunism, was aimed at defeating extreme leftism and Islamism by force, and remaining in power. Daoud's founding of a one-party state (his party of National Revolution) after a trip to Iran in December 1975 is one of the milder examples of his undemocratic tendencies. He aimed to destroy the fledgling Islamist groups of Gulbuddin Hekmatyar, Ahmad Shah Massoud and Abdul Rasoul Sayyaf through arrest and harassment. Many Islamists fled the country to the welcoming arms of Pakistan's premier, Zulfiqar Ali Bhutto, and it was in this period that the Islamist resistance to a Soviet-backed government in Kabul began to take shape, albeit mostly in Peshawar and Kabul, being organised around the personalities of future leaders of the anti-Soviet *jihad*, and drawing on the popular student support that the Islamist groups had in Kabul. An Islamist uprising in July 1975 was largely a disaster, resulting in a crackdown on Islamist groups. The uprising was organised with Pakistani assistance and aimed

to infiltrate small bands of fighters to agitate and spread the revolutionary gospel of Islamism and anti-Soviet propaganda. Given the small
figures involved, it is difficult to know how seriously to take the ambitions of this episode, and it was quickly crushed. In Herat, the early
Islamists were led by Sayfuddin Nasratyar, a teacher from Ghorband,
who played a key part in the formation of Islamist ideology in Kabul's
university campuses. In truth, Herat's 1975 Islamist uprising barely
registered in the public's consciousness, and many struggle to recall it
taking place. Nasratyar was arrested on arrival in the city, and the insurrection finished there, leaving Herat bewildered but warned.[130]

Despite the many treaties of friendship, both new and reaffirmed,
between the USSR and Kabul during this period, Daoud's flirtatious
foreign policy and his visits, particularly those in 1977 to Egypt (the
Soviets were especially worried at the prospect of Daoud 'doing a Sadat'
and jumping ship to the other side of the Cold War), Pakistan and Saudi
Arabia, earned him a summons to Moscow in April 1977. During the
course of these meetings, Soviet party leader Leonid Brezhnev sharply
criticised Daoud for allowing 'NATO experts' into Afghanistan, alleging
that they were spies, and demanding that he dismiss them from the country. Daoud responded with the irritation of a proud nationalist that
Brezhnev's remarks were 'unacceptable interference' in Afghanistan's
internal affairs.[131] Unfortunately for Daoud, he failed to heed this concealed warning from Moscow and went on to conclude economic deals
with Saudi Arabia and the US. He even goaded Moscow with overt dalli-
ances with non-aligned states such as Yugoslavia.

These public shows of disobedience in Moscow and elsewhere sealed
Daoud's fate. His removal came not in the form of a coup, as had
heralded his own ascent to power, but of a 'revolution', the Saur Revolution (named after the month in which it occurred). The Saur
Revolution was orchestrated with help from alienated Khalq and
Parcham communists within Afghanistan, and Moscow. The same individuals who had put Daoud in power, Colonel Abdul Qader and
Captain Aslam Watanjar, carried out the Saur Revolution on 27 April
1978; Afghanistan lurched further towards the left, further towards the
Soviet Union, as it announced to the world the creation of the Democratic Republic of Afghanistan (DRA).

These years in question, which had begun with the departure of
English mappers and soldiers to the sound of falling Timurid masonry,

ended with the arrival of Khalq thugs who sought to uproot yet more of Herat's historical fabric: its culture, religion, peace and ways of life. The era of 1887 and the work of the Afghan Boundary Commission had effectively sealed Herat from the rest of Afghanistan, later incubating its conservative, Sufi, artistic tendencies against torrents of modernism that washed over Kabul and the rest of the country. But this tendency would in turn give way to a violent return to the front line of global wars of ideas and hubris. The unbroken lines of culture and music and poetry and architecture would be torn up and ripped apart by ideology and conflict, and many would be exiled from their homes, executed, conscripted, tortured or brainwashed. The Herat of Bagher Kazemi, Dervla Murphy, Ismail Siyah, John and Veronica Baily, *Herat Bastan* and hippies nodding off to The Doors would be lost forever.

6

HERAT IN A TIME OF LEFTISTS, ISLAMISTS
AND OPPORTUNISTS, 1978–2001

The Saur Revolution of April 1978 brought the Khalq faction of the People's Democratic Party of Afghanistan (PDPA) into power. The description of the Khalq by the noted scholar of Afghanistan and Political Islam, Olivier Roy, as 'driven by a suicidal and destructive lust for violence', is an accurate one.[1] At its head was Nur Mohammad Taraki, a founding member of both the Khalq party and the PDPA itself; in his post-revolutionary guise he became General Secretary of the party and President of the Revolutionary Council of the Democratic Republic of Afghanistan (DRA). Behind him stood Hafizullah Amin, an opportunistic strongman who quickly ordered the arrest of hundreds of his opponents: score settling masquerading as enlightened revolutionary zeal. An assessment that the events of April 1978 were a 'natural and inevitable outcome of the steadily growing antagonistic contradictions between the overwhelming majority of the Afghan population and a tiny handful of exploiters' was Soviet propaganda at its most delusionary.[2]

In a similar fashion to Herat's rather antipathetic attitude to Daoud's 1973 coup, many in Herat saw the Saur Revolution as distant, despite the flurry of radio announcements and proclamations of the end of 'despotism and tyranny' in Afghanistan.[3] After all, the membership of the PDPA at this time stood at little more than 12,000 people, mostly teachers and students, and their impact in Herat was not nearly as pronounced as other left-wing groups, in particular the Maoist group Shola-ye Jawid.[4] A few hundred idealist young Khalq members could have little impact on a city of roughly 250,000. What the Khalqis lacked in numbers and manpower, they seemed intent on making up with violence, fear and coercion.

For many in Herat looking back at this time, the Soviet Union and their protégés in Kabul were little more than moral, political and social frauds with whom hypocrisy and incompetence were synonymous. This can be seen in the extraordinarily ambitious and utterly impracticable programme of reforms announced through various presidential decrees by Hafizullah Amin on 30 April 1978. The reforms, largely based on the Khalq Manifesto of 1977, were aimed at dragging 'feudal' Afghanistan out of its supposed backwardness and bringing the Saur Revolution to the heart of the Afghan countryside. Amin's reforms had three main branches: agrarian reform, the elimination of illiteracy and the elimination of debt in the market (debt was an essential component of Afghan rural life, for everything from buying seed to paying for a dowry in marriage). The first major decree to be issued in the direction of reform was Decree Six, issued on 12 July 1978, in which the mortgage system was abolished along with debt and usury. The impact of this decree was either limited or almost entirely negative, and Khalqi teams sent to enforce it were often attacked by angry mobs.[5] Decree Eight, of November 1978, addressed the redistribution of land; behind it stood the intention to create a class of peasants loyal to the Khalqis by giving away the land held by large landowners, or by relocating landless families to new plots. Land was simply redistributed along pre-ordained lines, with families often being transported to areas either unfertile or already occupied, with devastating consequences. Rural Afghans found themselves the owners of title deeds to worthless land; by the spring of 1979, agricultural production had plummeted.[6]

Decree Seven of October 1978 addressed issues of under-age marriage and inflated dowry prices for brides. The price was fixed at 300 Afghanis, a relatively small sum (approximately $50 in today's money), and marriage was forbidden under the age of eighteen for men and women. Whilst this was a laudable attempt to address the appalling abuses to which young girls are subjected in rural Afghanistan, the decree was seen as unacceptable interference in the mores of conservative Afghan society, and it was bitterly opposed, echoing the opposition to Amanullah's own attempts at societal and educational reform. A common theme of all these decrees, and one which is echoed when speaking with both their supporters and enemies, is that whilst they might have been well-intentioned, such was the disdain they held for the rural and conservative context in which they were operating that they were bound to fail.[7]

Another ideological pillar of the Khalqi government was an admirable drive to end illiteracy in Afghanistan. Given the secular inclinations of those tasked with its implementation, it is unfortunate that the title given to this bold initiative was a '*jihad*'. Its acolytes began in May 1978 by fanning out across the country, and particularly into Herat's rural districts, armed with textbooks and a reforming zeal that would have done Luther proud. They promised that a man or woman could learn to read and write in 150 hours. The books showed cartoon tropes of men and women leaving behind their pasts of conservatism and Islam, and marching to a glorious future in the city, full of factories. Sentences were learned through the ideological medium of progress and a rejection of the values and traditions that underpinned rural life. One Herati I interviewed told me that 'Many people actually supported the notion of education and literacy for all in Herat; we are, after all, a city famed for its poetry and cultural greatness, but it was the humiliation of elders and the lack of respect which upset so many of us.'[8] Stories of village elders and khans being humiliated and shamed for their illiteracy are a commonplace accompaniment to this *jihad* to end illiteracy. Humiliation seemed to be part of the deal. Herat's sense of social propriety was also impinged upon by these lessons, for in highly conservative rural Herat, young men and women were taught together by city-dwelling young Khalqi men from Kabul, a revolutionary move for classes more at home with segregation of the sexes. The trope of a Khalqi teacher falling in love with one of his female students and then being killed by the young girl's family is told often in Herat.

But perhaps the most risky social experiments took place in the field of religion. Religion was, for the Khalqis, as for all committed communists, a barrier blocking progress to a perfect society. As such, it should be stamped out, or at the very least sidelined. In the most complete and eloquent Persian account of the events that took place in Herat during this period, Ahmad Shah Farzan, himself imprisoned by the Khalqis in Herat for his allegiances to Shola-ye Jawid, tells the following, highly emblematic, story about an incident he witnessed in his village:

> One Friday, as the worshipers were leaving the mosque after evening prayers, a young teacher, recently recruited to the party, approached the mullah and said to him; "How much longer are you going to have that ridiculous bushy beard? How much longer are you going to pray for? How much longer will you insist on these people following your path? Leave this path and come build a new society with our friend Taraki. Come and be with us, work with us. This society has no need for *Akhunds* [religious leaders]. We will kill you, but if you follow our society and be with us, you will be protected."[9]

The thought of standing outside a mosque in rural Herat, as a young, secular and presumably beardless teacher, and saying such things out loud is a terrifying one. It came as no surprise to read that this same teacher was later, on account of his continued insults to Islam, hacked to death. Whilst such actions are in no way to be condoned, one must surely question the advisability of uttering such words in the vicinity of a mosque in rural Herat. The utter rejection of Afghanistan's history and societal norms could not fail to give rise to anger and opposition amongst conservative and staunchly religious Heratis, young and old. As with so many reforms across the Muslim world which aimed to drag society 'forwards', the speed and violence of this pull only served to anger. Deracination is rarely a smooth process.

On Saturday 10 June 1978, Nur Mohammad Taraki, the Chairman of the Revolutionary Council and Prime Minister of Afghanistan, was in an ebullient mood. He was busy extolling the virtues of the PDPA to a journalist from Iraq. The Khalq party was the 'sole nationwide, powerful, national, revolutionary, patriotic and democratic party… the true speaker for the interests of workers, peasants, intelligentsia, small and middle bourgeoisie or national bourgeoisie'.[10] By every assessment, this was a grandiose boast. (Such statements might well have been amusing were it not for the appalling tragedy that ultimately resulted from the PDPA's idealism.) Herat, too, was forced to sit through similar displays of red theatre. Images of Daoud Khan had been replaced with ones of Taraki, and his personality cult reached absurd levels. Herat's radio pulsed with paeans to the Great Leader, Nur Mohammad Taraki. The city was quite literally stopped in its tracks to praise his far-sighted benevolence and wisdom. Herat's shopkeepers, farmers, teachers and bakers were coerced into largely pointless marches through the streets of the city in praise of Afghanistan's Great Leader, and ministries had to close to deal with the logistics. After Herat's comparatively quiet experience of the twentieth century, this bombastic intrusion must have appeared shocking, to say the least. Farzan notes how 'Farmers were forbidden to go into the meadows, being forced instead into the stupid marches and slogan-shouting in support of the Taraki regime, flags above their heads.'[11] The *khiaban* of Herat and the alleyways of the Old City rang out with half-hearted damnations of imperialism, tyranny and feudalism as, by all accounts, ragged bunches of workers held aloft red banners and placards of Taraki, chivvied along by enthusiastic Khalqi ideologues. A stinging irony of this ideological charade was that most of the slogans being recited were utterly unknown to the illiterate farmers and labourers who shouted them to passers-by. These imported terms such as feudalism, ideology, imperialism and so on were not ones with which the men and women of Karokh, Obeh, Injil and Ghurian were familiar, or could pronounce.[12] Kabul and its Khalqi puppets had come to Herat in the form of ideological pageantry, disturbing the rhythms of city and province and mystifying its inhabitants. A thin veil of coerced legitimacy was spread over the city, artificial and painted red, or covered with a photo of Taraki.

If the people found the land and education reforms ill-informed but somehow admirable, the pressures to venerate Taraki ridiculous and the changes to dowry requirements an assault on convention, it was the brutality of the repression that pushed Herat to violent insurrection. In many respects, Taraki's forced marches, red doors and grinning face plastered everywhere were simply a biting parody of Soviet tendencies to bombast and delusion. Yet this theatre had a darker side of violence for the people of Herat. A war of control was being conducted, and its battlegrounds were, increasingly, the streets and teahouses of Herat, and the prisons in which men and boys were radicalised by torture or executed for resistance, real or imagined. There were secret prisons to which Heratis were taken and executed. Names such as Bagh-e Forushan, an AGSA (Afghanistan's security services, the Department for Safeguarding the Interests of Afghanistan) compound outside Herat, and Bagh-e Shahi, from which detainees rarely left with their lives, struck real fear into the hearts of Heratis. Herat's old Timurid gardens had become prisons and torture chambers. AGSA's informants and the arrests they caused created an atmosphere of unbridled fear in the city and province, and the price for speaking out against the government was simply disappearance. As in Kabul, pits were dug on the outskirts of the city in which to tip executed political prisoners, often in their thousands.[13] That the walls of these prisons and government offices were painted with slogans such as 'Respect for humanity is our party slogan' and 'A democratic government guarantees our just and fair society' was surely of little comfort to those being beaten and executed.

These were the same prisons, overcrowded, dank and full of despair, in which I would work, thirty years later. What I saw there echoed Herat's past: Islamists, real or imagined, tortured by Soviet-educated and KGB-trained employees of an Afghan state supported by a foreign power, the USA, for the purposes of stamping out an insurgency which refuses to be stamped out. The reports from Khalqi Herat, of threats to families, electrocuted limbs, savage beatings and broken limbs could have been the very same reports I would write about the same prisons decades later. When researching this chapter in Herat and Kabul, I had the strong impression of a historical cycle, still unbroken, which menaces Afghanistan: an open wound which will struggle to heal as long as the cycle is repeated. In Khalqi Herat, prisons were stretched to capacity, and prisoners were electrocuted, whipped, frozen, had their fingernails torn out and were beaten to the last inch of their lives. Detainees were forced to confess to crimes they had rarely committed, and the presence of informants in the city gave the AGSA plenty of opportunities to pounce on unsympathetic comments made towards the government. Detainees were beaten for information on links with Iran or with Pakistan, and this fear of Afghanistan's Islamist neighbours became increasingly pronounced, as Iran's own political situation deteriorated and Imam Khomeini's revolutionary and powerful anti-Shah rhetoric became more vocal. Phantom infiltrations from Pakistan terrified Kabul. And yet, these accusations are clearly indicative of Kabul's lack of understanding about Herat at this time, for Islamism at this time was negligible in its potency or even its reputation in Herat, as is seen by the failed 1975 Islamist uprising. The politicised Islamism of Hekmatyar and Massoud in Kabul did not fit with Herat's Sufi-inspired shrine culture of tolerance and tradition. Yet the repression continued.

Islamists, real or perceived, were not the only victims of this period of extraordinary brutality, in which an estimated 50,000–100,000 Afghans were said to have been executed, or disappeared.[14] Herat's Maoists, Parchamis, teachers, intellectuals, farmers, shopkeepers, labourers, electricians and students were all targeted by the Khalqi purges. Members of Herat's great families, the Mojadeddi and Mohmandi, were executed in their hundreds; when I visited a leading member of Herat's Mojadeddi family in Herat in the summer of 2014, the wall of his office was dedicated to photos of his antecedents who had died during Khalqi purges. Photos of young teenagers, mustachioed sunglass-wearing youths, older and bearded religious figures, all attest to the indiscriminate nature of the AGSA's campaign of terror aimed at silencing dissent and targeting existing elites, families and groups of potential influence. The exile from Herat of its prominent figures began during this period of Khalqi terror; 'It was as if we could sense the onset of a war, or that the war had already started.'[15]

* * *

In March 1979, the dam of frustration, rage and anger finally broke, unleashing a torrent of chaos. Herat's districts and city, aided by a mutinous army, rose up in a chaotic and violent unison which placed Herat on the front line of hostilities against the Afghan government in Kabul and the Soviet Union. The event is known as Qiyam-e 24 Hout (The Uprising of 24 Hout), corresponding to 15 March 1979.

In the early spring of 1979, much of Herat city and the districts had been experiencing a tense, febrile atmosphere. Night-letters castigating the Khalqi government made their way around the city, and murmurs of more frequent disappearances and torture in prisons and villages became louder. Occasional disturbances were reported, though scarce.[16] Like the creation myths of Herat itself, the exact beginnings of the *qiyam* are difficult to discern with any accuracy, and as with many other myths, they have become shared amongst the province, each district claiming some sort of agency in the beginnings. 'It all started in Pashtun Zarghun', runs one account; 'It was a beaten mullah in Ghurian', runs another; 'It all started because of that article in *Ettefaq-e Islam* saying that God did not create the world and that man comes from a monkey' runs a third.[17] I have stuck close to Farzan's own account, and cross-checked it with interviews I conducted in Herat.

In the district of Pashtun Zarghun, 25 kilometres to the east of Herat, in early March, with prisons reportedly bursting with inmates, a local mullah at Friday prayers exhorted his flock to resistance against the communists, to defend their faith, customs, honour and dignity.[18] Reprisals against this treacherous sermon were swift, and arrests made. By way of response, the people of Pashtun Zarghun, led by the mullah, rose up against the Khalqis. In their first and most sustained attack, they launched their hatred against the AGSA compound, the heart of the Khalqi presence in Pashtun Zarghun. A green flag of Islam was placed on the roof of the AGSA offices, and chaotic and violent riots ensued. To the west of Herat, in the district of Ghurian, on 9 March, a similar uprising took place, with rushing attacks on the district centre and spontaneous acts of violence, directed at the regime and their representatives; from here, horses were sent east to Zendah Jan, closer to Herat city, with a young soldier by the name of Nur Ahmad Ghuriani, to spread the news of these events in the districts. Farzan writes of Zendah Jan's prisons being forced open, although not before AGSA men had executed some detainees, and we hear of sporadic violence and uprisings in the villages of Shakiban.[19] The language used in Farzan and others' accounts brings to mind Sayfi's breathless retelling of Mongol atrocities: the canals of Ghurian ran with tulip-red blood; heroic resistance faced off against 'infidel invaders'. Herat had defiantly woken from its century-long slumber.

Word of these uprisings soon made its way to Herat city, its bearers passing from east to west, inflaming the city with talk of revolution. The villages of Teyzan, Ziyarat-Gah, Kart, Siyoshan all added their voices to the chorus of opposition, and a ragged force marched to Guzarah, poised to enter Herat under the leadership of a Sufi *pir* by the name of Ghulam Nabi. Whilst Farzan paints a picture of a vaguely organised and coherent assembling of protesters under the control of future Mujahideen commanders (those who would go on to fight the Russians), accounts from oral testimonies of eyewitnesses reveal a more chaotic scene in which anything approaching coherence or organisation is absent. The only unifying factor was hatred for the Khalq regime. Common to all accounts is the fact that on the evening of 14 March, as Heratis shouted '*Allah-u Akbar*' (God is greatest) from the rooftops in passing imitation of Iran's Islamic revolutionaries and in defiance of the Khalqis, Herat was on the verge of an uncontrollable and unpredictable event of real significance. The government responded to the tensions by increasing their presence in the city. In some ways, this was the nervous 'calm before the storm'.[20]

On the morning of 15 March 1979, the sun rose over Herat in a clear blue sky with scattered clouds visible to the west. Herat was tense. Protesters had massed at the Iraq Gate to the west of the city, arrived from Ghurian, Shakiban and Zendah Jan. These men faced tanks, lined up to repel any popular onslaught, and they were armed with little more than their bare hands, shovels, hammers and pitchforks. With rushes and charges from the protesters, the *qiyam* in Herat began. People came from the Qandahar Gate, the Malek Gate and from the Iraq Gate, flooding the small streets of the Old City and literally falling upon anyone they could see who might be construed as foreign or a Khalqi. 'Bare-headed people' (*sar luchi*) were set upon as possible infidels or foreigners, and indiscriminate violence and chaos ruled. This was raw and uncompromising rage at the Khalqis and their forced import of a hated and false revolution to Herat. One man interviewed by the journalist Radek Sikorski (who would later become Polish Foreign Minister) in Herat in 1987 recalls how two men with Kabuli accents were mistaken for foreigners, and quite literally torn limb from limb by the mob which had descended on the city.[21] If Soviet advisers were found in the city, they were killed. The number of such victims varies, but a sensible estimate is that a handful of foreign advisers were killed during the uprising.[22] One Soviet wool merchant named Yuri Bogdanov was hacked to death by the mob, but his wife was saved by being thrown over their garden wall, breaking her leg in the fall; she was looked after by their Afghan neighbours.[23] The mood of mindless anger is accurately summed up by Farzan when he says, 'People were out of their minds with anger and rage. All fear of pain had left their hearts and they were fearless.'[24] A good friend and former ICRC colleague from Herat, Hedayatullah, himself a participant in the uprising, described a scene of chaos and utter pandemonium:

People were just running every which way, screaming 'Death to the Khalqis', 'Death to Russia', looting stores and setting abandoned vehicles on fire. It was chaos, angry chaos, and I had no idea, really, what was going on. I remember one old man, mad with rage, coming up to a group of us and screaming, 'Give me a gun! I want to find a Khalqi and kill him and then be killed so as I can go to heaven a martyr!'[25]

Tales of citizens attacking manned barricades armed with little more than pitchforks and shovels are in no way exaggerations: guns were hardly used in the uprising simply because there was almost no military expertise amongst the protesters, and AK-47s were discarded by the mob in favour of shovels and other heavy implements. Sayyed Abdul Wahhab Qattali, a prominent figure in Herat's Mujahideen and builder of Herat's Mujahideen Museum, recalls how he and his fellow protesters stormed Herat's citadel (heirs to a fine tradition of Heratis storming the citadel, Qalah-ye Ekhtiar al-Din) and came across a cache of weapons; after a few bemused moments attempting to work out how to load the guns, they cast them aside.[26] Fighting erupted in the small streets of the Old City, at the foot of the citadel, and in the wide streets of Herat's avenues running north towards the Gawhar Shad Mausoleum.[27] Some government forces, mostly police and army, fired on the rebels to disperse them, but others simply tore off their government uniforms, burned them and fled the scene. Few were willing to die for the Khalqis; most were more concerned with saving their skin and surviving the mob.

As had occurred in the villages, in Herat the protesters, the rebels, attacked the symbols of Khalq power—photos of Taraki, posters of the party, the newly adopted red flags—as if they were living beings. These symbols of power were destroyed; banks, government buildings and the prison were all attacked. Contact had been made between the protesters and prison guards prior to the attack on the prison, 'the epicentre of torture and death', in which sympathetic guards of the political wing assisted the protesters and released the political prisoners. Yet tanks barred the protesters' way, and they were beaten back with continuous bursts of gunfire.[28] The fighting continued through an afternoon of heavy rain until nightfall. Dusk settled on Herat; government forces were still in control of the Friday Mosque and some key strategic points of the city, and the charred streets were effectively a no-man's-land. Bodies were strewn at the places of the most intense fighting: the Malek Gate, the Qandahar Gate and the Iraq Gate. It had been a day of rage and a day of retribution from which Herat had emerged bloody and divided; it would never be the same again. Once again cries of '*Allah-u Akbar*' rang out over the rooftops as government troops that had remained in the city repaired their defences and readied themselves for another day of fighting. Groups of mourners wandered the rain-soaked streets, dressed in black.[29]

The Sovietisation of the Afghan army had begun in 1973 with the arrival of Soviet advisers who, in the words of Ismail Khan, caused immediate suspicion and fear amongst Herat's soldiers. He remarked to Radek Sikorski in 1987 how 'in Herat we had five Russians, and they enquired into every secret'.[30] Such was the extent to which those Afghans sent to Moscow for training returned brainwashed that Ismail Khan recalled 'it was difficult even to talk to them because they used strange long words with which we were unfamiliar'.[31] After the Saur Revolution, the education of the soldiers intensified, focusing on Soviet tactics and historical 'stages of development'; those with party sympathies were elevated to high positions of responsibility, although in the interests of good financial housekeeping those who joined the party found their party membership fee deducted from their salaries. Non-members were overlooked for promotion.

On 17 March, as Herat's villages and countryside rose up in anger and rebellion, and chaos reigned on the streets of the city, news of the unfolding drama reached Herat's 17th Army Division, stationed in Zalmay Kot. The 17th Division was duly ordered to put down the uprising through any means possible. This never happened. A mutiny by the 17th Division turned Herat's *qiyam* into a takeover of the city, an unlikely triumph against a hated government. There are dramatic accounts of Ismail Khan and Sardar Khan Rasoul making rousing and eloquent speeches to the 17th Division, inciting their fellow soldiers to join the rebellion, turning on their superiors and freeing political prisoners held on the base in awful conditions.[32] This group then led an attack on the city to take over key governmental offices and checkposts.[33] What started as an inchoate uprising was now a full-blown insurrection, possibly even a revolution. Intelligence shared with the Politburo in Moscow suggests that of the total number of approximately 9,000 soldiers at Herat's garrison, the vast majority deserted; the 17th Division's Artillery Regiment, of which Ismail Khan was a member, fired on its own troops and 'went to the insurgents'.[34] The 17th Division then took up strategic positions on the Takht-e Safar and in the north of Herat, at Gazurgah to the north-east; from there they could both hide from air strikes and also control the city. Officers and soldiers loyal to the regime fled, mostly to the safety of Herat's airport, where Farzan describes Herat's mayor, General Mokaram and a Russian adviser engaging in a discussion about the failure of the Khalqi project in Afghanistan and averring Iranian involvement in the *qiyam*.[35] Herat had fallen to a disjointed assortment of rebels, ranging from mullahs to farmers, Sufi *pirs* to teachers, ex-soldiers to ex-policemen. But just as in 1221 and 1381, their independence was to be short-lived.

What exactly happened during these few days of independence is difficult to assess with any accuracy. Conflicting reports abound. The most convincing picture is one of ungovernable chaos and a lack of clarity as to either who ruled the city, or in whose name they could claim to do so. The unity of the *qiyam* was fragile, and its genesis had provided no blueprint for a unified political response, save for broad anti-Khalqi sentiment. Shir Agha Shongar, a reckless and impulsive man with a fondness for male and female prostitutes, and the bandit Kamar-e *Dozd* (*dozd* means thief in Dari) played key roles in the formation of a committee which would govern Herat, or at least attempt to, for the short period of time that it remained 'free'.[36] This committee never achieved anything other than fleeting power, and it was quickly swept away in the chaos. The majority of the rebels who had entered Herat from the surrounding areas simply returned to their villages and district centres at nightfall, more concerned with avoiding government reprisals than with political experimentation or ruling committees.

With Herat now in rebel hands, urgent secret discussions began to take place in Moscow and Kabul about the immediate fate of Herat. How on earth had everything unravelled so alarmingly quickly? Such was the potential seriousness of the situation that some in Moscow and Kabul feared the end of the Soviet project in Afghanistan. In a meeting of the Politburo on 17 March 1979, the Soviet high command saw events in Herat as the work of 'bands of saboteurs and terrorists, having infiltrated from the territory of Pakistan, trained and armed not only with the participation of Pakistani forces but also of China, the United States of America, and Iran'. According to Moscow's analysis, these bands were 'committing atrocities in Herat'.[37] Russia's alarmist response was entirely at odds with the 'Olympian tranquillity' of Afghan politicians, and in particular Foreign Minister Hafizullah Amin, whose initial assessment to his Soviet masters was that the situation in Herat was quite literally nothing to worry about.[38] The *qiyam* forced the Soviet hierarchy to ask some difficult questions with regard their military assistance and training in Afghanistan, and the conclusions were bleak. The assessment by Andrei Kirilenko, a high-ranking Soviet official, on 17 March reflects the prevailing opinion in Moscow at this time:

> The government of Afghanistan itself has done nothing to secure the situation. And it has a 100 thousand-man army at that [*sic*]. What has it done? What good has it accomplished? Essentially nothing. And after all, Comrades, we gave very, very good support to Afghanistan... We gave them everything. And what has come of it? Nothing of any value. After all, it was they who executed innocent people for no reason and told us that we also executed innocent people in Lenin's time. You see what kind of Marxists we have found.[39]

After this elegiac lament for the failure of their Afghan project, the Politburo turned to discussing practical matters. Kosygin immediately suggested raising the price at which Russia bought their gas from Afghanistan from 15 roubles per 1,000 cubic metres to 25 roubles, and requested that wheat be sent to Afghanistan to counter economic hardships in the country which had arisen from the disastrous land and fiscal reforms. Military assistance, in the form of technical expertise and specialist advisers, was approved, although very much within the framework that whilst Afghanistan must not be lost to Iran and Pakistan's Islamism, direct military intervention was simply not an option for the Soviet Union in Afghanistan. Afghanistan was not to be lost, but troops would not be sent in to prevent it from falling.

One day later, on 18 March, Taraki and Kosygin discussed the uprising over the telephone with rather more urgency. Kabul's position had shifted from the sunny optimism of the previous day. When asked by Kosygin about the situation in Herat, Taraki responded in the following stark terms: 'There is no active support on the part of the population. It [Herat] is almost wholly under the influence of Shiite slogans—follow not the heathens, but follow us.'[40] Taraki saw in the fall of Herat the end of the entire Saur Revolution, and for this reason he persistently requested tanks, pilots and weapons. He was desperate, and gambled on hoodwinking the Politburo into cleaning up the mess that his rule had created. He went on, 'Iran and Pakistan are working against us, according to the same plan. Hence, if you now launch a decisive attack on Herat, it will be possible to save the revolution.'[41] The tactic was to terrify the Soviets into military intervention, playing on Moscow's fear of Chinese Maoists and Islamists. Kosygin's refusal to send in Russian troops, despite Taraki's insistence that the entirety of Herat's officers trained in Moscow had since switched their allegiance to the Muslim Brotherhood, caused the Afghan leader to switch tack, demanding that the Soviets send in Russians disguised as Afghans: 'In our view, no one will be any wiser.'[42] The responses from Kosygin become more wearied as the conversation developed, to a point where one can almost sense his irritation. His final response to yet another request for pilots and soldiers was, 'I expected this kind of reply from you.'[43] Moscow was worried, Herat was rebellious and Taraki was in despair.

A strained discussion between Gromyko, Chairman of the Council of Ministers, Alexi Kosygin and KGB chief Yuri Andropov reveals the almost total confusion as to how to react to the events in Herat. It was clear that no one wanted war, but it soon became apparent that a war might be necessary if they were to maintain their influence in Afghanistan. Gromyko echoed Andropov's hesitancy on the advisability of a Soviet invasion of Afghanistan, insisting on supporting Kabul to rid the country of reactionary mullahs instead of military action. He also advised Taraki to curb his violence against innocent Afghans. He went on, 'I fully support Comrade Andropov's proposal to exclude a measure as the introduction of our troops into Afghanistan. The [Afghan] army there is unreliable. Thus our army if it enters Afghanistan will be an aggressor. Against whom will it fight? Against the Afghan people first of all, and it will have to shoot at them.' This theme of disastrous unintended consequences was taken up with alacrity by Kosygin, who feared a collapse of Soviet policy in Afghanistan, but also saw a global backlash against Russia should the Soviet Union respond to Herat's *qiyam* with troops and tanks. He talks of a 'whole bouquet of countries' grouping together to condemn Soviet policy as a whole. In a further discussion on 20 March 1979 between Taraki, Kosygin and the Minster for Defence, Dmitry Ustinov, Kosygin uttered the fateful words that hang over foreign interventions in Afghanistan before and since: 'One cannot deny that our troops would have to fight not only with foreign aggressors, but also with a certain number of your people. And a people does not forgive such things.'[44] Herat's *qiyam* had begun Moscow's reluctant drift to war, for it forced Moscow to confront the unreliability of its Afghan allies, and simultaneously to recognise the importance they attached to keeping Afghanistan within the Soviet sphere of influence.

Sitting on the Takht-e Safar on 20 March, the rebels from the 17th Division and others who had joined their cause saw government tanks rolling into Herat along the Herat–Qandahar highway.[45] Green flags of Islam fluttered on their turrets; the men shouted Islamic slogans. The rebels' initial thought was that word of Herat's rebellion had spread to Qandahar, to Kabul and to Paktiya, and that the country had risen up in solidarity with Herat's rebels. The reality, however, was entirely different. The 300 soldiers at the head of thirty tanks were in fact from Qandahar, loyal to the Khalqi cause, come to punish the citizens of Herat for their *qiyam*.[46] Pockets of the 17th Division in Herat had returned to their government paymasters, but many had begun their lives as Mujahideen. Herat was still an ungoverned space, damaged from the fighting and nervous as to how its government would respond. The tanks attacked enfeebled rebel positions in the city, and an aerial bombing campaign took out posts taken by rebels on the Rignah bridge and other strategic points in the city. The aircraft, Ilyushin Il-28s, sent in from Shindand air base, were effective in scattering the resistance, and caused damage to people and buildings alike. Many who had pledged their allegiance to the rebels decided to melt into the background, wary of the government's superior firepower and resources. Within a week, the *qiyam* had ended. Retribution was to follow.

In the months of crackdowns and arrests which came in the wake of the *qiyam*, it has been alleged by Ismail Khan and other Mujahideen that over 24,000 Heratis were killed.[47] This number was given some credence with the 1992 discovery of a mass grave to the north of Herat, in which 2,000 bodies were found. Many Heratis I discussed this with maintain that these were actually bodies killed before the *qiyam* had erupted, and as such cannot count amongst the supposed figure of 24,000.[48] What is clear, however, is that the government response was brutal and swift, even if the numbers are unsure. The executions, torture and repression continued as before. Taraki was not, it seems, heeding the advice of his Soviet paymasters to cut down on violent repression. These days of spring in Herat saw a gradual entrenchment of positions as each side retreated further into positions of war and intransigence. Violent repression engendered violent response, which was in turn met with violent repression; the cycle continued. Elsewhere across Afghanistan there were more massacres in the spring of 1979, notably in the north-eastern province of Kunar, where over a thousand men and young boys were killed simply for refusing to shout Khalqi slogans.[49] Assadullah Sarwari, Afghanistan's intelligence chief whose nicknames included 'King Kong' and 'The Butcher', chose the following chilling response to the nationwide uprisings: 'Those who plot against us in the dark will vanish in the dark.'[50]

The *qiyam* was an enigmatic phenomenon: a noble alliance of city and country, civilian and soldier, which triumphed for a brief and glorious few days. It suffered the absence of a leader or a vision. It galvanised and yet divided, raised hopes and saw them crushed. It also celebrated Herat's urban–rural links. These routes through Herat, from Zendah Jan in the west to Pahtun Zarghun in the east, on which trade, water, rumours and war had been carried for centuries, were used to carry a unified cry of resistance, albeit temporarily. The *qiyam*'s message moved without obstruction from place to place along the tracks and ways which Beheshti had immortalised in his travelogue. In a cruel irony, the war to which the *qiyam* gave life largely destroyed these urban–rural links so cherished in Herat's history and memory. Nik Siyar, one of Herat's leading poets and intellectual figures of recent times, emphasised this when we discussed the *qiyam*. He described a city and surrounding rural area long unified by trade, culture, religion and the water that floods the oasis, and he passionately lamented the fact that war has damaged this harmonious urban–rural interaction.[51]

One question so many Heratis seek to answer is 'Why did the *qiyam* fail?' Why could their efforts not have led to something more stable, permanent and peaceful, instead of the cycle of exile and bloodshed which has followed so relentlessly since those days? Whilst in Herat and conducting interviews for the book, or just discussing in teahouses, I was constantly asked why I thought the *qiyam* had failed. I became more and more convinced that I was being shown an allegorical key to Herat's understanding of Afghanistan's problems, as if the *qiyam* were a leitmotif for a country's struggles. The direction of conversations so often went towards the *qiyam*'s lack of a leader or ideology behind which to unite. Despite Herat's urban–rural harmony, the *qiyam* had come and gone before ideology or leaders could be found; there was no time to formulate a body of ideas which might outlast the chaos on the streets. Consequently the unity, although useful for inciting the uprising, was essentially fragile and easily shattered by the might of government tanks from Qandahar. The rebels had few aims beyond destruction of Khalqi symbols of terror; they sought not to create, but to tear down. Shir Agha Shongar and Kamar *Dozd*'s committee was stillborn, the 17th Division remained on Takht-e Safar, and the ordinary rebels returned to Zendah Jan, Pashtun Zarghun and Ghurian to await the next phase of the war they had begun.

The significance of the uprising within the minds of Herat's people, the impact it had on the lives of so many and its place in the city's history cannot be overestimated. It has defined Herat as a centre of resistance to tyranny: another incarnation of the city's legacy of thwarting, and being thwarted by, imperial advances. Herat was seemingly fulfilling some of its age-old traditions of resistance and of defending Islam. The province came alive in the *qiyam* after the sleepy decades of the twentieth century when it had slipped into total obscurity. Local accounts of the *qiyam* make conscious links to the events of 1221, when Herat tried disastrously to throw off the yoke of Chingiz Khan, and to Herat's role in the Battle of Maiwand of 1880, joining the threads of heroism in the face of tyranny, most often a foreign tyranny.[52] It was celebrated in Taliban-edited editions of Herat's daily paper, *Ettefaq-e Islam*, as an example of resistance to imperialism and foreign-backed invasions of Afghanistan. The anniversary of the uprising is celebrated with solemnity in Herat's mosques to this day.

Yet there is a subtler legacy of the *qiyam*, and it concerns Herat's relationship with Kabul. Herat's isolation from Kabul has its roots in the nineteenth century, but the *qiyam* highlighted this sense of distance between Herat and Kabul, whilst also deepening suspicions between the two cities. Kabul, as the Politburo documents suggest, had very little idea of what was actually occurring in Herat, a city which now found itself at the front line of the resistance to Soviet-backed tyranny. This combination of Kabul's misunderstanding of Herat and Herat's new-found significance presented a threat to Kabul. But how could a city so removed from Kabul be effectively controlled when so little was understood about it? Soviet Defence Minister Ustinov accurately summed up the situation when he remarked, 'in Afghanistan ... there are no ties between Herat and Kabul'.[53] Perhaps this explains Amin's total miscalculation of what had transpired in Herat? Yet after the *qiyam* it was as if Herat had quite literally thrown off the previous mantle of faded imperial outpost, and was now at the centre of a national struggle against Soviet interference and Khalqi savagery; it had become, as Farzan stated, the 'beating heart of the Afghan nation', yet its palpitations were still a long way from Kabul.[54]

At a roundabout which was once the Qandahar Gate, the southern entrance to the Old City, stands a memorial to the *qiyam*. A captured Soviet tank is assailed by men in traditional Herati clothes of *pirhan tonban*. They are armed with pitchforks, shovels and axes. All the men are heavily bearded; all are wearing turbans. They have 'taken' the tank and are both celebrating and gesticulating with their makeshift weapons. Time and war have not, however, been kind to this memorial: Herat's brave assailants are falling to pieces. The clothes of the figures, sculpted from a now faded and disintegrating plaster of sorts, appear frayed and ragged, and one man's back is all but torn away revealing thin girders where his spine should be. The hand of the man standing on the top of the tank, a hand raised in triumph, has decayed to leave a collection of crazed wires pointing to the sky. Ghoulish kitsch meets dystopian Jeff Koons. Another figure, on top of the tank, has fallen backwards and lies awkwardly, his legs snapped at the shin, in a pose not dissimilar to that adopted by Saddam Hussein's statue as US soldiers tried to drag it from its plinth in 2003. Around his pitchfork, fixed to his crumbling hand by bailer twine, someone has draped a faded Afghan flag. In these crumbling figures we see the crumbling influence of the Mujahideen and their declining relevance to the youth of today's Herat, many of whom were in exile when the war raged. Occasionally one sees sombre-looking men having their photos taken next to one of the broken heroes, but most drive past, indifferent or dismissive. It is an awful irony that the Soviet tank which the figures assail has endured these long years without so much as a scratch. Does this monument embody Herat's centuries-long history of resistance to tyranny, or perhaps is it subtler than that? Perhaps it functions both as a celebration and a castigation of resistance: an eloquent tribute to the self-defeating nature of resistance and conflict? Or maybe it is just a monument to a war that some have tried to forget and others refuse to forget.

* * *

As Herat and its people faced a rising tide of terror and government oppression, events in Washington, Moscow and Kabul decided the fate of Afghanistan. Taraki, on his return from Havana in September 1979, was overthrown by his erstwhile ally Hafizullah Amin in a coup, strangled and left to die.[55] In a grim reminder that all revolutions, even fake ones, kill their children, Amin was killed by Soviet Special Forces. Moscow decided to replace Amin with the more pliant and pro-Soviet figure of Babrak Karmal (a Parchami), and plans were put in place for the invasion of Afghanistan. Moscow had succumbed to the inevitable process which had begun in Herat. The Soviet decision to invade Afghanistan was motivated by fear: fear of losing Afghanistan to Islamists and Maoists who could, the Soviets anticipated, quite literally rip the Central Asian underbelly from underneath them; and fear of losing face on the world stage. The main Soviet operation started in the afternoon of 25 December 1979: airborne troops from the 103rd and 105th air divisions landed in Kabul and Bagram, and units from the 5th and 108th motorised rifle divisions crossed the northern border at Kushka and at Termez. Within a week of the initial invasion, over 50,000 Soviet troops were in Afghanistan, and the bases of Qandahar, Shindand and Kabul were quickly stocked with military hardware and Soviet soldiers. The Khalqi reign over Afghanistan was finished, and in its place the Soviet Union gave Afghanistan a war in which over a million Afghans would be killed and in which nearly half of the city of Herat would be destroyed. The vast majority of its people would be forced to flee to Iran.

For Herat's rural communities, the psychological impact of seeing columns of Soviet tanks flood south from Turghundi to Shindand, skirting Herat and running through villages and meadows, was profound. Not since the late nineteenth century had Herat seen such an influx of foreign troops. The buzz of helicopters and fighter jets overhead merely served to add to a sense of impending disaster.[56] Over the summer and autumn of 1979, Herat had seen demonstrations and pockets of resistance, but the arrival of Soviet troops sharpened the focus of both sides, of all sides. In this cold winter of post-invasion, Herat's streets and gutters were strewn with Mujahideen propaganda leaflets. Bakbrak Karmal, Afghanistan's pro-Soviet ruler in Kabul, was termed a *gondi* (puppet), a *watanforoush* (nation-seller) and a *dast-e neshan da* (pawn). He was compared to the nineteenth-century puppet ruler, Shah Shujah. In the wake of these incendiary leaflets, KHAD (AGSA underwent a name change in 1979) intelligence officers prowled and eavesdropped to find the perpetrators and bring them to justice. History, in the form of biting satire, was now used in the service of the Mujahideen, which was something of an irony given the Khalqi and Parchami disdain for much of what had gone before in Afghanistan. The resistance's decision to pursue an ideological attack on the regime, based on their supposed betrayal of Afghanistan and its values, is a telling example of the momentum of the perception of this war in Herat and beyond.

The *qiyam* had avenged assaults on Islam and conservative Afghan values; now it was the very sovereignty of Afghanistan that was threatened. The soil of Guzarah and Obeh, the canals of Injil and the monumental heritage of Herat's ancient structures were at the mercy of Soviet weaponry. The fight had moved from the souls and minds of Heratis to the realm of physical geography. Foreign troops were now stationed in Shindand, and KGB and Soviet soldiers occupied Herat's districts and patrolled its meadows and cornfields.

It was hardly surprising that state media outlets sought to challenge the Mujahideen version of the truth, fighting ideological fire with ideological fire along the very same lines, decrying the Mujahideen as foreign imports in the service of the United States, Pakistan or Saudi Arabia, infected by Muslim Brotherhood propaganda and only concerned with the destabilisation of Afghanistan for their own imperialist or reactionary ends. The Mujahideen were referred to in derogatory terms as *monafeqin* (hypocrites), and successive editions of the *Kabul Times* lambasted their supposed backwardness and their seeming desire to keep Afghanistan stuck in the past, refusing to embrace the light of progress which was said to guide the government in Kabul. Nationalism, for both sides, had become a defining issue in the conflict. Both sides sought to answer the question of who could really claim to speak for Afghanistan.[57]

Shortly after the beginning of the war, in the winter of 1980, Afghan Defence Minister Abdul Qader made a trip to Herat with a selection of high-ranking Afghan officials to speak with the city's elders, requesting them to bring their influence to bear on the citizens of Herat and its surrounds to end the resistance, to lay down their arms and join the government. He promised in exchange a full investigation into the events of the *qiyam*.[58] That he did so in the presence of Afghan intelligence and army officials who had so violently oppressed the people of Herat would have seemed unusual to Herat's assembled elders. These negotiations appeared to many as a last-ditch attempt to forestall further fighting. As elders and *ulema* gathered in Herat's governor's hall, it was clear that the government in Kabul had little to offer Herat beyond empty promises, delivered down the barrel of a gun. There would be no investigation into the *qiyam*. It was as if Kabul had already accepted a defeat of sorts and saw that now was the time to try to persuade, cajole and pay their way to victory, or at least a settlement. Needless to say, Herat's *ulema* and elders were not convinced. Similarly, on a global level, Soviet negotiations with Pakistan aimed at ending the war began almost immediately after the start of the war, in response to the overwhelming global condemnation of the invasion. Even Fidel Castro, as early as 1980, offered his services as a mediator between Kabul and Pakistan.[59]

The momentum of the resistance, which had flowered briefly and chaotically in the spring of 1979, had stalled by the summer of 1979. Arms and money plundered in the *qiyam* could only last so long. And so, in the summer of 1979 representatives from the major Mujahideen parties in Pakistan and Iran came to Herat on a series of clandestine missions to enlist the support of Herat's resistance groups and to turn the disconnected rebels into cohesive fighting units. Representatives from Jamiat-e Islami (Islamic Society), a Tajik-dominated party under the auspices of Burhanuddin Rabbani (whose doctoral thesis was on Herat's most famous poet, Jami), came and discussed resistance, weapons and money with those representing the Mujahideen in Herat, as did representatives from Hezb-e Islami (Islamic Party), under the control of the CIA and Pakistan's ruthless darling Gulbuddin Hekmatyar. Shia parties, Mahaz-e Melli (National Movement) and Harakat-e Enghelab-e Islami (Movement for the Islamic Revolution), also made trips from Iran in an attempt to secure patronage of coreligionist groups in Herat. Jamiat-e Islami had an office in Mashhad, and Iran's nascent Islamic Republic was seeking to influence the war. In reality, however, the real funding and patronage was mostly to be found in the Pakistani city of Peshawar, many difficult miles from Herat. The parties gathered in Peshawar had been receiving assistance from Iran and Saudi Arabia, as well as from the CIA and Pakistan's intelligence services, ISI, since the beginning of the conflict, and an atmosphere of intense rivalry between Rabbani of Jamiat-e Islami and Hekmatyar's stridently revolutionary Hezb-e Islami had begun to play a part in the dynamic of resistance. From the outset the resistance was sharply divided, and these rivalries brewing in Peshawar would eventually give Afghanistan's post-Soviet civil war its destructive energy. (Hekmatyar, for example, took to imprisoning his rivals in Peshawar, or simply executing them as he saw fit.) In Herat, it was the Jamiat-e Islami party that dominated matters, striking up an alliance with the former army captain, Ismail Khan, in Mashhad in the aftermath of the *qiyam*. It was Jamiat that would fund Ismail Khan and his band of fifteen horsemen who rode into Injil in the winter of 1980.[60]

During the early years of the war, 1980–84, the fighting took on predictable patterns of insurgent and guerrilla warfare. Yet as the respective positions became entrenched, it became more accurate to talk of an insurgent war of front lines, with the Soviets gaining control over the country's logistical veins, its roads and byways, and the Mujahideen controlling rural areas and the increasingly desolate western parts of the city. The Mujahideen focused their attacks on these arterial supply lines, attacking the Herat–Qandahar road, harrying convoys from Turghundi on their southward passage to Herat or Shindand. Each successful attack on a Soviet convoy yielded more weapons and a few more soldiers to the cause, and each botched Soviet air strike, each tortured family member brought more fighters to the cause of resistance. In these early passages of the war, Herat's Mujahideen managed to achieve notable early gains, and by 1981, as assistance began to trickle into Herat, large swathes of rural Herat had fallen to the rebels.

The war then took on an energy of its own. Soviet and government forces would respond to Mujahideen ambushes and raids by sending in troops, fighter jets and heavy artillery to pummel villages into submission and to shell Mujahideen positions in remote mountainous or rural areas. Having been on the back foot in terms of a war of ideas, Kabul and Moscow now found themselves playing a military game dictated by ambushes; they responded with annihilation. The Soviets also launched large-scale offensives, with questionable results, against Mujahideen positions in Chesht, Obeh and Pashtun Zarghun. One such operation in March 1985 resulted in heavy loss of civilian and Mujahideen life.[61] The results of such operations were to drive civilians either abroad to Iran, or simply to the government-controlled parts of Herat, and in so doing separated the Mujahideen from the rural communities who gave them support. Examples of these engagements can be found in a remarkable selection of documents, stored in the archives of Nancy Hatch Dupree's library in Kabul. The publications detail cases of alleged human rights abuses and violations of the Geneva Convention perpetrated by the Soviets during the war in Afghanistan, as taken by the National Committee of Human Rights in Afghanistan (NCHRA), based in Peshawar. Whilst these documents possess a clearly anti-Soviet bias—the war is referred to as the 'Just Jehad' [sic]—these accounts of events in Herat are invaluable for painting a picture of the abuses of life during the war.[62] Having written similar documents for the ICRC in Herat and Khost, reading them brought back memories of speaking with traumatised victims of conflict. Below are just some examples of the conflict and its impact on Herat's civilians.

On the morning of 20 July 1980 in the village of Adraskan, to the south of Herat, a convoy of Russian tanks and armoured vehicles entered the village from Shindand. Soldiers spread out into the surrounding fields before setting up camp. As had become the norm in the fighting, a small band of Mujahideen attacked the Russians during the night, causing minor casualties. The Soviet troops, as told to the NCHRA in Peshawar, reacted by killing some 250 civilians of Adraskan, burned in their houses or bombed from the skies.[63]

The village of Chesht, in Obeh, was once the home of the Sufi order who had, through mediation, helped the Kart *malek*s and

Il-Khanids avoid bloodshed. In May 1981, fifty-five Afghans, including women and children, were cut down in a series of strafing helicopter runs over the village, hitting mud houses with gun-ship helicopters and missiles. The attack was in response to a night raid by the Mujahideen on the Soviets, in which a number of Soviet and Afghan government soldiers lost their lives.

In October 1984, a series of Soviet attacks in Ghurian was said to have caused the death of 872 Heratis. This was, as ran the insurgent pattern, provoked by a raid on the Russians by a smallish band of Mujahideen, possibly thirty men, with a retaliation of untold slaughter on civilian and Mujahideen alike.[64]

For those unlucky enough to have to remain in Herat, this was the currency of daily life: caught between two equally ruthless sides in a war of faith and nation. The English scholar and polymath Bruce Wannell recalls witnessing such a shelling in Herat during his time in the province with Ismail Khan in 1988. Such was the noise, ferocity and proximity of the attack that Bruce made his peace with God, fully expecting to be dead before sunrise.

The Mujahideen's rural tactics of harrying and ambushing found their urban counterpoint in a battle for Herat's streets. Tunnels and assassinations were the tactics of this urban conflict. Highlighting the government's inability to control Herat's streets was just as much a victory as any territorial gains in the districts, much as is the case today. Assassinations of key government figures demonstrated the Mujahideen's ability to operate in places the government had declared safe. These bold operations in Herat's bazaars and streets challenged assurances that Kabul was 'winning' against the Mujahideen and providing a safer city and country for Afghanistan's people. Mirroring tactics used by the Taliban, these assassinations, then carried out with guns and knives, had a deep psychological impact on those in government. They turned Herat into pockets of nervous spaces where government writ could not be confidently said to run.

On 22 January 1985, Shir Agha Shongor (the prostitute-loving rebel who had briefly ruled over a burning post-*qiyam* Herat) was assassinated by a member of Ismail Khan's Jamiat. His Russian adviser was also killed in this stabbing. Ever the opportunist, Shir Agha had defected to the government and renounced his erstwhile insurrectionary ideology in favour of the lure of opportunism. At the time of his death he was visiting a hospital in Herat to see soldiers who had been wounded fighting the Mujahideen. Shir Agha's assassination was reported with glee in a selection of pro-Mujahideen news articles, edited by Jamiat in Peshawar. One article in question, however, goes on to make the less credible claim that, after his assassination, seventy-five villages previously under his control willingly and warmly received the Mujahideen.[65] In the winter of 1984–5, in response to government offensives in Herat's troublesome districts, the Mujahideen stepped up this campaign of assassinations, targeting government officials from within the feared KHAD, such as the ruthless intelligence officer Qalandar Baybani.[66] The Mujahideen also used tunnels as a way to infiltrate the city and inflict more psychological and real damage on Soviet and Afghan enemies. One such tunnel ran through swathes of priceless Timurid and earlier archeological remains, under the Gawhar Shad gardens, from the Fakhrul Madares *madrasa* to the ruined minarets which had formed part of the Sultan Bayqara complex, and another from Payeen-e Ab to the shrine of Sultan Agha. These tunnels enabled the Mujahideen to conduct operations inside the city at night without passing through the Soviet checkpoints which by 1983 encircled the city.

Complementing their urban assaults on government figures and Soviet advisers, the Mujahideen also infiltrated the Afghan state, playing on the unpopularity of the war even amongst those Afghans who had joined the army. Each defection weakened the morale of the government and swelled the ranks of the Mujahideen. One of Ismail Khan's most significant successes in this field was reported in an article written in *Foreign Affairs* in the summer of 1986 at the height of the war:

> The Afghan air force, previously considered the most loyal service, has experienced increased defections and sabotage. Heightened vulnerability to mujahedeen [sic] air defense has steadily eroded morale. In June 1985 about 20 Afghan fighter planes were destroyed by sabotage at Shindand Air Base [in Herat] near the Iranian border—the largest loss of aircraft in any single incident of the war. The accused saboteurs (DRA officers who were later executed) were unhappy over the disciplining of pilots who dropped their bombs in the desert instead of on a village.[67]

Mujahideen tactics of assassination and ambushes had a profound psychological impact on Herat's Soviet occupiers. Their response involved placing greater emphasis on the security of the city itself. Rings, or more accurately arcs, of 'safety' were set up in Herat, to protect it from Mujahideen attacks and the destruction that inevitably followed. The first arc, running from the northern *Khiaban* down to the Iraq Gate of the Old City and then joining the shrine of Sultan Agha, sliced its way through Herat's archeological remains with mines, so as to prevent the Mujahideen from entering into the city. These arcs aimed to make Herat safer, yet they simply showcased the government's inability to venture out of the city; the Mujahideen saw an opportunity to attack a sitting target at will.[68]

What remained of the Old City walls was mined. Herat's western suburbs, where Mujahideen control ringed the Soviet check-posts, became a treacherous minefield with thousands upon thousands of mines. Trips to buy bread for Mujahideen factions would involve serious risks to life, each trip into town potentially fatal.[69] A documentary by filmmaker Leon Flamholc entitled *A Winter in Herat*, shot over five months in 1985, shows a young Herati boy being sent into the city to buy bread and provisions and the utterly destroyed state of Herat at this time.[70] The young boy is seemingly fearless about the dangers he faces and heads off into the city without the slightest hesitation and a large grin across his face. The film shows us Herat's suffering under the Soviets, the destruction and the fear that informed daily life in the city. It is, in so many ways, a grim antithesis to John Baily's films of an idyllic pre-1978 Herat.

Herat had become a city of suspended reality, where legitimacy was sought through coercion and mines, and where the press still spoke glowingly about the success of the Saur Revolution as the city went through the motions of what approximated to normality. Mullahs were no longer free to speak their mind, as they were either in the pay of the government or threatened with death if they criticised the Mujahideen. More often than not, this would entail a death every bit as gruesome as that which Soviet soldiers meted out to the Mujahideen.[71] Herat's streets retained a semblance of activity, of trade, yet the rubble of war, the parrot-like Friday sermons, Soviet tanks and the menacing minefields, for which government and Mujahideen bore an equal share of the blame, told another story.[72] Herat's ancient citadel housed Russian troops, and the radio buzzed with government sermons telling Herat that this was a war foisted upon them by the English and Americans, appealing to their 'brothers', the Mujahideen, for peace. During government bombing raids, the Mujahideen joked amongst themselves, 'this is no way to treat your brothers!'[73]

* * *

Amidst the rhetoric of resistance and Cold War politics, Herat at war became a city of conflicted loyalties. Family and self-interest often trumped nation, Marx or Allah. Opportunism, necessity and self-preservation became key motivating factors, used by all sides to cajole and persuade. The vast majority of those who fought with the Afghan army did so not out of a firm ideological commitment to a communist Afghan nation, nor out of strong hostility to the Mujahideen and their backers; this was a choice made of necessity. Many who either fought or worked for the government during this war shrug their shoulders as if to say 'What choice did I have?' Exile was costly, resistance was dangerous and inaction left one jobless or, yet worse, under suspicion from Kabul's intelligence agencies. Financial incentives motivated some, revenge others. These were an unenviable set of circumstances facing Heratis in a harsh world that was not nearly as black and white as much of the caricatured heroism literature of this period would suggest.

Possibly sensing these grey areas, the Soviets created 'militia' groups, who would be directly responsible to KHAD and KGB officers, and who would in theory take the insurgent and unorthodox fight to the insurgents. These groups were made up of ruthless opportunists, swayed by promises of cash and guns. The militia became just as feared as the KHAD and KGB. In Ghurian, for example, militia groups settled into a life of drug smuggling and criminality in the pay of the KGB.[74] Yet as the war became ever more entrenched, the need for communication between KHAD, KGB, militia and Mujahideen became all the more apparent. Towards the end of the conflict back-channel communications were thriving. In this atmosphere, the lines between intelligence gathering, deal making and fraternising with the enemy became blurred, as fluid alliances, or relationships of convenience, were mixed up in a nether world of smuggling and exchange of weapons for hashish or opium. The militia were emblematic of this black market for loyalty, a black market into which disgruntled Soviet soldiers, or simply those bored by fighting a conflict in which they had no interest, were only too willing to enter. Stories of Russian soldiers swapping their weapons for drugs or electronics not available in the USSR were confirmed to me by both ex-Mujahideen and ex-Soviet servicemen.[75] Some Soviet troops in Herat even took to adopting local customs and dress. Major General Vitaly Babneski, serving in Herat with Russian Special Forces in the late 1980s, struck up relations with a Mujahideen faction, ostensibly to gain intelligence, but just as likely as a conduit for illicit trade. Babneski took to wearing Afghan clothing, a gas mask, carrying hand grenades on his belt and generally adopting the habits of local Heratis.[76] His story was by no means unique. So serious was the problem of Soviet soldiers defecting to the Mujahideen, or engaging in drug or gun-running, that Kabul's largest prison, Pul-e Charkhi, even contained a specific section for Soviet soldiers who had attempted desertion or engaged in criminal activities. There were as many as 2,000 Soviet soldiers imprisoned there at one point.

For many Soviet soldiers, this war lacked the ideological certainty that America's war in Afghanistan would later offer its troops, and the treatment of young Soviets coming into the army was notoriously harsh and violent. Savage beatings were used as a tool of discipline and dissent was muzzled.[77] First-hand Soviet accounts of the war in Afghanistan reveal a conflict of truly horrific proportions: Soviet soldiers' lives were endangered as much by the appalling treatment they received at the hands of their superiors as they were by the conflict they were waging against the Mujahideen. One account of a Soviet soldier serving in Shindand is particularly harrowing. It talks of water mixed with chlorine, meat rations dating from the 1950s, letters never sent home for fear of the truth of this war emerging into Russian society, drunken officers torturing their own troops, drug addiction and the casual mass executions of Afghans captured on patrol.[78]

For many young Soviet soldiers, a life with the Mujahideen was a more attractive prospect than fighting for the USSR, or life back home. It was for these reasons that the Soviet forces employed KGB officers to spy on their own, to prevent the soaring desertion rates.[79] In the heat of the 1988 summer, one such KGB officer was shot in the head during a Mujahideen ambush whilst on patrol in Adraskan. At the time of the shooting his name was Bakhretdin Khakimov. He survived the shooting (but still shakes from his injuries), and was taken in by the

Mujahideen as a prisoner of war. While he was a prisoner he was guarded closely and given the relevant medical care, but unusually the Mujahideen did not execute him, as happened to many captured Soviet soldiers. During his convalescence he became gradually convinced, although in reality he had little choice, of his desire to switch sides and join the Mujahideen. I went to visit Khakimov in Herat's Mujahideen Museum on a snow-covered day in February 2014. He works there as a tour guide, an extremely excitable tour guide, for foreign 'dignitaries'. Afghanistan has taken him in, moulded him into an ersatz Afghan, although traces of his Russian heritage still show through. If one looks closely enough, beneath the beard and *pakol* (the hat favoured by the Mujahideen), a Russian man is visible. Khakimov's spoken Dari is both unmistakably Herati and yet also clearly Russian, with an attention to grammatical detail that strongly reminded me of my own Russian Pashtu teacher, himself a former interpreter for Dr Najibullah.

Attached to the museum is a zoo, of which Khakimov is extremely proud, and as we made an obligatory pass by the monkeys, he said of his decision to convert to Islam, 'Why wouldn't I want to join these men who had saved my life, who had shown me humanity? Why wouldn't I want to convert to their religion and adopt their ways of life?'[80] It was only when he converted to Islam (at which point he changed his name to Abdullah—as he will be referred to from now on) that he was to be fully trusted with an AK-47, and he soon proved himself loyal to his new comrades. When he had learned enough Dari, he translated intercepted Soviet communications on the radio and passed on information on Soviet military tactics to the Mujahideen. Abdullah became a respected fighter, but he recalls that there were some in the Mujahideen who never fully trusted him, who always eyed him suspiciously. When I asked him if he had killed any Russians, he shrugged his shoulders and replied evasively and with a smirk that no one really knows what's going on in a battle. With no experience of such things, I nodded assent. Abdullah's loyalty to Herat and his gratitude to Ismail Khan and the museum are unshakable, but I could not escape the sense that some Afghans were still unsure about this foreigner in their midst. Hajji Qattali, the founder and director of the museum, would look shiftily across at his Russian friend, still curious.

With the end of the war, Abdullah decided to remain in Herat, as a Muslim and with an Afghan wife. He worked closely with the repatriation of returning exiles from Mashhad, and even fought for the Taliban for a time, but later renounced his loyalty to them after a friend of his was unjustly imprisoned. I asked Abdullah if he felt any urge to return to Russia to see his family, and he replied that his home was Herat. He is happy in Herat. Yet as our conversation went on, he admitted that he does sometimes miss home, and he deals with this by reading Russian literature, particularly Tolstoy and Dostoevsky. Abdullah is by no means the only such example, and the number of Soviet soldiers who remained in Afghanistan after the war numbers in the hundreds. Abdullah is in occasional contact with a Russian friend, settled in Ghur during the war. He says they speak Russian together.

* * *

It was a repeated lament amongst Herat's resistance that few Western journalists ever crossed to Khorasan to cover the war and bear witness to the horrors unfolding, in contrast to the massed throngs gathered in Peshawar. The perils of travelling overland through Paktiya, Qandahar and then Baluchistan to reach the south of Herat were considerable. Iran's own violent instability and anti-Western bent precluded floods of truth-hungry journalists from entering Herat via Mashhad. Those who did make it, and back again, in whatever guise—be it humanitarian, journalist or adventurer—often wrote or filmed excellent and detailed accounts; Leon Flamholc's documentary is a powerful visual account of life with the Mujahideen, the suffering, privations and struggle of that war. Two written accounts of Herat at war in this period that stand out are those by Afghanaid employee Radek Sikorski, and the photojournalist Nick Danziger. Nick Danziger's description of his entry into Herat in the summer of 1984, a summer in which the fighting in Herat intensified as Moscow looked to drive the insurgents from their strongholds, is an apocalyptic one. For its description of Herat in ruins, it is worth quoting in full:

> The western part of the city was devastated. It was far worse than any pictures I had seen of Dresden or London: it called the total wreck of Nagasaki to mind. The great city of Herat, which has stood for 2500 years and witnessed the passage of Alexander the Great, Genghis Khan and Tamerlane, is being reduced to rubble. I looked aghast at the destruction. Twisted timber beams jutted from collapsed walls like arms reaching out

for help from a buried body. Embedded in walls were rockets, still unexploded, their fuses clearly visible in their tail-sections. Everywhere was the litter of modern warfare, and across it ranged the mujahedeen [*sic*], scavenging for reusable weaponry.[81]

These accounts tell of how life had become almost impossible for those who stayed behind, aside from the secluded eastern enclave of the city in which, as Danziger recalls, Mujahideen would take 'holiday' time away from the fighting.[82] Such was the devastation of farming and trade that local bazaars barely functioned; also, the exile of Herat's people to Iran was estimated by the end of the war to be around 80 per cent, so the demand for basic foodstuffs and goods had withered. People still speak of the daily experiences of fighting this war: the forced marches from village to village to avoid aerial bombardments which could quite literally tear men limb from limb, the experience of walking through a minefield to catch a glimpse of Herat's ruined Timurid remains, and the complexities of a war in which the Mujahideen fought amongst themselves for influence and guns. Meals were provided in villages, and hospitality was not dimmed by war; the *ta'arof* (roughly translated as 'etiquette', encompassing a set of rules which outline the way in which one behaves towards those who are guests, irrespective of rank or importance of either party) of Persian life appears to be indestructible. The support shown to the Mujahideen humbled and astounded all those who were lucky enough to witness it.

As the conflict plumbed the depths of human evil and depravity, Herat was not forgotten by the spirit world, its beloved saints and shrines. Mysticism, and the intercessions of Herat's most important saint, Abdullah Ansari, shone through in Herat's war. In one brilliant instance, John Baily was interviewing for his 1994 film a calligrapher and artist, while his guest, shaky, grey-bearded and with a full head of silver hair, sat before a miniature painting: heir to Herat's Timurid traditions. The miniature depicted a Russian bombardment of Gazur Gah: rubble and earth swirled and eddied in the awful attack as helicopters hovered overhead. Yet amidst this, a shaft of light reaching into the sky from the tomb of Ansari at Gazur Gah can be seen, clear and brilliant.[83] During the bombardment, as the calligrapher explains, somehow this beam of white light surged up into the sky and was accompanied by a few minutes of miraculous peace and calm, as if

Ansari himself had taken control of the mayhem and calmed the vio-lence. The voice of the calligrapher retelling this miracle is stretched somewhere between otherworldly grief and the awe reserved for mar-velling at the wonders of the spirit world. It hovers on the edge of a torrent of emotion, yet is held in check by Herat's patron saint, just as the conflict for a few minutes had been. In another clip from Baily's 1994 film, the same man retells the story of a Soviet bombardment in which there was no divine intervention; the river ran red with blood, so red that it was renamed Blood River.[84]

* * *

A point on which Danziger and Sikorski's accounts agree is the impor-tance of Ismail Khan's leadership to Herat's Jamiat Mujahideen. He was a popular and able, charming and compassionate leader, utterly dedi-cated to his cause, and his humanity comes across in many accounts of this time. Yet this picture of a benevolent Islamic nationalist fighting a just war must be tempered by an understanding of Ismail Khan's ruth-lessness, shown in his quick ascent to power. In 1980, Ismail Khan was leading a small band of no more than fifteen men in the border district of Gulran, nominally loyal to Jamiat, then run by the thuggish but brave former-criminal, Kamal Gulbagaz (he was assassinated by a rival, Mir Ali Khan Jamju). Ismail Khan's organisational abilities and focus on discipline marked him out as a future commander, and in 1981–2 he was offered charge of Ali Khan's larger troop of 'a few hundred men', a post he accepted and which bought him influence.[85] In 1984, Ismail Khan had Mir Ali Khan Jamju assassinated, an event which in turn brought him to the head of Jamiat's military operations in Herat and cemented his place as undisputed leader of a yet larger group of men. This was not the dedicated Islamic nationalist of popular accounts, but rather, as Giustozzi shows us, the ruthless Machiavellian Prince, win-ning at all costs, a role which he plays to this day. Indeed, such was the ruthlessness Ismail Khan showed in eliminating his Mujahideen rivals that Ghulam Yahya of Siyoshan was the only resistance or militia leader of note to survive.[86]

To his ruthlessness, we can add an extraordinary efficiency and skill. Ismail Khan's Jamiat were more than simply a top-down grouping of insurgents; they aspired to be a working political and social entity, with a number of different departments which would provide basic services for the districts where Jamiat were present. Their work included setting up hospitals, one of which, at Zendah Jan, was described by a *Médecins Sans Frontières* doctor as being an example of the 'best help from a commander he'd seen in all his time'.[87] A United Nations team, visiting Herat in December 1988, reported on the existence of 'ten or eleven' committees in Ismail Khan's self-styled Emirate. These included Finance, Agriculture, Culture, Justice, Political Affairs (dealing with Iran), Military, Intelligence and so on.[88] In this Emirate, the prominence of mullahs, as opposed to educated 'intellectuals' or those with a technocratic background, gives one an idea as to the tenor of Ismail Khan's governance. He was suspicious of intellectuals and technocrats; mullahs exerted 'moral authority' in the villages and provided guidance on how society was to be ordered.[89] The use of Mujahideen courts and justice systems was in place from 1982–3 onwards, yet their speed and supposed efficiency was the price paid for a passing interest in the accused's representation.[90]

The Mujahideen of Herat were to some extent cut off from the national, or even international, aspects of the conflict, unplugged from the political dialogue going on in Peshawar and, by the later 1980s, in international capitals of the world under the auspices of the UN and International Community. A ceasefire in 1985, negotiated by Ahmad Shah Massoud from the Panjshir, saw a supply line open up across the north of Afghanistan, through which weapons and supplies could still reach Ismail Khan. Other than this brief opening for Herat, its Mujahideen were forced to send for guns via the route on which occasional journalists and adventurers had travelled from Peshawar. Despite listening to the BBC Persian service to glean news of the conflict, an almost blanket lack of information on the direction of the war in the rest of the country, and the political process as a whole, is apparent from this time. Ismail Khan lamented Herat's isolation to anyone who cared to listen, and to this day he is proud of the fact that he only went to Peshawar on a handful of occasions, preferring to remain and fight a forgotten war in Herat. Yet our image of a province totally cut off from the outside should be tempered by the fact that Ismail Khan was more connected than he let on. It is almost certain that the ISI was paying Ismail Khan a $500,000 annual subsidy,[91] and

Danziger's account, based on discussions with the fighters, suggests that weapons were brought in from China.[92] Ismail Khan also had representatives in Pakistan, Salahuddin in Quetta and Qari Fazl Ahmad in Peshawar, through whom he communicated to the outside world. The picture of a totally isolated resistance fighting a single war is not entirely accurate, but in its inaccuracies it forms part of Herat's complicated relationship with the rest of Afghanistan during this time.[93] The tensions between Herat's seeming irrelevance and its simultaneous importance—an orphan of the twentieth century—still persisted in the Soviet conflict.

Ismail Khan's relations with Iran are a constant source of intrigue to Western watchers of Herat. This intrigue is an example of both the West's fascination with Iran, but also of our lack of understanding of what was going on in Herat, then and now. The echoes from confused nineteenth-century diplomacy are difficult to ignore in this regard. In reality, the exact nature of Jamiat's links to Iran varies from account to account. For example, Ismail Khan suggested to Nick Danziger that Iran's Revolutionary Guards fought against his Mujahideen, yet in another account, an interview Ismail Khan gave to Jamiat representatives in Peshawar, he is reported as saying, in response to the question of whether or not he would accept money and weapons from Iran, 'Yes, why not? We want to receive money and weapons from all Islamic countries.'[94] Such readiness to receive support from Iran is, in turn, undermined by a later report, written in 1988 by a United Nations mission to Herat, in which Ismail Khan specifically made it a condition that he would not allow UN offices to come under the influence of Iran during that time, and forbade Iranian influence in the conception and implementation of UN assisted programmes.[95] Iran's Foreign Ministry at this time did have a devoted Afghan Cell from which it would liaise with all Mujahideen parties who were using Mashhad as a base from which to launch their operations, but in reality Iranian involvement was more interested in backing Shia parties operating in the Hazarajat. Iran had come to rely on Russia for weapons in their own military quagmire against Saddam Hussein, and so trod carefully in Afghanistan's conflict. Ismail Khan's response to my own questioning about links to Iran was a bristly one, resenting the implication that Herat needed outside help.[96] From his time in the Afghan army, he was keenly aware that foreign assistance was rarely altruistic and often betokened a form of obligation. He was keen to keep his backers at arm's length.

* * *

During Radek Sikorski's time with the Mujahideen in the summer of 1987, he was privileged to observe one of the most significant meetings to have occurred in western Afghanistan during the war. This meeting took place over a number of days in Sagah district of Ghur province in July 1987, and was convened on the orders of Ismail Khan as a way of gathering representatives of the main Mujahideen parties in Herat and beyond to discuss the future of their fight and their country.[97] Tellingly, the majority of those present at this Mujahideen conclave in Ghur were from Jamiat, with Hezb-e Islami only having a small representation among the estimated 1,200 present. The meeting showed Ismail Khan in a more expansive mode, attempting to use his credibility as one of the few leading Mujahideen commanders, along with Ahmad Shah Massoud, who remained in Afghanistan to fight and avoided the circus of sycophants and swindlers in Peshawar. Ismail Khan's vision was founded on the Mujahideen's successes and demanded that Afghanistan be rid of both Soviets and Afghan communists, that it receive reparations from the Soviets for war, and a government of Mujahideen in the name of Islam. Ismail Khan called for exiled doctors to return to begin to treat the injured, and for greater cooperation amongst those Mujahideen parties fighting in Afghanistan. His Jamiat party sought to establish national legitimacy for itself by positioning itself as the sole defender of an independent and Islamic Afghanistan which had shed blood in the service of those values. Ismail Khan's belief was that these were the people to whom to entrust the future of the country. Yet history would relate that the impressive words and gathering of Mujahideen commanders could not unite the disparate groups outside Jamiat any more than the war had done so far.

By 1986 the war appeared to both sides as unwinnable. Stalemates across the country, and particularly in Herat, had set in with the Mujahideen in a sort of ascendancy and the militia showing worrying signs of opportunistic criminality. Mikhail Gorbachev's decision in February 1986 to extricate a tired Soviet Union from an impossible war reflected this fact. Gorbachev referred to the crisis in Afghanistan as a 'bleeding wound', yet he would still commit Soviet money and expertise to continue the defence of Moscow's protégé, the Afghan President Dr Najibullah.[98] Talks to bring about a political solution to the conflict, or at least to resolve key issues such as the return of Afghan refugees, had been ongoing across the world since 1982 (mostly between Kabul and Islamabad). It was only in April 1988, when Afghanistan and Pakistan signed the Afghan Geneva Accords, co-signed and guaranteed by the USSR and the US, that the war could be said to be entering its final stages. The Geneva Accords comprised four main obligations: non-interference agreements between Pakistan and Afghanistan; Soviet commitment to withdraw its troops by 15 February 1989; safe repatriation of Afghan refugees in Pakistan (Iran was not included); and guarantees from Washington and Moscow to respect the terms.[99] Any provisions for peace were absent; the Geneva Accords aimed solely at a respectful exit for the Soviets. Weapons would still be supplied by Moscow, at rates of three to four times that which its standing army required, and support for the KHAD remained strong. The bleeding wound would continue to bleed, but the blood would now be entirely Afghan.

Washington, meanwhile, was more concerned with the grander narrative of the Cold War than their 'freedom fighters' whose transition to 'terrorists' would later present the US with a headache every bit as serious as Moscow's. In a startling oversight, although possibly a reflection of the heterogeneous and fickle nature of the groups, the Mujahideen had not been invited to the talks. Their lack of participation caused outrage in Peshawar. Ismail Khan's response to the Geneva Accords was as one might expect: 'I don't believe that anyone who has been fighting the Russians and the government for ten years will accept any coalition. What would be the point of fighting for ten years and then handing over power?'[100] Most people in Herat just wanted peace, and the hundreds of thousands in Mashhad wanted to return to their beloved city.

Amidst the breakdown of Soviet support for Kabul and an 'end' to the conflict, stirrings of coming conflicts can be discerned. Fundamentalists dominated the formation in 1988 of the Afghan Interim Government (AIG), with Sebghatullah Mojadeddi as President and Abdul Rassoul Sayyaf as Prime Minister. Amidst the lines being drawn for the next conflict, the Mujahideen had become hopelessly divided and ready to fight amongst themselves. The cry from within the AIG was that Dr Najibullah was the main impediment to peace, but the reality was closer to home, for the Mujahideen themselves, and their blood feuds, would erupt into a civil war every bit as deadly as the conflict it replaced. That the Geneva Accords were signed with US and USSR cooperation pushed the more radical of the Mujahideen to turn their ire towards the US, and Washington became bracketed with the Soviets as enemies of an independent and free Afghanistan. One Afghan writer reminded his fellow Mujahideen that 'Equal struggle against East or West imperialism is considered by us as the fundamental obligation of nations and, in order to put an end to this, we will use all the means at our disposal.'[101] Amidst the infighting and the backbiting, recorded with excellent detail in *Afghan Jihad*, we see again these worrying signs of a creeping fundamentalism amongst the Mujahideen parties. One issue of *Afghan Jihad*, from September 1990, carries with it allegations against Mujahideen parties of executed civilians and beheaded villagers. It is in these pages that we see glimpses of 'Afghan Arabs', those same men who would go on to form al-Qaeda, and 'extremist' elements are blamed for attacks in and around Herat in 1988.[102] Some in the West saw the danger of creeping fundamentalism and a broken Afghanistan, but such fears were simply waved away by Thatcher and Reagan for whom the Cold War's final victory trumped everything. The defeat of the Soviet Union was, surely, more important than a handful of Islamic fundamentalists in Afghanistan?

The Soviet withdrawal from Shindand and the outlying posts began on 26 July 1988. By the autumn of that year Herat was Soviet-less, but still at war with itself. Reports written in 1988–90 by Afghanaid and UN workers indicate a multitude of groups operating in Herat, along with government-affiliated militia, all fighting each other. In 1990, a team of UN staff travelled to Herat from Pakistan to begin documenting the state of the province. The team wrote the following highly perceptive observations about an increasingly complex conflict:

> There are two wars in Herat, one between the Resistance and the DRA [Government of Afghanistan] and a more subtle struggle between traditional influences and the emergence of new and independent influences. Ismail Khan dominates in the west of Herat, where tribal influence is low

and education is high. In the east and north-west of the city, where tribal leaders and Sufi influence is great, Ismail Khan has had to work through these people. Hajji Malang, killed in April 1990, was the son of a religious leader who instigated the Herat Uprising of 1979 and despite his known connections with the government, continued to command popular respect, thus showing that this was not a simple political makeup, but more complex and deeper than we have thought. The resistance is divided. Ismail Khan controls Enjil and Zindajan and partly the other provinces, save Pashton [*sic*] Zarghun, which is in the hand of the militia and *Hezb-e Islami Gulbuddin*.[103]

Herat had become splintered. Dangerous ethnic divisions were emerging. Herat's Alizai and Nurzai Pashtuns sided with the government and fought with the militia in the later phases of the war, as Shia parties looked to do Iran's bidding. Other militia figures had renounced their loyalty to Ismail Khan's Jamiat and sided with the government's militias. Pockets of militia activity dotted the province; groups of former Mujahideen commanders had sided with the government by the late 1980s and were actively challenging Ismail Khan's provincial hegemony with attacks on his supply lines.[104] By 1990 the militia were 24,000 strong and had begun to control criminal activities such as smuggling, kidnapping and extortion along the roads leading out of Herat. Stories of the Mujahideen themselves looting, extorting and murdering their way through what remained of Herat are a common counterpoint to the militias' own criminal opportunism. In a Persian pun referring to this time, Ismail Khan's Jamiat group is referred to as '*Jam kilim*', meaning 'to roll up a carpet'. The implication was that when they looted, they took everything you had. The certainty of the conflict had dissipated; opportunism reigned. One *mujahed* was asked by the filmmaker Leon Flamholc in 1985 what he was fighting for, and replied with conviction that 'we are fighting to free our country from the Russians, to liberate Afghanistan'. The next question, 'then what?', was met with less certainty: 'we'll work that out when we come to it.'[105] Working it out was proving more difficult than freeing Afghanistan of Soviet soldiers.

* * *

On 21 April 1992 Herat's daily newspaper, *Ettefaq-e Islam*, was published in green ink and adorned with photos of Ismail Khan, radio in

LEFTISTS, ISLAMISTS AND OPPORTUNISTS

hand, to celebrate the triumph of the Jamiat-e Islami troops against the forces of Dr Najibullah. The war had officially ended in Herat with the victory of Ismail Khan's forces. They had withstood a 312-day long siege at Zendah Jan.[106] The fight for Zendah Jan had been drawn out and difficult. That much is revealed in Ismail Khan's frantic letters to Kabul: handwritten notes desperately requesting ever more assistance against Najibullah's forces.[107] In this green and celebratory edition of *Ettefaq-e Islam*, a letter from Rabbani to the people of Herat, the 'long-suffering and grief-stricken' Heratis and their martyrs and injured, firmly puts Herat's efforts at the front of all the troubles of the nation. Herat was a city that had not only begun the war with its fearless and brazen uprising, but had also sustained heavy fighting throughout. Perhaps there is also some envy in Rabbani's words, as he himself surveyed the mess that Kabul was soon to experience in the coming civil war; perhaps he was envious of Herat's distance from central government? This victory for Herat was rubber-stamped by a swearing-in ceremony the following month which took place in Herat's Friday Mosque. The captain in the Afghan army with leanings towards revolutionary Maoism had returned as a devout *mujahed* with a solid claim over Herat, Farah and Badghis and a reputation enhanced by his defeat of the Soviet Union. In his own words:

> I swear on the Holy Quran that my aim is towards serving the nation, pleasing God, honouring the dead martyrs, the freedom of beloved Afghanistan, the rule of the Quran over Afghanistan, and until my final breath I will fight for the freedom of Afghanistan and the rule of the Quran and in the service of the faithful people of Afghanistan; I will always remain faithful to the faithful people of Afghanistan and will stand shoulder to shoulder with you, brothers, in this endeavour.[108]

In the summer of 1984, Nick Danziger had entirely correctly observed, 'So devastating was the war that there would soon be nothing left for the victors to inherit.'[109] Even to speak of victors in this war is a misnomer. How Herat suffered can be seen from humanitarian reports of the time and articles on the destruction of Herat's cultural heritage, its Timurid and Safavid gardens and buildings, the chaotic alleyways and houses of the Old City, and the cisterns that had survived since the fall of the Safavid empire. The province as a whole experienced what one might call a first-tier level of destruction. Incident-reporting from the NCHRA from both 1985 and 1986 shows that Herat experienced the highest casualty rates of any province, and the highest number of incidents. For example, in 1986 the number of cases of Soviet attacks in Herat was recorded at 686, the next highest being Parwan at 534.[110] One English visitor to Herat in the autumn of 1988 estimated the district of Injil to be the 'most damaged few square miles of Afghanistan'.[111] The list of buildings and gardens, bazaars and mosques of historical interest which were destroyed is long and depressing; what remained of Herat's cultural heritage was irrevocably damaged.[112] Individual districts suffered untold damage. For example in Ghurian, cultivation of wheat fell by over 50 per cent, 80 per cent of its buildings were destroyed and the same percentage of its people fled to Iran.[113] By 1990 its 500-shop bazaar had become a five-shop bazaar.[114] Education 'all but collapsed' throughout the province, save for the schools within Herat city's eastern suburbs, which along with the main city hospital and mosque became centres for city life. Roughly 40 per cent of the city of Herat was destroyed in the fighting, and 60 per cent of its trees were cut down to prevent the Mujahideen from hiding amongst them. The western section of the city, winding alleys about which the *Kabul Times* had waxed so lyrical, were flattened, as were the southern suburbs. They still remained ruins in the winter of 1995. In 1998, almost a decade after Herat had seen the last of the fighting, a visitor to Herat wrote the following observations: 'Virtually all the buildings along the first 15 km of the main roads leading to Herat have been destroyed as a precautionary measure. Of the 1,300 villages in Herat Province, 600 have either been seriously damaged or totally destroyed.'[115]

Life shrank to the bare bones of subsistence. The sweet waters of Herat, and the canals and *kareze*s that had watered Herat's homes and villages, were all but destroyed; 'In ten years of war, 1,500 km of irrigation, 200 km of rural roads and 120 bridges and culverts and 200 canals and wells were destroyed.'[116] The very essence of Herat's fertility had been bombed into submission, to a degree that recalled Chingiz Khan or Tamerlane. Cotton production, so long a staple crop, was reduced to one-sixth of its pre-war level. The diversity of pre-1979 Herat became a memory. Herat's thriving 3,000-strong Jewish community, with their shops and homes in the Old City and the Iraq Bazaar, had chosen to flee to Jerusalem in 1979–80; Sikhs and Hindus had also fled. Returning refugees wept openly on seeing their ruined province and shattered city. Herat's identity, as a functioning province with cohesive urban–rural relations and trade, was no longer.

* * *

In the spring of 1993, Jane Thomas, a British aid worker with a Danish NGO, reported on a city moving cautiously from the horrors of conflict to a more positive future. Herat was rebuilding as only it can.[117] This lively and entertainingly written report shows Heratis grouping together to rebuild a shattered society, countryside and city. The promise of spring is infused with Herat's innate ability to regenerate and rebuild after traumatic experiences of conflict and exile. Summing up the mood of post-war recovery, she notes, 'What Herat has most going for it, unlike other places in the country, is a government, peace and security.'[118] Thomas makes the point that owing to the fact that Herat was isolated from the 'aid centre' of Peshawar during the Soviet war, it 'did not build up an aid-dependent culture', and therefore had the ability to stand on its own feet.[119] The report goes on to note that:

> [the] tradition of *hashar* (work bees to do large community jobs or help and individual harvest, repair storm damage) is alive and well in Herat. The anjoman [a collective or association] system is also providing help to the community. In many places pre-war anjomans were begun by the villagers and supervised by the maleks and in the cities there were anjomans specifically doing charitable work for women and children.[120]

The bazaars are described as being full of electronic goods, 'Hong Kong watches, Sony colour TVs and VCRs, German shampoo, colognes, cosmetics', and the author wonders how people can afford to buy the goods, so incongruous and contradictory is the picture of devastation and seeming plenty in Herat's bazaars.[121] Classes in basic literacy were given to the Mujahideen, both those returning from war and those recently released from prison, in a 'night-school'. Herat's university profited from the peace and stability that Ismail Khan's governance created, and a delegation from a German university even visited Herat in early 1993 to discuss curricula. Yet they faced an uphill task: when the university's then president, Nur al-Haq Saba, was asked about the university's facilities after years of war, he replied, 'we have only a few art books'.[122]

A video of Herat in 1994 by John Baily echoes this sense of a city going about its business, thriving despite the hardships and not for one second losing its sense of humour. Each interview conducted by the brilliant musician and mischievous raconteur Rahim Khushnawaz uses jokes and playful innuendo. Like his earlier films, this footage is a visual celebration of Herat's ability to triumph over adversity. Gone is the calm elegance of Herat's pre-war Golden Age, yet Herat's mischief and humour have scarcely been blunted. Rahim Khushnawaz's interviews show a rare sense of comic timing and skill, and his interaction with an old man from a village outside Herat, for example, gives me the giggles every time I see it. The city keeps building, making, weaving, laughing storytelling and living despite what it experienced during the Soviet conflict; sounds of hammers, and carvers and masons and builders have replaced the gunfire and shelling of the 1980s. There is a quiet determination amongst the blacksmiths, weavers, tailors and builders. A joke of some sort invariably hovers at the edge of each turn of phrase, as if to break the rhythm of work.

This notion of a convalescent Herat has political parallels, gleaned from local accounts of the time, albeit accounts which are largely pro-Ismail Khan. One such book by the Herati historian Mohammad Yusuf Qawam Ahrary contains a fascinating collection of documents on Ismail Khan's Emirate. A 1993 manifesto for Ismail Khan's rule in the Western Zone opens with the stipulation that the government in Herat should be constantly striving for 'the realisation of the aims of an Islamic Revolution and the institution of an Islamic government'. In the sphere of culture, Herat saw something of a revival, and a section of Ahrary's book entitled 'Services Rendered [to Herat]', lists the reopening of the Cultural Association, which had been closed during the war, and highlights the rebuilding programme undertaken by Ismail Khan. Buildings and cultural regeneration helped Herat to get back on its feet. Ahrary's comparison between the buildings of Ismail Khan and the Timurid renaissance is far-fetched, however, since the recent additions are generally gaudy and not always of the highest quality. Education was also seen as key to the province's revival, and by 1993 over 260 schools and high schools had been set up in Herat; amongst this number were girls' schools, as Ismail Khan encouraged girls' education, cautiously. Herat's university, opened during the early 1980s, was given fresh impetus and direction, stripped of any communist educational material or content. Islam was to be the 'cornerstone' on which the 'new' university was to be founded. A Sharia faculty was established there, as well as an engineering faculty, and exiled Afghan teachers were invited back to teach Herat's post-war generation.[123] The repatriation of refugees from Iran was also a priority, supported by organisations and individuals including Abdullah Khakimov, the ex-KGB-turned-*mujahed*. These organisations also housed and fed those fleeing the civil war in Kabul and seeking sanctuary in the stability of Herat. In a letter written as the city languished under the Taliban, Ismail Khan referred to Herat at this time rather wistfully as the 'valley of peace', for it provided a sanctuary for refugees fleeing the civil war in Kabul.[124] Much as Herat had functioned as a haven for those fleeing Mongol atrocities in the fourteenth century, it performed the same function at the end of the twentieth century.

And yet, for all the committees set up to deal with drug-runners, to honour women's rights or to promote Mujahideen education, there is a hollowness to this utopian vision. This was not rule by committee or enlightened technocrats; rather this was Ismail Khan's Emirate, and as such it bore the hallmarks of patrimony and highly conservative Islam. Consequently, there is some distance between the portrayals of Herat's idyllic and industrious convalescence and the reality of Ismail Khan's rule. The Emirate that Ismail Khan created, in reality, was a poorly functioning mini-state of limited competence. When the highly respected scholar of contemporary Afghanistan, Antonio Giustozzi, talks of a 'political culture which did not put much store by the role of political organisations', he is entirely correct.[125] Ismail Khan maintained, and still does, that the suffering of the Mujahideen elevated them to a position whereby they, and only they, were qualified to govern Afghanistan; and yet the reality suggested otherwise, and Mujahideen in positions of government were often unqualified for the role, irrespective of their heroism in ridding Afghanistan of the Soviet Union. There was a weakness to Ismail Khan's Emirate, a weakness found in its lack of inclusivity, which in turn encouraged a nepotism founded on shared experiences in the war. Rule by Mujahideen, for Mujahideen. He was suspicious of those who had fled Herat, the intellectuals and technocrats, and found he could only trust those who had fought along-side him. An oft-quoted saying of Ismail Khan runs, 'One obedient uneducated person is better than 100 disobedient intellectuals.' His mistrust for technocrats and intellectuals bears this out to this very day.

Amidst the repression and the bazaars selling Casio and Sony elec-tronics, under Ismail Khan's rule there was a flourishing of Herati nationalism.[126] Pride in Herat's peaceful oasis was expressed through songs about being a Herati, and songs expressed in new musical com-positions as if to signal a new departure and a new start for the city. As Kabul's civil war raged, Herat turned to celebrating its isolation and its ability to regenerate itself after yet another war. It is likely that this surge of civic pride was given some impetus from Ismail Khan, as well as being a natural expression of Herat's own civic pride. He forced musicians, who had been muzzled under his strict Islamic rule, to play at concerts celebrating his retaking of Herat in the spring of 1992. Yet musicians wanting to practise had to possess a licence from Ismail Khan's government, a strange state of affairs for a city through whose veins music runs as water. Veronica Baily recalls the strange contradic-tion of seeing gory banners depicting scenes of heroic victories by the Mujahideen, one glorious spring morning in Herat.[127]

If the departure of Herat's Jews in 1979 sounded a death knell for cosmopolitan Herat, then the war, and the Mujahideen victory, paved the way for the triumph of Islamism and strictly enforced conserva-tism, the first of which sat uneasily with Herat's intelligentsia and cul-tural elites, not to mention its women. A 1993 manifesto for Ismail Khan's rule in the Western Zone opens with the stipulation that the government in Herat should be constantly striving for 'the realisation of the aims of an Islamic Revolution and the institution of an Islamic government'. Respecting the property and livelihood of all Muslims in Afghanistan and making Allah proud are ancillary aims of this constitu-tion of sorts.[128] If Islam had won the war, why not put it to good use in peacetime? The war had radicalised certain sections of the Mujahideen, and a struggle for a free Herat had become an almost eschatological battle for the rule of the Quran over all the earth, as per Ismail Khan's letters from the front line.[129] The veiling of women and the beating of those who refused to wear a long beard presaged the arrival of the Taliban in Herat. Edicts on women's rights were every bit as harsh under Ismail Khan's first Emirate as they would become later under the

Taliban. Whilst Islam had always played a dominant role in Herat, the *jihad* infused it with the political Islamism of Hezb-e Islami and the Muslim Brotherhood, and gave to Herat's Islamic culture an edge which it had previously lacked. Islam had been a powerful tool for wartime, but its coercive use in peacetime alienated many who felt they had not suffered exile for the rule of saints on earth, but rather for a fairer, freer Afghanistan. That their heroic, and it was truly heroic, struggle should end in yet another form of tyranny was for many a source of genuine sadness.

* * *

By 1994, Pakistan had become worried about the failure of their protégé and Hezb-e Islami leader, Gulbuddin Hekmatyar. His power and influence had dwindled during the civil war he waged with Shah Ahmad Massoud for control of Kabul. Pakistan now looked for a new group to do their bidding in Afghanistan, to secure their troublesome borders.[130] This proxy force or, as Ismail Khan saw them, the 'Sindhis, Punjabis and Arabs, [working] at the behest of the ISI', was the Taliban, an ultra-conservative Pashtun fighting group. (Ismail Khan's assertion that the Taliban was little more than an offshoot of the ISI is by no means an exaggeration.)[131] The Taliban's initial popularity and success was largely founded on popular dislike of and disillusionment with the Mujahideen who, in the eyes of many Afghans, had turned from a respected and popular fighting force waging a noble cause to little more than a gang of self-interested and rapacious thugs whose ruthlessness had done huge damage to Afghanistan in a few short years.[132] Men such as Hekmatyar, Sayyaf and Massoud, once darlings of a respected resistance movement, had become Afghanistan's worst nightmare. The shelling of Kabul, the sectarian divides and the flickering remnants of the militia–Mujahideen struggle convinced some Afghans that the Taliban could rise above it all, and bring peace.[133] By early 1995 the Taliban had made extraordinary gains through the south and east of the country, astonishing many with their rapid advances, bringing large swathes of the country under their control, and being guided every step of the way by Pakistan's military, political and intelligence institutions.

In the high summer of 1995, as Herat faced a second wave of Taliban attacks from Qandahar and Helmand (a Taliban assault on Shindand in

February 1995 had proved unsuccessful and was beaten back with ease by Ismail Khan's forces),[134] the government in Kabul, still held together by the troubled guidance of Rabbani and Massoud, sent a commission to Herat to aid the city with its defences. This commission was a veritable case study in troubled Herat–Kabul relations. Its demands on Herat for money and its 'disrespectful' attitudes towards Ismail Khan were said to have 'subverted the morale of the city'.[135] Ismail Khan responded in kind, playing power games with Kabul. One eyewitness writes that 'Ministers from Kabul had to wait sometimes for days until they were granted a meeting with the local military commanders, let alone Ismail Khan himself.'[136] This sort of behaviour can hardly have endeared Ismail Khan to the Jamiat and ex-Mujahideen leaders in Kabul, who were keenly aware of the need to confront the Taliban as a united and coherent military force. Meanwhile, Taliban forces had reached the Farah river and were threatening the safety of Shindand airbase and the entry points to the south of Herat city. The Taliban were strangling Herat and threatening its military heart. At a point when Herat was in mortal danger, especially given the poor state of Ismail Khan's forces and the internal divisions within his polity, the commission was playing out old rivalries between Kabul and Herat, arguing old scores. Herat's isolation, once its saviour, would now prove to be its undoing.

A first-hand account of the fall of Herat tells of Jamiat defences being breached by the Taliban, of hastily ordered retreats and of soldiers simply walking off into the distance to the safety of Iran with little desire to stay and fight as they had done in the 1980s. The baton of suicidal devotion to a cause had, seemingly, been passed to the younger and more extreme generation. The axial points running into Herat were defended by various Mujahideen, either from Herat or those sent to Herat from Kabul, and roads leading to Qandahar from the city were guarded against the expected attack. Yet the retreat of Jamiat troops was chaotic, with no real direction or coordination. The army that finally did face the Taliban, or more accurately fled from the Taliban, was a rabble with little or no organisation or cohesion.[137] Bitter divisions and infighting which had characterised Afghanistan since the departure of the Soviets rendered the country almost totally inept at dealing with more foreign-backed invaders. Herat had yet again fallen victim to its troubling relationship with Kabul and its isolating independence.

The Taliban began their attack on Herat at 9 a.m. on 4 September.[138] The southern districts of Adraskan and Shindand had already fallen; the city was almost defenceless. The arrest of around 400 Helmandi and Qandahari men whom Ismail Khan suspected of being a potential fifth column for the Taliban was a largely pointless endeavour.[139] As it turned out, the Taliban were so well advised and well stocked with munitions that fifth columnists, however numerous, would have been of little use. In a telling indication of the state of morale and military expectation in Herat, many senior intelligence and military figures had taken the precaution of moving their families from the city; previously heroic figures of the resistance against the Soviets had secured themselves visas to Iran. From 11 a.m. on the day the city fell, the flight to the border began. General Azimi describes men previously loyal to Ismail Khan simply leaving their tanks and walking away. By 2 a.m. on the morning of 5 September, Herat had effectively been abandoned, leaving its terrified inhabitants, many of whom had only recently returned after years of exile, to contemplate their fate at the hands of what was feared to be a violent anti-Tajik mob. Herat had essentially ceased to be defendable when Shindand airbase fell to the Taliban prior to their advance on the city from Adraskan; the city's defences had been remotely punctured. The city's traditional fortress, Qalah-ye Ekhtiar al-Din, had ceased to be of any strategic relevance.

* * *

Walking around Qala-ye Naw (the capital of the province of Badghis) on a hot July afternoon in 2010, I was chatting with Yousoufi, a friend from Herat. The conversation turned, as most eventually do in Afghanistan, to the Taliban. As he recalled the beatings in the streets for supposedly immoral behaviour, the men hanged from lampposts, the closure of schools and the strangulation of their curricula and the unremittingly drab and violent pall that the Taliban had spread over the city, he began to cry. The force of his grief, nearly ten years on, was the closest I could come to understanding fully the horrors of life under the Taliban in Herat; this was as moving a testament to the destructive force of extremism as I have ever heard. The city became grey and uniform. Herat was ruled largely, although not exclusively, by illiterate Pashtuns in the name of an extremist Islam much at odds with Herat's more tolerant Hanafite traditions.

When I was in Herat, as a way of understanding quite how soulless the city became during those years of nihilism, I would often walk around and make a mental note of all the things—the music one hears, the photos on shop walls, the brightly dressed children, the shops and the sense of a city at work and play—that would simply not have been allowed under the Taliban's rule. Very little remains once one has stripped away those aspects of life deemed un-Islamic. One Taliban commander was once asked what people are supposed to do for entertainment in a world without music, dancing or song. The answer was that people should either read the Quran or look at flowers.[140] The city's cheer and lilt was stripped to its very barest bones and joy became a thing of the past. As if to reinforce this sense of despair, in December 1996 a commission from Qandahar's Vice and Virtue Squad (usually bands of young men sent around to beat those whose dress, behaviour, laughter or manner of walking were deemed to transgress Islamic norms) came to Herat to teach its people about respect for Islam. The edicts to be enforced covered the correct fashion for the wearing of the *hejab* (an indication that Herat's women had not immediately succumbed to the *burqa*), the length of men's beards, the prohibition of women walking unaccompanied through Herat's streets, the prohibition of flying kites, the prohibition of music, and the absolute prohibition of any representation of the human form. They stuck to their task as only zealots can. The work of these young men was given the most fulsome praise imaginable by the writer of an editorial in *Ettefaq-e Islam*.[141] Yet these prohibitions on the representation of human forms caused huge problems, especially for baby food and medicines which naturally carried on their packaging happy photos of young children or mothers. Even the silhouettes of human forms were outlawed, thus depriving Herat of a particular brand of soap.[142]

The BBC journalist John Simpson produced a documentary for *Newsnight* in 1998 on Afghanistan. During this documentary, he interviewed Herat's then governor, a Qandahari man. The mullah, seated at an entirely empty desk, made some extraordinarily grandiose and wildly incorrect claims about the Taliban's popularity, not least that the

'Kings' of America and England are keen to come to Afghanistan to observe, and ultimately learn from, the Taliban's peaceful governance of Herat and Afghanistan. This is a small, but highly instructive, insight into the ruling elite of Herat under the Taliban, frightening both in its almost total incomprehension of the world outside and also the absolute certainty with which this belief is poured forth. The man displayed not even the faintest flicker of doubt at the existence of American or English kings. The Taliban might have been the antithesis of their Marxist ancestors in ideological terms, but in overblown rhetoric they were every bit as false as the Khalqis in whose footsteps of violent extremism they were so ably following.

With Herat's writers and poets muzzled, it fell to the city's exiles to tell the story of their city. The journalism of Herat's diaspora, based in Mashhad and the US, mostly written through a publication called, appropriately enough, *Omid* (Hope), is filled with elegies for a broken province. Articles lament the almost total descent into colourless squalor, violent extremism and opium production. In an article written in Virginia about the state of Herat in the spring of 2001, the author laments the Hari Rud valley's descent from a green and fertile valley to a set of fields for opium cultivation: 'opium is everywhere; in the fields, in the minds of Heratis, in the mosques, in religion itself...'[143] According to this diaspora literature, Herat had become totally and utterly devastated by the influx of Pakistani-backed Islamists who had destroyed the province they knew and loved. A light had gone out in the cultural bastion of Herat; every article written from exile resonated with the themes of despair and devastation. The fertility of the province was being subverted to cultivate opium, its waters polluted, and the people of Herat's natural and ingrained piety and devotion was being poisoned by fundamentalism, foreign fundamentalism.

Possibly one of the most remarkable stories about Afghanistan's resistance to Taliban nihilism occurred in Herat. The Taliban not only banned education for young girls and women, but also circumscribed the curriculum for those allowed to learn. Herat's library was stripped of all its books, aside from those relating to Islam, and the books were carried away, ostensibly to be burned, although according to the maverick Herati intellectual, Mayel Heravi, despite the Taliban's conviction of the poison of enlightened education, the lure of money persuaded them to sell the books. The money was used to buy weapons.[144] Opportunism trumps ideology; money trumps spiritual reward. The Taliban's prohibition on female education and the restrictions on women leaving their houses unless accompanied by a male relative had effectively imprisoned thousands on thousands of young girls and women who had previously enjoyed the relative freedoms and education of Ismail Khan's Emirate. Owing to the crackdown on literature deemed to be un-Islamic, these women were denied the intellectual or literary space to explore in their captivity. By way of resisting the Taliban's oppressive dictates on education, a group of girls under the guidance of Naser Rahiab, a generous and charming Herati intellectual, began to organise classes for young girls who wished to learn the secrets of literature and poetry. These classes were run under the guise of sewing circles, one of the few activities which the Taliban had not proscribed. A young boy would stand guard outside the house, ready to alert the students should the Taliban pay them a visit whilst they read Rumi or Nabokov, Saadi or Shakespeare. Christina Lamb's moving account of this time, written through interviews with those who took part, gives the reader an excellent insight into the power of learning and culture in Herat, and also the lengths to which the Taliban would go to deny people the oxygen of literature and the escapism of good writing.[145] Many of those girls who took part in the Golden Sewing Circle went on to achieve fame in Afghanistan's literary circles, their obvious literary merit being burnished by the courage of their resistance to a hated regime of nihilists, and their education in the literary classics giving their work a sense of context it might never have had. Nadia Anjoman, a celebrated Herati poet who was killed in 2005 by her husband, learned in these classes. Her poems are simple and beautiful, capturing the horrors of captivity under the Taliban. One poem, entitled 'In Vain' is taut with the energy of a caged animal desperate to be set free. The final two quatrains are as powerful as any poem written in Herat, and have been excellently translated by Farzana Marie:

> One thought of the day I will break the cage
> makes me croon like a carefree drunk until
>
> they can see I am no wind-trembled willow tree—
> an Afghan woman wails and sings, and wail and sing I will.[146]

When I met with Naser Rahiab in January 2014, he spoke with real pride at the achievements of those girls for whose education he had risked his life. The simple act of reading Joyce or Persian poets such as Shahzadeh Momtaz was defiance, a defiance and resistance which was every bit as celebrated and every bit as typically 'Herati' as the *qiyam* of March 1979.[147]

The Golden Sewing Circle was not the only form of resistance to the Taliban during this time. Men such as Abdul Ghani 'Nik Seyar', born in 1942 in Herat, a pensive man whose life has been filled with worthwhile and notable cultural achievements, was part of Herat's Literary Association (*Annojman-e Adabi*) during the Taliban era (Nadia Anjoman took her pen name from this association). He still continues to write a regular blog on cultural and historical topics relating to Herat, looking at Herat's arts and artists of calligraphy, masonry and poetry. Under the Taliban, the Literary Association ran a magazine called *Aurang-e Hashtom*, a publication dedicated purely to cultural matters and fittingly named after a line of Herat's most famous poet, Jami. Nik Seyar and Mr Rahiab asked the Taliban if they could publish this magazine for cultural issues, and the Taliban representatives from the Ministry of Information and Culture granted permission only if Herat's intellectuals and poets contented themselves with writing purely on cultural and literary matters; politics was to be off-limits. Nik Seyar recalls the Taliban representative requesting that the name be changed to a Pashtu name, and asking the representatives of the Cultural Association and those running the magazine why they bothered with literature when all the beauty they could wish for was to be found in the Quran. That was as far as the interference went, and Herat retained a lifeline to its heritage as a city of poets and wits and aesthetes. True to their word, the magazine never strayed from the realm of the cultural, publishing 'nothing in favour of Mullah Omar, and nothing against him'.[148] From this grew poetry recitals, much needed gatherings through which to resist and oppose the nihilism of extremism, the emptiness of fundamentalism. The magazine was published weekly, and Nik Seyar estimates that there were approximately 500 printed during the years 1996–2001.[149] This was an endeavour unique in Afghanistan, and one which fused Herat's traditions of cultural greatness with their love of resistance to foreign-backed tyranny.

The Taliban's representative in the Ministry of Information and Culture in Herat, Ltifullah Hakimi (a man about whom Naser Rahiab is complimentary, distinguishing him from the other Taliban 'robots' who stalked the streets, cane in hand), recognised Herat's place as Afghanistan's cultural guardian. He gave Herat an outlet for their poetry and literature and appealed to the city's cultural and religious past as a way of showing the Taliban in a more positive light. This can be seen in the pages of Herat's daily paper *Ettefaq-e Islam*, in which the city's cultural and historical identities were used as ways to appeal to Heratis, or ways to celebrate the city's past. One article makes the clear link between Herat's waters and the city's cultural legacies and is clearly a celebration, albeit muted, of Herat as a city of culture and fertility.[150] Other articles in *Ettefaq-e Islam* quote Taliban leadership figures actively looking to appeal to Herat's historical and renowned piety, through its shrines and the natural intelligence of its people. These articles seem to plead with Herat to put their intelligence and capacity for religious observance to good use in the service of doing God's will on earth and implementing the Sharia in Herat. It is as if Herat's buildings and people were seen as one, indivisible, and it is also clear that the Taliban were fully conscious of having to approach the citizens of Herat in a language they might understand. And yet these must be set against the strict line the Taliban propagandists took with Herat's hearts and minds. The editorial of 26 January 1997 in Herat's Taliban-run paper *Ettefaq-e Islam*, entitled 'Resistance is futile', stresses that at no point should the people of Herat even consider joining the anti-Taliban resistance. This was for the good of their immortal souls as well as for their continued existence in this life.

* * *

Whilst Herat laboured under the strangulation and starvation of the Taliban's nihilism, and its young girls and cultured elites read Nabokov and Saadi in secrecy, the city's erstwhile 'saviours', Ismail Khan and his chastened Mujahideen, were secluded in Iran as guests of a nervous Islamic Republic. They were plotting another triumphant entry into Herat. Iran, fearful of the Taliban's virulent Sunni ideology, assisted in a number of half-hearted attempts to recapture Herat.[151] In early November 1997, with the help and apparent blessing of Iran's

Revolutionary Guards, Ismail Khan planned an attack on Herat to dislodge the Taliban and return to the city in triumph. The operation was a disaster. Ismail Khan was arrested, along with 1,700 of his fighters, and taken to the Taliban's prison in Qandahar, betrayed by one of his erstwhile allies, General Malek, a Jamiat turncoat. A diaspora news bulletin from 3 November 1997 announced the duplicity of General Malek, describing it as a betrayal of Islam and a betrayal of the people of Afghanistan.[152] The arrest was a cause for concern for many who had seen Ismail Khan as a vague figure of hope in the fight against the Taliban; in articles published by Herat's diaspora his incarceration was lamented with florid Persian sighs, and requests to the Taliban that his treatment be worthy of his esteemed status as a respected *mujahed*.[153] The Taliban, in turn, were keen to highlight the fact that Ismail Khan's arrest signalled the end of resistance to their rule.

In the winter of 2000, Ismail Khan's supporters in Iran discussed plans to spring their erstwhile commander. A number of previous attempts to bribe him out had met with little success; the Taliban simply took the money and sat tight. Khan himself had identified a willing Talib, Abdul Razzaq Hekmatullah, through whom to engineer his flight. A cash offer was made to Hekmatullah, and it is a testament to Ismail Khan's nerve and his ability to influence people that he could so utterly bring under his control a Taliban guard.[154] Much as the Qajars did in the nineteenth century, members of Hekmatullah's family were spirited out of Qandahar to Iran, where they acted as surety for Hekmatullah's continued cooperation.

In the small hours of 19 March 2000, Hekmatullah was on duty in the prison guarding Ismail Khan's cell. Ismail Khan shared this cell with two fellow escapees, a man simply referred to as 'the General' and Hajji Zaher, the son of the former governor of Nangahar, Hajji Abdul Qader. Hekmatullah had arranged for his father to park the getaway car in a small lane behind the prison so as to avoid Taliban police on the prowl for anyone breaking the curfew. Ismail Khan and his fellow jailbirds were given 'Taliban clothes'. Hekmatullah, by all accounts a resourceful man, even sprayed oil on the hinges of the cell doors so to silence any rusty creaks which might have alerted the guards. Keys had been smuggled to Ismail Khan inside a book; there were to be no doors left ajar. As Hekmatullah's duty began, Ismail Khan and his companions quite literally walked out of the Taliban's Qandahar prison, heading for the back streets where Hekmatullah's father was waiting to drive them into the deserts of Baluchistan. Hekmatullah showed real nerve in remaining on duty, telling those who replaced him not to disturb Ismail Khan and his cellmates as they had already done their ablutions and morning prayers and were now sleeping again. He later slipped out of the prison.

From Qandahar they followed the ordinary road to Helmand until they reached Lashkar Gah. From there they took the dusty track through the desert to Nimruz. They reached their destination on the Iran–Afghanistan border in Baluchistan despite running over a mine, which exploded with some force and caused damage to their party. As the news of Ismail Khan's daring escape broke across Afghanistan, for a full week Mirwais, Ismail Khan's son, denied any knowledge of the escape, so as to toy with the Taliban. An interview with Mirwais notes how he took delight in 'watching the Taliban rush here and there' after sending them on wild goose chases into mountains and deserts.[155] The Taliban, in turn, reacted with a blanket search of the border between Iran and Afghanistan. Radio Sharia, the Taliban's official radio channel in Kabul, announced that the people of Afghanistan should do every-thing in their power to help catch those who had escaped. This appeal to the people of Afghanistan was repeated hourly, and so serious was the announcement on the radio that Hajji Saheb Qader Khan announ-ced that they would even be prepared to search under the veil of Afghan women.[156]

Ismail Khan's release from prison offered some hope for those in Herat (and its exiled community in Mashhad and America) who suf-fered under the Taliban. As soon as he had escaped from prison, he set about lobbying powerful friends he had met during the *jihad*, such as the then Polish Foreign Minister, Radek Sikorski, for help in defeating the Taliban. Ismail Khan's calls for help were, it must be said, some-thing of a departure for a fiercely nationalist figure whose default set-ting had been suspicion of foreign interventions. A letter written to Minister Sikorski in April 2001 talks of ridding Afghanistan of extrem-ism and heroin, of establishing a nation along the lines of democracy and transparency. In short, it reads like a UN document from the post-Taliban era when the regeneration of Afghanistan had become a global priority.[157] Interestingly, this letter also seeks to place Herat at the centre of a post-Taliban revival of Afghanistan's fortunes, citing the city's 'social, economic, political, military, bureaucratic and geographical' advantages, which would mean it could take the lead in this project of renewing Afghanistan.[158] These boasts bear the hallmark of an ambitious man, yet the truths inherent in his claims that Herat and its surrounds have the requisite assets to help the country flourish are difficult to refute. When it came to a domestic audience, however, Ismail Khan's first public pronouncement was one of angry determination to defeat the Taliban, far from the neat ideals of liberal democracy and freedom of expression. He calls the exiled people of Afghanistan back to their country to wage a *jihad* against the 'forces of colonialism and the influences of heroin and Pakistan'.[159] At every turn, for all his faults, Ismail Khan has proved himself to be a survivor, just like Herat, with genuine talent for saying the right things at the right time to the right people, and yet somehow not compromising or diluting his core messages. Like Yar Mohammad before him, Ismail Khan was an opportunist with a weakness for his city of Herat.

* * *

A little while after the working day had finished on 11 September 2001, a group of ICRC employees sat in their compound watching the awful events in New York unfold as al-Qaeda's attacks against America were broadcast to the world. One of their number was drinking a beer. At some point during the broadcast, a senior member of the Taliban government in Herat entered the compound and demanded to watch the tragedy live. The Taliban had, after all, banned televisions and the ICRC owned one of the only televisions in the city. The staff member drinking a beer managed to wedge the can between leg and chair, a position from which he did not dare move until the Taliban official had departed. It was, for many reasons, an uncomfortable hour or so. I was told that the Taliban figure was as shocked, or nearly as shocked, as the ICRC staff members with whom he was watching the events.[160] It is unlikely that he knew that within six weeks his government would be driven from Herat.

Herat reacted with a muted sense of disbelief to the attacks on the United States. The increasingly anti-Western presence of Osama bin

Laden in Khost and Abu Musa Zarqawi in Herat and the assassination of Ahmad Shah Massoud by two al-Qaeda suicide bombers on 9 September 2001 left the city in little doubt as to the identity of the hijackers. Herat's radio and press had been full of anti-US and anti-Western messages since the arrival of the Taliban, and even before. Zarqawi and his al-Qaeda followers had set up camp near the Takht-e Safar and were unpopular extremists for their time in Herat, adding to the anti-US and anti-Western sentiments of the Taliban. Consequently, the thought of an anti-Taliban backlash, with overwhelming support from the US, gave many in Herat cause for cautious optimism that the Taliban and their extremist guests would finally be driven from Afghanistan. Since Ismail Khan's escape from Qandahar prison in March 2000, he had been making contact with resistance figures in Ghur and the Panjshir, and so in some senses Herat had been preparing for this moment for over a year. Yet it was with the support, both money and technical assistance, provided to Northern Alliance figures from the CIA team inserted into Afghanistan in October 2001 and the positive impact this had on the fight against the Taliban, that Ismail Khan, along with erstwhile Mujahideen figures, could retake Herat on 12 November 2001.[161]

The fall of Herat to the Taliban had been as swift as their arrival. Their departure was as ragged as the Jamiat forces' withdrawal had been in 1995. Joy erupted on the streets and the Pashtun Qandaharis and Helmandis who had so oppressed Herat since 1995 ran south as forces from the Shia Hezb-e Wahdat, in consort with the Iranian Revolutionary Guard's figures under the control of General Yahya Safavi, drove the Taliban from the city and Ismail Khan's forces pushed up from the south through Shindand and Adraskan.[162] Herat had been freed from Taliban oppression. Eyewitnesses recall the Taliban being literally chased from the city; Ismail Khan was, once again, proclaimed as Herat's leader, as he had been in the spring of 1992.[163]

The British writer and historian Christopher de Bellaigue was one of the first Westerners to visit Herat after its liberation. The article he wrote for the *New Yorker* about his entry into Herat paints a fascinating and characteristically eloquent picture of a broken city trying to rejoice. De Bellaigue writes that Heratis had driven their cars into the railings of a spot used by the Taliban for hangings, both as an expression of their rage and yet also in celebration of the Taliban's fall. As de Bellaigue walked through the streets, an old Herati man approached him to ask who he'd come to see. When the old man realised he didn't know the man de Bellaigue sought, he 'wandered off, saying that he didn't know him but that the city had changed so much, so many new people had arrived from the villages, that no one really knew anyone any more'.[164]

* * *

In the frozen depths of January 2014, I went to meet with Hajji Abdul Wahhab Qattali, the owner of Herat's Mujahideen Museum. The museum is a towering monument to the conflict which had driven out the Russians and, so they thought, achieved its final victory in the ousting of the Taliban in 2001. Hajji Qattali is a man who played his part in the *jihad*, and whose fortune was made in the post-Taliban days of reconstruction and logistical support for the new Karzai government and its US backers. The museum sits in the foothills of the city, next to the US Consulate, perched on a hill overlooking Herat. A Soviet helicopter and MIG jet are displayed nearby, almost like stuffed animals that adorn the walls of a hunting lodge or stately home. The walls are covered with the names of the martyrs who perished in the fighting, civilian and *mujahid* alike. One room is devoted to photos of martyrs, and I walked around it alone, as the weather had covered the city in a thick blanket of snow and shut most of its shops; the photos showed an almost endless sea of bodies, lifeless faces and young men who were killed during the war. The sheer numbers of the victims brought to mind the sense of waste, the flower of youth being gunned down in Herat's war with the Soviets. In the museum's entrance hall are lifelike wax statues of Afghan men and women dressed in traditional garments, and glass cases showing weapons and shells. The weapons are now decommissioned, Qattali told me, but in case anyone should doubt their potency, they are accompanied by descriptions of their use and range. As one moves further inside, the corridor is lined with thickly coloured paintings of Mujahideen figures who played significant roles in the *jihad*. Kindly eyes and luxurious beards stare down on the visitor. A spiral staircase, all shiny glass and ornate tiling, leads upwards to a panoramic depiction of significant events in Herat, from the *qiyam* of

March 1979 to the departure of Soviet troops from Herat ten years later. The shelling of mosques and killing of women are all depicted through these scaled-down figures and models with disquieting accuracy; one can almost sense the frenzied violence that swept the city during the heady days of March 1979 and hear the bombs thudding into villages and mosques. Babies are cradled in wailing mothers' arms; houses shot through with shells and bullets. Russian soldiers die agonising deaths by the side of abandoned tanks. The pagoda around which this orgy of violence unfolds is a commemoration of Ismail Khan's heroic resistance to the Soviet troops and his final victory at Zendah Jan. The names listed on plaques celebrate different stages of the resistance to the Soviets.

I discussed the war with Hajji Qattali as we both warmed our hands on the heater in his office, talking about Herat and drinking tea in an attempt to stave off the cold from outside. After the usual jingoism and patriotism had been covered, something in Hajji Qattali changed, and the conversation changed tone dramatically. 'War achieves nothing', he said, with an almost apologetic arc of his hand towards the museum, as if to say that the millions he has made and his magnificent Mujahideen Museum (unique in Afghanistan) are nothing when set against the horrors of warfare. He went on, 'It just tears people apart and destroys everything.'[165] This brief, but alarmingly eloquent, testament was powerful in its implicit castigation of warfare and conflict, particularly when contrasted with the simultaneously jingoistic and solemn glorification of the *jihad* as depicted in his museum. The contrast made for a powerful point and I sensed a real and deeply ingrained sense of sadness and vulnerability, one that had been arrived at through reflection and not just a numb response to the violent shock of violence. He was still in mourning for his lost city, his lost friends and, as so many of the photos of the dead young men showed, for a lost age. The futility of war, a war which in so many ways defined Herat and continues to define men like Hajji Qattali and Ismail Khan, hangs like a pall over the city.

EPILOGUE

HERAT AS IT FACES THE FUTURE

The sense of optimism and relief which engulfed Afghanistan in the autumn and winter of 2001–2 was short-lived in Herat. Afghanistan was caught between the Scylla of the US war machine, let off its leash and seeking to destroy its attackers, and the Charybdis of that same war machine seeking to co-opt men like Ismail Khan into doing their bidding in the interests of short-term strategic objectives. Ismail Khan was, on account of his martial and organisational skills, chosen to resume his tenure as Herat's Amir. Unfortunately those most suited to hunt al-Qaeda and the Taliban were not necessarily those around whom one could build the type of government being dreamt up in Bonn, where international leaders and Afghan powerbrokers were meeting in the winter of 2001 to decide Afghanistan's future. In the heady and bruised atmosphere of a post-9/11 world, political concerns trumped human rights and the rule of law, and the country is living with the consequences of this. Blame, however, is never a one-way street; Afghan culpability in this is clear, for it was that nation's politicians and leaders who decided to syphon off money meant for worthier causes than penthouses in Dubai and private militias.

Two *Human Rights Watch* reports from 2002, one entitled 'All Our Hopes are Crushed', and another entitled 'We Want to Live as Humans: Repression of Women and Girls in Western Afghanistan', are damning indictments of Ismail Khan's second Emirate and what followed the fall of the Taliban in Herat.[1] 'All Our Hopes are Crushed' speaks of ill-treatment at the hands of Ismail Khan's Jamiat men, of shaven-headed criminals paraded around Herat and of the swift and violent punishment of political dissent. In this open and hopeful atmosphere to which the Taliban's fall had briefly given rise, different political factions and new ideas on how to govern Herat emerged. One such faction was in favour of the return of the exiled King Zahir Shah, then in Rome, and the Bonn Conference which outlined the future political make-up of Afghanistan. This faction staged a rally outside the Friday Mosque after having been barred by Ismail Khan from holding a press conference in Herat's Mowfaq Hotel. The rally occurred on 21 November 2001: it was not the peaceful pro-democracy event its organisers had envisioned, as Ismail Khan himself punched the head of the movement's leader, Abu Bakr Barez, a respected elder of Herat, and then had him arrested. Jamiat troops surrounded the rally and beat and arrested as they pleased. Barez was later savagely beaten by Ismail Khan's troops with whips, thorny branches and rifle butts, and ten months later he still showed livid scars on his head and torso from the assaults. His release from prison was conditional on his promise not to discuss the incident with international journalists. Ismail khan was clearly fearful of his reputation amongst Westerners, a reputation he had been careful to cultivate over the years.[2] The benevolent freedom fighter of the 1980s had hardened, and gone were his earlier appeals to create a democratic state in Herat.

The values of inclusivity, transparency and freedom of association were nowhere to be seen in Herat's post-Taliban Emirate. This was rule by Mujahideen. Ismail Khan was angry at his exile, out for revenge and vowing never to let go of power again. As a result, Herat was thrown back into the nightmare of repression and authoritarian rule. In 2002 he re-introduced the Taliban's 'vice and virtue police' and transgressions of Islamic law were punishable by shaved heads, beatings and blackening with coal, as had been the case under the Kart *malek*s. Women were banned from walking in parks after dark, and colourful clothing was deemed sacrilegious; the sale of taped media and music in public was prohibited. Ismail Khan even tried to ban females from taking driving lessons, and tailors were not allowed to measure women for clothes.[3] Journalists were threatened and beaten; those whose candidacy in the provincial elections of 2002 might have challenged Ismail

Khan's own were threatened with death and severely beaten to force them not to run. Ismail Khan and his brand of ruthless efficiency very much chimed with the American intentions of ridding Afghanistan of al-Qaeda and Taliban affiliates, whatever the cost. In the process, Herat became a 'virtual mini-state… with little allegiance to Kabul'. It was a closed society where freedom was muzzled, law a fiction and the hope of a post-Taliban Afghanistan largely dead in the water.[4]

If the world after 9/11 saw a chance to bring Afghanistan forwards into the light of a democratic utopia, Ismail Khan saw the situation rather differently; this was a chance to reassert his authority and to do things his way. He ruled, as the English writer, businessman and Kabul resident Matthew Leeming told me, like a Central Asian Khan, dispensing patronage, justice and funds from a table in Herat's gubernatorial hall. When problems were brought to his attention, he cut through any bureaucratic niceties or requirements and simply passed down judgement or handed out money. One such occasion involved a woman who had lost her husband in the fight against the Taliban; she was unable to provide for her family, and her pleading was understandably heading in the direction of financial assistance. Ismail Khan's response, however, was to assign her to one of his fellow Mujahideen as a wife. Whilst this solved the immediate problems of penury, it might not have been the desired outcome for the widow.[5]

Such was the triumphalism of Ismail Khan's return to Herat that he decided to instigate a culture of forced political rallies. The rallies themselves were occasioned by holidays celebrating the deeds of the Mujahideen, or the death of *mujahed* Ahmad Shah Massoud. One shopkeeper was 'savagely' beaten for his tardiness in attending one such rally in September 2002. The parallels with the forced political marches in support of the Khalqi leader Taraki are too striking to ignore, a point made to me during my time in the city. Why, so many ask, would one have to resort to forced political rallies if one enjoyed genuine popular support? One doesn't force one's own wife to walk around the kitchen professing her love for you, as one Herati friend told me.

It would, however, be wrong to demonise Ismail Khan as a one-dimensional tyrant, for he has had an undoubtedly positive impact on the city of Herat. The tales of his ruthless suppression of political opposition and the cronyism which went with his return to power must be set against the real prosperity which Herat enjoyed at this time and the energetic programme of building works and reconstruction, not all of it tasteful, that he put in motion in the years after 2001. Aside from mosques and *madrasas*, whose construction Herat's Taliban newspaper *Ettefaq-e Islam* was so fond of reporting, the Taliban were never one of Herat's great builders or makers; Ismail Khan was and is. A saying in Herat is that whilst he was 20 per cent corrupt (by keeping the taxes from the Islam Qala border crossing to Iran), the other 80 per cent of revenue went on building, schools, parks, roads, hospitals and so on. Ahrary's book *Sardar-e Aria* is full of photos of the many buildings Ismail Khan built during his Second Emirate. Whenever Ismail Khan was interviewed after the Taliban's fall and since, he always spoke expansively about his work of rebuilding the city, both after the fall of the Soviet regime in Kabul and in the days after the flight of the Taliban. A popular refrain in his interviews was to ask the interviewer about the appalling state of the roads in Kabul compared with those in Herat; the answer would invariably reflect well on Herat's Amir.

Yet despite this atmosphere of repression, Herat did not totally capitulate. For many, they had not endured the Taliban years to let this opportunity to refashion Afghan society pass them by. Rafiq Shahir, a good friend and civil society activist, along with Engineer Salahi, sought to capitalise on this sense of openness and possibility which they sensed in Kabul and beyond. The founding of the Professional Shurah, a collection of doctors, intellectuals, businessmen and lawyers, was intended as an independent body through which education, learning and association could help to contribute to a better society in Herat and beyond. Rohullah Amin, a leading intellectual in Kabul, assessed Herat's contribution to Afghanistan's development in the following terms, with the Professional Shurah very much in mind: 'They have been, since 2001, at the forefront of ideas of political inclusivity, diversity and were at the vanguard of a realistic and optimistic discussion on the future of the country.'[6] The Shurah published, and still continues to do so, a journal called *Takhasos* (Specialisation), in which writings of a political, cultural and historical nature are covered.[7] The journal is well received and popular amongst Herat's educated. However, Ismail Khan's arrest and beating of Rafiq Shahir, both for his role in the Professional Shurah (an organisation which Ismail Khan regularly criticises) and for his decision to run in the 2002 elections to the Loya Jirga, forced the publication of *Takhasos* into a more pliant pose. Gone were criticisms of the government or even discussions of political freedoms, and in their place came bland praise for Ismail Khan's rule.[8] The journal runs to this day, and continues to provide a space for learning and discussion.

Just when Afghanistan needed to unite after the ravages of war and exile and rebuild their nation, old rivalries were being played out between Kabul and Herat. Ismail Khan's rule of Herat as a semi-independent fiefdom angered the newly minted government in Kabul; Hamid Karzai and his Pashtun clique were suspicious of Ismail Khan, his private militia, rural support base and the relative prosperity the city enjoyed. The Taliban had never really enjoyed anything approaching popular support in Herat, save for the southern districts of Shindand and the province of Farah, and Ismail Khan's return to power, albeit with Iranian and US support, had put him in a position of real strength, both financial and military. Instead of harnessing this strength, Kabul sought to undermine it, as became apparent in the interviews I conducted in Herat. They aimed to destabilise the province so as to have a pretext for sending in troops and setting up a military presence in the dormant base at Shindnand, once the home of the Soviet troops during the *jihad*. Ismail Khan replied that Herat was not menaced by al-Qaeda and Taliban figures; they had all fled, or been captured. Herat was at peace and did not need Kabul's assistance, was the message that Herat's leader sent to Kabul. Troops loyal to Ismail Khan, and those loyal to the Kabul government and the US, clashed during 2004 as the tensions between Herat's semi-independence and Kabul's efforts to build a new nation came into conflict. The very real culmination of this period of Herat–Kabul tension was the death of Ismail Khan's son, Mirwais Sadiq, then Minister for Civil Aviation and Tourism, in March 2004, an event which caused widespread fighting and violence throughout Herat.[9] Such divisions had troubled the city's nineteenth-century entry into an Afghan nation, and still separated Kabul from Herat. At a time when Herat sought to embrace a new Afghan future, history and suspicion thwarted their attempts.

Eventually Kabul's patience snapped and the situation came to a head in 2005. Ismail Khan was removed from his throne in Herat and transferred to Kabul, where he took up the position of Minister for

Energy and Water. Herat's Amir had seen his son killed, his power taken away from him and his removal to a ministerial backwater in Kabul. Ismail Khan's waxing and waning influence, his difficulty in influencing the country as a whole, in so many ways epitomised Herat's awkward inclusion in the Afghan nation. It was Afghanistan's current president, Ashraf Ghani, who had led the charge to neuter Ismail Khan, and to force him to submit his taxes to Kabul. A hero of the Soviet conflict had become, temporarily, a minor player, unlike so many of his erstwhile Mujahideen who went on to figure prominently in this new post-2001 world. Like Herat itself, Ismail Khan struggled to find a place within Afghanistan's polity.

* * *

In other ways, too, Herat's history and past still inform how it faces the future. Culture still moves the city forwards, just. Poets meet in dwindling groups, although historical journals such as *Herat Bastan* have long since ceased publication. Herati intellectual Nik Seyar told me that he feared for Herat's cultural future, as the young were less interested in what once made Herat one of the most extraordinary cities in the world; many of Herat's young now prefer a route out of Afghanistan, to Iran, or Europe. The tile workshop where coloured tiles are made for the Friday Mosque limps along, and Sayfuddin blows glass in a corner of the gardens of Gawhar Shad's mausoleum.

One of the most fascinating aspects of Herat's post-2001 cultural landscape is the flourishing of a group of female poets. This is celebrated in an excellently translated anthology of female poets' work, including the tragic case of Nadia *Anjoman*, a talented poet who was killed by her husband for her refusal to give up her writing.[10] Nearly all of these girls were students in Herat's Taliban-era Golden Sewing Circle, where girls studied literature in secret, away from the Taliban's nihilistic interference. One particularly harrowing poem by Somaya Ramesh celebrates the life of Nadia *Anjoman* and mourns her passing with a haunting precision of words and emotion:

> The sky died
> for the wind that split open its chest
>
> We all died for you
> though fate's sleight of hand snuck you from us

And you smiled from the sky
for us

and for the moments we carry away
from our memories.[11]

These poems by celebrated female poets talk of unrequited love, the
frustrations of being enslaved in a conservative Islamic society and of
the pain of growing up surrounded by conflict. They speak of domestic
violence and the futility of conquest. One poem, 'Tulips' by Roya
Sharifi, takes aim at Afghanistan's martial valour, its reputation for
repelling invaders. The Mujahideen who liberated in the name of Islam
also destroyed as they went, leaving nothing where they had claimed to
have saved, so the poem goes. The Mujahideen were not all the starched
white souls fighting a noble resistance against Soviet evil; they too
destroyed, raped, pillaged and burned and harried Herat into a mess of
bone and rubble, destroying Herat's flowers in the process. It is typically Herati in its swiftness to see something for what it is:

Don't speak of the zeal of those bleeding tulips;
their destroyers' slogans were all Islam and Liberation
but they came in anything but peace.
And now the world thinks it knows us
by the famous "valor" of the Afghan nation.[12]

* * *

Herat faces an uncertain future. Its monumental links to a golden
Timurid age are daily disappearing amid the gaudy Pakistani-style palaces and high-rise buildings. The Taliban, along with criminal gangs, are
slowly creeping back into the city itself. Shindand, to the south of the
city, suffers from its easy links both to the drug smuggling routes that
wind their way from Helmand, through Farah and Nimruz, and also to
the Taliban and ISIL fighters spilling into Herat from the south. Herat
is consequently menaced by criminality, and kidnappings are increasingly common. The time I spent in Herat from 2009 to 2014 saw
friends killed, others kidnapped and the historical skyline encroached
upon by high-rise blocks. Today it is a city changing, almost unrecogni-
sable from the charming tourist attraction of the 1960s and 70s, or
even from the dark days of the Taliban rule. Much of its historical

monuments are being knocked down, space being made for commercial ventures in which government and commerce profit at the expense of a city's cultural and monumental heritage. Working in Herat for UNESCO, focusing on the restoration of the Gawhar Shad mausoleum and the remaining minarets from the Mosalla complex, showed me the challenges facing a city which has been so brutally cut off from its own history through exile and war.

Looking to the future, how can Herat reconcile its orthodox Sunni Islamic beliefs with its heritage as a city home to poetry and song, Sufism, music and dance? How will it move out from the shadow of a war of local, regional and global proportions which has engulfed so much and destroyed so many lives? How will it face off against the rise of ISIL in Farah to the south and to the east, and how will it provide jobs and livelihoods for its people so as to lessen the appeal of insurgent groups and Islamic fundamentalism? Corruption has spread like a cancer through the Afghan states and it infects every step the government tries to take, making crime and insurgency a more attractive bet for the young, idle and downtrodden. No easy answer can be found for how Herat and Afghanistan will recover from these years of horrific suffering and misrule. So many I speak to in Herat are pessimistic for the city and what it faces; departing international money and soldiers leave Afghanistan to stand on its own feet again. This spectacle recalls uncomfortable memories of the precarious early 1990s when the country slid into civil war, sectarian and ethnic conflict, a period which gave the world the Taliban. In other ways, too, the current period echoes the uncertainties Herat saw at different points in its history: the precarious post-Mongol apocalypse, the frantic uncertainty of clashing Safavid and Uzbek armies and the nineteenth-century tumult.

And yet, amidst it all, there has to be hope; there is always hope in Herat. As a province and city it has a sense of community, a sense of togetherness that cannot be found elsewhere in Afghanistan. Cultural organisations, literary societies, education and a pride in their identity all mark out Herat as a place which will always bounce back, no matter the damage that people inflict. The Hari Rud will continue to flow, the springs will always dazzle and inspire and the tiles on the mosque will shimmer in the summer heat. The raucous energy which infuses the bazaars and weddings and streets and homes will never dwindle. The time I have spent with Herat's young and dynamic educated classes convinces me that there is a generation of Heratis who embody the very best that the city has to offer: educated, sensible, energetic, and with a healthy balance between compassionate Islamic values and a critical eye, all that is needed to take the city forward.

* * *

Herat in 2016 is still as misunderstood as it was in the nineteenth century, yet not as isolated and forgotten as it was during the Golden Age it experienced in the 1950s, 60s and 70s.[13] The years of outright opposition to Kabul under Ismail Khan during 2001–5 have turned to a sense of accepting accommodation between the two cities; Herat submits its taxes and is largely left alone. Yet Heratis both question why they have so little say in the running of their country, and are simultaneously wary of the power games that go on in the capital. The shadow of Ismail Khan looms over the city, his private militia poised to step into any security crises that arise. He still commands respect and still wields just enough power to make him an important figure in the future of the city; yet he is now yesterday's man for many, a relic of the *jihad*, a crumbling statue out of kilter with ideas and trends which push the nation forwards and away from its bloody conflicts of the 1980s and their legacy.

Herat has recovered from the Mongol atrocities, slid from the Timurid glories, risen from the ashes of Safavid and Uzbek conquests and slipped again from the heady heights of its nineteenth-century importance. Today it is not the 'God forsaken' mess of the 1950s, the elegant cultured haven it was in the 1960s, nor the rubble-strewn wreck of the 1980s. Its Old City walls have crumbled; the citadel has been restored to a pitch of ersatz strength, more like a museum piece; the old *Khiaban* is a mass of new buildings and clogged gutters. The Pul-e Malan still ferries traffic south into Pashtun country. Gone are the running messengers noted by the Chinese diplomat in the fifteenth century, but Heratis' fondness for baggy, colourful clothing still persists. Herat today is an amalgam of its history: its isolation, its cultured refinement, its Sufi shrines and its life-giving fertility. Hazaras, Pashtuns, Tajiks and Farsi-speaking young Heratis all mix together in a city which has played host to all the region's greatest conquerors and empires. In so many respects it is still a city of contradictions and a city apart—Herati friends tell me that when they go to Kabul they have to modify their accents so as to be understood—yet Afghan flags are proudly displayed on car bonnets and in shop windows, and scarves in the red, black and green of the flag warm necks or shade faces from the sun. Children, on whose shoulders the future of this country rests, rush and giggle their way through the city, totally unaware of the problems they will one day inherit. Perhaps these children embody Herat's essence, if such a thing is possible: fearless in the face of what awaits it, full in the knowledge that it has survived and prospered through more difficult times. How Herat evolves will depend on so many things out-side its control—Kabul, Pakistan, unemployment and the rising tide of fundamentalism—but we can be sure that Herat will survive and, eventually, prosper again.

Herat's most famous poet, mystic and scholar, Jami, penned the lines below. They are carved on his tombstone in Herat. These lines perfectly describe Herat's tortured history, its perpetual struggle between the forces of light and darkness, war and peace, whilst also hinting at the importance of poetry as a medium for making sense of the world. This sentiment goes to the very heart of Herat's identity, its history and the way it sees the world: 'Asia without the inferiority complex'. They speak to the city's cyclical sackings and to the triumph of art over the forces of evil, echoing the disdain men of letters have had for the hubris of rule and the folly of empire.

> Behold, the palaces in ruins,
> The wrath of rulers disappeared in vain,
> No trace of pomp and glory remains,
> But poets live on in glory through the ages.

When I walked the streets of Herat and worked in its prisons, on the conservation of the city's crumbling Timurid buildings and in its librar-ies, those lines would run and run in my head like an echoing refrain, sad and yet hopeful, temporary and yet eternal, wisdom and folly, beauty and destruction: Herat.

APPENDIX 1

THE KARTID DYNASTY OF HERAT

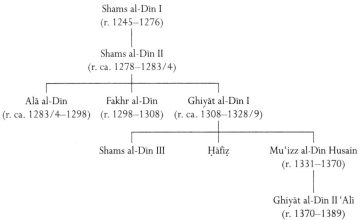

Souce: Noelle-Karimi, *The Pearl in its Midst*.

APPENDIX 2

THE TIMURID DYNASTY

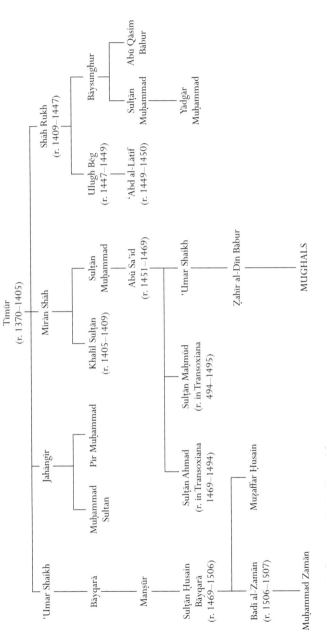

Source: Noelle-Karimi, *The Pearl in its Midst*.

APPENDIX 3

THE SAFAVID DYNASTY

Ismā'īl I
(r. 1501–1524)

- Sultān Murād
(d. 1545)
- Tahmāsp I
(r. 1524–1576)
  - Muhammad Khudābanda
(r. 1578–1587)
    - 'Abbās I
(r. 1587–1629)
      - Muhammad Bāqir (Safī Mirzā)
(d. 1615)
        - Safī
(r. 1629–1642)
          - 'Abbās II
(r. 1642–1666)
            - Safī II, later Sulaimān
(r. 1666–1694)
              - Sultān Husain
(r. 1694–1722)
                - Tahmāsp II
(r. 1729–1732)
- Sām
(d. 1576)
  - Ismā'īl II
(r. 1576–1577)
- Ilqās
(d. 1550)
  - Sultān Muhammad
- Bahrām
(d. 1549)
  - Sultān Husain
(d. 1576)
    - Badi' al-Zamān
  - Muzaffar Husain

Source: Noelle-Karimi, *The Pearl in its Midst.*

APPENDIX 4

THE SADOZAI DYNASTY

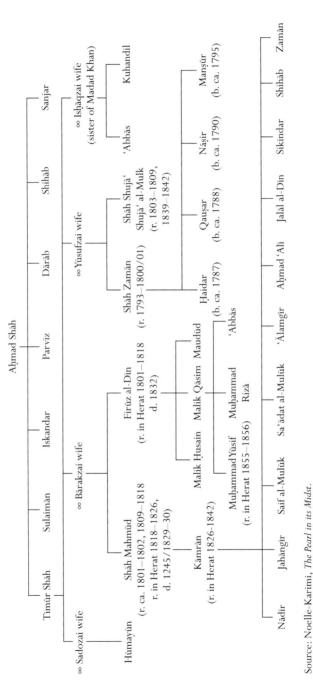

Source:: Noelle-Karimi, *The Pearl in its Midst.*

CHRONOLOGY

BC

800s   Assyrian empire moves eastwards, pushing tribes into the Hari Rud. Herat is mentioned in the Avesta and Artocoana by Greek writers.

500s   Achaemenid armies pass through Herat, then a frontier province.

c.330   Alexander the Great founds his city and fortress at Herat.

129   Scythian troops from Chinese Turkestan invade and occupy Herat.

123   Parthian tribes take Herat.

AD

c.60   Kushans capture Herat from the Parthian tribes, setting up an empire which they rule from Kabul and Peshawar.

226   Sassanian empire extends to Herat, reducing Herat again to the status of a frontier city.

425   Hephthalites establish themselves north of Herat, north of the Hindu Kush, using Badghis as a capital.

5th century   Herat suffers from warring parties splitting into different factions. Herat comes under control of Hephthalites.

652   Sassanian dynasty falls to Arab Muslim armies and Herat's Hephthalite rulers submit.

673	Khorasan submits to Arab Muslim armies and is used as a base from which to push into Central Asia.
8th–9th centuries	Herat resists Arab Muslim invasions, setting the stage for local ruling dynasties, such as the Taherids, Saffarids and Samanids.
c.900	Herat's Malan bridge, running south into Farah and Qandahar, is supposedly built by local female saint, Bibi Nur.
994	Sebuktigin founds the Ghaznavid dynasty, taking Khorasan from the Samanids.
1000	Mahmud of Ghazni becomes governor of Khorasan.
1006	Khwajah Abdullah Ansari, Herat's patron saint and most famous son, is born in Herat.
1036	Herat's citadel is strengthened against the rising Seljuk Turkic empire to the north-west.
1040	Seljuk forces defeat the Ghaznavids in Khorasan and Herat's citadel is destroyed, leaving the city to be taken by the Seljuks and ruled in their name.
1150	Fakhr al-Din Razi, famous Herati theologian for whom Herat's Friday Mosque was rebuilt, born in Herat.
12th century	Local Ghurid dynasty gathers power to the east of Herat in present-day Ghur province.
1153	Sultan Ghias al-Din Ghuri begins his reign in Ghur.
1159	Seljuk power begins to wane with the death of Sultan Mohammad II ibn Mahmud; in the same year Herat is captured by Sultan Ghias al-Din Ghuri of the Ghurid dynasty.
1200	Sultan Ghias al-Din Ghuri rebuilds Herat's Friday Mosque.
1200s	Kartid family gains prominence in Herat as government officials and local rulers.
1203	Sultan Ghias al-Din Ghuri dies; Herat is weaker because of his death.
1206	Herat is captured by Shah Mohammad of the Khwarazm dynasty; the city is ruled from Khorasan's

	city of Merv, and suffers from misrule and local warlords.
1221–2	Mongol armies move through Khorasan, burning and sacking as they go; Herat is captured, but spared the worst atrocities. A local uprising against Mongol rule results in the city's utter devastation, leaving only 16 male survivors.
1221–40	Herat languishes as a broken relic, but gradually, through luck, fertility and the skill of its artisans, it manages to revive itself.
1245	The Kart Maleks, beginning with Shams al-Din Kart, are set to rule over Herat in the name of the Mongols, giving rise to Herat's most successful local dynasty, paving the way for the city's ultimate revival from the depths of 1222.
1256	The Mongol empire divides, and the Mongol Il-Khans of Persia under Hulagu Khan rule over Herat from Tabriz.
1258	Mongol forces sack Baghdad, bringing to an end the Abbasid Caliphate and leaving Islam without a regional leader.
1284	Nikudari leader Hindu Noyin seeks refuge at Kheisar with Shams al-Din Kahin Kart, beginning decades of tension between the Il-Khans and the Karts. Kahin remains in self-imposed imprisonment in the Ghurid fortress of Kheisar.
1288–92	Herat is sacked by Nikudari hordes, at one point being totally emptied of its inhabitants.
1291	Il-Khanid general, Amir Nawruz, arrives in Herat to seize Kahin from Kheisar and bring Herat again into the Il-Khanid fold. Kahin's son, Fakhr al-Din, is in turn his father's prisoner in Kheisar; Nawruz sets about prising them apart. Fakhr al-Din Kart accedes to his patrimony in Herat.
1297	Amir Nawruz flees to Herat expecting aid from Fakhr al-Din, and besieges the city, but is betrayed and executed in the citadel.

1299–1303	Fakhr al-Din, after military exchanges with Il-Khan Oljeitu, sets out to rebuild Herat and its citadel. It is from this spate of building that the citadel gets its current name, Ekhtiar al-Din. Fakhr al-Din also undertakes reforms of Herat's social life, banning alcohol and requiring more complete observation of Islamic values in daily life.
1305	Fakhr al-Din refuses to attend Il-Khanid coronation ceremony in Persia, causing Il-Khan Ghazzan, Oljeitu's successor, to turn Il-Khanid armies on Herat again.
1306	Il-Khanid military general Amir Daneshmand Bahador meets his death in Herat's citadel when trying to subdue Fakhr al-Din Kart. Thousands of Mongol troops are slain in the citadel in a pre-planned attack.
1308	After two years of chaos, Ghias al-Din Kart assumes rule over the city, setting to work rebuilding damaged fortifications and bazaars. Ghias al-Din spends four years away from Herat, convincing the Il-Khans of his loyalty.
1321	Sayfi makes his last entry into his Herati chronicle, the History Book of Herat.
1327	Another prominent Il-Khanid military commander, Amir Chupan meets his death in Herat.
1335	Il-Khan Abu Said, the last Il-Khan, dies, bringing to a close the Mongol empire in Persia, rendering the Kartid dynasty independent and Herat a de facto regional capital. Herat becomes a refuge for those fleeing the chaos surrounding the collapse of the Il-Khanate.
1352	Moezz al-Din Kart returns to Herat after internal tensions had forced him to flee to Transoxania; Herat flourishes as a centre for cultural and artistic excellence.
1370	Moezz al-Din Kart dies, splitting Herat's patrimony into two, between Sarakhs and Herat (Pir

	Ali Kart and Mohammad Kart). This causes rival factions within the Kart family to emerge, paving the way for the dynasty's eventual fall to Timur, or Tamerlane.
1376	Timur sends envoys to Herat to sound out the city's loyalty to his expanding empire; a Kartid prince marries a Timurid princess in Herat in 1378.
1380–81	Timurid–Kartid relations break down, and Timur sends 50,000 troops to take the city; Herat falls to Timur and the armies of his son, Miran Shah, bringing to a close the Kartid hold over the city. The city is sacked twice, as in 1221–2.
1405	Timur dies in Otrar, and in the succession struggle Shah Rukh comes to the fore, seeking to govern his newly won empire from Herat, not Samarqand. Herat enjoys some peace and prosperity as an imperial capital; Shah Rukh spends until 1420 campaigning in Central Asia and Persia to secure his empire.
15th century	Herat becomes a centre of artistic, academic and theological excellence, attracting artists and scholars from the region and equalling European Renaissance cities for majesty and beauty.
1410	Shah Rukh and his wife Gawhar Shad begin a Timurid building boom in Herat, constructing religious institutions, repairing defences and restoring Gazur Gah, Herat's holiest shrine and resting place of Abdullah Ansari, the city's patron saint. Herat begins to take shape as one of the region's most enchanting and beautiful cities.
1414	Chinese diplomat Chen Cheng visits Herat, recording his observations and beginning a rich Chinese–Herati cultural and political dialogue.
1427	Shah Rukh survives an assassination attempt outside Herat's Friday Mosque at the hands of a Sufi dervish of the Hurufiya movement, Ahmad Lur.

	The investigation into this attempted assassination continues for over five years, culminating in a trial in Gawhar Shad's religious establishment in the north of Herat.
1435	Herat is struck down with a variant of the Black Death, killing many thousands.
1447	Shah Rukh dies in Shiraz.
1448–58	Khorasan descends into chaos and Herat is tossed back and forth between rival claimants to the imperial throne.
1460s	Herat sees a measure of recovery under the Timurid Sultan Abu Said.
1467–8	Under Abu Said, Herat's northern areas are irrigated, paving the way for the construction of gardens, mosques and palaces from the Old City walls to the foothills of Gazur Gah.
1470	Timurid Sultan Husain Bayqara, grandson of Shah Rukh, enters and takes Herat.
1470–1506	Under Husain Bayqara, Herat becomes one of the world's most captivating and sophisticated cities.
1501	Uzbek power, under Mohammad Shaybani, gathers north of the Oxus; Shah Ismail I Safavid in Persia begins to expand his fledgling Shia empire; Herat's Timurid empire begins to shrink as a result of corruption and mismanagement.
1506	Sultan Husain Bayqara dies, leaving two squabbling princes to rule over Herat, as had been the case towards the end of the Kart dynasty's rule over Herat.
1506	Emperor Babur, founder of the Mughal dynasty and Timurid descendant, enters Herat, recording his observations of a decadent city and dynasty collapsing on itself.
1507	Herat falls to Mohammad Shaybani Khan's Uzbek armies, bringing to an end Herat's most glorious period of cultural brilliance and political stability.

1510	Safavid armies move into Khorasan and take Herat into their control, thus beginning a century of contested rule between Shia Safavids and Sunni Uzbek Shaybanids.
1513	The first years of Safavid control are marked by conquest, siege at the hands of the Uzbeks and famine.
1529	Herat succumbs to the Uzbeks and is taken by Ubaidullah Khan from Safavid control, but is quickly wrested back into Safavid hands by Shah Tahmasp I.
1536	Herat revolts against Safavid Shia control after years of famine, misrule and warfare against the Uzbeks. Herat suffers greatly and is taken over by Uzbeks.
1537	Safavid forces reclaim Herat after a calamitous year of Uzbek tyranny.
1540s	Some rebuilding takes place in Herat, taking advantage of peace.
1544	The 2nd Mughal emperor, Humayoun, arrives in Herat after fleeing from a succession of conflicts in the Mughal empire relating to disputed inheritances. Herat provides the backdrop for Humayoun's lavish reception and carefully orchestrated stay as the Safavids' guest.
1580	With Khorasan in chaos, against the backdrop of a fading Safavid empire, Herat suffers siege after siege as rival families compete to hold Khorasan's pearl.
1581	Herat briefly becomes an imperial capital again with the coronation of a young Safavid prince; power reverts quickly back to Esfahan.
1587	Uzbek forces, acting on intelligence of Herat's weakened and divided state, march to Khorasan and take Herat in 1588. It remains in their hands for a decade.
1588	Shah Abbas I comes to the Safavid throne, to

365

	become the Shia empire's greatest shah, reviving its fortunes.
1591	Abdali Sadozai Pashtun families first emerge in Herat, coming west from Kabul.
1598	Shah Abbas I takes Herat back under Safavid control; Herat gradually loses regional importance relative to Mashhad and Qandahar.
17th century	Against the backdrop of Mughal and Safavid decline, the Abdali Pashtuns of Herat and Qandahar and Multan begin to assume political power, thanks to money earned from acting as mercenaries, traders and serving two competing empires: Safavid and Mughal.
1717	Herat's Abdali Sadozai Pashtuns expel the city's last Safavid governor, bringing an end to Persian dominance and paving the way for Herat's eventual inclusion in an Afghan nation ruled from Kabul or Qandahar.
1732	Herat falls to the brilliant, psychotic and mercurial conqueror, Nader Shah Afshar.
1740	Nader Shah's troops march through Herat on their way to Persia, noting the utter decline the city had experienced since the fall of the Timurids.
1747	Nader Shah Afshar is executed in his tent near Mashhad, inadvertently giving rise to the Sadozai Abdali Pashtun dynasty of Afghanistan. Ahmad Khan Abdali plays a leading role in the aftermath of Nader Shah's execution and takes his troop of Pashtuns south-east to Qandahar to found his dynasty.
1750	Ahmad Shah Abdali changes his family name to Durrani, and after having been crowned in Qandahar, takes Herat, subduing Uzbek, Tajik and Hazara tribes in present-day Afghanistan. Herat becomes a gateway to Persian Khorasan, and is linked to Qandahar and India by roads kept safe by Pashtun forces.

1775	Timur Shah Durrani designates Kabul as the capital of his empire, stretching from Herat into India. Durrani power is weakened by familial feuding and corruption. Qandahar, Kabul and Herat all become semi-independent fiefdoms, bases from which family feuds can be prosecuted. The Afghan state is consequently hopelessly divided.
1781	George Forster, an East India Company civil servant, enters Herat on his way back to England after service in Bengal. His observations are the first of their kind, and the first of a long line of European adventurers to pass through Herat in the ensuing 19th century.
1796	The Persian Qajar dynasty conquer Mashhad, and look further into Khorasan to take Herat back under Shia Persian control.
Early 19th century	Control of Herat remains in Sadozai hands, but chaos reigns in Afghanistan and Khorasan. British and Russian imperial ambitions take shape in India and Central Asia; Herat assumes a key strategic importance as 'The Gateway to India'. The Great Game, a colonial war of information between British and Russian forces, marks Herat as one of its most important cities. Britain wishes to protect India; Russia seeks strategic advantage in Central Asia, and to upset British control over India.
1807	Herat rebels against Shia incursions into Khorasan.
1828	Russian military successes in the Caucasus force Qajar Persia to sign a humiliating treaty, the Treaty of Turkmanchai, by which Qajar Persia becomes beholden to Russian demands. Persia, shorn of Caucasus lands, looks to Khorasan for conquest, to Herat.
1834	Amir Dost Mohammad Khan takes Kabul from the ruling Durrani family; the Abdali Sadozais continue to hold Herat as a semi-independent

	enclave, hovering between Afghan and Persian sovereignty.
1837–8	Herat is besieged by Qajar Persian troops, acting in consort with Russian advisers. A young English soldier, Eldred Pottinger, helps to save Herat from Qajar dominance; the siege is called off in March 1838. Two English officers remain in Herat in an attempt to rebuild the city; they are chased out in 1841 by Yar Mohammad Khan Alikozai, the governor of Herat.
1839–42	First Anglo-Afghan War begins with a disastrous return to power for the puppet ruler, Shah Shujah al-Mulk, to replace Dost Mohammad Khan. This ends in chaos and a massacre of British troops and hangers-on in the passes from Kabul to Jalalabad. Herat is largely cut off from this conflict.
1853	British diplomat Justin Sheil conducts a treaty with the Qajars, by which Tehran would refrain from interfering in the affairs of Herat.
1855	Qajars receive a plea from Herat that they save it from an Afghan attack; this leads to another siege of Herat at the hands of Qajar forces.
1856	Qajar troops surround Herat; Britain declares war on Persia, making Persian withdrawal from Herat a condition of peace between the two powers. Herat suffers greatly in the process.
1857	Treaty of Paris signed in March. Persia agrees to renounce formal claims to sovereignty over Herat and refrains from interfering in Herat's internal affairs. A Qajar puppet rules over Herat, in direct violation of the terms of the Treaty of Paris.
1863	Amir Dost Mohammad takes Herat and dies soon after. He is buried at Gazur Gah, and whilst some see this as the inclusion of Herat in an Afghan nation, in reality Herat remains an isolated enclave within a fractured Afghan polity.
1880	Amir Abdur Rahman Khan begins his rule over

	Afghanistan; British and Russian tensions still inform a Great Game in Central Asia and Persia.
1885	A military skirmish in Pajndeh, north of Herat, threatens to erupt into a World War between Britain and Russia, but tensions are reduced by diplomacy and a promise to draw the boundaries, south of which Russian influence cannot encroach.
1887	Afghan Boundary Commission sets to work on defining the borders separating Afghanistan and Iran, effectively relegating Herat to the status of forgotten outpost. In large part, Herat ceases to be Britain's 'Gateway to India'.
1901	Abdur Rahman Khan dies and is succeeded by his son, Habibullah Khan, a reform-minded ruler with vague secular leanings and a penchant for luxury and Rolls Royce motor cars. Herat is largely left to its own devices as Afghanistan enters into a phase of modernisation which takes its lead from Turkish and British influences.
1915	Herat plays host to the arrival of German spies come to stir up a jihad against the British in India, starting in Afghanistan. The Germans spend a few weeks in Herat, and one of their number, Oscar von Niedermayer, records his visit with a selection of extremely beautiful photographs.
1919	Habibullah Khan is assassinated whilst hunting in Laghman; tensions mount between Young Afghan reformers and conservative elites. He is succeeded by Amanullah Khan. Herat remains enigmatic, on the sidelines.
1919	On 24 August, Herat's newspaper, Ettefaq-e Islam, is published for the first time.
1927	The Knowledge Printing House opens in Herat, bringing reformist and educative texts to a select number of educated Heratis.
1929–31	Nationwide revolution brings to power the Tajik ruler Habibullah Kalakani after the abdication of

Amanullah Khan; Herat succumbs to Kalakani, but remains secluded from the worst of the fighting taking place in the east and south-east of the country. The revolution is seen by many as a reaction to Amanullah's modernist reforms, and is supported by rural and religious conservative elites. The revolution ends with Kalakani's execution and the arrival of the Musahebin dynasty, with Nader Shah as their first king.

1930s   Herat sees some modernisation: the urban spaces are widened and a New City created to the north and north-east of the Old City; some Old City walls are torn down to allow this expansion. Herat is largely peaceful, cut off and isolated. Herat sees a revival of poetry and theatre.

1933   Nader Shah dies in November, bringing to power his son, Zaher Shah, who presides over one of the most peaceful and prosperous eras in Afghanistan's history until his removal from power in 1973 in a coup.

1933–4   British architectural historian and travel writer Robert Byron makes two trips to Herat, recording his observations in the celebrated travel book, The Road to Oxiana.

1935   In June, Herat's Jewish communities rise up against persecution at the hands of Herat's Shia population.

1960s   Herat becomes a firm fixture on the hippy trail and enters a mini Golden Age of relative prosperity and calm.

1973   Daoud Khan comes to power in a leftist-backed coup to remove Zaher Shah from the throne and begin a ruinous slide to war. Communist and Islamist ideologies fight for supremacy and Afghanistan's Communist parties, Khalq and Parcham, wage bitter underground conflicts.

1978   Daoud Khan is removed from power in the 'Saur

Revolution', essentially a Soviet-backed coup to
bring to power the Khalq faction of the People's
Democratic Party of Afghanistan, PDPA. Widespread oppression and torture turn Herat and its
people against the government in Kabul.

1979 Herat erupts in a three-day uprising of anti-Khalqi
violence, known as the Qiyam-e 24 Hout; the city
falls to a ragtag group of opportunists, would-be
Mujahideen, Maoists and rural workers. The city
is taken back by the government in Kabul, beginning the slide to war.

1979 Soviet troops invade Afghanistan, answering calls
to save a beleaguered and unpopular regime in
Kabul, beginning the Afghan–Soviet War. Herat
assumes a front line position in this conflict, suffering higher casualties than almost any other
province. Large parts of the city are flattened;
millions flee to Iran and Pakistan.

1980s Herat suffers gravely in the conflict. Whole villages disappear under Soviet bombardment.

1989 Soviet troops leave Afghanistan a broken and warring country; a Soviet puppet, Dr Najibullah, rules.

1992 Ismail Khan, a Mujahideen commander with
Jamiat-e Islami, takes power in Herat.

1990–94 Afghanistan suffers from a Civil War between rival
Mujahideen factions; Herat is able to rebuild
itself, away from the worst of the fighting. Ismail
Khan undertakes a largely positive programme of
building and regeneration.

1994 The Sunni Deobandi fundamentalist Islamic group,
the Taliban, take power in Kabul.

1995 Ismail Khan's Jamiat-e Islami forces melt away in
the face of a concerted Taliban attack on Herat;
Herat falls to the Taliban, bringing to the city a
repressive and ultra-conservative form of Islamic
rule and Pashtun nationalism. Taliban rule scars
Herat.

1997	Ismail Khan captured by Taliban forces, having been betrayed by an erstwhile ally; he is imprisoned in Qandahar. Herat's hopes of dislodging the Taliban fade with Ismail Khan's incarceration.
2000	Ismail Khan escapes from Qandahar prison with the help of a sympathetic Talib, Hekmatullah. He begins to push for international assistance in driving the Taliban from Afghanistan, working with old contacts from the Soviet conflict whilst in exile in the Islamic Republic of Iran.
2001	Attacks on the Twin Towers in New York and on the Pentagon by al-Qaeda lead to the removal of the Taliban from Afghanistan in Operation Enduring Freedom; Herat is quickly liberated from Taliban oppression. Ismail Khan again assumes control over the city as an independent fiefdom, and eyewitnesses claim his rule proves to be as oppressive as the Taliban.
2005	Ismail Khan is forced to Kabul to serve as Minister for Energy and Water as a way of loosening his control on Herat. Prior to his removal, his forces repeatedly clash with government and American troops; his son, Mirwais Sadiq, is killed in fighting, further worsening Herat–Kabul relations. Ashraf Ghani, then Minister of Finance, was instrumental in forcing Ismail Khan to leave Herat and come to Kabul. He also forced Ismail Khan to remit long overdue customs duties and taxes to the central government in Kabul.
2014	Ashraf Ghani becomes Prime Minister of Afghanistan after a contested election campaign in which he agrees to a division of powers between himself and the Tajik Dr Abdullah Abdullah.

NOTES

INTRODUCTION

1. It must be noted that the image of Macedonian nobles seated on carpets and floors, ready to discuss matters of state, has been invented by the historian in this case, for the ancient Greeks were not a floor culture; they sat on stools and chairs. Persian courtly culture, on the other hand, was a floor culture, and this detail says more about its author than it does about Alexander the Great. I am grateful to Bruce Wannell for this point.

2. Sayf ibn Mohammad ibn Yaqub al-Heravi, *Tarikh namah-ye Harat* (hereafter, Sayfi, *Tarikh namah*), ed. Muhammad Zubayr al-Siddiqi, Calcutta: Baptist Mission Press, 1944, pp. 25–35.

3. W. J. Vogelsang, 'Herat ii, History, Pre-Islamic Period', *Encyclopaedia Iranica*, Iranica Online, 15 December 2003, at http://www.iranicaonline.org/articles/herat-ii, accessed on 15.12.2015.

4. The British historian and linguist Bruce Wannell recalls local Heratis in the 1980s pronouncing *Hari* as *Haray*, a fact which hints at the earliest Persian word from which we derive Herat.

5. See Bijan Omrani and Matthew Leeming, *Afghanistan, A Companion and Guide*, Hong Kong: Airphoto International Ltd, 2003, p. 313.

6. Note by Major-General P. S. Lumsden on the Aspect of Affairs at Herat and in Central Asia, 1885, British Library, IOR/L/PS/18/A68.

7. See Sayfi, *Tarikh namah*.

8. J. P. Ferrier, *History of the Afghans*, London: John Murray, 1858, p. 172.

9. See W. Barthold, *An Historical Geography of Iran*, Princeton: Princeton University Press, 1984; and C. Edmund Bosworth, "ERĀQ-E ʿAJAM(Ī)', *Encyclopaedia Iranica*, Vol. VIII, Fasc. 5, December 1998, p. 538. See also X. de Planhol, 'ARAK', *Encyclopaedia Iranica*, Vol. II, Fasc. 3, December 1986, pp. 247–8.

10. 'The Appearance of the Mahdi', *Sunan Ibn Majah*, Vol. I, Book 36, Hadith 4084.

11. Mir Ghulam Muhammad Ghubar, *Khorasan*, Kabul: Kabul Printing House, 1937.

12. On the death of the Prophet Muhammad on 8 June AD 632, Islam faced a succession crisis. In the ensuing debates and conflicts on who might follow Muhammad as leader of Islam, the competing claims of bloodline and competence were the lines along which a long-running and debilitating war would be waged, dividing Islam into two camps: Sunni and Shia. One group, referring to the fol-

lowers of the *sunna*, or 'way' in Arabic, opposed political succession based on Muhammed's bloodline and favoured a more elective approach which saw suitability to rule as a more fitting criterion for choosing a leader of the Islamic community; they chose to select Abu Bakr, a companion of Muhammad, to be the first caliph, or leader of the Islamic community. The other group favoured Ali ibn Abi Talib, Muhammad's cousin and son-in-law, and from this they were given the name, *shi'atu Ali*, Arabic for 'partisans of Ali', because of their belief that Ali and his descendants represent a divine order and succession of authority in the Islamic community, as opposed to Abu Bakr.

13. See Chapter 5.
14. Nancy Dupree, *Afghanistan*, Princeton: Princeton University Press, 1973, p. 180.
15. For the best account of Herat's shrines, see Fekri Seljuki, *Resalah-ye mazarat-e Herat*, Herat: Hajji Abdul Halim Mohammady, 1386 AH.
16. An interesting look at Ansari and other Sufis of Afghanistan can be found in Unknown, 'Abdullah Ansari and other Sufis of Afghanistan', *Afghanistan Journal (Special Issue) published on the Occasion of the Millennium of Abdullah Ansari of Herat*, Kabul: Ministry of Information and Culture, Department of Culture and Arts, Historical Society of Afghanistan, April 1979.
17. Robert Byron, *The Road to Oxiana*, 1937; London: Pimlico edition, 2004, p. 105.
18. I am grateful to Bruce Wannell for telling me this phrase. It is a more pleasing couplet in the original Persian.
19. Paul English, 'The Traditional City of Herat, Afghanistan', in L. Carl Brown, ed., *From Medina to Metropolis, Heritage and Change in the Near Eastern City*, Princeton: Darwin Press, 1973, p. 77.
20. For accounts of Herat's urban morphology, see English, 'The Traditional City of Herat'; Rafi Samizay, *Islamic Architecture in Herat: A Study Towards Conservation*, Kabul: Research Section of International Project for Herat Monuments, Ministry of Information and Culture, Democratic Republic of Afghanistan, 1981; Abdul Wassay Najimi, *Herat: The Islamic City: A Study in Urban Conservation*, Scandinavian Institute of Asian Studies, occasional papers, July 1987. For an excellent account of Herat during the Timurid period, see Terry Allen, *Timurid Herat*, Wiesbaden: Reichert, 1983. See also Nancy Hatch Wolfe, *Herat, A Pictorial Guide*, Kabul: Afghan Tourist Organization, 1966.
21. Najimi, *Herat: The Islamic City*, p. 39.
22. English, 'The Traditional City of Herat', p. 75.
23. Ibid., p. 80.
24. Ibid., p. 77.
25. Ibid., p. 81.
26. Wolfe, *Herat*, p. 58.
27. Sayfi, *Tarikh namah*, p. 36.
28. See W. J. Vogelsang, 'Herat ii, History, Pre-Islamic Period', *Encyclopaedia Iranica*.
29. The best account of Persia's long history is the *Cambridge History of Iran*, all volumes. See the Chronology in this book for a quick outline.

1. DESTRUCTION AND RENEWAL: HERAT IN THE SHADOW OF THE MONGOLS AND BEYOND, 1221–1381

1. For good literature on the Mongols, see David Morgan, *The Mongols*, 2nd edn, London: Wiley-Blackwell Press, 2007; J. J. Saunders, *The History of the Mongol*

Conquests, London: Routledge, 1971; Peter Jackson, *The Mongols and the West, 1221–1410*, Edinburgh: Pearson Education, 2005; and for the Mongol Empire in its Iranian context, see *Cambridge History of Iran, Vol. 5, The Seljuk and Mongol Periods*, Cambridge: Cambridge University Press, 1968. For translated primary sources, see Ala al-Din Ata-Malik Juvaini, *Genghis Khan, The History of the World Conqueror*, trans. J. A. Boyle, Manchester: UNESCO Publishing, 1997; and Bertold Spuler, *History of the Mongols; Based on Eastern and Western Accounts of the Thirteenth and Fourteenth Centuries*, London: Routledge & Kegan Paul, 1972.

2. This initial envoy is described in lurid detail by the Persian and Ghurid thirteenth-century chronicler Juzjaini, who in his *Tabaqat-e Nasiri* written at the court of the Delhi Sultanate, having fled the worst of the Mongol atrocities, describes the Khwarazm Shah envoys journeying through northern China, amidst rotting flesh and passing towers of skulls, so high as to have appeared like a snow-peaked mountain. See *Cambridge History of Iran*, Vol. 5, pp. 303–4.

3. Ata al-Din Juvaini, *The History of the World Conqueror*, trans. J. A. Boyle, Manchester University, UNESCO Publishing, 1997, p. 80.

4. Ibid., p. 86.

5. Ibid., p. 105.

6. Ibid., p. 152. The province was Bamiyan.

7. Sayfi, *Tarikh namah*, p. 50. The present-day province of Bamiyan in central Afghanistan is home to the Hazara people, whose Asiatic appearance and their name (Hazara, from the Persian for a thousand, and thought to be directly linked to the well-known military practice of the Mongols for organising their troops along decimal lines) strongly suggest descent from Chingiz Khan. For a more detailed discussion of Hazara history, see Elizabeth E. Bacon, 'The Inquiry into the History of the Hazara Mongols of Afghanistan', *Southwestern Journal of Anthropology*, Vol. 7, No. 3, Autumn 1951, pp. 230–47.

8. Sayfi, *Tarikh namah*, p. 68.

9. Ibid., p. 69.

10. Ibid., p. 71.

11. Ibid., p. 71.

12. Ibid., p. 73.

13. Ibid., p. 74.

14. Ibid., p. 76.

15. Ibid., p. 80.

16. Ibid., p. 80.

17. Lawrence Potter, in his excellent PhD thesis on the Kartid Dynasty, suggests figures of 60,000 for the city of Herat, 140,000–160,000 for the province (*welayat*), and for the Herat quarter of Khorasan 300,000–400,000 (Lawrence Potter, *The Kartid Dynasty of Herat: Religion and Politics in Medieval Iran*, PhD diss., Columbia University, 1992, pp. 210–16. It is interesting to note that Sayfi alludes to a census from the year 1241 in which 6,900 people were counted in Herat city, a credible figure if we take into account the repopulation of the city from 1236 onwards.

18. Sayfi, *Tarikh namah*, p. 83.

19. Ibid., p. 85.

20. Ibid., p. 86.

21. Ibid., p. 95.

22. Throughout this and the next two chapters, we shall see capitals moving from place to place as the court moves from winter to summer pastures, and from bat-

tlefield to fresh campaign. Within the imperial lands power moves with the court. The centre of power was the court, so patronage, law and justice moved with the sovereign and the court as they travelled through their realms.

23. Sayfi, *Tarikh namah*, p. 107.

24. Ibid., pp. 95–110. For an excellent discussion of the significance of *qanat*s, *karezes* and water irrigation in Iranian cities, see M. Kheirabadi, *Iranian Cities: Formation and Development*, Austin. TX: University of Texas Press, 1991, pp. 91–4; T. Allen, *Timurid Herat*, Wiesbaden: Reichert, 1983, p. 12.

25. Sayfi, *Tarikh namah*, p. 115.

26. Ibid., p. 117.

27. Ibid., p. 120.

28. Ibid., pp. 120–21.

29. Ibid., p. 121.

30. Chingiz Khan died in 1227, having previously split his empire into four distinct parts amongst his sons. Ogodei became the Great Khan, with lands in Eastern Asia and China; Tolui received the original homeland in Mongolia; Jochi was given the remote eastern pasturelands that would later form the Golden Horde of Russia and Eastern Europe (his death, however, caused these lands to go to Jochi's son Batu); Chagatai took northern Iran and Central Asia.

31. For a detailed survey of the secondary literature relating to the Karts, see Potter, *Kartid Dynasty*, pp. 10–13.

32. Sayfi, *Tarikh namah*, p. 165.

33. For the dating of this episode, I have relied on Potter, who rightly cites Allsen in correcting the dates of Sayfi with regard to these years. Potter, *Kartid Dynasty*, p. 41.

34. An appealing description of the gifts and lands bestowed on the Kart *malek* can be found in the Timurid source of Moin al-Din Mohammad Esfezari, *Rawdat al Jannat fi Ausaf Madinat Herat* (The Gardens of Paradise in Herat), Vol. I, Tehran: Moalem Danesgah Tehran, 1338, p. 411.

35. For an excellent outline of the Chagataid Dynasty, see Peter Jackson, 'Chaghatayid Dynasty', *Encyclopaedia Iranica*, Vol. V, Fasc. 4, December 1991, pp. 343–6.

36. Sayfi, *Tarikh namah*, p. 304.

37. Ibid., p. 311.

38. Ibid., p. 314.

39. Ibid., p. 315.

40. Ibid., p. 315.

41. Ibid., p. 321. For an article on the significance of this battle and its consequences, see Michael Biran, 'The Battle of Herat (1270): A Case of Inter-Mongol Warfare', in Nicola Di Cosmo, ed., *Warfare in Inner Asian History (1500–1800)*, Leiden: Brill, 2002, pp. 175–219.

42. Sayfi, *Tarikh namah*, p. 331.

43. Ibid., p. 331.

44. This was Shams al-Din Juvaini.

45. Sayfi, *Tarikh namah*, p. 332.

46. Ibid., p. 344.

47. Ibid., p. 361.

48. Esfezari, *Gardens of Paradise*, Vol. I, p. 424.

49. Sayfi, *Tarikh namah*, p. 368.

50. Ibid., p. 368.

51. Ibid., p. 374.
52. Relating to the Nikudaris, Christine Noelle-Karimi offers a detailed summation of the differing primary sources and secondary analysis for this topic. Christine Noelle-Karimi, *The Pearl in its Midst: Herat and the Mapping of Khorasan (15th–19th Centuries)*, Wien: Verlag der Österreichischen Akademie der Wissenschaften, 2013a, pp. 70–72.
53. Sayfi, *Tarikh namah*, p. 377.
54. Ibid., p. 378.
55. Ibid., p. 379.
56. For a more detailed discussion of these issues, see Ann K. S. Lambton, 'Concepts of Authority in Persia: Eleventh to Nineteenth Centuries A.D.', *Iran*, Vol. 26, 1988, pp. 95–103.
57. See, Sayfi, *Tarikh namah*, pp. 377–82.
58. Ibid., p. 381.
59. Ibid., p. 382.
60. Ibid., p. 383.
61. Ibid., p. 383.
62. Ibid., p. 384.
63. Ibid., p. 384.
64. Ibid., pp. 387–8.
65. Ibid., p. 391.
66. It was common, in such buildings, as can be seen in Herat's citadel, for there to be an upper fort for prisoners and important business.
67. Sayfi, *Tarikh namah*, p. 393.
68. Ibid., pp. 393–400.
69. For a further discussion on the relations between the Karts and the Sufis of Jam and Chisht, see Potter, *Kartid Dynasty in Herat*, pp. 82–123.
70. Sayfi, *Tarikh namah*, p. 397.
71. Ibid., p. 397.
72. Esfezari, *Gardens of Paradise*, Vol. I, p. 433. The word *fetnah* has particularly strong Islamic connotations relating to strife and a disorder which threatens the Muslim polity, and can be compared with the use of the word *qiyam*, simply meaning insurrection.
73. For an excellent overview of the Mamluk Sultanate and its relations with the Mongols, see Reuven Amitai-Preiss, *Mongols and Mamluks: The Mamluk-Ilkhanid War, 1260–1281*, Cambridge: Cambridge University Press, 1995.
74. Sayfi, *Tarikh namah*, p. 423.
75. Ibid., p. 424. However, it must be noted that it is only in Sayfi, not Esfezari, that we have this story of Nawruz having designs on the throne of Herat. Esfezari simply writes that Fakhr al-Din had concerns which caused him to kill Nawruz. Esfezari, *Gardens of Paradise*, Vol. I, p. 434.
76. Esfezari, *Gardens of Paradise*, Vol. I, p. 434.
77. Sayfi, *Tarikh namah*, p. 429.
78. Esfezari, *Gardens of Paradise*, Vol. I, p. 425.
79. It was Il-Khan Ghazan who set about reforming Khorasan, left desolate after the cumulative effect of years of warfare and pillage. From the tender age of ten, he was governor of Khorasan, and he made strident his opposition to the introduction of paper money, the *cho*, by his dissolute and drunken predecessor Il-Khan Geikhatu. The reforms of Ghazan are dealt with in excellent detail in *Cambridge History of Iran*, Vol. 5, pp. 494–505.

80. Sayfi, *Tarikh namah*, p. 433.
81. An excerpt from a poem by Rabii of Fushanj, quoted in Sayfi, *Tarikh namah*, p. 437.
82. Sayfi, *Tarikh namah*, p. 438.
83. Ibid., p. 440.
84. Esfezari, *Gardens of Paradise*, Vol. I, p. 438.
85. Sayfi, *Tarikh namah*, p. 440.
86. Ibid., p. 440.
87. Ibid., pp. 440–1.
88. Ibid., p. 441.
89. Guya Etemadi, 'Darbar-e Malouk-e Kart' [The Court of the Kartid Maleks], *Aryana*, Vol. 2, No. 4, Sawr 1323/May 1944, p. 46.
90. See Khwandamir, *Habib al-Siyar*, trans. W. M. Thackston, London: I. B. Tauris, 2012, p. 212.
91. Sayfi, *Tarikh namah*, p. 449.
92. Ibid., p. 450.
93. Ibid., p. 450.
94. Ibid., p. 456.
95. Khwandamir, *Rajal*, quoted in Etemadi, 'Rabii-e Fushang, Sha'er-e Darbar' (Rabii of Fushang: Courtly Poet), *Ariana*, Vol. 5, No. 12, Jedi 1326/December 1947, pp. 1–8.
96. Oljeitu was known as 'The Servant of God' (*Khodabandah*) and during his lifetime he flitted between Nestorian Christianity, Buddhism and Sunni Islam before finally, in the winter of 1307–8, declaring his allegiance to Shia Islam.
97. Sayfi, *Tarikh namah*, p. 462.
98. Sayfi, *Tarikh namah*, pp. 462–5, and Esfezari, *Gardens of Paradise*, Vol. I, pp. 442–3.
99. Esfezari, *Gardens of Paradise*, Vol. I, p. 447.
100. Esfezari, *Gardens of Paradise*, Vol. I, p. 449.
101. Sayfi, *Tarikh namah*, p. 495.
102. Ibid., p. 495.
103. Ibid., pp. 504–5.
104. Guya Etemadi, 'Darbar-e Malouk-e Kart' (The Court of the Kartid Maleks), *Aryana*, Vol. 2, No. 4, Sawr 1323/May 1944, p. 48.
105. Sayfi, *Tarikh namah*, p. 533.
106. Ibid., p. 533
107. Ibid., p. 542.
108. We know this detail as Sayfi himself was captured by the Mongols in the aftermath of this siege for writing poems in praise of the rebellious Mohammad Sam, and was himself chained to Mohammad Sam on their march north to Shiburghan. Sayfi, *Tarikh namah*, p. 542, and see George Lane, *Early Mongol Rule in Thirteenth-Century Iran: A Persian Renaissance*, London: Routledge Curzon, 2003, p. 159.
109. Sayfi, *Tarikh namah*, pp. 550–51.
110. Ibid., p. 556.
111. Ibid., p. 575.
112. Ibid., p. 571.
113. Ibid, p. 562.
114. Ibid., p. 615.
115. Ibid., p. 619.

116. Ibid., p. 624.
117. Ibn Batuta, *The Travels of Ibn Batuta, AD 1325—1354*, 3 Vols., Vol. III, trans. H. A. R. Gibb, Cambridge: Cambridge University Press, 1971, p. 574.
118. Ibid., pp. 609–14.
119. Ibid., p. 715.
120. Ibid., pp. 742–4.
121. Ibid., p. 747.
122. Esfezari, *Gardens of Paradise*, Vol. I, p. 507.
123. Sayfi, *Tarikh namah*, p. 748.
124. Ibid., p. 776.
125. Ibid, pp. 782–6.
126. Khwandamir, *Habibu-s-Siyar*, Thackston, p. 119.
127. Hafez Abru, *Chronique des Rois Mongols en Iran*, trans. K. Bayani, Paris: Librairie d'Amerique et d'Orient Adrien-Maisonneuve, 1936, p. 92.
128. Khwandamir, *Habibu-s-Siyar*, Thackston, p. 120.
129. Hafez Abru, *Rois Mongols*, p. 92.
130. The downfall of Amir Chupan is dealt with in the detail it deserves by Charles Melville's excellent article on the matter. Professor Melville rightly locates this incident within the context of the decline of the Il-Khanate. Charles Melville, 'The Fall of Amir Chupan and the Decline of the Ilkhanate, 1327–37: A Decade of Discord in Mongol Iran', *Papers on Inner Asia*, No. 30, Bloomington: Indiana University, Research Institute for Inner Asian Studies, 1999.
131. Hafez Abru, *Rois Mongols*, p. 105.
132. Ibid., p. 110.
133. For a more detailed account of this complicated episode in a complicated period of history, see *Cambridge History of Iran*, Vol. 5, pp. 413–17.
134. Hafez Abru, *Cinq Opuscules de Hafez Abru*, ed. Felix Tauer, Prague, 1959, p. 32.
135. For an excellent discussion of Kartid coinage, see Potter, *Kartids in Herat*, pp. 50, 160–2.
136. See John Limbert, *Shiraz in the Age of Hafez; The Glory of a Medieval Persian City*, Washington, DC: University of Washington Press, 2004.
137. Khwandamir, *Habibu-s-Siyar*, Thackston, p. 220. See also Hafez Abru, *Cinq Opuscules*, p. 31.
138. Mohammad Ismail Moballegh Gharjestani, 'Malek Moezz al-Din Hussein', *Aryana*, Vol. 17, No. 7 [misprint: says 6], Saratan 1338/June 1959, pp. 25–8.
139. For Persian takes on the Sarbedars, see Dr A. Rakhlataber, 'Aya Abdul Razzaq aghazgar-e sarbedaran ast? (Is Abdul Razzaq the founder of the Sarbedars?), *Shenakht*, No. 2, Summer 1365/1987, pp. 80–94; Mardaiy Nasb, 'Dowlat-e Sarbedaran wa tahavolat-e siasi, ejtemaiey wa farhangi dar qarn hashtom' (The governance of the Sarbedars and the political, social and cultural upheavals of the eighth century), *Tarikh dar Aianeh-ye Pozuhesh*, No. 4, Winter 1382/2004, pp. 143–66; and Mehdi Fathi Nia, 'Rabeta-ye din wa dowlat nazd-e sarbedaran' (Mosque and state relations under the Sarbedars), *Tarikh dar Aianeh-ye Pozuhesh*, No. 23, Autumn 1388/2008, pp. 181–208. The dynasty is dealt with excellently in *Cambridge History of Iran*, Vol. 6, pp. 16–41; and J. Masson Smith Jr, *The History of the Sarbadar Dynasty 1336–1381 A.D. and its Sources*, The Hague and Paris: Mouton, 1970.
140. E. G. Browne, *Literary History of Persia*, 4 vols., Cambridge: Cambridge University Press, 1920, Vol. III, p. 179.

141. *Cambridge History of Iran*, Vol. 6, pp. 16–41.

142. Ibn Batuta, *The Travels of Ibn Batuta*, Vol. III, p. 574.

143. Mardaiy Nasb, 'Dowlat-e Sarbedaran wa tahavolat-e siasi, ejtemaiey wa farhangi dar qarn hashtom' (The governance of the Sarbedars and the political, social and cultural upheavals of the eighth century), *Tarikh dar Aianeh-ye Pozuhesh*, No. 4, Winter 1382/2004, p. 153.

144. Hafez Abru, *Cinq Opuscules*, p. 32.

145. Ibid., p. 32.

146. Ibid., pp. 32–6.

147. Khwandamir, *Habibu-s-Siyar*, Thackston, p. 221.

148. Ibid., p. 221.

149. Ibid., p. 221.

150. Hafez Abru, *Cinq Opuscules*, pp. 32–6.

151. Ibid., p. 43.

152. Qasem bin Yusuf Abu Nasri Heravi, *Rasalah-e tariq-e qesmat-e ab-e qolub va mard-e juy va arazi-e bolukat-e velayat* (Study on the division of water and canal networks in the localities and district) ed. Mayel Heravi, Tehran, 1347/1967, p. 34.

153. Hafez Abru, *Cinq Opuscules*, p. 48.

154. See Ali Bahrani Pour, 'The Trade in Horses between Khorasan and India in the 13th to 17th Centuries', at https://www.academia.edu/5516297/THE_TRADE_ IN_HORSES_BETWEEN_KHORASAN_AND_INDIA_IN_THE_13TH_-_17TH_CENTURIES, accessed on 18.12.2013.

155. Hafez Abru, *Cinq Opuscules*, p. 49.

156. Ibid., p. 49.

157. Ibid., p. 49.

158. Mohammad Ismail Gharjestani, 'Malek Moezz al-Din Hussein', *Aryana*, Vol. 17, No. 6 [misprint: says 5], Saratan 1338/June 1959, p. 25.

159. Hafez Abru, *Cinq Opuscules*, p. 51.

160. Ibid., p. 52.

161. Ibid., p. 52.

162. Ibid., p. 53.

163. Ibid., p. 54. See also Esfezari, *Gardens of Paradise*, Vol. II, p. 30.

164. Esfezari, *Gardens of Paradise*, Vol. II, p. 31.

165. For a good account of Timur and his life, see Justin Marozzi, *Tamerlane, Sword of Islam, Conqueror of the World*, London: Harper Collins, 2004.

166. Esfezari, *Gardens of Paradise*, Vol. II, p. 32.

167. Ibid., pp. 58–60.

168. Ibid., p. 60.

169. Ibid., p. 60.

170. Ibid., p. 60.

171. Ibid., p. 60.

172. Ibid., p. 62.

173. See A. K. S. Lambton, 'Early Timurid Theories of State: Hafiz Abru and Nizam al-Din Sami', *Bulletin d'Études Orientales*, Vol. XXX, 1978, pp. 1–9.

174. Hafez Abru, *Cinq Opuscules*, p. 62.

175. Ibid., p. 62.

176. Ibid., p. 67.

177. The events of the first sack of Herat are told in Hafez Abru, Cinq Opuscules, pp. 66–72.

2. HERAT IN AN AGE OF HIGH ART, IMPERIAL FAVOUR AND LOW POLITICS,
    1381–1510

1. For an eloquent and succinct account of Timur's many campaigns, see
    E. G. Browne, *A Literary History of Persia*, Vol. 6, Cambridge: Cambridge University
    Press, 1920, pp. 185–99.
2. Samarqandi, for example, in his *Takhdirat al-Shuara*, describes the death with ref-
    erence to a verse from the Quran: 'O thou soul which art at rest, return unto
    thy Lord, well pleased with thy reward, and well pleasing unto God.' Dawlatshah
    Samarqandi, *Takhdirat al-Shuara*, in W. M. Thackston, *A Century of Princes: Sources
    on Timurid History and Art, Selected and Translated by W. M. Thackston, Published in
    Conjunction with the Exhibition 'Timur and the Princely Vision', Washington, DC and Los
    Angeles, 1989*, Cambridge, MA: Aga Khan Program for Islamic Architecture, 1989,
    p. 18. For an opposing view, an official historian of Timur's reign, Ibn Arabshah,
    saw it in slightly less exalted terms, describing Timur as being 'carried to the
    cursing and punishment of God'; quoted in Thomas W. Lentz and Glenn D. Lowry,
    Timur and the Princely Vision: Persian Art and Culture in the Fifteenth Century, Washington,
    DC: Smithsonian Press, 1989, p. 67.
3. For the succession struggle consequent on Timur's death, see Beatrice F. Manz,
    The Rise and Rule of Tamerlane, Cambridge: Cambridge University Press, 1989,
    pp. 128–47.
4. Hafez Abru, *Zubadat-e Tawarikh*, Vol. I, ed. Kamal Hajji Sayyed Javadi, Tehran:
    Sazman-e chap wa entesharat-e vezarat-e farhang wa ershad-e Islami, 1372 AH,
    p. 14.
5. Ibid., p. 16. Interestingly, at the moment when Hafez Abru is discussing the city's
    preparations for the conflict, he takes that opportunity to quote the famous lines
    from Mostowfi about Herat as the pearl within the oyster, a verse which so cel-
    ebrates the fame and majesty of the city, somehow presaging its Timurid glories.
    He also cites a different, but equally pleasing, poem which celebrates this act of
    building occasioned by the instability caused by Timur's passing in Otrar.
6. Samarqandi, in Thackston, *Century of Princes*, p. 25.
7. 'His transfer of the Timurid capital from Samarqand to Herat, "the dome of Islam,"
    in 812/1409, represented a conscious shift in focus away from Transoxania and
    toward the Khorasanian centers [sic] of Islamic law, learning, and piety thus sig-
    naling the start of a new era of accommodation and acculturation.' Maria Eva
    Subtelny and Anas B. Khalidov, 'The Curriculum of Islamic Higher Learning in
    Timurid Iran in the Light of the Sunni Revival under Shah-Rukh', *Journal of the
    American Oriental Society*, Vol. 115, No. 2, 1995, p. 211.
8. Lentz and Lowry, *Timur and the Princely Vision*, p. 27.
9. Samarqandi, in Thackston, *Century of Princes*, p. 35.
10. Subtelny and Khalidov, 'The Curriculum of Islamic Higher Learning in Timurid
    Iran', p. 212.
11. Ibid., p. 213.
12. Samarqandi, in Thackston, *Century of Princes*, p. 19.
13. Ibn Arabshah, quoted in Lentz and Lowry, *Timur and the Princely Vision*, p. 81.
14. Lentz and Lowry, *Timur and the Princely Vision*, pp. 100, 102.
15. *Cambridge History of Iran*, Vol. 6, p. 102.
16. For an excellent discussion of Shah Rukh's travels, and the significance of this for
    our understanding of the Timurid court and administration, see Charles Melville,

'The itineraries of Shahrukh b. Timur (1405–47)', in D. Durand-Guédy, ed., *Turko-Mongol Rulers, Cities and City Life*, Leiden: Brill, 2013, pp. 285–315.

17. Samarqandi, in Thackston, *Century of Princes*, p. 19.
18. For a breathless contemporary description of Samarqand by a European traveller, see Clavijo's account: Ruy Gonzales de Clavijo, *Narrative of the Embassy of Ruy Gonzalez de Clavijo to the Court of Timûr at Samarkand. A.D. 1403–6*, 1859, trans. Clements R. Markham, London: Hakluyt Society. Clavijo was sent from the court of King Henry III of Spain to the court of Timur for diplomatic purposes, and he talks with awestruck wonder about the magnificence of Timur's court and the buildings in Samarqand. See, Guy Le Strange, *Narrative of the Spanish Embassy to the Court of Timur at Samarkand in the Years, 1403–1406*, New York: 1928. For Timur's use of the symbolism of power, see B. F. Manz, 'Tamerlane and the Symbolism of Sovereignty', *Iranian Studies*, Vol. 21, Nos. 1–2, 1988, pp. 105–22.
19. Khwandamir, in Thackston, *Century of Princes*, p. 132.
20. *Cambridge History of Iran*, Vol. 6, p. 86.
21. For a good summary of her life and work, see Beatrice Forbes Manz, 'Gowhar-Sad Aga', *Encyclopaedia Iranica*, at http://www.iranicaonline.org/articles/gowhar-sad-aga, accessed on 13.02.2015.
22. For an excellent discussion of Shirazi and his works, see Donald Wilber, 'Qavam al-Din ibn Zayn al-Din Shirazi: A Fifteenth Century Timurid Architect', *Architectural History*, Vol. 30, 1987, pp. 31–44.
23. Major C. E. Yate, *Northern Afghanistan, or Letters from the Afghan Boundary Commission*, London: William Blackwood and Sons, 1888, p. 32.
24. *Cambridge History of Iran*, Vol. 6, p. 748.
25. Robert Byron, *The Road to Oxiana*, 1937; London: Pimlico edition, 2004, p. 96.
26. *Cambridge History of Iran*, Vol. 6, p. 748.
27. Mohan Lal, quoted in Byron, *Road to Oxiana*, p. 221.
28. Ibid., p. 219.
29. It must be stated that this area was not totally empty at the time of the Karts, and *khaneqah*s built during Kartid rule could be found on this stretch of land, directly to the north of the Old City walls and the Bagh-e Shah.
30. Terry Allen, *Timurid Herat*, Wiesbaden: Reichert Verlag, 1983, p. 18.
31. The Timurid gardens of Herat, mostly located on the upward sloping ground to the east and the north of the city, heading towards Gazur Gah and the Kuh-e Mukhtar, were spaces of size and extraordinary luxury. The Bagh-e Zaghan, for example, which sat to the north-west of the Old City became Shah Rukh's main residence, a place from which he conducted imperial business, entertained diplomats and held court. Many of Herat's illustrations and portraits of Timurid Sultans, princes and viziers have them seated in a garden, wine cup in hand, courtiers looking on nervously. Hafez Abru, *Zubadat al-tawarikh*, Vol. 4, p. 897.
32. Morris Rossabi, 'Two Ming Envoys to Inner Asia', *T'oung Pao*, 2nd Series, Vol. 62, Nos. 1/3, 1976, pp. 1–34. For the text of his account of his time in Herat, see Morris Rossabi, 'A Translation of Ch'en Ch'eng's *Hisi-yü Faukuo Chih*', *Ming Studies*, Fall 1983, pp. 49–59. See also Felicia J. Hecker, 'A Fifteenth-Century Chinese Diplomat in Herat', *Journal of the Royal Asiatic Society*, 3rd Series, Vol. 3, No. 1, 1993, pp. 85–98.
33. Quoted in Hecker, 'A Fifteenth-Century Chinese Diplomat in Herat', p. 87.
34. *The Bondage and Travels of Johann Schiltberger, A Native of Bavaria, In Europe, Asia and Africa, 1396–1427*, trans. Commander J. Buchan Telfer, RN, London: Hakluyt Society, 1879, p. 44.

35. Rossabi, 'A Translation of Ch'en Ch'eng's *Hsi-yü Faukuo Chih*', p. 49.
36. Ibid., p. 51. Here we have a nice contrast to the observations of Herat's envoy to Peking in 1420, who remarked on the use of stone for buildings.
37. Ibid., p. 50.
38. Ibid., p. 54.
39. In 2006, a UNESCO team working on a restoration of the Gawhar Shad Mausoleum sought to put coloured glass into a space for the window, in a continuation of the traditions of the Timurid era and most likely earlier. However, a local mullah refused this, saying that the mausoleum would resemble a Christian church if coloured glass were put in the windows of the mausoleum.
40. Rossabi, 'A Translation of Ch'en Ch'eng's *Hsi-yü Faukuo Chih*', p. 54.
41. Ibid., p. 53.
42. Ibid., p. 53.
43. Ibid., p. 52.
44. A Herati doctor once told me that a regular intake of coffee can stave off the H1N1 virus, and commanded that I should drink 'at least 10 litres of water a day' during the summer months.
45. Rossabi, 'A Translation of Ch'en Ch'eng's *Hsi-yü Faukuo Chih*', p. 52.
46. Oscar von Niedermayer and Ernst Diez, *Afghanistan, Bearbeitet von Oscar von Niedermayer und Ernst Diez*, Leipzig: Verlag Karl W. Hiersemann, 1924, plate no. 102.
47. Rossabi, 'A Translation of Ch'en Ch'eng's *Hsi-yü Faukuo Chih*', p. 52.
48. Ibid., p. 53.
49. Ibid., p. 52.
50. Ibid., p. 51.
51. Ibid., p. 51.
52. Ibid., p. 53.
53. The envoy was clearly a success, with those retuning to China rewarded with silver, silk and banquets in honour of their safe return from the 'barbarian' Western lands. Chen Cheng returned to Herat on a number of occasions, but none of these return journeys was marked with a similarly fulsome account of his travels. Shah Rukh was even considered as a political equal to the Yung-le Emperor, a change from the vassalage earlier claimed by the Ming Emperor over Timur. The 1418 missive talked of Shah Rukh as 'enlightened, perceptive, knowing, mature, sensible and greater than all the Muslims', a reflection both of Shah Rukh's image as presented to Chen Cheng, and also of a distinctly improved relationship between the two men. Herat responded, in 1420, with an embassy of a number of Timurid artists and nobles to the Ming court in Beijing. One of those present, Ghiath al-Din Naqash, sent by Prince Baysanghur, wrote an equally fascinating account of his travels east. For a translation of the envoy's report, see Thackston, *Century of Princes*, pp. 289–97.
54. It is important to note that Shah Rukh's diplomatic outreach was not solely in the direction of China. Shah Rukh exchanged letters with Ottoman sultans and initiated contacts with Indian and Egyptian trading partners. In 1439, Herat welcomed the ambassador of the Mamluk rulers of Egypt and Syria, entertaining their ambassador, Chechak Buqa, with great extravagance in Herat's gardens and halls. See Khwandamir, in Thackston, *Century of Princes*, pp. 145–6.
55. A chronicler's description of his death contains a suggestion that the Timurid sovereigns probably spoonfed the citizens of Herat a varnished version of the truth,

for it notes that 'The people of Herat supposed his death was due to a stroke.' See Samarqandi, in Thackston, *Century of Princes*, p. 23.

56. Dawlatshah, in Thackston, *Century of Princes*, p. 22.

57. The most thorough description and analysis of the *ketabkhana* can be found in Lentz and Lowry, *Timur and the Princely Vision*, pp. 159–236.

58. Baysanghur also had a role to play in the administration of Herat, occupying a position within the *diwan* (bureaucracy) which reflected his royal status. Hafez Abru, *Zubadat al-tawarikh*, Vol. 4, p. 926.

59. Arzadasht, in Thackston, *Century of Princes*, p. 323.

60. Ibid., p. 323.

61. Ibid., p. 325.

62. Carpets and textiles were also produced and designed in this atelier. Lentz and Lowry, *Timur and the Princely Vision*, pp. 218–19.

63. Arzadasht, In Thackston, *Century of Princes*, pp. 323, 325.

64. For an excellent discussion of Baysanghur's *Shahnama* in comparison with that of Ibrahim Sultan, see Eleanor Sims, 'The Illustrated Manuscripts of Firdausi's "Shahnama" Commissioned by Princes of the House of Timur', *Ars Orientalis*, Vol. 22, 1992, pp. 42–68.

65. Ibid., pp. 44–5.

66. Ibid., p. 55.

67. Lentz and Lowry, *Timur and the Princely Vision*, p. 125.

68. Ibid., p. 125.

69. Babur in his visit to Herat; see Thackston, *Century of Princes*.

70. Khwandamir, in Thackston, *Century of Princes*, p. 145.

71. Ibid., p. 145.

72. Samarqandi, in Thackston, *Century of Princes*, p. 24.

73. Ibid., p. 23.

74. Ibid., p. 23.

75. From Samarqandi's *Matla al-sadayn*, quoted in Lentz and Lowry, *Timur and the Princely Vision*, p. 1.

76. The world of religion and politics in Timurid Iran is a complex one, best analysed in Beatrice Forbes Manz, *Power, Politics and Religion in Timurid Iran*, Cambridge: Cambridge University Press, 2010. Owing to the strictures of time and space, my analysis on this fascinating subject is topical at best.

77. Moin al-Din Mohammad Zamchi Esfezari, *Rawdat al Jannat fi Ausaf Madinat Herat* (The Gardens of Paradise in Herat), Vols. I and II, Tehran: Moalem Danesgah Tehran, 1338 AH, Vol. I, pp. 101–2.

78. Manz, *Power, Politics and Religion in Timurid Iran*, p. 205.

79. Khwandamir, in Thackston, *Century of Princes*, p. 153.

80. Dawlatshah, in Thackston, *Century of Princes*, p. 19.

81. Abdullah Sani, known as Beheshti Heravi, *Nur al-mashreqain* (The Light of the Two Easts), ed. Mayel Heravi, Mashhad: Mosesse-ye chap wa entesharat-e astan-e quds rezawi, 1377/1957, p. 200.

82. Manz, *Power, Politics and Religion in Timurid Iran*, p. 219.

83. Ibid., pp. 208–44.

84. For an excellent study of various aspects of Ansari's shrine, see Lisa Golombek, *The Timurid Shrine at Gazur Gah*, Toronto: Royal Ontario Museum, 1969.

85. Khwandamir, in Thackston, *Century of Princes*, p. 143.

86. For the most comprehensive discussion of the different accounts of this seminal

event, see Ilkber Evrim Binbas, 'The Anatomy of a Regicide Attempt: Shahrukh, the Hurufis, and the Timurid Intellectuals in 830/1426–7', *Journal of the Royal Asiatic Society*, 3rd Series, Vol. 23, Part 3, July 2013, pp. 391–428.

87. For all, see Evrim Binbas, 'The Anatomy of a Regicide Attempt: Shahrukh, the Hurufis, and the Timurid Intellectuals in 830/1426–7', *Journal of the Royal Asiatic Society*, 3rd Series, 2013, Vol. 23, No. 3.
88. Esfezari, *Zubadat al-Tawarikh*, Vol. II, p. 262.
89. The notion of plague burning and being of an incendiary nature is found in other poems of this time. See, for example, a poem by Katibi of Herat in which he makes this allusion through his poems. Browne, *Literary History of Persia*, Vol. 3, p. 488.
90. Quoted in Dr Sayyed Husain Mojtaboue, *Herat dar ahd-e Timurian* (Herat in the Timurid Era), Herat: Entesharat-e Ahrary, 1389/2011, p. 90.
91. See Allen, *Timurid Herat*.
92. Samarqandi, in Thawkston, *Century of Princes*, p. 39.
93. Khwandamir, *Century of Princes*, p. 147.
94. Ibid., p. 39.
95. Shah Rukh would have preferred to see Mohammad Juki, then 40 years old and serving as governor in Balkh, as his successor despite not having made any detailed provision for the succession. During the waning years of his power, Sultan Mohammad, his boisterous grandson, had moved to control much of present-day Iran, and had shown signs of acting with a dangerous streak of independence. Gawhar Shad's favourite, Ala al-Dawla, a son of Baysanghur whom she had brought up herself, had been given control of Herat whilst Shah Rukh was on his campaign against Sultan Mohammad.
96. Manz, *Power, Politics and Religion in Timurid Iran*, p. 259.
97. Two years of chaos saw the division of Shah Rukh's lands. Ulugh Beg was ruling over Transoxania; Abul Qasim Babur took Khorasan, and Ala al-Dawla controlled areas in the present day south west of Afghanistan. Central Persia and Fars were under the control of Sultan Mohammad. Shah Rukh's conquests in north-west Persia and Anatolia were rendered obsolete by the chaos; the Qara Qoyunlu tribes took back land they had lost to Shah Rukh's campaigning.
98. Manz, *Power, Politics and Religion in Timurid Iran*, pp. 263–4.
99. The most detailed treatment of this complicated period can be found in Manz, *Power, Politics and Religion in Timurid Iran*, pp. 245–75.
100. Ibid., p. 268.
101. These years are nicely summed up by Khwandamir: 'It is an amazing and strange thing that during this year throughout the regions and fortresses of Khurasan there were several effective rulers, none of whom was in obedience to another: Amir Jahanshah held from Astarabad to Sabzawar in his mighty grip; Mirza Sultan Abu-Said governed in Balkh; Mirza Sultan Ibrahim sat in Herat and bowed to no one else; Mawlana Ahmad Yasaul [*sic*] had made fast Ikhtiaruddin [*sic*] Fort and took no notice of any of the sultans; Mirza Sultan Sanjar resided in Merv [*sic*]; Mirza Shah Mahumud dreamed of independence in Tus; Berka the Mughul held the Tiratu fortress; and Amir Abdullah Pirzada defended the citadel at Sarakhs; Malik Qasim son of Iskandar Yusuf, along with Amir Khalil, controlled the kingdom of Sistan as far as Farah and Isfizar [*sic*]; in Kabushan fort Hasan Shaykh-Temur was commandant; and the fort at Tabas was under the control of Amir Uways b. Khawandshah.' Khwandamir, in Thackston, *Century of Princes*, p. 196.

102. Khwandamir, in Thackston, *Century of Princes*, p. 191.
103. Ibid., p. 193. See also, Esfezari, *Gardens of Paradise*, Vol. II, p. 203.
104. Khwandamir, in Thackston, *Century of Princes*, p. 193.
105. Ibid., p. 199.
106. Ibid., p. 203.
107. Ibid., p. 205.
108. Samarqandi, quoted in Allen, *Timurid Herat*, pp. 23–4.
109. Allen, *Timurid Herat*, p. 24.
110. Husain Bayqara's accession to the throne of Herat was by no means uncontested. Uzun Hassan (Hassan 'the tall') looked to take advantage of the precariousness of the political situation—a continuation of the post-Shah Rukh turbulence—and he backed a descendant of Shah Rukh, Yadgar Mohammad. A brief victory for Husain Bayqara over Yadgar Mohammad at the battle of Chinaran in September 1469 was not enough to secure total control; Uzun Hassan sent more supplies in the form of his own sons to Yadgar Mohammad, resulting in Husain Bayqara being compelled to retreat and abandon Herat in July 1470. However, this occupation of Herat by the 'vile, foul-mouthed Turcomans' lasted a mere six weeks. See Dawlatshah, in Thackston, *Century of Princes*, p. 56.
111. Ibid., p. 57.
112. An excerpt from Sultan Husain's *Apologia*, quoted in Lentz and Lowry, *Timur and the Princely Vision*, p. 254.
113. Majboue, *Herat dar ahd-e Timurian*, p. 88.
114. Dawlatshah, in Thackston, *Century of Princes*, pp. 54–9. Babur also alludes to Husain Bayqara's strong reputation as a military figure of some note. Babur, in Thackston, *Century of Princes*, p. 254.
115. This may, however, have simply been a convenient excuse for Husain Bayqara to avoid his religious duties, for Islam allows prayers to be said in a manner of positions so as to allow for the sick and injured to say their prayers. Thank you to Bruce Wannell for pointing this out to me.
116. Babur, in Thackston, *Century of Princes*, p. 252.
117. Ibid., p. 252.
118. Ibid., p. 258.
119. Hans R. Roemer, 'Hosayn Bayqara', *Encyclopaedia Iranica*, at http://www.iranicaonline.org/articles/hosayn-bayqara, accessed on 14.15.2015.
120. Husain Bayqara had a scribe place his family into a Uighur and Arabic genealogy so as to connect him visibly to Timur, and by commissioning a special copy of Yazi's epic *Zafarnama*, a book celebrating the life and victories of Timur, Husain Bayqara was clear in showing the locus of his political inspirations. Lentz and Lowry, *Timur and the Princely Vision*, p. 260.
121. Khwandamir, in Thackston, *Century of Princes*, p. 227.
122. Yate, *Northern Afghanistan*, p. 32.
123. Byron, *The Road to Oxiana*, p. 96.
124. Ibid.
125. Allen, *Timurid Herat*, p. 24.
126. Esfezari, *Gardens of Paradise*, Vol. II, pp. 317–19.
127. Lentz and Lowry, *Timur and the Princely Vision*, p. 286.
128. Browne, *Literary History of Persia*, Vol. 3, p. 505.
129. Babur, in Thackston, *Century of Princes*, p. 259.
130. *Cambridge History of Iran*, Vol. 6, pp. 123–4.

131. Lentz and Lowry, *Timur and the Princely Vision*, p. 254.

132. Khwandamir, in Thackston, *Century of Princes*, p. 224.

133. Mirza Mohammad Dughlat, in Thackston, *Century of Princes*, p. 359.

134. Babur, in Thackston, *Century of Princes*, p. 265.

135. Ibid., p. 266.

136. Browne, *Literary History of Persia*, Vol. 4, p. 94.

137. Khwandamir tells us that he built 'more than 135 structures including 52 caravansaries or *ribats*, 19 cisterns, 20 mosques, 14 bridges, 9 baths, 7 khanaqahs and a madrasa'. Quoted in Lentz and Lowry, *Timur and the Princely Vision*, p. 255.

138. See Browne, *Literary History of Persia*, Vol. 3, pp. 437–9.

139. M. Yaqub Wahidy Juzjaini, ed., *Diwan-e Sultan Husain Mirza Bayqara ba enzemam-e resala-ye u* (A Collection of Literary Works of Sultan Husain Mirza Bayqara), Kabul: Book Publication Department, 1968.

140. Khwandamir, in Thackston, *Century of Princes*, p. 219.

141. Babur, in Thackston, *Century of Princes*, pp. 265–6.

142. Lentz and Lowry, *Timur and the Princely Vision*, p. 284.

143. E. H. Gibb, quoted in Browne, *Literary History of Persia*, Vol. 3, p. 422.

144. Browne, *Literary History of Persia*, Vol. 3, p. 507.

145. Ibid., p. 511.

146. For a more detailed look at Jami's output, with extracts and analysis, see Browne, *Literary History of Persia*, Vol. 3, pp. 507–48.

147. Lentz and Lowry, *Timur and the Princely Vision*, p. 276.

148. Babur, in Thackston, *Century of Princes*, p. 267.

149. Esfezari, *Gardens of Paradise*, Vol. II, p. 308.

150. The Shaybanid Uzbeks were a tribal confederacy which claimed descent from the fifth son of Jochi, himself a grandson of Chingiz Khan. During the fifteenth century, the Shaybanids had been in conflict with regional powers, menacing the edges of Timurid authority in and around the Oxus river, and beyond into Samarqand and Bukhara. For a lively account of their advance through Khorasan and Transoxania, see Khwandamir, in Thackston, *Century of Princes*, pp. 220–23.

151. See Riazul Islam, ed., *A Calendar of Documents on Indo-Persian Relations (1500–1750)*, Vol. I, Karachi: Institute of Central and West Asian Studies, 1982, pp. 57–8. This is a letter between Husain Bayqara and Shah Ismail I, in which Husain Bayqara cuts a rather grovelling figure in contrast with the dynamic Safavid.

152. Quoted in Babur, in Thackston, *Century of Princes*, p. 269.

153. For a good account of Babur and the Mughal Empire to which he gave birth, see John F. Richards, *The Mughal Empire (The New Cambridge History of India)*, Cambridge: Cambridge University Press, 1995.

154. Babur, in Thackston, *Century of Princes*, p. 250.

155. Ibid., p. 268.

156. Ibid., p. 272.

157. Ibid., pp. 271–2.

158. Ibid., p. 249.

159. Ibid., p. 263.

160. Ibid., p. 274.

161. Ibid., p. 272.

162. Khwandamir, in Thackston, *Century of Princes*, p. 227.

163. Ibid., p. 228.

164. Ibid., p. 228.
165. These men were as follows: the Shaykh al-Islam, the Dean of Saids Amir Kamal al-Din Attaullah al-Husaini, Amir Abdul Qadir, Amir Ghiath al-Din Mohammad, Sayyed Sadruddin Yunus, Qazi Ikhtiar al-Din Hassan, Qazi Sadruddin Mohammad al-Imami, Sayyed Raziuddin Abdul al-Awal, Khwaja Jamal al-Din Attaullah and Khwaja Nizam al-Din Abdulhai Sahib Iyar. Khwandamir, in Thackston, *Century of Princes*, p. 231.
166. Ibid., pp. 232–3.

3.　SAFAVIDS TO PASHTUNS AND THE DECLINE OF A TIMURID JEWEL, 1510–1747

1. Amir Mahmud Khwandamir, *Habib al-Siyar*, trans. W. M. Thackston, London: I. B. Tauris, 2012, p. 556.
2. For a comprehensive account of the Safavid empire, its beginnings and evolution, see *Cambridge History of Iran*, Cambridge: Cambridge University Press, 1968, Vol. 6, pp. 189–411.
3. Ibid., p. 199. The Safavid empire and its religious philosophy is a fascinating field of study, and English readers are best advised to read this volume for an introduction to this dynasty and various aspects of their rule in the sixteenth and seventeenth centuries.
4. This is especially the case for official Safavid court historians, such as Hasan Rumlu. See Hasan Rumlu, *A Chronicle of the Early Safawis, being the Ahsanut tawarikh*, Vol. I, ed. C. N. Seddon, Baroda: Oriental Institute, 1931.
5. Quoted in E. G. Browne, *Literary History of Persia*, 4 vols., Cambridge: Cambridge University Press, 1920, Vol. 4, pp. 50–51.
6. One Safavid historian has the Shaybanid army in a chaotic retreat from Herat to Merv, where they would be defeated by the Safavid armies. Rumlu, *Ahsanut tawarikh*, Vol. I, pp. 118–25.
7. Khwandamir, *Habibu's-Siyar*, p. 593.
8. Rumlu, *Ahsanut tawarikh*, Vol. I, p. 124.
9. Khwandamir, *Habibu's-Siyar*, p. 593.
10. Ibid., p. 593.
11. See M. Szuppe, 'Entre Timourides, Uzbeks et Safavides: questions d'histoire politique et sociale de Hérat dans la première moitié du XVIe siècle', *Studia Iranica*, Cahier 12, 1992, Paris, pp. 121–32.
12. Khwandamir, *Habibu's-Siyar*, pp. 593–4.
13. One of the first such sieges was in 1513. Ubaidullah Khan, an Uzbek leader, and a military commander by the name of Jani Beg invaded Khorasan and launched a siege on Herat during which the city was defended at all four quarters of the city by various Herati and Safavid nobles and military figures. The siege was bitter, coming in the middle of winter, and grain supplies had been low since 1511; hardship for Herat's surrounding areas became commonplace and the city itself was besieged, and attacked with rushing thrusts at the Firuzabad, Iraq and Malek Gates by the Uzbek forces. The invaders eventually called off the attack after a dispute arose between them, but this was soon followed by the city being taken by Mohammad Temur Sultan, then ruling in Samarqand, along with Ubaidullah Khan, both of whom ruled over a fractious city in which Sunni–Shia tensions regularly spilled over into violence and executions.

14. Browne, *Literary History of Persia*, Vol. 4, p. 65. Browne also lists letters between Ottoman and Uzbek leaders in which the language used to refer to the Safavids is high on invective and insults.

15. These are the main sieges suffered by the city during the first half of the sixteenth century: January–March 1513, May–June 1521, winter of 1525–6, and from 1528. Uzbek troops occupied Herat from the winter of 1528 until August 1530. In 1533 Uzbek forces occupied large parts of Khorasan: Ubaidullah's final occupation of Herat lasted from August 1536 to January 1537. See Eskandar Beg Monshi, *History of Shah 'Abbas the Great (Tarikh-e Alamaray-ye Abbasi)*, Vol. I, trans. Roger M. Savory, Boulder, CO: Westview Press, 1978, pp. 84–109.

16. See Rumlu, *Ahsanut tawarikh*, Vol. I, p. 171.

17. The regional political context for this chaos visited on Herat was the crushing defeat of the Safavid army at the hands of the Ottoman forces under Sultan Selim (r.1512–29) at the battle of Chaldiran (in modern day Iran's north-west) on 23 August 1514. Consequent on this defeat, Ismail lost an aura of military invincibility and the divinely sanctioned sense of the Safavid expansionist *jihad* went with it. Chaldiran forced Ismail, in effect, to turn his attentions to the Iranian plateau, away from their natural Anatolian heartlands. 'Despite all Ismail's conquests as far as Khurasan [*sic*], it was by no means clear in the first phase of his rule whether his realm, whose western frontier with the Ottoman empire was marked by the upper stretches of the Euphrates, would develop into an Iranian state with a Turkish glacis to the west, or into a Turkish state with an Iranian perimeter to the east.' See *Cambridge History of Iran*, Vol. 6, p. 228.

18. Rumlu, *Ahsanut tawarikh*, Vol. I, p. 150.

19. Ibid., p. 226.

20. Ibid., pp. 225–32.

21. Ibid., p. 267.

22. Ibid., p. 269.

23. Ibid., p. 269.

24. Ibid., p. 269.

25. Ibid., p. 269.

26. Khwandamir, *Tarikh-e shah ismail va shah Tahmasp safavi (zil-e tarikh-e habib al-siyar)*, ed. Dr Mohammad Ali Jarahi, Tehran: Sherkat-e qalam va sina, 1375/1996, p. 167.

27. Rumlu, *Ahsanut tawarikh*, Vol. I, p. 272.

28. Ibid., p. 271.

29. Ibid., p. 272.

30. Quoted in Christine Noelle-Karimi, *The Pearl in its Midst: Herat and the Mapping of Khorasan (15th-19th Centuries)*, Wien: Verlag der Österreichischen Akademie der Wissenschaften, 2013a, p. 59.

31. Szuppe, *Entre Timourides, Uzbeks et Safavides*.

32. Rumlu, *Ahsanut tawarikh*, Vol. I, p. 276.

33. Qasim b. Yusuf Abu Nasri Heravi, *Resale-ye tariq-e qesmat-e qoloub-e ab* (A Treaty on the Ways of Water), ed. Mayel Heravi, Tehran: Entersharat-e Bonyad-e Farhang-e Iran, 1347, pp. 95–6.

34. Mohammad Khan Sharaf al-Din Takkalu's governorship also signalled a phase of territorial consolidation and even expansion. In 1537–8, Shah Tahmasp I made expeditions into Qandahar, even conquering that city.

35. The Mughal empire's political evolution is a fascinating but highly complicated story. Excellent treatments can be found in John F. Richards, *The Mughal Empire*,

Cambridge: Cambridge University Press, 1996; and P. Robb, *A History of India*, London: Palgrave, 2001.

36. Abu al-Fazl Allami, *Akbar namah*, ed. and trans. H. Beveridge, Vol. I, Fasc. VIII, Calcutta: Asiatic Society of Bengal, New Series, No. 1036, 1903, p. 413.

37. Colin P. Mitchell, *The Practice of Politics in Safavid Iran, Power, Religion and Rhetoric*, London: I. B. Tauris, 2009, p. 94. The political benefits of a Mughal being in the debt of the Safavids were enticing to Shah Tahmasp and his ambitions to push his empire further east, to Qandahar.

38. The text of the *firman* can be found in Anonymous, *Majmuah, MS*, London, British Library, I. O. Islamic 379, ff. 95–102. An English translation can be found in Abu al-Fazl Allami, *Akbar namah*, pp. 418–31; and for an account of the stay, see idem, pp. 412–52.

39. Anon., *Majmuah*, f. 96; and Abu al-Fazl Allami, *Akbar namah*, p. 419.

40. Riazul Islam, *A Calendar of Documents on Indo-Persian Relations (1500–1750)*, Vol. I, Karachi: Iranian Culture Foundation, 1982, p. 78.

41. Anon., *Majmuah*, f. 93; and Abu al-Fazl Allami, *Akbar namah*, p. 421.

42. Anon., *Majmuah*, f. 93, and Abu al-Fazl Allami, *Akbar namah*, pp. 420–21.

43. The use to which Herat's Timurid *bagh*s were put in the Safavid era is addressed in an excellent article by Maria Szuppe, 'Les résidences princières de Herat: questions de continuité fonctionnelle entre les époques timouride et safavide (1ᵉ moitié du XVIᵉ siècle)', in Jean Calmard, ed., *Etudes Safavides*, Paris and Tehran: Institut Français de Recherche en Iran, Bibliothèque iranienne 39, 1993, pp. 266–86.

44. Anon., *Majmuah*, f. 98.

45. Khwandamir, *Tarikh-e Shah Ismail*, p. 213.

46. The distance was 'the flight of one arrow'.

47. John Baily, *Music of Afghanistan, Professional musicians in the city of Herat 1973–77*, London: Silk Road Books and Photos Publications, 2nd edn, 2012, p. 15.

48. Mitchell, *The Practice of Politics in Safavid Iran*, p. 94.

49. Browne, *Literary History of Persia*, Vol. 4, pp. 24–9.

50. Quoted in Mitchell, *The Practice of Politics in Safavid Iran*, p. 94.

51. See Louis Dupree, *Afghanistan*, Princeton: Princeton University Press, 1973.

52. A good contemporary account of these years can be found in Eskandar Beg Monshi, *History of Shah Abbas*, Vol. I, pp. 283–514.

53. R. N. Savory, 'Ali-Qoli Khan Shamlu', *Encyclopaedia Iranica*, http://www.iranica-online.org/articles/ali-qoli-khan-samlu-b, accessed on 2.05.2015.

54. Eskandar Monshi, *History of Shah Abbas*, Vol. I, p. 363.

55. Browne, *Literary History of Persia*, Vol. 4, p. 99.

56. The subtext for this conflict was a bitter internal Safavid–Qizilbash rivalry which in the late-1570s threatened to split the Safavid empire in two, and which effectively set Khorasan's two most significant cities, Herat and Mashhad, against each other.

57. The battle lines of this conflict are sketched out with McChesney's characteristic academic rigour and precision. R. D. McChesney, 'The Conquest of Herat 995–96/1587–88: Sources for the Study of Safavid/qizilbāsh—Shībānid/Uzbak Relations', in Jean Calmard, ed., *Etudes safavides*, Paris and Tehran: Institut Français de Recherche en Iran, Bibliothèque iranienne 39, 1993, pp. 76–84. Broadly speaking, the lines along which these conflicts ran were as follows: the Takkalu/Turcoman Qizilbash opposed the Shamlu/Ustajlu Qizilbash, and the Safavid court

in Qazvin sought to control all Qizilbash tribes by holding family members to ransom, a tactic with mixed results.

58. Audrey Burton, 'The Fall of Herat to the Uzbegs [sic] in 1588', *Iran*, Vol. 26, 1988, p. 119.
59. See McChesney, 'The Conquest of Herat', *Etudes Safavides*, pp. 93–8.
60. Ibid., pp. 93–8.
61. For an interesting account of the historiographical and chronological debates surrounding the fall of Herat to the Uzbeks, see Burton, 'The Fall of Herat to the Uzbegs in 1588'.
62. McChesney, 'The Conquest of Herat', *Etudes Safavides*, pp. 102–3.
63. There are different versions of his end, and for these, see ibid., pp. 105–6.
64. Eskandar Beg Monshi, *History of Shah Abbas*, Vol. II, pp. 559–60.
65. For a more comprehensive account of Safavid administrative and military reform during this period, see R. N. Savory, 'Abbas I', *Encyclopaedia Iranica*, at http://www.iranicaonline.org/articles/abbas-I, accessed on 18.06.2015.
66. This complicated year, the year of the Dog, 1598–9, is well documented by Eskandar Beg Monshi in *History of Shah Abbas*, Vol. II, pp. 727–76.
67. Eskandar Beg Monshi, *History of Shah Abbas*, Vol. II, pp. 752–3.
68. A. Olearius, *The Voyages and Travels of J. Albert de Mendelso (A Gentleman belonging to the Embassy, sent by the Duke of Holstein to the great Duke of Muscovy and the King of Persia) into the East Indies. Begun in the year MDCXXXVIII and finished in MDCXL. Containing a particular description of The great Mogul's Empire, the Kingdoms of Decan, Calicut, Cochim, Zeilon, Coromandel, Pegu, Siam, Cambodia, Malacca, Summatra, Java, Amboina, Banda, The Molucca's, Philippine and other Islands, Japan, the Great Kingdom of China, the Cape of Good Hope, Madagascar, etc.*, ed. and trans. John Davies, London: J. Starkey and T. Basset, 1669, p. 223.
69. Another exquisite account of Safavid Esfahan was by the seventeenth-century Italian traveller Pietro Della Valle, who wrote widely of his experiences in Safavid Esfahan and beyond. Pietro Della Valle, *Viaggi di Pietro Della Valle il pellegrino, con minuto ragguaglio di tutte le cose notabili osservate in essi: descritti da lui medesimo in 54 lettere familiari all'erudito suo amico Mario Schipano, divisi in tre parti cioè: la Turchia, la Persia e l'India. Colla vita e ritratto dell'autore. Roma 1650–1658*, Torino, 1843.
70. The English were given 'halfe the spoile of Ormus (when taken)', the other half going to the Safavids. The castle at Hormuz, too, was to be divided between Persian and English interests. See *Afghan Tribes*, Oriental Manuscripts, British Library, 1861, f. 4, IOR/G/29/1, *PRO, State Papers, Colonial East Indies*, pp. 234–9.
71. An introduction to the text can be found in Riazul Islam, 'Travelogue of Mahmud B. Amir Wali', *Journal of the Pakistan Historical Society*, Vol. XXVII, Part I, January 1979, pp. 88–120.
72. Ibid., pp. 89–90.
73. Ibid., p. 102.
74. The Safavids conquered Qandahar in 1622, beginning a competition with the Mughals, and later Abdali Pashtuns, for the city.
75. Abdullah Sani, known as Beheshti Heravi, *Nur al-mashreqain* (The Light of the Two Easts), ed. Mayel Heravi, Mashhad: Mosesse-ye chap wa entesharat-e astan-e quds rezawi, 1377/1957, p. 26.
76. The arrival of the Ottomans towards Hamadan with a certain Khusraw Pasha (whom Beheshti calls '*jahan shumi*' [bad omen of the world]) forced his departure back east towards India and back through the provinces of Farah and Sistan. The

account was not well known at the time of its writing, and as a poet Beheshti featured little in contemporary anthologies.

77. Showcasing a poet's talent for self-effacement, Beheshti devotes the longest poem to his own life story. Beheshti, *Nur al-mashreqain*, pp. 180–95.

78. Mayel Heravi, the noted twentieth-century Herati intellectual, makes this point in his introduction to the *Nur al-mashreqain*, p. 31.

79. Beheshti, *Nur al-mashreqain*, p. 196.

80. Ibid., pp. 197–8.

81. One *jerib* is approximately 144 yards, as per the Indian measurement. Given the familiarity between Herat and India at this time, it is likely that this is the measurement in mind. See F. J. Steingass, *A Comprehensive Persian-English Dictionary*, 1892, p. 361.

82. Beheshti, *Nur al-mashreqain*, p. 196.

83. Ibid., p. 199.

84. Ibid., p. 200.

85. Ibid., p. 225.

86. Beheshti was not entirely carefree on his tranquil idyll, for on one occasion he came face to face with Pashtun brigands, whom he terms *Afghanha*: most likely feuding Pashtuns who at that time plied their trade in the territories of Qandahar and those bordering present-day Afghanistan and Pakistan.

87. Noelle-Karimi, *The Pearl in its Midst*, p. 62.

88. The standard account of the decline and fall of the Safavid empire to the Afghans is Laurence Lockhart, *The Fall of the Safavi [sic] Dynasty and the Afghan Occupation of Persia*, Cambridge: Cambridge University Press, 1958. A more recent treatment of the Safavid decline can be found in Michael Axworthy's biography of Nader Shah, the seventeenth-century Persian conqueror of much of Khorasan and Iran: *The Sword of Persia, Nader Shah, from Tribal Warrior to Conquering Tyrant*, London: I. B. Tauris, 2009.

89. Sir John Chardin, *Voyages*, quoted in Lockhart, *Fall of the Safavi Dynasty*, p. 16.

90. *Cambridge History of Iran*, Vol. 6, p. 302.

91. Ibid., p. 308.

92. Quoted in Lockhart, *The Fall of the Safavi Dynasty*, p. 30.

93. This field of Pashtun anthropology and sociology is complicated and often theoretical. It is covered in detail by scholars such as James Caron, Shah Mahmoud Hanifi and Jamil Hanifi. See, for example, Shah Mahmoud Hanifi, *Connecting Histories in Afghanistan: Market Relations and State Formation on a Colonial Frontier*, Stanford: Stanford University Press, 2011; and Shah Mahmoud Hanifi, 'The Pashtun Counter-Narrative', in Amin Tarzi, Arthur E. Karell, Stephanie E. Kramer and Adam C. Seitz (eds), *Arguments for the Future of Afghanistan: Competing Narratives on Afghanistan*, Quantico: Marine Corps University Press, 2012.

94. *Afghan Tribes*, Oriental Manuscripts, British Library, 1861, f. 4.

95. Balland, 'Dorrani', *Encyclopaedia Iranica, Iranica Online*, http://www.iranicaonline.org/articles/dorrani-1, accessed on 16.06.2015.

96. R. Leech, 'An Account of the Early Abdalees', *Journal of the Asiatic Society of Bengal*, Vol. 14, No. 162, 1845, pp. 445–70. See also Mohammad Hayat Khan, *Hayat-e afghan*, trans. H. Priestly, as *Afghanistan and its Inhabitants*, Lahore, 1874.

97. Descendants of Pashtun groupings are denoted by the suffix–*zai*, meaning son of: Ahmadzai, Popalzai, Sadozai and so on. These lines are united into clans or *kheil*: Suleiman-kheil, Jani-Kheil; and these clans are themselves descended from the

four main Pashtun groupings: Abdalis, Ghilzais, Gurgusht and those who currently reside in the North West Frontier Province of Pakistan and areas of Khost
and Loya Paktia, the Karlanri.

98. Noelle-Karimi, *The Pearl in its Midst*, p. 81.
99. Nicholas Sanson, *Estat present du royaume de Perse*, Paris: La veuve de Jacques
    Langlois; Jacques Colombat, 1694, pp. 164–5.
100. Quoted in Noelle-Karimi, *The Pearl in its Midst*, p. 74.
101. George Forster, *A Journey from Bengal to England through the Northern Parts of India,
     Kashmire, Afghanistan and Persia, and into Russia, by the Caspian-Sea*, 2 vols., London:
     R. Faulder, 1798, p. 74.
102. See Noelle-Karimi, *The Pearl in its Midst*, pp. 74–83.
103. Ibid., pp. 77–8.
104. Noelle-Karimi, *The Pearl in its Midst*, p. 79.
105. Mirza Muhammad Khalil Marashi Safavi, *Majma al-tawarikh dar tarikh-e enqeraz-e
     safavieh va vaqaeh-ye baad ta sal-e 1207 hejri qamari*, ed. Abbas Eqbal Ashtiyani,
     Tehran: Sanai-e Tahuri, 1362 AH.
106. Marashi, *Majma al-tawarikh*, p. 19.
107. Ibid., p. 20.
108. Lockhart, *Fall of the Safavi Dynasty*, p. 99.
109. The best biography of Nader is the recent work by Michael Axworthy, op. cit.
110. For a good summary of this intensely complicated period, see Noelle-Karimi,
     The Pearl in its Midst, pp. 89–90.
111. Forster, *A Journey from Bengal*, p. 152.
112. *Bayan-e vaqi*, quoted in Noelle-Karimi, *The Pearl in its Midst*, p. 94.
113. See Riazul Islam, *Calendar of Documents*, pp. 102–3 for such a letter.

4. HERAT, THE KEY TO INDIA: HERAT, KHORASAN'S BROKEN PEARL,
   1747–1863

1. Michael Axworthy, *Nader Shah, Sword of Islam*, London: I. B. Tauris, 2009.
2. For an excellent biography of Ahmad Shah, see Ganda Singh, *Ahmad Shah Durrani:
   Founder of Modern Afghanistan*, Bombay: Asia Publishing House, 1979. For the assassination of Nader Shah, see Singh, *Ahmad Shah*, p. 20.
3. Ibid., p. 20.
4. Fayz Muhammad Katib Hazarah, *Siraj al-tawarikh, Vol. 1, The Saduzai Era 1747–1843*,
   trans. R. D. McChesney, Khorrami, Leiden: Brill, 2013, p. 13.
5. Some sources state that Ahmad Khan took the diamond from the finger of the
   prone Nader, but I find it hard to believe that the Persian executioners, opportunistic and hardened by battle, would not have seen fit to take such a rare jewel
   themselves.
6. Singh, *Ahmad Shah*, pp. 22–3.
7. Ahmad Khan styled himself Ahmad Shah Durrani, an appellation with unclear origins, but which is thought to have originated with the decision of the dervish to
   crown him Ahmad Shah, 'Pearl of the Age', *dur-e dowran*, and from which Ahmad
   Shah himself created 'Pearl of Pearls', *dur-e durrani*. The name of the Abdali tribe
   was thus changed to Durrani, yet despite the seemingly consensus-driven nature
   of his election, the state created by Ahmad Shah Durrani was a largely Sadozai/
   Abdali affair, sidelining Ghilzai Pashtuns, entrenching divisions between Ghilzai and
   Abdali Pashtuns which would add extra layers of contest and conflict to the Afghan

nation. For an excellent précis of the Durrani tribes in Afghanistan, see Henry C. Rawlinson, 'Report by Lieutenant (now Sir) Henry C. Rawlinson, on the Dooranee Tribes. Dated 19th April 1841', in British Library India Office Archives L/PS/20/MEMO.21.

8. For an excellent summary of Ahmad Shah's campaigns in India, see Christine Noelle-Karimi, *The Pearl in its Midst, Herat and the Mapping of Khorasan (15th-19th Centuries)*, Wien: Verlag der Österreichischen Akademie der Wissenschaften, 2013a, pp. 111–13.

9. Hazarah, *Siraj al-tawarikh*, Vol. 1, trans. McChesney, Khorrami, p. 22.

10. Another similarly opportunistic attack in 1796 on Qandahar from Herat by Mahmud Mirza resulted in the latter being exiled from Herat by his own soldiers' rebellion and heading to Mashhad where he sought refuge.

11. There are numerous good English-language accounts of this era of Afghan history, skated over in this book for reasons of length. For an excellently well researched such account, see Noelle-Karimi, *The Pearl in its Midst*, pp. 101–41.

12. George Forster, *A Journey from Bengal to England through the Northern Parts of India, Kashmire, Afghanistan and Persia, and into Russia, by the Caspian-Sea*, 2 vols., London: R. Faulder, 1798, p. 115.

13. Forster, *A Journey from Bengal*, p. 115.

14. Ibid., pp. 134–5.

15. Ibid., p. 133.

16. Ibid., pp. 133–4.

17. Ibid., p. 119.

18. Ibid., p. 131.

19. Ibid., pp. 120–1.

20. Ibid., p. 142.

21. For the best biographical account of Riyazi, see R. D. McChesney, 'Historiography in Afghanistan', in Charles Melville (ed.), *Persian Historiography*, London: I. B. Tauris, 2012, ch. 11.

22. Mohammad Yuusof Riyazi 'Heravi', *Ain al-waqaye, tarikh-e Afghanistan dar salha-ye 1207–1324 Q*, ed. Mohammad Fekrat Heravi, Tehran, 1369 AH, p. 21.

23. Riyazi, *Ain al-waqaye*, pp. 21–2.

24. There exists a large body of literature on the Qajars, ranging from E. G. Browne's masterful *A Year Amongst the Persians, Impressions as to the Life, Character & Thought of the People of Persia received during Twelve Months' Residence in that Country in the Years 1887–1888*, London: A & C Black Ltd, 1893; to more detailed works on the Constitutional Revolution which ended their hold on the Peacock Throne: in particular Abbas Amanat *Pivot of the Universe: Nasir al-Din Shah Qajar and the Iranian Monarchy, 1831–1896*, Berkeley: University of California Press, 1997; and Homa Katouzian, *The Persians: Ancient, Medieval and Modern Iran*, New Haven, MA: Yale University Press, 2010. For an excellent general account, see Nikki R. Keddie, *Qajar Iran and the Rise of Reza Khan, 1796–1925*, Costa Meesa: Mazda, 1999.

25. Aziz al-Din Fufalzai, *Durrat al-zaman fi tarikh-e Shah Zaman*, Kabul: Matbua-ye Daulati, 1958, quoted in Noelle-Karimi, *The Pearl in its Midst*, p. 199.

26. J. P. Ferrier, *History of the Afghans*, London: John Murray, 1858, p. 153.

27. Riyazi, *Ain al-waqaye*, pp. 7–9.

28. For information on his shrine, see R. Samizay, *Islamic Architecture in Herat: A Study Towards Conservation*, Kabul: Research Section of International Project for Herat Monuments, Ministry of Information and Culture, Democratic Republic of Afghanistan, 1981, pp. 50–52.

29. Hazarah, *Siraj al-tawarikh*, Vol. 1, McChesney, Khorrami, p. 135.
30. Recent studies of the period have stressed that local agency in the Great Game should be more widely acknowledged, and have doubted the validity of the use of the term Great Game for its colonialist connotations. Benjamin D. Hopkins, *The Making of Modern Afghanistan*, New York: Palgrave Macmillan, 2008.
31. For a late-nineteenth-century summary of the Great Game, see British Library India Office Archives, L/PS/20/MEMO/21, pp. 141–91.
32. Quoted in *Cambridge History of Iran*, Vol. 6, p. 377.
33. Sir Harford Jones Brydges, *An Account of the Transactions of His Majesty's Mission to the Court of Persia in the years 1807–11*, London: James Bohn, 1834, p. 221.
34. I am grateful for Melissa Neckar for this translation.
35. Peter Hopkirk, *The Great Game, On Secret Service in High Asia*, Oxford: Oxford University Press, 1991, p. 3.
36. Brydges, *An Account*, p. 225.
37. Hopkirk, *The Great Game*, p. 35.
38. G. J. Alder, 'The Key to India? Britain and the Herat Problem 1830–63, Part 1', *Middle Eastern Studies*, Vol. 10, No. 2, p. 189.
39. See Hopkirk, *The Great Game*, pp. 42–4.
40. Quoted in Alder, 'Key to India, Pt 1', p. 187.
41. *Cambridge History of Iran*, Vol. 6, p. 391.
42. For an in-depth overview of British policies in India, Afghanistan and Iran during these years, see Malcolm Yapp, *Strategies of British India, Britain, Iran and Afghanistan, 1798–1850*, Oxford: Clarendon Press, 1980.
43. Arthur Conolly, *Journey to the North of India*, 2 vols., London: Richard Bentley, 1834, Vol. II, pp. 20–21.
44. Ibid., p. 10.
45. Ibid., p. 2.
46. Ibid., p. 3.
47. Ibid., p. 3.
48. Ibid., pp. 3–4.
49. Ibid., p. 5.
50. Hazarah, Siraj al-tawarikh, McChesney, Khorrami, pp. 195–4.
51. Noelle-Karimi, *The Pearl in its Midst*, p. 225.
52. Mohan Lal, *Travels in the Punjab, Afghanistan and Turkistan, to Balk, Bokhara and Herat, and a Visit to Great Britain and Germany*, London: W. H. Allen, 1846, p. 213.
53. Ibid., p. 216.
54. Ibid., p. 268.
55. Ibid., p. 233.
56. Ibid., p. 238.
57. Ibid., p. 265.
58. Ibid., p. 239. For the Chinese diplomat in Herat, see Chapter 2.
59. Lal, *Travels*, pp. 272–3.
60. Ibid., p. 276.
61. Professor Michael Chossudovsky, 'The War is Worth Waging: Afghanistan's Vast Reserves of Minerals and Natural Gas,' *Global Research*, June 2010, at http://www.globalresearch.ca/the-war-is-worth-waging-afghanistan-s-vast-reserves-of-minerals-and-natural-gas/19769, accessed on 12.06.2016.
62. Lal, *Travels*, pp. 275–7.
63. Ibid., p. 271.

64. Ibid., p. 272.
65. Mohan Lal to MacNeil describing Herat, British Library, IOR: MSS EUR C941.
66. Lal, *Travels*, p. 213.
67. Hasan-e Fasai, *Farsmana-ye Naseri*, or, *History of Persia Under Qajar Rule*, translated from the Persian by Heribert Buse, New York: Columbia University Press, 1972, pp. 253–4.
68. Riyazi, *Ain al-waqaye*, p. 31.
69. Ibid., p. 27.
70. Riyazi, *Ain al-waqaye*, p. 28.
71. Hazarah, *Siraj al-tawarikh*, McChesney, Khorrami, pp. 226–7.
72. Ibid., p. 227.
73. Ferrier, *Afghans*, pp. 227–8.
74. Riyazi, *Ain al-waqaye*, p. 31.
75. Pottinger, quoted in John William Kaye, *A History of the War in Afghanistan*, 2 vols., London: Richard Bentley, 1857, Vol. I, p. 226.
76. Hazarah, *Siraj al-tawarikh*, McChesney, Khorrami, p. 129.
77. Ferrier, *Afghans*, pp. 229–30; see also Riyazi, *Ain al-waqaye*, p. 30.
78. McNeill to Palmerston, Camp before Herat, 11 April 1838, IOR, L/PS/9/106.
79. Mirza Atta Mohammad Shikapuri, *Nawai-ye maarek*, Kabul, 1952, p. 189.
80. Atta Mohammad, *Nawai-ye maarek*, p. 189.
81. Ferrier, *Afghans*, p. 231.
82. Pottinger, quoted in Kaye, *A History of the War in Afghanistan*, Vol. I, p. 229.
83. Ferrier, *Afghans*, p. 226.
84. Maud Diver, *The Hero of Herat, Frontier Epic in Romantic Form*, London: Constable, 1915.
85. Atta Mohammad, *Nawai-ye maarek*, p. 189.
86. Hazarah, *Siraj al-tawarikh*, Vol. 1, McChesney, Khorrami, p. 22.
87. Atta Mohammad, *Nawai-ye maarek*, p. 190.
88. Pottinger, quoted in Kaye, *A History of the War in Afghanistan*, Vol. I, pp. 214–15.
89. Hopkirk, *The Great Game*, p. 176; Kaye, *A History of the War in Afghanistan*, Vol. I, p. 223.
90. McNeill to Pottinger, June 3 1838, IOR, L/PS/9/106.
91. Ibid.
92. Pottinger, quoted in Kaye, *A History of the War in Afghanistan*, Vol. I, p. 232.
93. An excellent account of the 1838 negotiations can be found in Kaye, *A History of the War in Afghanistan*, Vol. I, pp. 250–99.
94. British actions were constrained by Article 9 of an 1814 Anglo-Persian treaty which denied the British government the right to get involved with either of the warring parties unless their mediation to bring about peace were official requested by both parties. In 1837 this criterion was clearly not satisfied.
95. Pottinger, quoted in Kaye, *A History of the War in Afghanistan*, Vol. I, pp. 247–9.
96. Hazarah, *Siraj al-tawarikh*, McChesney, Khorrami, p. 218.
97. 19 March 1838, IOR, L/PS/9/106.
98. McNeill to Palmerston, Camp before Herat, 12 May 1838, IOR, L/PS/9/106.
99. Count Simonitch, to Mohammad Shah Qajar, concerning 'The intentions of Mohammad Shah towards conquering Herat and the Russian request that such an intention be put off', July 1837, in *Gazideh-ye asnad-e siasi-ye Iran wa Afghanistan, Jeld-e awal, Massaleh-ye Herat dar ahdMohammad Shah Qajar* [A Selection of Political Documents of Iran and Afghanistan, Vol. 1, Relating to issues pertaining to Herat

during the reign of Mohammad Shah Qajar], ed. Mohammad Nader Nasir Moqaddam, Tehran: Vahed Nashr-e Asnad, 1374, p. 20.

100. See Mohammad Ali Bahmani Qajar, *Iran wa Afghanistan: az yekganegi ta tayin-e marzha-ye siasi* (Iran and Afghanistan: From Unity to the Defining of Political Boundaries), Tehran: Markaz-e Asnad-e Tarikh-e Diplomasi, 1385 AH.
101. Ferrier, *Afghans*, p. 217.
102. Pottinger, quoted in Kaye, *A History of the War in Afghanistan*, Vol. I, p. 256.
103. Riyazi, *Ain al-waqaye*, pp. 27–8.
104. Ibid., p. 29.
105. McNeill to Palmerston, Camp before Herat, 11 April 1838, IOR, L/PS/9/106.
106. McNeill to Palmerston, Camp before Herat, 12 May 1838, IOR, L/PS/9/106.
107. Ibid.
108. Hazarah, *Siraj al-tawarikh*, McChesney, Khorrami, p. 242.
109. McNeill to Persian Ministers, 1 May 1838, IOR, L/PS/9/106.
110. McNeill to Palmerston, Mashhad, 25 June 1838 IOR, L/PS/9/106.
111. Kaye, *A History of the War in Afghanistan*, Vol. I, p. 282.
112. Ibid., p. 281.
113. Fasai, *Farsnama*, p. 258.
114. Stoddart to McNeill, Camp near Herat, 8 a.m., 9 September 1838, IOR, L/PS/9/108.
115. Stoddart to McNeill, quoted in Kaye, *A History of the War in Afghanistan*, Vol. I, p. 285.
116. Atta Mohammad, *Nawai-ye maarek*, p. 190.
117. Riyazi, *Ain al-waqaye*, p. 35.
118. Todd to Macnaghten, Herat, 2 October 1839, L/PS/5/144.
119. Ibid.
120. Ibid.
121. Ferrier, *Afghans*, p. 258.
122. In particular, see Kaye, *War in Afghanistan*; William Dalrymple, *Return of a King*, London: Bloomsbury, 2011; and J. A. Norris, *The First Afghan War 1838–1842*, Cambridge: Cambridge University Press, 1967.
123. Ranjit Singh and his fearsome Sikh armies had seized Multan in 1810, Kashmir in 1819, Peshawar in 1823.
124. Conolly, *Journey to the North of India*, Vol. II, p. 13.
125. For Burnes' extensive account of his 1831–2 travels in Central Asia and 'into Bokhara [*sic*]', see Lieut. Alexander Burnes, *Travels into Bokhara: Containing the Narrative of a Voyage on the Indus from the Sea to Lahore, with Presents from the King of Great Britain; And an Account of a Journey from India to Cabool, Tartary, and Persia. Performed by the order of the Supreme Government of India, in the years 1831, 32 and 33, Three Volumes*, London: John Murray, MDCCCXXXV. For an edited version, see Kathleen Hopkirk's excellent edition, Alexander Burnes, *Travels into Bokhara*, ed. Kathleen Hopkirk, London: Eland, 2012. For his later expeditions to Kabul of 1836–8, see Lieut. Col. Sir Alexander Burnes, *Cabool, A Personal Narrative of a Journey to and Residence in That City, in the years 1836, 7, and 8*, Philadelphia: Carey and Hart, 1843.
126. The plan was made official by the Simla Manifesto of 1 October 1839.
127. Hazarah, *Siraj al-tawarikh*, McChesney, Khorrami, p. 232.
128. Quoted in Hopkirk, *The Great Game*, pp. 190–91.
129. Hopkirk, *The Great Game*, p. 192.

130. Hazarah, *Siraj al-tawarikh*, McChesney, Khorrami, p. 252.
131. Riyazi, *Ain al-waqaye*, p. 37.
132. Ferrier, *Afghans*, p. 407.
133. Todd to Macnaghten, Herat, 2 October 1839, L/PS/5/144.
134. Ferrier, *Afghans*, p. 259.
135. Kamran Mirza to Mohammad Shah, Spring 1841, L/PS/9/119.
136. Kamran Shah to Shah of Persia, 17 June 1840, L/PS/9/115.
137. Copy of a letter from Yar Mohammad Khan to Qajar King, Spring 1841, L/PS/9/119.
138. Memorandum by McNeill, 30 November 1841, L/PS/9/120.
139. Ferrier, *Afghans*, p. 408.
140. Ibid., p. 437.
141. Memorandum on affairs at Herat, Sheil, 30 November 1841, L/PS/9/120.
142. Todd to Secret Committee, 8 December 1840, L/PS/9/117.
143. Hazarah, *Siraj al-tawarikh*, McChesney, Khorrami, p. 325.
144. Todd to Secret Committee, 14 November 1840, L/PS/9/117.
145. Abbott to Todd, Khiva, 14 February 1840, L/PS/9/115.
146. Riyazi, *Ain al-waqaye*, p. 37.
147. For an account of the killing of Macnaghten, the English army's ill-fated march to Jalalabad, the massacre along the way and its rendering in an Afghan source, see Hazarah, *Siraj al-tawarikh*, McChesney, Khorrami, pp. 293–305.
148. Hazarah, *Siraj al-tawarikh*, McChesney, Khorrami, pp. 308–10.
149. Sheil to Palmerston, 17 September 1851, L/PS/20/A7/VOL/2.
150. Hazarah, *Siraj al-tawarikh*, McChesney, Khorrami, p. 326.
151. Atta, *Nawa-e maarek*, p. 190.
152. Ferrier, *Afghans*, p. 479.
153. Ferrier, *Afghans*, p. 481.
154. Lieutenant Colonel Lewis Pelly, *Journal of a Journey from Persia to India, through Herat and Candahar*, Bombay: Education Society's Press, 1866, p. 68.
155. Sheil to the Sedr Azim, 7 February 1852, L/PS/20/A7/VOL/2.
156. Riyazi, *Ain al-waqaye*, p. 54.
157. Ibid., p. 56.
158. Lieutenant Sheil to Viscount Palmerston, 18 September 1851, L/PS/20/A7/VOL/2.
159. Riyazi, *Ain al-waqaye*, p. 55.
160. Sheil to Seyd Mahomed Khan, February 1853, L/PS/20/A7/VOL/2.
161. *Engagement Contracted by the Persian Government relative to Herat*, 25 January 1853, Inclosure 5 in No. 25, L/PS/20/A7/VOL/2.
162. Quoted in Barbara English, *John Company's Last War*, London: Collins, 1971.
163. Riyazi, *Ain al-waqaye*, p. 60.
164. Ibid., p. 60.
165. A letter from Essa Khan Bardurrani to a Pashtun amir, quoted in David Charles Champagne, 'The Afghan Iranian Conflict over Herat Province and European Intervention 1796–1863: A Reinterpretation', PhD diss., Austin, TX: University of Texas, p. 374.
166. Stevens to Clarendon, Tehran, 8 October 1856, L/PS/20/A7/VOL/2.
167. Noelle-Karimi, *The Pearl in its Midst*, p. 163.
168. Essan Khan to Mr Murray, 12 August 1856, L/PS/20/A7/VOL/2.
169. Acting-Commissioner in Scinde to Lord Elphinstone, Kurrachee, 29 May 1856, L/PS/20/A7/VOL/2.

170. Stevens to Clarendon, Tehran, 2 October 1856, L/PS/20/A7/VOL/2.
171. Riyazi, *Ain al-waqaye*, p. 61. See also J. F. Standish, 'The Persian War of 1856–1857', *Middle Eastern Studies*, Vol. 3, 1966, pp. 28–9.
172. Stevens to Clarendon, Tehran, 8 October 1856, L/PS/20/A7/VOL/2.
173. Stevens to Earl of Clarendon, Camp Near Tehran, 22 June 1856, L/PS/20/A7/VOL/2.
174. Riyazi, *Ain al-waqaye*, p. 63.
175. Lieutenant-Colonel Edwardes to the Secretary to the Chief Commissioner for the Punjab, Camp Nowshera, 16 May 1856, L/PS/20/A7/VOL/2.
176. J. Calmard, 'Anglo-Persian War, 1856–7', *Encyclopaedia Iranica*, Iranica Online, at http://www.iranicaonline.org/articles/anglo-persian-war-1856–7, accessed on 17.9.2015.
177. Earl of Clarendon to the Sedr Azim, Foreign Office, 11 July 1856, L/PS/20/A7/VOL/2.
178. A text of the treaty can be found in the British Library, Treaty of Peace with Persia, 4 March 1857, L/PS/20/C2.
179. A Persian Minister, *Herat and Great Britain*, London: W. H. Allen, 1880, p. 9.
180. Riyazi, *Ain al-waqaye*, p. 66.
181. Ibid., p. 68.
182. Quoted in Mohammad Ali Bahmani Qajar, *Iran wa Afghanistan: az yekgani to ta'in-e marzha-ye siasi* (Iran and Afghanistan: From Unity to the Defining of Political Boundaries), Tehran: Markaz-e Asnad-e Tarikh-e Diplomasi, 1385 AH, p. 108.
183. 'Note by Mr. Willoughby, Abstract of Despatches and Memoranda on Asiatic Politics and European Diplomacy in the countries between India and Russia, and especially in Afghanistan; and as to the establishment of a British Agent at Herat, to watch the progress of events on the Perso-Afghan frontier and in other parts of Central Asia; and further as to the continuance of the subsidy to Dost Muhammmad', L/PS/18/C3.
184. See G. J. Alder, 'The Key to India? Britain and the Herat Problem, 1830–1863, Part II', *Middle Eastern Studies*, Vol. 10, No. 3, 1974, pp. 287–311.
185. Pelly to Allison, Herat, 11 October 1860, L/PS/9/161.
186. Pelly to Allison, Herat, 11 October 1860, L/PS/9/161.
187. Pelly to Canning, Herat, 27 October 1860, L/PS/9/161.
188. Ibid.
189. Pelly, *Journal of a Journey*, p. 57.
190. Iraj Afshar, *Shasht o Chahar sanad dar barayae waqeah-e Herat wa Khorasan* (64 documents relating to the events of Herat and Khorasan), Tehran: Daneshiar-e Daneshgah-e Tehran, 1349 AH, p. 4.
191. Ibid., p. 5.
192. Riyazi, *Ain al-waqaye*, p. 69.
193. Ibid., p. 71.
194. Qajar, *Iran wa Afghanistan*, pp. 269–72.
195. Quoted in Qajar, *Iran wa Afghanistan*, p. 129.
196. Qajar, *Iran wa Afghanistan*, pp. 124–5.
197. 15 Shaban 1279, from Nasr al-Din Shah Qajar to Nasr al-Din Molk, Iranian ambassador in London, concerning a 'Handwritten note from Nasr al-Din Shah to Nasr al-Din Molk regarding the discussions with the English authorities.' Qajar, *Iran wa Afghanistan*, p. 272.
198. See Qajar, *Iran wa Afghanistan*, pp. 126–7.

199. 14 Safar 1279, from Mirza Sayyed Khan, Foreign Minister, to Mirza Hossein Khan, Special Qajar Representative in London, in Qajar, *Iran wa Afghanistan*, p. 260.
200. See 15 Shaban 1279, from the Iranian Foreign Minister to Nasr al-Din Molk, Iranian ambassador in London, concerning 'An Order from the Foreign Ministry to Nasr al-Din Molk Concerning Discussions with the English Government about Dost Mohammad's Attack on Herat'. Qajar, *Iran wa Afghanistan*, p. 271.
201. 8 Ramazan 1274, Iranian Foreign Ministry to Farakh Khan Amin al-Molk, concerning 'Political Advice to the Authorities of the English Government about Afghanistan', Qajar, *Iran wa Afghanistan*, p. 247.
202. Qajar, *Iran wa Afghanistan*, p. 251.
203. Riyazi, *Ain al-waqaye*, p. 73.
204. Arminius Vambéry, *Travels in Central Asia*, London: John Murray, 1864, p. 296.

5. HERAT IN AN EMERGING AFGHANISTAN: ISOLATED, SLEEPY AND REVOLUTIONARY, 1863–1978

1. For an exceptionally detailed and interesting look at Afghanistan's railways, see Andrew Grantham, *Railways of Afghanistan*, at http://www.andrewgrantham.co.uk/afghanistan/, accessed on 27.1.2016.
2. Vartan Gregorian, *The Emergence of Modern Afghanistan: Politics of Reform and Modernization, 1880–1946*, Stanford, CA: Stanford University Press, 1969, p. 148.
3. After death of Dost Mohammad in 1863, his son Shir Ali Khan set off from Herat for Kabul to take possession of the capital, leaving Yaqub Khan, his eldest son, as governor of Herat, tipping his hat to Safavid policies perhaps. In 1867 a royal uncle, Afzal Khan, took Herat; Shir Ali became a fugitive to the north and Yaqub headed south. Yet Yaqub, through force of arms and gold, retook Herat in 1868, marking the start of his reign. A grandson of Dost Mohammad Khan, Ayyub Khan, was to flit between Afghanistan and Iran, inflicting defeats here and there, one in particular to the British at the Battle of Maiwand in 1879.
4. 'Afghanistan', British Library India Office Archives, L/PS/18/A.21–42, p. 7.
5. 12 June 1880, Sir H. Rawlinson, L/PS/18, A.21–42, p. 7.
6. A Persian Minister, *Herat and Great Britain*, London: W. H. Allen, 1880, p. 4.
7. Thomson to Marquis Salisbury, Tehran, December 1878, in 'Further Correspondence respecting Affairs in Central Asia, 1879', British Library, BP 24/(9).(3).
8. See L/PS/20/MEMO.21.
9. For an Afghan account of these years, see Mohammad Yuusof Riyazi 'Heravi', *Ayn al-waqaye, Tarikh-e Afghanistan dar salha-ye 1207–1324 Q*, ed. Mohammad Fekrat Heravi, Tehran, 1369 AH, pp. 111–19.
10. Quoted in Thomas Barfield, *Afghanistan, A Cultural and Political History*, Princeton: Princeton University Press, 2010, p. 142.
11. The Battle of Maiwand is a sacred part of Afghan history; nearly all the Taliban fighters I met never hesitated to remind me of this Afghan victory against the infidel English. It was a battle in which the actions of a young girl, Malala, shamed the Afghan men to deeds of military bravery and heroism.
12. Frank A. Martin, *Under the Absolute Amir of Afghanistan*, New Delhi: Bhavana Books & Prints, 2000, pp. 161–2.
13. D. P. Singhal, *India and Afghanistan, 1876–1907: A Study in Diplomatic Relations*, Brisbane: University of Queensland Press, 1963, p. 107.

14. Charles Marvin, *Russians at the Gates of Herat*, London: Frederick Warne, 1885, p. 58.
15. Major Charles E. Yate, *Northern Afghanistan, or Letters from the Afghan Boundary Commission*, Edinburgh: William Blackwood and Sons, 1888, p. 2.
16. Ibid., p. 16.
17. Ibid., p. 11.
18. 'Correspondence respecting the demarcation of the North-Western Frontier of Afghanistan from the Heri Rud to the Oxus', L/PS/18, A.48–53, p. 4.
19. Yate, *Northern Afghanistan*, p. 14.
20. Ibid., p. 14.
21. Ibid., pp. 20–21.
22. Ibid., p. 28.
23. Ibid., p. 29.
24. Riyazi, *Ain al-waqaye*, p. 171.
25. Captain Durand, 30 May 1885, L/PS/20/MEMO/13.
26. Singhal, *India and Afghanistan*, p. 120.
27. Ibid., p. 121.
28. Riazi, *Ain al-waqaye*, p. 164.
29. Riyazi, *Ain al-waqaye*, p. 174.
30. Ibid., p. 174.
31. Ibid., p. 172.
32. Lieutenant Arthur C. Yate, *England and Russia face to face: Travels with the Afghan Boundary Commission*, London: William Blackwood, 1887, p. 330.
33. Lumsden to Granville, 4 May 1885, L/PS/20/MEMO/13.
34. Surgeon-Lieutenant Colonel T. S. Weir, *From India to the Caspian, or, Journeys with and after the Afghan Boundary Commission*, Bombay: Times of India, 1893, p. 104.
35. Yate, *Northern Afghanistan*, p. 77.
36. See the maps in Yate, *Northern Afghanistan* for the exact routes of the different boundaries.
37. Takki Khan Mirza Mohammad, *Report on the City and Province of Herat*, 1885, IOL, L/PS/7/49, pp. 1175–1270.
38. Yate, *Northern Afghanistan*, p. 16.
39. Riyazi, *Ain al-waqaye*, p. 179.
40. Nancy Hatch Dupree, *Afghanistan, An Historical Guide*, Kabul: Afghan Air Authority, Afghan Tourist Organization, 1970, p. 180.
41. Afghan Boundary Commission, *18 plates of ornamental tiles collected by the Afghan Boundary Commission*, India: Afghan Boundary Commission, publication date unknown.
42. Robert Byron, *Road to Oxiana*, 1937; London: Pimlico edition, 2004, p. 96.
43. Persian Minister, *Herat and Great Britain*, p. 15.
44. Major Lumsden's Report, 1859, IOR, L/PS/18/C3, p. 11.
45. Quoted in Gregorian, *Modern Afghanistan*, p. 187.
46. Gregorian, *Modern Afghanistan*, p. 248.
47. See Abdul Rasoul Rahin, *Matbuat-e Afghanistan, az shams al-nazar ta jomhuriyat, 1863–1973* (The History of Afghanistan's Media, from *Shams al-nazar* to a republic), Kabul: Shurah-ye farhangi-ye Afghanistan, 2008.
48. Gregorian, *Modern Afghanistan*, p. 170.
49. May Schinasi, *Afghanistan at the Beginning of the Twentieth Century: Nationalism and Journalism in Afghanistan, A study of Seraj ul-akhbar (1911–1918)*, Naples: Istituto Universitario Orientale, 1979, p. 35.

50. For an extremely comprehensive and eloquent account of the publication of *Siraj al-Akhbar*, see Rahin, *Matbuat-e Afghanistan*, pp. 111–214.
51. Gregorian, *Modern Afghanistan*, p. 171.
52. Quoted in Gregorian, *Modern Afghanistan*, p. 170.
53. 'Herat', *Siraj al-Akbar*, 17 March 1915, 4th Year, No. 13, p. 3.
54. Herat Agent to Consul-General, Mashhad, August 1904, L/PS/18/C29, p. 141.
55. Rahin, *Tarikh-e matbuat*, p. 90.
56. Ursula Sims-Williams, 'The Afghan Newspaper Siraj al-Akhbar', *Bulletin (British Society for Middle Eastern Studies)*, Vol. 7, No. 2, 1980, pp. 118–22.
57. *Harper's Weekly*, 11 December 1915, quoted in Gregorian, *Modern Afghanistan*, p. 216.
58. The best account of this scheme can be found in Peter Hopkirk's *On Secret Service East of Constantinople: The Plot to Bring Down the British Empire*, London: John Murray, 1994. See also Thomas L. Hughes, 'The German Mission to Afghanistan, 1915–16', *German Studies Review*, Vol. 25, No. 3, 2002, pp. 447–76. See also Jules Stewart, *The Kaiser's Secret Mission to Kabul*, London: I. B. Tauris, 2014.
59. Hughes, 'The German Mission to Afghanistan, 1915–16', p. 458.
60. Ibid., p. 463.
61. Ibid., p. 463.
62. Mir Mohammad Sadiq Farhangi, *Afghanistan dar panj qarn ahker, jeld-e awal* (Afghanistan in the last five centuries, Vol. 1), Mashhad: Entesharat-e darakhshash, 1371 AH, p. 461.
63. Oscar von Niedermayer and Ernst Diez, *Afghanistan, Bearbeitet von Oscar Von Niedermayer und Ernst Diez*, Leipzig: Verlag Karl W. Hiersemann, 1924, with 243 photogravure plates.
64. L/PS/11/157/p. 5815/1919.
65. For the Third Anglo-Afghan War and the Treaty of Rawalpindi, see C. U. Aitchison, *A Collection of Treaties, Engagements and Sanads* XIII: *Persia and Afghanistan*, Calcutta, 1933; and *The Third Afghan War, 1919. Official Account*, Calcutta, 1926.
66. *Ettefaq-e Islam* underwent a brief name change, to the more combative title of *Jarida-ye Fariad* (Scream Publication), but after one year it reverted to its current title, which it has kept since then.
67. See Nassereddin Parvin, 'Ettefaq-e Eslam', *Encyclopaedia Iranica*, Vol. IX, 15 December 1998, Fasc. 1, p. 1.
68. Rahin, *Matbuat-e Afghanistan*, p. 254.
69. Ibid., p. 256.
70. See Rahin, *Matbuat-e Afghanistan*.
71. Ibid., p. 234.
72. Ibid., p. 270.
73. Ibid., p. 271.
74. For further reforms undertaken under Amanullah Khan, see Gregorian, *Modern Afghanistan*, pp. 234–56.
75. Gregorian, *Modern Afghanistan*, p. 333.
76. For a highly entertaining, if possibly embellished, account of his reign, see Amir Habibullah Kalakani, *My Life: From Brigand to King*, London: Octagon Press, 1990. Another account of this period, equally excitable and fascinating, is Rhea Talley-Stewart, *Fire in Afghanistan, 1914–29, Faith Hope and the British Empire*, London: Doubleday, 1973.
77. Gregorian, *Afghanistan*, p. 280.

78. Rahin, *Matbuat-e Afghanistan*, p. 291.
79. I am eternally grateful to Khanom-e Ettehadieh for giving me a copy of these diaries when I was in Tehran. Baqer Kazemi (Mohazab al Dowleh), *Yaddashtha-ye az zendegi-ye Baqer Kazemi, Jeld-e sewom* (The Memoirs of Baqer Kazemi, Vol. 3), ed. Dr Daoud Kazemi and Mansoureh Ettehadieh (Nezam Mafi), Tehran: Nashrat Tarikh-e Iran, 1390/2011, p. 10.
80. Kazemi, *Yaddashtha*, p. 43.
81. Ibid., p. 40.
82. Ibid., pp. 40–41.
83. Ibid., p. 49.
84. Ibid., p. 80.
85. Ibid., p. 81.
86. Ibid., p. 49.
87. Ibid., p. 52.
88. Ibid., p. 80.
89. Ibid., p. 83.
90. Ibid., p. 153.
91. Ibid., p. 155.
92. Ibid., p. 52.
93. Ibid., pp. 100–101.
94. Ibid., p. 93.
95. Ibid., p. 104.
96. Ibid., pp. 100–103.
97. Ibid., p. 103.
98. Ibid., p. 106.
99. Ibid., p. 152.
100. A. L. P. Burdett, ed., *Afghanistan Strategic Intelligence, British Records, 1919–1970, Vol. 2: 1928–1939, From the End of the Civil War to the Declaration of Neutrality in World War Two*, Chippenham: Archive Editions, 2002, p. 355.
101. Burdett, *Afghanistan Strategic Intelligence*, Vol. 2, p. 355.
102. Ibid., p. 359.
103. For a good summary of Nader Shah's reign, see May Schinasi, 'Mohammad Nader Shah', *Encyclopaedia Iranica*, 7 April 2008, at http://www.iranicaonline.org/articles/mohammad-nader-shah-king-of-afghanistan, accessed on 24.11.2015.
104. Byron, *Road to Oxiana*, p. 88.
105. Ibid., p. 87.
106. Byron, *Road to Oxiana*, p. 88. Nicholas Shakespeare, *Bruce Chatwin*, London: Harvill, 1999, p. 149.
107. Byron, *Road to Oxiana*, p. 251.
108. Sayyed Qasem Rishtiya, ed., *Salnamah-ye Kabul, 1316/1937–8*, Kabul: Motebah-ye omoumi-ye Kabul, 1938, plates after p. 128.
109. Rahin, *Matbuat-e Afghanistan*, pp. 348–9.
110. Interviews in Herat, February 2014.
111. Interview with John and Veronica Baily, Brighton, November 2015.
112. National Archives, *Note by Mr Franklin on Conditions in Herat*, 21 March 1952, FO 371/100962.
113. Ibid.
114. Interview with John Baily, Brighton, November 2015.
115. Dervla Murphy, *Full Tilt, Ireland to India with a Bicycle*, London: Eland, 2010, p. 45.

116. Peter Levi, *The Light Garden of the Angel King*, London: Eland, 2013, p. 100.

117. Levi, *Light Garden*, p. 103.

118. *Kabul Times*, Herat, 2 May 1973, p. 3.

119. Nancy Hatch Dupree, *Afghanistan*, pp. 243–69.

120. For more information on the coup, see Barfield, *Afghanistan*, pp. 195–225. See also Amin Saikal, *Modern Afghanistan, A History of Struggle and Survival*, I. B. Tauris, London: 2012, p. 175.

121. Safa Akhwan, ed., *Tarikh-e Shafaye-e Afghanistan (1900–1992)* (Oral History of Afghanistan [1900–1992]), Tehran: Markaz-e Asnad wa Tarikh-e Diplomasy, 1389 AH, p. 122.

122. Barfield, *Afghanistan*, p. 215.

123. Interview with Hedayatullah in Herat, February 2014.

124. For a brief summary of the speech, as per Wikileaks' *Kissinger Files*, see https://wikileaks.org/plusd/cables/1975KABUL02834_b.html, accessed on 18.6.2015.

125. Saikal, *Modern Afghanistan*, p. 181.

126. The film can be seen at https://www.youtube.com/watch?v=BMY E83DJU4Q, accessed on 4.6.2015.

127. John Baily, *The Herat Trilogy*, *The Cycle of Music in Herat*, author's collection.

128. Shola-ye Jawed (The Eternal Flame) was the name for the quickly splitting Maoist movement which is sometimes referred to as Sazman-e Jawanan-e Mutaraqi (SaJaM, Progressive Youth Organisation) or Jamiat-e Dimukrasi-ye Nawin (New Democracy Movement, a reference to Mao Zedong's concept of 'new democracy'). *Shola-ye Jawed* was the title of the movement's short-lived periodical, founded in April 1968. See Niamatullah Ibrahimi, 'Ideology without Leadership: The Rise and Decline of Maoism in Afghanistan', Afghan Analysts Network, at http://www.afghanistan-analysts.org/wp-content/uploads/downloads/2012/09/NIbr-Maoists-final.pdf, accessed on 12.3.2015.

129. Steve Galster, *Afghanistan: the Making of US Policy, 1973–1990*, National Security Archive, Vol. II: Afghanistan: Lessons from the last war, 9 October 2001, at http://www2.gwu.edu/~nsarchiv/NSAEBB/NSAEBB57/essay.html#docs, accessed on 19.9.2014.

130. Interviews in Herat, February 2014 and June 2014.

131. Abdul Samad Ghaus, *The Fall of Afghanistan: An Insider's Account*, London: Pergamon-Brassey's Ltd, 1988, pp. 179–80. Abdul Samad Ghaus' analysis and retelling of this period is excellent for its detail and authenticity.

6. HERAT IN A TIME OF LEFTISTS, ISLAMISTS AND OPPORTUNISTS, 1978–2001

1. Olivier Roy, *Islam and Resistance in Afghanistan*, 2nd edn, Cambridge: Cambridge University Press, 1990, p. 34.

2. Ghulam Muradov, 'The Democratic Republic of Afghanistan: A New Stage of the April Revolution', *Afghanistan: Past and Present*, Moscow: Oriental Studies in the USSR, No. 3, 1981, p. 180.

3. 'Remnants of Monarchy Wiped', *Kabul Times*, Vol. XVII, No. 33, 4 May 1978, p. 1.

4. Mark Urban, *War in Afghanistan*, London: Macmillan, 1990, p. 12; and Ahmad Shah Farzan, *Qiyam-e Herat* (Herat's Uprising), Mashhad: Entesharat-e Farbad, 1995, p. 24.

5. Interviews in Herat, February 2014.

6. See Roy, *Islam and Resistance in Afghanistan*, p. 89.

7. For an English translation of the decrees, see Louis Dupree, *Red Flag over the Hindu-Kush*, Part 3, American Universities Field Staff Report, South Asia Series, 1980.

8. Interviews in Herat, February 2014.

9. Farzan, *Qiyam-e Herat*, p. 25.

10. 'Afghan People Unanimous in Supporting Revolution', *Kabul Times*, Vol. XVII, No. 63, Saturday 10 June 1978, 20 Jauza 1357 SH, p. 1.

11. Farzan, *Qiyam-e Herat*, p. 25.

12. Interviews in Herat, February 2014.

13. Interviews in Herat, January 2014.

14. Amnesty International, *Violations of Human Rights and Fundamental Freedoms in the Democratic Republic of Afghanistan* (AI Index ASA 11/04/79), and Olivier Roy. Despite the release in 2013 of a document of nearly 5,000 names of those executed under the Taraki and Amin regime, there is no official recognition of the scale of this slaughter; families to this day remain unaware of the fate of their loved ones. Whilst the majority of reports from the time focus on the abuses which occurred in Pul-e Charkhi, Afghanistan's largest prison located just outside Kabul, reading accounts of Herat's prisons also gives one a vivid and often graphic impression of the Khalqi regime's atrocities. For an excellent article on the publication of this list and the legacy of torture in Afghanistan, see Kate Clark, 'Death List Published: families of disappeared end a 30 year wait for news', 26 September 2013, Afghan Analysts Network, at https://www.afghanistan-analysts.org/death-list-published-families-of-disappeared-end-a-30-year-wait-for-news/, accessed on 19.9.2014.

15. Interview in Herat, February 2014.

16. Interviews in Herat, January 2014.

17. The most comprehensive account of the uprising is found in Farzan's *Qiyam-e Herat*, and English readers should look especially at Radek Sikorski, *Dust of the Saints: A Journey to Herat in a Time of War*, London: Chatto & Windus, 1989, pp. 222–36 for an account which stresses the Islamist nature of the rising and places Ismail Khan at the centre of the military response.

18. Farzan, *Qiyam-e Herat*, p. 43.

19. Ibid., pp. 44–51, and interviews in Herat, January 2014.

20. Farzan, *Qiyam-e Herat*, p. 60.

21. Sikorski, *Dust of the Saints*, p. 124.

22. Interviews in Herat, February 2014.

23. Rodric Braithwaite, *Afgantsy: The Russians in Afghanistan, 1979–89*, London: Profile Books, 2011, p. 45.

24. Farzan, *Qiyam-e Herat*, p. 68.

25. Interview with Hedayatullah, ICRC offices, Herat, January 2014.

26. Interview with Hajji Sayyed Wahhab Qattali, Herat, January 2014.

27. Interviews in Herat, January 2014.

28. Farzan, *Qiyam-e Herat*, p. 89.

29. Interviews in Herat, January 2014.

30. Sikorski, *Dust of the Saints*, p. 229.

31. Ibid., p. 229.

32. Farzan, *Qiyam-e Herat*, p. 98.

33. Ibid. p. 98.

34. 'Concerning the Situation in "A", New Russian Evidence on the Soviet Intervention in Afghanistan', in 'Documents on the Soviet Invasion of Afghanistan, e-Dossier No. 4', *Cold War International History Project*, Woodrow Wilson International Centre for Scholars, Washington, DC, November 2001 (hereafter, 'E-Dossier'), at http://

www.wilsoncenter.org/sites/default/files/e-dossier_4.pdf, pp. 26, 32, accessed on 8.12.13. For an excellent account of the conflict from a Soviet vantage point, see Braithwaite, *Afgantsy*.

35. Farzan, *Qiyam-e Herat*, p. 101.
36. Giles Dorronsoro, *Revolution Unending: Afghanistan 1979 to the Present*, translated from the French by John King, London: Hurst & Co., 2005, p. 100.
37. 'E-Dossier', p. 137.
38. Ibid., p. 32.
39. Ibid., pp. 26, 37.
40. Ibid., p. 40.
41. Ibid., p. 41.
42. Ibid., p. 41.
43. It is interesting that many of the Soviet and PDPA worries at this moment saw China as a party of real danger in funding and arming the Mujahideen, a fact which is often overlooked in Western analysis of this period, and most likely suggests the importance that policy-makers attached to the Maoist group Shola-ye Jawid, whose presence in Herat was significant during this time.
44. 'E-Dossier', p. 41.
45. The date of this is disputed, but referring to the Politburo discussion of 22 March, in which Kosygin states that Herat was then 'more or less' under government control, then 21 March makes sense as a date for the arrival of government troops. 'E-Dossier', p. 45.
46. The 4th and 15th Divisions, stationed at Pul-e Charkhi in Kabul, had been detailed to put down the uprising, but such was the seriousness and urgency of the situation that soldiers were sent from Qandahar to make sure that the rebels' hold on the city did not become permanent.
47. Interview with Ismail Khan, Herat, February 2014.
48. Dorronsoro, *Revolution Unending*, p. 101.
49. Anthony Hyman, *Afghanistan under Soviet Domination, 1964–83*, London: Macmillan, 1984, p. 127.
50. *Kabul Times*, 9 April 1979, p. 1.
51. Interview with Nik Siyar, Herat, January 2014.
52. Sayyed Sharif Yosoufi, *Qiyam-e Golgun-e Kafnan-e 24 Hout-e Herat* (The Blood-Soaked Uprising of Herat of 24th Hout), Kabul, 1985, p. 7.
53. 'E-Dossier', p. 33.
54. Farzan, *Qiyam-e Herat*, p. 80.
55. For the Russian take on these events, see 'E-Dossier', p. 49.
56. See Farzan, *Qiyam-e Herat*, pp. 138–42.
57. The first backward step in this argument was taken by the government: almost immediately concessions were made to Islam. Babrak Karmal's speeches embraced Islamic phrases, and attempts were made to claw back an ideological advantage through condemnation of the Khalqi regime's violent oppression.
58. For an impassioned denunciation of KHAD's oppression in Herat and more on this incident, see Farzan, *Qiyam-e Herat*, pp. 136–42.
59. 'E-Dossier', pp. 62–8. Much as the Soviet hierarchy had feared in the hectic days after Herat's *qiyam*, the world's reaction to their invasion of Afghanistan was unanimous in its condemnation. The UN Security Council confirmed this by passing a resolution calling for the immediate and unconditional withdrawal of Soviet troops, and an emergency session on 14 January 1980 voted overwhelmingly in favour of an immediate Soviet withdrawal.

60. Antonio Giustozzi, 'Genesis of a "Prince": the rise of Ismail Khan in western Afghanistan, 1979–1992', Crisis States Research Centre, LSE, September 2006, p. 5.
61. Interviews in Herat, January 2014.
62. See also Farzan, *Qiyam-e Herat*, pp. 162–72, for a more florid account of Soviet military tactics and their consequences.
63. National Committee for Human Rights in Afghanistan, *Russia's Barbarism in Afghanistan*, Vol. II, July 1985, Peshawar, p. 66.
64. Ibid., p. 66.
65. *Afghan News*, A Biweekly Bulletin of Jami'at Islami Afghanistan, Vol. 1, 1985, p. 5.
66. Ibid., p. 5.
67. Craig M. Karp, 'The War in Afghanistan', in *Foreign Affairs*, Summer 1986, at http://www.foreignaffairs.com/print/41061
68. M. Yosouf Qawwam Ahrary, *Sardar-e Aria*, Herat, 1383/2004, p. 371.
69. Nick Danziger recalls a partisan conscientious objector in Herat, Gholalam, who would contribute to the cause by undertaking these dangerous trips for bread. Nick Danziger, *Danziger's Travels, Beyond Forbidden Frontiers*, London: Grafton Books, 1987, p. 128.
70. Leon Flamholc, *A Winter in Herat*, 1985, at https://www.youtube.com/playlist?list=PL4BC35ABC9405BDA4, accessed on 18.11.2015.
71. Interviews in Herat, January 2014.
72. The resistance groups used mines extensively to target Soviet convoys, and the districts of Ghurian and Zendah Jan, in particular, were heavily mined by Ismail Khan's Jamiat. UNHCR Background Report, *Herat Province, Prepared by the Data Collection for Afghan Repatriation Project*, *15 April 1990*, Islamabad, 1990, p. 6.
73. Flamholc, *Winter in Herat*.
74. These groups had their modern equivalent in the form of CIA-backed militia such as the Khost Protection Force, the Qandahar Strike Force and the Afghan Local Police. Allegations of involvement in criminality and executions against these groups are similarly legion.
75. Interviews in Herat, January 2014.
76. Star General Alexander Mayiurof, *Dar Afghanistan chi gozasht* (What Happened in Afghanistan), trans. Doctor Daoud Jonbesh, Peshawar: Anjoman-e Nesharati-ye Danesh, 1379/2001, p. 239.
77. See Sikorski, *Dust of the Saints*, pp. 44–8.
78. Anna Heinäma, Maija Leppänen and Yuri Yurchenko, *The Soldiers' Story: Soviet Veterans Remember the Afghan War*, trans. A. D. Haun, Berkeley: University of California Press, 1994. For the Shindand account, see pp. 59–69.
79. It is hard to imagine US or UK soldiers of today readily joining the Taliban and deciding to live their lives amongst them until old age, but then the cruelty of the Soviet military must have been a strong push factor in so many decisions. Many Soviet soldiers spoke Afghan languages as their mother tongues, and the worlds inhabited by an Afghan farmer and one from, say, Soviet Tajikistan were in no way diametrically opposed.
80. Interview with Abdullah Khakimov, Herat Mujahideen Museum, 6 January 2014.
81. Danziger, *Danziger's Travels*, pp. 127–8.
82. Ibid., p. 141.
83. John Baily, *A Portrait of Herat*, 1994, author's collection.
84. Ibid.

85. Antonio Giustozzi, 'Genesis of a "Prince"', p. 5.
86. Ibid., p. 9.
87. Habib Kawyani and Jonathan Tinker, *Report of a Journey to Herat, 1988: For Afghanaid*, Autumn 1988, p. 27.
88. United Nations Humanitarian and Assistance Programmes relating to Afghanistan, *Salam 1*, 8–14 December 1988, Tehran, p. 6.
89. United Nations Humanitarian and Assistance Programmes relating to Afghanistan, *Salam 1*, p. 6.
90. Interviews in Herat, January 2014.
91. Barnett R. Rubin, *The Fragmentation of Afghanistan: State Formation and Collapse in the International System*, Yale: Yale University Press, 1995, p. 260.
92. Danziger, *Danziger's Travels*, p. 130.
93. Ismail Khan was represented in Iran by Jan Agha in Tehran and Masun in Mashhad. United Nations Humanitarian and Assistance Programmes relating to Afghanistan, *Salam 1*, p. 31.
94. *Afghan News*, Vol. 1, 1985, p. 5.
95. United Nations Humanitarian and Assistance Programmes relating to Afghanistan, *Salam 1*, p. 6.
96. Interview with Ismail Khan, January 2014.
97. Sikorski, *Dust of the Saints*, pp. 104–5.
98. Quoted in Saikal, *Modern Afghanistan*, p. 202.
99. For an extremely erudite discussion of the Accords, and the text of the Accords themselves, see Rosanne Klass, 'Afghanistan: The Accords', *Foreign Affairs*, Summer 1988.
100. Habib Kawyani and Jonathan Tinker, *Report of a Journey to Herat*, p. 35.
101. *Afghan Jihad*, Vol. 1, No. 4, April–June 1988, Islamabad, p. 60.
102. *Afghan Jihad*, Vol. 3, No. 4, July–September 1990, Islamabad, p. 34.
103. UNHCR Background Report, *Herat Province, Prepared by the Data Collection for Afghan Repatriation Project, 15 April 1990*, Islamabad, 1990, p. 2.
104. Ibid., p. 8.
105. Flamholc, *Winter in Herat*.
106. *Ettefaq-e Islam*, 21 April 1992, pp. 1–3. Two articles, one carrying a message of congratulation from Rabbani in Kabul, and one titled 'Herat Conquered'.
107. See M. Yosouf Qawwam Ahrary, *Sardar-e Aria*, Herat, 1383/2004.
108. Ahrary, *Sardar-e Aria*, p. 20
109. Danziger, *Danziger's Travels*, p. 150.
110. National Committee for Human Rights in Afghanistan, *Russia's Barbarism in Afghanistan*, Vol. II, p. 123.
111. Habib Kawyani and Jonathan Tinker, *Report of a Journey to Herat*, p. 7.
112. For more detail on the loss to Herat's monumental historical and cultural legacy, see Olivier Tirard-Collet, 'After the War. The Condition of Historical Buildings and Monuments in Herat, Afghanistan', *Iran*, Vol. 36, 1998, pp. 123–38.
113. UNHCR Background Report, *Herat Province, Prepared by the Data Collection for Afghan Repatriation Project, 15 April 1990*, Islamabad, 1990, p. 15.
114. Ibid.
115. United Nations Humanitarian and Assistance Programmes relating to Afghanistan, *Salam 2, Mission to Herat, 31 August–4 September 1988*, Tehran, pp. 8–10.
116. Ibid., p. 12.

117. Jane Thomas, *Herat, Afghanistan Community Profile Report, 1993*, Peshawar, 1993.
118. Ibid., p. 7.
119. Ibid., p. 7.
120. Ibid., p. 8.
121. Ibid., p. 12.
122. Ibid., p. 12.
123. Ahrary, *Sardar-e Aria*, pp. 24–5.
124. Ahrary, *Sardar-e Aria*, p. 441.
125. Antonio Giustozzi, *Empires of Mud: Wars and Warlords in Afghanistan*, London: Hurst & Co., 2009, p. 213.
126. On 24 April 1992, the Peshawar Accords were signed, a deal which provided for an interim government under the leadership of Sebghatullah Mojadeddi, set to hold power for two months, after which Rabbani would head a leadership council for a further four months. Hekmatyar was unhappy with his brief as Prime Minister and Massoud's appointment to Minister of Defence, so decided to shell Kabul into submission, a bombardment which lasted until 1996, destroying Kabul as a functioning city and leaving over 40,000 civilians dead and countless more maimed or exiled.
127. Interview with John and Veronica Baily, Brighton, November 2015.
128. Ahrary, *Sardar-e Aria*, p. 25.
129. Ibid., p. 280.
130. Dorronsoro deals with this highly complicated period in *Revolution Unending*, pp. 227–72. Pakistan's concern at having their eastern border controlled and Kabul in their pocket is founded in their intense rivalry with Indian ambitions in the region. Whatever the cost or consequences, Pakistan's interests will always support a pliant government in Kabul and the Taliban movement, an ultra-conservative Sunni fundamentalist movement, the product of a damaged generation of Afghans who sought solace in an ahistorical, acultural and dehumanised ideology of religion and violence.
131. Ahrary, *Sardar-e Aria*, p. 79.
132. The most comprehensive account of the Taliban's rise to power can be found in Ahmed Rashid's peerless study, *Taliban: Islam, oil and the new great game in central Asia*, London: I. B. Tauris, 2002.
133. Here, it is worth noting that the Taliban's first noteworthy act was the brutal murder and hanging of two corrupt Mujahideen commanders in Qandahar who were engaged in a destructive battle for the sexual rights over a young Pashtun boy. The people of Qandahar were happy to see a force unafraid of the commanders and one acting in accordance with strict moral codes of both Islam and Pashtunwali (the Pashtun honour code).
134. This first attack was not directed by ISI, and therefore militarily less successful or well-organised. Interviews in Herat, January 2014.
135. Azimi, *Taliban chegune amadand?* (How did the Taliban Emerge?), Germany: Afghan Association, 1377 AH, p. 114.
136. Ibid., p. 113.
137. Ibid., pp. 117–18.
138. Ibid., p. 124.
139. Ibid., p. 117.
140. Interview in Kabul, Winter 2010.
141. *Ettefaq-e Islam*, 16 December 1996, p. 1.

now

142. Interviews in Herat, January 2014.
143. Ahrary, Sardar-e Aria, p. 77.
144. This story was told to me when I was working in Herat's Public Library in February 2014. Ismail Khan built the library after his return to power in 2001, and it houses many books and a ragged selection of old newspapers and ephemera dating back to the mid twentieth century.
145. Christina Lamb, The Sewing Circles of Herat, London: HarperCollins, 2002.
146. Nadia Anjoman, 'Makes no Sense', Load Poems Like Guns, Women's Poetry from Herat, Afghanistan, ed. Farzana Marie, Minnesota: Holy Cow! Press, 2015, pp. 38–9.
147. Interviews in Herat, January 2014.
148. Nik Seyar, Interviews in Herat, January 2014.
149. Interviews in Herat, January 2014.
150. Ettefaq-e Islam, 1 November 1996, p. 1.
151. In 1998 Iran very nearly invaded Afghanistan, via Herat, as a result of the Taliban's execution of a number of Iranian diplomats in the northern city of Mazaar-e Sharif.
152. Ahrary, Sardar-e Aria, p. 40.
153. Ahrary, Sardar-e Aria, p. 48.
154. Despite his obvious lack of sympathy with the Taliban, Hekmatullah was later arrested by the US and sent to Guantanamo, where he died of cancer. He remained in Guantanamo despite Ismail Khan's avowal of his innocence. Carlotta Gall and Andy Worthington, 'Time Runs Out for an Afghan Held by the US', New York Times, at http://www.nytimes.com/2008/02/05/world/asia/05gitmo.html?_r=0&ei=5087&em=&en=69559dc1ec42361a&ex=1202360400&pagewanted=all, accessed on 19.9.2014.
155. Ahrary, Sardar-e Aria, p. 72.
156. Ibid., p. 73.
157. Ibid., p. 441.
158. Ibid., p. 441.
159. Ibid., p. 84.
160. Interview in Herat, August 2009.
161. For an entertaining account of the CIA's involvement in the early days of the war in Afghanistan, see Gary Schroen, First In: An Insider's Account of How the CIA Spearheaded the War on Terror in Afghanistan, New York: Random House, 2005.
162. For Herat's fall, see Susan Glasser and Molly Moore, 'Rebel Forces Claim Key City of Herat, Seize Road to Kabul; Area's Former Ruler Returns in Victory Six Years After His Defeat by Taliban', Washington Post, 13 November 2001; Soraya Sarhaddi Nelson, 'Ousting Taliban from Herat relatively easy', Chicago Tribune, 15 November 2001; Ahmed Rashid, 'The Lion returns to his old haunts', Daily Telegraph, 13 November 2002.
163. Interviews in Herat, January 2014.
164. Christopher de Bellaigue, 'Letter from Herat', New Yorker, January 2002.
165. Interview with Abdul Sayyed Qattali, Herat, February 2014.

EPILOGUE: HERAT AS IT FACES THE FUTURE

1. Human Rights Watch, 'All Our Hopes Are Crushed: Violence and Repression in Western Afghanistan', Vol. 14, No. 7, November 2002, New York; Human Rights Watch, 'We Want to Live as Humans: Repression of Women and Girls in Western Afghanistan', New York, December 2002.

2. *Human Rights Watch*, 'All Our Hopes are Crushed', pp. 15–17.
3. Interviews in Herat, January 2014.
4. *Human Rights Watch*, ''All Our Hopes are Crushed, p. 4.
5. Interview with Waheed Wafa, Kabul, January 2014.
6. Interview in Kabul with Rohullah Amin, January 2014.
7. Interviews in Herat with Rafiq Shahir and Engineer Salahi, January 2014.
8. See *Human Rights Watch*, 'All Our Hopes are Crushed', pp. 30–2.
9. Al-Jazeera, 'Afghan Minister Killed in Herat Shootout', at http://www.aljazeera.com/archive/2004/03/20084914449768186.html, accessed on 21.12.2014.
10. Farzana Marie, *Load Poems Like Guns, Women's Poetry from Herat, Afghanistan*, Minnesota: Holy Cow! Press, 2015.
11. Somaya Ramesh, 'For Nadia Anjoman', in *Load Poems Like Guns*, pp. 122–3.
12. Roya Sharifi, 'Those Bleeding Tulips', in *Load Poems Like Guns*, pp. 152–3.
13. Charlie Gammell, 'The Place of Herat in a Modern Afghanistan: Lessons from the March 1979 Uprising', *Asian Affairs*, Vol. XLVI, no. 1, pp. 51–67.

BIBLIOGRAPHY

Abbott, James (1843), *Narrative of a Journey from Heraut to Khiva, Moscow and St. Petersburgh*, 2 vols., London: W. H. Allen.

Abru, Hafez (1936), *Chronique des Rois Mongols en Iran*, tr. K. Bayani, Paris: Librairie d'Amerique et d'Orient, Adrien-Maisonneuve.

———— (1959), *Cinq Opuscules de Hafez Abru*, ed. Felix Tauer, Prague.

———— (1372 AH), *Zubadat-e Tawarikh, Vol. I*, ed. Kamal Hajji Sayyed Javadi, Tehran: Sazman-e chap wa entesharat-e vezarat-e farhang wa ershad-e Islami.

Adamec, Ludwig (1972–85), *Historical Gazetteer of Iran*, 6 vols., Graz: Akademische Druk- u. Verlagsanstalt.

———— (1975), *Who's Who of Afghanistan*, Graz: Akademische Druk- u. Verlagsanstalt.

Afshar, Iraj (1349 AH), *Shasht o Chahar sanad dar barayae waqeah-e Herat wa Khorasan* (64 documents relating to the events of Herat and Khorasan), Tehran: Daneshiar-e Daneshgah-e Tehran.

Ahrary, M. Yosouf Qawwam (1383 AH), *Sardar-e Aria*, Herat.

Aitchison, C. U. (1983), *A Collection of Treaties, Engagements, and Sanads Relating to India and Neighbouring Countries* IV and XIII, Calcutta, 1909; 5th edn, rev. and cont. to 1929, Calcutta, 1929–33, repr. Delhi, 1983.

Akhwan, Safa (ed. 1389 AH), *Tarikh-e shafaye-e Afghanistan (1900–1992)* (Oral History of Afghanistan [1900–1992]), Tehran: Markaz-e Asnad wa Tarikh-e Diplomasy.

Al-Daoud, Sayyed Ali (ed. 2000), *Asnad va namehha-ye Amir Kabir* (Amir Kabir's Letters and Records), Tehran: Iran National Archives Organisation.

Alam, Muzaffar and Subrahmanyam, Sanjay (2007), *Indo-Persian Travels in the Ages of Discoveries, 1400–1800*, Cambridge: Cambridge University Press.

Alder, G. J. (1974a), 'The Key to India? Britain and the Herat Problem 1830–63, Part 1', *Middle Eastern Studies*, Vol. 10, No. 2, pp. 186–209.

BIBLIOGRAPHY

———— (1974b), 'The Key to India? Britain and the Herat Problem 1830–63, Part II', *Middle Eastern Studies*, Vol. 10, No. 3, pp. 287–311.

Allami, Abu al-Fazl (1903), *Akbar namah*, ed. and trans. H. Beveridge, Vol. I, Fasc. VIII, Calcutta: Asiatic Society of Bengal, New Series, No. 1036.

Allchin, F. R. and Hammond, N. (1978), *The Archaeology of Afghanistan. From Earliest Times to the Timurid Period*, London: Palgrave.

Allen, Terry (1981), *The Catalogue of the Toponyms and Monuments of Timurid Herat*, Cambridge, MA.

———— (1983), *Timurid Herat*, Wiesbaden: Reichert Verlag.

Amanat, Abbas (2004), 'Historiography viii. Qajar Period', in *Encyclopaedia Iranica, XII*, pp. 369–77.

———— (1997), *Pivot of the Universe: Nasir al-Din Shah Qajar and the Iranian Monarchy, 1831–1896*, Berkeley: University of California Press.

Amitai-Preiss, Reuven (1995), *Mongols and Mamluks: The Mamluk-Ilkhanid War, 1260–1281*, Cambridge: Cambridge University Press.

Amnesty International, *Violations of Human Rights and Fundamental Freedoms in the Democratic Republic of Afghanistan* (AI Index ASA 11/04/79).

Anonymous, *Majmuah, MS*, London, British Library, I. O. Islamic 379, ff. 95–102.

Arunova, M. R. (1960), 'The Herat Rising of 1716–32', *Central Asian Review*, Vol. 8.

Aubin, Jean (1963), 'Comment Tamerlan prenait les villes', *Studia Islamica*, Vol. 19, pp. 83–122.

———— (1970), 'Éléments pour l'étude des agglomérations urbaines dans l'Iran médiéval', in Albert Habib Hourani and Samuel Miklos Stern, eds, *The Islamic City*, Oxford: Oxford University Press, pp. 65–76.

———— (1971), 'Réseau pastoral et réseau caravanier: les grand'routes du Khurassan à l'époque mongole', *Le Monde Iranien et l'Islam*, Vol. 1, pp. 105–30.

———— (1976), 'Le khanat de Chagatai et le Khorassan (1334–1380)', *Turcica*, Vol. 8, No. 2, pp. 16–60.

Axworthy, Michael (2009), *The Sword of Persia, Nader Shah, from Tribal Warrior to Conquering Tyrant*, London: I. B. Tauris.

Azimi, Zaher (1377 AH), *Taliban chegune amadand?* (How did the Taliban Emerge?), Germany: Afghan Association.

Baali, Fuad (1988), *Society, State and Urbanism: Ibn Khaldun's sociological thought*, New York: State University of New York Press.

Bacon, Elizabeth E. (1951), 'The Inquiry into the History of the Hazara Mongols of Afghanistan', *Southwestern Journal of Anthropology*, Vol. 7, No. 3, pp. 230–47.

Bahmani Qajar, Mohammad Ali (ed., 1385 AH), *Iran va Afghanistan: az yekganegi ta tayin-e marzha-ye siasi* (Iran and Afghanistan: From Unity to the

Defining of Political Boundaries), Tehran: Markaz-e Asnad-e Tarikh-e Diplomasi.

Bahrani Pour, Ali, 'The Trade in Horses between Khorasan and India in the 13th to 17th Centuries', at https://www.academia.edu/5516297/THE_ TRADE_IN_HORSES_BETWEEN_KHORASAN_AND_INDIA_IN_ THE_13TH_-_17TH_CENTURIES

Baily, John (2012), *Music of Afghanistan, Professional musicians in the city of Herat 1973–77*, London: Silk Road Books and Photos Publications, 2nd edn, p. 15.

——— (2015), *War, Exile and the Music of Afghanistan. The Ethnographer's Tale*, Surrey: Ashgate.

Ball, Warwick (1981), 'The Remains of a Monumental Timurid Garden Outside Herat', *East and West*, N.S. 31, Nos. 1–4, pp. 79–82.

——— (1982) (with the collaboration of Jean-Claude Gardin), *The Archaeological Gazetteer of Afghanistan: Catalogue des sites archéologiques d'Afghanistan*, 2 vols., Paris.

Balland, Daniel (1988), 'Bacca-ye Saqqa', *Encyclopaedia Iranica*, Vol. III, Fasc. 3–4, pp. 336–9.

——— (1995), 'DORRĀNĪ', *Encyclopaedia Iranica*, Vol. VII, Fasc. 5, pp. 513–19.

Barbier de Meynard, Casimir (1860–62), 'Extraits de la chronique persane d'Herat,' *Journal Asiatique*, 5, Séries, 16 (1860), pp. 461–520, 17 (1861), pp. 473–522, 20 (1862), pp. 268–319.

Barfield, Thomas (2004), 'Problems in establishing legitimacy in Afghanistan', *Iranian Studies*, Vol. 37, No. 2, pp. 263–93.

——— (2010), *Afghanistan, A Cultural and Political History*, Princeton: Princeton University Press.

Barthold, V. (1956–62), *Four Studies in the History of Central Asia*, tr. V. and T. Minorsky, 3 vols., Leiden: Brill.

——— (1968), *Turkestan down to the Mongol Invasion*, new edn revised by Clifford E. Bosworth, London: Luzack & Co.

——— (1984), *An Historical Geography of Iran*, Princeton: Princeton University Press.

Batuta, Ibn (1971), *The Travels of Ibn Batuta AD 1325–1354*, 3 vols., Vol. III, trans. H. A. R. Gibb, Cambridge: Cambridge University Press.

Bayat, Mangol (1982), *Mysticism and Dissent. Socioreligious Thought in Qajar Iran*, New York: Syracuse University Press.

Beall, Jo and Esser, Daniel (2005), *Shaping Urban Futures: Challenges to Governing and Managing Afghan Cities*, AREU Issues Paper, Kabul: Afghanistan Research and Evaluation Unit.

Bearden, Milt (2003), *The Main Enemy: The Inside Story of the CIA's Final Showdown with the KGB*, New York: Random House.

'Beheshti Heravi', Abdullah Sani (1377 AH), *Nur al-mashreqain* (The Light of the Two Easts), ed. Mayel Heravi, Mashhad: Mosesse-ye chap wa entesharat-e astan-e quds rezawi.

de Bellaigue, Christopher (2002), 'Letter from Herat', *New Yorker*, January.

Binbas, Evrim (2013), 'The Anatomy of a Regicide Attempt: Shahrukh, the Hurufis, and the Timurid Intellectuals in 830/1426–7', *Journal of the Royal Asiatic Society*, 3rd Series, Vol. 23, No. 3, pp. 391–428.

Biran, Michael (2002), 'The Battle of Herat (1270): A Case of Inter-Mongol Warfare', in Nicola di Cosmo, ed., *Warfare in Inner Asian History (1500–1800)*, Leiden: Brill, pp. 175–219.

Bosworth, C. E. (1998), "ERĀQ-E 'AJAM(Ī)', *Encyclopaedia Iranica*, Vol. VIII, Fasc. 5, December, p. 538.

Braithwaite, Rodric (2011), *Afgantsy: The Russians in Afghanistan, 1979–89*, London: Profile Books.

Brandenburg, Dietrich (1977), *Herat: Eine timuridische Hauptstadt*, Graz: Akademische Druk- u. Verlagsanstalt.

Browne, E. G. (1893) *A Year Amongst the Persians, Impressions as to the Life, Character & Thought of the People of Persia received during Twelve Months' Residence in that Country in the Years 1887–1888*, London: A & C Black Ltd.

——— (1920), *A Literary History of Persia*, 4 vols., Cambridge: Cambridge University Press.

Brydges, Harford Jones (1833), *The Dynasty of the Kajars, Translated from the Original Persian Manuscript Presented to Sir H. J. Brydges*, New York.

——— (1834), *An Account of the Transactions of His Majesty's Mission to the Court of Persia in the years 1807–11*, London: James Bohn.

Burdett, A. L. P. (ed., 2002), *Afghanistan Strategic Intelligence, British Records, 1919–1970, Volume 2: 1928–1939, From the End of the Civil War to the Declaration of Neutrality in World War Two*, Chippenham: Archive Editions.

Burnes, Alexander (1843), *Travels into Bokhara: Containing the Narrative of a Voyage on the Indus from the Sea to Lahore, with Presents from the King of Great Britain; And an Account of a Journey from India to Cabool, Tartary, and Persia. Performed by the order of the Supreme Government of India, in the years 1831, 32 and 33, Three Volumes*, London: John Murray.

——— (1843), *Cabool, A Personal Narrative of a Journey to and Residence in That City, in the years 1836, 7, and 8*, Philadelphia: Carey and Hart.

Burton, Audrey (1988), 'The Fall of Herat to the Uzbegs in 1588', *Iran*, Vol. 26, pp. 119–23.

Busse, Heribet (1972), *History of Persia under Qajar Rule, Translated from the Persian of Hasan-e Fasa'i's, Farsnama-ye Naseri*, New York: Columbia University Press.

Byron, Robert (1937), *The Road to Oxiana*, London: Pimlico edition, 2004.

Cambridge History of Iran (1968), 6 vols., Cambridge: Cambridge University Press.

BIBLIOGRAPHY

Caroe, Olaf and Howell, Evelyn (1963), *The Poems of Khushal Khan Khatak*, Peshawar: Pashto Academy.

Chossudovsky, Professor Michael (2010), 'The War is Worth Waging: Afghanistan's Vast Reserves of Minerals and Natural Gas', *Global Research*, June, at http://www.globalresearch.ca/the-war-is-worth-waging-afghanistan-s-vast-reserves-of-minerals-and-natural-gas/19769, accessed on 12.06.2016.

Clark, Kate (2013), 'Death List Published: families of disappeared end a 30 year wait for news', 26 September, Afghan Analysts Network, at https://www.afghanistan-analysts.org/death-list-published-families-of-disappeared-end-a-30-year-wait-for-news/

de Clavijo, Ruy Gonzales (1859), *Narrative of the Embassy of Ruy Gonzalez de Clavijo to the Court of Timûr at Samarkand. A.D. 1403–6*, trans. Clements R. Markham, London: Hakluyt Society.

Coll, Steve (2004), *Ghost Wars. The Secret History of the CIA, Afghanistan and Bin Laden, From the Soviet Invasion to September 10 2001*, New York: Penguin Press.

Conolly, Arthur (1834), *Journey to the North of India*, 2 vols., London: Richard Bentley.

——— (1840), *Journal of Captain Arthur Conolly's expedition in 1840 from Afghanistan to Bokhara*, IOL, BL, 1947, b. 560.

Curzon, George N. (1892), *Persia and the Persian Question*, 2 vols., London: Frank Cass.

——— (1889), *Russia in Central Asia and the Anglo-Russian Question*, London: Frank Cass.

Dalrymple, William (2011), *Return of a King*, London: Bloomsbury.

Daniel, E. L. (1979), *The Political and Social History of Khurasan under Abbasid Rule, 747–820*, Minneapolis and Chicago: Bibliotheca Islamica.

Danziger, Nick (1987), *Danziger's Travels, Beyond Forbidden Frontiers*, London: Grafton Books.

Dasti, Humaira (1998), *Multan, a Province of the Mughal Empire*, Karachi: Royal Book Company.

Della Valle, Pietro (1843), *Viaggi di Pietro Della Valle il pellegrino, con minuto ragguaglio di tutte le cose notabili osservate in essi: descritti da lui medesimo in 54 lettere familiari all'erudito suo amico Mario Schipano, divisi in tre parti cioè: la Turchia, la Persia e l'India. Colla vita e ritratto dell'autore. Roma 1650–1658*, Torino.

Dickson, Martin B. (1958), 'Shàh Ṭahmàsp and the Uzbeks: The Duel for Khuràsàn with 'Ubayd Khàn, 930–946/1524–1540', PhD diss., Princeton University.

Dorronsoro, Giles (2005), *Revolution Unending: Afghanistan 1979 to the Present*, trans. from French by John King, London: Hurst & Co.

Dupree, L. (1973), *Afghanistan*, Princeton: Princeton University Press.

———— (1980), *Red Flag over the Hindu-Kush*, Part 3, American Universities Field Staff Report, South Asia Series.

Durrani, Asheq Mohammad Khan (1999), *Tarikh-e Afghanistan*, Lahore: Sang-e Meel.

Eastwick, Edward B. (1864), *Journal of a Diplomat's Three Years Residence in Persia*, 2 vols., London: Blackwood & Sons.

Edwards, David Busby (1996), *Heroes of the Age. Moral Fault Lines on the Afghan Frontier*, Berkeley: University of California Press.

Elliot, Jason (1999), *An Unexpected Light: Travels in Afghanistan*, London: Picador.

Elphinstone, Mountstuart (1815), *An Account of the Kingdom of Kabul*, London: John Murray.

Elsmie, G. R. (1863), *Epitome of Correspondence regarding our relations with Afghanistan and Herat*, Lahore: Government Press.

English, Barbara (1971), *John Company's Last War*, London: Collins.

English, Paul (1973), 'The Traditional City of Herat, Afghanistan', in L. Carl Brown, ed., *From Medina to Metropolis, Heritage and Change in the Near Eastern City*, Princeton: Darwin Press.

Esfezari, Moin al-Din Mohammad Zamchi (1338 AH), *Rawdat al Jannat fi Ausaf Madinat Herat* (The Gardens of Paradise in Herat), Vols. I and II, Tehran: Moalem Danesgah Tehran.

Etemadi, Guya (1322 AH), 'Sayfi al-Heravi,' *Aryana*, Vol. 1, No. 10, pp. 16–20.

———— (1944), 'Darbar-e Malouk-e Kart' (The Court of the Kartid Maleks), *Aryana*, Vol. 2, No. 4, Sawr 1323, pp. 42–9.

———— (1947) 'Rabii-e Fushang, Sha'er-e Darbar' (Rabii of Fushang: Courtly Poet), *Ariana*, Vol. 5, No. 12, Jedi 1326, pp. 1–8.

Ettehadieh, Mansoureh (Nezam Mafi) (2002), *Enfesal-e Herat, Goushe-ha-ye az ravabet-e khareji-ye iran (1280–1399 hijri qamri)*, Tehran: Ketab-e Siyamak and Nashr-e Tarikh-e Iran.

Farhangi, Mir Mohammad Sadiq (1371 AH), *Afghanistan dar panj qarn ahker, jeld-e awal* (Afghanistan in the last five centuries, Vol. 1), Mashhad: Entesharat-e darakhshash.

Farzan, Ahmad Shah (1995), *Qiyam-e Herat* (Herat's Uprising), Mashhad: Entesharat-e Farbad.

Farzana, Marie (ed., 2015), *Load Poems Like Guns, Women's Poetry from Herat, Afghanistan*, Minnesota: Holy Cow! Press.

Fatahi, Fath al-Din (1370 AH), *Herat dar qalamro-ye este'emar* (Herat in the Colonial Age), Tehran: Entesharat-e mostawfi.

Ferdinand, K. (1963), 'The Horizontal Windmills of Western Afghanistan', *Folk*, Vol. 5, pp. 71–90.

BIBLIOGRAPHY

Ferrier, J. P. (1858), *History of the Afghans*, London: John Murray.

———— (1857), *Caravan journeys and wanderings in Persia, Afghanistan, Turkistan, and Beloochistan: with historical notices of countries lying between Russia and India*, London: John Murray.

Fikrat, Mohammad Asaf (ed. 2002), *Pirasta-ye tarikhnamah-ye Herat*, Tehran: Bonyad-e Mawqefat-e Doktor Mahmud Afshar Yazdi.

Forster, G. (1798), *A Journey from Bengal to England through the Northern Parts of India, Kashmire, Afghanistan and Persia, and into Russia, by the Caspian-Sea*, 2 vols., London: R. Faulder.

Franklin, H. E. (1952), *Note By Mr. Franklin on Conditions in Herat*, The National Archives, London, FA 1016/1.

Fraser, James Baillie (1825), *Narrative of a Journey into Khorasan in the Years 1821 and 1822*, London: Longman.

Fraser-Tytler, W. K. (1953), *Afghanistan. A Study of Political Developments in Central and Southern Asia*, 2nd edn, Oxford: Oxford University Press.

Frye, Richard (1948), 'Two Timurid Monuments at Herat', *Artibus Asiae*, Vol. 11, pp. 206–11.

Gall, Carlotta and Worthington, Andy (2008), 'Time Runs Out for an Afghan Held by the U.S.', *New York Times*, at http://www.nytimes.com/2008/02/05/world/asia/05gitmo.html?_r=0&ei=5087&em=&en=69559dc1ec42361a&ex=1202360400&pagewanted=all

Gall, Sandy (2012), *War Against the Taliban, Why it all went wrong in Afghanistan*, London: Bloomsbury.

Galster, Steve (2001), *Afghanistan: the Making of US Policy, 1973–1990*, The National Security Archive, Vol. II: Afghanistan: Lessons from the last war, 9 October 2001, at http://www2.gwu.edu/~nsarchiv/NSAEBB/NSAEBB57/essay.html#docs

Gammell, Charlie (2015), 'The Place of Herat in a Modern Afghanistan: Lessons from the March 1979 Uprising', *Asian Affairs*, Vol. XLVI, No. 1, pp. 51–67.

———— (2015), 'Failings of Inclusivity: The Herat Uprising of March 1979', Afghan Analysts Network, at https://www.afghanistan-analysts.org/failings-of-inclusivity-the-herat-uprising-of-march-1979/

Gaube, Heinz (1979), *Iranian Cities*, New York: New York University Press.

Ghani, Ashraf (1982), 'Production and Domination: Afghanistan, 1747–1901', PhD diss., Columbia University.

Gharjestani, Mohammad Ismail (1959), 'Malek Moezz al-Din Husain', *Aryana*, Vol. 17, No. 6 [misprint: says 5], Saratan 1338, pp. 20–26.

Ghaus, Abdul Samad (1988), *The Fall of Afghanistan: An Insider's Account*, London: Pergamon-Brassey's Ltd.

Ghaznavi, Abu Zar Pirzadeh (1389 AH), *Tarikh-e siyasi-ye Afghanistan: coudetay-e 24 saratan 1352 wa jomhuriyat-e Daoud Khan*, Tehran: Nashr Ehsan.

BIBLIOGRAPHY

Ghohari, D. M. J. (1998), *Taliban: Ascent to Power*, Oxford: Oxford Logos Society.

Ghubar, Mir Ghulam Mohammad (1937), *Khorasan*, Kabul: Kabul Printing House.

———— (1968), *Afghanistan dar masir-e tarikh*, Qum: Payam-e Muhajer.

Gignoux, P. (2001), 'Une croix de procession de Hérat inscrite en pehlevi', *Le Muséon*, Vol. 114, Nos. 3–4, pp. 291–304.

Giustozzi, Antonio (2000), *War, Politics and Society in Afghanistan, 1978–1992*, London: Hurst & Co.

———— (2006), 'Genesis of a 'Prince': the rise of Ismail Khan in western Afghanistan, 1979–1992', Crisis States Research Centre, LSE, September.

———— (2007a), *Koran, Kalashnikov and Laptop: The neo-Taliban Insurgency in Afghanistan*, London: Hurst & Co.

———— (2007b), 'War and Peace Economies of Afghanistan's Strongmen', *International Peacekeeping*, Vol. 14, No. 1, pp. 75–89.

———— (2009), *Empires of Mud: Wars and Warlords in Afghanistan*, London: Hurst & Co.

Glasser, Susan and Moore, Molly (2001), 'Rebel Forces Claim Key City of Herat, Seize Road to Kabul; Area's Former Ruler Returns in Victory Six Years after his Defeat by Taliban', *Washington Post*, 13 November.

Goldsmid, Frederic J. (ed. 1876), *Eastern Persia, an Account of the Journeys of the Persian Boundary Commission 1870–1872*, 2 vols., London: Macmillan.

Golombek, Lisa (1969), *The Timurid Shrine at Gazur Gah*, Toronto: Royal Ontario Museum Occasional Paper 15.

Grantham, Andrew, *Railways of Afghanistan*, at http://www.andrewgrantham.co.uk/afghanistan/

Gregorian, Vartan (1969), *The Emergence of Modern Afghanistan: Politics of Reform and Modernization, 1880–1946*, Stanford, CA: Stanford University Press.

Grönhaug, Reidar (1978), 'Scale as a Variable in Analysis: Fields in Social Organization in Herat, Northwest Afghanistan', in Fredrik Barth, ed., *Scale and Social Organization*, Oslo: Universitetsforlaget, pp. 78–121.

Gronke, Monika (1992), 'The Persian Court between Palace and Tent: From Timur to 'Abbas I', in Lisa Golombek and Maria Subtelny, eds, *Timurid Art and Culture: Iran and Central Asia in the Fifteenth Century*, Leiden: Brill, pp. 18–22.

Grossman, Patricia (2001), 'Afghanistan in the Balance', *Middle East Report*, No. 221, Winter, pp. 8–15.

Hanifi, Shah Mahmoud (2011), *Connecting Histories in Afghanistan: Market Relations and State Formation on a Colonial Frontier*, Stanford, CA: Stanford University Press.

———— (2012), 'The Pashtun Counter-Narrative', in Amin Tarzi, Arthur E. Karell, Stephanie E. Kramer and Adam C. Seitz (eds), *Arguments for the*

BIBLIOGRAPHY

Future of Afghanistan: Competing Narratives on Afghanistan, Quantico: Marine Corps University Press.

Hatch Dupree, Nancy (1970), *An Historical Guide to Afghanistan*, Kabul: Afghan Air Authority, Afghan Tourist Organization.

———— (1966), *Herat, A Pictorial Guide*, Kabul: Afghan Tourist Organization.

Hayat Khan, Mohammad (1874), *Hayat-e afghan*, trans. H. Priestly as *Afghanistan and its Inhabitants*, Lahore.

Hecker, Felicia J. (1993), 'A Fifteenth-Century Chinese Diplomat in Herat', *Journal of the Royal Asiatic Society*, 3rd Series, Vol. 3, No. 1, pp. 85–98.

Heinäma, Anna, Leppänen Maija and Yurchenko, Yuri (1994), *The Soldiers' Story: Soviet Veterans Remember the Afghan War*, trans. A. D. Haun, Berkeley: University of California Press.

Heravi, Qasim b. Yusuf Abu Nasri (1347 AH), *Resale-ye tariq-e qesmat-e qoloub-e ab* (A Treaty on the Ways of Water), ed. Mayel Heravi, Tehran: Entersharat-e Bonyad-e Farhang-e Iran.

Hillenbrand, Robert (1999), *Islamic Art and Architecture*, London: Thames and Hudson.

Holdich, Thomas Hungerford (1909), *The Indian Borderland, 1880–1900*, London: Methuen & Co.

———— (1910), *The Gates of India*, London: Macmillan.

Hopkins, Benjamin D. (2008), *The Making of Modern Afghanistan*, New York: Palgrave Macmillan.

Hopkirk, Kathleen (ed. 2012), *Alexander Burnes, Travels into Bokhara. A Voyage up the Indus to Lahore and a Journey to Cabool, Tartary & Persia*, London: Eland.

Hopkirk, Peter (1991), *The Great Game, On Secret Service in High Asia*, Oxford: Oxford University Press.

———— (1994), *On Secret Service East of Constantinople: The Plot to Bring Down the British Empire*, London: John Murray.

Hughes, Thomas L. (2002), 'The German Mission to Afghanistan, 1915–16', *German Studies Review*, Vol. 25, No. 3 pp. 447–76.

Human Rights Watch (2001), 'Afghanistan: Crisis of Impunity?' New York, July.

———— (2002a), 'All Our Hopes Are Crushed: Violence and Repression in Western Afghanistan', Vol. 14, No. 7, New York, November.

———— (2002b), 'We Want to Live as Humans: Repression of Women and Girls in Western Afghanistan', New York, December.

Hyman, Anthony (1984), *Afghanistan under Soviet Domination, 1964–83*, London: Macmillan.

Ibrahimi, Niamatullah (2012), 'Ideology without Leadership: The Rise and Decline of Maoism in Afghanistan', Afghan Analysts Network, at http://www.afghanistan-analysts.org/wp-content/uploads/downloads/2012/09/NIbr-Maoists-final.pdf

Ingram, Edward (1979), *The Beginning of the Great Game in Asia, 1828–1834*, Oxford: Oxford University Press.

———— (1981), *Commitment to Empire: Prophesies of the Great Game in Asia 1797–1800*, Oxford: Oxford University Press.

Islam, Riazul (1982), *A Calendar of Documents on Indo-Persian Relations (1500–1750)*, Vol. I, Tehran: Iranian Culture Foundation; Karachi: Institute of Central and West Asian Studies.

———— 'Travelogue of Mahmud B. Amir Wali', *Journal of the Pakistan Historical Society*, Vol. XXVII, Part I, pp. 88–120.

Ismail Seyar, Mohammad (1388 AH), *B'ezm-e neshat*, ed. Ghulam Haydar Kabiri 'Heravi', Herat: Entesherat-e momeni.

Jacob, J. (1858), *Letters on the Persian War*, London: W. H. Allen.

Jackson, Peter (1991), 'Chaghatayid Dynasty', *Encyclopaedia Iranica*, Vol. V, Fasc. 4, December, pp. 343–6.

———— (1999), 'From *Ulus* to Khanate: The Making of the Mongol States c. 1220–1290', in Reuven Amitai-Preiss and David O. Morgan, eds, *The Mongol Empire and its Legacy*, Leiden: Brill, pp. 12–38.

———— (2005), *The Mongols and the West, 1221–1410*, Edinburgh: Pearson Education.

Juvaini, Ata al-Din (1997), *The History of the World Conqueror*, trans. J. A. Boyle, Manchester University, UNESCO Publishing.

Juzjaini, M. Yaqub Wahidy (ed. 1968), *Diwan-e Sultan Husain Mirza Bayqara ba enzemam-e resala-ye u* (A Collection of Literary Works of Sultan Husain Mirza Bayqara), Kabul: Book Publication Department.

Kakar, Hassan K. (2006), *A Political and Diplomatic History of Afghanistan, 1863–1901*, Leiden: Brill.

Kalakani, Amir Habibullah (1990), *My Life: From Brigand to King*, London: Octagon Press.

Karp, Craig M. (1986), 'The War in Afghanistan', in *Foreign Affairs*, Summer 1986, at http://www.foreignaffairs.com/print/41061

Kashani-Sabet, Firoozeh (1999), *Frontier Fictions. Shaping the Iranian Nation, 1804–1946*, Princeton: Princeton University Press.

Katib Hazarah, Fayz Muhammad (2013), *Siraj al-tawarikh, Vol. 1, The Saduzai Era 1747–1843*, trans. R. D. McChesney, Khorrami, Leiden: Brill.

———— (1912), Ibid., Kabul.

Kawyani, Habib and Tinker, Jonathan (1988), *Report of a Journey to Herat, 1988: For Afghanaid*, Autumn 1988.

Kaye, John William (1857), *A History of the War in Afghanistan*, 2 vols., London: Richard Bentley.

Kazemi, Baqer (Mohazab al Dowleh) (2011), *Yaddashtha-ye az zendegi-ye Baqer Kazemi, Jeld-e sewom* (The Memoirs of Baqer Kazemi, Vol. 3), ed. Dr Daoud Kazemi and Mansoureh Ettehadieh (Nezam Mafi), Tehran: Nashrat Tarikh-e Iran.

Keddie, Nikki R. (1999), *Qajar Iran and the Rise of Reza Khan, 1796–1925*, Costa Meesa: Mazda.

BIBLIOGRAPHY

Kempiners, Russel G. (1985), 'The Struggle for Khurâsân: Aspects of Political, Military and Socio-Economic Interaction in the Early 8th/14th Century', PhD diss., University of Chicago.

Khalili, Khalilullah (1309 AH), *Asar-e Herat*, Herat: Mohammad Ibrahim Shariati Afghanistan.

Khan, Ansar Zahid (1990–93), 'Bahr al-Asrar', partial translation in *Journal of Pakistan Historical Society*, Vol. 38, No. 2, pp. 125–41; Vol. 39, No. 2, pp. 5–25; Vol. 40, pp. 337–59; Vol. 41, pp. 13–30 and pp. 235–54.

Khanikoff, Nicolas de (1866), *Mémoire sur l-ethnographie de Perse*, Paris: Société de Géographie.

Kheirabadi, Masoud (1991), *Iranian Cities: Formation and Development*, Austin, TX: University of Texas Press.

Khwandamir, Amir Mahmud (1375/1996), *Tarikh-e shah ismail va shah Tahmasp safavi (zil-e tarikh-e habib al-siyar)*, ed. Dr Mohammad Ali Jarahi, Tehran: Sherkat-e qalam va sina.

——— (2012), *Habib al-Siyar*, trans. W. M. Thackston, London: I. B. Tauris.

Klass, Rosanne (1988), 'Afghanistan: The Accords', *Foreign Affairs*, Summer.

Krusinski, Judasz Tadeusz (1973 [1740]), *The History of the Revolutions of Persia: taken from the Memoirs of Father Krusinski*, 2 vols., New York: Arno Press.

Lal, Mohan (1846), *Travels in the Punjab, Afghanistan and Turkistan, to Balk, Bokhara and Herat, and a Visit to Great Britain and Germany*, London: W. H. Allen.

——— (1834), 'A Brief Description of Herat', *Journal of the Asiatic Society of Bengal*, Vol. 3, pp. 9–18.

——— Lal to MacNeil describing Herat, British Library, IOR: MSS EUR C941.

Lamb, Christina (2002), *The Sewing Circles of Herat*, London: HarperCollins.

——— (2015), *Farewell, Kabul: From Afghanistan to a More Dangerous World*, London: HarperCollins.

Lambton, Ann K. S. (1978), 'Early Timurid Theories of State: Hafiz Abru and Nizam al-Din Sami', *Bulletin d'Études Orientales*, Vol. XXX, pp. 1–9.

——— (1988), 'Concepts of Authority in Persia: Eleventh to Nineteenth Centuries A.D.', *Iran*, Vol. 26, pp. 95–103.

——— (1988), *Qajar Iran*, Austin, TX: University of Texas Press.

Lane, George (2003), *Early Mongol Rule in Thirteenth-Century Iran: A Persian Renaissance*, London: Routledge Curzon.

Le Strange, Guy (1905), *The Land of the Eastern Caliphate*, Cambridge: Cambridge University Press.

——— (transl. 1919), *The Geographical Part of the Nuzhat-al-Qulub Composed by Hamd-Allah Mustawfi of Qazvin in 740 (1340)*, repr. Frankfurt am Main: Institute for the History of Arabic-Islamic Science at Johann Wolfgang Goethe University.

BIBLIOGRAPHY

———— (1928), *Narrative of the Spanish Embassy to the Court of Timur at Samarkand in the Years, 1403–1406*, New York.

Lee, Jonathan (1987), 'The History of Maimana in North-Western Afghanistan 1731–1893,' *Iran*, Vol. 25, pp. 107–24.

———— (1996), *The 'Ancient supremacy': Bukhara, Afghanistan and the Battle for Balkh, 1731–1901*, Leiden: Brill.

Leech, R. (1845), 'An Account of the Early Abdalees', *Journal of the Asiatic Society of Bengal*, Vol. 14, No. 162, pp. 445–70.

Lentz, Thomas W. and Lowry, Glenn D. (1898), *Timur and the Princely Vision: Persian Art and Culture in the Fifteenth Century*, Washington, DC: Smithsonian Press.

Levi, Peter (2013), *The Light Garden of the Angel King*, London: Eland.

Limbert, John (2004), *Shiraz in the Age of Hafez: The Glory of a Medieval Persian City*, Washington, DC: University of Washington Press.

Lockhart, Laurence (1938), *Nadir Shah*, London: Luzac & Co.

———— (1958), *The Fall of the Safavi [sic] Dynasty and the Afghan Occupation of Persia*, Cambridge: Cambridge University Press.

———— (1960), *Persian Cities*, London: Luzac & Co.

McChesney, Robert D. (1991), *Waqf in Central Asia*, Princeton: Princeton University Press.

———— (1993), 'The Conquest of Herat 995–96/1587–88: Sources for the Study of Safavid/qizilbāsh—Shībānid/Uzbak Relations', in Jean Calmard, ed., *Etudes safavides*, Paris and Tehran: Institut Français de Recherche en Iran, Bibliothèque iranienne 39, pp. 69–107.

———— (2012), 'Historiography in Afghanistan', in Charles Melville, ed., *Persian Historiography*, London: I. B. Tauris, ch. 11.

MacGregor, Charles M. (1879), *Narrative of a Journey through the Province of Khorassan in 1875*, 2 vols., London: John Murray.

Macintyre, Ben (2004), *Josiah the Great, the True Story of the Man Who Would be King*, London: HarperCollins.

Magnus, Ralph H. and Naby, Eden (2002), *Afghanistan, Mullah, Marx and Mujahid*, Oxford: Westview Press.

Malleson, George (1880), *Herat: The Granary and Garden of Central Asia*, London: W. H. Allen.

Mandeville, Peter (2005), *Global Political Islam*, London: Routledge Curzon.

Manz, Beatrice Forbes (1989), *The Rise and Rule of Tamerlane*, Cambridge: Cambridge University Press.

———— (1988), 'Tamerlane and the Symbolism of Sovereignty', *Iranian Studies*, Vol. 21, Nos. 1–2, pp. 105–22.

———— (2001), 'Gowhar-Sad Aga', *Encyclopaedia Iranica*, at http://www.iranicaonline.org/articles/gowhar-sad-aga

———— (2010), *Power, Politics and Religion in Timurid Iran*, Cambridge: Cambridge University Press.

BIBLIOGRAPHY

Marozzi, Justin (2004), *Tamerlane, Sword of Islam, Conqueror of the World*, London: Harper Collins.

———— (2015), *Baghdad, City of Peace, City of Blood*, London: Penguin.

Marsh, Hippisley Cunliffe (1877), *A Ride Through Islam: Being a Journey through Persia and Afghanistan to India via Meshed, Herat and Kandahar*, London: Tinsley Brothers.

Martin, Frank A. (2000), *Under the Absolute Amir of Afghanistan*, New Delhi: Bhavana Books & Prints, 2000.

Marvin, Charles (1880), *Colonel Grodekoff's Ride from Samarcand to Herat through Balkh and the Uzbek States of Afghan Turkestan*, London: W. H. Allen.

———— (1881), *Merv, Queen of the World; and the Scourge of the Man-Stealing Turcomans*, London: W. H. Allen.

———— (1883), *The Russians at the Gates of Herat*, London: W. H. Allen.

———— (1884), *Reconnoitring Central Asia: Pioneering Adventures in the Region Lying between Russia and India*, London, W. Swan Sonnenschein.

Masson Smith Jr, J. (1970), *The History of the Sarbadar Dynasty 1336–1381 A.D. and its Sources*, The Hague and Paris: Mouton.

Mayiurof, Star General Alexander (1379 AH), *Dar Afghanistan chi gozasht* (What Happened in Afghanistan), trans. Dr Daoud Jonbesh, Peshawar: Anjoman-e Nesharati-ye Danesh.

Mehdi Fathi Nia (2008), 'Rabeta-ye din wa dowlat nazd-e sarbedaran' (Mosque and State Relations under the Sarbedars), *Tarikh dar Aianeh-ye Pozuhesh*, No. 23, Autumn 1388, pp. 181–208.

Melville, Charles (1990), 'The Itineraries of Sultan Oljeitu, 1304–16', *Iran*, Vol. 28, pp. 55–70.

———— (ed. 1996), 'Shah Abbas and the Pilgrimage to Mashhad', *Safavid Persia, Pembroke Persian Papers*, Vol. 4, London: I. B. Tauris, pp. 191–229.

———— (1999), 'The Fall of Amir Chupan and the Decline of the Ilkhanate, 1327–37: A Decade of Discord in Mongol Iran', *Papers on Inner Asia*, No. 30, Bloomington: Indiana University, Research Institute for Inner Asian Studies.

———— (2008), 'Between Tabriz and Herat: Persian Historical Writing in the 15th Century', in Markus Ritter, Ralph Kauz und Brigitt Hoffmann, eds, *Iran und iranisch geprägte Kulturen. Studien zum 65. Geburtstag von Bert G. Fragner*, Wiesbaden: Reichert Verlag, pp. 28–38.

Melikian-Chirvani, Assadullah Souren (1970), 'Eastern Iranian Architecture: a Propos of the Ghurid Parts of the Great Mosque of Harāt', *Bulletin of the School of Oriental and African Studies*, Vol. 33, No. 2, pp. 322–37.

———— (1982), *Islamic Metalwork from the Iranian World, 8th-18th Centuries*, London: Victoria and Albert Museum Catalogue.

Mitchell, Colin P. (2009), *The Practice of Politics in Safavid Iran, Power, Religion and Rhetoric*, London: I. B. Tauris.

BIBLIOGRAPHY

Mojtaboueh, Sayyed Husain (1379 AH), *Herat dar ahd-e Timourian*, Herat: Entesharat-e Ahrary.

Mojtahed-Zadeh, Pirouz (1994), 'The Eastern Boundaries of Iran', in Keith McLachlan, ed., *The Boundaries of Modern Iran*, London: UCL Press, pp. 128–39.

———— (2004), *Small Players of the Great Game. The Settlement of Iran's Eastern Borderlands and the Creation of Afghanistan*, London and New York: Routledge Curzon.

Monshi, Eskandar Beg (1978), *History of Shah 'Abbas the Great (Tarikh-e Alamaray-ye Abbasi)*, Vols. I and II, trans. Roger M. Savory, Boulder, CO: Westview Press.

Moqaddam, Mohammad Nader (ed. 1374 AH), *Gazideh-ye asnad-e siasi-ye Iran wa Afghanistan, Jeld-e awal, Massaleh-ye Herat dar ahd-e Mohammad Shah Qajar* (A Selection of Political Documents of Iran and Afghanistan, Vol. 1, Relating to issues pertaining to Herat during the reign of Mohammad Shah Qajar), Tehran: Vahed Nashr-e Asnad.

Morgan, David (1988), *Medieval Persia 1040–1797*, London: Longman.

———— (2007), *The Mongols*, 2nd edn, London: Wiley-Blackwell Press.

Muradov, Ghulam (1981), 'The Democratic Republic of Afghanistan: A New Stage of the April Revolution', *Afghanistan: Past and Present*, Moscow: Oriental Studies in the USSR, No. 3, 1981.

Murphy, Dervla (2010), *Full Tilt, Ireland to India with a Bicycle*, London: Eland.

Najimi, A. W. (1982), 'The Cistern of Char-suq: A Safavid Building in Herat, built after 1634', *Afghanistan Journal*, No. 2, pp. 38–41.

———— (1987), *Herat: The Islamic City: A Study in Urban Conservation*, Scandinavian Institute of Asian Studies, occasional papers.

Nasb, Mardaiy (2004), 'Dowlat-e Sarbedaran wa tahavolat-e siasi, ejtemaiey wa farhangi dar qarn hashtom' (The Governance of the Sarbedars and the Political, Social and Cultural Upheavals of the 8th Century), *Tarikh dar Aianeh-ye Pozuhesh*, No. 4, Winter 1382, pp. 143–66.

Nasr, Vali (2006), *The Shia Revival: How Conflicts within Islam Will Shape the Future*, New York and London: W. H. Norton & Co.

Nelson, Soraya Sarhaddi (2001), 'Ousting Taliban from Herat relatively easy', *Chicago Tribune*, 15 November.

von Niedermayer, Oscar and Diez, Ernst (1924), *Afghanistan, Bearbeitet von Oscar von Niedermayer und Ernst Diez*, Leipzig: Verlag Karl W. Hiersemann.

Noelle-Karimi, Christine (1997), *State and Tribe in Nineteenth-century Afghanistan: The Reign of Amir Dost Muhammad Khan (1826–63)*, London: Curzon.

———— (2004), 'Historiography Afghanistan', *Encyclopaedia Iranica*, XII, pp. 390–95.

———— (2013a), *The Pearl in its Midst: Herat and the Mapping of Khorasan*

(15ᵗʰ–19ᵗʰ Centuries), Wien: Verlag der Österreichischen Akademie der Wissenschaften.

———— (2013b), 'The Abdali Pashtuns between Multan, Qandahar and Herat in the Sixteenth and Seventeenth Centuries', in Benjamin Hopkins and Magnus Marsden, eds, *Beyond Swat: History, Society and Economy along the Afghanistan–Pakistan Frontier*, London: Hurst & Co., pp. 31–8.

Norris, J. A. (1967), *The First Afghan War 1838–1842*, Cambridge: Cambridge University Press.

North, Charles and Sanders, Edward (1842), *Plan of Herat Fort, 1842*, Public Record Office, FO 925/2149.

O'Kane, Bernard (1987), *Timurid Architecture in Khurasan*, California: Costa Mesa.

Olearius, A. (1669), *The Voyages and Travels of J. Albert de Mendelso (A Gentleman belonging to the Embassy, sent by the Duke of Holstein to the great Duke of Muscovy and the King of Persia) into the East Indies. Begun in the year MDCXXXVIII and finished in MDCXL. Containing a particular description of the great Mogul's Empire, the Kingdoms of Decan, Calicuth, Cochim, Zeilon, Coromandel, Pegu, Siam, Cambodia, Malacca, Summatra, Java, Amboina, Banda, The Molucca's, Philippine and other Islands, Japan, the Great Kingdom of China, the Cape of Good Hope, Madagascar, etc.*, ed. and trans. John Davies, London: J. Starkey and T. Basset.

Olesen, Asta (1996), *Islam and Politics in Afghanistan*, Oxford: Routledge.

Omrani, B., and Leeming, M. (2005), *Afghanistan, A Companion and Guide*, Hong Kong: Airphoto International Ltd.

Parvin, Nasserddin (1998), 'Ettefaq-e Eslam', *Encyclopaedia Iranica*, Vol. IX, Fasc. 1, 15 December.

Paul, J. (2000), 'The Local Histories of Herat', *Iranian Studies*, Vol. 33, Nos. 1–2, pp. 93–115.

Pelly, Lewis (1866), *Journal of a Journey from Persia to India, through Herat and Candahar*, Bombay: Education Society's Press.

Persian Minister, A (1880), *Herat and Great Britain*, London: W. H. Allen.

de Planhol, X. (1986), 'ARAK', *Encyclopaedia Iranica*, Vol. II, Fasc. 3, December, pp. 247–8.

Potter, Lawrence Goddard (1992), 'The Kart Dynasty of Herat: Religion and Politics in Medieval Iran', PhD diss., Columbia University.

———— (1994), 'Sufis and Sultans in Post-Mongol Iran', *Iranian Studies*, Vol. 27, No. 1, pp. 77–102.

Pottinger, Eldred (1839), *Memoir on the Country between Herat and Kabul, the Paropamisian Mountains and the River Amoo*, India Office Library, L/PS/5/145 No. 7, Enc. 20.

Pouhian, Rasoul (1388 AH), *Jughrafiya-ye Omomi-ye Herat*, Mashhad: Entesharat-e terana.

BIBLIOGRAPHY

Rakhlataber, Dr A. (1987), 'Aya Abdul Razzaq aghazgar-e sarbedaran ast? (Is Abdul Razzaq the founder of the Sarbedars?), *Shenakht*, No. 2, Summer 1365, pp. 80–94.

Rashid, Ahmad (2002), *Taliban: Islam, oil and the new great game in central Asia*, London: I. B. Tauris.

————— (2002), 'The Lion returns to his old haunts', *Daily Telegraph*, 13 November.

Raverty, H. G. (1902), *The History of Hiri or Herat, and its Dependencies*, India Office Library, 7 vols., MSS. Eur. C. 83–89.

————— (1830) 'Route from Meshed to Cabul by Herat and Candahar', L/PS/19/59.

Richards, John F. (1996), *The Mughal Empire*, Cambridge: Cambridge University Press.

Rishtiya, Sayyed Qasem (ed. 1938), *Salnamah-ye Kabul, 1316/1937–8*, Kabul: Motebah-ye omoumi-ye Kabul.

Riyazi 'Heravi', Mohammad Yuusof (1369 AH), *Ayn al-waqaye, Tarikh-e Afghanistan dar salha-ye 1207–1324 Q*, ed. Mohammad Fekrat Heravi, Tehran.

Robb, Paul (2001), *A History of India*, London: Palgrave.

Robinson, Francis (2007), *The Mughal Emperors and the Islamic Dynasties of India, Iran and Central Asia*, London: Thames and Hudson.

Roemer, Hans R. (2004), 'Hosayn Bayqara', *Encyclopaedia Iranica*, Vol. XII, Fasc. 5, pp. 508–11.

Rossabi, Morris (1976), 'Two Ming Envoys to Inner Asia', *T'oung Pao*, 2nd Series, Vol. 62, Livr. 1/3, 1976, pp. 1–34.

————— (1983), 'A Translation of Ch'en Ch'eng's *Hisi-yü Faukuo Chih*', *Ming Studies*, Fall, pp. 49–59.

Roy, Olivier (1990), *Islam and Resistance in Afghanistan*, 2nd edn, Cambridge: Cambridge University Press.

Rubin, Barnett S. (1995), *The Fragmentation of Afghanistan: State Formation and Collapse in the International System*, Yale: Yale University Press.

Rumlu, Hasan (1931), *A Chronicle of the Early Safawis being the Ahsan-ut Tawarikh of Hasan-i Rumlu*, ed. Charles N. Seddon, Baroda: Oriental Institute.

————— (1934), *A Chronicle of the Early Safawis being the Ahsan-ut Tawarikh of Hasan-i Rumlu*, trans. Charles N. Seddon, Baroda: Oriental Institute.

Safavi, Mirza Mohammad Khalil Marashi (1362 AH), *Majma al-tawarikh dar tarikh-e enqeraz-e safavieh va vaqaeh-ye baad ta sal-e 1207 hejri qamari*, ed. Abbas Eqbal Ashtiyani, Tehran: Sanai-e Tahuri.

Saikal, Amin (2012), *Modern Afghanistan, A History of Struggle and Survival*, London: I. B. Tauris.

Samizay, R. (1981), *Islamic Architecture in Herat: A Study Towards Conservation*, Kabul: Research Section of International Project for Herat Monuments, Ministry of Information and Culture, Democratic Republic of Afghanistan.

Sanson, Nicholas (1694), *Estat present du royaume de Perse*, Paris: La veuve de Jacques Langlois; Jacques Colombat.

Sarshar, Houman M. (ed. 2015), *The Jews of Iran: The History, Religion and Culture of a Community in the Islamic World*, London: I. B. Tauris.

Saunders, J. J. (1971), *The History of the Mongol Conquests*, London: Routledge.

Savory, R. M. (1985), 'Ali-Qoli Khan Shamlu', *Encylopaedia Iranica*, Vol. I, Fasc. 8, pp. 875–6.

———— (1965), 'The Struggle for Supremacy in Persia after the Death of Timur', *Der Islam*, Vol. 40, pp. 35–65.

———— (1969), 'A 15th-Century Safavid Propagandist at Herat', in Dennis Sinor, ed., *Semi-centennial Volume, American Oriental Society, Middle West Branch*, Bloomington: Indiana University Press.

Sayf ibn Mohammad ibn Yaqub al-Heravi (1944), *Tarikh Namah-ye Harat*, ed. Muhammad Zubayr al-Siddiqi, Calcutta: Baptist Mission Press.

Schinasi, May (2008), 'Mohammad Nader Shah', *Encyclopaedia Iranica*, at http://www.iranicaonline.org/articles/mohammad-nader-shah-king-of-afghanistan

———— (1979), *Afghanistan at the Beginning of the Twentieth Century: Nationalism and Journalism in Afghanistan, A study of* Seraj ul-akhbar *(1911–1918)*, Naples: Istituto Universitario Orientale.

Schroen, Gary (2005), *First In: An Insider's Account of How the CIA Spearheaded the War on Terror in Afghanistan*, New York: Random House.

Seljuki, Fekri (1386 AH), *Resalah-ye mazarat-e Herat*, Herat: Hajji Abdul Halim Mohammady.

———— (1962), *Gazorgah*, Kabul.

———— (1964), *Khiaban: ba monasebat-e ehtefal-e panjsad wa panjahumin sal-e weladat-e Mawlana Nur al-Din Abdul Rahman Jami Herawi*, Kabul: Anjoman-e Kabul.

———— (1390 AH), *Herat namah*, Herat: Matbuah-ye Afghanistan tamiz.

Shakespeare, Nicholas (1999), *Bruce Chatwin*, London: Harvill.

Shikapuri, Mirza Atta Mohammad (1952), *Nawai-ye maarek*, Kabul.

Shujah, Shah (*c.*1842/1954), *Waqeat-e Shah Shujah*, ed. Ahmad Ali Kohzad, Kabul: Entesharat-e Anjoman-e Tarikh-e Afghanistan.

Sikorski, Radek (1989), *Dust of the Saints: A Journey to Herat in a Time of War*, London: Chatto & Windus.

Sims, Eleanor (1992), 'The Illustrated Manuscripts of Firdausi's "Shahnama" Commissioned by Princes of the House of Timur', *Ars Orientalis*, Vol. 22, pp. 42–68.

Sims-Williams, Ursula (1980), 'The Afghan Newspaper *Siraj al-Akhbar*', *Bulletin of British Society for Middle Eastern Studies*, Vol. 7, No. 2, pp. 118–22.

Singh, Ganda (1979), *Ahmad Shah Durrani: Founder of Modern Afghanistan*, Bombay: Asia Publishing House.

BIBLIOGRAPHY

Singhal, D. P. (1963), *India and Afghanistan, 1876–1907: A Study in Diplomatic Relations*, Brisbane: University of Queensland Press.

Spuler, Berthold (1972), *History of the Mongols; Based on Eastern and Western Accounts of the Thirteenth and Fourteenth Centuries*, London: Routledge & Kegan Paul.

Stack, Shannon Caroline (1975), 'Herat: a Political and Social Study', PhD diss., UCLA.

Standish, J. F. (1966), 'The Persian War of 1856–1857', *Middle Eastern Studies*, No. 3, pp. 28–9.

Stewart, C. E. (1886), 'The Herat Valley and the Persian Border from Hari-Rud to Sistan', *Proceedings of the Royal Geographical Society*, No. 8, pp. 137–55.

Stewart, Jules (2014), *The Kaiser's Secret Mission to Kabul*, London: I. B. Tauris.

Subtelny, Maria Eva, (1988), 'Centralizing Reform and Its Opponents in the Late Timurid Period', *Iranian Studies*, Vol. 21, Nos. 1–2, pp. 123–51.

————— (1991), 'A Timurid Educational and Charitable Foundation: the Ikhlâsiyya Complex of ʿAlî Shîr Navâ'î in 15th-Century Herat and its Endowment', *Journal of African and Oriental Studies*, Vol. 111, No. 1, pp. 38–61.

————— (1993), 'A Medieval Persian Agricultural Manuel in Context: The *Irshād al-zirāʿa* in Late Timurid and Early Safavid Khorasan', *Studia Iranica*, Vol. 22, No. 2, pp. 167–217.

————— (1994a), 'The Cult of 'Abdullah Ansari under the Timurids', in Alma Giese and J. Christoph Bürgel, eds, *God is Beautiful and He Loves Beauty*, Frankfurt: Peter Lang, pp. 377–406.

————— (1994b), 'The Symbiosis of Turk and Tajik', in Beatrice Manz, ed., *Central Asia in Historical Perspective*, Boulder, CO: Westview Press, pp. 45–61.

————— (2007), *Timurids in Transition. Turko-Persian Politics and Acculturation in Medieval Iran*, Leiden: Brill.

Subtelny, Maria Eva and Khalidov, Anas B. (1995), 'The Curriculum of Islamic Higher Learning in Timurid Iran in the Light of the Sunni Revival under Shah-Rukh', *Journal of the American Oriental Society*, Vol. 115, No. 2, pp. 210–36.

Sykes, Percy (1930), *A History of Persia*, 2 vols., London: Macmillan.

————— (1940), *A History of Afghanistan*, 2 vols., London: Macmillan.

Szuppe, M. (1992), 'Entre Timourides, Uzbeks et Safavides: questions d'histoire politique et sociale de Hérat dans la première moitié du XVIe siècle', *Studia Iranica*, Cahier 12, Paris.

————— 'Herat, iii. History, Medieval Period; iv. Topography and Urbanism', *Encyclopaedia Iranica*, 12, pp. 211–17.

————— (1993), 'Les résidences princières de Hérat: questions de continuité fonctionnelle entre les époques timouride et safavide, première moitié du XVIe siècle', in Jean Calmard, ed., *Etudes safavides*, Paris and Tehran: Institut Français de Recherche en Iran, Bibliothèque iranienne 39, pp. 267–86.

———— (1999), 'The Bazaar and Urban Life of Herat in the Middle Ages', in Rika Gyselen and Maria Szuppe, eds, *Matériaux pour l'histoire économique du monde iranien*, Paris: Studia Iranica, Cahier 21, pp. 277–85.

———— (2004), 'Historiography v. Timurid Period', *Encyclopaedia Iranica*, Vol. XII, pp. 356–63.

Takki Khan Mirza Mohammad (1885), *Report on the City and Province of Herat*, India Office Library, L/PS/7/49, pp. 1175–1270.

Talley-Stewart, Rhea (1973), *Fire in Afghanistan, 1914–29, Faith Hope and the British Empire*, London: Doubleday.

Tarzi, Shah M. (1993), 'Afghanistan in 1992: A Hobbesian State of Nature', *Asian Survey*, Vol. 33, No. 2, A Survey of Asia in 1992: Part II (February).

Tavernier, Jean Baptiste (1679), *Les Six Voyages de Jean Baptiste Tavernier, Ecuyer Baron d'Aubone, En Turquie, En Perse, Et Aux Indes*, 2 vols., Paris.

Taylor, R. L. (1858), *Narrative of Events at Herat from the Death of Yar Muhammad Khan to the Present Time*, India Office Library, L/PS/5/144, pp. 420–65.

Thackston, W. M. (1989), *A Century of Princes: Sources on Timurid History and Art, Selected and Translated by W. M. Thackston, Published in Conjunction with the Exhibition 'Timur and the Princely Vision', Washington, DC and Los Angeles*, Cambridge, MA: Aga Khan Program for Islamic Architecture.

———— (1994), *Khwandamir Habibu's-Siyar*, Vol. 3, *The Reign of the Mongol and the Turk. Pt I, Genghis Khan—Amir Temür; Pt II, Shahrukh Mirza—Shah Ismail*, Cambridge, MA: Department of Near Eastern Languages and Civilizations, Harvard University.

———— (1996), *The Baburnama. Memoirs of Babur, Prince and Emperor*, trans., ed. and annotated by Wheeler M. Thackston, New York: Oxford University Press.

Thesiger, Wilfred (1955), 'The Hazaras of Central Afghanistan', *Geographical Journal*, Vol. 121, pp. 312–19.

Thomas, Jane (1993), *Herat, Afghanistan Community Profile Report, 1993*, Peshawar.

Tirard-Collet, Olivier (1998), 'After the War. The Condition of Historical Buildings and Monuments in Herat, Afghanistan', *Iran*, Vol. 36, pp. 123–38.

Todd, D'Arcy (1844), 'Report of a Journey from Herat to Simla, via Candahar, Cabool and the Punjab, Undertaken in the Year 1838', *Journal of the Asiatic Society of Bengal*, Vol. 13.

Unknown author (1979), 'Abdullah Ansari and other Sufis of Afghanistan', *Afghanistan Journal (Special Issue) published on the Occasion of the Millennium of Abdullah Ansari of Herat*, Kabul: Ministry of Information and Culture, Department of Culture and Arts, Historical Society of Afghanistan.

Urban, Mark (1990), *War in Afghanistan*, London: Macmillan.

BIBLIOGRAPHY

Vambéry, Arminius (1864), *Travels in Central Asia. A Journey from Tehran across the Turkoman Desert on the Eastern Shore of the Caspian to Khiva, Bokhara, and Samarcand Performed in the Year 1863*, London: John Murray.

———— (1865), 'The Geographical Nomenclature of the Disputed Country between Merv and Herat', *Proceedings of the Royal Geographical Society*, Series 2, 7, pp. 591–6.

Vogelsang, W. J. (2003), 'Herat ii, History, Pre-Islamic Period', *Encylopaedia Iranica*, Iranica Online, at http://www.iranicaonline.org/articles/herat-ii.

———— (2002a), *The Afghans*, Oxford: Oxford University Press.

———— (2002b), 'The Ethnogenesis of the Pashtuns', in Warwick Ball and Leonard Harrow, eds, *Cairo to Kabul. Afghan and Islamic Studies Presented to Ralph Pinder-Wilson*, London: Melisende, pp. 228–35.

Wannell, Bruce (2002), 'Echoes in a Landscape—Western Afghanistan in 1989', in Warwick Ball and Leonard Harrow, eds, *Cairo to Kabul. Afghan and Islamic Studies Presented to Ralph Pinder-Wilson*, London: Melisende, pp. 236–47.

Weir, Surgeon-Lieutenant Colonel T. S. (1893), *From India to the Caspian, or, Journeys with and after the Afghan Boundary Commission*, Bombay: Times of India.

Wide, Dr Thomas (2014), 'The Refuge of the World: Afghanistan and the Muslim Imagination 1880–1922', DPhil diss., Oxford University.

Wilber, Donald (1987), 'Qavam al-Din ibn Zayn al-Din Shirazi: A Fifteenth Century Timurid Architect', *Architectural History*, Vol. 30, pp. 31–44.

Woods, John E. (1990), *The Timurid Dynasty*, Bloomington: Research Institute for Inner Asian Studies.

Wright, Dennis (1977), *The English Among the Persians. Imperial Lives in Nineteenth-Century Iran*, London: I. B. Tauris.

Wright, Lawrence (2007), *The Looming Tower: Al-Qaeda's Road to 9/11*, London: Penguin.

Yapp, Malcolm E. (1980), *Strategies of British India; Britain, Iran and Afghanistan 1798–1850*, Oxford: Oxford University Press.

Yate, Lieutenant Arthur C. (1887), *England and Russia Face to Face in Asia: Travels with the Afghan Boundary Commission*, Edinburgh: William Blackwood and Sons.

———— (1891) *The Trans-Caspian Railway and the Power of Russia to Occupy Herat*, Simla: Government Central Printing House.

Yate, Major Charles E. (1887), 'Notes on the City of Hirát', *Journal of the Asiatic Society of Bengal*, Vol. 56, No. 1, pp. 84–106.

———— (1888), *Northern Afghanistan, or Letters from the Afghan Boundary Commission*, Edinburgh: William Blackwood and Sons.

———— (1900), *Khurasan and Sistan*, Edinburgh: William Blackwood and Sons.

Yosoufi, Sayyed Sharif (1985), *Qiyam-e Golgun-e Kafnan-e 24 Hout-e Herat* (The Blood-Soaked Uprising of Herat of 24th Hout), Kabul.

British Library India Office Archives

L/PS/5/144
L/PS/5/145
L/PS/7/83
L/PS/9/106
L/PS/9/108
L/PS/9/114
L/PS/9/115
L/PS/9/116
L/PS/9/117
L/PS/9/119
L/PS/9/120
L/PS/9/161
L/PS/11/157
L/PS/14/1
L/PS/18/C3
L/PS/20/A7/1
L/PS/20/A7/2
L/PS/20/A7/VOL/2
L/PS/20/MEMO/21
Curzon Papers (1884–86), *Papers on the Afghan Boundary Commission*, 7 vols., India Office Library, MSS Eur., F. 111/60
Treaty of Paris, 4 March 1857 (1857), *Treaty of Peace with Persia, 1857*, L/PS/20/C/2
'Henry C. Rawlinson, on the Dooranee Tribes. Dated 19th April 1841', in L/PS/20/MEMO.21
Kabul Times, British Library
Parcham, British Library
Seraj al-Akhbar, British Library
Khalq, British Library
Afghan Tribes, Oriental Manuscripts, British Library, 1861, f. 4, IOR/G/29/1, *PRO, State Papers, Colonial East Indies*
National Archives, *Note by Mr Franklin on Conditions in Herat*, 21 March 1952, FO 371/100962

Miscellaneous sources

Afghan Jihad, publication from Peshawar which ran until the end of the civil war, 1992.

———— Vol. 1, No. 4, April–June, 1988, Islamabad, p. 60.

———— Vol. 3, No. 4, July–September, 1990, Islamabad, p. 34.

Afghan News, A Biweekly Bulletin of Jami'at Islami Afghanistan, Vol. 1, 1985.

Al-Jazeera, 'Afghan Minister Killed in Herat Shootout', 21 March 2004, at http://www.aljazeera.com/archive/2004/03/20084914449768186.html

'Concerning the Situation in "A"', New Russian Evidence on the Soviet Intervention in Afghanistan', in 'Documents on the Soviet Invasion of Afghanistan, e-Dossier No. 4', *Cold War International History Project*, Woodrow Wilson International Centre for Scholars, Washington, DC, November 2001, at http://www.wilsoncenter.org/sites/default/files/e-dossier_4.pdf

Ettefaq-e Islam, Herat's daily paper from 1930 to the present day, Herat Public Library.

National Committee for Human Rights in Afghanistan, *Russia's Barbarism in Afghanistan*, Vol. II, July 1985, Peshawar.

United Nations Humanitarian and Assistance Programmes relating to Afghanistan, *Salam 1*, 8–14 December 1988; *Salam 2, Mission to Herat*, 31 August–4 September 1988, Tehran.

UNHCR Background Report, *Herat Province, Prepared by the Data Collection for Afghan Repatriation Project, 15 April 1990*, Islamabad, 1990.

Wikileaks, *Kissinger Files*, https://wikileaks.org/plusd/cables/1975KABUL 02834_b.html

Videos

Baily, John (1978), *The Herat Trilogy*.

———— (1995), *A Portrait of Herat, 1994*.

Flamholc, Leon (1985), *A Winter in Herat*, at https://www.youtube.com/playlist?list=PL4BC35ABC9405BDA4

Simpson, John (1996), 'Soldiers of Allah', BBC *Newsnight* documentary, at https://www.youtube.com/watch?v=Ekyrv3sSZQQ

INDEX

INDEX

INDEX